# ZAGAT
# U.S. HOTEL, RESORT AND SPA SURVEY

D0067106

### Edited by
### Joan Lang and Susan Safronoff

Published and Distributed by

ZAGAT SURVEY
4 Columbus Circle
New York, New York 10019
212-977-6000

# ACKNOWLEDGMENTS

We would like to thank the following for all their help: Richard Altman, Stan Arnold, Sherry Atnip, Candace and Rick Beinecke, Bill Bennett, Karen Berk, Joe Brancatelli, Kimmy and Steve Brauer, Ellen and Al Butts, Millard Cohen, Suzanne and Norman Cohn, Ellen and George Conant, Cass Davies, Lanny Davis, Pat Denechaud, Margot and John Ernst, Donna and Ken Eshelman, Jim Farnham, Joel Fleishman, Hal Foster, Gerry Frank, Randall Gates, Kay Goldstein, Mimi and Beverly Head, Marilyn and Bob Johnson, Carolyn Jones, Ivan Karp, Clay and Garrett Kirk, Jane Heald Lavine, William Levit, Jr., Marjorie and Milton Levy, Ursula and Edward McCracken, Leroy Meshel, Donald Mooney, Kitty Morgan, Maureen and Tom Myers, Neil Peck, Duane Peterson, Eric Redman, Robert Rich, Jeannie and John Russell, Ashley Safronoff, Peter Safronoff, Brenda and Earl Shapiro, Barbara and Stewart Sims, Louise Slominsky, Heather Stantic, Su Stevens, Bill St. John, Howard Stravitz, Paul Uhlmann III and Gerald Wald.

We would also like to thank the following for their editorial assistance: Olga Boikess, Robert Bone, Denise Brennan, Paul Camp, Judy Colbert, Katharine Colton, Laura Daily, Audrey Farolino, Valerie Hart, Sam Hughes, Elin Jeffords, Bill Kent, Lea Lane, Audrey Lee, Chuck Malody, M.F. Onderdonk, Todd Persons, Joe Pollack, Elizabeth Rhein, Ron Ruggless, Matthew Sade, Merrill Shindler and Joanne Timmins.

# TO ORDER

**ZAGAT U.S. HOTEL, RESORT, SPA SURVEY**

**ZAGAT SURVEY: AMERICA'S
TOP RESTAURANTS**

**ZAGAT SURVEY: AMERICA'S
BEST VALUE RESTAURANTS**

**ZAGAT RESTAURANT SURVEYS**
Atlanta; Atlantic City; Boston; Chicago;
Dallas–Fort Worth; Hawaii; Houston; Kansas City;
London; Los Angeles–Southern California;
Miami–Southern Florida; Montreal; New Orleans;
New York City; Orlando–Central Florida;
Pacific Northwest; Philadelphia;
San Francisco; Southwest; St. Louis;
Tri-State–CT/NJ/NY; Washington, D.C.–Baltimore

**ZAGAT NYC MARKETPLACE SURVEY**
covering food, wine and entertaining sources

**ZAGAT/AXXIS CityGuides™**
for desktop, notebook and handheld computers.
Comprehensive mapping software fully integrated
with Zagat restaurant and hotel ratings; available
by city on disk or nationwide on CD-ROM.

Call (212) 977-6000 • (800) 333-3421

or Write to:

Zagat Survey
4 Columbus Circle
New York, New York 10019

**Regarding
Corporate Gifts and
Deluxe Editions, call
(212) 977-6000
or (800) 333-3421**

# CONTENTS

**Top Hotels In Other Cities**

# DIRECTORY OF RESORTS AND INNS BY STATE

**Names, Addresses, Phone Numbers,
Ratings and Commentary**

## DIRECTORY OF SPAS

## INDEXES

# INTRODUCTION

Here are the results of our new *U.S. Hotel, Resort and Spa Survey*, covering more than 1,500 hotels, resorts, spas and hotel chains across the country, as well as major airlines and car rental companies. By surveying large numbers of regular travelers, we think we have achieved a uniquely current and reliable guide. We hope you agree. On the assumption that most people want a "quick fix" on the places at which they are considering staying, we have also tried to be concise and to provide handy indexes.

Over 7,000 people participated in this *Survey*. Since these participants stayed at hotels an average of 38 nights per year, the *Survey* is based on roughly 265,000 nights at hotels per year. Knowing that the quality of this *Survey* is the direct result of their thoughtful voting and commentary, we sincerely thank each participant. Among the surveyors, there were many meeting planners and travel agents who brought their combined expertise to this project. This book is dedicated to all of you.

We are especially grateful to Joan Lang and Susan Safronoff, our editors. They made the daunting job of surveying the constantly changing travel industry almost seem easy and made sure that the information contained in this guide is as current as possible. The factual information, including addresses, phone numbers and facilities, was gathered directly from the hotels, resorts and spas.

**We invite you to be a reviewer in our next *Survey*.** So that we may contact you, send a stamped, self-addressed, business-size envelope marked "Travel" to ZAGAT SURVEY, 4 Columbus Circle, New York, NY 10019. Each participant will receive a free copy of the next *U.S. Hotel, Resort and Spa Survey* when it is published. Your comments, suggestions and criticism of this *Survey* are also solicited. There is always room for improvement – with your help.

New York, New York                          Nina and Tim Zagat
January 25, 1993

# FOREWORD

It's a "buyer's market" out there when it comes to booking a hotel room or planning a vacation in the United States. Never before has such a wealth of hotels and resorts been available. Never before have there been such bargains. At the very least, travelers now have their pick of clean, comfortable, reasonably priced accommodations. And at the very most, you can stay in a first-rate hotel or resort, the kind of marvelous place that's guaranteed to make any travel experience memorable.

As a result of the overbuilding of hotels in the 1980s followed by a recession, American hoteliers are aggressively marketing frequent-stay programs, weekend packages, midweek specials and other promotions, as well as low off-season and off-peak rates. Even negotiated rates have become common. A willingness to shop around can result in complimentary upgrades, lots of special amenities, better accommodations and lower prices. Fallout from the overbuilding of the past decade means that competition in the '90s is likely to remain fierce. And the hotel developer's loss is the traveler's gain.

Today, the U.S. has more good hotels, resorts and spas to choose from than at any time in its history, with even secondary cities offering first-class modern or renovated accommodations. All these facilities are accompanied by more and more services: there are conference centers, meeting rooms and state-of-the-art business facilities including computers and even secretaries available.

And personal services are expanding rapidly, too: fast fading from the scene is the traditional Norman Rockwell–like hotel barber shop; replacing it is a full-scale unisex body-pampering center where customers can get spruced up between business meetings or city tours, and also indulge in relaxed self-improvement. Massages, facials, whirlpool baths, running tracks, weight machines and even indoor swimming pools are commonplace in hotels. Indeed, city hotels have become quasi-resorts.

It should come as no surprise that the hotels with the best service tend to be the most appreciated. As a result, many places now offer concierge service on special floors. These "club floors" provide complimentary breakfast and cocktails, morning newspapers and a better level of service.

Resort-owners haven't been exactly idle either. As you study this book you'll find a dazzling variety of resorts that compete with the natural wonders that surround them, from the islands of Hawaii to the coast of Maine. Besides the works of nature, there are man-made lakes for fishing, trails for horseback riding or hiking, tennis courts and sometimes not just one championship golf course, but five of them, all beautifully manicured – and waiting. No more is a resort vacation necessarily dictated by geography and season. Whatever form of diversion or sport you crave is available nearly everywhere.

As for food, the best restaurants in many cities are found in hotels, starting with the high-rated Ritz-Carltons of Atlanta through Washington, D.C.'s Four Seasons. Hoteliers have come to realize that it takes a first-class restaurant to be a first-class hotel.

In the final analysis, it all comes down to more options for the traveler. A generation ago the world's best hotels were in Europe, and you took your chances in the U.S., especially outside big cities. In many small cities and towns your choice was limited to roadside motels or the local "Overnighter Arms." Now, there isn't a city or region in America that doesn't have an abundance of new hotel rooms, and the prices are unbelievably low – by world standards.

In fact – let's be bold about it – the United States has the best and most affordable lodging facilities of any country in the world. And they're all yours.

New York, New York
January 25, 1993

Joan Lang
Susan Safronoff

11

# TRAVEL TIPS

Before you begin your trip, take a few minutes to review these travel tips:

- Unless you simply want to make a reservation, call the hotel itself rather than its toll-free 800 number. The 800 operators are often part of a central-reservation service, thus they may be far removed from the hotel that interests you. By calling the hotel's direct number you can make the best deal and ask specific questions about facilities from the people on the scene.

- Don't hesitate to negotiate when reserving. Begin by asking about the "corporate rate" (traditionally up to a 20-percent discount based on corporate use) and then ask about other discount rates that may be available.

- Typically, hotels in cities are busy during the week but not on weekends; with resorts it's usually the reverse. Of course, seasonal places are eager to develop off-season business. All this spells opportunity for you, the traveler. In all three instances, discounts of as much as 50 percent may be available.

- When it makes sense, book your room as close as possible to your date of arrival. Low occupancy may encourage the front desk to slash rates, provide upgrades or both, but you can't be shy about asking for such breaks.

- Be sure to check your room immediately. If not satisfied, you should not be embarrassed to ask to be moved to a different one.

- Special services such as secretarial help or babysitting are often available for the asking. Many city hotels now feature "business centers" that supply guests with a complete range of office services. Ask about those services that concern you.

- Inquire about taxes and extra charges when you book a room, so you aren't surprised at check-out time. For rooms above $100, New York City adds taxes that run to a preposterous 21 percent.

- Check in advance on the hotel's policy regarding standard telephone and fax charges. Don't forget about surcharges on collect or credit card calls. They can add up very quickly.

■ Access for the handicapped has become a matter of law, with the result that almost all newer hotels have facilities such as ramps and wider doors. Still, it's advisable to check when you reserve regarding those facilities that concern you.

## CAR RENTAL

■ When it comes to car rentals, read the contract carefully. And keep in mind that declining the insurance options offered by the rental companies may make sound business sense. For example, the "collision damage waiver" may be unnecessary if you are covered by your personal auto insurance. In addition, you can receive similar coverage by charging the rental to a major "gold issue" credit card or to American Express. Get your insurance agent's advice on which coverage you should take.

■ Return rental cars with a full tank of gas to avoid the outlandishly high markups charged on refueling.

■ Return the rental car on time. Whopping hourly fees can be assessed if you return the vehicle even an hour late; you may even incur a higher daily rate if you return the car too early.

## AIRLINE TRAVEL

■ It's difficult to assess the impact of recent price wars on the airline industry. Long-term prices are still very much "up in the air", so it still makes a lot of sense to shop around for the best deal.

■ Remember, frequent-flyer programs often tie in with hotel and car rental companies (see Frequent Flyer Index), but participation in some programs requires long-term planning and is limited by complex rules. Once again, read the contract and shop the market.

## TRAVEL AGENTS

■ Many travelers make their arrangements simply by calling a travel agent. That's fine; we have only one word of advice in this regard: you should pick your travel agent as carefully as you would your lawyer or doctor to make sure the agent acts in your interest and not based on which hotel pays the biggest commission. Don't be shy about asking for references.

# EXPLANATION OF RATINGS AND SYMBOLS

**ROOMS, SERVICE, DINING** and **PUBLIC FACILITIES** are reflected on a scale of 0 to 30 in columns marked **R, S, D** and **P**:

> 0–9  = poor to fair
> 10–19 = good to very good
> 20–25 = very good to excellent
> 26–30 = extraordinary to perfection

The **COST** column, headed by a **$**, reflects our surveyors' estimate of the price of a double room for one night. **VI** (Very Inexpensive) = less than $65; **I** (Inexpensive) = $65 to $99; **M** (Medium-Priced) = $100 to $149; **E** (Expensive) = $150 to $199; **VE** (Very Expensive) = $200 and up.

**Best Places** are listed in the front of each Directory section, with **Best Values** derived by dividing the cost of a room into the hotel's **Overall Rating**, i.e. the average of it's **R, S, D** and **P** ratings. The names of lodgings with overall ratings of 23 or above are printed in solid capital letters, e.g., "**THE WINDSOR COURT**."

An **Asterisk** (*) after a hotel's name means the number of persons who voted on it is too low to be reliable. The **Number of Rooms and Suites** in each hotel, resort and spa is indicated after its name. For example, **100R(20S)** means the place has 100 Rooms, 20 of which are Suites, Villas, Condos or Cabins.

By way of **Commentary**, we attempt to summarize the comments of our participants, occasionally retaining a prior year's *Survey* comment where appropriate. The prefix **U** means comments were basically uniform; **M** means they were mixed. **(Pr)**, used in a few instances, means the review is based on a previous *Survey*.

If we do not show ratings, the entry is either an important **newcomer** or a popular **write-in**; however, comments are included and the estimated cost is indicated. Occasionally, **separate food ratings appear** regarding a hotel's top restaurant. Such ratings are drawn from that city's *Zagat Restaurant Survey*.

# KEY 800 NUMBERS AND RATINGS

## AIRLINES
(Overall ratings are derived by averaging surveyors' ratings
for comfort, service, timeliness/reliability and food)

| AIRLINE | OVERALL | COST | 800 NUMBER |
|---|---|---|---|
| Aeroflot | 6 | M | 535-9877 |
| Air Canada | 19 | E | 776-3000 |
| Air France | 21 | E | 237-2747 |
| Alaska Airlines | 22 | E | 426-0333 |
| Alitalia | 17 | E | 223-5730 |
| American | 18 | E | 433-7300 |
| America West | 16 | M | 247-5692 |
| ANA | 23 | E | 235-9262 |
| British Airways | 21 | E | 247-9297 |
| Cathay Pacific | 24 | E | 233-2742 |
| Continental | 14 | M | 525-0280 |
| Delta | 18 | E | 221-1212 |
| El Al | 17 | E | 223-6700 |
| JAL | 23 | E | 525-3663 |
| KLM | 22 | E | 374-7747 |
| Lufthansa | 22 | E | 645-3880 |
| Midwest Express | 19 | M | 452-2022 |
| Northwest | 15 | E | 225-2525 |
| Olympic | 13 | E | 223-1226 |
| Qantas | 22 | E | 227-4500 |
| SAS | 22 | E | 221-2350 |
| Singapore | 26 | E | 742-3333 |
| Southwest | 15 | I | 531-5601 |
| Swissair | 24 | E | 221-4750 |
| TWA | 13 | M | 221-2000 |
| United | 17 | E | 241-6522 |
| USAir | 15 | M | 428-4322 |
| Varig | 19 | E | 468-2744 |
| Virgin Atlantic | 22 | M | 862-8621 |

## CAR RENTALS
(Overall ratings are derived by averaging surveyors' ratings
for vehicle condition, service, location and availability)

| RENTAL COMPANY | OVERALL | COST | 800 NUMBER |
|---|---|---|---|
| Alamo | 17 | I | 327-9633 |
| Avis | 22 | E | 331-1212 |
| Budget | 19 | M | 527-0700 |
| Dollar | 18 | M | 800-4000 |
| Hertz | 23 | E | 654-3131 |
| National | 21 | E | 328-4567 |
| Payless | 16 | I | 237-2804 |
| Rent-A-Wreck | 11 | I | 535-1391 |
| Thrifty | 17 | I | 367-2277 |

## RAILROAD

| Amtrak | NA | NA | 800-872-7245 |
|--------|----|----|--------------|

## BUS LINES

| Bonanza | NA | NA | 800-556-3815 |
|---------|----|----|--------------|
| Greyhound/Trailways | NA | NA | 800-531-5332 |

## HOTEL CHAINS
(Overall ratings are derived by averaging surveyors' ratings
for rooms, service, dining and public facilities)

| HOTEL CHAIN | OVERALL | COST | 800 NUMBER |
|-------------|---------|------|------------|
| Clarion | 15 | I | 252-7466 |
| Comfort Inns | 13 | VI | 228-5150 |
| Courtyard by Marriott | 17 | I | 321-2211 |
| Crown Sterling Suites | 18 | M | 433-4600 |
| Days Inn | 11 | VI | 325-2525 |
| Doubletree | 18 | M | 528-0444 |
| Econo Lodge | 11 | VI | 446-6900 |
| Embassy Suites | 18 | M | 362-2779 |
| Fairfield Inns | 15 | VI | 228-2800 |
| Four Seasons | 26 | E | 332-3442 |
| Guest Quarters | 19 | M | 424-2900 |
| Hampton Inn | 16 | VI | 426-7866 |
| Hilton | 18 | M | 445-8667 |
| Holiday Inn | 14 | I | 465-4329 |
| Howard Johnson | 12 | I | 654-2000 |
| Hyatt | 21 | M | 228-9000 |
| Inter-Continental | 21 | E | 327-0200 |
| La Quinta Inns | 14 | VI | 531-5900 |
| Leading Hotels † | 25 | VE | 223-6800 |
| Loews Hotels | 22 | E | 235-6397 |
| Marriott | 19 | M | 228-9290 |
| Omni | 19 | M | 843-6664 |
| Preferred Hotels† | 24 | E | 323-7500 |
| Quality Inns | 14 | I | 228-5151 |
| Radisson | 18 | M | 333-3333 |
| Ramada | 14 | I | 276-6232 |
| Red Lion Hotels & Inns | 17 | M | 547-8010 |
| Red Roof Inns | 12 | VI | 843-7663 |
| Relais & Chateaux † | 27 | VE | *212-856-0115 |
| Residence Inns | 18 | M | 331-3131 |
| Ritz-Carlton | 26 | E | 241-3333 |
| Sheraton | 17 | M | 325-3535 |
| Stouffer | 20 | M | 468-3571 |
| Super 8 | 11 | VI | 843-1991 |
| Travelodge/Viscount | 12 | VI | 255-3050 |
| Westin | 21 | E | 228-3000 |
| Wyndham | 19 | M | 822-4200 |

*Not a toll-free number.
†Indicates a marketing/reservations service, rather than a chain.

# DIRECTORY OF
# HOTEL CHAINS

# TOP NATIONAL RATINGS

## (In order of rating)

### BEST OVERALL*

26 – Four Seasons
     Ritz-Carlton
22 – Loews Hotels
21 – Inter-Continental
     Westin
     Hyatt
20 – Stouffer
19 – Marriott
     Wyndham
     Omni

### BEST VALUES**

I  – Fairfield Inns
     Hampton Inns
     La Quinta Inns
     Red Roof Inns
     Super 8
M – Residence Inns
     Radisson
     Guest Quarters
     Embassy Suites
     Doubletree

\*           \*           \*

### Best Rooms

27 – Four Seasons
     Ritz-Carlton
22 – Loews Hotels
     Inter-Continental
     Westin
     Residence Inns
21 – Guest Quarters
     Hyatt
     Embassy Suites
     Stouffer

### Best Service

27 – Four Seasons
     Ritz-Carlton
22 – Inter-Continental
21 – Loews Hotels
     Westin
     Hyatt
20 – Stouffer
     Marriott
     Wyndham
19 – Omni

### Best Dining

26 – Ritz-Carlton
     Four Seasons
21 – Loews Hotels
     Inter-Continental
20 – Westin
19 – Hyatt
     Stouffer
18 – Marriott
     Wyndham
17 – Guest Quarters

### Best Public Facilities

26 – Four Seasons
     Ritz-Carlton
21 – Loews Hotels
     Inter-Continental
     Westin
     Hyatt
20 – Stouffer
19 – Marriott
     Omni
     Wyndham

---

\*Excluding Leading Hotels, Preferred Hotels and Relais & Chateaux, three fine marketing/reservation services that are not chains.
\*\*The five Best Values under $100 are indicated by an "I", the five Best Values over $100 are indicated by an "M."

# HOTEL CHAIN REVIEWS

| R | S | D | P | $ |
|---|---|---|---|---|

### Clarion
(800) 252-7466

| 17 | 16 | 14 | 15 | $88 |

*M* – *"Average everything"* characterizes this group of more than 110 full-service locations; most of our surveyors judge Clarion *"good for an inexpensive night on the road"* and praise the *"accommodating service"* and *"exceptional deals"* at breakfast, but others say it's *"overpriced for what you get."*

### Comfort Inns*
(800) 228-5150

| 15 | 14 | 11 | 15 | $63 |

*U* – *Limited-service inns that deliver the 4C's: i.e. "cheap", "comfortable", "clean" and "convenient"; with "nice extras for a budget chain", it's a "good, predictable" value that "delivers what it promises"; in addition to the 800-odd inns now open, the company also has 50 mini-suite properties under its trademark.*

### Courtyard by Marriott
(800) 321-2211

| 19 | 17 | 15 | 16 | $84 |

*U* – *A "fresh Marriott idea", this good-value concept (said to be designed by businesspeople, for businesspeople) offers a "nice, well-furnished and well-maintained room" (with separate sleeping, sitting/work and dressing areas) at a "reasonable price"; with over 200 properties, this chain receives solid marks for rooms and service, but you "may need a car" since many are in the suburbs; critics say they're "drab" and serve "airline" chow.*

### Crown Sterling Suites
(800) 433-4600

| 20 | 18 | 16 | 18 | $102 |

*U* – *"A good value", these "very pleasant" all-suiters with kitchenettes are especially "good with children" or for extended stays; thriftniks of all kinds like such perks as "free breakfast", "workout rooms" and pools, and in-room wet bars and microwaves; with only 22 locations, you may have to hunt to find one.*

---

*Not all hotels in this chain have food service.

## Days Inn
| 13 | 12 | 9 | 10 | $60 |

(800) 325-2525

*M – "Tsk, tsk"; surveyor comments vary almost as much as the quality of the hotels themselves; "could have paid a lot more for less" vs. "don't care if it's cheap, I'd pay good money not to stay in one"; you may "get what you pay for", but with "no standards among locations" and with 1,300 franchised operations, you're taking your chances.*


## Doubletree
| 19 | 19 | 17 | 18 | $108 |

(800) 528-0444

*U – This company got a big boost when it joined forces with Canadian Pacific Hotels in 1990, adding 26 luxury hotels in Canada to its U.S. base of 38 full-service Doubletree Hotels and 20 more competitively priced Doubletree Club locations (formerly Compris); "innovative cuisine", "comfortable and attractive rooms" and the most "eager-to-please staff anywhere" yield "pleasant surprises" at this "very good hotel" chain.*


## Econo Lodge*
| 12 | 12 | 9 | 10 | $52 |

(800) 446-6900

*M – "The name says it all": "good value for the price", making "family travel affordable", is the main advantage of this "low-priced typical motel" with about 700 locations in 48 states and Canada; though some say "you could do worse" and "reliable for a night", others say "don't bother" or "save your money."*


## Embassy Suites
| 21 | 18 | 16 | 18 | $107 |

(800) 362-2779

*U – One of the first all-suite groups, now nearly 100 units strong, still offers "good value" for a "home-away-from-home" package that includes "extra space for extra comfort"; the "rooms are nicely appointed", the cooked-to-order breakfast "very generous" and the complimentary cocktail hour "well attended"; it's "a reasonable choice with kids" (children under 12 stay free) and a "bargain for business" trips.*


## Fairfield Inns
| 17 | 16 | – | 14 | $61 |

(800) 228-2800

*U – "The price is right" for "simple, clean and cheap" rooms with handy work desks and "consistently attentive, upbeat personnel"; if you must travel "economy class", "you can't beat" these Marriott-owned "bargain" locations; our surveyors only "wish there were more of them"; no food service.*

# HOTEL CHAIN REVIEWS | R | S | D | P | $ |

### Four Seasons
(800) 332-3442

| 27 | 27 | 26 | 26 | $196 |

*U – "Pamper me and book me here", since "luxury is perfected" at Four Seasons; the Canada-headquartered chain wins all-American high marks for its "exquisite food", "marvelous service", "always-fine" rooms, "outstanding" facilities and "elegant" public spaces – "tops in all departments"; the company operates 16 hotels and resorts stateside, with new properties in development in Carlsbad, CA, and the Big Island of Hawaii; each and every one is pricey but "worth every penny."*

### Guest Quarters
(800) 424-2900

| 21 | 19 | 17 | 18 | $112 |

*U – "Excellent facilities for both families and businessmen" characterize this growing chain of 27 all-suiters boasting accommodations that are "roomy, airy and well laid out"; the "basic comforts" are augmented by handy "writing desks" and in-room kitchenettes with "large refrigerators and ovens"; complimentary breakfast is a "nice touch", and the employees "try hard."*

### Hampton Inn
(800) 426-7866

| 18 | 17 | – | 15 | $64 |

*U – "Budweiser quality at Meisterbrau prices" makes these no-frills inns the "best of the genre" for many travelers; the chain is growing fast, with more than 300 U.S. locations, mostly east of the Mississippi; "excellent breakfasts", "spacious, clean rooms", "convenient locations" and "reasonable rates" add up to "value in economy lodging"; no food service.*

### Hilton
(800) 445-8667

| 18 | 18 | 17 | 18 | $122 |

*M – "Variability from Hilton to Hilton" with hotels and resorts ranging from "superb" and "a good bet" to "outdated" and "coasting", and with more than 400 properties in 50 countries (240 in the U.S.), that's a lot of variability; hope widespread "recent renovations" will restore a once great name; N.B. almost all the U.S. properties are run by the LA-based Hilton Hotels Corp., while London-based Hilton International runs most of the foreign hotels; thankfully, there's a single reservation service.*

### Holiday Inn
(800) 465-4329

| 15 | 14 | 12 | 13 | $83 |

*M – "Does anybody need these described?"; probably not – with more than 1,600 properties in the U.S. alone, Holiday Inn is the most ubiquitous brand in the business – "you can't spit without hitting one"; for many, this "cliché that works" means "cheap, clean hotels" that are usually a "safe bet on the road"; quality, however, depends on location.*

| R | S | D | P | $ |

## Howard Johnson
(800) 654-2000

| 13 | 13 | 11 | 11 | $76 |

*M – Time and competition are catching up to these familiar blue and orange roadside "motor lodges"; "erratic from state to state", HoJos range from "reasonable family hotels" to the "last resort in a small town"; opinions vary from "good quality for the price, much like their ice cream", to a blunt "yuck"; not unawares, the company is replacing many of the typical orange-roofs with a more sophisticated selection of low-priced entrants.*

## Hyatt
(800) 228-9000

| 21 | 21 | 19 | 21 | $139 |

*U – "When in doubt, Hyatt is 99-percent perfect"; for the majority of our surveyors, "excellent food", "wonderful resorts", "always-reliable rooms" and "spectacular lobbies" and public facilities make Hyatt, with 162 hotels worldwide (104 in North America), "the best of the mass-market chains" for "business or pleasure" travel; "there's a lot to be said for consistency", though a "not always competent" staff get some complaints.*

## Inter-Continental
(800) 327-0200

| 22 | 22 | 21 | 21 | $164 |

*M – "Generally good all over", this midsize chain of approximately 100 higher-priced properties, many of them abroad, provides a "step up" from the Hyatt-Hilton-Marriott triumvirate, with "good rooms and service" and some "unforgettable properties"; world travelers say the "overseas hotels are better than the domestic ones", so "why not fly to one?"*

## La Quinta Inns*
(800) 531-5900

| 16 | 15 | 11 | 13 | $59 |

*U – Offering motel lodging "with a Spanish accent", this "quite nice" budget-priced chain of 213 properties in 19 states (mostly in the Southwest) checks in with "good value" on a "clean and comfortable room"; they may be "Spartan", but they're "consistent" and "cheap."*

## Leading Hotels
(800) 223-6800

| 25 | 25 | 25 | 25 | $208 |

*U – "The best of the best", this marketing and reservation service for 260 "quite unique properties" (about 50 in the U.S.) sets a "standard to which all else should be held"; "style, service and warmth" are yours in any of these "always-excellent" "high-end products", that offer "top-notch" facilities to sophisticated travelers who don't mind paying top dollar for quality; because they are independently run, you can expect "a discovery every time."*

| R | S | D | P | $ |

| 22 | 21 | 21 | 22 | $151 |

## Loews Hotels
(800) 235-6397

*U – "High above the commonplace", this well-managed New York–based group of 14 "first-class hotels" strikes fans as "a great chain", with "nice rooms", well-trained staff and a "wide variety" of types of properties; on the other hand, its diversity may also be a weakness in that the chain hasn't developed a clear identity"; solid scores across the board indicate it's worth searching out the next time you're in town, especially in Dallas, LA, NYC and Tucson.*

| 20 | 20 | 18 | 19 | $125 |

## Marriott
(800) 228-9290

*U – Marriott's Mormon roots show in such comments as "very efficient", "friendly service" and "consistent quality and value" – probably the reason boosters say "when in doubt, go Marriott"; scoring extra points as a "good business hotel" with a staff that "works a little harder", Marriott also gets compliments for its "frequent-stay program" (and with 230 properties located around the world, that's saying a lot); a few dissenters say it's "like Wonder Bread, predictable and bland", but that's probably another reason why so many like it.*

| 20 | 19 | 18 | 19 | $135 |

## Omni
(800) 843-6664

*M – "Innovative" Omni is "reaching for the top" but sometimes stumbles, if our surveyors' comments are any indication; though most laud the "nice, clean rooms" and "good food and service", some say the Omni experience is "variable"; the bottom line seems to be "nice hotels for the money"; with only 40 properties worldwide (34 in the U.S.), there are "not too many around."*

| 24 | 24 | 24 | 24 | $179 |

## Preferred Hotels
(800) 323-7500

*U – Another marketing-and-reservations organization for a "quirky collection" of "excellent" hotels, judged "usually superior to the others in the area"; though the selection is "somewhat limited", with only 58 in the U.S. (105 altogether around the world), our travelers prefer Preferred when they have the choice, thanks to the "many outstanding properties" offering luxurious accommodations, "great service" and that feeling of "tasteful" "old elegance."*

### Quality Inns
(800) 228-5151

| 15 | 14 | 13 | 13 | $69 |

*U – "Adequate for late-night stopovers", this midline group of hotels, with 500 worldwide locations, checks in as "clean, safe and dull" with value-conscious surveyors; "reasonable prices", "surprisingly nice" rooms and "usually dependable" quality make for a "comfortable overnight stay", but not much more.*

### Radisson
(800) 333-3333

| 19 | 18 | 17 | 17 | $104 |

*M – Radisson covers "a big swing, ranging from magnificent to mediocre, depending on the city"; its "suite hotels" are especially "great", but others "could take lessons"; overall, they offer a "more upscale" experience than most of the chains and are "an increasingly good choice", particularly "for business travel"; with 270 properties open already and one of the most aggressive expansion plans in the industry, they are increasingly handy.*

### Ramada
(800) 272-6232

| 15 | 14 | 13 | 13 | $78 |

*M – "Inconsistency" plagues this massive chain of some 600 midmarket hotels: guest experiences here range from "good" to the "worst ever"; the handful of upgraded Renaissance units earn higher marks for "excellent guest rooms, nice dining and grounds", but the rest can be "pretty spotty" in quality; about all you can count on are "comfortable rooms" and "fairly reasonable" prices.*

### Red Lion Hotels & Inns*
(800) 547-8010

| 18 | 18 | 16 | 17 | $103 |

*U – "Large rooms and friendly service" coupled with handy locations and "modern", "functional architecture" make this moderately priced Western U.S. regional chain a "very attractive" choice "where available"; it may offer no bells and whistles, but "you know you'll get a good night's stay" that's "terrific for the money."*

### Red Roof Inns
(800) 843-7663

| 14 | 13 | – | 11 | $52 |

*M – An "exercise in minimalism", Red Roof's "cheap", "very plain" "no-frills" properties are "no incentive to tarry"; although some judge this "budget-all-the-way" chain (200-plus units in the Midwest, East and South) a "reliable place to sleep" and a "good value", more demanding travelers rank it among the "lowest of the low"; no food service.*

| R | S | D | P | $ |

### Relais & Chateaux
| 27 | 27 | 27 | 26 | $220 |

(212) 856-0115

*U – "Expensive but worth it" is the consensus on what is an association, not a chain, of "wonderful", "small", "intimate", "luxurious" and "friendly hotels" that specialize in "outstanding dining"; of these 387 privately owned properties, sadly only 21 are in the U.S., but these include The Point, Inn at Little Washington, Little Palm Island, Blantyre and Sherman House, all of which made our Top 10 lists in their respective categories; altogether this group epitomizes "class."*

### Residence Inns
| 22 | 18 | 14 | 17 | $104 |

(800) 331-3131

*U – Extended-stay business travelers and families with kids appreciate the "home-away-from-home amenities" of these Marriott-owned "lovely" and "spacious" "condo-style" hotels; they offer "lots of room for a great price", and the 180-odd "good locations" offer "easy access" to highways and surrounding attractions; you can't keep anything this good a "best-kept secret" for long.*

### Ritz-Carlton
| 27 | 27 | 26 | 26 | $196 |

(800) 241-3333

*U – "Heaven with a front desk"; Ritz-Carlton "spoils it for the rest", with "excellent food", "wonderful" rooms and handsome, formal English facilities, plus "always-excellent service" and "marvelous attention to privacy"; it's difficult to find fault with a chain about which the only complaint is "too much service"; to date, there are 27 Ritz-Carltons, leading some surveyors to wish there were more; "when money is no object", "pamper yourself" and check into "the most luxurious of all the chains."*

### Sheraton
| 18 | 18 | 16 | 17 | $121 |

(800) 325-3535

*M – "Big and brassy" Sheraton, with 427 properties worldwide (284 of them in the U.S.) is "fine for the popular-priced category", with "nice facilities and rooms" and "generally good restaurants and service"; our surveyors say some of the "franchised hotels are real losers, but the nice ones are really nice"; others think the chain has "lost touch with what American business expects."*

### Stouffer
| 21 | 20 | 19 | 20 | $136 |

(800) 468-3571

*U – A "good dependable chain", 40-unit Stouffer seems to be getting better; its flagship properties and resorts are deemed "great", with facilities that are "lovely and elegant" and "a step above the rest"; the company also gets high marks for the "friendliest service", but a few think the chain "wants to be in the major leagues" but "fails more than it succeeds."*

| R | S | D | P | $ |
|---|---|---|---|---|

### Super 8
| 13 | 12 | 8 | 10 | $49 |
|---|---|---|---|---|

(800) 843-1991

*M – Definitely not a super experience, some say "these should be outlawed",
but others report they're "fine for the night on the way to somewhere else"
and offer rock-bottom prices for a "clean room", "comfortable bed" and
"no frills at all"; "each is operated independently, so check it out first" –
there certainly are plenty to choose from, with 924 across the country.*

### Travelodge/Viscount*
| 13 | 13 | 11 | 11 | $64 |
|---|---|---|---|---|

(800) 255-3050

*M – If "typical" "basic lodging" is your need, these bare-bones hotels are
"not bad for the price" and "ok for a brief stay"; our more demanding
surveyors complain of "old beds", "thin sheets" and "poor service"
concluding it "shouldn't even be an option."*

### Westin
| 22 | 21 | 20 | 21 | $150 |
|---|---|---|---|---|

(800) 228-3000

*U – "Always acceptable and sometimes excellent", this international chain
is "still not abundant" (just 30 stateside locations); they generally offer
"large", "attractive rooms", "attentive staff", "some terrific restaurants",
"good locations" and "top-quality amenities" that can take the sting out of
a grueling business trip; in sum, "a professional organization with pride."*

### Wyndham
| 20 | 20 | 18 | 19 | $120 |
|---|---|---|---|---|

(800) 822-4200

*M – This 37-unit Dallas-based chain is trying to upgrade its image; while
it elicits diverse comments ranging from "unpleasant" to "really first class";
solid scores seem to indicate that the company is achieving its goals,
and its new Wyndham Gardens Hotels are establishing a reputation for
solid value.*

# ALPHABETICAL
# DIRECTORY OF
# HOTELS BY CITY

# TOP 50 U.S. HOTELS*

## (In order of rating)

| | | |
|---|---|---|
| **27** – | Windsor Court Hotel | New Orleans |
| | Mansion on Turtle Creek | Dallas |
| | Hotel Bel-Air | Los Angeles |
| | Sherman House | San Francisco |
| | Halekulani | Honlolulu |
| | Ritz-Carlton, Laguna Niguel | Orange County |
| **26** – | Four Seasons | Chicago |
| | Ritz-Carlton, Buckhead | Atlanta |
| | Ritz-Carlton | Houston |
| | Ritz-Carlton, Huntington | Los Angeles |
| | Ritz-Carlton | San Francisco |
| | Four Seasons | Boston |
| | Four Seasons | Philadelphia |
| | Phoenician | Phoenix/Scottsdale |
| | Four Seasons | Los Angeles |
| | Ritz-Carlton | Chicago |
| **25** – | Peninsula Beverly Hills | Los Angeles |
| | Hotel Crescent Court | Dallas |
| | Ritz-Carlton | Philadelphia |
| | Ritz-Carlton | St. Louis |
| | Ritz-Carlton, Rancho Mirage | Palm Springs |
| | Ritz-Carlton | Phoenix/Scottsdale |
| | Four Seasons | Dallas |
| | Mandarin Oriental | San Francisco |
| | Grand Bay Hotel | Miami/Miami Beach |
| | Kahala Hilton | Honolulu |
| | Omni | Houston |
| | Four Seasons, Newport Beach | Orange County |
| | Ritz-Carlton, Marina del Rey | Los Angeles |
| | Regent Beverly Wilshire | Los Angeles |
| | Four Seasons Olympic | Seattle |
| | Hotel Plaza Athenee | New York City |
| | Ritz-Carlton | Atlanta |

---

*Based on overall ratings derived by averaging ratings for rooms, service, dining and public facilities, this list excludes places with voting too low to be reliable.

| | |
|---|---|
| Four Seasons | Washington, D.C. |
| Ritz-Carlton, Pentagon City | Washington, D.C. |
| Scottsdale Princess | Phoenix/Scottsdale |
| Four Seasons | Houston |
| Disney's Grand Floridian | Orlando |
| 24 – Hyatt Regency Grand Cypress | Orlando |
| St. Regis | New York City |
| Ritz-Carlton | Kansas City |
| Hotel Nikko | Atlanta |
| Four Seasons Hotel | Austin |
| Ritz-Carlton | Cleveland |
| La Colombe d'Or | Houston |
| Boston Harbor Hotel | Boston |
| Turnberry Isle Club | Miami/Miami Beach |
| Willard Inter-Continental | Washington, D.C. |
| Carlyle | New York City |

# ATLANTA†

## TOP HOTELS
## (In order of rating)

### BEST OVERALL

26 – Ritz-Carlton, Buckhead
25 – Ritz-Carlton, Atlanta
24 – Nikko Atlanta
22 – Swissotel Atlanta
    J.W. Marriott at Lenox
    Stouffer Waverly
21 – Evergreen Conf. Ctr.
20 – Aberdeen Woods Center

### BEST VALUES

Courtyard by Marriott
Marriott Suites Perimeter
Embassy Suites Perim. Ctr.
Holiday Inn Crowne Plaza
Holiday Inn Buckhead
Swissotel Atlanta
Doubletree at Concourse
Terrace Garden Inn

\*      \*      \*

### Best Rooms

26 – Ritz-Carlton, Buckhead
25 – Ritz-Carlton, Atlanta
    Nikko Atlanta
23 – J.W. Marriott at Lenox
    Swissotel Atlanta
22 – Stouffer Waverly
    Marriott Suites Perimeter
21 – Marque of Atlanta

### Best Dining

26 – Ritz-Carlton, Buckhead
24 – Ritz-Carlton, Atlanta
23 – Hotel Nikko Atlanta
22 – Swissotel
    Stouffer Waverly
20 – J.W. Marriott at Lenox
19 – Peachtree Exec. Conf. Ctr.
    Westin Peachtree Plaza

### Best Service

27 – Ritz-Carlton, Buckhead
26 – Ritz-Carlton, Atlanta
24 – Nikko Atlanta
22 – Swissotel Atlanta
21 – J.W. Marriott at Lenox
    Stouffer Waverly
20 – Peachtree Exec. Conf. Ctr.
19 – Doubletree at Concourse

### Best Public Facilities

26 – Ritz-Carlton, Buckhead
25 – Nikko Atlanta
24 – Ritz-Carlton, Atlanta
23 – Evergreen Conf. Ctr.
    Aberdeen Woods Center
22 – Stouffer Waverly
    J.W. Marriott at Lenox
21 – Swissotel Atlanta

†For restaurants, see *Zagat Atlanta Restaurant Survey*.

## ATLANTA HOTELS

| R | S | D | P | $ |
|---|---|---|---|---|

**Aberdeen Woods Conference Center\*** 150R   | 18 | 21 | 21 | 23 | $121 |
201 Aberdeen Pkwy., Peachtree City; (404) 487-2666; FAX 487-1063
*U – "Heaven for meetings", this Marriott conference center with "college dorm
rooms" has a "good, casual atmosphere" for retreats; reviewers praise its
"comfort food" and "outstanding staff", and are glad it's expanding in 1993.*


**Ansley Inn** 33R (2S)   | – | – | – | – | M |
253 15th St. NE; (800) 446-5416; (404) 872-9000; FAX 892-2318
*This charming Tudor mansion built in 1907 in the historic Ansley Park area
is a quiet bed-and-breakfast for those doing business in the Midtown area;
the pleasant staff attends to your every need, and rooms – some with
fireplaces and four-posters – have cable TVs, wet bars and whirlpool
baths; in sum, this is an unusually nice alternative to the modern chains.*


**Atlanta Hilton & Towers** 1224R (40S)   | 18 | 18 | 17 | 18 | $126 |
255 Courtland St. NE; (800) HILTONS; (404) 659-2000; FAX 222-2967
*M – "Southern hospitality" is praised by some, but others complain that
despite the "soaring Atlanta atrium-style architecture", this big, "standard
Downtown hotel" "needs to be remodeled"; it offers "nice gym facilities", a
MARTA connection to the airport, and the "popular" Nikolai's rooftop restaurant
with city views, but the consensus is "not good, not bad – just a Hilton."*


**Atlanta Marriott Marquis** 1674R (64S)   | 20 | 19 | 18 | 20 | $135 |
265 Peachtree Ctr. Ave.; (800) 228-9290; (404) 521-0000; FAX 586-6299
*U – "Wow" say reviewers about the "cavernous" atrium lobby at this
popular convention hotel – it's the world's largest; the location near
Underground Atlanta and sports complexes is a plus; "flashy", "first-class"
and recently renovated, it's called a "space odyssey", and with conference
capacity for 3,000, it's a regular meeting machine.*


**Atlanta Marriott Perimeter Center** 400R (4S)   | 18 | 18 | 16 | 18 | $105 |
246 Perimeter Ctr. Pkwy.; (800) 228-9290; (404) 303-7202; FAX 913-9440
*M – "Southern hospitality abounds" at this midsize hotel in the growing
Perimeter Business District; it has pools and a game room (only one
restaurant) and "great shopping nearby", but detractors say this "very
average" place is a "cookie-cutter hotel."*

# ATLANTA HOTELS

| R | S | D | P | $ |

**Atlanta Penta Hotel\***   504R (24S)      | 18 | 18 | 17 | 15 | $118 |
(fka Sheraton)
590 W. Peachtree St. NW; (800) 633-0000; (404) 881-6000; FAX 815-5010
*M – Despite a recent management change and renovation, critics claim
this business hotel near the convention center is "standard throughout",
and despite the balconies, there's "nothing special about the rooms"
(although four suites have private pools, and much of the place has
wheelchair access); the service gets the most praise.*

**Biltmore Suites, The** 60S (fka Biltmore Inn)    | – | – | – | – | M |
30 Fifth St. NE; (800) 822-0824; (404) 874-0824; FAX 874-2913
*This classic Georgian inn, built in 1924 in the heart of Downtown Atlanta,
has been converted to a small all-suites hotel with full kitchens; details like
10-foot ceilings, crown moldings and exposed brick walls are combined
with modern appointments and whirlpool baths; "nice rooms", to say the
least, plus a new meeting area, free shuttle, complimentary breakfast and
interesting packages make it appealing for long stays.*

**Courtyard by Marriott**   129R (20S)      | 20 | 18 | 14 | 17 | $80 |
5601 Peachtree-Dunwoody Rd.; (800) 321-2211; (404) 843-2300; FAX 851-1938
*U – "A great combination of service and price" is offered at this "clean,
comfortable, functional and convenient" "cookie-cutter" hotel on Atlanta's
northern perimeter; a fine health club, free parking, "fantastic views" and
"comfy beds" are praised, but critics put it down as "sterile."*

**Doubletree Hotel at Concourse**   370R (21S)   | 20 | 19 | 17 | 19 | $108 |
7 Concourse Pkwy.; (800) 528-0444; (404) 395-3900; FAX 395-3918
*U – A much-praised health club (next door, for a small fee) and "great
chocolate-chip cookies" are counterbalancing trademarks at this recently
renovated, "beautifully decorated" North Atlanta hotel "near the Perimeter
Mall" between Sandy Springs and Dunwoody; its "lovely setting" with
jogging trails is "easy to take."*

**Embassy Suites Perimeter Center**   225S     | 20 | 18 | 15 | 18 | $98 |
1030 Crown Pointe Pkwy.; (800) 362-2779; (404) 394-5454; FAX 396-5167
*U – This popular midsize suburban all-suites hotel "packs amenities business-
people love", including complimentary breakfast and cocktails; families say
it's "good to have the extra room during long stays."*

**Evergreen Conference**    | 20 | 21 | 21 | 21 | $132 |
**Center & Resort\***  249R (11S)
Stone Mountain Park, 1 Lakeview Dr., Stone Mountain; (800) 722-1000;
(404) 879-9900; FAX 469-9013
*U – "Beautiful grounds" and "pretty views" are pluses at this "luxurious"
lakeside conference center on 3,200 acres of parkland, offering 27 holes
of golf, "a good working environment" and a "very good" buffet; it's a great
place for a weekend getaway, but one can't help but wonder why
"everything is green, including the soap and towels."*

**French Quarter Suites Hotel\***  155S   | 18 | 18 | 17 | 16 | $102 |
2780 Whitley Rd.; (800) 843-5858; (404) 980-1900; FAX 980-1528
*M – Lots of honeymooners frequent this New Orleans–style suburban
all-suites hotel – maybe that's because newlyweds don't care so much
about an atmosphere that less-romantic surveyors call "dark, dull and
musty", and focus on the double-size whirlpool bath in each room; a
weekend jazz band helps make this a "good value."*

**Holiday Inn Buckhead**  221R (11S)   | 17 | 16 | 15 | 14 | $89 |
3340 Peachtree Rd.; (800) 241-7078; (404) 231-1234; FAX 231-5236
*U – "Disappointingly tacky" to some, to fans this "better-than-typical
Holiday Inn" offers good value and proximity to Buckhead businesses and
shopping; "institutional" atmosphere doesn't inspire more than "average"
comments from reviewers; current renovation should perk the place up.*

**Holiday Inn Crowne Plaza Ravinia**  492R (43S)  | 19 | 17 | 15 | 19 | $99 |
(fka Hyatt Regency Ravinia)
4355 Ashford-Dunwoody Rd.; (800) HOLIDAY; (404) 395-7700; FAX 392-9864
*U – "Exotic birds in the lobby" are the most striking feature of this North
Atlanta suburban hotel; aside from the tropical atrium, it features "great
trails for hiking", a "nice" indoor pool and "good service"; some say it's "still
a Holiday Inn at heart", but a recent $4 million renovation has spruced up
its guest rooms.*

**HOTEL NIKKO ATLANTA**  440R (21S)   | 25 | 24 | 23 | 25 | $152 |
3300 Peachtree Rd.; (800) NIKKO-US; (404) 365-8100; FAX 233-5686
*U – This "world-class", "exceptionally beautiful" Buckhead hotel is giving
the neighboring Ritz-Carlton a run for its money; it offers "delicate simplicity",
with a "cold, crisp Oriental efficiency", and its "wonderful service", sweeping
views, top restaurants, Cassis (Continental) and Kamogawa (Japanese),
three concierge floors and three-story outdoor Japanese gardens – complete
with waterfall – account for its high ratings.*

**Hyatt Regency Atlanta**   1278R (56S)      | 20 | 19 | 18 | 20 | $132 |
265 Peachtree St.; (800) 233-1234; (404) 577-1234; FAX 588-4137
*M – Still offering "the best elevator ride in America", this "granddaddy" of
all Hyatt atrium hotels, designed by John Portman, has "'70s architecture
that's still cool in the '90s"; some praise the "old South service", others
report it's "erratic"; critics say "noisy", others note the "beautifully appointed
rooms" and "good" Downtown location; a recent face-lift makes a difference.*

**J.W. Marriott at Lenox**   371R (43S)      | 23 | 21 | 20 | 22 | $130 |
3300 Lenox Rd. NE; (800) 228-9290; (404) 262-3344; FAX 262-8603
*M – An "excellent" midsize suburban business hotel next to Lenox Square
shopping and the MARTA rail station, this less-refined competitor of the Ritz-
Carlton is "comfortable, well located and quiet", with "a great view of the city."*

**Lanier Plaza Hotel &**                     | 19 | 18 | 17 | 16 | $116 |
**Conference Center***   349R (13S)
415 Armour Dr. NE; (800) 554-8444; (404) 873-4661; FAX 872-1292
*M – Opinions vary about this moderately priced establishment that's big on
training seminars; some feel it "makes Howard Johnson look upscale", but
others claim it's "a great place to do business" and perfectly "ok", with
"good" accommodations – including suites with fireplaces.*

**Marque of Atlanta**   278R (122S)          | 21 | 19 | 17 | 16 | $104 |
(fka Guest Quarters – Perimeter Center)
111 Perimeter Ctr. W.; (800) 683-6100; (404) 396-6800; FAX 399-5514
*U – "All the comforts of home", including china, glassware and an ironing
board in "spacious, clean" suites (many of which have full kitchens, too),
make this suburban hotel a "good place to crash" for "long-term stays";
the "staff goes out of its way" and "gets the job done."*

**Marriott Suites Atlanta Midtown***   254S   | 21 | 19 | 15 | 17 | $104 |
35 14th St.; (800) 228-9290; (404) 876-8888; FAX 876-7727
*M – "Homey" and "comfortable", this new Midtown all-suiter near MARTA
and the Arts Center has recently doubled its meeting space; some praise,
others pan, the service, but the "gracious", low-key atmosphere is an
alternative to its glitzy Downtown hotel neighbors.*

**Marriott Suites Perimeter**   224S          | 22 | 18 | 14 | 18 | $100 |
6120 Peachtree-Dunwoody Rd.; (800) 228-9290; (404) 668-0808; FAX 668-0008
*U – How suite it is at this "comfortable" and "relaxing" Perimeter hotel, which
is perfect for "overnight recharging"; "light and airy" rooms are "great" to
work in, and special packages and price deals make it a notable "value";
as ratings reflect, you don't come here to eat.*

# ATLANTA HOTELS

| R | S | D | P | $ |

**Omni Hotel at CNN Center**  465R (12S)  | 19 | 18 | 17 | 18 | $132 |
100 CNN Ctr.; (800) THE-OMNI; (404) 659-0000; FAX 525-5050
*M – "Reminiscent of Gone With the Wind" – or at least near its continuous showings – this "massive" convention hotel is located within a huge enclosed mall housing Turner Broadcasting, and near the new Georgia Dome; to a few it's a "tony cattle pen for conventioneers"; to most it's "comfortable and pleasant."*

**Peachtree Executive**  | 21 | 20 | 19 | 21 | $141 |
**Conference Center**  250R (3S)
2443 Hwy. 54 W., Peachtree City; (800) 732-2411; (404) 478-2000; FAX 487-4428
*U – The "lagoon in the lobby out-Hyatts Hyatt" at this contemporary Southside conference center, but it's so far from Downtown "you could be In Cleveland"; glass elevators and "Portman overkill" abound, but "superb accommodations", golf and lots of activities help make it popular with meeting planners – "a peach."*

**Radisson Hotel Atlanta**  754R (22S)  | 16 | 15 | 15 | 14 | $97 |
Courtland St. & Int'l Blvd.; (800) 333-3333; (404) 659-6500; FAX 524-1259
*M – Still not up to the standard of other Radissons, this motelish Downtowner gets bad-mouthed by reviewers who say it "looks like a basement" and is "nothing special"; some do praise the "busy, attractive lobby", but most advise "shop for better."*

**Ramada Hotel Dunwoody***  390R (24S)  | 15 | 14 | 15 | 18 | $92 |
(fka Dunwoody Hotel & Conference Center)
1850 Cotillion Dr.; (800) 272-6232; (404) 394-5000; FAX 394-5114
*M – This low-priced conference facility, which has changed hands several times in the past few years, offers "great prices" and a "nice area" with convenience to the Perimeter Highway and Business District, but its middling scores indicate that our surveyors are underwhelmed by it.*

**RITZ-CARLTON, ATLANTA**  447R (22S)  | 25 | 26 | 24 | 24 | $171 |
181 Peachtree St.; (800) 241-3333; (404) 659-0400; FAX 688-0400
*U – "Southern hospitality in a world-class wrapper" is yours at this "wonderful hotel", which our surveyors say is "the best Downtown"; reasons range from "luxurious accommodations" and "impeccable service" to a "location that can't be beat" and "excellent food" at The Restaurant (food rating, 25) and The Cafe (food rating, 24) – even the "best ice cubes in the USA"; "top-notch" and "truly elegant."*

## ATLANTA HOTELS

| R | S | D | P | $ |
|---|---|---|---|---|

**RITZ-CARLTON, BUCKHEAD**   553R (29S)   | 26 | 27 | 26 | 26 | $174 |

3434 Peachtree Rd.; (800) 241-3333; (404) 237-2700; FAX 233-5168
*U* – *"Puttin' on the Ritz" at this midsize suburban "jewel in the middle of nowhere" delights our reviewers, who cite sumptuous "Oriental vases, flowers and carpets", a "great pool with skylights", the "shiniest lobby floors", afternoon tea and top-rated, world-class "elegant dining" at The Dining Room (food rating, 28) or the less-formal Cafe (food rating, 24) for the perfect "power brunch"; nearby Buckhead shopping is also lauded; to most it's "a little bit of England with a Southern accent."*

**Sheraton Colony Square Hotel***   461R (33S)   | 17 | 16 | 12 | 15 | $94 |

(fka Colony Square Hotel)
Peachtree & 14th Sts.; (800) 325-3535; (404) 892-6000; FAX 876-3276
*U* – *This modern, "basic business hotel" near the Arts Center "on the nice side" of Midtown is attached to a mall complex and is "well located" near the MARTA lines; it has ample meeting facilities and a nearby health club; a recent renovation freshened things up.*

**Stouffer Waverly Hotel**   521R (24S)   | 22 | 21 | 20 | 22 | $130 |

2450 Galleria Pkwy.; (800) HOTELS-1; (404) 953-4500; FAX 953-0740
*U* – *"Away from the hubbub" of Downtown and part of Atlanta's suburban Galleria complex, this "handsome" "outer-fringe" hotel offers "great meeting space", "good-size" rooms (newly renovated for $6 million), well-liked Continental fare at the Waverly Grill, and "service with a smile"; some call the "huge" public spaces "cold."*

**Summerfield Suites**   122S   | – | – | – | – | M |

760 Mt. Vernon Hwy. NE; (800) 833-4353; (404) 250-0110; FAX 250-9335
*"Homely" – in the best sense – this traditional suburban all-suites hotel has full kitchens and a complimentary continental breakfast and cocktails, all of which add up to good value for long-stayers; "charming" rooms make one reviewer compare it to another Georgia charmer: simply "Marla-velous."*

**Swissotel Atlanta**   348R (17S)   | 23 | 22 | 22 | 21 | $126 |

3391 Peachtree Rd.; (800) 253-1397; (404) 365-0065; FAX 233-7664
*U* – *An award-winning restaurant (Opus) with "smashing" Contemporary American cuisine and a less-formal cafe (Cafe Germany), "lovely rooms", "caring staff", a "fabulous spa" and European-style atmosphere and management are why this "sophisticated" new Buckhead hotel is "first-class in every way"; some find the contemporary style "stark", but most call it "elegant."*

## ATLANTA HOTELS

| R | S | D | P | $ |
|---|---|---|---|---|

**Terrace Garden Inn – Buckhead**  371R (12S)  | 18 | 18 | 17 | 18 | $104 |
3405 Lenox Rd.; (800) 241-8260; (404) 261-9250; FAX 848-7391
*U – "Low-rise and low-key", this motel-like establishment has one great virtue:
it's next to Lenox Square and Phipps Plaza – "shopping heaven"; guests praise
the "comfortable rooms and service" and "pleasant ambiance"; free parking,
weekend packages and an indoor swim/racquet center help make it a "good value."*


**Westin Peachtree Plaza, The**  1068R (48S)  | 20 | 19 | 19 | 20 | $136 |
210 Peachtree St.; (800) 228-3000; (404) 659-1400; FAX 589-7424
*M – "Pie-shaped rooms" in a round, "ludicrously tall building" with revolving
restaurants make this Downtown hotel a "wild-looking place"; the view from the
80th floor – while endless – is of "nothing in particular"; "circuslike" public rooms
and "monstrous" conventions make this, for some, a "hotel from hell", but to
others all this adds to the excitement of the place; N.B. be sure to ask for a
renovated room.*


**Wyndham Garden Hotel – Vinings***  159R (6S)  | 20 | 17 | 11 | 16 | $109 |
2857 Paces Ferry Rd.; (800) 822-4200; (404) 432-5555; FAX 436-5558
*U – Across the Chattahoochee River in a historic town outside Atlanta, this
new, turn-of-the-century-style hotel with lovely landscaped grounds has
well-appointed rooms with coffeemakers, hair dryers and well-lit work areas;
weekend rates make it a "good value" for a romantic getaway.*


**Wyndham Garden – Midtown***  191R (5S)  | 18 | 16 | 17 | 15 | $100 |
125 10th St.; (800) 822-4200; (404) 873-4800; FAX 877-7377
*U – "Great style for the price" is found at this modern Midtown high rise sibling
of the other Atlanta-area Wyndhams; some feel the lobby is "tiny", but the lobby
bar is pleasant, the rooms are efficient, and the health club includes a lap pool
and massage facilities.*


**Wyndham Perimeter Center**  143R (39S)  | – | – | – | – | E |
800 Hammond Dr. NE; (800) 822-4200; (404) 252-3344; FAX 843-1228
*Catering to business travelers and located just off I-285 in Atlanta's major
suburban corporate neighborhood, this modern, midsize low rise has attractive
rooms with desks designed for work; a connecting indoor-outdoor pool and
exercise area, lounge with fireplace and library, and complimentary shuttle
service all help to make this a comfortable destination.*


### ● OTHER HOTEL-CHAIN CHOICES
*You will find one or more additional locations of the following hotel chains in the
Atlanta area: Courtyard by Marriott, Days Inn, Embassy Suites, Hampton Inn,
Hilton, Howard Johnson, Hyatt, La Quinta Inns, Marriott, Residence Inn,
Stouffer and Travelodge/Viscount; for reservations or information, see the
toll-free 800 phone listings on page 16.*

# ATLANTIC CITY†

## TOP HOTELS
## (In order of rating)

### BEST OVERALL

22 – Marriott's Seaview
19 – Bally's Grand
    Harrah's Marina
18 – Trump Castle
    Caesars
    Trump Taj Mahal

### BEST VALUES

Harrah's Marina
TropWorld
Bally's Grand
Sands Hotel
Caesars
Marriott's Seaview

\*    \*    \*

### Best Rooms

22 – Marriott's Seaview
21 – Bally's Grand
20 – Harrah's Marina
19 – Trump Taj Mahal
    Bally's Park Place
    Trump Castle

### Best Dining

21 – Marriott's Seaview
18 – Harrah's Marina
    Bally's Grand
    Caesars
    Trump Castle
17 – Sands Hotel

### Best Service

22 – Marriott's Seaview
19 – Bally's Grand
    Harrah's Marina
18 – Caesars
17 – Trump Castle
    Trump Taj Mahal

### Best Public Facilities

22 – Marriott's Seaview
19 – Bally's Grand
18 – Trump Taj Mahal
    Harrah's Marina
    Trump Castle
17 – Caesars

---

†For restaurants, see *Zagat Atlantic City Restaurant Survey.*

**Bally's Grand Hotel & Casino**  518R (160S)  | 21 | 19 | 18 | 19 | $126 |
Boston & Pacific Aves.; (800) 257-8677; (609) 347-7111; FAX 340-4858
*M – Our surveyors like the fact that Bally's second, smaller casino hotel,
located at the southern end of the Boardwalk "away from the honky tonk",
"doesn't have the feel of a large hotel"; early risers rave about the breakfast
buffet but warn "you'll starve before they seat you"; suites are "overblown
and tacky but fun", but be wary of standard rooms that are "small with
poor ventilation"; the best dining bet is the steak-and-seafooder, The Oaks
(food rating, 23).*

**Bally's Park Place Casino**              | 19 | 17 | 16 | 17 | $127 |
**Hotel & Tower**  1300R (110S)
Park Place & Boardwalk; (800) 772-7777; (609) 340-2000; FAX 340-2595
*U – Bally's largest casino hotel still gets high marks for its lavish spa, which
offers a separate meal plan and exercise regimen; "well-appointed" rooms
in the hotel's new tower offer "views second to none", our surveyors
suggest that some are already "starting to look a little worn" – but they're
better than the "small, dark and uncomfortable" quarters in the older
section; while service overall is "good", the "front desk is a nightmare."*

**Caesars Atlantic City**  636R (26S)      | 18 | 18 | 18 | 17 | $121 |
2100 Pacific Ave.; (800) 257-8555; (609) 348-4411; FAX 348-8830
*M – "You get the rush of a gambling hotel" at this "excessive" casino hotel
that's a "poor copy of Caesars in Vegas"; it's a bastion of "cheesy decor"
and "plastic glitz", with "tremendous statues in the hallways"; still, some
find it "opulent" and "one-of-a-kind"; its center-of-the-Boardwalk location a
block from the convention center is a plus, as is the "really splendid buffet";
service, especially for the high rollers, is "the royal treatment all the way."*

**Claridge Casino Hotel**  501R (73S)      | 17 | 17 | 15 | 15 | $113 |
Indiana Ave. & Boardwalk; (800) 257-8585; (609) 340-3400; FAX 340-3875
*M – Atlantic City's smallest casino hotel, located one block from the
Boardwalk facing Brighton Park, is "slightly less tacky" than the competition
but still has rooms that are "dark, dreary and dysfunctional"; while some
call it "second-rate", the lower prices, "varied" restaurants and "pleasant
staff working hard to please" are "like the old Atlantic City, and that's nice."*

## ATLANTIC CITY HOTELS

| R | S | D | P | $ |

**Harrah's Marina Hotel & Casino**  750R (240S)  | 20 | 19 | 18 | 18 | $108 |
1725 Brigantine Blvd.; (800) 2HARRAHS; (609) 441-5000; FAX 344-2974
*M – A mile and a half away from the Boardwalk -- and proud of it – this massive self-contained universe on the Absecon Channel sports its own marina; it gets raves for the views from the guest rooms ("lovely" and "luxurious" if you "spend the extra bucks" for the Atrium Tower, small and "Holiday Inn"–like if you don't) and for its top-notch French eatery, The Meadows (food rating, 25); most find Harrah's "friendlier" and more "family oriented" than the Boardwalk places, but being "off the Boardwalk is a drawback" if you want to spread your bets around.*

**Holiday Inn Diplomat***  220R (8S)  | 14 | 12 | 12 | 9 | $106 |
(fka Diplomat Hotel)
Chelsea Ave. & Boardwalk; (800) 548-3030; (609) 348-2200; FAX 345-5110
*M – Though "clean and modern", the Diplomat falls short of its competition in just about every other area; a half-block from the Boardwalk and the beach, it's connected to TropWorld by skywalk; with lower prices and a less frenetic pace, it's adequate for business travelers on a budget and families who want to be near the casinos but not in them.*

**Marriott's Seaview Resort**  299R (34S)  | 22 | 22 | 21 | 22 | $147 |
401 S. New York Rd., Absecon; (800) 228-9290; (609) 652-1800; FAX 652-2307
*U – With two on-site golf courses, you might expect that "golfers prevail" at this former private club, now a "graceful", "quiet" resort in a "serene" setting on the mainland, 15 minutes away from Atlantic City – nongolfers enjoy free shuttle service to the casinos; "smallish" rooms in the older wing "feel like an old folks' home" and are not as good as those in the newer wing, but the food and service get better marks than anywhere else in town.*

**Merv Griffin's Resorts**  | 16 | 16 | 15 | 16 | $111 |
**Hotel & Casino**  722R (53S)
1133 Boardwalk; (800) 336-MERV; (609) 344-6000; FAX 340-6349
*M – Atlantic City's first casino hotel (the renovated Haddon Hall) now under the ownership of entertainer Merv Griffin, "still needs work" according to our surveyors, who complain of "peeling paint" and "dingy rooms" in a building that's "worn, outdated and cheap"; then why is it "so crowded"? -- "good location", "five-cent slot machines", reasonable room rates and a buffet that's one of the cheapest in town.*

## ATLANTIC CITY HOTELS     | R | S | D | P | $ |

**Sands Hotel & Casino**   500R (50S)     | 17 | 17 | 17 | 16 | $111 |
Indiana Ave. & Brighton Park; (800) 257-8580; (609) 441-4000; FAX 441-4180
*M – Visitors are unusually undecided about this "older hotel on the
Boardwalk in the middle of the action"; detractors (in the majority, it seems)
say it's "overpriced" and "trying unsuccessfully to keep up with the big
guys", while boosters think it's "the best hotel in Atlantic City"; special
mention for the Plaza Club concept, with its "personal staff", "beautiful"
suites and "private keys" (other rooms are "a bore").*

**Showboat Hotel Casino**   516R (90S)     | 18 | 17 | 15 | 17 | $117 |
Boardwalk at Delaware & Pacific Aves.; (800) 621-0200; (609) 343-4000;
FAX 345-2334
*M – At the northern end of the Boardwalk in the shadow of the Taj, this
nautically themed hotel/casino (still the only one in town with its own
bowling alley) is deemed "too carnival-like" and "trying to improve but still
strictly small-time"; fans and families like the "friendly, fun atmosphere", but
critics suggest "if you're going to lose money, do it in better surroundings."*

**TropWorld Casino &**                     | 17 | 17 | 15 | 16 | $104 |
**Entertainment Resort**     1014R (300S)
Brighton Ave. & Boardwalk; (800) 843-8767; (609) 340-4000; FAX 340-4295
*M – "Coney Island lives" at TropWorld's indoor Tivoli Pier amusement park,
with its impressive Ferris wheel and quickie roller coaster – there's "more
here for kids than at any other AC hotel"; adults, however, may find it "very
glitzy, gaudy and loud", "but not out of place"; the "ocean-view rooms are
delightful", but service varies: "they knocked themselves out" vs. "clueless."*

**Trump Castle Resort**   703R (95S)     | 19 | 17 | 18 | 18 | $123 |
Huron Ave. & Brigantine Blvd.; (800) 365-8786; (609) 441-2000;
FAX 441-8541
*U – Across Brigantine Boulevard about a mile and a quarter from the
Boardwalk, this "glitzier" neighbor of Harrah's is connected to the Farley State
Marina by an enclosed skywalk and offers summertime sightseeing by boat,
and berths for gamblers and their yachts; though some think it's "all show
and no substance", for most this is an "all-around nice place to stay", with
"comfortable" rooms, "convenient parking" and a "flashy" lobby and casino.*

## ATLANTIC CITY HOTELS

| R | S | D | P | $ |

**Trump Plaza Hotel & Casino**  556R (74S)  | 18 | 17 | 16 | 17 | $126 |
Mississippi Ave. at Boardwalk; (800) 677-RESV; (609) 441-6000; FAX 441-6249
*M – The most "convenient casino hotel to Convention Hall" – access is
from an enclosed walkway – this "noisy and impersonal" place gets mixed
reviews for everything else; fans say it's "more upscale and elegant" than
most, with "good restaurants", an "above-average spa" and "glamorous"
atmosphere; but for others it's "commercial and cold"; N.B. Ivana's (food
rating, 24) restaurant is well known locally and considered very good.*

**Trump Regency Hotel**  500R (24S)  | 15 | 14 | 13 | 13 | $113 |
Virginia Ave. & Boardwalk; (800) 234-5678; (609) 344-4000; FAX 344-1377
*U – The former Atlantis Casino Hotel and now part of Donald Trump's AC
dynasty, this casino-free hotel has one thing going for it: location – it's right
on the Boardwalk and adjoins the Convention Hall (via a rather grim stairwell);
although some of our surveyors consider it "good for just a room without a
casino", to most it's "tired", "dumpy" and "overpriced."*

**Trump Taj Mahal**  | 19 | 17 | 16 | 18 | $130 |
**Casino & Resort**  1250R (270S)
2500 Boardwalk; (800) 825-8786; (609) 449-1000; FAX 449-6818
*U – The biggest and most expensive casino hotel in Atlantic City – and,
quite possibly, the world – the "tacky" Taj is "wonderfully silly", with a "touch
too much glitter and glitz", but "what a showplace!"; the scale is so huge
that "you can die walking from one end of the casino to the other", and the
public areas are "so crowded that you fall over all the people" gawking;
there's so much "flashy fun" that it's easy to forget that it's "a cut above"
"sultan Donald's" other digs.*

## ● OTHER HOTEL-CHAIN CHOICES
*You will find one or more additional locations of the following hotel chains in
the Atlantic City area: Days Inn, Hampton Inn, Howard Johnson, Ramada,
Residence Inn and Travelodge/Viscount; for reservations or information,*
*see the toll-free 800 phone listings on page 16.*

# BALTIMORE†

## TOP HOTELS
### (In order of rating)

### BEST OVERALL

24 – Harbor Court
22 – Peabody Court
20 – Stouffer Harborplace
19 – Hyatt Regency
    Sheraton Inner Harbor
    Admiral Fell Inn

### BEST VALUES

Marriott's Hunt Valley
Sheraton Baltimore North
Admiral Fell Inn
Cross Keys Inn
Stouffer Harborplace
Peabody Court

\*     \*     \*

### Best Rooms

25 – Harbor Court
22 – Peabody Court
    Stouffer Harborplace
21 – Admiral Fell Inn
20 – Hyatt Regency
    Baltimore Marriott Inner Harbor

### Best Dining

23 – Harbor Court
    Peabody Court
19 – Stouffer Harborplace
18 – Hyatt Regency
    Sheraton Inner Harbor
    Marriott's Hunt Valley

### Best Service

24 – Harbor Court
22 – Peabody Court
21 – Stouffer Harborplace
20 – Hyatt Regency
19 – Sheraton Baltimore North
    Sheraton Inner Harbor

### Best Public Facilities

24 – Harbor Court
21 – Stouffer Harborplace
    Peabody Court
19 – Hyatt Regency
    Sheraton Baltimore North
    Sheraton Inner Harbor

---

†For restaurants, see *Zagat Washington D.C./Baltimore Restaurant Survey.*

**Admiral Fell Inn**  37R

| 21 | 19 | 17 | 18 | $111 |

888 S. Broadway; (800) 292-INNS; (410) 522-7377; FAX 522-0707
*U – A "romantic", "quaint" inn with modern conveniences; its "hip" Fells Point locale retains the salty flavor of the "original Baltimore harbor" (but also echoes its rowdy nighttime bar scene); you can sleep in a four-poster bed, have a drink in the cozy pub and "catch a reading of Dickens's* A Christmas Carol *in the lobby" in season – and still be "near Baltimore sites" and Downtown businesses.*

**Baltimore Marriott Inner Harbor**  525R (26S)

| 20 | 19 | 17 | 18 | $124 |

110 S. Eutaw St.; (800) 228-9290; (410) 962-0202; FAX 962-8585
*M – The "opening of Camden Yards" (home of the Orioles) made this neighboring convention hotel "the place for visiting teams (and out-of-town fans) to stay"; since it's also near the Civic Center and relatively near the aquarium, Harborplace and the convention center, it stays "very busy" year-round despite what strikes some as "lackluster" rooms, spotty service and "boring" public spaces.*

**Brookshire Hotel**  90S

| 18 | 19 | 16 | 14 | $116 |

120 E. Lombard St.; (800) 647-0013; (410) 625-1300; FAX 625-0912
*U – Try this Business District all-suiter "when the major hotels are sold out" – it's well-intentioned, "well-appointed" and "very convenient to Harborplace"; if you're in the mood for pasta, there's a penthouse restaurant, or better still, take the trolley outside to nearby Little Italy.*

**Celie's Waterfront Bed-and-Breakfast**  7R

| – | – | – | – | M |

1714 Thames St.; (410) 522-2323
*Seek out this antique-filled bed-and-breakfast in historic Fells Point for a delightful change of pace; a roof deck overlooking the seaport, private balconies, whirlpools and a cloistered garden explain why it's the "summum bonum" of its genre; N.B. they go out of their way for handicapped travelers.*

**Clarion Hotel – Inner Harbor***  71R (5S)

| 20 | 18 | 18 | 20 | $111 |

(fka Harrison's Pier 5)
711 Eastern Ave.; (800) 252-7466; (410) 783-5553; FAX 783-1787
*M – Staying at this seaport hotel–restaurant–shopping complex beside the aquarium can feel like sailing on an ocean liner (minus seasickness); the experience includes a "beautiful view", smallish rooms, and seasonal dining on fishing boats docked pierside; though only a few years old, it shows "signs of wear."*

**Cross Keys Inn**   148R (16S)     | 19 | 18 | 16 | 18 | $108 |
5100 Falls Rd.; (800) 532-KEYS; (410) 532-6900; FAX 532-2403
*U – This mecca for shoppers, racing buffs and "power-breakfasters" is set
in a large, boutique-filled complex near Pimlico Racetrack, with highway
access to the rest of town; it underwent a much-needed makeover in late
'92, updating "the '70s decor" but keeping its "feel-at-home" appeal and
pleasant service; locals like it for brunch and "professional meetings."*


**Doubletree Inn at the Colonnade**  125R (30S)  | – | – | – | – |  M  |
(fka Inn at the Colonnade)
4 W. University Pkwy.; (800) 456-3396; (410) 837-3630; FAX 837-4654
*Well known locally for its see-and-be-seen bar and restaurant power
scene, this classy, easy-to-reach hotel/condominium across from the Johns
Hopkins campus offers luxurious rooms with spa bathrooms, executive
work areas and excellent conference and banquet facilities.*


**HARBOR COURT HOTEL**   203R (25S)     | 25 | 24 | 23 | 24 | $162 |
550 Light St.; (800) 824-0076; (410) 234-0550; FAX 659-5925
*U – Rated No. 1 in Baltimore in nearly all categories, this is a "favorite of
international travelers", who consider it "one of the best hotels in the
country"; its "splendid" lobby and "roomy", "comfortable" guest rooms with
"commanding views" of the Inner Harbor from upper floors, "wonderful
service" and "stylish" Contemporary American food at the "formal" Hampton's
(food rating, 26) win near-universal praise; weekend bargains tempt
Baltimoreans to vacation close to home.*


**Hyatt Regency Baltimore**   489R (26S)     | 20 | 20 | 18 | 19 | $133 |
300 Light St.; (800) 233-1234; (410) 528-1234; FAX 685-3362
*M – "A slick, practical Hyatt" distinguished by an ideal location bridging
Harborplace and the convention center, a "wonderful VIP floor" and a
"great" rooftop bar and restaurant, Berry & Elliot's (food rating, 18)
"overlooking all that's worth seeing in Baltimore"; assessments range from
"solid convention hotel" to "rough around the edges", "weird-shaped
rooms" and "too much chrome."*


**Inn at Henderson's Wharf**  72R (34S)     | – | – | – | – |  M  |
1000 Fell St.; (800) 522-2088; (410) 522-7777; FAX 522-7087
*Those few surveyors who have discovered this Fells Point delight rave
about the "absolutely beautiful waterfront location, gorgeous furnishings"
and formal English garden; it combines in-town convenience, "comfortable
rooms", corporate amenities and small-hotel charm.*

## BALTIMORE HOTELS | R | S | D | P | $ |

**Johns Hopkins Inn, The\***   145R (6S)   | 14 | 14 | 11 | 11 | $106 |
400 N. Broadway; (800) 858-1700; (410) 675-6800; FAX 276-1131
*M – "When one needs to be close" to Johns Hopkins Hospital across the
street, this hotel is "serviceable", offering a "cordial" welcome and low tariff;
however, the not-so-hot ratings for service, food and comfort confirm one
surveyor's quip that it's "no place to recuperate."*

**Marriott's Hunt Valley Inn**   392R (8S)   | 19 | 19 | 18 | 18 | $102 |
245 Shawan Rd., Hunt Valley; (800) 228-9290; (410) 785-7000; FAX 785-0341
*U – The fast-growing Hunt Valley area's need for conference and convention
facilities is met by the area's No. 1 "best value", a "sprawling" "resort-type
complex"; weekdays, it's filled with "too many product managers", but on
weekends it's a "painless visit" for families; in sum, it's good but "a yawner."*

**Omni Inner Harbor Hotel**   702R (19S)   | 18 | 17 | 16 | 16 | $120 |
101 W. Fayette St.; (800) THE-OMNI; (410) 752-1100; FAX 752-0832
*M – It's "a long walk to Inner Harbor via the skyway" from this 1990
rehabbed "commercial hotel", but it's still a useful "Downtown location";
however, reports ranging from "hospitable" and "comfortable" to "sterile
and pretentious" signal "wild inconsistency in room quality and size";
P.S. the formal Grill Room is popular.*

**Peabody Court Hotel, The**   104R (7S)   | 22 | 22 | 23 | 21 | $148 |
612 Cathedral St.; (800) 732-5301; (410) 727-7101; FAX 789-3312
*U – A lovely grande dame with new "old-world" public spaces, "beautiful"
rooms "sealed from street noise" and a glittering view of the city lights
below Mount Vernon Square from the rooftop lounge, Peabody's Grill (food
rating, 19) and formal French restaurant, The Conservatory (food rating, 26);
although "new management" took over while this Survey was in the works,
chances are she'll keep her high ratings – after all, "class remains class."*

**Sheraton Baltimore North**   284R (3S)   | 19 | 19 | 17 | 19 | $109 |
(fka Sheraton Towson Conference Hotel)
903 Dulaney Valley Rd., Towson; (800) 433-7619; (410) 321-7400; FAX 296-9534
*U – This suburban high rise is just about the "only show in town", and a
pretty good one at that if you need a "nice place to stay" or to hold a
conference in North Baltimore; a pool and gym, "convenient shopping" in
the mall across the street and nearby restaurants augment its "regular"
convention and dining facilities.*

## BALTIMORE HOTELS | R | S | D | P | $ |

**Sheraton Inner Harbor Hotel**  339R (20S)  | 20 | 19 | 18 | 19 | $128 |
300 S. Charles St.; (800) 325-3535; (410) 962-8300; FAX 962-8211
*M – Surveyors agree that the "best things" about this "very average"
business-class hotel are its Inner Harbor "location" near the convention
center and aquarium and the "view", with an honorable mention for the
"very helpful" staff; the rooms are "comfortable", the facilities fine, and the
food is deemed "fair" – if approached with moderate expectations.*

**Society Hill Hotel**  60S  | – | – | – | – | M |
58 W. Biddle St.; (800) 676-3630; (410) 837-3630; FAX 837-4654
*This chic bed-and-breakfast across from Myerhoff Symphony Hall blends
Euro-sophistication with local charm; guest rooms are large and filled with
antiques, while downstairs there's pleasant dining.*

**Stouffer Harborplace Hotel**  622R (62S)  | 22 | 21 | 19 | 21 | $135 |
202 E. Pratt St.; (800) 468-3571; (410) 547-1200; FAX 783-9676
*U – At "one of the best of the Inner Harbor hotels", a "dynamic location"
near "food, fish, fun", plus "shops and more shops", is helped by spacious
rooms, "super service", a "great-for-kids" indoor pool and "excellent harbor
views" from the Windows Bar and Restaurant (food rating, 18); despite a
few swipes ("long corridors", "touristy"), most say "surprisingly good."*

**Tremont Hotel\***  60S  | 20 | 18 | 18 | 16 | $114 |
8 E. Pleasant St.; (800) 638-6266; (410) 576-1200; FAX 685-4215
*U – An ambiance of "calm" and "quality" pervades this "understated"
Downtown all-suiter; it's a small, "comfortable" place with personalized
service that makes it a good choice for longer stays – and a "favorite of
visiting actors" performing at the nearby Morris-Mechanic Theater; try the
"lovely, Oriental-feeling" restaurant for breakfast or a casual bite.*

**Tremont Plaza Hotel\*** 230S (aka Tremont Suite)  | 21 | 20 | 17 | 17 | $98 |
222 St. Paul Place; (800) TREMONT; (410) 727-2222; FAX 685-4215
*U – Value-conscious tourists and conventioneers willingly trade a few extra
blocks' walk to the convention center or Harborplace for "generally nice,
spacious rooms" and the feeling of "being in your own living room" at this
Center City all-suites hotel; a "good deli" and exercise room are on board.*

## ●OTHER HOTEL-CHAIN CHOICES
*You will find one or more additional locations of the following hotel chains
in the Baltimore area: Days Inn, Embassy Suites, Guest Quarters, Hampton
Inn, Hilton, Holiday Inn, Howard Johnson, Marriott, Omni, Radisson,
Ramada, and Super 8; for reservations or information, see the toll-free
800 phone listings on page 16.*

# BOSTON†

## TOP HOTELS
## (In order of rating)

### BEST OVERALL

26 – Four Seasons
25 – Ritz-Carlton
24 – Boston Harbor Hotel
22 – Le Meridien
     Bostonian
21 – Charles Hotel
     Swissotel Boston
20 – Westin Copley Place

### BEST VALUES

Boston Marriott Peabody
Cambridge Center Marriott
Boston Park Plaza
Royal Sonesta Hotel
Guest Quarters Suite Hotel
Lenox Hotel
Copley Square Hotel
Marriott Copley Place

\*     \*     \*

### Best Rooms

26 – Four Seasons
25 – Boston Harbor Hotel
     Ritz-Carlton
22 – Bostonian
     Le Meridien
     Charles Hotel
21 – Westin Copley Place
     Swissotel Boston

### Best Dining

25 – Four Seasons
24 – Ritz-Carlton
23 – Boston Harbor Hotel
     Bostonian
     Le Meridien
21 – Swissotel Boston
     Charles Hotel
20 – Copley Plaza

### Best Service

26 – Four Seasons
     Ritz-Carlton
24 – Boston Harbor Hotel
23 – Bostonian
22 – Le Meridien
21 – Swissotel Boston
     Charles Hotel
20 – Westin Copley Place

### Best Public Facilities

25 – Four Seasons
24 – Boston Harbor Hotel
     Ritz-Carlton
22 – Le Meridien
21 – Bostonian
     Charles Hotel
     Westin Copley Place
     Copley Plaza

---

†For restaurants, see *Zagat Boston Restaurant Survey.*

# BOSTON HOTELS                    | R | S | D | P | $ |

**Back Bay Hilton**   337R (3S)            | 17 | 17 | 15 | 15 | $134 |
40 Dalton St.; (800) 874-0663; (617) 236-1100; FAX 236-1506
*M – Despite "comfortable rooms", "good value" and a "central location"
near the Prudential Center and Copley Square, this business-intensive
Hilton has "never caught on" with our surveyors; perhaps that's because
it's so "average", with "ordinary" dining, merely "serviceable" facilities, the
"usual" chain amenities and service that's "not what it should be."*


**Best Western Boston\***   152R (14S)        | 14 | 15 | 12 | 11 | $104 |
342 Longwood Ave.; (800) GOT-BEST; (617) 731-4700; FAX 731-6273
*M – The main advantages offered by this small chain hotel are low rates
and a location "wonderfully convenient" to the Longwood Medical Area
and Harvard Medical School (alas, not Boston's finest neighborhood);
it's considered "comfortable" by some, but "marginally habitable" and
"claustrophobic" by others.*


**BOSTON HARBOR HOTEL**   230R (28S)       | 25 | 24 | 23 | 24 | $191 |
70 Rowes Wharf; (800) 752-7077; (617) 439-7000; FAX 330-9450
*U – "Near the water and close to perfection"; popular for business
meetings – in part because of the speedy water-shuttle service to Logan
Airport – this "gorgeous", "first-class" hostelry "captures the feel of Boston";
it affords "beautiful views" – especially from harborfront suites – "excellent
service", "very good" New England fare at Rowes Wharf (food rating, 20)
and "the best health club in Boston."*


**Bostonian Hotel, The**   152R (12S)        | 22 | 23 | 23 | 21 | $180 |
Faneuil Hall Marketplace; (800) 343-0922; (617) 523-3600; FAX 523-2454
*U — Distinguished by its European flair and philosophy, this chic, "small
and intimate" contemporary is charmingly located next to Faneuil Hall
Marketplace, near Government Center and the North End; its "rooms vary
in size" and may possess "strange angles", but the "junior suites" boast
"fireplace and whirlpool bath"; it gets high marks for "super service" and
"splendid food" at its renowned Seasons Restaurant (food rating, 26), but
"don't get a room over the fruit stands."*


**Boston Marriott Peabody**   259R (3S)       | 19 | 19 | 18 | 18 | $103 |
8A Centennial Dr., Peabody; (800) 228-9290; (508) 977-9700;
FAX 977-0297
*M – This "comfortable suburban" hotel, located in an industrial complex on
the North Shore, features all the usual facilities and "fairly new, fairly nice
rooms"; the "No. 1 best value" in the Boston area, it appeals to middle-
management types with business north of Boston, but basically it's "in the
middle of nowhere."*

# BOSTON HOTELS

**Boston Park Plaza**     | 16 | 18 | 17 | 17 | $124 |
**Hotel & Towers**   980R (20S)
64 Arlington St.; (800) 225-2008; (617) 426-2000; FAX 423-1708
*M – All the charm of Boston Common and Back Bay lie just outside the
door of this venerable, moderately priced hotel, but, alas, it "needs
redecoration ASAP"; "courteous" service ("the restaurant operators double
as babysitters") and "large, homey" rooms do much to make up for a
certain aura of "faded glory"; having Boston's favorite fish house, Legal
Seafoods, on the premises is a boon.*

**Cambridge Center Marriott**   431R (13S)   | 20 | 18 | 17 | 18 | $127 |
2 Cambridge Ctr., Cambridge; (800) 228-9290; (617) 494-6600; FAX 494-0036
*M – Adjacent to MIT, this "understated" and "well-run" high rise is
considered "a good value for a good location" – "near the universities" and
within easy reach of Downtown Boston by the MTA; though its food is
mundane, the hotel scores points for "very comfortable rooms" and "the
best concierge."*

**Charles Hotel in**     | 22 | 21 | 21 | 21 | $162 |
**Harvard Square, The**   296R (44S)
1 Bennett St., Cambridge; (800) 882-1818; (617) 864-1200; FAX 864-5715
*U – Built less than a decade ago, this stylish, well-located luxury hotel
manages to combine homey comfort (Shaker furniture and patchwork
quilts in the "pleasant", "spacious" rooms) and sophistication (a "wonderful"
jazz club, "two fine in-house restaurants", "accommodating" service and full
health club/spa facilities) in one "neat" package; it's "a first-class hotel", "far
above anything else Cambridge offers."*

**Colonnade Hotel, The**   288R (11S)   | 19 | 19 | 18 | 18 | $150 |
120 Huntington Ave.; (800) 962-3030; (617) 424-7000; FAX 424-1717
*M – Near Newbury Street, Symphony Hall and the Museum of Fine Arts,
this Back Bay contemporary with "large, beautiful rooms" is a "great bargain
in the heart of Boston"; "good dining", "nice amenities", a welcoming
"European feel", and (yes, it's true) "rubber ducks in the bathtubs" add
that "personal touch"; detractors say "ho-hum."*

**Copley Plaza Hotel, The**   373R (52S)   | 20 | 20 | 20 | 21 | $157 |
138 St. James Ave.; (800) 826-7539; (617) 267-5300; FAX 267-7668
*M – Recent renovations have "given this grande dame back some of her
former stature", though a few still insist she's "showing her age"; to her many,
many fans, she's "nicely stuffy", with "ornate and elegant" public spaces
and "sophisticated, caring service"; the "restaurant and piano bar are tops",
and a "great location" means that the rest of Boston is right here, too.*

## BOSTON HOTELS

| R | S | D | P | $ |

**Copley Square Hotel**   143R (11S)    | 18 | 18 | 17 | 17 | $131 |
47 Huntington Ave.; (800) 225-7062; (617) 536-9000; FAX 267-3547
*M – "Yes, Virginia, there is a good, moderately priced hotel in Back Bay";*
*this small, "quirky" Victorian near Exeter Street is "not elegant, but it's*
*comfortable" and has "lots of character"; "their best rooms are good –*
*others are not so great"; all in all, however, it offers a "fantastic location*
*and real value."*

**Eliot Hotel, The\***   93R (82S)    | 19 | 20 | 15 | 17 | $122 |
370 Commonwealth Ave.; (800) 443-5468; (617) 267-1607; FAX 536-9114
*M – Some of our surveyors may be annoyed by the "lack of a restaurant, a*
*gym and the other amenities of chain hotels", but the moderate prices and*
*"old-world charm" of this "touch of Paris in Beantown" – not to mention a*
*fine location in the best part of town – have won a loyal following, including*
*many guest artists who stay here when performing with the Boston*
*Symphony and the Pops.*

**FOUR SEASONS HOTEL**   288R (13S)    | 26 | 26 | 25 | 25 | $200 |
200 Boylston St.; (800) 332-3442; (617) 338-4400; FAX 482-9751
*U – Superlatives abound for this "splendid hotel in a splendid location"*
*overlooking Boston's beautiful Public Garden; whether you consider it*
*"perfect" or just "almost perfect", it's the top-rated Boston hotel in our*
*Survey; "exquisite rooms" and "exceptional formal dining" at Aujourd'hui*
*(food rating, 26) and "lovely teas" at the Bristol Lounge (food rating, 20) are*
*matched by service that "bends over backward to accommodate"; "a class*
*act across the board," though "you'd better have a liberal expense account."*

**Guest Quarters Suite Hotel**   310S    | 20 | 17 | 15 | 17 | $129 |
400 Soldiers Field Rd., Cambridge; (800) 424-2900; (617) 783-0090;
FAX 783-0189
*M – Picturesquely, if not ideally, located on the Charles – of course, the*
*river views are "stunning" – this Cambridge all-suiter offers good value on*
*clean, comfortable rooms and is rumored to be the busiest hotel in the*
*Guest Quarters chain (advance booking is thus advised); though the*
*Sunday brunch can be "awesome", you're otherwise advised to eat out;*
*"if you don't have a car, you'll wait a long time for a taxi."*

**Harvard Manor House\***   72R    | 14 | 13 | 10 | 13 | $103 |
110 Mt. Auburn St.; (800) 458-5886; (617) 864-5200; FAX 864-2409
*M – By changing two letters, the Harvard Motor House of years back*
*became the Harvard Manor House, small in size and price, long on*
*"shabby" convenience; it offers "great motel values in the middle of*
*Harvard Square", though dining is limited to a coffee shop, and other*
*amenities and service are Spartan.*

**Hyatt Regency Cambridge**   469R (33S)   | 19 | 19 | 18 | 19 | $141 |
575 Memorial Dr., Cambridge; (800) 233-1234; (617) 492-1234; FAX 491-6906
*M – On the Charles River "close to nothing but MIT", this big, pyramid-shaped
contemporary endeavors to close its location gap with a complimentary
shuttle to destinations in Boston and Cambridge; an "Ivy League atmosphere"
and "great pool area" do not compensate for food "below par" – though
there is a "great view from the restaurant"; cheers for the "striking architecture"
and "beautiful public areas" are met by jeers for "expensive parking" and
"unpredictable" service.*

**Le Meridien Boston**   326R (22S)   | 22 | 22 | 23 | 22 | $174 |
250 Franklin St.; (800) 543-4300; (617) 451-1900; FAX 423-2844
*M – A delightfully converted former Federal Reserve Bank in the midst of
Boston's Financial District, this landmark "European-style" hotel was again
updated in Renaissance revival style a few years ago; an "excellent French
restaurant", Julien (food rating, 26), "great facilities for meetings" and
"courteous service" make it "truly a delight"; still, some complain of a "cold,
distant feeling" and "small and boxy" rooms.*

**Lenox Hotel, The**   222R (3S)   | 17 | 17 | 14 | 15 | $118 |
710 Boylston St.; (800) 225-7676; (617) 536-5300; FAX 267-1237
*U – A "comfortable Downtown hotel" that offers "good value in the middle
of Boston"; it's especially praised for the "homey" corner rooms, which
"have been beautifully restored with working fireplaces"; though the dining
and service are "limited", the hotel sports a "fantastic" piano bar and
exemplary location; in short, "a bargain."*

**Marriott Copley Place**   1147R (77S)   | 20 | 20 | 18 | 20 | $146 |
110 Huntington Ave.; (800) 228-9290; (617) 236-5800; FAX 236-5885
*M – Vast and bustling, this "excellent full-service hotel" is known for "one of
the best concierge staffs in the chain" and a "convenient location attached
to a beautiful mall"; the rhapsodies over nearby Neiman-Marcus, Tiffany and
Lord & Taylor all but overwhelm praise for the "nice views from rooms", "great
health club" and "beautiful furnishings"; still, to some it remains "too big,
too modern, too corporate", i.e. "a dressed-up Marriott in an ideal locale."*

**Marriott Hotel Long Wharf**   400R (11S)   | 19 | 19 | 18 | 19 | $156 |
296 State St.; (800) 228-9290; (617) 227-0800; FAX 227-8595
*M – This waterfront hotel gets more raves for its "unbeatable" location and
"great view of the harbor" than for its dependable service and food, "smart,
modern rooms" and "festive atmosphere"; detractors say it's "overrated" and
"overpriced", but solid numbers suggest the contrary; convenient to the airport,
it's "dependable for Boston meetings", and with the aquarium and historic
North End nearby, it's also "an excellent location for a family tour of Boston."*

## BOSTON HOTELS | R | S | D | P | $ |

**Midtown Hotel\*** 160R  | 13 | 13 | 11 | 13 | $98 |
220 Huntington Ave.; (800) 343-1177; (617) 262-1000; FAX 262-8739
*U – Room prices "lower than some" make this Back Bay hotel work for the
budget-minded; a location convenient to Copley Square, Symphony Hall
and the museums, free parking and a subway stop also help compensate –
but probably not enough – for the "underwhelming" ambiance, "very poor
service" and badly rated food.*


**Omni Parker House** 541R (57S)  | 16 | 18 | 18 | 17 | $140 |
60 School St.; (800) THE-OMNI; (617) 227-8600; FAX 227-2120
*M – "Charles Dickens stayed here – why not you?"; the Omni touch at this
"historically rich" old hotel – once a Boston byword for sophistication –
rates an "A for effort", but problems still abound; while "the muffins may be
great, the rooms aren't much bigger", and service is "sometimes good,
sometimes not"; though "it's gone to seed a bit", the "lobby has enough
old-world ambiance to make you forgive it."*


**RITZ-CARLTON, BOSTON** 278R (48S)  | 25 | 26 | 24 | 24 | $212 |
15 Arlington St.; (800) 241-3333; (617) 536-5700; FAX 536-9340
*U – In the tradition that has made the word ritz a synonym for elegance,
excellence and expensiveness, this "Boston Brahmin" of hotels is "the last
of a breed", from its elevators manned by white-gloved operators and
"beautiful rooms with views of the Public Garden", to "great afternoon teas"
and the "patina that only time will give"; moreover, the Ritz Dining Room
(food rating, 23) is "superb, with a wine list that is truly outstanding."*


**Royal Sonesta Hotel – Boston** 400R (28S)  | 19 | 19 | 19 | 19 | $140 |
5 Cambridge Pkwy., Cambridge; (800) SONESTA; (617) 491-3600;
FAX 661-5956
*M – While catering mostly to businesspeople and college affiliates, this
riverfront hotel also does right by summertime tourists, with free boat rides
on the Charles, use of bicycles, complimentary ice cream and a fully
equipped health club; expect "friendly", "courteous staff", and "good food"
at the Italian restaurant Davio's (food rating, 23).*


**Sheraton Boston Hotel & Towers** 1250R (85S)  | 18 | 18 | 17 | 17 | $139 |
Prudential Ctr. at Mass. Tpke.; (800) 325-3535; (617) 236-2000; FAX 236-1702
*M – Boasting a big indoor/outdoor pool and health club, this "mammoth",
"serviceable" convention hotel "could be anywhere", but it's adjoining
Hynes Auditorium; "no surprises" for business travelers, who approve the
"convenient location," "friendly service" and "great facilities"; there's a
"super view" from the towers, but watch out for that "factory feeling" and
the "convention crowd with a 'me' attitude"; the word on food is "eat out."*

## BOSTON HOTELS

| R | S | D | P | $ |
|---|---|---|---|---|

**Sheraton Commander Hotel**    176R (24S)    | 16 | 15 | 14 | 14 | $126 |
16 Garden St., Cambridge; (800) 325-3535; (617) 547-4800; FAX 868-8322
*M – "Cozy", "quaint" and convenient to Harvard, this '30s vintage hotel may
be a little "tired", but it's judged "not bad for those on a budget"; "the
location makes it a find", though dining can prove "limited"; it conveniently
answers the question "where else is there when the Charles is full?"*

**Swissotel Boston**    497R (41S)    | 21 | 21 | 21 | 19 | $157 |
(fka Lafayette Hotel, The)
1 Ave. de Lafayette; (800) 621-9200; (617) 451-2600; FAX 451-0054
*M – The closing of its flagship restaurant, Le Marquis de Lafayette, bodes
ill for this European-style hotel, stuck with a problematical location in
central Boston on the declining edge of the old-line retail shopping district;
still, "superb service", "pleasant rooms and public areas", and nice
amenities make this worth considering, but "don't walk out after dark."*

**Westin Hotel Copley**    | 21 | 20 | 19 | 21 | $156 |
**Place Boston, The**    804R (46S)
10 Huntington Ave.; (800) 228-3000; (617) 262-9600; FAX 424-7483
*M – A renovation is imminent for this "luxury businessperson's hotel",
favored for its "excellent location" convenient to the top-notch retailers of
Copley Place ("the Rodeo Drive of Boston"); food and service are
"consistent", and from the upper floors, "the view is beautiful"; special
touches include a gourmet express coffee wagon; a few detractors sniff
that they "can't tell the difference between the mall and the hotel."*

### ● OTHER HOTEL-CHAIN CHOICES
*You will find one or more additional locations of the following hotel chains
in the Boston area: Courtyard by Marriott, Days Inn, Doubletree, Hilton,
Holiday Inn, Howard Johnson, Hyatt, Marriott, Radisson, Ramada,
Residence Inn and Super 8; for reservations or information, see the
toll-free 800 phone listings on page 16.*

# CHICAGO†

## TOP HOTELS
## (In order of rating)

### BEST OVERALL

26 – Four Seasons
Ritz-Carlton
24 – Hotel Nikko Chicago
Park Hyatt
Fairmont Hotel
23 – Stouffer Riviere
Mayfair Hotel
Le Meridien
22 – Drake Hotel
Sheraton Chicago

### BEST VALUES

Chicago Marriott Stes. O'Hare
Hotel Sofitel Chicago
Sheraton Chicago
Talbott Hotel
Forum Hotel Chicago
Knickerbocker Chicago
Best Western Inn of Chicago
Westin Hotel O'Hare
Hotel Nikko Chicago
Stouffer Riviere

\*        \*        \*

### Best Rooms

27 – Four Seasons
26 – Ritz-Carlton
25 – Fairmont Hotel
24 – Le Meridien
Hotel Nikko Chicago
Stouffer Riviere
Hyatt Regency Suites
Park Hyatt
23 – Mayfair Hotel
Swissotel

### Best Dining

26 – Four Seasons
25 – Ritz-Carlton
24 – Park Hyatt
23 – Hotel Nikko Chicago
Fairmont Hotel
Mayfair Hotel
22 – Le Meridien
Drake Hotel
Stouffer Riviere
21 – Hotel Sofitel Chicago

### Best Service

27 – Four Seasons
26 – Ritz-Carlton
25 – Park Hyatt
24 – Mayfair Hotel
Stouffer Riviere
Hotel Nikko Chicago
23 – Fairmont Hotel
Le Meridien
Drake Hotel
22 – Hyatt Regency Suites

### Best Public Facilities

26 – Four Seasons
25 – Ritz-Carlton
23 – Hotel Nikko Chicago
Fairmont Hotel
Stouffer Riviere
22 – Sheraton Chicago
Drake Hotel
Park Hyatt
Mayfair Hotel
Hotel Inter-Continental

†For restaurants, see *Zagat Chicago Restaurant Survey*.

55

## CHICAGO HOTELS

| R | S | D | P | $ |

**Allerton Hotel**   380R (75S)   | 12 | 13 | 14 | 12 | $102 |
701 N. Michigan Ave.; (800) 621-8311; (312) 440-1500; FAX 440-1819
*U – "Great location", low prices and "one of Chicago's better French restaurants", L'Escargot (food rating, 23; not to be confused with the hotel's overall low food rating), recommend this otherwise "drab", "rickety" Michigan Avenue dowager; still, few can overlook "facilities sorely in need of new fashions"; the "Windy City is not windy enough" to clear away this stale standby.*


**Barclay Chicago, The**   119S   | 19 | 18 | 17 | 16 | $133 |
166 E. Superior St.; (800) 621-8004; (312) 787-6000; FAX 787-4331
*M – Many praise this small all-suites hotel off Michigan Avenue for its relatively reasonable prices, "views of Lake Michigan" (from some rooms) and "full amenities" such as minikitchens that save on restaurant bills; ratings slipped a notch in this year's* Survey, *apparently because the "smallish rooms" really "need refurbishing."*


**Best Western Inn of Chicago**   357R (26S)   | 16 | 16 | 14 | 13 | $103 |
(fka Inn of Chicago)
162 E. Ohio St.; (800) 528-1234; (312) 787-3100; FAX 787-8236
*M – Located just one block off Michigan Avenue, this low-budget hotel is described as a "sort of Red Roof Inn of Downtown", offering an "inexpensive alternative" to its upscale rivals; the staff is exceedingly "friendly", and while it offers little "character" or "charm", "good value" and "great location" make most travelers overlook these failings.*


**Bismarck Hotel**   510R (20S)   | 14 | 15 | 14 | 13 | $105 |
171 W. Randolph St.; (800) 643-1500; (312) 236-0123; FAX 236-3177
*U – This "grand old lady" has a "good central location" in the Loop but has been looking "a little tired" lately and much in need of an "overhaul"; that's just what it's getting – a complete renovation already in process should help restore some luster to this convenient art deco charmer.*


**Blackstone Hotel, The**   305R (30S)   | 11 | 12 | 11 | 11 | $107 |
2636 S. Michigan Ave.; (800) 622-6330; (312) 427-4300;
FAX 427-4300 x7182
*M – Stalwarts hold that this Loop landmark, which was "good enough for Truman, is good enough for us", others moan that if it were "any darker and damper it would be a dungeon" – reflecting the fact that despite a 1987 renovation, little seems to have changed since Truman's day; still, this place exhibits considerable "Chicago charm", with the city's premier jazz club, Jazz Showcase, just off the lobby.*

| R | S | D | P | $ |

**Chicago Hilton & Towers**  1543R (149S)  | 20 | 19 | 18 | 20 | $144 |
720 S. Michigan Ave.; (800) HILTONS; (312) 922-4400; FAX 922-5240
*M – While most travelers agree that this South Loop behemoth is
"surprisingly nice for a Hilton", with "fabulous views of Lake Michigan",
"excellent service" and "great" rooms, thanks to a "wonderful renovation",
others dismiss it as a "noisy" "anthill with private rooms"; insiders say go for
the Tower suites and the "authentic" Irish bar in the lobby.*

**Chicago Marriott Downtown**  1137R (37S)  | 18 | 18 | 17 | 18 | $139 |
540 N. Michigan Ave.; (800) 228-9290; (312) 836-0100; FAX 836-6139
*M – One either appreciates the "convenience" and efficiency of
"industrial-strength" convention hotels like this one or hates the "sterile"
environment; a $12 million complete renovation in 1992 toned down the
"flashy" Las Vegasesque lobby and dramatically improved the rooms; of
course, the "great" Michigan Avenue location and lake views from the
upper – and more expensive – floors are unchanged.*

**Chicago Marriott O'Hare**  685R (22S)  | 16 | 17 | 16 | 15 | $120 |
8535 W. Higgins Rd., Rosemont; (800) 228-9290; (312) 693-4444; FAX 714-4297
*U – As airport hotels go, this is about as good – or as bad – as it gets,
depending on one's point of view: "big and noisy" vs. "convenient" for
meetings and seminars"; a $5 million guest-room renovation in 1992 greatly
"improved" the ambiance, but at heart this is still a "typical airport hotel."*

**Chicago Marriott Suites O'Hare**  256S  | 23 | 20 | 18 | 19 | $124 |
6155 N. River Rd., Rosemont; (800) 228-9290; (708) 696-4400; FAX 696-2122
*U – If you don't mind sleeping to the "roar of jet engines", the "surprisingly
nice" suites and "friendly staff" make this "great little business hotel" near
the airport more than acceptable for a "quick stay"; it's not Downtown, but
with a comfort and value like this, who cares?*

**Claridge Hotel of Chicago, The**  175R (7S)  | 16 | 16 | 15 | 15 | $114 |
1244 N. Dearborn Pkwy.; (800) 245-1258; (312) 787-4980; FAX 266-0978
*U – The "excellent" Gold Coast location, "fair value" and "very nice staff"
are enough to make most visitors overlook the "somewhat small" rooms at
this "charming hotel"; still, ratings slipped a notch in this year's Survey,
perhaps because of the "dingy hallways" and decor that "could be brighter."*

**Congress Hotel, The**  850R (60S)  | 12 | 13 | 12 | 12 | $107 |
520 S. Michigan Ave.; (800) 635-1666; (312) 427-3800; FAX 427-3972
*M – Located across from Buckingham Fountain, this Loop "classic" built in
1893 elicits wildly divergent opinions, ranging from "dreadful", "it's a pit"
and "stay at your own risk" to "small but tasteful rooms", "reliable" and "a
bargain for visitors"; take your pick – and your chances.*

## CHICAGO HOTELS

| R | S | D | P | $ |

**Drake Hotel Chicago, The**   535R (56S)   | 22 | 23 | 22 | 22 | $169 |
140 E. Walton Place; (800) 55-DRAKE; (312) 787-2200; FAX 787-1431
*U – Survey participants sing the praises of this "lovely" "grande dame",
with its "old-world charm", "elegant" sense of "tradition" and "perfect
location" on Lake Michigan at the beginning of the Magnificent Mile; its Cape
Cod Room (food rating, 21) is a seafood "classic", and, of course, afternoon
tea is served in the Palm Court.*

**Executive Plaza**   417R (67S)   | 17 | 15 | 13 | 14 | $118 |
(fka Executive House)
71 E. Wacker Dr.; (800) 621-4005; (312) 346-7100; FAX 346-1721
*M – The "rooms are enormous" and "what a view" exclaim fans of this
blue-sheathed hotel overlooking the Chicago River; most agree it's a good
spot for "traveling businesspeople", but others complain the place tends to
be "seedy", although a stunning new lobby may change their minds.*

**FAIRMONT HOTEL, THE**   692R (66S)   | 25 | 23 | 23 | 23 | $170 |
200 N. Columbus Dr.; (800) 527-4727; (312) 565-8000; FAX 856-9020
*U – "Great views of the lake", solid service and a feeling of "class" and
"elegance" combine to make this neoclassic "CEO's delight" on the
emerging East Side of Downtown "one of Chicago's finest"; it also offers
"great weekend packages", and this hotel's restaurants, Entre Nous (food
rating, 23) and Primavera (food rating, 21) also win applause.*

**Forum Hotel Chicago**   523R (6S)   | 18 | 19 | 17 | 18 | $124 |
525 N. Michigan Ave.; (800) 628-2112; (312) 944-0055; FAX 944-1320
*U – Although the rooms are perhaps "too small to read* Playboy*" in, most
agree that this North Michigan Avenue spot may be "bland" but offers
"great value" on a "great location"; service and food can be uneven but
are generally solid.*

**FOUR SEASONS CHICAGO**   343R (185S)   | 27 | 27 | 26 | 26 | $205 |
120 E. Delaware Place; (800) 332-3442; (312) 280-8800; FAX 280-1748
*U – Generally considered "the best in town", this postmodern North
Michigan Avenue tower is built over the multilevel shopping mall that houses
Bloomingdale's, Bendel's and various other luxury specialty stores; some
find the "hunting-lodge-in-the-sky" lobby a bit overdone, but the "great
location", "elegantly appointed" rooms, "best-trained" staff and fine restaurant,
Seasons (food rating, 26), make it a winner for all seasons and reasons.*

**CHICAGO HOTELS**                                    | R | S | D | P | $ |

**Holiday Inn City Centre**  500R (9S)    | 16 | 15 | 13 | 14 | $115 |
300 E. Ohio St.; (800) HOLIDAY; (312) 787-6100; FAX 787-6259
*M – Upstairs from the Apparel Mart and connected by a skywalk to the
massive Merchandise Mart – no wonder "convenience" and "efficiency" are
the words favored to recommend this "good", "no-frills" Downtown hotel
located on the Chicago River; but despite a "great health club" and a 1992
renovation of the seventh-floor lobby and all public areas, many find it "all
cheap chrome and glass" with no class.*

**Hotel Inter-Continental Chicago**  338R (36S)   | 22 | 21 | 20 | 22 | $163 |
505 N. Michigan Ave.; (800) 628-2468; (312) 944-4100; FAX 944-1320
*U – Swimmers and romantics should not miss the "greatest pool in
Chicago" at this "beautifully" restored "historic" building in a prime location
near the Chicago Tribune on Michigan Avenue; it's "convenient to business,
shopping and restaurants", with "outstanding food" at its French-Continental
restaurant, The Boulevard.*

**HOTEL NIKKO CHICAGO**  421R (18S)    | 24 | 24 | 23 | 23 | $167 |
320 N. Dearborn Ave.; (800) NIKKO-US; (312) 744-1900; FAX 527-2650
*M – People use words like "ascetic" and "very Shinto" to describe this
contemporary Downtown hotel and either find the "minimalist" gray-and-
black decor "dazzling", "peaceful" and "spectacular" or simply "cold" and
"sterile"; virtually everyone agrees that "exceptional thought" went into this
place – thought topped off by "excellent service" and "great" river views,
making it worth every bit of the price; Benkay (food rating, 22) and
Celebrity Cafe offer excellent dining.*

**Hotel Sofitel Chicago**  305R (8S)    | 23 | 22 | 21 | 21 | $136 |
5550 N. River Rd., Rosemont; (800) 233-5959; (708) 678-4488; FAX 678-4244
*M – High ratings notwithstanding, our travelers warn that this near-O'Hare
business hotel has inconsistent service, with comments ranging from
"good" to "if the French are known for service, they forgot to tell the
Chicago staff"; still, most surveyors appreciate the foreign "flair" and
"European charm" of the Country French decor and "fine" food service,
especially compared to its airport neighbors.*

**Hyatt Printers Row**  161R (4S)    | 20 | 19 | 21 | 17 | $140 |
(fka Morton Hotel)
500 S. Dearborn St.; (800) 843-6678; (312) 986-1234; FAX 939-2468
*U – Although ratings have slipped a notch since Hyatt took over the former
Morton Hotel in historic Printers Row near the South Loop Financial
District, this is still a "nice place to hide when you have work to do", with an
award-winning restaurant (Prairie) that's worth a visit "even if you don't
stay" at this "intimate" European-style hotel.*

**Hyatt Regency Chicago** 2194R (175S)  | 19 | 18 | 18 | 19 | $151 |
151 E. Wacker Dr.; (800) 233-1234; (312) 565-1234; FAX 565-2966
*M – This "lakeside bivouac for conventioneers" has "breathtaking views of
Downtown" and nine food and beverage facilities, including Big, a "great
bar" with live entertainment; "big" pretty much sums up this mammoth
convention facility, but what amazes people most is that "a hotel this large
can make one feel so important"; others moan that "you feel most
comfortable wearing a convention name tag" here.*

**Hyatt Regency O'Hare** 1160R (60S)  | 17 | 17 | 16 | 16 | $131 |
9300 W. Bryn Mawr Ave., Rosemont; (800) 233-1234; (708) 696-1234;
FAX 696-0139
*M – Some praise the "unique" multilevel atrium and characterize this hotel
as "pretty", while others dismiss it as a "dump" with the most "peculiar
layout"; almost all agree that the chief asset of this "massive sardine can"
is its location "oh, so close to O'Hare" and acknowledge that though it's a
bit like a "factory", they "make it work."*

**HYATT REGENCY SUITES** 347S  | 24 | 22 | 21 | 20 | $166 |
676 N. Michigan Ave.; (800) 233-1234; (312) 337-1234; FAX 698-0139
*U – A "brilliant new kid on the block", this Magnificent Mile all-suiter has
visitors wondering "why Hyatt doesn't have more of these"; the "gorgeous",
"Ralph Lauren"–style suites win praise even though they are small;
"first-rate service", an "unexpectedly" "superb" restaurant (Jaxx) and an
"excellent" location make this "a find."*

**Knickerbocker Chicago Hotel** 256R (26S)  | 19 | 20 | 19 | 18 | $131 |
163 E. Walton Place; (800) 621-8140; (312) 751-8100; FAX 751-0370
*M – Although renovated in 1989, this art deco hotel in the "shadow of the
Drake" still seems "somewhat tired" to some – "comfortable" but just a tad
"seedy"; others find it "gracious" and full of "old-world" charm; in either
case its location just off Michigan Avenue is a shopper's delight.*

**LE MERIDIEN HOTEL CHICAGO** 247R (41S)  | 24 | 23 | 22 | 21 | $166 |
21 E. Bellevue Place; (800) 543-4300; (312) 266-2100; FAX 266-2141
*M – The novelty of a "high-tech" hotel with trendy splashes of black may
have worn off, as ratings slipped a notch in this Survey, but most of our
surveyors appreciate such "elegant" touches as CD players (and CDs),
VCRs and "gorgeous" bathrooms in every spacious room and say "you'll
feel like a rock star" at this "original-looking", "very special place."*

**Lenox House Suites**  325S       | 16 | 16 | 14 | 15 | $115 |
616 N. Rush St.; (800) 44-LENOX; (312) 337-1000; FAX 337-7217
*M – The suites are small at this "low-budget" Downtowner, but the
redecorating currently under way should spruce up the "very drab rooms";
given the kitchenettes, "good location" and relatively low prices, budget-
minded visitors appreciate this place.*

**MAYFAIR HOTEL, THE**  201R (30S)       | 23 | 24 | 23 | 22 | $194 |
(fka Mayfair Regent Hotel)
181 E. Lake Shore Dr.; (800) 545-4000; (312) 787-8500; FAX 664-6194
*U – A recent change in management and a rumored conversion into
condos have not dampened enthusiasm for this Edwardian Gold Coast
jewel; "service beyond the call" of duty, "elegance", "charm" and ambiance
you simply "can't fake", combined with well-rated food and a "fabulous
location", make this a welcome "oasis."*

**McCormick Center Hotel**  650R (50S)       | 13 | 13 | 12 | 12 | $128 |
Lake Shore Dr. & 23rd St.; (800) 621-6909; (312) 791-1900; FAX 791-0634
*U – The only reason to stay at this "very ugly" monstrosity is its location
across from the convention center; its captive audience of conventiongoers
offer comments like "dingy and disgusting", "horrid" and "very uninviting" –
yet they keep coming back for more.*

**Midland Hotel, The**  257R (4S)       | 14 | 18 | 15 | 14 | $117 |
172 W. Adams St.; (800) 621-2360; (312) 332-1200; FAX 332-5909
*U – An old-fashioned London taxi will whisk guests around town, and
breakfast and cocktail hour are included in the price, so this "European-
style" beaux-arts Loop hotel is a good bet for travelers "not looking for
extravagance"; but insiders warn that the cheapest rooms are so tiny that
you can almost "touch two opposite walls with arms outstretched" – and
the recent renovation didn't correct that.*

**Omni Ambassador East**  275R (52S)       | 19 | 20 | 21 | 18 | $149 |
1301 N. State Pkwy.; (800) THE-OMNI; (312) 787-7200; FAX 787-4760
*M – Renaming this Gold Coast institution the Pump Room Hotel might be
appropriate, because the legendary see-and-be-seen restaurant (food
rating, 21) received nearly as many comments as the hotel, which is either
a "charming" "grande dame", still "going strong", or a bit "shabby" and
"showing its age", depending on whom you ask; Survey participants agree
that the "genuinely gracious service" and affluent neighborhood are pluses.*

## CHICAGO HOTELS                    | R | S | D | P | $ |

**Palmer House Hilton**   1634R (90S)   | 18 | 18 | 18 | 19 | $141 |
(fka Palmer House Hotel & Towers)
17 E. Monroe St.; (800) 445-8667; (312) 726-7500; FAX 263-2556
*M – Admirers and detractors split about evenly over the merits and failings
of this historic Loop dowager; despite an ongoing $118 million renovation,
some wish the rooms looked "as good as the lobby", while others praise
the "refurbished" facilities and "old-world" charms.*


**PARK HYATT CHICAGO**   255R (38S)   | 24 | 25 | 24 | 22 | $187 |
800 N. Michigan Ave.; (800) 233-1234; (312) 280-2222; FAX 280-1963
*M – Overlooking the historic old Water Tower just off Michigan Avenue,
this "small" European-style hotel is a civilized "refuge" known for "superior
service" and its top-notch French restaurant, La Tour (food rating, 25);
despite high ratings, many feel the "claustrophobic" rooms make this great
only "for midgets", and insiders urge you to spring for a suite.*


**Quality Inn & Clarion**   | 13 | 13 | 12 | 12 | $112 |
**Hotel at O'Hare**   463R (20S) (fka Sheraton International at O'Hare)
6810 N. Mannheim Rd., Rosemont; (800) 221-2222; (708) 297-1234;
FAX 297-5287
*M – A recent change in ownership split this former Sheraton into two
different hotels under one roof and may improve the ratings, but our
surveyors divide evenly between those who "avoid" this "highly overrated"
"dump" like the plague and those who say it's an "oasis" for stranded
travelers, a "great value."*


**Radisson Plaza Ambassador West**   267R (50S)   | 18 | 19 | 18 | 18 | $133 |
(fka Ambassador West)
1300 N. State Pkwy.; (800) 621-8090; (312) 787-7900; FAX 787-2067
*M – "Willie Loman would like" this "very quaint" small hotel for its
"businesslike" atmosphere, "good prices" and affluent Gold Coast location,
but expect nothing exceptional and be forewarned that some people think
this landmark is simply "worn out."*


**Radisson Suite Hotel – O'Hare Airport**   296S   | 19 | 16 | 14 | 15 | $118 |
5500 N. River Rd., Rosemont; (800) 333-3333; (708) 678-4000; FAX 671-3059
*U – If you must stay near O'Hare, then this may be the place; there's a
microwave, refrigerator and wet bar in every suite, a skywalk to the O'Hare
Expo Center, and breakfast and cocktail hour included in the price; value,
"comfort" and convenience rate high, making this "the best" some have
found near the airport.*

# CHICAGO HOTELS

| R | S | D | P | $ |

**Raphael Hotel**   172R (80S)   | 20 | 21 | 17 | 16 | $130 |
201 E. Delaware Place; (800) 821-5343; (312) 943-5000; FAX 943-9483
*M – Currently undergoing a total renovation, this "quiet", "cozy" European-style hotel charms most with its "reasonable prices", "great weekend packages", "excellent" service and location near Michigan Avenue; still, a few complain of "cloying cuteness."*

**Richmont Hotel**   193R (15S)   | 15 | 17 | 16 | 14 | $114 |
162 E. Ontario St.; (800) 621-8055; (312) 787-3580; FAX 787-1299
*M – A recent $2 million renovation should improve the room ratings at this "small" off–Michigan Avenue facility; there's "great" value for the price and location, but insiders say expect lackadaisical service and go for the "sweet suites", despite the additional cost, because some rooms are "teeny"; the Rue St. Clair restaurant offers pleasant outdoor dining in season.*

**RITZ-CARLTON, CHICAGO**   431R (85S)   | 26 | 26 | 25 | 25 | $205 |
160 E. Pearson St.; (800) 621-6906; (312) 266-1000; FAX 266-1194
*U – Its name notwithstanding, this Ritz is part of the Four Seasons chain; to many it represents the "epitome of luxury" and just "what a hotel should be", thanks to a $17 million renovation in 1991; it's also a "shopper's paradise", being connected to the Water Tower Place Mall; most reviewers are more than content with its "superior service", "incomparable ambiance" and "fabulous" dining at The Cafe (food rating, 22) and The Dining Room (food rating, 27).*

**Sheraton Chicago**   | 23 | 22 | 21 | 22 | $145 |
**Hotel & Towers**   1200R (54S)
301 E. North Water St.; (800) 325-3535; (312) 464-1000; FAX 464-9140
*U – The new kid on the block is turning heads as an "exciting addition to the skyline" along the Chicago River and emerging River Walk district; "beautiful public areas", a "friendly staff" and spectacular views of the city and lake give this large, freshly minted convention hotel an "old established feeling" and "easy elegance" that visitors seem to enjoy.*

**Sheraton Plaza Hotel**   334R (88S)   | 17 | 18 | 16 | 15 | $133 |
160 E. Huron St.; (800) 346-2591; (312) 787-2900; FAX 787-6093
*M – There's nothing too exciting about this somewhat aging (some say "run-down") Downtown high rise near the Magnificent Mile, but there's nothing wrong here either; expect "good, solid accommodations" near "great shopping", and a "quiet" atmosphere – and take advantage of the good weekend packages.*

**CHICAGO HOTELS**                          | R | S | D | P | $ |

**STOUFFER RIVIERE**   565R (40S)          | 24 | 24 | 22 | 23 | $163 |
1 W. Wacker Dr.; (800) HOTELS1; (312) 372-7200; FAX 372-0834
*U – This noteworthy newcomer situated at the north end of the Loop on the Chicago River offers "great views" of the lake and cityscape; the "modern" lobby and meeting spaces please visitors with their "beauty", and though a few find the facility a bit "corporate" and "sterile", most agree it's a welcome – and good-value – addition in a "very convenient" location.*

**Swissotel Chicago**   630R (30S)         | 23 | 21 | 20 | 20 | $149 |
323 E. Wacker Dr.; (800) 654-7263; (312) 565-0565; FAX 565-0540
*U – Swiss chocolates strategically placed in bowls throughout the hotel set an indulgent tone at this contemporary East Side high rise; "breathtaking views" of Lake Michigan from the higher floors, "great service" and "comfortable", "well-appointed" rooms lend a "European flavor" to what could have been just another large business hotel.*

**Talbott Hotel, The**   175R (28S)        | 18 | 19 | 15 | 16 | $115 |
20 E. Delaware Place; (800) 621-8506; (312) 944-4970; FAX 944-7241
*U – Just off the Magnificent Mile, this "charming" little Gold Coast hotel offers a "pleasant", if basic, experience at "cheap" prices for an area in the center of the shopping and entertainment action; "simple, genteel" service makes guests feel "like they are in Europe" instead of the Windy City.*

**Tremont Hotel**   127R (6S)              | 20 | 22 | 21 | 19 | $163 |
100 E. Chestnut St.; (800) 621-8295; (312) 751-1900; FAX 280-2111
*U – The consensus is that this "small", European-style Gold Coast "gem" is "nice" but "used to be nicer"; the "tiny", "dark" rooms and hallways remind some of a "rabbit warren", yet myriad charms – from the "cozy fireplace" and "homey" lobby to the "tasteful" appointments and "great antiques" – keep ratings fairly high; Cricket's restaurant downstairs remains a favorite too.*

**Westin Hotel, Chicago**   740R (43S)     | 18 | 18 | 16 | 16 | $143 |
909 N. Michigan Ave.; (800) 228-3000; (312) 943-7200; FAX 943-9347
*M – While some consider this an "above-average" commercial hotel that's "dependable" and "comfortable", others report that the great Magnificent Mile location is the only thing "that keeps the doors open" at this "tired" spot; sports fanatics may catch a glimpse of their favorite players because "pro baseball and football" teams frequent the place.*

| R | S | D | P | $ |

**Westin Hotel O'Hare**   525R (29S)       | 19 | 19 | 18 | 19 | $130 |
6100 River Rd., Rosemont; (800) 228-3000; (708) 698-6000; FAX 698-4591
*U – Business travelers say this airport property is "a cut above" the
garden-variety "been-to-one, been-to-'em-all" airport hotel; a bit more "ritzy
and glitzy" than most, yet "quiet", with "many amenities" and "discount"
rates, this spot wins the vote of many as "best-run hotel at O'Hare."*

● **OTHER HOTEL-CHAIN CHOICES**
*You will find one or more additional locations of the following hotel chains in
the Chicago area: Courtyard by Marriott, Days Inn, Embassy Suites, Guest
Quarters, Hampton Inn, Hilton, Holiday Inn, Howard Johnson, Hyatt, La
Quinta Inns, Marriott, Preferred Hotels, Radisson, Ramada, Residence Inn,
Super 8, Travelodge/Viscount and Wyndham; for reservations or
information, see the toll-free 800 phone listings on page 16.*

# CINCINNATI†

## TOP HOTELS
## (In order of rating)

### BEST OVERALL

22 – Cincinnatian Hotel
19 – Omni Netherland Plaza
   Westin Hotel
   Hyatt Regency

### BEST VALUES

Omni Netherland Plaza
Cincinnatian Hotel
Westin Hotel
Cincinnati Marriott

\*     \*     \*

### Best Rooms

22 – Cincinnatian Hotel
20 – Westin Hotel
   Hyatt Regency
18 – Cincinnati Marriott

### Best Dining

22 – Cincinnatian Hotel
19 – Omni Netherland Plaza
   Westin Hotel
18 – Hyatt Regency

### Best Service

22 – Cincinnatian Hotel
20 – Omni Netherland Plaza
   Westin Hotel
19 – Hyatt Regency

### Best Public Facilities

21 – Cincinnatian Hotel
   Omni Netherland Plaza
19 – Hyatt Regency
   Westin Hotel

| R | S | D | P | $ |
|---|---|---|---|---|

**Cincinnatian Hotel, The**   145R (5S)   | 22 | 22 | 22 | 21 | $139 |
601 Vine St.; (800) 942-9000; (513) 381-3000; FAX 651-0256
U – A "nice blend of old and new", this beautifully restored 1882 hotel combines Second Empire elegance (a stately exterior and "grand" marble-and-walnut staircase) with attractive postmodern decor; add "well-designed" rooms, a "superb" restaurant (The Palace, featuring gourmet American cuisine) that's the place for Cincinnati power lunch and a generally "high level of service", and you've got the "best hotel in town"; a Downtown location puts it right in the heart of the business/entertainment action.

---

†For restaurants, see *Zagat Ohio Restaurant Survey* (to be published mid-1993).

| R | S | D | P | $ |

**Cincinnati Marriott**   352R (5S)   | 18 | 17 | 16 | 16 | $113 |
11320 Chester Rd.; (800) 950-8883; (513) 772-1720; FAX 772-6466
*M – Located 20 minutes north of Downtown, this suburban mid-rise "looks, feels and smells like a hotel built for conventioneers"; though quite serviceable if you find yourself in the area on business, it's not especially appealing otherwise.*


**Cincinnati Terrace Hilton, The**   336R (40S)   | 17 | 17 | 16 | 14 | $114 |
(fka Terrace Hilton)
15 W. Sixth St.; (800) HILTONS; (513) 381-4000; FAX 381-5158
*M – "Utilitarian" describes everything about this Downtown Hilton, which is most appreciated for its "good location" close to Riverfront Stadium and the Coliseum; critics say the hotel was "never great" and isn't getting better, though some floors have been renovated recently.*


**Clarion Hotel Cincinnati**   887R (64S)   | 14 | 15 | 13 | 14 | $104 |
141 W. Sixth St.; (800) 876-2100; (513) 352-2110; FAX 352-2148
*M – "Ok for a business stay" or as a pit stop for the "long-distance driver", this hotel has two main assets: convenience to the convention center, and easy-on-the-wallet prices; "accommodating" service is another plus, but beyond that, the food's "terrible" and critics advise "check in elsewhere."*


**Holiday Inn I-275**   280R (5S)   | 15 | 16 | 16 | 14 | $90 |
(fka Cincinnati Hilton Inn North)
3855 Haurk Rd., Sharonville; (800) 465-4329; (513) 563-8330;
FAX 563-8330 x223
*M – Like many of its Holiday Inn brethren, this suburban high rise has few distinguishing characteristics (the rooms are described as "ok" and the food as "decent"), but at these prices, we don't hear many complaints; there's "always a room available", and it's only a few miles from Downtown; "average" is a good way to sum it up.*


**Hyatt Regency Cincinnati**   485R (22S)   | 20 | 19 | 18 | 19 | $128 |
151 W. Fifth St.; (800) 233-1234; (513) 579-1234; FAX 579-0104
*U – A "typical Hyatt", this modern Downtown hotel may be "impersonal", but it has "all the amenities", including "comfortable" rooms, warm service and a convenient location sandwiched between Saks and the Convention Center; it's "basic, clean and functional – what do you want?" but critics would at least like better food: they "can't make fajitas to save their lives."*

**Kings Island Inn &**          | 17 | 19 | 16 | 16 | $131 |
**Conference Center\***   288R (2S)
5691 Kings Island Dr., Kings Island; (800) 727-3050; (513) 398-0115;
FAX 398-1095
*M – "Sort of tacky" but "nice", this sprawling, chalet-style resort and
conference center is right across from Kings Island theme park, making it
a popular family destination; both the food and rooms are "average", but
there's no lack of distractions nearby, including golf and tennis facilities.*

**Omni Netherland Plaza**   621R (12S)          | 18 | 20 | 19 | 21 | $121 |
35 W. Fifth St.; (800) THE-OMNI; (513) 421-9100; FAX 421-4291
*M – A Downtown "art deco palace" that's part of the new mall, Tower Place,
this beautifully restored historic hotel makes you "feel like you're back in the
'30s", especially in the "breathtaking" restaurant and a ballroom that "looks
like the set of* Metropolis*"; critics complain that the plumbing is also vintage
'30s and that the rooms, though recently renovated, can be "small and dark."*

**Vernon Manor Hotel, The\***   169R (57S)          | 18 | 17 | 16 | 15 | $100 |
400 Oak St.; (800) 543-3999; (513) 281-3300; FAX 281-8933
*U – "Off the beaten track" (in the university district north of Downtown) but a
candidate for "best value in Cincinnati", this "old-fashioned" hotel – built in
1924 to resemble a stately English manor house – offers a taste of "faded
but comfortable" Victorian elegance; rooms are "huge" and nicely appointed,
and long-term stays can be arranged; dining options range from the elegant
Forum Room to an English pub–style lounge.*

**Westin Hotel**   448R (18S)          | 20 | 20 | 19 | 19 | $128 |
At Fountain Square; (800) 228-3000; (513) 621-7700; FAX 421-6869
*U – "Efficient but not memorable", this modern glass house in the heart of
Downtown is considered a "first-rate business hotel", thanks to "very
comfortable" rooms, "good food", reliable service and a "convenient"
location; it's a "solid" performer and "well priced" for the quality offered.*

● **OTHER HOTEL-CHAIN CHOICES**
*You will find one or more additional locations of the following hotel chains in
the Cincinnati area: Courtyard by Marriott, Days Inn, Embassy Suites,
Guest Quarters, Hampton Inn, Hilton, Howard Johnson, Hyatt, La Quinta
Inns, Marriott, Radisson, Ramada, Renaissance Inn, Super 8 and
Travelodge/Viscount; for reservations or information, see the toll-free 800
phone listings on page 16.*

# CLEVELAND†

## TOP HOTELS
## (In order of rating)

### BEST OVERALL

24 – Ritz-Carlton
19 – Stouffer Tower City
17 – Sheraton City Centre
16 – Cleveland Marriott East

\*

### BEST VALUES

Holiday Inn Lakeside
Ritz-Carlton
Cleveland Marriott East
Sheraton City Centre

\*　　\*

### Best Rooms

25 – Ritz-Carlton
20 – Stouffer Tower City
18 – Sheraton Cleveland
17 – Cleveland Marriott East

### Best Dining

23 – Ritz-Carlton
18 – Stouffer Tower City
16 – Sheraton City Centre
15 – Cleveland Marriott East

### Best Service

25 – Ritz-Carlton
20 – Stouffer Tower City
18 – Sheraton Cleveland
17 – Cleveland Marriott East

### Best Public Facilities

24 – Ritz-Carlton
18 – Stouffer Tower City
15 – Sheraton City Center
　　Cleveland Marriott East

| R | S | D | P | $ |
|---|---|---|---|---|

**Cleveland Marriott East**　403R (8S)　　| 17 | 17 | 15 | 15 | $104 |
3663 Park East Dr., Beachwood; (800) 334-2118; (216) 464-5950; FAX 464-8935
*M – Opinion is split on this contemporary suburban sprawler; to some it's "the best choice in Cleveland's fashionable East suburbs", with a good range of facilities (pool, health club, executive floor) and "friendly, helpful" service; to others it's "really a motel, with run-down rooms and a singularly undistinguished, uncaring staff"; a recent renovation may have brightened appearances, but with such a discrepancy in opinion, there's room for improvement.*

**Cleveland Marriott Society Ctr.**\*　416R (15S)　| 22 | 21 | 21 | 22 | $107 |
127 Public Square; (216) 696-9200; FAX 696-8615
*U – "Brand-new" and "great for business", this contemporary Cesar Pelli–designed luxury convention hotel scores high marks in every category; with a convenient Downtown location, it offers easy access to museums, nightlife and other attractions, and has a full complement of facilities (fitness center, sauna) as well as a winning concierge level.*

†For restaurants, see *Zagat Ohio Restaurant Survey* (to be published mid-1993).

## CLEVELAND HOTELS                    | R | S | D | P | $ |

**Cleveland South Hilton Inn, The\*** 198R (3S)   | 15 | 16 | 16 | 16 | $101 |
(fka Cleveland Hilton South)
6200 Quarry Lane; (800) HILTONS; (216) 447-1300; FAX 642-9334
*M – "Struggling to make a comeback" but not there yet, this "no-surprises"
Hilton is convenient to the airport and Downtown but still suffers from "poor
service" and "dreary" decor; pluses include plenty of meeting rooms and a
range of athletic facilities (tennis, sauna, whirlpool baths, indoor/outdoor
pool); warning: it's "overrun with Browns fans on Sunday."*


**Glidden House, The\***  60R (8S)         | 22 | 19 | 21 | 22 | $98 |
1901 Ford Dr.; (216) 231-8900; FAX 231-2130
*U – "Quaint and comfortable" bed-and-breakfast located in a "lovely"
1910 eclectic French gothic–style mansion; it's "right in the middle" of the
University–cultural center action and, with its good food and service, gives
"great value" for the money.*


**Holiday Inn Lakeside City Center** 378R (7S)   | 15 | 15 | 15 | 13 | $89 |
1111 Lakeside Ave.; (800) HOLIDAY; (216) 241-5100; FAX 241-1831
*M – "Not great but always adequate" sums up the prevailing view of this
touristy hotel near the convention center; the nice lake view is a plus, as
are low prices; recently rehabbed rooms get mixed reviews, from "ok" to
"incredibly, the best rooms in Cleveland."*


**Omni International Hotel\***  317R (24S)      | 19 | 19 | 17 | 15 | $108 |
(fka Clinic Center Hotel, The)
2065 E. 96th St.; (800) THE-OMNI; (216) 791-1900; FAX 791-7065
*M – Formerly the Clinic Center Hotel, this modern high rise has long
"served a purpose" for families of clinic patients, and now that it has joined
the Omni chain and undergone a room-and-lobby rehab, ratings have risen
significantly across the board – "excellent" service is singled out for special
praise; penthouse suites include full butler service, limo and meals.*


**Pierre Radisson Inn –**              | 20 | 17 | 15 | 17 | $101 |
**Cleveland East**   117R (4S)
3695 Orange Place, Beachwood; (800) 333-3333; (216) 765-1900;
FAX 765-1841
*U – It may be located in the "middle of nowhere", but this suburban hotel is
"surprisingly pleasant", with "nice rooms", "friendly service" and moderate
prices; it's "an excellent value" and good for business travelers.*

## CLEVELAND HOTELS

|   | R | S | D | P | $ |

**Radisson Plaza Hotel Cleveland\***  252S   | 21 | 20 | 17 | 18 | $108 |
1701 E. 12th St.; (800) 333-3333; (216) 523-8000; FAX 523-1698
*U – A "great location" (convenient to the convention center, stadium and Galleria shopping), "nice rooms" and "good prices" make this all-suites hotel a pleasant Downtown option; an indoor lap pool and exercise room add to its value, as do the usual special packages.*

**RITZ-CARLTON, CLEVELAND**  208R (21S)   | 25 | 25 | 23 | 24 | $153 |
1515 W. Third St.; (800) 241-3333; (216) 623-1300; FAX 623-0515
*U – "How much better can you get?" ask those who've experienced this "classic example" of Ritz-Carlton luxury, conveniently linked to a new urban shopping mall, The Avenue at Tower City Center; most pronounce it "excellent in all areas", from its "lovely and elegant" rooms and public areas to its outstanding food and service; this is clearly the "best in town" and the "place to be seen when making a splash" in Cleveland; the club floors with complimentary food and beverages are "like a second home, only better."*

**Sheraton Cleveland**   | 18 | 17 | 16 | 15 | $119 |
**City Centre Hotel**  515R (45S)
777 St. Clair Ave.; (800) 321-1090; (216) 771-7600; FAX 771-5129
*M – It's "not too special", but this recently renovated Downtown tower at least has "comfortable rooms" and a "good location" near the Convention Center, making it a good option for business stopovers; critics are less kind: "scary", "lacks everything except a lobby."*

**Stouffer Tower City Plaza Hotel**  491R (50S)   | 20 | 18 | 18 | 18 | $134 |
24 Public Square; (800) HOTELS-1; (216) 696-5600; FAX 696-0432
*M – Admirers of this renovated grande dame located in the vintage Terminal Tower call it "a jewel" in the middle of Downtown, praising its "beautiful lobby", "extremely comfortable rooms", "wonderful views of the Square" and "service that goes out of the way to help"; a minority remains unconvinced, however, finding it "big and impersonal", with all the "ambiance of a nursing home, and food to match."*

### ● OTHER HOTEL-CHAIN CHOICES
*You will find one or more additional locations of the following hotel chains in the Cleveland area: Days Inn, Embassy Suites, Hampton Inn, Holiday Inn, Howard Johnson, Radisson, Ramada, Residence Inn, Super 8, Travelodge/Viscount; for reservations or information, see the toll-free 800 phone listings on page 16.*

# DALLAS[†]

---

## TOP HOTELS
## (In order of rating)

### BEST OVERALL
27 – Mansion on Turtle Creek
25 – Hotel Crescent Court
     Four Seasons
24 – Adolphus
21 – Loews Anatole
     Omni Mandalay
     Grand Kempinski
     Fairmont Hotel

### BEST VALUES
Wyndham Garden Hotel
Doubletree Park West
Dallas Marriott Park Central
Stoneleigh Hotel
Sheraton Park Central
Omni Mandalay
Dallas Parkway Hilton
Melrose Hotel

\*        \*        \*

### Best Rooms
27 – Mansion on Turtle Creek
26 – Four Seasons
     Hotel Crescent Court
24 – Adolphus
22 – Omni Mandalay
     Loews Anatole
     Grand Kempinski
21 – Fairmont Hotel

### Best Dining
28 – Mansion on Turtle Creek
25 – Hotel Crescent Court
24 – Four Seasons
     Adolphus
21 – Grand Kempinski
     Fairmont Hotel
     Loews Anatole
20 – Omni Mandalay

### Best Service
28 – Mansion on Turtle Creek
25 – Hotel Crescent Court
     Four Seasons
24 – Adolphus
22 – Grand Kempinski
21 – Fairmont Hotel
     Westin Hotel Galleria
     Loews Anatole

### Best Public Facilities
27 – Mansion on Turtle Creek
26 – Hotel Crescent Court
25 – Four Seasons
24 – Adolphus
23 – Loews Anatole
22 – Omni Mandalay
21 – Grand Kempinski
     Westin Hotel Galleria

---

†For restaurants, see *Zagat Dallas/Fort Worth Restaurant Survey*.

## DALLAS HOTELS | R | S | D | P | $ |

**ADOLPHUS, THE**   432R (20S)   | 24 | 24 | 24 | 24 | $167 |
1321 Commerce St.; (800) 325-3535; (214) 742-8200; FAX 747-3532
*U – Built in 1912 by beer baron Adolphus Busch, this hotel provides
"old-world ambiance" and "a touch of Dallas at its turn-of-the-century
finest"; an "exquisite remodeling" and "warm and personable" staff provide
"the ultimate in comfort", "only two blocks from Neiman Marcus"; the
recently renovated French Room (food rating, 28), its highly touted
Contemporary American restaurant, is downright "gorgeous", and the
beautiful lobby, with "museum-quality tapestry", plays host to "refined
afternoon teas."*

**Aristocrat Hotel of Dallas***   172R (122S)   | 24 | 21 | 20 | 22 | $113 |
1933 Main St.; (800) 231-4235; (214) 741-7700; FAX 939-3639
*U – "Good value" and a "great location" Downtown make this circa-1925
old-timer (renovated in 1986) a popular spot for working travelers; business
gladiators find it "convenient" to their offices and a "great buy", thanks to
"minisuites and free breakfast"; "very nice rooms" are well priced for
week-long stays or "weekend bargains", though a few complain about the
"Sunday-night invasion of business types."*

**Dallas Grand***   710R (30S)   | 16 | 17 | 15 | 15 | $88 |
(fka Dallas Park Plaza Hotel)
1914 Commerce St.; (800) 421-0011; (214) 747-7000; FAX 742-1337
*U – Conference-goers make up the lion's share of the clientele at this
businesslike '50s-modern hotel, located near the convention center and
the West End Historic District; extended-stay businesspeople also find
it an affordable, reasonable spot, though they say it "needs a face-lift
inside and out.*

**Dallas Marriott Park Central**   445R (4S)   | 17 | 19 | 17 | 16 | $103 |
7750 LBJ Frwy.; (800) 228-9290; (214) 233-4421; FAX 233-4421 x1599
*M – "Middle of the road" and "nothing extraordinary", this chain link does
offer a "great location" and "easy access" to the LBJ Loop and nearby
hospitals and corporations; a 1992 renovation updated some of the rooms,
but it's basically "just a place to stay."*

**Dallas Marriott Quorum**   547R (15S)   | 20 | 21 | 18 | 18 | $123 |
14901 Dallas Pkwy.; (800) 228-9290; (214) 661-2800; FAX 991-1376
*U – "Solid and reliable", this "typical Marriott" offers "spacious rooms",
"attentive and gracious" service and a "great location next to Dallas
Tollway" in the northern reaches of the city; the well-outfitted exercise room
appeals to fitness buffs, and shop-till-you-droppers note that it's "close to
three malls"; overall, a reliable place when you want "a good night's sleep
with no disappointments."*

## DALLAS HOTELS | R | S | D | P | $ |

**Dallas Parkway Hilton\*** 310R (14S)  | 17 | 17 | 15 | 16 | $103 |
4801 LBJ Frwy.; (800) 356-3924; (214) 661-3600; FAX 385-3156
*U – Convenient to the Galleria shopping complex and North Dallas
commerce, this "average one-night business hotel" is nonetheless "nothing
remarkable"; a complimentary van transports guests to the many shopping
malls, restaurants and offices within five miles of the hotel, and "an
extra-nice staff makes up for any other weaknesses."*

**Doubletree Hotel at**  | 16 | 17 | 15 | 15 | $103 |
**Campbell Centre** 302R (19S)
8250 N. Central Expwy.; (800) 528-0444; (214) 691-8700; FAX 696-5601
*U – Sandwiched between the trademark golden towers at a major traffic
crossroads, this competitively priced place is "popular for bar mitzvahs,
weddings and business", but it doesn't win any special kudos for rooms or
service; "close to mall shopping" at nearby NorthPark, and near SMU, it's
known as much for its convenience as for its appointments.*

**Doubletree Hotel at Lincoln Centre** 500R (15S)  | 18 | 18 | 17 | 17 | $113 |
5410 LBJ Frwy.; (800) 528-0444; (214) 934-8400; FAX 701-5244
*U – "A good night's sleep" in a "good-size" room helps make this "the place
to stay for business", especially if your business is with nearby J.C.
Penney; it's "not real close to Downtown Dallas", but it's near the Galleria
and offers a complimentary shuttle for shoppers; despite a recent $3.5
million renovation, some still consider this a "standard highway hotel."*

**Doubletree Hotel at Park West** 339R (15S)  | 20 | 19 | 18 | 20 | $111 |
1590 LBJ Frwy.; (800) 528-0444; (214) 869-4300; FAX 869-3295
*U – "Good for business travelers", this hotel is convenient to the DFW
Airport, North Dallas business corridor and Las Colinas office park, but it's
"not located near anything to do or see"; fans laud the "great atmosphere"
and appreciate the extensive grounds (complete with lake and jogging
paths), but without your own transportation, it's easy to feel "isolated."*

**Embassy Suites\*** 280S (fka Park Suite)  | 23 | 20 | 16 | 19 | $105 |
13131 N. Central Expwy.; (800) EMBASSY; (214) 234-3300; FAX 437-4247
*U – Guests find this a sweet suite deal, citing "comfy" accommodations
and "quality and service at a reasonable price"; budget business travelers
and conventioneers are grateful for the free cocktail hours and complimentary
breakfast; the "tropical-looking" atrium with "greenery hanging from each
floor" gets extra points.*

## DALLAS HOTELS                    | R | S | D | P | $ |

**Fairmont Hotel**  550R (51S)                 | 21 | 21 | 21 | 21 | $158 |
1717 N. Akard St.; (800) 527-4727; (214) 720-2020; FAX 720-5269
*M – This "lovely old-style" "landmark" has a "wonderful location" Downtown
near the Arts District, but there are those who consider it "a rather soulless
commercial hotel" that "has seen better days"; recent renovations have
produced an "impressive" lobby that's "long on the glitz", but rooms, though
"comfortable", have "failed to keep up with the times"; service is "typical
Fairmont, gracious and staid", and perks for execs like limo service and
access to the YMCA across the street make it "great for the dollars";*
N.B. *The Pyramid Room restaurant (food rating, 25) is a local favorite.*


**FOUR SEASONS**                              | 26 | 25 | 24 | 25 | $173 |
**RESORT & CLUB**  315R (10S)
4150 N. MacArthur Blvd., Irving; (800) 332-3442; (214) 717-0700; FAX 717-2428
*U – The "unbelievable facilities" make this an "athlete's delight", with a
"country-club atmosphere" that includes a "fantastic health club", a "great
spa", a "nice location on a golf course", tennis and a pretty dining room,
Cafe on the Green; being in Las Colinas is "bad for Downtown access", but
the "simple and classy" "Ralph Laurenish" ambiance and "Immaculate"
service get high marks.*


**Grand Kempinski Dallas, The**  529R (37S)   | 22 | 22 | 21 | 21 | $143 |
15201 Dallas Pkwy.; (800) 426-3135; (214) 386-6000; FAX 991-6937
*M – "Surprisingly charming" for such a large place, this "true Texas hotel"
offers "personalized service", "good value" and "lovely" French-Italian
dining at the Monte Carlo (food rating, 23) in a setting that's "bigger than
life"; its North Dallas location is "a little out of the way", but it's "not a bad
alternative for the outskirts of town", offering "modern glitz" combined with
"understated elegance"; detractors consider it an "utterly boring business
hotel", but they're outvoted.*


**HOTEL CRESCENT COURT**  216R (28S)          | 26 | 25 | 25 | 26 | $191 |
400 Crescent Court; (800) 654-6541; (214) 871-3200; FAX 871-3272
*U – "Understated Texas elegance" (read Versailles with a twang), "beautiful
public rooms" and "Southern hospitality" make a stay at the Crescent a
"divine experience" according to our surveyors; like its celebrated sister,
The Mansion, it's "in the Rosewood tradition of excellence", with
"well-appointed" rooms, "superior service and amenities" and a "fabulous
health club"; its north-of-Downtown location offers "excellent shopping",
two fine restaurants, Beau Nash (food rating, 22) and The Conservatory
(food rating, 25) and a bar that's a "true social experience"; it "doesn't get
much better than this."*

## DALLAS HOTELS

| R | S | D | P | $ |
| --- | --- | --- | --- | --- |

**Hotel St. Germain** 7S

| – | – | – | – | VE |
| --- | --- | --- | --- | --- |

2516 Maple Ave.; (214) 871-2516; FAX 841-0740
*A 1906 Victorian residence near the Crescent has been transformed into
this "lovely small bed-and-breakfast", which boasts a "good location" and
suites that are "reasonably priced for the quality"; grouchy nonbuffs may
think the place is "overpreserved", but the beautiful parlor and library with
their 14-foot ceilings, the New Orleans–style walled courtyard and meals
served by a butler on 75-year-old Limoges certainly set it apart.*

**Hyatt Regency Dallas at Reunion** 943R (49S)

| 20 | 19 | 18 | 19 | $127 |
| --- | --- | --- | --- | --- |

300 Reunion Blvd.; (800) 233-1234; (214) 651-1234; FAX 742-8126
*M – There's no accounting for taste: while many call this Dallas skyline
icon your "typical atrium-type Hyatt" and a "standard convention hotel",
others cite it for "impressive architecture" and a "luxurious labyrinth" of
public spaces; certainly it's a "good location for business travel", and those
seeking diversions will be pleased that it's "close to West End nightspots",
but some consider it "too large for the staff to handle" and, as for the
"rotating restaurant" (Antares), it's too bad you can't eat the "great view."*

**Loews Anatole Hotel** 1620R (145S)

| 22 | 21 | 21 | 23 | $145 |
| --- | --- | --- | --- | --- |

2201 Stemmons Frwy.; (800) 23LOEWS; (214) 748-1200; FAX 761-7520
*M – This top-of-the-line convention hotel is "just like Texas – big, open and
spacious"; "lots of art", "friendly staff", "upscale decor" and a "superior
health club" please most, but some find this "city within a city" just "too big",
"impersonal and "confusing"; at Nana Grill (food rating, 24) the "food is
super and the view fabulous", and a deli in one of the atriums provides
"great 24-hour food, and the service ain't bad."*

**MANSION ON
TURTLE CREEK, THE** 141R (13S)

| 27 | 28 | 28 | 27 | $218 |
| --- | --- | --- | --- | --- |

2821 Turtle Creek Blvd.; (800) 527-5432; (214) 559-2100; FAX 528-4187
*U – Mix "European elegance with Texas hospitality" and you get this
"sublime" "top hotel", rated best in the city, the state, the SW...you get the
picture; "the ultimate" in service and "pampering" – "everything is there
when you want it" – and "top-of-the-line luxury" make The Mansion "a
refined oasis" that "seems more like a residence than a hotel" – at least
until you get the bill; the eponymous restaurant (food rating, 27) provides
"world-class dining in a historic setting."*

**Melrose Hotel, The**   184R (34S)   | 20 | 21 | 20 | 20 | $126 |
(fka Omni Melrose)
3015 Oak Lawn Ave.; (800) MELROSE; (214) 521-5151; FAX 521-2470
*U – This "lovely old hotel", built in the '20s Chicago style and renovated
with "Southern charm", remains a "classic despite frequent changes of
ownership"; "rooms are spacious but not luxuriously appointed" – "warm
and homey" to boosters, "but a little run-down" to others; new owners are
renovating the public areas; P.S. "be sure to stop in the Library Bar."*

**Omni Mandalay Hotel**   | 22 | 21 | 20 | 22 | $133 |
**at Las Colinas**   420R (96S) (fka Marriott Mandalay)
221 E. Las Colinas Blvd.; (800) OMNIRES; (214) 556-0800; FAX 556-0729
*M – A "quiet", "solid" hotel with "beautiful grounds" and a "fun" setting on a
"canal waterway" in the Las Colinas Urban Center; while some say the rooms
are "among the most spacious, well furnished and interestingly designed"
in the city, critics think they "need sprucing up"; there's "quaint shopping
nearby", but an "out-of-the-way" location leaves some feeling "stranded."*

**Plaza of the Americas Hotel**   403 (36S)   | 19 | 19 | 18 | 19 | $138 |
650 N. Pearl St.; (800) 255-3050; (214) 979-9000; FAX 953-1931
*U – A "Texas extravaganza" (complete with lobby ice-skating rink), this
"business hotel" connected to a "fine retail and office complex" Downtown
features "urbane, polished service" and a "great view of the yuppie
briefcase brigade"; fans cite "wonderful big bathtubs", a "helpful concierge
staff" and a location within "walking distance of the Arts District"; the $17
million update of the atrium and skating rink is now complete, and the new
restaurant, 650 North, draws "very good" comments.*

**Sheraton Park Central**   545R (22S)   | 19 | 19 | 19 | 19 | $118 |
12720 Merit Dr.; (800) 325-3535; (214) 385-3000; FAX 991-4557
*U – Though the rooms are "nice" and "comfortable", "the lobby is like an
airport terminal", and critics say that "if you like noise, this is the place; still,
a location at the busy crossroads of I-635 and U.S. 75 is a boon, and you
get "the best nighttime views of Dallas" from the 20th-floor restaurant,
Laurels (food rating, 27); in sum, a "better-than-average Sheraton."*

**Sheraton Suites**   253S   | 19 | 17 | 16 | 16 | $134 |
(fka Marriott Dallas Market Center Suites)
2101 Stemmons Frwy.; (800) 228-9290; (214) 747-3000; FAX 742-5713
*M – Agreement eludes our reviewers, except concerning this Sheraton's
handy location in the Market Center area; some call it "very popular and
sophisticated", while others sniff "nothing sensational", "a glorified motel –
and not a charming one at that"; hopefully, the recent ownership change
will address this.*

| R | S | D | P | $ |
| --- | --- | --- | --- | --- |

**Southland Center Hotel***   502R (54S)      | 12 | 11 | 9 | 11 | $94 |
400 N. Olive St.; (800) 272-8007; (214) 922-8000; FAX 969-7650
*U – It's right near the city center, but that hasn't prevented disgruntled guest reaction: "outdated rooms", "rude staff", "one of the worst"; even the Southwestern-style Cafe Verde draws zingers: "the slowest service ever."*

**Stoneleigh Hotel, The**   105R (23S)      | 19 | 19 | 17 | 18 | $112 |
2927 Maple Ave.; (800) 255-9299; (214) 871-7111; FAX 871-9379
*U – "An oldie but goodie" that is "evocative of a past era"; although "a little rough around the edges", it's "certainly acceptable", offering "comfort without the chain-hotel feel"; a "wonderful location" "close to the Market" is an attraction; Ewalds, the long-established Continental restaurant, adds points.*

**Stouffer Dallas Hotel**   540R (30S)      | 19 | 18 | 17 | 17 | $123 |
2222 Stemmons Frwy.; (800) 468-3571; (214) 631-2222; FAX 905-3814
*U – "Despite routine decor and dining" this 30-story tower gets respectable ratings; also it's "close to the Apparel Mart" and has a "nice lobby, but everything else pales by comparison."*

**Westin Hotel Galleria Dallas, The**   430R (14S)   | 21 | 21 | 19 | 21 | $140 |
13340 Dallas Pkwy.; (800) 228-3000; (214) 934-9494; FAX 851-2869
*M – A "serviceable hotel adjacent to a huge mall" (the upscale Galleria) means "no need for a car" – you can "shop and drop at the same location"; "for the sports-minded", a pool, tennis and jogging are offered at the "complete fitness-tennis facility" (for an extra charge); traveling families should note that "kids love this place" – "they can skate, shop and play" without ever leaving their parents' sight.*

**Wyndham Garden Hotel**   168R (6S)      | 20 | 21 | 19 | 20 | $115 |
110 W. John Carpenter Frwy., Irving; (800) 822-4200; (214) 650-1600; FAX 541-0501
*U – Residential-style design and convenience in the Las Colinas area make for a "pretty hotel" and a "good value"; the landscaped garden area lends a feeling of home (without the lawn to mow) for road-weary executives, while proximity to DFW Airport is an added advantage.*

## ● OTHER HOTEL-CHAIN CHOICES
*You will find one or more additional locations of the following hotel chains in the Dallas/Fort Worth area: Courtyard by Marriott, Crown Sterling Suites, Days Inn, Hampton Inn, Hilton, Holiday Inn, Howard Johnson, La Quinta Inns, Marriott, Omni, Preferred Hotels, Radisson, Ramada, Relais & Chateaux, Residence Inn, Travelodge/Viscount and Wyndham; for reservations or information, see the toll-free 800 phone listings on page 16.*

# DENVER†

## TOP HOTELS
## (In order of rating)

### BEST OVERALL
22 – Loews Giorgio
21 – Brown Palace
    Westin Tabor Center
20 – Oxford Hotel
19 – Burnsley Hotel
    Stouffer Concourse

### BEST VALUES
Doubletree Hotel
Embassy Suites
Oxford Hotel
Loews Giorgio
Hyatt Regency Tech Center
Residence Inn

\*      \*      \*

### Best Rooms
23 – Loews Giorgio
22 – Oxford Hotel
21 – Westin Tabor Center
    Embassy Suites
    Brown Palace
20 – Burnsley Hotel

### Best Dining
21 – Loews Giorgio
    Brown Palace
20 – Warwick
19 – Westin Tabor Center
    Oxford Hotel
18 – Burnsley Hotel
    Hyatt Regency – Denver

### Best Service
22 – Loews Giorgio
    Brown Palace
21 – Oxford Hotel
    Burnsley Hotel
    Westin Tabor Center
20 – Warwick

### Best Public Facilities
22 – Brown Palace
    Loews Giorgio
21 – Westin Tabor Center
19 – Stouffer Concourse
    Oxford Hotel
18 – Hyatt Regency Tech Center

†For restaurants, see *Zagat Rocky Mountains Restaurant Survey* (to be published mid-1993).

**Brown Palace Hotel, The**   230R (25S)   | 21 | 22 | 21 | 22 | $147 |
321 17th St.; (800) 321-2599; (303) 297-3111; FAX 293-9204
M – This "old-style historic Downtown hotel in the heart of the Business
District" "remains faithful to its grand past as it gracefully ages"; though
it's considered "a classic", some feel the "dark, depressing rooms" need
updating; still, a "fabulous" glass-domed lobby, "friendly service" and
"elegant dining" keep the Brown "everyone's sentimental favorite."

**Burnsley Hotel, The**   82S   | 20 | 21 | 18 | 17 | $146 |
1000 Grant St.; (800) 231-3915; (303) 830-1000; FAX 830-7676
U – Business executives favor this "comfortable little place" that's
considered ideal for extended stays, thanks to its all-suites concept; a
few find the property "a bit shopworn", but most praise the "elegant suites"
and "good value"; though the ratings don't show it, some think "the dining
room makes this place."

**Cambridge Hotel\***   27S   | 21 | 20 | 19 | 16 | $141 |
1560 Sherman St.; (800) 877-1252; (303) 831-1252; FAX 831-4724
U – A "small, intimate" all-suiter considered "very comfortable" because
of the oversize one- and two-bedroom suites, attentive service,
complimentary continental breakfast and the French cuisine of The Profile
restaurant downstairs.

**Denver Marriott City Center**   612R (28S)   | 19 | 18 | 17 | 17 | $120 |
1701 California St.; (800) 228-9290; (303) 297-1300; FAX 298-7474
M – "Good but unremarkable" business hotel "within an easy walk of
Downtown attractions"; rooms are "boxy and boring" but clean and
comfortable, and there are "beautiful views from the upper floors"; the
staff receives mixed reviews for service.

**Doubletree Hotel**   254R (4S)   | 18 | 18 | 15 | 16 | $94 |
13696 E. Iliff Place, Aurora; (800) 243-3112; (303) 337-2800; FAX 337-9691
U – Great if business takes you to Southeast Denver, otherwise "nothing
special, just another place with no personality" – though it does represent
"good value" compared to Downtown; hotel guests can take advantage of
golf and tennis privileges at nearby Heather Ridge Country Club.

**Embassy Suites Denver Downtown**   337S   | 21 | 19 | 17 | 16 | $103 |
1881 Curtis St.; (800) 733-3366; (303) 297-8888; FAX 298-8046
U – "Rooms are always comfortable" and "spacious" at this all-suites hotel
in Downtown Denver; with its atrium design, "rooms on lower floors can be
noisy"; health-conscious travelers find "a very good athletic club attached",
featuring a swimming pool, indoor track, cardio and weight equipment and
aerobics classes.

## DENVER HOTELS

**Hyatt Regency – Denver**   511R (25S)   | 20 | 19 | 18 | 18 | $129 |
1750 Welton St.; (800) 228-3336; (303) 295-1200; FAX 293-2565
*M – A "reliable business and convention hotel" that's "serviceable" but not*
*terribly exciting; the "convenient location" makes up for what some call a*
*"dingy lobby"; highest praise is reserved for the "excellent health club and*
*tennis court on the roof."*

**Hyatt Regency**   | 19 | 19 | 18 | 18 | $110 |
**Tech Center Denver**   450R (12S)
7800 E. Tufts Ave.; (800) 233-1234; (303) 779-1234; FAX 850-7164
*M – Mostly used by businesspeople, this hotel is called "good for*
*conventions" and "well priced", with a "youthful, enthusiastic staff", though*
*its standard rooms draw some criticism; the "excellent" rooftop restaurant,*
*Centennial, offers "beautiful views" of the surrounding Rocky Mountains.*

**Loews Giorgio Hotel**   196R (20S)   | 23 | 22 | 21 | 22 | $129 |
4150 E. Mississippi Ave.; (800) 345-9172; (303) 782-9300; FAX 758-6542
*U – Only its location away from Downtown mars a stay at this*
*"European-style jewel"; still, shoppers delight in its proximity to the chic*
*Cherry Creek Shopping Center, and its "grand" Tuscany restaurant is "just*
*like a night in Italy"; complimentary continental breakfast is a nice extra.*

**Marriott Southeast**   595R (17S)   | 16 | 17 | 15 | 15 | $104 |
I-25 & Hampden Ave.; (800) 228-9290; (303) 758-7000; FAX 691-3418
*M – This run-of-the-mill Marriott catering to a business clientele is*
*somewhat "isolated" between Downtown and the DTC; recent renovations*
*may dispel the "motel-like" ambiance – still, reviewers are unenthusiastic.*

**Oxford Hotel**   81R (12S)   | 22 | 21 | 19 | 19 | $116 |
(fka Oxford Alexis Hotel)
1600 17th St.; (800) 228-5838; (303) 628-5400; FAX 628-5413
*U – A "nice restoration" of a Downtown landmark featuring "cozy" rooms*
*with "luxurious" "19th-century decor"; fans rave about the "fabulous art*
*deco bar" and McCormicks' seafood restaurant; guests can firm up or cool*
*down at the adjacent Oxford Aveda Salon & Fitness Center.*

**Radisson Hotel Denver**   739R (30S)   | 17 | 16 | 14 | 15 | $109 |
1550 Court Place; (800) 333-3333; (303) 893-3333; FAX 623-0303
*M – A typical convention hotel, "big and impersonal"; after extensive*
*renovation, some find the rooms "extremely comfortable", while others*
*classify them as "small" and "mediocre"; still, it has a "good location" on*
*the 16th Street Mall, and "the price is right."*

## DENVER HOTELS

| R | S | D | P | $ |
|---|---|---|---|---|

**Red Lion**  515R (9S)  | 18 | 16 | 14 | 14 | $99 |
(fka Registry Hotel)
3203 Quebec St.; (800) 547-8010; (303) 321-3333; FAX 329-5233
*M – As airport hotels go, this one is "average" and "dependable"; fans call it "charming", but critics say it's "crowded and noisy"; all agree it's priced right, however; amenities include an indoor pool, an outdoor hot tub and a business center.*

**Residence Inn**  156S  | 19 | 16 | 13 | 16 | $96 |
2777 Zuni St.; (800) 331-3131; (303) 458-5318; FAX 458-5318
*U – "A lower-priced alternative", this all-suites hotel is especially suited to families and those planning an extended stay; it's also "convenient" to Downtown and Larimer Square; there's no restaurant, but there is a cocktail hour and a complimentary continental breakfast.*

**Scanticon Denver, The\***  302R (40S)  | 22 | 22 | 20 | 23 | $119 |
200 Inverness Dr. W., Englewood; (800) 346-4891; (303) 799-5800; FAX 799-5874
*U – "Clean, attractive, modern" business-oriented hotel located far south of Downtown; "superb" conference facilities "make working there a pleasure"; between meetings, take advantage of three restaurant possibilities, the indoor and outdoor pools, tennis courts and 18-hole golf course.*

**Sheraton Denver Tech Center**  625R (10S)  | 17 | 16 | 16 | 16 | $99 |
4900 DTC Pkwy.; (800) 552-7030; (303) 779-1100; FAX 779-1100 x396
*U – In Southeast Denver, this "generic conference hotel" is a little "off the beaten path" but considered "fine for business" despite "small rooms"; the Cafe in the Park serves an "excellent breakfast", and there are "good running trails nearby."*

**Stouffer Concourse Hotel**  400R (10S)  | 20 | 18 | 17 | 19 | $114 |
3801 Quebec St.; (800) HOTELS1; (303) 399-7500; FAX 321-1966
*U – With an ultramodern atrium "building that looks like it's going to blast off", this "great airport hotel" is a Denver "favorite"; a common complaint is excessive noise, and respondents suggest you "request a mountainside room" both for the views and the quiet; "dining is a pleasant surprise" in the Concorde restaurant.*

**Warwick Hotel**  194R (49S)  | 19 | 20 | 20 | 18 | $99 |
1776 Grant St.; (800) 525-2888; (303) 861-2000; FAX 832-0320
*U – This "nondescript but comfortable" business hotel with good service is well situated near the Financial District; the nicely appointed rooms are done in antiques; a complimentary European-style buffet and free limo service to Downtown are provided with the cost of a room.*

**Westin Hotel Tabor Center, The**   420R (13S)   | 21 | 21 | 19 | 21 | $138 |
1672 Lawrence St.; (800) 228-3000; (303) 572-9100; FAX 572-7288
*U – In the heart of Denver, "modern rooms", "cheerful service" and an
"informed concierge" mean good marks from businesspeople and tourists
alike; respondents applaud this midsize hotel's "great location" "close to
restaurants, shopping and sightseeing", including a direct connection to the
shops at Tabor Center, the 16th Street Mall and Tabor Athletic Club.*

● **OTHER HOTEL-CHAIN CHOICES**
*You will find one or more additional locations of the following hotel chains in
the Denver area: Courtyard by Marriott, Days Inn, Doubletree, Embassy
Suites, Hampton Inn, Hilton, Holiday Inn, Howard Johnson, La Quinta Inns,
Marriott, Radisson, Ramada, Residence Inn and Super 8; for reservations
or information, see the toll-free 800 phone listings on page 16.*

# DETROIT

## TOP HOTELS
### (In order of rating)

**BEST OVERALL**

23 – Ritz-Carlton
    Townsend Hotel
    Dearborn Inn Marriott
19 – Hyatt Regency Dearborn
18 – Radisson Plaza

**BEST VALUES**

Dearborn Inn Marriott
Radisson Plaza
Townsend Hotel
Ritz-Carlton
Hyatt Regency Dearborn

\*    \*    \*

**Best Rooms**

24 – Townsend Hotel
    Ritz-Carlton
20 – Dearborn Inn Marriott
19 – Radisson Hotel Pontchartrain
    Hyatt Regency Dearborn

**Best Dining**

23 – Ritz-Carlton
21 – Townsend Hotel
20 – Dearborn Inn Marriott
18 – Hyatt Regency Dearborn
16 – Radisson Hotel Pontchartrain

**Best Service**

23 – Ritz-Carlton
    Townsend Hotel
21 – Dearborn Inn Marriott
19 – Hyatt Regency Dearborn
18 – Radisson Hotel Pontchartrain

**Best Public Facilities**

24 – Ritz-Carlton
22 – Townsend Hotel
21 – Dearborn Inn Marriott
19 – Hyatt Regency Dearborn
17 – Radisson Plaza

| R | S | D | P | $ |
|---|---|---|---|---|

**Atheneum Suites**　175S　　　　| – | – | – | – | VE |
1000 Brush Ave.; (800) 772-2323; (313) 962-2323; FAX 962-2424
*The same entrepreneurs who turned the lights on in Greektown with Trapper's Alley Festival Marketplace bring hope to the moribund Downtown area with the opening of this luxurious all-suites hotel, the first new hotel to open in Detroit in years; classic deco architecture combines with all the possible comforts of a grand hostelry to create a city within a city.*

## DETROIT HOTELS

| R | S | D | P | $ |
|---|---|---|---|---|

**Dearborn Inn Marriott**   222R (20S)   | 20 | 21 | 20 | 21 | $127 |
20301 Oakwood Blvd.; (800) 228-9290; (313) 271-2700; FAX 271-7464
*M – A "fortune" was spent in restoring this 1930s vintage "beautiful old-fashioned resort" across from the Henry Ford Museum in Greenfield Village; fans call it "historic and classy", with "excellent service" and an "outstanding restaurant"; it's a "quiet and comfortable", "quaint standby" that gives a "good stay."*

**Hotel St. Regis\***   221R (15S)   | 14 | 13 | 13 | 12 | $109 |
3071 W. Grand Blvd.; (800) 848-4810; (313) 873-3000; FAX 873-2574
*M – Direct skywalks to the General Motors World Headquarters and Fisher Theatre provide "a good location for business execs" at New Center's French Regency style older hotel; though detractors – and the numbers – say it's "slightly shabby", fans say it has brought a "touch of class to Motown."*

**Hyatt Regency Dearborn**   771R (22S)   | 19 | 19 | 18 | 19 | $134 |
Fairlane Town Ctr., Dearborn; (800) 233-1234; (313) 593-1234; FAX 593-3366
*M – The rooms are "up to the usual Hyatt standards" and the "location on the grounds of a shopping mall is fun", making this "beautiful hotel" a "fine facility for meetings and trade shows"; in spite of "roomy and spacious" renovated suites on the club penthouse level, however, some feel "isolated" in a "remote location out of the mainstream."*

**Mayflower Bed &**   | – | – | – | – | M |
**Breakfast Hotel, The**   89R (8S)
827 W. Ann Arbor Trail, Plymouth; (800) 456-1620; (313) 453-1620; FAX 453-0775
*Small-town charm is yours at this comparatively large bed-and-breakfast located about 20 minutes from the airport, providing a warm contrast to Detroit's convention-oriented chain hotels; pleasant rooms, friendly service and good value make it a winner if you don't have to be in town.*

**Novi Hilton**   236R (5S)   | 15 | 15 | 15 | 14 | $109 |
21111 Haggerty Rd., Novi; (800) HILTONS; (313) 349-4000; FAX 349-4066
*M – Twenty minutes from Downtown Detroit and "adjacent to an industrial park" is Hilton's "nice business hotel" "in the middle of nowhere"; despite recent renovations, our surveyors say it's still "nothing special" – a "serviceable place", nothing more, nothing less.*

**DETROIT HOTELS**                          | R | S | D | P | $ |

**Omni Detroit Hotel**   255R (17S)          | 18 | 17 | 15 | 17 | $131 |
333 E. Jefferson Ave.; (800) THE-OMNI; (313) 222-7700; FAX 222-6509
*M – "Centrally located" across from the Renaissance Center in Downtown
Detroit, this "pleasant, modern hotel" is judged "standard for the chain";
some critics cite "inattention to detail" and the need for more staff.*


**Radisson Hotel Pontchartrain**   415R (34S)  | 19 | 18 | 16 | 16 | $128 |
2 Washington Blvd.; (800) 333-3333; (313) 965-0200; FAX 965-9464
*U – "If you must stay Downtown", this solid but "ordinary" midsize Financial
District hotel is certainly "convenient for business"; however, some suggest
it's "not what it used to be" and warn the location is "great for a mugging."*


**Radisson Plaza Hotel**   385R               | 20 | 18 | 17 | 17 | $113 |
1500 Town Ctr., Southfield; (800) 333-3333; (313) 827-4000; FAX 827-1364
*U – Fans say "the rest of the chain should take notes" on this "good solid,
efficient business hotel"; set in a "nice location" in suburban Detroit, it's
within "close proximity of outstanding restaurants" and many Fortune 500
companies; all in all, a "classy addition" to the area.*


**RITZ-CARLTON, DEARBORN**   308R (15S)       | 24 | 23 | 23 | 24 | $162 |
300 Town Center Dr., Dearborn; (800) 241-3333; (313) 441-2000; FAX 441-2051
*U – Adjacent to Fairlane Plaza Shopping Center and five minutes from
historic Greenfield Village, Dearborn's Ritzy "oasis" offers the "ultimate
luxury and pampering" from the "best staff anywhere", making it "a
quantum leap better than other hotels in the area"; though perhaps "not up
to par" with the rest of the Ritz group, this "welcome hideaway" makes
"dreary" Detroit "bearable."*


**River Place Inn\* (CLOSED)**   108R (22S)   | 22 | 20 | 21 | 21 | $132 |
1000 Stroh River Place; (800) 999-1466; (313) 259-2500; FAX 259-1248
*U – For a change of pace, try this "first-class hotel" in the restored Historic
District on the river overlooking Canada; built in 1902, it has undergone
recent renovations to revive its "charming, fresh country-inn decor", giving
this "excellent hotel" a "romantic feeling"; amenities include a health club,
complimentary valet parking and good package deals.*


**TOWNSEND HOTEL**   87S                      | 24 | 23 | 21 | 22 | $152 |
100 Townsend St., Birmingham; (800) 548-4172; (313) 642-7900;
FAX 645-9061
*U – If you can stay in the suburbs, this "charming small hotel" (suites only)
in the town of Birmingham is a "very pleasant surprise", "almost worth
going to Detroit" for; expect "excellent value" on "lovely suites", "pleasant
service", "English-countryside" ambiance and "afternoon tea in the lobby",
making it a "real find" for Motown.*

**Westin Hotel, The**   1400R (52S)          | 18 | 16 | 15 | 16 | $128 |
Renaissance Center; (800) 228-3000; (313) 568-8000; FAX 568-8146
*M – "A fortress in the middle of no-man's-land", this "stark" tower with great
views of the "concrete jungle" inspires discord among our surveyors; fans
call this hotel "convenient" with extra praise for the "spectacular views of the
river and Canada" and "lots of dining choices"; critics say it's "noisy" and "in
need of repair", and "you'll need a tour guide to find your room."*

● **OTHER HOTEL-CHAIN CHOICES**
*You will find one or more additional locations of the following hotel chains in
the Detroit area: Courtyard by Marriott, Days Inn, Embassy Suites, Guest
Quarters, Hampton Inn, Hilton, Holiday Inn, Howard Johnson, Marriott,
Preferred Hotels, Radisson, Ramada, Super 8, Travelodge/Viscount and
Wyndham; for reservations or information, see the toll-free 800 phone
listings on page 16.*

# FORT LAUDERDALE†

## TOP HOTELS
### (In order of rating)

**BEST OVERALL**

22 – Marriott's Harbor Beach
20 – Westin Cypress Creek
19 – Lago Mar
     Fort Lauderdale Marina Marriott
     Pier 66

**BEST VALUES**

Westin Cypress Creek
Crown Sterling Suites
Sheraton Design Center
Fort Lauderdale Marriott North
Fort Lauderdale Marina Marriott

\*    \*    \*

**Best Rooms**

22 – Marriott's Harbor Beach
     Westin Cypress Creek
21 – Lago Mar
20 – Crown Sterling Suites
     Pier 66

**Best Dining**

20 – Marriott's Harbor Beach
     Westin Cypress Creek
19 – Lago Mar
18 – Sheraton Design Center
     Fort Lauderdale Marina

**Best Service**

22 – Marriott's Harbor Beach
21 – Westin Cypress Creek
20 – Lago Mar
19 – Fort Lauderdale Marina
     Sheraton Design Center

**Best Public Facilities**

22 – Marriott's Harbor Beach
20 – Westin Cypress Creek
     Pier 66
19 – Fort Lauderdale Marina
     Crown Sterling Suites

†For restaurants, see *Zagat Miami/South Florida Restaurant Survey.*

### Bahia Mar Resort & Yachting Center   307R (9S)

| 18 | 17 | 16 | 17 | $126 |

801 Seabreeze Ave.; (800) 327-8154; (305) 764-2233; FAX 524-6912
*U – "Yachts of fun by the sea" describes this "boater's delight" on the Intracoastal Waterway; "undemanding tourists" opting for the "less pretentious" find this "old facility with its great location on the beach and marina" appealing, but they still advise staying in the renovated main building to avoid "run-down rooms."*

### Crown Sterling Suites Fort Lauderdale/ Cypress Creek   254S (fka Embassy Suites)

| 20 | 18 | 16 | 19 | $111 |

555 NW 62nd St.; (800) 433-4600; (305) 772-5400; FAX 772-5400
*M – "Great free breakfast and booze", "free parking" and a choice of "wonderful" suites are pluses for budget-minded travelers at this "comfortable" Mediterranean-style "family place"; close proximity to the railroad tracks, however, means it may get "extremely noisy", and critics suggest "this crown be dethroned."*

### Fort Lauderdale Marina Marriott   580R (17S)

| 19 | 19 | 18 | 19 | $135 |

1881 SE 17th St.; (800) 433-2254; (305) 463-4300; FAX 527-6205
*U – With one of the largest free-form pools in Lauderdale, this "resortlike" modern Port Everglades hotel is right across the street from the new convention center for businessfolk; "large, comfortable rooms in the tower with private balconies" and a "beautiful view of the waterway" go a long way toward counteracting a "so-so", "basically mass-appeal" hotel.*

### Fort Lauderdale Marriott North   321R (fka Cypress Creek)

| 17 | 17 | 16 | 17 | $110 |

6650 N. Andrews Ave.; (800) 228-9290; (305) 771-0440; FAX 771-0440 x6608
*U – This "clean and friendly but institutional" "cookie-cutter Marriott" offers appealing, "less expensive" weekend specials and a convenient location half a mile from the airport; it's a "good hotel for the business traveler" – nothing more, nothing less.*

### Lago Mar Resort & Club   180R (150S)

| 21 | 20 | 19 | 18 | $150 |

1700 S. Ocean Lane; (800) 255-5246; (305) 523-6511; FAX 523-6511
*U – "Your club-away-from-home" provides "real elegance" and "excellent amenities" in a "secluded" setting a water-taxi-ride away from town; respondents say this newly renovated low-rise Mediterranean is a "gorgeous property" with a "lovely isolated beach", much-appreciated "play areas for kids" and "service like hotels used to give"; all in all, about "the nicest resort you can get for the money."*

## FORT LAUDERDALE HOTELS | R | S | D | P | $ |

**Marriott's Harbor Beach Resort**   624R (35S) | 22 | 22 | 20 | 22 | $164 |
3030 Holiday Dr.; (800) 228-9290; (305) 525-4000; FAX 766-6165
*U – "Just a super hotel", with a "stunning waterfall pool setting", "elegant
and spacious suites" and "pampering service" – a "huge class-act on
the beach"; "wonderful grounds" and "great food in the gourmet dining
room" make this No.1 Fort Lauderdale property a "vacation dream" in a
"romantic tropical oasis" for most; however, a few complain that it's "pricey"
and "overcrowded."*

**Ocean Manor Resort Hotel***   110R (25S) | 14 | 15 | 14 | 16 | $107 |
(fka Radisson Resort)
4040 Galt Ocean Dr.; (800) 955-0444; (305) 566-7500; FAX 564-3075
*M – Built in 1957 and renovated in 1991, this resort offers a good vacation
value for sports lovers visiting the busy Lauderdale strip, with golf, tennis
and deep-sea fishing available close by; to critics it offers "basic seaside
glitz" with "no imagination."*

**Pier 66 Resort & Marina**   388R (8S) | 20 | 19 | 18 | 20 | $142 |
2301 SE 17th St. Causeway; (800) 327-3796; (305) 525-6666; FAX 728-3551
*M – Enjoy cocktails with "a spectacular view from the rotating lounge on
the top floor" or call room service from one of the "wonderful rooms newly
decorated with reproduction antiques and beautiful Pierre Deux fabrics";
but service lapses and unrefurbished rooms around the pool leave some
guests dissatisfied.*

**Riverside Hotel***   117R (5S) | 18 | 21 | 18 | 19 | $100 |
620 E. Las Olas Blvd.; (800) 325-3280; (305) 467-0671; FAX 462-2148
*U – Since 1936, this "charming, old-world", "funky chic" Downtown
landmark with antique furnishings and European ambiance has been
"great for the businessperson" attending small corporate meetings; despite
a redo to bestow the public areas and some of the hotel rooms with a
brighter, cleaner look, it retains that quaint feeling so loved by travelers
who'd walk an extra mile to stay anywhere but in a chain hotel.*

**Sheraton Design Center**   258R (7S) | 19 | 19 | 18 | 18 | $116 |
1825 Griffin Rd., Dania; (800) 325-3535; (305) 920-3500; FAX 920-3571
*M – "Terrific conference facilities" and "good value" are assets, but for
businesspeople visiting the adjacent Design Center of the Americas, the
location is this hotel's principle strength; critics say it has a "hectic
atmosphere" and "front rooms like sleeping on a speed raceway."*

## FORT LAUDERDALE HOTELS          | R | S | D | P | $ |

**Sheraton Yankee Clipper**   504R (7S)          | 14 | 14 | 12 | 13 | $108 |
1140 Seabreeze Blvd.; (800) 325-3535; (305) 524-5551; FAX 523-5376
*U – "Be sure to get a room on the ocean side of the road", where the
"reasonably priced" but "average rooms" are at least "clean" and "quiet";
the "great location", and "good facilities" help save an otherwise "tired and
worn-out" but "reliable older hotel", now in the process of refurbishing
rooms that our surveyors say "haven't been fixed up since the* Yankee
Clipper *sailed."*

**Westin Hotel, Cypress Creek**   293R (33S)          | 22 | 20 | 20 | 20 | $117 |
400 Corporate Dr.; (800) 228-3000; (305) 772-1331; FAX 772-6867
*U – Thanks to its "proximity to the highway and airport", "excellent service"
and "pleasant, roomy rooms", this "beautifully decorated", "supermodern"
hotel with an "outstanding restaurant", Cypress Room (food rating, 23), and
"beautiful pool and gardens" is "perfect for business or pleasure"; though
"out of the way" when it comes to the beach, its setting in a "corporate
park" on the north end of Fort Lauderdale makes it very popular for
"secluded meetings."*

## ●OTHER HOTEL-CHAIN CHOICES
*You will find one or more additional locations of the following hotel chains in
the Fort Luaderdale area: Courtyard by Marriott, Crown Sterling Suites,
Days Inn, Embassy Suites, Guest Quarters, Hampton Inn, Hilton, Holiday
Inn, Howard Johnson, Ramada, Travelodge/Viscount; for reservations or
information, see the toll-free 800 phone listings on page 16.*

# HONOLULU*†

## TOP HOTELS
## (In order of rating)

### BEST OVERALL

27 – Halekulani
25 – Kahala Hilton
23 – Hawaii Prince Waikiki
22 – Sheraton Moana Surfrider
  Royal Hawaiian
21 – Hyatt Regency Waikiki
20 – Hilton Hawaiian Village
  New Otani

### BEST VALUES

Hawaii Prince Waikiki
Outrigger Waikiki
New Otani
Sheraton Princess
Sheraton Moana Surfrider
Turtle Bay Hilton
Hilton Hawaiian Village
Ala Moana Hotel

\*        \*        \*

### Best Rooms

27 – Halekulani
25 – Kahala Hilton
23 – Hawaii Prince Waikiki
  Sheraton Moana Surfrider
22 – Royal Hawaiian
21 – Hyatt Regency Waikiki
  Hawaiian Regent
  Colony Surf

### Best Dining

27 – Halekulani
24 – Kahala Hilton
23 – Hawaii Prince Waikiki
22 – Colony Surf
21 – Sheraton Moana Surfrider
  Hyatt Regency Waikiki
20 – New Otani
  Royal Hawaiian

### Best Service

27 – Halekulani
25 – Kahala Hilton
23 – Hawaii Prince Waikiki
22 – Sheraton Moana Surfrider
  Royal Hawaiian
21 – Hyatt Regency Waikiki
  New Otani
20 – Hilton Hawaiian Village

### Best Public Facilities

26 – Halekulani
25 – Kahala Hilton
23 – Sheraton Moana Surfrider
  Royal Hawaiian
22 – Hawaii Prince Waikiki
  Hyatt Regency Waikiki
  Hilton Hawaiian Village
20 – Hawaiian Regent

---

\*See also: Hawaii Resorts.
†For restaurants, see *Zagat Hawaii Restaurant Survey*.

**Ala Moana Hotel**   1172R (67S)   | 20 | 19 | 17 | 19 | $153 |
410 Atkinson Dr.; (800) 367-6025; (808) 955-4811; FAX 947-7338
*M – Not by any stretch of the imagination a Waikiki hotel, this behemoth
(often confused with the Sheraton Moana Surfrider) instead appeals to
shoppers for its proximity to the tony Ala Moana Shopping Center, and to
business types with no interest in beaching and bronzing; fans mention
"convenience" and a "homey" yet "efficient" atmosphere; detractors dismiss
it as "very commercial."*


**Colony Surf Hotel**   101S   | 21 | 19 | 22 | 17 | $193 |
2895 Kalakaua Ave.; (800) 252-7873; (808) 923-5751; FAX 922-8433
*U – Technically just outside Waikiki, across from Kapiolani Park, this well-
liked all-suiter boasts a "beautiful setting on the beach" "a little away from
the crowd"; praise for the "elegant restaurant", Michel's (food rating, 24),
"very big rooms", "great bathrooms" and "good kitchens" more than offsets
random grumblings about needed refurbishments; all in all, a "fine value."*


**HALEKULANI**   456R (44S)   | 27 | 27 | 27 | 26 | $245 |
2199 Kalia Rd.; (800) 367-2343; (808) 923-2311; FAX 926-8004
*U – "Expensive but worth it", this "outstanding", well-managed hotel (the
top vote-getter on Oahu) is generally acknowledged as "the only truly
elegant place in Honolulu" and "an oasis of highest luxury in the middle of
crowded Waikiki"; a cordial, perfectly trained staff, a "great pool", lovely
rooms and public facilities, and the "indescribably" wonderful restaurants,
La Mer (food rating, 25) and Orchids (food rating, 23), all add up to "an
enchanting experience" – "like being in heaven."*


**Hawaiian Regent**   1346R   | 21 | 19 | 19 | 20 | $160 |
2552 Kalakaua Ave.; (800) 367-5370; (808) 922-6611; FAX 921-5255
*M – An "excellent location" across the street from the beach and "great
views" make the very big and no-longer-new Regent good for groups,
but it's less praised by individual travelers; "good value" is also cited,
but those in search of quiet repose may want to pass on this "ok, not
o lei" hotel; N.B. The Secret restaurant (food rating, 24) has an
"exceptional" reputation locally.*


**Hawaiian Waikiki Beach Hotel\***   715R (41S)   | 19 | 18 | 17 | 18 | $148 |
(fka Holiday Inn Waikiki)
2570 Kalakaua Ave.; (800) 877-0889; (808) 922-2511; FAX 926-3656
*M – A change in management has improved the scores – if not our
surveyors' recognition – of this well-located and reasonably priced "family
resort" across from the legendary beach at Waikiki; though critics say it still
"falls short of its reputation", fans are happy to book a room here and say
"push for a Diamond Head view."*

## HONOLULU HOTELS

| R | S | D | P | $ |

**HAWAII PRINCE HOTEL WAIKIKI** 521R (57S)  | 23 | 23 | 23 | 22 | $152 |
100 Holomoana St.; (800) 321-6284; (808) 956-1111; FAX 946-0811
*U – Waikiki may be in the name, but this Prince is a considerable hike from
the famous beach; nonetheless, guests are pleased with the "well-trained
personnel", "fabulous view" "overlooking the yacht harbor" and "gorgeous
rooms" that make for a "refreshing change" from the madding crowds;
there are six restaurants (two Japanese) and an outdoor pool; room rates
escalate with the floor level, but it's still the city's top value.*


**Hilton Hawaiian Village**   2542R (365S)   | 21 | 20 | 20 | 22 | $165 |
2005 Kalia Rd.; (800) HILTONS; (808) 949-4321; FAX 947-7898
*U – The largest hotel in Hawaii and a mainstay of the Hilton chain, this
"overwhelming" "minicity" "busy convention hotel" boasts "gorgeous
grounds" on the widest part of Hawaii's "most famous beach" and lots of
shopping in the 'village'; "despite the size", it's "comfortable" and "friendly",
with a "beautiful setting", "superb public areas", two big pools, nine
restaurants, one coffee shop, plus two excellent dining rooms, Golden
Dragon (food rating, 23) and Bali by the Sea (food rating, 24) so "you
don't ever need to leave the grounds."*


**Hyatt Regency Waikiki**   1230R (21S)   | 21 | 21 | 21 | 22 | $180 |
2424 Kalakaua Ave.; (800) 882-1234; (808) 923-1234; FAX 923-7935
*M – "You're in the middle of it all but so far above" the crush in this
"stunning" across-the-street-from-Waikiki high rise, with its "drop-dead"
lobby, "wonderful views of Diamond Head" and "two floors of mall stores
for shopping"; though most call it a "class act of Waikiki", there are those
who say it's "all glitter and no substance", and "if you don't speak
Japanese, they're not interested"; N.B. the Regency Club, with its rooftop
deck and whirlpool, is Honolulu's best-kept secret.*


**Ilikai Hotel Nikko Waikiki**   852R (52S)   | 19 | 18 | 17 | 18 | $155 |
1777 Ala Moana Blvd.; (800) 367-8434; (808) 949-3811; FAX 947-0892
*M – "The Ilikai" for short, this "serviceable old-timer" is described as "beautiful
and exotic" by some, a "Travelodge that took vitamins" by others; "Hawaii
5-0 to the bone", it's got a "great location" off the beach but handy to Ala
Moana Center, along with "large rooms"; a recent takeover by the highly
rated Nikko group bodes well for this '60s-era hotel in need of a shakeup.*

**KAHALA HILTON**   369R (33S)              | 25 | 25 | 24 | 25 | $226 |
5000 Kahala Ave.; (800) 367-2525; (808) 734-2211; FAX 737-2478
*U – Think of it as "an outer island property 15 minutes from Waikiki"; "just
far enough" from the "hubbub" "to be perfect", this Hilton International Hotel
is judged "older-but-aging-gracefully" and the "epitome of what a Hawaii
hotel should be"; a beach setting, "wonderful" grounds complete with
dolphins and turtles in the pools, and staff that "treats guests like royalty"
make this, for some, "the only place to stay in Honolulu"; you can't miss
dining at any of the three fine dining rooms, Maile Room (food rating, 26),
Plumeria Cafe (21) or Hala Terrace (20).*

**New Otani Kaimana**                       | 19 | 21 | 20 | 19 | $149 |
**Beach Hotel, The**   125R (31S)
2863 Kalakaua Ave.; (800) 733-7949; (808) 923-1555; FAX 922-9404
*U – A small, "underrated", low-key property that's one of Honolulu's best
values is "away from the crowds" of Waikiki on a "quiet" "nontourist beach"
near the famous Colony Surf; the rooms are "tiny" but "elegant", and the
Hau Tree Lanai (food rating, 20) ("under the big tree") restaurant may be
"the best place for breakfast in Honolulu" – or for another meal.*

**Outrigger Waikiki**   530R (195S)         | 17 | 16 | 15 | 16 | $116 |
2335 Kalakaua Ave.; (800) 733-7777; (808) 923-0711; FAX 921-9749
*M – The flagship of the home-grown Outrigger fleet, this well-located
"beach hotel" is good "if you're on a budget", and "right where the action
is"; though the unconverted suggest that it's "just a place to leave your
luggage", at least you can "watch the ongoing beach show from your balcony."*

**Pacific Beach Hotel***   850R (8S)        | 17 | 18 | 15 | 16 | $114 |
2490 Kalakaua Ave.; (800) 367-6060; (808) 922-1233; FAX 922-8061
*U – Famous for the 280,000-gallon "oceanarium" in the lobby but not much
else, this older twin-towered hotel is also conveniently located near the
beach and shopping; a 1990 renovation hasn't cured our surveyors of the
conviction, however, that it's "nothing special."*

**Park Plaza Waikiki***   313R (45S)        | 21 | 20 | 17 | 16 | $112 |
(fka Waikiki Marina Hotel)
1956 Ala Moana Blvd.; (800) 367-6070; (808) 941-7275; FAX 951-3114
*U – Too new to call in its present incarnation, this little-known, smallish
hotel, slightly off the beaten path, just got a $37 million renovation, with
"excellent" guest rooms and a new business center and exercise facilities;
the restaurant, Roy's Park Bistro, is a branch of the highly popular Roy's.*

## HONOLULU HOTELS

| R | S | D | P | $ |
| --- | --- | --- | --- | --- |

**Royal Hawaiian Hotel**   526R (50S)   | 22 | 22 | 20 | 23 | $203 |
(fka Sheraton Royal Hawaiian Hotel)
2259 Kalakaua Ave.; (800) 325-3535; (808) 923-7311; FAX 924-7098
*U – This revered "classic pink palace of Waikiki" was built in 1927 and is
still "a beautiful, lavish getaway"; fans love this "club from the old days of
Waikiki glory", with its "beautiful" flower-filled grounds (now somewhat
truncated by a shopping mall) and "old-fashioned comfort" (in the original
building) and service; it's a "grand old lady" in a "sea of faceless high rises."*

**Sheraton Makaha Resort &**   | 18 | 18 | 16 | 18 | $150 |
**Country Club**   200R (8S)
84-626 Makaha Valley Rd., Waianae; (800) 325-3535; (808) 695-9511; FAX 695-5806
*M – In a distant valley 45 minutes from Waikiki, this hotel is the least known
of Sheraton's many Oahu properties, and it's not everyone's cup of tea: for
every booster who calls it a "beautiful refuge" and the perfect place "for honeymooners", there's a critic who thinks it's "really in need of some serious
remodeling"; the fact that it's got golf, tennis, hiking and nearby surfing is a plus.*

**SHERATON MOANA SURFRIDER**   793R (44S) | 23 | 22 | 21 | 23 | $179 |
2365 Kalakaua Ave.; (800) 325-3535; (808) 922-3111; FAX 923-0308
*U – A "romantic bit of history" is yours at this "brilliant" restoration of a
"national treasure", the 1901 Moana Hotel; her full "face-lift put this hotel in
the front row" again, with a "wonderful veranda" ("so special for breakfast"),
"beautiful pool area" and grounds, and a "lovely" oceanfront atmosphere;
book a suite for "incredible two-way views" at "Hawaii's Tara on the beach",
infinitely better than rooms in the newer high rises.*

**Sheraton Princess Kaiulani Hotel**  1150R (6S) | 17 | 18 | 17 | 17 | $134 |
120 Kaiulani Ave.; (800) 325-3535; (808) 922-5811; FAX 924-7210
*M – One of Honolulu's first high rises, "P.K." holds fond memories for many,
even if she's now outclassed by younger rivals; all agree on the "great
location" (across the street from the beach and next to the International
Marketplace) and "beautiful open lobby", but the disenchanted complain of
"ugly, claustrophobic rooms"; hey, it's cheap – what d'ya want?*

**Sheraton Waikiki Hotel**   1900R (125S)   | 20 | 18 | 18 | 19 | $165 |
2255 Kalakaua Ave.; (800) 325-3535; (808) 922-4422; FAX 923-8785
*M – Sheraton's island flagship poised on the edge of the beach at Waikiki
is "big, bold and beautiful" according to some, "too huge and impersonal"
to others; "rooms vary greatly", and you may encounter "a zoo of tour
groups" in the "colorful", if "chaotic", lobby; of course, "the views are what
every first-timer thinks of: Waikiki Beach and Diamond Head" – and for
fans, they more than "make up for any deficiencies."*

## HONOLULU HOTELS

| | R | S | D | P | $ |
|---|---|---|---|---|---|

### Turtle Bay Hilton Golf & Tennis Resort   486R (26S)

| 19 | 18 | 17 | 19 | $147 |

57-091 Kamehameha Hwy., Kahuku; (800) HILTONS; (808) 293-8811; FAX 293-9147

*M – Being about an hour "away from the hustle of Honolulu" is a great advantage to some, "an utter disappointment" to others; seclusion and "superb landscaping and layout" make this hotel "great for honeymooners", while golf, tennis, horseback riding and other "country" sports unavailable in Waikiki are a bonus for the health-conscious traveler.*

### Waikiki Beachcomber Hotel*   498R (4S)

| 17 | 17 | 15 | 16 | $129 |

2300 Kalakaua Ave.; (800) 622-4646; (808) 922-4646; FAX 923-4889

*M – This tourist hotel located above the Liberty House department store is "one of the best-kept secrets in Honolulu" to travelers interested in a basic, "inexpensive" package with a "good location across from the beach"; those with more demanding expectations, however, call it just "adequate" and "plain for the tropics."*

### Waikiki Joy*   93R (44S)

| 20 | 19 | 16 | 17 | $126 |

320 Lewers St.; (800) 733-5569; (808) 923-2300; FAX 924-4010

*U – This boutique hotel, a five-minute walk from the beach, is a joy to most who check in; it's "beautiful and serene", with "good clientele and free breakfast and coffee", at prices that are extremely reasonable for Waikiki; there's a pool, an attractive little restaurant (Cappuccinos), whirlpool baths in many rooms and even karaoke party rooms.*

### ●OTHER HOTEL-CHAIN CHOICES

*You will find one or more additional locations of the following hotel chains in the Honolulu area: Holiday Inn and Ramada; for reservations or information, see the toll-free 800 phone listings on page 16.*

# HOUSTON†

## TOP HOTELS
## (In order of rating)

### BEST OVERALL
26 – Ritz-Carlton
25 – Omni Houston
     Four Seasons
24 – La Colombe d'Or
23 – Lancaster
21 – Wyndham Warwick
20 – Westin Oaks
     J.W. Marriott

### BEST VALUES
Holiday Inn Crowne Plaza
Lancaster
Adam's Mark Hotel
Marriott Medical Center
Wyndham Greenspoint
J.W. Marriott
Guest Quarters
Omni Houston

\*          \*          \*

### Best Rooms
26 – Ritz-Carlton
25 – Four Seasons
     Omni Houston
     La Colombe d'Or
24 – Lancaster
21 – Wyndham Warwick
     Guest Quarters
     Westin Oaks

### Best Dining
26 – La Colombe d'Or
     Ritz-Carlton
25 – Omni Houston
     Four Seasons
23 – Lancaster
21 – Wyndham Warwick
19 – Westin Oaks
18 – J.W. Marriott

### Best Service
26 – Ritz-Carlton
25 – Omni Houston
     Four Seasons
24 – La Colombe d'Or
     Lancaster
21 – Wyndham Warwick
20 – Westin Oaks
     J.W. Marriott

### Best Public Facilities
26 – Ritz-Carlton
25 – Omni Houston
24 – Four Seasons
23 – La Colombe d'Or
22 – Lancaster
21 – Wyndham Warwick
     Woodlands Exec. Conf. Ctr.
20 – Houstonian Hotel

†For restaurants, see *Zagat Houston Restaurant Survey*.

| R | S | D | P | $ |

**Adam's Mark Hotel**   604R (49S)   | 19 | 17 | 18 | 17 | $110 |
2900 Briarpark Dr.; (800) 444-ADAM; (713) 978-7400; FAX 735-2726
*U – If you can overlook that aura of "leftover disco glitz", you'll find yourself
in the "only luxury hotel in Far West Houston"; its premium restaurant, The
Marker (food rating, 22), is a "cut above the usual", and the "lively" bar is a
fun place to "take a friend"; "good food and service" plus "comfortable
rooms" add up to "a great businessperson's hotel."*

**Allen Park Inn***   263R (24S)   | 11 | 13 | 11 | 11 | $80 |
2121 Allen Pkwy.; (800) 231-6310; (713) 521-9321; FAX 521-9321
*M – Reasonable prices and a location five minutes from Downtown seem
to be the draw of this low-key, family-run motel that a few of our surveyors
say provides a "nice atmosphere for regulars"; to others, however, it's
"uninspired and inconvenient", maybe even "a dump."*

**Doubletree at Post Oak**   450R (37S)   | 20 | 19 | 18 | 20 | $122 |
2001 Post Oak Blvd.; (800) 528-0444; (713) 961-9300; FAX 623-6685
*U – "Texas-showy but nice" describes this "starkly elegant" hotel designed
by I.M. Pei; "impressive public areas and beautiful rooms" are "posh
without pretentiousness", and the service, yes, "compassionate"; bring your
appetite for the "fabulous Sunday brunch."*

**Doubletree Hotel at Allen Center**   341R (16S)   | 18 | 17 | 17 | 18 | $124 |
400 Dallas St.; (800) 528-0444; (713) 759-0202; FAX 752-2734
*U – "Nice public space", "good rooms" and "great cookies" – not
necessarily in that order – characterize this convenient midsize
Downtowner; although one surveyor says the food "needs some work",
for most this is a "good reliable."*

**Fit Inn Charlie Club**   86R (6S)   | – | – | – | – | E |
(fka Charlie Fitness Club & Hotel)
9009 Boone Rd.; (713) 530-0000; FAX 530-3701
*Few have discovered this West Houston health club–with–guest rooms,
where the bedrooms take second place to the 100,000-square-foot (count
'em) sports emporium, complete with jogging track, two pools, exercise
facilities and whirlpool baths (all at guests' disposal).*

## FOUR SEASONS　　　　　| 25 | 25 | 25 | 24 | $159 |
### HOTEL HOUSTON　399R (12S)
1300 Lamar St.; (800) 332-3442; (713) 650-1300; FAX 650-8169
*U – "A true oasis in the desert", this East Side "country club, Texas style" is molded in the Four Seasons tradition: "always elegant, always expensive"; what some call a "desolate location" is also a welcome refuge from" the standard convention center scene of other hotels; but the consensus among surveyors is "don't ever leave" – you'll miss the "excellent" SW food at Deville (food rating, 28), "sharp" service and "rich, warm feeling" of the hotel.*

## Guest Quarters　335S　　| 21 | 19 | 16 | 18 | $117 |
(fka Guest Quarters – Galleria West)
5353 Westheimer Rd.; (800) 424-2900; (713) 961-9000; FAX 877-8835
*U – "Time will tell" if recent owner changes and refurbishment will lift this "so convenient", Galleria-handy all-suiter above the ranks of "big, clean and practical"; in the meantime, "you can't beat the square feet per dollar."*

## Harvey Suites Houston　　| – | – | – | – | I |
### Medical Center*　284R (212S)
6800 S. Main St.; (800) 922-9222; (713) 528-7744; FAX 528-6983
*"Spacious" rooms and "all the comforts of home" and then some, including a library, an outdoor pool and complimentary transportation to the medical center; prices are right, too.*

## Holiday Inn Crowne Plaza　477R (9S)　| 19 | 19 | 16 | 16 | $96 |
2222 West Loop S.; (800) 327-6213; (713) 961-7272; FAX 961-3327
*M – "Top-notch" or "ho-hum"? – it depends on whom you ask; detractors say it's a "Holiday Inn upgrade, but not much"; admirers say management "really tries and it shows"; no one's arguing with the fact that it's one of the "best values in the Galleria area" and in all of Houston.*

## Holiday Inn Houston West*　353R (5S)　| 16 | 16 | 14 | 14 | $107 |
14703 Park Row; (800) 465-4329; (713) 558-5580; FAX 496-4150
*M – An atrium pool and views of nearby golfers from this modern West Houston high rise, plus convenient access to businesses along the Energy Corridor and to nearby highways are all pluses, but they don't convince surveyors, who suggest that it has been "in decline" for several years.*

## Holiday Inn West Loop　　| 17 | 17 | 15 | 14 | $79 |
### Near the Galleria*　318R (4S)
3131 West Loop S.; (800) HOLIDAY; (713) 621-1900; FAX 439-0989
*M – A "great location" right near the Galleria recommends this decent "traveling salesman's hostelry", more so than the "nice rooms" and "good service"; convenient, yes, but "nothing to write home about."*

**Hotel Sofitel Houston**   337R (9S)          | 19 | 19 | 17 | 17 | $115 |
425 N. Sam Houston Pkwy. E.; (800) 221-4542; (713) 445-9000; FAX 445-9826
*M – "Comfortable" rooms and "good restaurants" offset this airport-area
modern's "cold, somber" mien; maybe it's "not up to the best of the Sofitel
group", but a "feeling of luxury" and thoughtful amenities warm things up.*

**Houstonian Hotel &**                         | 17 | 18 | 17 | 20 | $132 |
**Conference Center, The**   297R (17S)
111 N. Post Oak Lane; (800) 231-2759; (713) 680-2626; FAX 680-2992
*M – "If it's good enough for George Bush, is it good enough for you?" –
now, that's a complicated one; some respondents (Republicans, no doubt)
like the location that's "good for biz in the Galleria area", "nice setting and
grounds", and a "great spa" that's really "geared to athletes"; folks looking
for a change say it's "far from tops" and this "drab hotel is in much need of
a revamp"; well, now.*

**Houston Marriott Astrodome**   339R (4S)     | 15 | 16 | 13 | 14 | $95 |
2100 S. Braeswood Blvd.; (800) 228-9290; (713) 797-9000; FAX 799-8362
*U – Showing its age, this "mediocre" Marriott is "an antique" that many of
our surveyors say is "in desperate need of attention and TLC"; it gets further
brickbats for the name – "the Astrodome is a 20-minute drive away!" – and
the "dangerous neighborhood."*

**Houston Marriott**                           | 17 | 18 | 16 | 16 | $110 |
**West Loop by the Galleria**   302R (2S)
1750 West Loop S.; (800) 228-9290; (713) 960-0111; FAX 960-0111
*M – Although there's "Galleria shopping next door", this "typical" "business
hotel" rates only "satisfactory"; still, it's certainly "comfortable", and admission
to the Punchline Comedy Club downstairs is an added perk with the Two
for Breakfast weekend package – a "great value."*

**Houston Marriott Westside***   400R (20S)    | 19 | 18 | 16 | 18 | $96 |
(fka Hyatt Regency West Houston)
13210 Katy Frwy.; (800) 228-9290; (713) 558-8338; FAX 558-4028
*U – A "pleasant surprise" in Southwest Houston; its "great location in the
Energy Corridor" attracts "plenty of oil businessmen", ditto the "beautiful
modern design surrounded by pools and fountains" and the well-priced,
if standard, guest rooms.*

**Hyatt Regency Houston**   959R (52S)   | 18 | 18 | 17 | 18 | $125 |
1200 Louisiana St.; (800) 233-1234; (713) 654-1234; FAX 951-0934
*M – "A Hyatt is a Hyatt is a Hyatt" – and never more so than in Houston;
it's got a "great location for business" but "not much personal touch",
making it more appealing for dealmakers than vacation-takers; "watch out
for falling objects" (just kidding) in the atrium; N.B. more than a few people
find it "dreary" and say it's showing its age.*


**J.W. Marriott Hotel**   494R (18S)   | 21 | 20 | 18 | 19 | $124 |
5150 Westheimer Rd.; (800) 228-9290; (713) 961-1500; FAX 961-5045
*M – "Better than plain-vanilla Marriotts", this "solid and dependable"
performer is a "best bet for the Galleria area", especially when you just
can't wait to "spend some money" in the stores; though some say
everything is "out of a cookie cutter", others think of it as a "quiet refuge."*


**LA COLOMBE D'OR**   6S   | 25 | 24 | 26 | 23 | $223 |
3410 Montrose Blvd.; (713) 524-7999; FAX 524-8923
*U – "Old-world ambiance and decor in thoroughly modern facilities" combine
to create a "wonderful change of pace" in this "brilliant small hotel" with its
six theme suites, hewn from a former private mansion; the eponymous
restaurant (food rating, 24) is perfect for "romantic dining"; here, say
surveyors, it's possible to be "pampered to death" – but what a way to go!*


**LANCASTER, THE**   93R (9S)   | 24 | 24 | 23 | 22 | $140 |
701 Texas Ave.; (800) 231-0336; (713) 228-9500; FAX 223-4528
*U – "Small and clubby" and a "real gem", this "oasis" of "old-world charm"
"doesn't feel like Houston"; "wonderful service", "beautifully appointed
rooms", a "great location" and "excellent dining" at the Lancaster Grille
(food rating, 20) make this "English Manor in the middle of Downtown" –
an unexpected delight.*


**Marriott Medical Center**   389R (22S)   | 19 | 20 | 17 | 18 | $117 |
6580 Fannin St.; (800) 228-9290; (713) 796-0080; FAX 796-2201
*U – "Quiet elegance amid the bustle of a world-class medical center" sums
up the experience here; comfortable rooms and a "very caring" staff make
this particularly appropriate "for families with relatives in the hospital."*


**Nassau Bay Hilton & Marina***   244R (13S)   | 16 | 15 | 13 | 17 | $93 |
3000 NASA Rd. 1; (800) 634-4320; (713) 333-9300; FAX 333-3750
*M – A "nice location" on Clear Lake and easy access to the Space Center
recommend this otherwise out-of-the-way Hilton; fans suggest you "choose
a room with a bayside view", but detractors say it "needs to be updated";
try meals off-property.*

**OMNI HOUSTON HOTEL**   381R (35S)        | 25 | 25 | 25 | 25 | $159 |
(fka Four Seasons Inn on the Park)
4 Riverway St.; (800) THE-OMNI; (713) 871-8181; FAX 871-0719
*U – A staff that "truly cares" elevates service to "outstanding" at this "very plush" Galleria-area hotel; the new Omni management "tries hard to maintain its first-class" reputation – and succeeds admirably; the rooms and public areas are "lovely", the pool is "an artist's dream" and its Classic French restaurant, La Reserve (food rating, 26), is one of "Houston's very best-kept secrets."*

**Plaza Hilton, The\***   195R (145S)        | 16 | 16 | 16 | 15 | $102 |
(fka Houston Medical Center Hilton)
6633 Travis St.; (800) HILTONS; (713) 524-6633; FAX 529-6806
*U – "Special rates for medical-center visitors" and a complimentary shuttle do little to enhance this hotel's appeal; our surveyors, in fact, are distinctly underwhelmed: "Hyatt should run this place" – and a big slip in ratings since last we surveyed suggests that they may be right.*

**Ramada Kings Inn Hotel &**                 | – | – | – | – | M |
**Conference Center**   198R (4S)
1301 NASA Rd. 1; (800) 255-7345; (713) 488-0220; FAX 488-1759
*There is no middle ground here; fans call it "world-class", citing the attractive, extensive grounds (all rooms have private balconies), reasonable prices and convenience to NASA, but to detractors it's a "last resort" that has "seen better days – about 20 years ago."*

**RITZ-CARLTON, HOUSTON**   232R (24S)        | 26 | 26 | 26 | 26 | $179 |
(fka The Remington)
1919 Briar Oaks Lane; (800) 241-3333; (713) 840-7600; FAX 840-0616
*U – If the "royal treatment" is what you need to "endure the Galleria area", the Ritz provides it – that and "luxury to the max", with "impeccable service", "plush rooms" and restaurants that "rival the best in Houston"; although a few guests "miss the old Remington", most say the Ritz has "everything" one could ask for from a first-class hotel.*

**Sheraton Astrodome Hotel\***   832R (44S)        | 18 | 17 | 16 | 16 | $98 |
(fka Astro Village Hotel)
8686 Kirby Dr.; (800) 325-3535; (713) 748-3221; FAX 796-9371
*U – This "workhorse" of a hotel is "the only decent place close to the Astrodome" according to our surveyors; it's "very Texan", what with its large scale and the Star Brand Cattle Co. restaurant; also, the recent top-to-bottom renovation rates a "nice job."*

**HOUSTON HOTELS**                     | R | S | D | P | $ |

**Sheraton Grand Hotel by**            | 17 | 18 | 14 | 16 | $112 |
**Houston Galleria**   321R (6S) (fka Grand Hotel)
2525 West Loop S.; (800) 325-3535; (713) 961-3000; FAX 961-1490
*M – Members of Shoppers Anonymous should appreciate the Endless
Weekend package that offers coupons redeemable at Galleria-area shops
and restaurants; still, our surveyors seem ambivalent: "super service but
average rooms" and "just ok" typify their lack of enthusiasm.*

**Stouffer Presidente Hotel**   389R (9S)   | 20 | 19 | 17 | 19 | $127 |
6 Greenway Plaza E.; (800) HOTELS1; (713) 629-1200; FAX 629-4702
*M – "Good prices" may make this Greenway Plaza hostelry "the best value
in Houston", but others complain that it's "not up to their usual standards"
and the "employees have an attitude"; the bottom line seems to be:
"another large, comfortable hotel without personality."*

**Westin Galleria**   485R             | 20 | 20 | 18 | 19 | $134 |
5060 W. Alabama St.; (800) 228-3000; (713) 960-8100; FAX 960-6553
*M – It's easy to shop till you drop at this "compulsive shopper's heaven" in
the Galleria; while the location may be perfect, the facility itself is said to be
"getting shabby and overdue for a redo", and some even sniff that "a
shopping center is no place for a hotel"; never mind, it's "an enjoyable
place to stay", with "things to do, people to see," shops to empty....*

**Westin Oaks**   406R                 | 21 | 20 | 19 | 19 | $134 |
5011 Westheimer Rd.; (800) 228-3000; (713) 960-8100; FAX 960-6553
*U – Despite this hotel's "pea-in-a-pod" similarity to the Westin Galleria
next door, our surveyors seem less than enthusiastic: "basic" and "ok
but not memorable" are typical reactions; several suggest it "could use
some renovating."*

**Woodlands Executive**                | 19 | 17 | 17 | 21 | $137 |
**Conference Center & Resort**   268R (79S)
2301 N. Millbend Dr., The Woodlands; (800) 433-2624; (713) 367-1100;
FAX 367-2576
*U – If the changeable Houston weather cooperates, this out-of-the-way
conference resort/golf club is "worth it just for the location" – a "beautiful
setting in the woods"; our surveyors disregard service and dining
deficiencies in light of "great sports" and "beautiful grounds"; a "nice place
for a conference."*

**Wyndham Greenspoint**   472R (50S)        | 18 | 19 | 17 | 18 | $114 |
12400 Greenspoint Dr.; (800) 822-4200; (713) 875-2222; FAX 875-1652
*M – Fans "would love to move this hotel to another area", but if you're stuck
out at Intercontinental Airport, it's a "best bet"; room decor is deemed
"lovely", and the square-acre lobby is "exquisite", but the "completely
ordinary" restaurants are not.*

**Wyndham Warwick Hotel, The**   308R (76S)   | 21 | 21 | 21 | 21 | $140 |
5701 Main St.; (800) 822-4200; (713) 526-1991; FAX 639-4545
*U – "Classy", "romantic" and "elegant" are a few of the adjectives used to
describe this newly renovated "old charmer" located next to the Medical
Center in the heart of the city's Museum District; it may be "quirky" and
rather "Texas showy", but many of our surveyors really "like to stay here."*

● **OTHER HOTEL-CHAIN CHOICES**
*You will find one or more additional locations of the following hotel chains in
the Houston area: Days Inn, Doubletree, Embassy Suites, Hampton Inn,
Hilton, Howard Johnson, La Quinta Inns, Radisson, Residence Inn, Super 8
and Travelodge/Viscount; for reservations or information, see the toll-free
800 phone listings on page 16.*

# INDIANAPOLIS

## TOP HOTELS
## (In order of rating)

### BEST OVERALL
**24** – Canterbury Hotel
**19** – Holiday Inn Union Station
    Westin Hotel
**18** – Hyatt Regency

### BEST VALUES
Holiday Inn Union Station
Westin Hotel
Adam's Mark Hotel
Canterbury Hotel

\*    \*    \*

### Best Rooms
**25** – Canterbury Hotel
**20** – Holiday Inn Union St.
    Embassy Suites
    Westin Hotel

### Best Dining
**24** – Canterbury Hotel
**18** – Westin Hotel
**17** – Hyatt Regency
    Holiday Inn Union Station

### Best Service
**26** – Canterbury Hotel
**24** – Westin Hotel
**19** – Holiday Inn Union Station
**17** – Hyatt Regency

### Best Public Facilities
**22** – Holiday Inn Union Station
    Canterbury Hotel
**19** – Westin Hotel
**18** – Hyatt Regency

| R | S | D | P | $ |
|---|---|---|---|---|

**Adam's Mark Hotel** 407R (44S)

| 17 | 17 | 16 | 16 | $99 |
|----|----|----|----|-----|

2544 Executive Dr.; (800) 444-ADAM; (317) 248-2481; FAX 248-1670
*M – A 1989 room renovation did not improve the ratings for this "comfortable"
but "ordinary" airport hotel; some say it has the "best meeting space" in
town and like the "convenient" location, while others find it an "awful place"
that's "poorly managed" and "dirty."*

**CANTERBURY HOTEL, THE** 99R (25S)

| 25 | 26 | 24 | 22 | $144 |
|----|----|----|----|------|

123 S. Illinois St.; (800) 588-8186; (317) 634-3000; FAX 685-2519
*U – Ratings nudged upward at this "wonderful" small hotel near the Hoosier
Dome and convention center, which most consider Indianapolis's "best"; its
"old-world" ambiance and the romantic Beaulieu restaurant were impressive
enough to make one* Survey *participant proclaim, "Paris comes to Naptown!";
don't miss the afternoon tea here.*

## INDIANAPOLIS HOTELS

| R | S | D | P | $ |

**Embassy Suites Hotel –**   | 20 | 17 | 14 | 16 | $105 |
**Indianapolis Downtown**   360S
110 W. Washington St.; (800) EMBASSY; (317) 236-1800; FAX 236-1816
*M – People love to hate this Downtown all-suiter – "what's left after the free
breakfast?" and "a business hotel without room service is a hotel to avoid"
are typical put-downs – but the impressive 15-story atrium and 1991 room
renovation please most, who love the "nice big rooms" and "open-air" feel
of the place; there are good weekend packages, too.*

**Holiday Inn Union Station**   276R (7S)   | 20 | 19 | 17 | 22 | $109 |
123 W. Louisiana St.; (800) 465-4329; (317) 631-2221; FAX 236-7474
*U – Try to nab one of the 26 Pullman cars converted into suites at this
midsize Downtowner; attached to the renovated Union Station shopping,
restaurant and entertainment complex, it's an "exciting environment";
though the ordinary rooms can be "small" and the lobby "noisy", on balance
this nostalgia trip is "great fun" as well as a great value.*

**Hyatt Regency Indianapolis**   497R (27S)   | 19 | 17 | 17 | 18 | $123 |
1 S. Capitol Ave.; (800) 233-1234; (317) 632-1234; FAX 231-7569
*M – Most visitors to this Downtown hotel across from the Hoosier Dome
get what they expect from Hyatt – "good location", "no surprises" and
"functional" facilities, but some find the "small" rooms too "dark and musty"
and warn that service can be "sloppy and indifferent."*

**Indianapolis Hilton Downtown**   371R (45S)   | 15 | 16 | 14 | 14 | $108 |
(aka Hilton at the Circle)
31 W. Ohio St.; (800) 445-8667; (317) 635-2000; FAX 638-0782
*U – A "good" Downtown location and inexpensive weekend packages are
about all this hotel has going for it; "Hilton should be embarrassed" and
"needs renovation and cleaning" reflect reactions to this "mediocre" facility.*

**Indianapolis Marriott**   252R (3S)   | 17 | 17 | 16 | 16 | $105 |
7202 E. 21st St.; (800) 228-9290; (317) 352-1231; FAX 352-1231
*M – Ratings dropped a notch in this year's Survey, and our reviewers split
on the merits of this Northeast suburban business hotel; some appreciate
the "full-size desk-and-seating area in the rooms" and describe the 1989
refurbishing as "elegant", while others say this "tired" facility still "needs help."*

## INDIANAPOLIS HOTELS

| | R | S | D | P | $ |
|---|---|---|---|---|---|

**Omni Severin***   423R (38S)   | 23 | 24 | 22 | 21 | $127 |

40 W. Jackson Place; (800) THE-OMNI; (317) 634-6664; FAX 687-3612
*U – A soothing 20-foot waterfall flows into a marble pool in the skylit atrium
of this "surprisingly elegant" historic Downtown hotel located across from
Union Station; well-appointed, spacious rooms and "friendly service" help
most overlook such negatives as a "noisy ventilation" system and a few
"rough edges" remaining after a recent renovation.*

**Radisson Plaza & Suites Hotel***   559R (159S) | 19 | 20 | 18 | 19 | $103 |

8787 Keystone Crossing; (800) 333-3333; (317) 846-2700; FAX 846-2700 x402
*U – Up a bit in its ratings, this contemporary North Side high rise is "pretty
swanky for Indiana", with its sleek suite tower and attached shopping mall
and health spa; our reviewers like the "great location" and "good convention
facilities" and call this a good "home-away-from-home"; check out the
attractively priced weekend and family packages.*

**University Place***   278R (16S)   | 19 | 19 | 17 | 18 | $95 |

850 W. Michigan St.; (800) 627-2700; (317) 269-9000; FAX 231-5168
*U – The rooms may be a bit "Spartan", but they are also "comfortable", and
there's "great service"; located near Purdue's Indianapolis campus and
linked by a skywalk to the Indiana University Medical Center, this contemporary
conference center with 30 meeting rooms is reasonably priced.*

**Westin Hotel Indianapolis**   572R (38S)   | 20 | 20 | 18 | 19 | $112 |

50 S. Capitol Ave.; (800) 228-3000; (317) 262-8100; FAX 231-3928
*M – This slick, postmodern Downtowner across from the Hoosier Dome
wins kudos for its "central location", "very posh" accommodations and
"good comfort", but distresses others as a "monstrosity"; the 15-story
complex houses the state's largest meeting facilities.*

**Wyndham Garden Hotel**   172R (11S)   | – | – | – | – | I |

251 E. Pennsylvania Pkwy.; (800) 822-4200; (317) 574-4600; FAX 574-4633
*Business travelers appreciate the well-lit desk area, drip coffeemakers with
complimentary coffee and built-in hair dryers in every room at this suburban
newcomer, situated between Downtown (12 miles away) and the airport
(25 miles); but it's the "Hoosier hospitality" of the "friendly" staff and the low
prices that make this business hotel seem special.*

## ● OTHER HOTEL-CHAIN CHOICES

*You will find one or more additional locations of the following hotel chains
in the Indianapolis area: Courtyard by Marriott, Days Inn, Embassy Suites,
Guest Quarters, Hampton Inn, Howard Johnson, La Quinta Inns, Omni,
Ramada, Residence Inn and Super 8; for reservations or information, see
the toll-free 800 phone listings on page 16.*

# KANSAS CITY†

## TOP HOTELS
### (In order of rating)

**BEST OVERALL**

24 – Ritz-Carlton
21 – Westin Crown Center
20 – Raphael Hotel
19 – Hyatt Regency Crown Center
18 – Doubletree Hotel

**BEST VALUES**

Marriott Overland Park
Doubletree Hotel
Adam's Mark Hotel
Raphael Hotel
Westin Crown Center

\*     \*     \*

**Best Rooms**

25 – Ritz-Carlton
22 – Raphael Hotel
21 – Westin Crown Center
20 – Hyatt Regency Crown Center
19 – Doubletree Hotel

**Best Dining**

25 – Ritz-Carlton
20 – Westin Crown Center
19 – Raphael Hotel
     Hyatt Regency Crown Center
17 – Doubletree Hotel

**Best Service**

24 – Ritz-Carlton
22 – Raphael Hotel
21 – Westin Crown Center
19 – Hyatt Regency Crown Center
     Doubletree Hotel

**Best Public Facilities**

24 – Ritz-Carlton
22 – Westin Crown Center
20 – Hyatt Regency Crown Center
19 – Allis Plaza Hotel
18 – Marriott Overland Park

| R | S | D | P | $ |
|---|---|---|---|---|

**Adam's Mark Hotel**   374R (8S)   | 18 | 17 | 16 | 16 | $98 |
9103 E. 39th St.; (800) 444-ADAM; (816) 737-0200; FAX 737-4713
*M – Rated an "excellent value", this "reliable" Eastsider features service and facilities in an "interesting yet quiet part of town"; detractors say it's "in the middle of nowhere" and "you need wheels to get around" – but at least it's across from Truman Sports Complex (home of the Royals and the Chiefs), and has "free bus service to sporting events"; it also features a "fine restaurant", Remington's (food rating, 21).*

---

†For restaurants, see *Zagat Kansas City Restaurant Survey.*

## KANSAS CITY HOTELS

| R | S | D | P | $ |

**Allis Plaza Hotel**  573R (23S)    | 19 | 18 | 16 | 19 | $110 |
200 W. 12th St.; (800) 548-4782; (816) 421-6800; FAX 421-6800 x4418
*M – A "nice hotel for business", this newish Downtown high rise is
connected by an underground walkway to Bartle Hall convention center;
boosters laud its convenient location, "nice-size rooms" and pretty lobby
complete with splashing waterfall, but detractors say that without the
convention center, "it would have to work harder to please."*


**Americana Hotel on**    | – | – | – | – |  |  |
**Convention Square**  482R (4S)
1301 Wyandotte St.; (800) 325-9149; (816) 221-8800; FAX 472-7964
*Low prices, large rooms and proximity to Bartle Hall convention center
and KC's historic sites and sports stadium don't do anything to dispel the
ambivalence of our surveyors about this unatmospheric high rise.*


**Doubletree Hotel, The**  357R (17S)    | 19 | 19 | 17 | 18 | $103 |
10100 College Blvd., Overland Park, KS; (800) 528-0444; (913) 451-6100;
FAX 451-3873
*U – It's funny how many of our surveyors think of the "delicious" "chocolate-
chip cookies at turndown" when they think of Doubletree – those and
"comfy rooms", "pleasant staff" and well-rated sports facilities, including
bike and jogging trails; add a handy location and you get a winner.*


**Hilton Plaza Inn**  226R (10S)    | 15 | 16 | 15 | 14 | $94 |
1 E. 45th St.; (800) 525-6321; (816) 753-7400; FAX 753-4777
*U – This "small but adequate" low rise "close to Country Club Plaza" offers
fair prices and the usual amenities; otherwise our surveyors seem distinctly
underwhelmed: "ok, but nothing to write home about."*


**Holiday Inn Crowne Plaza**  296R (18S)    | 19 | 18 | 17 | 18 | $106 |
(fka Kansas City Marriott Plaza)
4445 Main St.; (800) 465-4329; (816) 531-3000; FAX 531-3007
*U – A "statement hotel", this towering flagship has a choice location near
the Crown Center complex and a dramatic "center-court atrium", plus
"great views of the Plaza" from many rooms; detractors report that the
guest rooms are "run-of-the-mill" and the desk staff "befuddled", but it's
still considered a "good value" and a "decent business hotel."*

## KANSAS CITY HOTELS | R | S | D | P | $ |

**Hotel Savoy**   90S   | – | – | – | – | I |
219 W. Ninth St.; (816) 842-3575; FAX 842-3575 x103
*Claiming to be the oldest continually operating hotel west of the
Mississippi, this 104-year-old art nouveau–style hostelry located in KC's
Historic District is currently undergoing a complete renovation, which
should address surveyors' concerns; amenities like a complimentary
made-to-order breakfast and limo service are appreciated.*

**Hyatt Regency Crown Center**   731R (42S)   | 20 | 19 | 19 | 20 | $122 |
2345 McGee St.; (800) 233-1234; (816) 421-1234; FAX 435-4190
*U – "Almost a legend", this imposing "modern" high rise "makes you forget
you are in Kansas", with "good service and location" in the "thick of Crown
Center activities" and a dramatic six-story atrium lobby connected by a
"skybridge to the mall"; BBQ fans say it's "too far from Arthur Bryant's" and
a little "sterile", but to most everyone else, it's a "quality hotel"; it gets extra
points for the popular Peppercorn Duck Club (food rating, 26) restaurant.*

**Marriott Overland Park**   397R (7S)   | 19 | 18 | 16 | 18 | $111 |
10800 Metcalf Ave., Overland Park, KS; (800) 228-9290; (913) 451-8000;
FAX 451-5914
*M – This moderately priced "family hotel" offers "dependable quality every
time" according to our surveyors; the suburban location is either
"accessible" or "no man's land" depending on whom you ask, but has
"good dining options" including Nikko Steak House (food rating, 23).*

**Quarterage Hotel**   123R (8S)   | – | – | – | – | I |
560 Westport Rd.; (800) 942-4233; (816) 931-0001; FAX 931-0001 x157
*Little known to our surveyors, this "cozy" and rather "European" hotel in
Midtown's historic Westport area offers a very reasonably priced
alternative to Downtown; room rates include a complimentary continental
breakfast and cocktail hour, plus the use of a mini-spa.*

**Radisson Suite Hotel –**   | 17 | 17 | 15 | 17 | $147 |
**Kansas City***   214R (198S)
106 W. 12th St.; (800) 333-3333; (816) 221-7000; FAX 221-7000 x387
*M – Once home to the city's smartest social scene, this 60-year-old all-suiter
(or nearly) was completely renovated in 1989 and appeals to businesspeople
who like its Downtown convenience, large in-room desks and a fully
equipped business center; detractors say "don't expect too much."*

## KANSAS CITY HOTELS | R | S | D | P | $ |

**Raphael Hotel**   123R (90S)   | 22 | 22 | 19 | 18 | $121 |
325 Ward Pkwy.; (800) 821-5343; (816) 756-3800; FAX 756-3800
*U – This "cozy" "former upscale apartment building" exudes "old-world
charm in a tidy package", with "spacious but not overdecorated rooms", a
"romantic" Continental restaurant, Raphael (food rating, 21), and a "perfect
location" in the "heart of Country Club Plaza"; "comfortable as an old shoe",
this "little gem" strikes our surveyors as "delightful."*


**RITZ-CARLTON, KANSAS CITY**   373R (28S)   | 25 | 24 | 25 | 24 | $153 |
401 Ward Pkwy.; (800) 241-3333; (816) 756-1500; FAX 756-1635
*U – A "luxurious, artistic reincarnation" of the old Alameda Plaza Hotel;
Kansas City is "putting on the Ritz" with "beautiful rooms", "superb staff"
and first-class facilities and restaurants with a "European flair"; in keeping
with the chain's high standards, this grand old hotel may have been
updated, but in ways that count most it's the "same as always – excellent."*


**Sheraton Suites Country Club Plaza***   259S   | 22 | 22 | 18 | 17 | $105 |
(fka Marriott Suites Country Club Plaza)
770 W. 47th St.; (800) 325-3535; (816) 931-4400; FAX 561-7330
*U – A "super location" close to Country Club Plaza and the Nelson Atkins
Art Museum, combined with a "fabulously friendly staff" and "terrific rooms",
makes this a solid, if seldom-mentioned, value.*


**Westin Crown Center, The**   725R (49S)   | 21 | 21 | 20 | 22 | $126 |
1 Pershing Rd. at Grand Ave.; (800) 228-3000; (816) 474-4400; FAX 391-4493
*U – "Wonderful architecture" featuring a "spectacular atrium" and a choice
location that puts shopping and attractions right at hand are the most
memorable features of this "cornerstone of Crown Center shops and
activities"; "great service", first-class dining at Bentons (food rating, 22),
Kabuki (22) and Trader Vic's (23), and very large rooms" help keep this
"top-notch" hotel at "the center of everything."*


## ● OTHER HOTEL-CHAIN CHOICES
*You will find one or more additional locations of the following hotel chains in
the Kansas City area: Courtyard by Marriott, Days Inn, Embassy Suites,
Hampton Inn, Hilton, Holiday Inn, Howard Johnson, Marriott, Ramada,
Residence Inn, Super 8 and Travelodge/Viscount; for reservations or
information, see the toll-free 800 phone listings on page 16.*

# LAS VEGAS

## TOP HOTELS
### (In order of rating)

### BEST OVERALL

22 – Mirage
21 – Caesars Palace
     Golden Nugget
19 – Alexis Park
     Desert Inn
18 – Bally's
     Las Vegas Hilton
16 – Tropicana Hotel

### BEST VALUES

Excalibur
Four Queens
Golden Nugget
Plaza Hotel
Showboat
Circus Circus
Frontier
Sahara

\*       \*       \*

### Best Rooms

22 – Caesars Palace
21 – Mirage
     Golden Nugget
     Alexis Park
20 – Desert Inn
19 – Las Vegas Hilton
     Bally's
17 – Flamingo Hilton

### Best Dining

21 – Mirage
20 – Caesars Palace
     Golden Nugget
19 – Alexis Park
18 – Desert Inn
17 – Four Queens
     Bally's
     Las Vegas Hilton

### Best Service

21 – Mirage
20 – Golden Nugget
     Caesars Palace
19 – Desert Inn
18 – Alexis Park
17 – Bally's
     Las Vegas Hilton
16 – Four Queens

### Best Public Facilities

24 – Mirage
22 – Caesars Palace
21 – Golden Nugget
19 – Desert Inn
     Alexis Park
18 – Bally's
     Las Vegas Hilton
17 – Tropicana Hotel

## LAS VEGAS HOTELS                    | R | S | D | P | $ |

**Aladdin Hotel**   1100R (253S)          | 14 | 14 | 12 | 13 | $82 |
3667 Las Vegas Blvd. S.; (800) 634-3424; (702) 736-0144; FAX 736-0283
*U – Expect "no magic" at this "mediocre" '60s survivor, which has "seen
better days" and "needs updating"; our surveyors complain of "rude"
service, a "shabby" casino and an "utterly disappointing" experience;
there's one bright spot, however: the hotel recently emerged from
bankruptcy, so things may improve with the genie out of the bottle.*


**Alexis Park Resort**   500S          | 21 | 18 | 19 | 19 | $128 |
375 E. Harmon Ave.; (800) 582-2228; (702) 796-3300; FAX 796-4334
*U – Sans gaming, the "beautiful" Alexis Park is considered a "welcome
relief from the Strip", "great for people avoiding casino hotels" – especially
those "business-minded" travelers who are "in Las Vegas because they
have to be"; it has "unbelievably luxurious grounds", above-average food
and service, and "tasteful" suites – a "diamond in the desert."*


**Bally's – Las Vegas**   2900R (265S)          | 19 | 17 | 17 | 18 | $97 |
3645 Las Vegas Blvd. S.; (800) 722-5597; (702) 739-4111; FAX 739-4405
*M – "Gamble, guzzle and graze" at this "huge" but "very typical" Strip hotel,
with its "football field" of a lobby and "large", "lively" casino; the "enormous"
rooms are "nice", but it's a "long walk" through "sometimes confusing
hallways" to reach them; fans are fond of the bathrooms in the suites –
"gaudy but fun" – so let's hope they're left alone in the remodeling now
taking place; phobes say "tacky" and "garish."*


**Binion's Horseshoe***   374R (8S)          | 13 | 15 | 14 | 12 | $68 |
128 E. Fremont St.; (800) 622-6468; (702) 382-1600; FAX 382-5750
*U – "The classic sawdust joint", this old-time Downtown Vegas hotel/casino
is "the place to be during national rodeo finals"; scores for service and
dining have crept up a bit since our last Survey, and best of all, room rates
are really cheap; check out the Skye Room for its views, if not its food.*


**Caesars Palace**   1500R          | 22 | 20 | 20 | 22 | $129 |
3570 Las Vegas Blvd. S.; (800) 634-6001; (702) 731-7110; FAX 731-7172
*U – "Still the best in Vegas", the "adult getaway" to what one surveyor calls
"spaceship Italiana – another world" is "all glitz", "the epitome of fantasy",
done up à la Ancient Rome; this "sprawling place" also has nine
restaurants, two pools, a health club and, of course, a "gaudy, shiny"
casino; upstairs, the guest rooms are "like a bordello", with circular beds
and overhead mirrors; Caesars' newest attraction is its "opulent but
elegant" Forum Shops, where you can spend your winnings, if any.*

## LAS VEGAS HOTELS

**Circus Circus Hotel**   2793R (126S)     | 14 | 14 | 13 | 15 | $66 |
2880 Las Vegas Blvd.; (800) 634-3450; (702) 734-0410; FAX 734-2268
U – "Strictly for families and those who love noise", this enormous, "hokey,
jokey and tacky" "zoo" is famed for almost-continuous circus acts on view
in the lobby; "bargain rates" buy "poor service" and "motel-type" rooms that
are "nothing special" (there's even an RV park on-site for the truly "budget-
minded"); the food is "horrible" except for The Steakhouse restaurant, but
the "pool is nice"; "it's great for kids, but adults should stay elsewhere"; the
casino itself is considered unremarkable, except for its size.

**Desert Inn Hotel & Country Club** 821R (95S)   | 20 | 19 | 18 | 19 | $113 |
3145 Las Vegas Blvd. S.; (800) 634-6906; (702) 733-4444; FAX 733-4774
M – "Not overwhelmed by the casino", the "most sedate of Strip hotels" has
a "good shopping location" and is famous for its "country-club atmosphere"
and Sunday champagne brunch; though rooms are "quiet" and service is
"friendly", some say it has "seen better days"; still, for most of our surveyors, it
"manages to maintain its old grandeur" – a touch of "class in Glitter Gulch."

**Dunes Hotel & Country Club**   1212R (98S)   | 14 | 14 | 14 | 14 | $80 |
3650 Las Vegas Blvd. S.; (800) 243-8637; (702) 737-4110; FAX 737-4110
U – The location facing both Caesars Palace and Bally's is "excellent", and
the "old-fashioned" casino can be "fun", but the "faded glitz" of the Dunes
badly "needs TLC"; "dreary atmosphere" and "not good" food put it "over
the hill"; however, its rates are "cheap" and "it'll do in a pinch", as long as
you know "you get exactly what you pay for."'

**Excalibur Hotel/Casino**   4032R     | 15 | 15 | 14 | 17 | $62 |
3850 Las Vegas Blvd.; (800) 937-7777; (702) 597-7777; FAX 597-7004
U – "Disneyland meets Vegas" via this "terrific bargain" masquerading as
a "make-believe medieval" castle; it's a "huge" "whole world", with 4,000
rooms, a Renaissance "jousting dinner show" and costumed minstrels
wandering about; the "service people seem to be having fun", but some
guests say only for "kids, knights, kids, wenches, kids" – and "parents
with no taste."

**Fitzgerald's Casino Hotel***   652R     | 12 | 11 | 10 | 11 | $59 |
301 E. Fremont St.; (800) 274-5825; (702) 388-2400; FAX 388-2230
M – A "typical old Vegas hotel" that draws mixed reviews from our
surveyors: one guest's "charming and rustic" is another's "old and dirty";
if you're tempted, it does have "simple decor", a convenient Downtown
location and a Micky D's on-site.

# LAS VEGAS HOTELS

**Flamingo Hilton – Las Vegas**   3530R (209S)   | 17 | 16 | 15 | 16 | $87 |
3555 Las Vegas Blvd. S.; (800) 732-2111; (702) 733-3111; FAX 733-3499
*M – The one that started it all; famous as "Bugsy Siegel's hotel", for more
than 40 years the Flamingo has been "the center of Strip action"; by
today's standards the public areas are "small" and "frenetic", but the casino
is "very active" (check out the "great bounce-back package"), and the
recently renovated guest rooms are "large"; many reviewers note problems
and delays at the registration desk, where flocks practice standing around
on one leg.*

**Four Queens Hotel & Casino**   700R (40S)   | 15 | 16 | 17 | 15 | $67 |
202 E. Fremont St.; (800) 634-6045; (702) 385-4011; FAX 385-3568
*U – Known for its "good entertainment", especially* Live at the Four Queens
*(a popular weekly PBS jazz show broadcast nationwide), this "comfortable"
Downtown "change from the Strip" boasts a "nice" casino and extremely
reasonable rates; Hugo's Cellar may be the "best restaurant in Las Vegas."*

**Frontier Hotel**   970R (384S)   | 16 | 14 | 14 | 14 | $72 |
3120 Las Vegas Blvd. S.; (800) 634-6966; (702) 794-8200; (702) 794-8326
*U – Despite a "good" Central Strip location and a new high-rise addition
that doubled its size, this "very average" place still "needs a spruce-up",
according to some of our surveyors; on the plus side, the "new suites are a
good value", it's "nice and quiet", and fans say it's "much friendlier than its
Vegas competition."*

**Golden Nugget Hotel & Casino**   1907R (102S)   | 21 | 20 | 20 | 21 | $90 |
129 E. Fremont St.; (800) 828-6206; (702) 385-7111; FAX 386-8362
*U – It's easy to see why this is a "favorite in Las Vegas" and the "best of
the Downtown" bunch; guests are "pampered", rooms are "palatial", the
buffet is top-rated, dealers are "friendly" and owner Steve Wynn "is the
best host" in town; "the only place in Vegas with class instead of glitz."*

**Hacienda Hotel & Casino**   1142R (52S)   | 14 | 14 | 11 | 12 | $86 |
3950 Las Vegas Blvd. S.; (800) 634-6713; (702) 739-8911; FAX 798-0632
*U – "Adequate and cheap" sums up the attitude here; fans think the old
tower rooms have been renovated "nicely" (a new 380-room tower opened
in 1991) but also say it offers "Las Vegas style without the grandeur or
amenities"; it may be "good to gamblers", but one surveyor jokes: "they test
fire alarms in rooms at 3 AM to keep you gambling."*

# LAS VEGAS HOTELS

| | R | S | D | P | $ |
|---|---|---|---|---|---|

**Imperial Palace Hotel & Casino** 2700R (225S) | 13 | 13 | 13 | 12 | $73 |
3535 Las Vegas Blvd. S.; (800) 634-6441; (702) 731-3311; FAX 735-8328
*U – The Antique Auto Collection gets the most raves at this "tacky" "value"
that's friendly and "well located" across from Caesars Palace and The
Mirage; rooms are only "fair", and the Asian-themed facilities have
definitely "seen better days" – "it's not imperial and it's not a palace";
die-hard handle-pullers take note of the "good payoff on slots."*

**Lady Luck Casino Hotel\*** 791R (130S) | 13 | 13 | 12 | 13 | $53 |
206 N. Third St.; (800) 634-6580; (702) 477-3000; FAX 384-2832
*M – The very reasonable room rates at this hotel-casino in the heart of
Downtown help make it hospitable to some, but to others it's just a "dump";
although you can watch the sun rise over the mountains from your tower
room, low scores in all categories suggest this place may be down on
its own luck.*

**Las Vegas Hilton** 3000R (300S) | 19 | 17 | 17 | 18 | $105 |
3000 Paradise Rd.; (800) 732-7117; (702) 732-5111; FAX 732-5834
*U – You'd better "drop bread crumbs to find your room" in this 3,000-room
behemoth one long block from the Strip; it may be "cold" and "impersonal",
but it's a "gambler's and conventioneer's paradise", right next to the
convention center and very "smoothly run"; of course, "everything's here",
including a "good sports book" and "lots of slots", "clean, neat" rooms,
"terrific" showrooms and a whole slew of "better-than-average" restaurants.*

**Maxim Hotel/Casino** 795R (38S) | 15 | 14 | 12 | 12 | $72 |
160 E. Flamingo Rd.; (800) 634-6987; (702) 731-4300; FAX 735-3252
*U – "Good value" for a "basic room" and a "good location" (just off the
Strip), nothing more; boosters say its "more human proportions" make it
a better bet than "many Strip hotels", and the slot machines seem to be
known for "good payoffs"; as one guest puts it, "how much time do you
spend in the room anyway?"*

**Mirage, The** 3049R (279S) | 21 | 21 | 21 | 24 | $126 |
3400 Las Vegas Blvd. S.; (800) 456-4564; (702) 791-7111; FAX 791-7446
*U – This "spectacular", "breathtaking" "tropical paradise in the desert" –
"what other hotel has dolphins, white tigers and an active volcano?" –
offers "surprising quality" and "wonderful service" despite its "immense"
size; on the downside, it's tough to find your room through "all the gawkers
in plaid shorts looking at the rain forest", but if you like "Vegas at its most
excessive", this is the place (of course, there are stiffs who shout "garish");
rooms, though "small", are "beautiful", and even the restaurants are
"surprisingly good"; "visit it even if you don't stay."*

**Plaza Hotel, The** 1037R (45S) (fka Union Plaza)   | 14 | 15 | 14 | 13 | $63 |
1 Main St.; (800) 634-6575; (702) 386-2110; FAX 382-8281
*M – Direct access to Amtrak doesn't necessarily offset the fact that "the
only good thing here is the price"; foes say "you get what you pay for – not
much", but there are fans who think it's "good if you want Downtown", and
one reviewer says the place even has a certain "ambiance, rare for Las
Vegas", proving once again that you get all kinds in a town like Vegas.*

**Riviera Hotel & Casino** 2100R (150S)      | 15 | 15 | 14 | 15 | $89 |
2901 Las Vegas Blvd. S.; (800) 634-3420; (702) 734-5110; FAX 794-9230
*M – "Dated but holding its own", this "big, old" convention center–area place
offers "reasonable rates and service" and a casino with "a comfortable
feeling, which says a lot for a casino"; food can be "overpriced and under-
flavored", and the rooms are just "average", but this "old Las Vegas" (1955!)
hotel has a "nice" staff; dissenters say it "typifies large- scale LV mediocrity."*

**Sahara Hotel & Casino** 1200R (50S)      | 16 | 16 | 15 | 15 | $76 |
2535 Las Vegas Blvd. S.; (800) 634-6078; (702) 737-2111; FAX 791-2027
*U – This "well-maintained" and "surprisingly nice" "older hotel" at the north
end of the Strip "needs refurbishing and more lights", but it's "still jumping"
and offering "good value"; rooms are "decent", but "just don't expect a real
dinner at the dinner show."*

**Sam Boyd's Fremont**                     | 15 | 17 | 12 | 12 | $75 |
**Hotel & Casino** 452R (24S)
200 E. Fremont St.; (800) 634-6460; (702) 385-3232; FAX 385-6229
*U – Built in the ancient times of 1956 and renovated in 1991, this "low-
budget" Downtown landmark has "good value" but "not much going for it";
rooms, though otherwise "clean", are "cramped", and the food is "terrible."*

**Sands Hotel & Casino** 716R (80S)      | 16 | 15 | 15 | 15 | $94 |
3355 Las Vegas Blvd. S.; (800) 446-4678; (702) 733-5000; FAX 733-5624
*U – A "good central location" doesn't make up for the fact that the Sands
"saw its best days 10 or more years ago"; the good news is that about a
third of the 720 rooms are under renovation and more work may follow.*

**Showboat Hotel, Casino &**               | 15 | 15 | 13 | 14 | $68 |
**Bowling Center** 500R (4S)
2800 Fremont St.; (800) 634-3484; (702) 385-9123; FAX 385-9154
*M – With an Old South/New Orleans theme, the Showboat recently spent
$25 million on four new restaurants, a new bingo hall, an expanded casino,
a new parking garage and the largest bowling center in North America (106
lanes); results are decidedly mixed: "I'd like to live there" vs. "I wouldn't
wave bon voyage if it floated away."*

## LAS VEGAS HOTELS

| R | S | D | P | $ |
|---|---|---|---|---|

**Stardust Resort & Casino**   2341R (130S)   | 14 | 14 | 14 | 15 | $71 |
3000 Las Vegas Blvd. S.; (800) 634-6757; (702) 732-6111; FAX 732-6557
*M – Although it's "one of the best bargains on the Strip" and recently
renovated, a lot of our surveyors think the Stardust "can never be improved
enough"; "shabby" quarters in its motel area and "abysmal" service have
given this place a reputation for being "long in the tooth" that may be hard
to shake – although, to be fair, with the newly built towers, ratings have
edged up since our last Survey.*

**St. Tropez\***   150S   | 18 | 17 | 14 | 16 | $93 |
(fka Ramada Suites St. Tropez)
455 E. Harmon Ave.; (800) 666-5400; (702) 369-5400; FAX 369-1150
*U – This newish all-suiter has a "useful location for business", convenient
to the convention center and as close to the University of Nevada as it is to
the Strip; "attentive service" and "nice rooms" make this a "good choice for
a nongaming" stay in Las Vegas.*

**Tropicana Hotel &**   | 17 | 16 | 16 | 17 | $86 |
**Country Club**   1913R (125S)
3801 Las Vegas Blvd.; (800) 468-9494; (702) 739-2222; FAX 739-2469
*M – An "older, well-kept property" that's "somewhat faded but still has
excitement"; it's best known for the "wonderful pool", complete with a "great
slide", and a "very tropical" decor with "live birds and plants all over" the
extensive grounds, but its near-airport location can be "too far" from the
Strip and convention center"; reviewers disagree on virtually everything
else, including food ("amazingly good" vs. "terrible"), rooms ("nicely
decorated" vs. "ugly") and service ("very good" vs. "forgot to hire staff").*

**Vegas World Hotel & Casino**   1000R   | 11 | 11 | 9 | 10 | $61 |
2000 Las Vegas Blvd.; (800) 634-6277; (702) 382-2000; FAX 383-0664
*U – Stay at this "strange place" with its "wacky" outer-space theme "only
for the rates", say most reviewers; the rooms are "plain" and the casino
and public areas "dingy"; "this is rock bottom", and apparently it shows, but
it's the Strip hotel closest to Downtown action, and if you're out all night
painting the town, a cheap room may be no problem.*

### ● OTHER HOTEL-CHAIN CHOICES
*You will find one or more additional locations of the following hotel chains
in the Las Vegas area: Courtyard by Marriott, Days Inn, Holiday Inn,
Howard Johnson, La Quinta Inns, Marriott, Ramada, Super 8 and
Travelodge/Viscount; for reservations or information, see the toll-free 800
phone listings on page 16.*

# LOS ANGELES†

## TOP HOTELS
## (In order of rating)

### BEST OVERALL

27 – Hotel Bel-Air
26 – Ritz-Carlton, Huntington
     Four Seasons
     Peninsula Beverly Hills
25 – Ritz-Carlton, Marina del Rey
     Regent Beverly Wilshire
24 – L'Ermitage
     Checkers Hotel Kempinski
23 – Tower at Century Plaza
     Westwood Marquis

### BEST VALUES

Warner Center Marriott
Industry Hills Sheraton
Westin Hotel – LAX
Sheraton Los Angeles Airport
Ritz-Carlton, Huntington
Marriott LAX
Le Parc Hotel
Biltmore Los Angeles
Ritz-Carlton, Marina del Rey
Los Angeles Airport Hilton

\*          \*          \*

### Best Rooms

28 – Hotel Bel-Air
26 – Four Seasons
     Peninsula Beverly Hills
     Ritz-Carlton, Huntington
     Regent Beverly Wilshire
25 – Ritz-Carlton, Marina del Rey
     L'Ermitage
24 – Tower at Century Plaza
     Hotel Nikko
     J.W. Marriott

### Best Dining

26 – Hotel Bel-Air
25 – Ritz-Carlton, Huntington
     Four Seasons
     Checkers Hotel Kempinski
     Peninsula Beverly Hills
24 – Regent Beverly Wilshire
     Ritz-Carlton, Marina del Rey
     L'Ermitage
23 – Westwood Marquis
     Tower at Century Plaza

### Best Service

27 – Hotel Bel-Air
26 – Four Seasons
     Ritz-Carlton, Huntington
     Peninsula Beverly Hills
25 – Ritz-Carlton, Marina del Rey
     Checkers Hotel Kempinski
     L'Ermitage
24 – Westwood Marquis
     Tower at Century Plaza
     J.W. Marriott at Century City

### Best Public Facilities

27 – Hotel Bel-Air
     Ritz-Carlton, Huntington
26 – Peninsula Beverly Hills
25 – Four Seasons
     Ritz-Carlton, Marina del Rey
24 – Regent Beverly Wilshire
23 – Tower at Century Plaza
     Biltmore Los Angeles
     Loews Santa Monica
     J.W. Marriott at Century City

---

†For restaurants, see *Zagat Los Angeles/So. California Restaurant Survey.*

# LOS ANGELES HOTELS

|  | R | S | D | P | $ |
|---|---|---|---|---|---|

**Barnabey's Hotel**   117R (7S)

|  | – | – | – | – | M |
|---|---|---|---|---|---|

3501 Sepulveda Blvd., Manhattan Beach; (800) 552-5285; (310) 545-8466;
FAX 545-8621
*Located in a coastal community just minutes from LAX, this family-owned
establishment is reminiscent of an old European country inn; amenities
include guest rooms with European antiques and canopy beds, a garden
terrace with tiered fountains, an enclosed heated pool and a free shuttle
service to the airport, beach and Manhattan Village mall; in sum, a relaxing
alternative to an airport hotel.*


**BelAge Hotel**   192S

|  | 23 | 22 | 22 | 21 | $201 |
|---|---|---|---|---|---|

1020 N. San Vincente Blvd., West Hollywood; (800) 424-4443;
(310) 854-1111; FAX 854-0926
*U – A "very elegant" luxury property owned by the ubiquitous (and
financially troubled) Ashkenazy family, just off the "rock 'n' roll" heart of the
Sunset Strip, creating an interesting cultural clash – "perfection and bliss"
just a few feet from heavy metal and in-your-face comedy clubs; the
French-Russian Diaghilev restaurant is considered among the most
"romantic" in town.*


**Beverly Hills Hotel**   268R (52S)

|  | – | – | – | – | VE |
|---|---|---|---|---|---|

9641 Sunset Blvd., Beverly Hills; (800) 283-8885; (310) 276-2251; FAX 271-0319
*Closed for renovation until 1994.*


**Beverly Hilton, The**   581R (91S)

|  | 20 | 20 | 19 | 19 | $175 |
|---|---|---|---|---|---|

9876 Wilshire Blvd., Beverly Hills; (800) HILTONS; (310) 274-7777;
FAX 285-1313
*M – This "glitzy" Merv Griffin–owned hotel at the intersection of Santa
Monica and Wilshire boulevards has one of the largest banquet rooms in
town (often used for celebrity benefits) and is home to Polynesian-retro
Trader Vic's (food rating, 20); extensive renovations have blessed this
centrally located "business hotel" with an "elegant lobby" lined with "lots of
marble", and the rooms run from "slightly run-down to excellent."*


**Beverly Pavilion Hotel**   110R (10S)

|  | 17 | 19 | 19 | 16 | $146 |
|---|---|---|---|---|---|

9360 Wilshire Blvd., Beverly Hills; (800) 441-5050; (310) 273-1400;
FAX 859-8551
*M – "Good-bargain", low-key small hotel in the heart of "high-rent" Beverly
Hills, with "standard rooms" that are compensated for by a "good location"
just two blocks from Rodeo Drive; a "quiet", "value" spot that some find
"disappointing" and un-BH "dowdy."*

## LOS ANGELES HOTELS

**Beverly Rodeo Hotel**   86R (12S)       | 16 | 16 | 16 | 14 | $170 |
360 N. Rodeo Dr., Beverly Hills; (800) 356-7575; (310) 273-0300;
FAX 859-8730
*M – Probably the strangest juxtaposition of hotel and location in LA, this
"functional" facility with "no ambiance" sits right on Rodeo Drive, surrounded
by Gucci, Armani, Tiffany and Cartier; for those who want "perfect
people-watching" and topflight shopping, this is a "great find" where "they
remember guests"; others find it "ho-hum", except for the bill.*

**Biltmore Los Angeles, The**   700R (40S)       | 20 | 21 | 22 | 23 | $164 |
506 S. Grand Ave.; (800) 245-8673; (213) 624-1011; FAX 612-1545
*U – The "grande old dame" of Downtown, "lovingly restored" to its "former
elegance" with lots of "old-world charm", offers a touch of "serenity" in the
"forgotten heart of the city"; this "touch of old LA" has the "best lobby in the
country", with "great public rooms" where you can meet and greet to your
heart's content (the Board of Governors of the Grammys throws its annual
post-show ball here); many praise the "great" food at Nouvelle French
Bernard's, but the neighborhood can be "dangerous at night", though it's
close to concerts and theater at the Music Center.*

**Century Plaza Hotel & Tower**   1072R (75S)       | 22 | 21 | 20 | 21 | $178 |
2025 Ave. of the Stars, Century City; (800) 228-3000; (310) 277-2000;
FAX 551-3355
*M – A "glitzy" "big hotel" with "a fabulous location" in the middle of Century
City between Beverly Hills and Westwood; with "thousands of lawyers"
in the towers and the "shop-till-you-drop" scene in the mall, this "great
businessman's hotel" is also fine for "families on vacation", though some
note that "things are kind of run-down" and "they have conventions and
meetings day in and day out."*

**Chateau Marmont**   63R (53S)       | 18 | 18 | 16 | 17 | $160 |
8221 Sunset Blvd.; (800) 242-8328; (213) 656-1010;
FAX 655-5311
*M – "Kooky" and "bohemian to the core", with a comfortably musty and
shabbily genteel lobby, this "European-style" hotel "just above the Sunset
Strip" has long been popular with visiting rock musicians and British actors,
who "like it because nothing works"; still famed after a decade as the place
where John Belushi spent "his last night"; those in the know prefer the
"homey bungalows" adjacent to this "possibly haunted" ersatz castle that's
"a must for movie buffs."*

**CHECKERS HOTEL KEMPINSKI**            | 23 | 25 | 25 | 22 | $192 |
**LOS ANGELES**   190R (15S) (fka Checkers Hotel)
535 S. Grand Ave.; (800) 426-3135; (213) 624-0000; FAX 626-9906
U – A "truly luxe", "meticulously run" branch of SF's prestigious Campton
Place; this "gem" is often called the "best hotel Downtown", thanks to its
"old-world comfort", "perfect location" and "lovely spa", along with its
"remarkable" Californian-French restaurant, also called Checkers (food
rating, 25) especially good for breakfast meetings; expect "smallish rooms
but tremendous ambiance" in an "intimate" setting that makes this "cozy",
"romantic" retreat "excellent for a naughty weekend."

**FOUR SEASONS HOTEL**            | 26 | 26 | 25 | 25 | $223 |
**AT BEVERLY HILLS**   285R (106S)
300 S. Doheny Dr.; (800) 332-3442; (310) 273-2222; FAX 859-3824
U – "Heavenly"; this "California rococo" branch of the "elegant and lovely"
Four Seasons chain provides "a real escape from reality" for visiting
celebrities who want to get away from the paparazzi; it's "the best and
keeps getting better", with "big bathtubs, balconies and two phone lines in
every room", along with "Sunday brunch fit for a king" at the Gardens
restaurant; for the "ultimate California experience", try "riding an exercise
bike at the edge of the pool" while looking out over Beverly Hills – you
never know who'll be riding next to you!

**Hollywood Roosevelt Hotel**   336R (28S)   | 14 | 15 | 14 | 16 | $125 |
7000 Hollywood Blvd., Hollywood; (800) 950-ROOS; (213) 466-7000;
FAX 462-8056
M – This "poorly refurbished", "nostalgic" Hollywood landmark across the
street from Mann's Chinese Theatre is considered "fun for movie buffs and
stargazers" who "want to relive the past"; don't miss the David Hockney–
painted pool and the lobby with its "real character"; otherwise, "like
Hollywood, it tries hard" but lives mostly in memory.

**HOTEL BEL-AIR**   91R (38S)            | 28 | 27 | 26 | 27 | $268 |
701 Stone Canyon Rd.; (800) 648-4097; (310) 472-1211;
FAX 476-5890
U – "Tranquillity, thy name is Bel-Air"; this top-rated, "near-perfect" "country-
in-the-city" "hideaway" in the midst of LA's richest community is, by all
accounts, "the best hotel on earth for love", "an oasis in the nouvelle glitz of
LA", a "Garden of Eden" including "suave service with a California smile"; add
on a landscape of "swans, brooks and trees" and "paradise leaves nothing to
be desired"; while you're here, don't miss The Restaurant (food rating, 25).

**Hotel Inter-Continental**                          | – | – | – | – | E |
**Los Angeles at California Plaza**   439R (4S)
251 S. Olive St.; (213) 617-3300; FAX 617-3399
*A $100 million luxury hotel – part of a lavish business-and-entertainment*
*complex in historic Bunker Hill, near Chinatown and the Music Center; it's*
*the first new hotel in Downtown LA in over a decade; floor-to-ceiling windows*
*bring in light and views from rooms high up in the 17-story tower; Californian*
*cuisine (what else?) is the feature of the elegant Angels Flight restaurant.*


**Hotel Nikko Beverly Hills**   304R (40S)    | 24 | 22 | 21 | 23 | $190 |
465 S. La Cienega Blvd.; (800) NIKKO-BH; (310) 247-0400; FAX 247-0315
*U – This "ultra high-tech" Japanese modernist hotel has a "great location"*
*on Restaurant Row in Beverly Hills (Morton's of Chicago on one side,*
*Matsuhisa on the other, and not far from Lawry's Prime Rib), plus an*
*"awesome" lobby complete with bridges and streams, and in-room*
*computers that allow you to make restaurant reservations through a*
*TV-phone interface; easily the most "stylish Oriental hotel" in town.*


**Hyatt at Los Angeles Airport**   594R (11S)   | 17 | 17 | 16 | 15 | $129 |
6225 W. Century Blvd.; (800) 233-1234; (310) 670-1234; FAX 641-6924
*M – "Standard meeting box" that's "good for airport layovers", with a "low*
*charm level" but "well-soundproofed rooms"; as with many airport hotels,*
*the location is the "only thing going for it", making it "fine for rolling out of*
*bed and into the plane", but for little else.*


**Hyatt on Sunset**   262R (2S)              | 14 | 14 | 12 | 12 | $123 |
8401 Sunset Blvd., West Hollywood; (800) 228-9000; (213) 656-4101;
FAX 650-7024
*M – A fabled "rock-and-roll hotel", celebrated in many a hard-rock anthem*
*for its permissive attitude toward trashed rooms and groupies, this "over-the-*
*hill" hilltop hotel on the Sunset Strip offers a fabulous view of the city and*
*little else, though the scene around the rooftop pool is "great if you like tattoos."*


**Hyatt Regency Los Angeles**   485R (41S)   | 19 | 18 | 17 | 18 | $151 |
711 S. Hope St.; (800) 233-1234; (213) 683-1234; FAX 629-3230
*M – "Greatly improved", this "gracious business hotel" is an "oasis in*
*Downtown LA", especially "if you're on the Regency Floor"; its stock-in-*
*trade is "consistent service for businesspeople" in an "excellent corporate"*
*setting with a "bustling lobby"; "not spectacular" but "good enough" except*
*at night, when Downtown is dead.*

**Industry Hills Sheraton Resort**   296R (31S)   | 17 | 17 | 15 | 18 | $112 |
1 Industry Hills Pkwy., City of Industry; (800) 524-4557; (818) 965-0861;
FAX 964-9535
*M – "Good basic suburban" hotel that's "great for functions", with a "nice golf course"; otherwise, it "needs work", especially the "not-overly-professional sales and catering staff"; still, it's "good for where it is."*

**J.W. Marriott at Century City**   367R (154S)   | 24 | 23 | 21 | 22 | $177 |
2151 Ave. of the Stars; (800) 228-9290; (310) 277-2777;
FAX 785-9240
*U – An "attempt at elegance" with "ambiance and glitz", this "cut-above" postmodern castle, glittering in the midst of high-rise Century City, is "as good as Marriott gets" (some even say it's "the best Marriott in the world"); expect "beautiful rooms" and "friendly service."*

**Le Dufy\***   103S   | 20 | 18 | 12 | 15 | $132 |
1000 Westmount Dr., West Hollywood; (800) 253-7997; (310) 657-7400;
FAX 854-6744
*U – "Home away from home", this "great in-town getaway" was carved out of "converted condos", making each suite "more like an apartment than a hotel"; this "great value" sits on a quiet West Hollywood side street, making it a "best bet in LA" and a "staple for business trips."*

**Le Parc Hotel**   150S   | 21 | 20 | 19 | 17 | $142 |
733 N. West Knoll Dr., West Hollywood; (800) 5-SUITES; (310) 855-8888;
FAX 659-7812
*U – "Roomy suites" and an "uncrowded pool" make this sibling of Le Dufy a "great family hotel"; expect "no lobby" and "no glitz"; instead, you get "private apartments with kitchenettes" in a "very quiet" "residential" setting; it's a "great find in a city of expensive hotels."*

**L'ERMITAGE HOTEL**   | 25 | 25 | 24 | 22 | $248 |
**DE GRANDE CLASSE**   112S
9291 Burton Way, Beverly Hills; (310) 278-3344; FAX 278-8247
*U – An "utterly luxurious", "wonderfully romantic" secluded retreat on a tree-lined Beverly Hills street, with "very elegant townhouse suites" and fireplaces in many rooms; "rooms are bigger than most apartments", with "totally understated elegance" and "service to the nines."*

## LOS ANGELES HOTELS

| R | S | D | P | $ |

**Loews Santa Monica**                            | 21 | 20 | 20 | 23 | $175 |
**Beach Hotel**   350R (31S)
1700 Ocean Ave., Santa Monica; (800) 223-0888; (310) 458-6700; FAX 458-6761
*M – "Charming" oceanfront hotel that "captures the fantasy of LA's beach
life" with its "very appealing" design, "gorgeous lobby" and "nice amenities";
this "nouvelle grand" hotel offers lots of "rooms with ocean views", but
good service may still need "attention"; it's got a "great location" as the only
major hotel on the beach.*

**Los Angeles Airport**                            | 16 | 16 | 15 | 15 | $121 |
**Hilton & Towers**   1279R (14S)
(aka Hilton LAX)
5711 W. Century Blvd.; (800) HILTONS; (310) 410-4000; FAX 410-6250
*M – A "quite comfortable" "place to sleep" at LAX for those who want to
avoid freeway traffic to the West Side and the "long trip to Downtown"; this
"basic", "unexceptional" business hotel is "convenient for the busy traveler",
with functional rooms and "average" service.*

**Los Angeles Hilton & Towers**   899R (36S)   | 18 | 17 | 17 | 17 | $144 |
930 Wilshire Blvd.; (800) 445-8667; (213) 629-4321; FAX 488-9869
*M – "Too big" say our surveyors of this Downtown chain hotel, with a lobby
so large you "need sneakers to get around"; still, this "efficient", "business-
oriented" facility is popular for conventions and meetings, thanks to
proximity to the LA convention center; detractors think its setting is "cold
and impersonal", the "best of Cleveland in LA."*

**Malibu Beach Inn**   47R (3S)                   | – | – | – | – | M |
22878 Pacific Coast Hwy., Malibu; (800) 4MALIBU; (310) 456-6444;
FAX 456-1499
*For those who dream of a beach house in Malibu, this newish small pink
hotel is the next best thing; water sports are the prime focus, but because
breakfast and round-the-clock nibbles are the only food service offered,
restaurant-hopping is also a popular pastime; all rooms have private
balconies with ocean views, as well as fireplaces, wet bars and VCRs.*

**Ma Maison Sofitel**   311R (13S)              | 20 | 19 | 18 | 19 | $162 |
8555 Beverly Blvd.; (800) 221-4542; (310) 278-5444; FAX 657-2816
*M – "European atmosphere" and "French country decor" are what you'll
find at this "charming" hotel with "very nice, tiny rooms" right across the
street from the massive bulk of the Beverly Center shopping mall; some
complain that the staffers are "too impressed with themselves", but most
approve of this Los Angeles branch of the French hotel operation, giving
extra nods for the "cozy" bistro (La Cajole Brasserie) on its ground floor.*

# LOS ANGELES HOTELS

| R | S | D | P | $ |

**Marriott LAX**   1012R (19S)   | 17 | 17 | 17 | 16 | $122 |
5855 W. Century Blvd.; (800) 228-9290; (310) 641-5700; FAX 337-5358
*M – An "oasis in a turbulent" setting and a "best choice" near LAX; "for an
airport hotel, this is better than most", though the wrong room can make it
seem "like sleeping in the runway terminal"; "glitzy Celtics stay here, and
so do fans"; regular airport shuttle service is popular with short-term
travelers with cars to leave.*

**Mondrian Hotel**   219S   | 21 | 19 | 18 | 17 | $175 |
8440 Sunset Blvd., West Hollywood; (800) 525-8029; (213) 650-8999;
FAX 650-5215
*U – On Sunset Strip, this Ashkenazy-owned hotel is famed for its exterior
painted to resemble (what else?) a geometric Mondrian work; a "kooky
but fun" structure, it's one of "LA's best-kept secrets" despite its central
location; an "ultrastylized" hotel for "deals and dreamers" that "oozes
rock 'n' roll chic."*

**New Otani Hotel & Garden, The**   435R (20S)   | 19 | 20 | 19 | 18 | $156 |
120 S. Los Angeles St.; (800) 421-8795; (213) 629-1200; FAX 622-0980
*M – Located on the north edge of Little Tokyo, this branch of a Japanese
chain offers such amenities as rooms made to look like Japanese country
inns, complete with large baths and cotton kimonos; this is a "charming"
refuge, with "superior" gardens hidden on upper floors and "great food" in
the Thousand Cranes restaurant (food rating, 24); "a taste of Japanese
elegance in a tacky section" of Downtown.*

**PENINSULA BEVERLY**   | 26 | 26 | 25 | 26 | $257 |
**HILLS, THE**   200R (48S)
9882 Santa Monica Blvd., Beverly Hills; (800) 462-7899; (310) 273-4888;
FAX 858-6663
*U – The new Big Guy in town has a "super elegant" restaurant, The Belvedere,
that's packed every morning with "agents, studio heads, stars and fellow
travelers"; this "new classic" is "a Peninsula in every sense of the word", with
"elegance on top of elegance", a "butler on every floor" and a rooftop pool
where "the stars shine during the day"; this is "a first-class place...and the
bill reflects it."*

**Radisson Bel-Air Summit Hotel**   161R (56S)   | 16 | 15 | 15 | 15 | $142 |
11461 W. Sunset Blvd.; (800) 333-3333; (310) 476-6571; FAX 471-6310
*M – This freeway-adjacent "good value" has "changed managements so
often" that it's hard to tell what state it's in; in its current incarnation, it's a
"small, noisy" hotel where you "shouldn't expect to get the room you made
a reservation for"; though some say the location is handy for West Side
business, critics insist "they could have done better on the renovation."*

## LOS ANGELES HOTELS

**Radisson Plaza Hotel &**                | 20 | 21 | 19 | 20 | $125 |
**Golf Course\***  380R (11S)
1400 Parkview Ave., Manhattan Beach; (800) 333-3333; (310) 546-7511;
FAX 546-7520
*M – "Good rooms and good service" are about the best you can expect at
this "nice" establishment south of the airport; though not close enough to
be in the LA loop", it offers "comfort for business travelers" with Long Beach
or Orange County destinations; critics complaion of "small, unimpressively
furnished rooms", but fortunately there's a golf course nearby.*

**REGENT BEVERLY**                        | 26 | 26 | 24 | 24 | $245 |
**WILSHIRE, THE**  300R (90S)
9500 Wilshire Blvd., Beverly Hills; (800) 421-4354; (310) 275-5200; FAX 274-2851
*U – "A unique hotel in a plastic world", this "handsome, masculine hotel"
has been "redone to perfection", transforming a "nostalgic old" Beverly Hills
dowager into what some call "the best hotel in town"; the "grand entrance
sets the mood" at this "veritable jewel" where "everyone feels like a movie
star"; don't forget to eat in "one of the best hotel restaurants in town", The
Dining Room (food rating, 24) – even the "coffee shop is fabulous"; many
praise the "elegant bathrooms" – "I could live in there" – and Rodeo Drive
is right across the street.*

**RITZ-CARLTON,**                         | 26 | 26 | 25 | 27 | $183 |
**HUNTINGTON HOTEL**  383R (27S)
1401 S. Oak Knoll Ave., Pasadena; (800) 241-3333; (818) 568-3900;
FAX 568-3700
*U – An "admirable restoration" of the "landmark" Huntington Hotel in the
old-money section of conservative Pasadena east of Downtown, this
"fabulous re-creation" is "even classier" than the original, with "marble
everywhere" and "weddings every weekend"; incredibly, from some rooms
there's "a view of Downtown LA"; "you'll want to stay for a month" and
should be able to if you get a good corporate rate.*

**RITZ-CARLTON,**                         | 25 | 26 | 24 | 25 | $193 |
**MARINA DEL REY**  306R (12S)
4375 Admiralty Way, Marina del Rey; (800) 241-3333; (310) 823-1700;
FAX 823-2403
*U – "Grand and elegant", this "palatial" property right on the water in the
Marina offers "the best view in town" from a "very impressive" "tie-and-
jacket hotel in a bikini-and-Rollerblade neighborhood" (a short non-freeway
drive from the airport); the "striking design" extends to the "outstanding
rooms", with their "very romantic view"; "expect to spend a lot of money"
in the "extremely proper" restaurants.*

**LOS ANGELES HOTELS**　　　　　　　| R | S | D | P | $ |

**Shangri-La**　55R (33S)　　　　　　| 18 | 16 | 14 | 15 | $140 |
1301 Ocean Ave., Santa Monica; (800) 345-STAY; (310) 394-2791;
FAX 451-3351
*U – You'll "feel like a character in a Phillip Marlowe mystery" at this "very
hip", "rock star"–intensive and celebrity-soaked (Al Pacino, Diane Keaton)
hideaway with its "funky, quaint, fun" rooms and "great location" overlooking
the Pacific; be sure to ask for one of the "suites with kitchens"; for those
who like a hotel with a few eccentricities, this West Side "art deco wonder"
is appealing.*

**Sheraton Grande**　469R (69S)　　　| 21 | 21 | 19 | 19 | $164 |
333 S. Figueroa St.; (800) 325-3535; (213) 617-1133; FAX 613-0291
*M – "Impeccable quality and service" are what draw throngs of "business
travelers" to this "very grand Sheraton" that's "convenient for Downtown
meetings" and "a good choice for out-of-towners"; this "high-quality" hotel
"tries hard to be luxurious", though sometimes it "misses the boat"; still, it's
a "superior Downtown hotel", complete with "limo service to the Music Center."*

**Sheraton Los Angeles Airport**　807R (93S)　| 18 | 16 | 16 | 17 | $116 |
6101 W. Century Blvd.; (800) 325-3535; (310) 642-1111; FAX 410-1267
*M – "Convenient" but "standard", this "impersonal" airport Sheraton is
judged "better than average" by many of our surveyors, with "well-
soundproofed rooms" and "pleasant public areas"; basically it's "just a
place to stay", with "convenient shuttle service" and, unexpectedly, "great
sushi" in Landry's Restaurant.*

**Sheraton Universal Hotel**　444R (28S)　| 18 | 17 | 16 | 17 | $138 |
333 Universal Terrace Pkwy., Universal City; (800) 325-3535;
(818) 980-1212; FAX 985-4980
*M – Nicknamed the "Sheraton Unusual", this "handy", "efficient" high rise is
adjacent to the very popular Universal City theme park, which means it's
"not near anything but Universal"; it's deemed "ok for tourists" "taking the
kids to see how movies are made", but some call it a "horror movie posing
as a hotel", with "nightmare parking", "shabby rooms" and "slow service."*

**Sportsmen's Lodge Hotel**　193R (13S)　| 13 | 13 | 13 | 13 | $106 |
12825 Ventura Blvd., North Hollywood; (800) 821-8511; (818) 769-4700;
FAX 877-3898
*M – "Faded" Valley "institution" that's "one step up from a Motel 6"; it's
been around for so long that one reviewer noted "my grandparents used
to fish in the pond there"; a sprawling motel that's "over the hill – literally",
"nice and nostalgic, but nothing more."*

**St. James's Club & Hotel**   63R (42S)        | 22 | 22 | 22 | 22 | $212 |
8358 Sunset Blvd., West Hollywood; (800) 225-2637; (213) 654-9287;
FAX 654-9287
*U – Journey into "another era" via this "art deco" landmark that's a "private
club" but also open to the public; located right on the Sunset Strip, it's got
an awesome view of Los Angeles, in a setting with "history in every room";
this is "something to experience...especially in Hollywood", offering a rare
"touch of British class in Tinseltown."*

**Sunset Marquis Hotel & Villas**   118S        | 21 | 21 | 19 | 19 | $179 |
1200 N. Alta Loma Rd., West Hollywood; (800) 858-9758; (310) 657-1333;
FAX 652-5300
*U – "Rock-and-roll is here to stay" – and also stays here, at this "heavy-
metal" hotel with lots of bankable faces lounging and dining around the
central "power pool"; this "classy", "motel-like" facility offers a wide choice
of "beautiful suites and villas" that are just right for notables who want to
get away from things – just one block below Sunset Boulevard; "if your
expense account can handle the room rates, then treat yourself."*

**TOWER AT CENTURY PLAZA, THE** 322R (9S)   | 24 | 24 | 23 | 23 | $200 |
2055 Ave. of the Stars; (800) 228-3000; (310) 277-2000; FAX 551-3355
*U – "Not to be confused with the Century Plaza next door", this "elegant"
Century City high rise was favored by Ronald Reagan during his presidency
and is "still the only place for a President to stay in LA"; expect a "different
world" of "beautiful views", and "wonderful down pillows and comforters" at
what some consider to be "among the best hotels in America."*

**Warner Center Marriott**   461R (14S)        | 20 | 20 | 19 | 19 | $127 |
21850 Oxnard St., Woodland Hills; (800) 228-9290; (818) 887-4800;
FAX 340-5893
*U – The primary hotel in the burgeoning West Valley, this chain outpost in
a business complex is considered "great for a Valley hotel", with "beautiful
public areas" and rooms that are "clean, if not fancy"; convenient to
shopping at "Nordstrom's and Saks", this is extra "pleasant" when you
consider that there's "nothing else around."*

**Westin Bonaventure, The**   1474R (66S)       | 17 | 17 | 17 | 17 | $160 |
404 S. Figueroa St.; (800) 228-3000; (213) 624-1000; FAX 612-4894
*M – Our surveyors love to criticize this "monolithic" "architectural disaster"
with its "awfully small", "pie-shaped rooms" and "Blade Runner–ish" lobby
that's been described as like being "inside a tooth"; this former "hotel of the
future" is "aging badly", and few are thrilled that "you need a tour guide to
find your way around"; modernists call it "spectacular", but to most it "looks
better in the opening shots of LA Law."*

## LOS ANGELES HOTELS                          | R | S | D | P | $ |

**Westin Hotel – LAX**   750R (47S)            | 19 | 18 | 18 | 18 | $125 |
(fka Stouffer Concourse)
5400 W. Century Blvd.; (800) 468-3571; (310) 216-5858; FAX 670-1948
*U – Generally considered to be the "best of the airport hotels", this
"pleasant surprise" is notable for its "beautiful lobby", "great corner suites"
and "excellent food"; it's "good for airport meetings" and the "perfect
stopover en route to Australia" or beyond, but watch out for changes under
the new Westin management.*

**WESTWOOD MARQUIS HOTEL**                     | 24 | 24 | 23 | 22 | $200 |
**& GARDENS**   258S
930 Hilgard Ave.; (800) 421-2317; (310) 208-8765; FAX 824-0355
*U – "Extremely elegant", this "jewel-like" "small European hotel" within
walking distance of the UCLA campus and Westwood shopping is "popular
with celebs who don't want to be seen"; expect "understated elegance" and
"great food", especially the legendary Sunday buffet brunch – one of the
"best in town" – at this "great alternative to big-city hotels."*

**Wilshire Plaza Hotel***   372R (29S)         | 14 | 15 | 15 | 14 | $140 |
(fka Hyatt Wilshire)
3515 Wilshire Blvd.; (800) 382-7411; (213) 381-7411; FAX 386-7379
*U – This business hotel located midway between Downtown and LA's West
Side strikes some as "convenient", but others find it "disappointing" and
in a "bad neighborhood to boot"; N.B. it's too soon to say whether a recent
switch to independent management will produce meaningful changes.*

### ● OTHER HOTEL-CHAIN CHOICES
*You will find one or more additional locations of the following hotel chains in
the Los Angeles area: Courtyard by Marriott, Crown Sterling Suites, Days
Inn, Doubletree, Embassy Suites, Hampton Inn, Hilton, Holiday Inn,
Howard Johnson, Hyatt, Preferred Hotels, Ramada, Relais & Chateaux,
Stouffer, Travelodge/Viscount; for reservations or information, see the
toll-free 800 phone listings on page 16.*

# MIAMI/MIAMI BEACH*†

## TOP HOTELS
## (In order of rating)

### BEST OVERALL

25 – Grand Bay Hotel
24 – Turnberry Isle Club
      Mayfair House
22 – Alexander
      Hyatt Regency Coral Gables
21 – Colonnade Hotel
      Doral Resort
20 – Hotel Place St. Michel
      Sonesta Beach Hotel
      Grove Isle Club

### BEST VALUES

Hotel Place St. Michel
Hyatt Regency Coral Gables
Biscayne Bay Marriott
Sheraton River House
Don Shula's Hotel
Mayfair House
Hyatt Regency Miami
Hotel Inter-Continental
Doubletree Coconut Grove
Omni International Hotel

\*       \*       \*

### Best Rooms

26 – Grand Bay Hotel
      Mayfair House
      Turnberry Isle Club
23 – Hyatt Regency Coral Gables
22 – Alexander
      Colonnade Hotel
21 – Doral Resort
20 – Grove Isle Club
      Hotel Inter-Continental
      Sonesta Beach Hotel

### Best Dining

24 – Grand Bay Hotel
23 – Turnberry Isle Club
22 – Mayfair House
      Alexander
21 – Hotel Place St. Michel
      Hyatt Regency Coral Gables
      Colonnade Hotel
19 – Doral Resort
      Sonesta Beach Hotel
18 – Grove Isle Club

### Best Service

25 – Grand Bay Hotel
24 – Mayfair House
23 – Turnberry Isle Club
22 – Hyatt Regency Coral Gables
21 – Alexander
      Hotel Place St. Michel
      Colonnade Hotel
      Doral Resort
20 – Sonesta Beach Hotel
18 – Doral Ocean Beach

### Best Public Facilities

25 – Turnberry Isle Club
      Grand Bay Hotel
23 – Mayfair House
22 – Doral Resort
      Grove Isle Club
      Alexander
      Colonnade Hotel
21 – Sonesta Beach Hotel
20 – Fontainebleau Hilton
      Hotel Inter-Continental

---

*See also: Florida Resorts.
†For restaurants, see *Zagat Miami/South Florida Restaurant Survey*.

# MIAMI/MIAMI BEACH HOTELS

| R | S | D | P | $ |

**Alexander All-Suite Luxury Hotel, The**   170S | 22 | 21 | 22 | 22 | $195 |
5225 Collins Ave., Miami Beach; (800) 327-6121; (305) 865-6500; FAX 864-8525
*M – Recommended for extended stays, this "condominium conversion run strictly as a hotel" receives high ratings for its "superb" "European elegance", "fabulous large suites", "beautiful gardens" and an "excellent restaurant", Dominique's (food rating, 24) where "the celebrities go" for the "best Sunday brunch on the Beach"; though it's "very expensive", high ratings suggest that this ambitiously named hotel isn't mere bravado.*

**Betsy Ross Hotel\***   77R (3S) | 17 | 20 | 24 | 18 | $122 |
1440 Ocean Dr., Miami Beach; (800) 755-4601; (305) 531-3934; FAX 531-5282
*U – The Deco District's "small but nice" Colonial-style hotel is best known for chef Norman Van Aken's top-rated restaurant, 'a Mano'; rooms that may be "not the best but not the worst" are not as important as the "relaxing atmosphere" in the center of South Beach's "in" area.*

**Biltmore Hotel**   270R (30S) | – | – | – | – | E |
1200 Anastasia Ave, Coral Gables; (800) 727-1926; (305) 445-1926; FAX 443-4607
*The grande dame returns with the recent reopening of this beautiful, luxurious circa-1926 Mediterranean-style palace that once hosted the likes of the Windsors, Eisenhowers and Howard Hughes, and is now under the Westin wing; with golf, tennis, a larger-than-life pool, full European spa and beautiful grounds and ocean views, it's sure to be on the social register of tony Coral Gables.*

**Biscayne Bay Marriott** | 19 | 18 | 18 | 18 | $129 |
**Hotel & Marina**   605R (21S)
1633 N. Bayshore Dr., Miami; (800) 228-9290; (305) 374-3900; FAX 579-0108
*M – If you're in town for "meetings and events" or need a "cruise-line stopover", this "better-than-average chain" hotel has a handy location adjacent to the Omni Shopping Center and Bayside Marketplace, plus a "romantic view" of the bay; it has "good service" and "adequate rooms", but watch out for the "rough neighborhood."*

**Colonnade Hotel, The**   157R (17S) | 22 | 21 | 21 | 22 | $171 |
180 Aragon Ave., Coral Gables; (800) 533-1337; (305) 441-2600; FAX 445-3929
*U – In the heart of Coral Gables, "within walking distance of Miracle Mile shops and Miami's best restaurants", sits this "charming" '20s-era hotel, "little known" yet "worshiped by regulars", who call it a "subdued return to elegance", citing complimentary champagne or orange juice on check-in, "comfortable" accommodations (the "bi-level suites" are "fabulous") and "wonderful service", all adding up to a "good, substantial value."*

**David William Hotel\*** 99R | 16 | 15 | 21 | 16 | $140 |
700 Biltmore Way, Coral Gables; (800) 327-8770; (305) 445-7821; FAX 445-5585
*M – Though known more as a condominium, this quiet alternative to more
touristy hotels offers 100 guest rooms that have been pleasantly modernized
in pastel colors and offer a "nice view of residential Coral Gables"; a handy
location within walking distance of elite shopping, and a charming Classic
French restaurant, Chez Vendôme (food rating, 20), are major bonuses.*

**Don Shula's Hotel & Golf Club** 342R (32S) | 17 | 18 | 18 | 18 | $126 |
Main St., Miami Lakes; (800) 247-4852; (305) 821-1150; FAX 821-1150 x1150
*U – "Shula knows hotels and food too" as this off-the-beaten-track "great
value" demonstrates; "golf's the thing" here, along with beautiful gardens
and a man-made lagoon, tennis, racquetball, a health club and lots of other
activities; though few of our surveyors know about it, those who do say it's
"a great place" for both families and corporate retreaters.*

**Doral Ocean Beach Resort** 420R (127S) | 19 | 18 | 18 | 18 | $160 |
4833 Collins Ave., Miami Beach; (800) 22-DORAL; (305) 532-3600;
FAX 532-7409
*M – "Scenic top-floor dining overlooking the ocean" at Alfredo's of Rome,
"a fitness center that rates well with locals" and complimentary shuttle
service to the Doral Resort & Country Club, with discount rates for golf, are
some of the advantages of this "rococo" "old-world" hotel, but that's not
enough to counteract the ravages of time on "older rooms" in "need of
renovation"; still, for its many fans it has that "old-time Miami feeling."*

**Doral Resort & Country Club** 650R (58S) | 21 | 21 | 19 | 22 | $169 |
4400 NW 87th Ave., Miami; (800) 22-DORAL; (305) 592-2000;
FAX 594-4682
*U – "A top-notch" resort if you're "sports-minded and like green"; five
championship golf courses in a "beautiful tropical setting" draw responses
of "golfer's paradise", with 15 tennis courts and a "world-class spa" (the
Doral Saturnia) across the street; be sure to ask for a "redone room" and
carry earplugs since the International Airport is nearby.*

**Doubletree Hotel at** | 17 | 17 | 15 | 16 | $129 |
**Coconut Grove** 190R (18S)
2649 S. Bayshore Dr., Coconut Grove; (800) 528-0444; (305) 858-2500;
FAX 858-5776
*M – "Pleasant and well priced", Coconut Grove's "vintage from the '70s" is
"small enough for personal service"; a "good" location, with access to the
marina across the road and an easy walk to the Mayfair and Cocowalk, is
an added benefit, but insiders advise "avoid top-floor rooms because of the
disco that pounds all night"; detractors insist "there are better choices."*

## MIAMI/MIAMI BEACH HOTELS

| | R | S | D | P | $ |
|---|---|---|---|---|---|

**Eden Roc Hotel & Marina**   351R (66S)   | 17 | 17 | 16 | 16 | $142 |
4525 Collins Ave., Miami Beach; (800) 327-8337; (305) 531-0000; FAX 531-6955
*U – "Still rolling along" with its reputation of "glitz and glamour" from the
'50s intact, "old Miami Beach's grand lady" is now a blue-haired has-been
despite a "top location" on the beach; however, given the resurgence of the
area, it's to be expected that the Eden Roc will inevitably be resurrected
and will, once again, be back on top.*

**Fontainebleau Hilton**   | 18 | 18 | 17 | 20 | $161 |
**Resort & Spa**   1206R (60S)
4441 Collins Ave., Miami Beach; (800) 548-8886; (305) 538-2000; FAX 532-8145
*M – Bus drivers in the '60s announced "Yankee Stadium" when they
stopped at this "famous landmark"; today this "vulgar but efficient" major
"convention facility" is still "wall-to-wall people"; a "recent renovation"
created the "fabulous lagoon pool", "fantastic health club" and "well-
appointed rooms" but "remodeled away" the "quirky charm"; though "garish"
and "gaudy", or perhaps because it is, the hotel is "making a comeback."*

**GRAND BAY HOTEL**   181R (49S)   | 26 | 25 | 24 | 25 | $202 |
2669 S. Bayshore Rd., Coconut Grove; (800) 327-2788; (305) 858-9600;
FAX 858-1532
*U – "Where the elite meet" for "European ambiance" and "luxury" "overlooking
Dinner Key Marina in Coconut Grove"; "first-class accommodations",
"impeccable personal service" and "the best of culinary experiences" provided
by chef Suki at Ciga's and Continental fare at Grand Cafe (food rating, 26)
make this "truly refined" hotel a "great alternative to the Beach or Downtown";
a few mutter that it's "pretentious", but most consider this hotel simply grand.*

**Grove Isle Yacht & Tennis Club**   49R (10S)   | 20 | 18 | 18 | 22 | $189 |
4 Grove Isle Dr., Coconut Grove; (305) 858-8300; FAX 858-5908
*U – Just "minutes from the hustle and bustle" of both Downtown Miami and
the center of Coconut Grove is this "secluded and private" enclave on an
exclusive island; its "gorgeous location and grounds" are complemented by
"comfortable suites" and "excellent service", making this ideal for tennis
players and yachters; the only complaints concern "unpredictable" food.*

**Hotel Inter-Continental Miami**   644R (34S)   | 20 | 18 | 18 | 19 | $144 |
100 Chopin Plaza, Miami; (800) 327-3005; (305) 577-1000; FAX 372-4720
*M – What some consider the "best choice for Downtown" attracts "lots of
wealthy South Americans" thanks to its "perfect location" in the heart of the
city and near Bayside Marketplace; its "nicely furnished" "rooms have great
views" of Biscayne Bay and the Port, and the "pricey" Le Pavillon restaurant
(food rating, 25) is a bastion of haute Continental dining; still, some Anglos
resent staff who appear to "only understand Spanish."*

**Hotel Place St. Michel**   27R (3S)   | 19 | 21 | 21 | 19 | $122 |
162 Alcazar Ave., Miami Beach; (800) 247-8526; (305) 444-1666; FAX 599-0074
*U – "Quaint" rooms filled with European antiques create an "eclectic and wonderful charm" in this 1926-vintage Mediterranean "bed-and-breakfast", known for "great service" and "fantastic food" at Restaurant St. Michel; though some say it's "no longer shiny", loyalists return to this "nice hotel in the city" for its dinner-and-a-room packages and "wonderful Sunday jazz brunch."*

**Hyatt Regency Coral Gables**   242R (50S)   | 23 | 22 | 21 | 21 | $151 |
50 Alhambra Plaza, Coral Gables; (800) 233-1234; (305) 441-1234; FAX 441-0520
*U – "Excellent service", "huge, clean" rooms and "good value", combine with "pleasant", Mediterranean-style surroundings to make this better-than-average Hyatt "very special all around"; it's the place to stay for businessfolk, who like its "access to the best restaurants in Coral Gables"; to say the "gym facilities could be improved" is a quibble.*

**Hyatt Regency Miami**   615R (34S)   | 19 | 18 | 17 | 18 | $139 |
400 SE Second Ave., Miami; (800) 233-1234; (305) 358-1234; FAX 374-1728
*M – "Great for meetings and events" but perhaps "not up to usual Hyatt standards", Downtown's "good, competent hotel" may be "functional for businesspeople", but it has "not much to offer" other than its central location; more attention to "employee training" and "housekeeping" may be needed.*

**Marlin, The***   11R   | 20 | 20 | 21 | 21 | $131 |
1200 Collins Ave., Miami Beach; (305) 673-8770; FAX 673-9609
*U – Though few yet know this new Deco District "avant garde" "disco hotel", its Caribbean-style hospitality, "great Jamaican food and tropical drinks", and charming "individually designed and hand-painted rooms" won't be a secret for long; the "great roof terrace" where "you can shower with your honey" also helps make it the "choicest"; watch for equally funky restorations of sister properties, the Cavalier and Leslie Hotels on Ocean Drive, soon.*

**MAYFAIR HOUSE HOTEL GRAND LUXE**   182S   | 26 | 24 | 22 | 23 | $175 |
3000 Florida Ave., Coconut Grove; (800) 433-4555; (305) 441-0000; FAX 447-9173
*U – For "a great, sexy getaway" featuring "wonderful outdoor whirlpools on every terrace" and "wacky art nouveau to the max", Coconut Grove's "first-class" "sweet all-suites hotel" offers "rooms and amenities second to none"; it's adjacent to Cocowalk shopping, restaurants and clubs, offering interesting "nightlife and ambiance"; for in-house dining, try the Contemporary American food at Mayfair Grill (food rating, 21).*

## MIAMI/MIAMI BEACH HOTELS

| R | S | D | P | $ |

**Occidental Parc Hotel***    135R (121S)    | – | – | – | – | M |
(fka Riverparc Hotel)
100 SE Fourth St., Miami; (800) 521-5100; (305) 374-5100; FAX 381-9826
*Tucked away behind Knight Convention Center in Downtown Miami, this little-known high rise affords Spanish cuisine and a well-priced suite overlooking the Miami River that can provide a charming experience; still, this comfortable hotel has not enjoyed financial success through several ownerships; N.B the health club was built in 1991.*

**Omni International Hotel**    531R (46S)    | 17 | 16 | 16 | 15 | $125 |
1601 Biscayne Blvd., Miami; (800) THE-OMNI; (305) 374-0000; FAX 374-0020
*U – Local charity and community events keep this "upscale hotel attached to a downscale mall" "busy", but our surveyors suggest that both the "area and hotel have passed their prime"; "don't walk the dangerous streets" when you can have "great food" inside the hotel at the Fish Market (food rating, 26).*

**Radisson Mart Plaza***    334R (21S)    | 19 | 19 | 17 | 19 | $121 |
711 NW 72nd Ave.; (800) 333-3333; (305) 261-3800; FAX 261-7665
*M – If you're in Miami strictly for business or need dependable overnight lodging by the airport, this first-class "commercial" hotel with big public areas is "the place"; adjacent to the "trade-only" Miami Merchandise Mart, it's popular with fashion and home-accessories types for its "large, good rooms" and heads-up service.*

**Sheraton Bal Harbour Hotel**    715R (30S)    | 18 | 17 | 16 | 18 | $149 |
9701 Collins Ave., Bal Harbour; (800) 325-3535; (305) 865-7511; FAX 864-2601
*M – Directly across from the "classy Bal Harbour Shopping Center" is this "beautifully landscaped" oceanfront "conventioneer"; "great views from really comfortable rooms" and an "upscale location", however, aren't enough to negate complaints that "the money spent on the public areas hasn't made a dent in what needs to be done."*

**Sheraton River House Hotel**    408R    | 16 | 17 | 15 | 14 | $111 |
3900 NW 21st St., Miami; (800) 325-3535; (305) 871-3800; FAX 871-0447
*U – "If you have to lay over at the airport, this is good"; it's known more as a "great place to meet", "exciting especially for lovers and singles" – wink, wink – than for anything else, but it happens to have "great service for an airport hotel" and a full health club and exercise facilities.*

## MIAMI/MIAMI BEACH HOTELS

| | R | S | D | P | $ |
|---|---|---|---|---|---|

**Sonesta Beach Hotel**   292R (5S)   | 20 | 20 | 19 | 21 | $173 |

350 Ocean Dr., Key Biscayne; (800) SONESTA; (305) 361-2021; FAX 361-3096
*U – The "beautiful Key Biscayne beach adorned with sea-grape trees"
offers "a quiet spot" with "fine facilities and dining" for those looking for a
"great family-oriented getaway"; critics say it's "too commercial" and in
need of renovation"; N.B. though damaged by Hurricane Andrew, the hotel
is expected to reopen in early 1993.*

**TURNBERRY ISLE RESORTS**   | 26 | 23 | 23 | 25 | $199 |
**YACHT & COUNTRY CLUB**   345R (30S)

19999 W. Country Club Dr., Aventura; (800) 327-7028; (305) 932-6200;
FAX 932-0528
*U – "You cannot improve on perfection" at "Florida's resort par excellence";
a "world unto itself", this newly renovated Mizner-Mediterranean makes
you "feel like you're in Europe" – but for the beautiful tropical setting; the
"best rooms in the South", "top-of-the-line sports action", "super shopping"
and "Miami's best gourmet dining experience" in the private Veranda
Restaurant (food rating, 22) make this a "totally indulgent" experience.*

### ● OTHER HOTEL-CHAIN CHOICES

*You will find one or more additional locations of the following hotel chains
in the Miami/Miami Beach area: Courtyard by Marriott, Crown Sterling
Suites, Days Inn, Embassy Suites, Hampton Inn, Howard Johnson, Hyatt,
La Quinta Inns, Marriott, Radisson, Ramada, Travelodge/Viscount and
Westin; for reservations or information, see the toll-free 800 phone listings
on page 16.*

# MILWAUKEE†

## TOP HOTELS
## (In order of rating)

### BEST OVERALL
21 – Wyndham Milwaukee Center
    Pfister Hotel
19 – Hyatt Regency
    Marc Plaza

### BEST VALUES
Marc Plaza Hotel
Pfister Hotel
Wyndham Milwaukee Center
Hyatt Regency

\*    \*    \*

### Best Rooms
22 – Wyndham Milwaukee Center
    Pfister Hotel
19 – Hyatt Regency
    Marc Plaza

### Best Dining
21 – Pfister Hotel
20 – Wyndham Milwaukee Center
18 – Hyatt Regency
    Marc Plaza

### Best Service
22 – Wyndham Milwaukee Center
    Pfister Hotel
20 – Hyatt Regency
    Marc Plaza

### Best Public Facilities
21 – Wyndham Milwaukee Center
    Pfister Hotel
19 – Hyatt Regency
    Marc Plaza

| R | S | D | P | $ |
|---|---|---|---|---|
| 14 | 15 | 17 | 14 | $91 |

**Astor Hotel\***   96R (30S)
924 E. Juneau St.; (800) 558-0200; (414) 271-4220; FAX 271-6370
*M – One person's "old and musty" is another's "turn-of-the-century comfort"
when it comes to this Easttown hotel listed on the National Register of
Historic Places; while it may not be suitable for fancy executive meetings,
many find the nice suites "enjoyable" at this "homey" refuge "away from
Downtown" – despite what some describe as a "junky exterior."*

---

†For restaurants, see *Zagat Chicago Restaurant Survey.*

## MILWAUKEE HOTELS

| R | S | D | P | $ |

**Embassy Suites, West\***  203S  | 23 | 21 | 23 | 21 | $99 |
1200 S. Moorland Rd., Brookfield; (800) 444-6404; (414) 782-2900;
FAX 796-9159
*U – With its proximity to Milwaukee's zoo, county stadium, medical complex
and state fair, this West suburban, located 15 miles from Downtown, is a
"great hotel for weekend getaways" and a "good family bargain"; during the
week, business travelers appreciate the "great" service and such usual
Embassy perks as free breakfast, cocktails and coffeemakers in the room;
insiders tout the "master suites" with a little conference room adjoining.*

**Hyatt Regency Milwaukee**  484R (19S)  | 19 | 20 | 18 | 19 | $117 |
333 W. Kilbourn Ave.; (800) 233-1234; (414) 276-1234; FAX 276-6338
*M – The "great" festive sports bar at this contemporary Downtown spot
may contribute to the hotel's biggest drawback: it's "noisy", especially when
"conventions take over"; still, its location adjoining Bradley Center and a
"marvelous" staff help make this a contender for "best in town."*

**Manchester Suites – Airport**  100S  | – | – | – | – | I |
200 W. Grange Ave.; (414) 744-3600; FAX 744-4188
*This "locally owned" plain-Jane all-suiter offers little in the way of luxury or
charm, but the traditionally furnished suites include a wet bar, refrigerator
and microwave that seem to please business travelers who need to stay
near the airport; the price is right, with breakfast included in the bargain.*

**Marc Plaza Hotel**  500R (18S)  | 18 | 18 | 17 | 18 | $97 |
509 W. Wisconsin Ave.; (800) 558-7708; (414) 271-7250; FAX 271-1039
*M – A 1988 update of this Downtown landmark was "not enough" for some,
who say this big old hotel, which looks "a bit like a bordello", is "showing its
age"; however, many love the "historic elegance" of its high-ceilinged
public areas and "comfortable" rooms and say this is the "nicest place to
stay Downtown", especially given the "reasonable" rates.*

**Milwaukee Marriott – Brookfield**  396R (3S)  | 17 | 18 | 17 | 15 | $94 |
375 S. Moorland Rd., Brookfield; (800) 228-9290; (414) 786-1100;
FAX 786-1100 x545
*M – Near the zoo, state fair, and county stadium, this "ordinary" West
suburban contemporary hotel wins few raves, but it's "good for business"
and "reliable"; critics call it "mediocre."*

## MILWAUKEE HOTELS                    | R | S | D | P | $ |

**Milwaukee River Hilton Inn***   169R (5S)   | 18 | 17 | 20 | 16 | $101 |
4700 N. Port Washington Rd.; (800) 445-8667; (414) 962-6040; FAX 962-6166
*M – Ratings have improved for this hotel since our last Survey, and our
reviewers laud the "nice river views", the "charming location" near Shorewood
and Whitefish Bay, and the Anchorage seafood restaurant overlooking the
river; critics complain of staff and facilities that are not up to par.*

**Park East Hotel***   160R (4S)   | 16 | 17 | 17 | 17 | $71 |
916 E. State St.; (800) 328-7275; (414) 276-8800; FAX 765-1919
*U – People like the "value" at this Downtown lakefront hotel, which is
perfectly situated for Milwaukee's many warm-weather festivals; a total
renovation begun in late 1992 should improve the ratings of what has long
been a sentimental favorite of so many.*

**Pfister Hotel, The**   307R (90S)   | 22 | 22 | 21 | 21 | $120 |
424 E. Wisconsin Ave.; (800) 558-8222; (414) 273-8222; FAX 273-0747
*U – Milwaukee's Downtown "grande dame" turns 100 in 1993, still looking
young thanks to a series of face-lifts that most agree retained its "old-world
charm" while adding a "more modern look" with the addition of the new
towers; the result is all "elegance" and "splendor", tempered by a sense of
midwestern "warmth" that makes visiting the Pfister "an event in itself";
insiders urge staying "in the old part" to experience "the good old days, but
in comfort"; dining in The English Room (food rating, 24) is also
recommended.*

**Wyndham Milwaukee Center**   221R (75S)   | 22 | 22 | 20 | 21 | $123 |
139 E. Kilbourn Ave.; (800) 822-4200; (414) 276-8686; FAX 276-8007
*U – This "quiet retreat" in the Downtown Theatre Complex adjoining the
Performing Arts Center wins raves for its "lovely" decor and excellent
service; though it's been open only a few years, many consider this to be
the "nicest hotel" in the city; the pasta bar at the well-regarded Kilbourn
Cafe is called a "must."*

## ● OTHER HOTEL-CHAIN CHOICES
*You will find one or more additional locations of the following hotel chains in
the Milwaukee area: Courtyard by Marriott, Days Inn, Hamptons Inn, Hilton,
Howard Johnson, Marriott, Ramada, Residence Inn and Super 8; for
reservations or information, see the toll-free 800 phone listings on page 16.*

# MINNEAPOLIS/ST. PAUL

## TOP HOTELS
### (In order of rating)

## BEST OVERALL

**22** – Whitney
    Saint Paul Hotel
**19** – Radisson Plaza
    Hotel Sofitel
    Marquette
    Hyatt Regency

## BEST VALUES

Hotel Luxeford Suites
Saint Paul Hotel
Radisson Hotel St. Paul
Radisson Plaza
Radisson Conference Center
Hotel Sofitel

*    *    *

## Best Rooms

**23** – Whitney
**22** – Saint Paul Hotel
**21** – Hotel Luxeford Suites
    Marquette
**20** – Radisson Plaza
**19** – Radisson Hotel St. Paul

## Best Dining

**22** – Whitney
**21** – Saint Paul Hotel
    Hotel Sofitel
**18** – Radisson Plaza
    Hyatt Regency
    Marquette

## Best Service

**24** – Whitney
**22** – Saint Paul Hotel
**20** – Radisson Plaza
**19** – Marquette
    Hotel Sofitel
    Hotel Luxeford Suites

## Best Public Facilities

**21** – Saint Paul Hotel
**19** – Radisson Plaza
**18** – Radisson Conference Center
    Hyatt Regency
    Radisson Hotel St. Paul
**17** – Whitney

## MINNEAPOLIS/ST. PAUL HOTELS

| R | S | D | P | $ |

### Crown Sterling Suites – Minneapolis*    218S    | 20 | 17 | 15 | 16 | $125 |
(fka Embassy Suites – Minneapolis)
425 S. Seventh St.; (800) 433-4600; (612) 333-3111; FAX 333-1178
*U – The closest hotel to the Metrodome Stadium, this Downtown all-suiter boasts a "great location" and a pleasing art deco style; though a change of ownership has left our surveyors unaware, those who know this spot appreciate the "nice" complimentary breakfast and Wall Street Journal after a comfortable night's sleep.*

### Crown Sterling Suites – St. Paul*    210S    | 17 | 16 | 15 | 15 | $108 |
(fka Embassy Suites – St. Paul)
175 E. 10th St., St. Paul; (800) 433-4600; (612) 224-5400; FAX 224-0957
*U – A cooked-to-order breakfast and complimentary cocktail hour make for "good hospitality" and solid value to those few surveyors who know this atrium Downtowner, located near the State Capitol.*

### Hotel Luxeford Suites    230S    | 21 | 19 | 16 | 17 | $102 |
1101 LaSalle Ave., Minneapolis; (800) 662-3232; (612) 332-6800; FAX 332-8246
*U – If you're in the market for a "nice all-suites" hotel in an interesting Downtown location rife with "great bars and restaurants nearby", this folksy place with its newly renovated rooms will give you all that, plus complimentary breakfast and a "comfortable" feeling "like home", all at a modest price.*

### Hotel Sofitel    282R (11S)    | 19 | 19 | 21 | 17 | $123 |
5601 W. 78th St., Minneapolis; (800) 876-6303; (612) 835-1900; FAX 835-2596
*U – A little bit of "Euroclass" on the Mississippi, this airport-convenient contemporary "feels like France" with "warmth and friendliness"; it's a "good choice" if you plan on visiting the nearby "mega" Mall of America, and the rooms and La Cafe Royal restaurant get high marks;* N.B. *collectively, the staff speaks 21 languages, which is either impossible or funny.*

### Hyatt Regency Minneapolis    | 19 | 19 | 18 | 18 | $129 |
on Nicollet Mall    533R (21S)
1300 Nicollet Mall, Minneapolis; (800) 233-1234; (612) 370-1234; FAX 370-1463
*U – "Typically Hyatt", this Downtown high rise is considered dependable "for business" and "convenient for shopping and strolling" – and for the convention center, to which it's connected by skyway; "the spacious rooms – many with nice views – and availability of the "superb" Greenway Athletic Club are valued benefits.*

**Marquette, The**   281R (13S)          | 21 | 19 | 18 | 17 | $135 |
Seventh St. & Marquette Ave., Minneapolis; (800) 445-8667; (612) 332-2351;
FAX 332-7007
*U – "Excellent" but a bit pricey, this center-of-everything Downtowner*
*boasts what some surveyors call the "best location in town"; large,*
*"comfortable" rooms – "corner rooms are best" – are a "good value", but*
*keep in mind that the executive floor "does not provide weekend service."*

**Minneapolis Marriott City Center**   583R (89S)   | 19 | 18 | 17 | 18 | $120 |
30 S. Seventh St., Minneapolis; (800) 228-9290; (612) 349-4000; FAX 332-7165
*M – "Small-town warmth" and "big-city conveniences" are mingled in this*
*heart-of-Downtown Marriott that's "convenient to everything", including a big*
*shopping center a skywalk away; though some say it's "nothing special" and*
*suffers from having its lobby on the fourth floor, it certainly is "dependable."*

**Northland Inn, The**   231S          | 18 | 16 | 16 | 16 | $122 |
7025 N. Northland Dr., Brooklyn Park; (800) 441-6422; (612) 536-8300;
FAX 536-8790
*U – "Beautiful suites" and a "quiet location" make for a "pleasant surprise" –*
*and a good spot for a business meeting – in this newish North suburban*
*conference center, which also targets weekenders with its special*
*packages and comprehensive exercise facilities; food and service ratings*
*suggest some improvement is needed.*

**Omni Northstar Hotel**   224R (4S)          | 17 | 17 | 17 | 16 | $133 |
618 Second Ave., S., Minneapolis; (800) 843-6664; (612) 338-2288;
FAX 338-6194
*M – It's an "easy walk to everything" from this "clean", "well-located" hotel*
*in the city's Financial District; no great shakes, but it's "comfortable" and*
*"well run", and the Rosewood Room restaurant is well regarded locally.*

**Radisson Hotel &**          | 18 | 18 | 17 | 18 | $115 |
**Conference Center**   243R (20S) (fka Scanticon)
3131 Campus Dr., Plymouth; (800) 333-3333; (612) 559-6600;
FAX 559-7516
*M – There's some disagreement about this newest Radisson, formerly*
*operated by Scanticon; fans call it an "excellent conference center and an*
*otherwise good hotel", while critics say "new management needs help"; a*
*concierge floor plus exercise facilities and solid comfort are appreciated.*

**Radisson Hotel Metrodome\***  304R (16S)  | 16 | 18 | 17 | 15 | $109 |
615 Washington Ave., SE, Minneapolis; (800) 333-3333; (612) 379-8888;
FAX 379-8888 x6008
*M – This well-outfitted business hotel (it just got a new workout facility)
on the U of M campus draws some heat as "depressing", "overrated",
"not worth it"; but on a more positive note, service is deemed "friendly,
responsive" and "they remember your name"; a few surveyors suggest
"better housekeeping" and "brighter lightbulbs."*

**Radisson Hotel St. Paul**  475R (58S)  | 19 | 19 | 17 | 18 | $110 |
11 E. Kellogg Blvd., St. Paul; (800) 333-3333; (612) 292-1900;
FAX 224-8999
*M – "Basic hotel" or "home away from home" – such is the controversy
regarding this circa-1960s "convention hotel" "ideally located" near the
Civic Center and World Trade Center; fans say it's a "classic St. Paul"
experience, while detractors say "adequate for a business stay, that's all."*

**Radisson Plaza Hotel**  357R (15S)  | 20 | 20 | 18 | 19 | $121 |
35 S. Seventh St., Minneapolis; (800) 333-3333; (612) 339-4900; FAX 337-9766
*M – "Altogether very nice", this newish Downtowner, connected to just
about everything by convenient skyways, offers "excellent" accommodations
for a "business hotel"; though some say the guest rooms are "rather
austere", this upgraded Radisson "breaks the company's mold" and
achieves uniformly good ratings.*

**Registry Hotel, The**  322R (8S)  | 20 | 20 | 17 | 17 | $115 |
7901 24th Ave. S., Bloomington; (800) 247-9810; (612) 854-2244; FAX 854-7183
*U – "If you have to be out there" in that middle-of-almost-nowhere by the
airport, this "charming and well-run" business hotel offers "good quality
for the price", as well as "the same facilities as if it were in the middle of
somewhere", i.e. a health club, 24-hour room service and secretarial
services; bonus points for being virtually across the street from the giant
new Mall of America.*

**Saint Paul Hotel, The**  254R (28S)  | 22 | 22 | 21 | 21 | $129 |
350 Market St., St. Paul; (800) 292-9292; (612) 292-9292; FAX 228-9506
*U – "The class of the Twin Cities", this "very beautiful" old European-style
hotel is "still in tip-top shape" thanks to a recent renovation; "great service"
and "very nice rooms", plus a "good location" overlooking a lovely park,
practically guarantee this as "the best hotel in St. Paul"; its new St. Paul
Grill is rated "excellent."*

**Sheraton Park Place\*** 298R (30S)    | 18 | 15 | 16 | 13 | $102 |
5555 Wayzata Blvd., St. Louis Park; (800) 542-5566; (612) 542-8600;
FAX 542-8068
*U – Our reviewers are distinctly unimpressed by this anonymous-looking
tower located in a suburb four miles southwest of Downtown; plentiful
packages and moderate prices ensure that it gets plenty of group business,
but surveyors suggest that it "needs help."*

**Whitney, The** 97R (43S)    | 23 | 24 | 22 | 17 | $148 |
150 Portland Ave., Minneapolis; (800) 248-1879; (612) 339-9300; FAX 339-1333
*U – Despite a "not-great" riverfront site that's a little out of the way, this
"charming and friendly" hotel in an "elegant", "historically renovated
granary" is a welcome "alternative to a standard hotel" and a top vote-
getter in Minneapolis; "free limo service" and plenty of charm make up for
any shortcomings in the location.*

### ● OTHER HOTEL-CHAIN CHOICES
*You will find one or more additional locations of the following hotel chains in
the Minneapolis/St. Paul area: Courtyard by Marriott, Crown Sterling Suites,
Days Inn, Doubletree, Embassy Suites, Hampton Inn, Hilton, Holiday Inn,
Marriott, Preferred Hotels, Radisson, Ramada, Residence Inn and Super 8;
for reservations or information, see the toll-free phone listings on page 16.*

## TOP HOTELS
## (In order of rating)

### BEST OVERALL

**21** – Union Station Hotel
    Opryland
**20** – Loews Vanderbilt
**19** – Sheraton Music City

### BEST VALUES

Union Station Hotel
Sheraton Music City
Nashville Airport Marriott
Holiday Inn Crowne Plaza

\*     \*     \*

### Best Rooms

**21** – Union Station Hotel
    Opryland
**20** – Stouffer
    Sheraton Music City

### Best Dining

**20** – Union Station Hotel
**19** – Opryland
**18** – Loews Vanderbilt
**17** – Sheraton Music City

### Best Service

**20** – Union Station Hotel
    Loews Vanderbilt
    Opryland
**19** – Sheraton Music City

### Best Public Facilities

**23** – Union Station Hotel
    Opryland
**19** – Sheraton Music City
    Loews Vanderbilt

| R | S | D | P | $ |

**Doubletree Hotel Nashville\***  337R (15S)     | 16 | 17 | 15 | 13 | $91 |
315 Fourth Ave. N.; (800) 528-0444; (615) 747-4818; FAX 747-4815
*M – A megabuck renovation, due for completion in 1993, came too late
to help this "très ordinaire" Downtown hotel for this Survey; however,
Doubletree's good reputation plus this hotel's convenient location and full
roster of amenities suggest that things may be looking up before long.*

**Embassy Suites Nashville\***  294S     | 22 | 19 | 17 | 21 | $99 |
(fka Park Suites Hotel)
10 Century Blvd.; (800) EMBASSY; (615) 871-0033; FAX 883-9245
*U – This "comfortable" hotel, "convenient to Vanderbilt" and the airport,
gets consistently solid ratings for its "huge suites" and "memorable" atrium
lobby, all made better by a recent "great renovation" and reaffiliation; free
breakfast and cocktail hour also make it a "good value."*

## NASHVILLE HOTELS

| R | S | D | P | $ |

**Hermitage Hotel\*** 112S    | 20 | 20 | 19 | 19 | $112 |
231 Sixth Ave. N.; (800) 251-1908; (615) 244-3121; FAX 254-6909
*M – Time seems to have taken its toll on this beaux-arts landmark that's "pleasant but seedy" and, "alas, slipping"; still, this all-suiter is one-of-a-kind in a chain-dominated city, with spacious accommodations, interesting architecture and views of the State Capitol, plus the "best lobby and bars in town."*

**Holiday Inn Crowne Plaza** 478R (14S)    | 16 | 16 | 15 | 16 | $97 |
(fka Hyatt Regency Nashville)
623 Union St.; (800) 447-9825; (615) 259-2000; FAX 742-6056
*M – Formerly Hyatt Regency, this Downtown high rise has had some remodeling, but surveyors say it's just a "typical Holiday Inn, nothing fancy"; the signature atrium and revolving rooftop restaurant fail to impress folks either way, but conventioneers like its central location.*

**Loews Vanderbilt Plaza Hotel** 338R (12S)    | 20 | 20 | 18 | 19 | $120 |
2100 West End Ave.; (800) 23-LOEWS; (615) 320-1700; FAX 320-0576
*M – A face-lift has given this "convenient" Midtown standby a dazzling new mien; our surveyors say it's "unusally good", with "nice rooms", "friendly service" and a well-liked "piano bar"; the location is "great" for access to Vanderbilt plus nearby shops and restaurants, and two concierge floors and a business center make it a "good business hotel."*

**Nashville Airport Marriott** 399R (9S)    | 19 | 19 | 17 | 18 | $107 |
1 Marriott Dr.; (800) 228-9290; (615) 889-9300; FAX 889-9315
*M – Marriott loyalists, a clear majority, give this one good marks for large, clean rooms, "friendly service", a "great health club" and "lots of extras"; dissenters say "undistinguished", even "totally plastic", but concede that it's "very convenient" to the airport.*

**Opryland Hotel** 1891R (160S)    | 21 | 20 | 19 | 23 | $131 |
2800 Opryland Dr.; (615) 889-1000; FAX 871-6942
*M – Music City USA's "middle-America fantasyland" inspires fierce debate: high notes include "country music everywhere", a "fabulous" lobby conservatory that's a "plant lover's paradise", tons of facilities (14 restaurants, 300,000 square feet of meeting space, a golf course) and "Southern hospitality supreme"; low notes: "too many gawkers", "toooo big" and "spread out"; the "Hawaiian steamboat gothic" decor reminds some of "Disneyland on steroids."*

148

**Regal Maxwell House\***   289R (14S)    | 19 | 18 | 18 | 18 | $98 |
(fka Clarion Maxwell House)
2025 Metrocenter Blvd.; (800) 457-4460; (615) 259-4343; FAX 242-4967
*U – Popular with the economy-minded business traveler who needs a
Downtown location with meeting space and free parking; respondents
praise the "super atmosphere" and "down-home" feel, while history buffs
like knowing it was Maxwell House (as in the coffee) in the 1800s and that
Jack Daniels Tennessee Whiskey was first served here.*

**Sheraton Music City**                 | 20 | 19 | 17 | 19 | $102 |
**Hotel Nashville**   412R (56S)
777 McGavock Pike; (800) 325-3535; (615) 885-2200; FAX 871-0926
*M – Most like the efficient, "wonderful service", "country-style decorating",
"abundant meeting space" and airport convenience of this ersatz Georgian
plantation, even if it's "touristy."*

**Stouffer Nashville Hotel**   707R (34S)    | 20 | 19 | 17 | 18 | $116 |
611 Commerce St.; (800) 468-3571; (615) 255-8400; FAX 255-8163
*M – This Downtown high rise offers "over-and-above service", "excellent
meeting facilities" and attractive rates to the convention set; the fact that it's
adjacent to the convention center and shopping and entertainment makes it
particularly popular, but to some it's just another "cold convention hotel."*

**Union Station Hotel**   126R (14S)    | 21 | 20 | 20 | 23 | $106 |
(fka Radisson Union Station)
1001 Broadway; (800) 331-2123; (615) 726-1001; FAX 248-3554
*U – It's worth the trip just to see the lobby of this "magnificent" top-rated
turn-of-the-century former train station, built in imposing Richardsonian
Romanesque style with a clock tower, mosaic floors, stained-glass windows
and ornate wooden paneling; Arthur's restaurant is said to be "excellent."*

● **OTHER HOTEL-CHAIN CHOICES**
*You will find one or more additional locations of the following hotel chains in
the Nashville area: Courtyard by Marriott, Days Inn, Hampton Inn, Hilton,
Howard Johnson, La Quinta Inns, Ramada, Residence Inn, Super 8 and
Wyndham; for reservations or information, see the toll-free 800 phone
listings on page 16.*

# NEW ORLEANS†

## TOP HOTELS
## (In order of rating)

### BEST OVERALL

27 – Windsor Court Hotel
22 – Hotel Maison de Ville
    Soniat House
    Westin Canal Place
21 – Omni Royal Orleans
    Le Meridien
    Hotel Inter-Continental
    Pontchartrain Hotel

### BEST VALUES

Le Richelieu
Dauphine Orleans
Le Pavillon Hotel
Place d'Armes Hotel
Hotel Inter-Continental
Cornstalk Hotel
Clarion Hotel
Doubletree Hotel

\*     \*     \*

### Best Rooms

28 – Windsor Court Hotel
24 – Soniat House
23 – Westin Canal Place
    Hotel Maison de Ville
22 – Hotel Inter-Continental
    Le Meridien
21 – Pontchartrain Hotel
    Royal Sonesta

### Best Dining

27 – Windsor Court Hotel
23 – Hotel Maison de Ville
22 – Pontchartrain Hotel
21 – Le Meridien
    Soniat House
    Omni Royal Orleans
    Westin Canal Place
20 – Hotel Inter-Continental

### Best Service

27 – Windsor Court Hotel
23 – Hotel Maison de Ville
    Soniat House
22 – Pontchartrain Hotel
    Westin Canal Place
    Hotel Inter-Continental
    Omni Royal Orleans
21 – Le Meridien

### Best Public Facilities

27 – Windsor Court Hotel
22 – Westin Canal Place
    Soniat House
21 – Hotel Maison de Ville
    Omni Royal Orleans
    Hotel Inter-Continental
20 – Le Meridien
    Royal Sonesta

---

†For restaurants, see *Zagat New Orleans Restaurant Survey*.

## NEW ORLEANS HOTELS                    | R | S | D | P | $ |

**Avenue Plaza Suite**                    | 14 | 12 | 13 | 13 | $89 |
**Hotel & Eurovita Spa\*** 239S
2111 St. Charles Ave.; (800) 535-9575; (504) 566-1212; FAX 566-1212 x7601
*M – A "terrific bargain" on the edge of the Garden District, this somewhat
threadbare hotel consists of "roomy apartments turned into hotel suites",
which fans describe as "old but comfortable"; low ratings suggest it's not
that great a bargain.*

**Bourbon Orleans Hotel** 211R (50S)     | 18 | 18 | 16 | 16 | $129 |
717 Orleans St.; (800) 521-5338; (504) 523-2222; FAX 525-8166
*U – Well-situated next to Jackson Square and within "the pulse of the
French Quarter", this "historic Creole-flavored property" features "large
bedrooms with lots of amenities" and a "quiet courtyard with pool";
some say "quaint but very noisy", but everything in the Quarter is just
outside your door.*

**Clarion Hotel New Orleans** 759R (23S)  | 14 | 14 | 13 | 13 | $94 |
1500 Canal St.; (800) 824-3359; (504) 522-4500; FAX 525-2644
*M – Special packages and affordable rooms compensate for the borderline
location and condition of this huge, convention-oriented hotel; a shuttle now
provides safe passage to most major attractions, and two restaurants –
one open 'round the clock – serve guests; the rooms are receiving a
much-needed renovation.*

**Columns Hotel, The\*** 19R              | 12 | 14 | 13 | 15 | $100 |
3811 St. Charles Ave.; (800) 445-9308; (504) 899-9308
*M – This Victorian mansion boasts a rustic-tropical setting, but that's not
always enough, even in the City That Care Forgot; the history-soaked bar
inside remains "very popular with locals", embodying "charm and character
newer places can't possibly capture"; but dusty antiques, smallish rooms
and scarce food turn "charming" to "seedy" for some.*

**Cornstalk Hotel, The** 14R             | 16 | 17 | 13 | 16 | $105 |
915 Royal St.; (504) 523-1515; FAX 522-5558
*M – Named for its fence of wrought-iron cornstalks, this early-1800s
landmark "piece of New Orleans" garners praise for its ideal French
Quarter location and "funky, spacious rooms"; some find it "in need of
renovation", yet others consider it "charming" and "restored with great
taste"; be prepared to find your dinner elsewhere.*

151

**NEW ORLEANS HOTELS**  | R | S | D | P | $ |

**Dauphine Orleans Hotel**   109R (9S)   | 19 | 19 | 17 | 18 | $111 |
415 Dauphine St.; (800) 521-7111; (504) 586-1800; FAX 586-1409
*U – This "cozy corner of cleanliness" is "a good place to rest after a late night on Bourbon Street"; in the morning try the "generous breakfast" served by an "extremely pleasant staff" before exercising in the fitness room or pool; as its ratings indicate, it's well-priced for such a well-run and well-located hotel.*

**Doubletree Hotel New Orleans**   367R (7S)   | 17 | 17 | 15 | 16 | $111 |
300 Canal St.; (800) 528-0444; (504) 581-1300; FAX 522-4100
*M – There are good views to be had from this towering "good convention hotel", whose Downtown location affords easy access to both Uptown and the French Quarter; primarily geared to pleasing touristy masses, it may be a "good value" and "a pleasant surprise", but some critics call it "a motel in disguise.", with "disorganized service."*

**Fairmont Hotel**   733R (65S)   | 19 | 20 | 20 | 19 | $143 |
University Place, 123 Baronne St.; (800) 527-4727; (504) 529-7111; FAX 522-2303
*M – Although it's bashed as "a grand dame in various stages of disintegration" most surveyors say this huge Downtown institution is still "full of grace", "old-world elegance" and "Southern hospitality"; join the many conventioneers for a good meal in its "elegant and romantic" Sazerac dining room or for something simpler in Bailey's, its 24-hour coffee shop popular with late-nighters.*

**Holiday Inn Crowne Plaza**   440R (8S)   | 18 | 17 | 15 | 16 | $118 |
333 Poydras St.; (800) 522-6963; (504) 525-9444; FAX 581-7179
*M – Slipping a bit since our last Survey, this "pretty basic", "standard" convention hotel rates better for its location near the convention center and Riverwalk (the Quarter's just a short stroll away) than for its dependable but unexciting accommodations; all in all, it's still a solid product.*

**Hotel Inter-Continental**   | 22 | 22 | 20 | 21 | $141 |
**New Orleans**   480R (32S)
444 St. Charles Ave.; (800) 445-6563; (504) 525-5566; FAX 523-7310
*U – "Luxurious but not stuffy", this Central Business District address is a "first-class location outside the French Quarter"; a "good, dependable Inter-Continental", with Angelo Donghia interiors and first-rate dining at the Veranda; insiders say it's "great for Mardi Gras", when the parades pass right before its doors; truly one of the "best of the biggies" in New Orleans.*

## NEW ORLEANS HOTELS

| R | S | D | P | $ |

**Hotel Maison de Ville**  23R (7S)    | 23 | 23 | 23 | 21 | $163 |
727 Toulouse St.; (800) 634-1600; (504) 561-5858; FAX 561-5858
*U – "Wonderfully romantic", this elite French Quarter hostelry is just made
for "breakfast in bed and port in the afternoon"; besides "terrific" privacy, its
courtyard and poolside accommodations offer tasteful furnishings, royal
treatment and the haute New Orleans cuisine of the premier Bistro restaurant
(food rating, 27); it's "like staying with rich friends who adore you."*

**Hotel Ste. Helene**  25R (9S)    | – | – | – | – | M |
508 Chartres St.; (800) 348-3888; (504) 522-5014; FAX 523-7140
*For a longer stay in the Crescent City, this small French Quarter hotel,
operated by Historic Inns of New Orleans, provides apartment suites with
kitchenettes plus a shady courtyard pool and patio; those few who know it
judge it "very pleasant", but plan on stepping out for dinner.*

**Hotel St. Marie**  93R (5S)    | – | – | – | – | M |
827 Toulouse St.; (800) 366-2743; (504) 561-8951; FAX 581-3802
*Just a block or two off the Mississippi riverfront and Bourbon Street, this
Spanish-influenced hotel is "great for staying in the Quarter"; its quaint
courtyard and pool are welcome after a day of sightseeing or revelry.*

**Hyatt Regency New Orleans**  1191R (100S)   | 20 | 19 | 17 | 18 | $131 |
500 Poydras Plaza; (800) 233-1234; (504) 561-1234; FAX 587-4141
*M – "Convention heaven", this all-around "good" high-rise Hyatt is praised
for its proximity to the Superdome and shopping at the adjoining New
Orleans Centre; naturally, it offers all the convention-going necessities,
including several in-house bars and restaurants, a new health club and a
"great shuttle to the French Quarter"; though "solid", it's "not New Orleans
style" and a bit "far from the action" (read: the Quarter).*

**Inn on Bourbon***  186R (2S)    | 17 | 16 | 15 | 14 | $96 |
541 Bourbon St.; (800) 535-7891; (504) 524-7611; FAX 568-9427
*U – If you've come to get "down and dirty" in New Orleans, this is the
place; on Bourbon Street in the heart of the French Quarter, it has a "great
location for people-watching", but don't expect to get much sleep if your
room overlooks the street; for the young, lively clientele, the courtyard pool,
singalong piano bar and Creole cafeteria more than compensate for
whatever else is lacking.*

## NEW ORLEANS HOTELS

| R | S | D | P | $ |

**LaMothe House\*** 20R (9S)  | 21 | 20 | 17 | 21 | $121 |
621 Esplanade Ave.; (800) 367-5858; (504) 947-1161; FAX 943-6536
*U – A "romantic hideaway" on the edge of the French Quarter, near the
action but "without the noise"; the essence of old New Orleans permeates
this "exclusive", aristocratic French Louisiana property; rooms vary in
character, so be sure to "select your room before" you unpack.*

**Le Meridien Hotel** 497R (5S)  | 22 | 21 | 21 | 20 | $147 |
614 Canal St.; (800) 543-4300; (504) 525-6500; FAX 586-1543
*U – The "French flavor works" at this "elegant" Downtown hotel, with its
"lovely rooms", "convenient location", "excellent service" and French
cuisine in the restaurant, La Gauloise (food rating, 21), as well as "great
jazz" in the attractive lobby; though a few say it's "typically" Gallic – "snooty
and cold" – for most, this "fine hotel" is "special."*

**Le Pavillon Hotel** 226R (7S)  | 18 | 19 | 17 | 18 | $115 |
833 Poydras St.; (800) 535-9095; (504) 581-3111; FAX 522-5543
*M – Newly renovated, this relic of the grand era of hotels has fans who say
it's the "best value in the Central Business District"; it may be "a bit off the
beaten path from the French Quarter", but it's on the upswing.*

**Le Richelieu in the French Quarter** 86R (16S)  | 19 | 20 | 16 | 16 | $100 |
1234 Chartres St.; (800) 535-9653; (504) 529-2492; FAX 524-8179
*U – Built at the behest of Louis XIII of France, this historic property
combining Greek Revival and French influences is frequented primarily by
vacationers and couples who enjoy its "old-world" Southern charm and
attentive service; it's very "reasonable for a good location" in the Quarter.*

**Maison Dupuy Hotel** 197R (7S)  | 19 | 19 | 17 | 17 | $126 |
1001 Toulouse St.; (800) 535-9177; (504) 586-8000; FAX 525-5334
*M – This "quiet hotel with courtyard and music" is a "charming oasis" amid
"all the action" of the French Quarter; while some find the place "cute but
pricey" and "showing signs of age", its solid service and "restful atmosphere"
are real assets, as is its Le Bon Creole restaurant.*

**Monteleone Hotel** 598R (36S)  | 17 | 18 | 16 | 16 | $122 |
214 Royal St.; (800) 535-9595; (504) 523-3341; FAX 528-1019
*M – The highlights of this historic hotel are a "fine French Quarter location"
and "very nice" rooftop pool; but despite its "old-world charm", there were
enough comments about "poor" service and rooms "a bit worn" to prove
that one surveyor's "aging gracefully" is another's "not so deluxe"; the
famous rotating carousel bar is judged "always good for a drunken laugh."*

## NEW ORLEANS HOTELS

| R | S | D | P | $ |

**New Orleans Hilton** | 20 | 19 | 19 | 20 | $136 |
**Riverside & Towers**  1602R (86S)
Poydras St. at the river; (800) HILTONS; (504) 561-0500; FAX 568-1721
*U – With its "great view of the river", "superb location" close to Riverwalk and the Quarter and "excellent conference facilities", it's no wonder this older Hilton is so "crowded"; folks who don't spend their days wearing a "funny hat" say it's "a zoo" and "too spread out"; even with decent rooms, dependable service and jazz celeb Pete Fountain at hand, it's a "convention hotel – no more, no less."*

**New Orleans Marriott**  1290R (54S) | 18 | 18 | 17 | 18 | $130 |
555 Canal St.; (800) 228-9290; (504) 581-1000; FAX 523-6755
*M – Frequented by conventioneers and tourists, this Downtown hotel is called a "usual vanilla Marriott", "not spectacular" but "nice"; the "typical decor", "adequate rooms" and "acceptable" service do less for our surveyors than the "fantastic location right beside the Quarter", "great view of the Mississippi" and jazz in the lobby – otherwise "you could be in Des Moines."*

**Omni Royal Orleans**  351R (25S) | 21 | 22 | 21 | 21 | $152 |
621 St. Louis St.; (800) THE-OMNI; (504) 529-5333; FAX 529-7089
*U – Heralded for "the best location in New Orleans", this "elegant", "gracious" hotel gives guests a chance to "swim atop the world while the French Quarter lies below" – or "lie in bed and hear a cornet player on the sidewalk"; while the "older rooms" may be small, the suites are downright "luxurious", and its Rib Room is ideal if you get tired of Creole food; in sum, a "quintessential New Orleans experience."*

**Place d'Armes Hotel**  79R (4S) | 19 | 19 | 17 | 19 | $100 |
625 St. Ann St.; (800) 366-2743; (504) 524-4531; FAX 581-3802
*U – Six beautiful French-provincial buildings frame a lush, "picturesque courtyard" complete with pool and patio; believe it or not, you have to be sure to "request a room with windows", but otherwise, the rooms are "lovely" and the French Quarter Jackson Square location, "perfect."*

**Pontchartrain Hotel, The**  100R (35S) | 21 | 22 | 22 | 18 | $144 |
2031 St. Charles Ave.; (800) 777-6193; (504) 524-0581; FAX 529-1165
*U – An "elegant old lady" with "more atmosphere than any marble-bathed high rise can hope for", this "unique" and "charming" hotel has been luring people "off the beaten path" to its Garden District location for generations; its comfort, "first-class service" and Caribbean Room restaurant (food rating, 22) all get high marks; its upscale coffee shop, Cafe Pontchartrain (food rating, 20) is where many locals come for their power breakfasts.*

**Radisson Suite Hotel New Orleans**  226S  | 17 | 17 | 14 | 14 | $117 |
315 Julia St.; (800) 333-3333; (504) 525-1993; FAX 522-3044
*U – Geared toward a business and convention-going clientele, this newly renovated Downtowner offers "spacious rooms" and a "friendly staff"; "the price is right", especially for longer stays; but being near the convention center makes it "too removed from other activities."*

**Royal Sonesta**  500R (32S)  | 21 | 21 | 20 | 20 | $149 |
300 Bourbon St.; (800) 766-3782; (504) 586-0300; FAX 586-0335
*U – This popular Bourbon Street hotel can be a "circus" at times but boasts an "unbeatable location", "excellent service" and "first-class" ratings; the "beautiful lobby" and popular Sunday buffet at Begue's (food rating, 19) are bonuses; to avoid the "noisy" street, reserve an interior room.*

**Saint Louis Hotel**  70R (32S)  | 21 | 21 | 20 | 19 | $163 |
730 Bienville St.; (800) 535-9111; (504) 581-7300; FAX 524-8925
*M – "A bit of left-behind Paris", this charming French Quarter hotel gets mostly raves for its central location and "elegant" mien, thanks in part to a beautiful courtyard and the French restaurant, Louis XVI; critics cite "tired" decor and "impersonal" service, but they're easily outvoted.*

**Sheraton New Orleans Hotel**  1100R (72S)  | 19 | 18 | 17 | 19 | $130 |
500 Canal St.; (800) 325-3535; (504) 525-2500; FAX 592-5615
*M – Our surveyors call this "functional but unexciting" Downtown hotel "fairly standard", although they judge the rooms "above average" and the service "friendly"; it may not have Southern charm or fabulous food, but with "excellent" business facilities, don't sell it short.*

**Soniat House**  24R (6S)  | 24 | 23 | 21 | 22 | $159 |
1133 Chartres St.; (800) 544-8808; (504) 522-0570; FAX 522-7208
*U – A "luxurious Southern retreat" exuding romance and "old-world charm", this intimate hotel in a renovated historic building with a courtyard occupies a plum location on a quiet French Quarter street, close to everything but away from the crowds; rooms vary from "hatbox to suite size", but all feature antiques and a Creole/Greco flavor; fans say it's the "best of old New Orleans."*

**St. Pierre**  70R (8S)  | – | – | – | – | M |
911 Burgundy St.; (800) 225-4040; (504) 524-4401; FAX 524-6800
*Though few know of it, this homey, small hotel, carved from a series of 18th-century Creole cottages in a tropical courtyard (with two swimming pools), boasts a quiet Lower Quarter location and moderate prices.*

**NEW ORLEANS HOTELS**                    | R | S | D | P | $ |

**Westin Canal Place, The**   438R (41S)    | 23 | 22 | 21 | 22 | $153 |
100 Iberville St.; (800) 228-3000; (504) 566-7006; FAX 523-5133
*U – "European grandeur and East Asian excellence" add up to one of the
best of New Orleans's high-rise hotels; its location on the "outskirts of the
Quarter" lets guests "live the seedy life but safely come home to elegance";
other pluses include a breathtaking view of the nearby Mississippi from the
cocktail lounge at night, "great" marble bathrooms, and Sunday brunch at
Le Jardin restaurant; don't be put off by the 11th-floor lobby (the hotel sits
atop the upscale Canal Place mall) – you can shop before registering.*

**WINDSOR COURT HOTEL**   315R (256S)    | 28 | 27 | 27 | 27 | $202 |
320 Gravier St.; (800) 262-2662; (504) 523-6000; FAX 596-4513
*U – Unquestionably the finest hotel in New Orleans, this royal – as in
Windsor– property combines the "charm of the South with the efficiency of
the North" and earns our surveyors' highest ratings with its "magnificent"
decor, "museum-quality art" and "stately" rooms; don't miss the Grill Room's
"superb cuisine" (food rating, 28); this is the No.1. rated U.S. hotel –
enough said.*

● **OTHER HOTEL-CHAIN CHOICES**
*You will find one or more additional locations of the following hotel chains
in the New Orleans area: Days Inn, Hilton, Holiday Inn, Howard Johnson,
La Quinta Inns, Ramada and Travelodge/ Viscount; for reservations or
information, see the toll-free 800 phone listings on page 16.*

# NEW YORK CITY†

## TOP HOTELS
## (In order of rating)

### BEST OVERALL

**25** – Hotel Plaza Athenee
**24** – St. Regis
    Carlyle Hotel
    Mayfair Hotel Baglioni
    Pierre
    Box Tree
**23** – Peninsula New York
    Lowell New York
    Mark
    Rihga Royal

### BEST VALUES

Paramount
Radisson Empire Hotel
Doral Court Hotel
Eastgate Tower Suites
Murray Hill East Suites
Salisbury Hotel
Hotel Macklowe
Beekman Tower Hotel
Holiday Inn Crowne Plaza
Dumont Plaza Hotel

*    *    *

### Best Rooms

**25** – Rihga Royal
    Lowell New York
    Carlyle Hotel
    Hotel Plaza Athenee
    St. Regis
**24** – Box Tree
    Waldorf Towers
    Mark
    Pierre
    Mayfair Hotel Baglioni

### Best Dining

**26** – Box Tree
**25** – Mayfair Hotel Baglioni
    Hotel Plaza Athenee
**24** – St. Regis
    Carlyle Hotel
    Pierre
    Mark
    Peninsula New York
**22** – Stanhope
    Plaza

### Best Service

**25** – Hotel Plaza Athenee
    Carlyle Hotel
    Lowell New York
    Pierre
    Mayfair Hotel Baglioni
**24** – St. Regis
    Box Tree
    Mark
    Peninsula New York
    Rihga Royal

### Best Public Facilities

**24** – St. Regis
    Hotel Plaza Athenee
**23** – Peninsula New York
    Plaza
    Pierre
    Carlyle Hotel
    Waldorf Towers
    Royalton
**22** – Paramount
    Mayfair Hotel Baglioni

---

†For restaurants, see *Zagat New York City Restaurant Survey.*

## NEW YORK CITY HOTELS

| R | S | D | P | $ |

**Algonquin Hotel, The**   165R (23S)   | 16 | 19 | 18 | 18 | $168 |
59 W. 44th St. (bet. 5th & 6th Aves.); (800) 548-0345; (212) 840-6800;
FAX 944-1419
*M – "History and ambiance" are the strong suits of this "legendary"
Midtown dowager, once a celebrated hangout for Parker, Benchley and
other literary lights; its "cozy" wood-paneled lobby/piano bar is still a
favorite meeting place for drinks, tea and "great people-watching", but as
for the rooms, despite a recent renovation, some are "so small you can't
change your mind once inside."*

**Barbizon, The**   365R (20S)   | 14 | 15 | 14 | 14 | $141 |
140 E. 63rd St., (Lexington Ave.); (800) 223-1020; (212) 838-5700; FAX 888-4271
*M – If the rooms weren't so "teeny", this East Side hotel could be a winner;
assets include a good location near Bloomie's, modest prices (by NYC
standards) and a "cooperative" staff; some call it a "good value", but others
would rather pay more for some breathing room.*

**Beekman Tower Hotel**   171S   | 19 | 17 | 17 | 15 | $152 |
3 Mitchell Place (1st Ave. & 49th St.); (800) ME-SUITE; (212) 355-7300;
FAX 753-9366
*U – "Far from the hustle but close to the bustle", this "understated"
all-suites hotel, near the U.N. in a pleasant residential area, features
spacious accommodations that "feel like home" and are especially "good
for long stays"; "great views" from the rooftop lounge and some of the
rooms also recommend it.*

**BOX TREE, THE**   12S   | 24 | 24 | 26 | 21 | $246 |
250 E. 49th St. (bet. 2nd & 3rd Aves.); (212) 758-8320; FAX 308-3899
*U – Extravagantly lush and romantic, this "jewel" of an inn, located above
the equally extravagant Box Tree restaurant, is a "genteel oasis in a hectic
world"; featuring 12 suites, each designed around a different theme, it's
"quirky but elegant", and even those who find the decor "a bit over the top"
admit that it's one of the "most special places in NYC"; though pricey, the
room rate does include a $100 credit in the restaurant.*

**CARLYLE HOTEL**   195R (69S)   | 25 | 25 | 24 | 23 | $281 |
35 E. 76th St. (Madison Ave.); (800) 227-5737; (212) 744-1600; FAX 717-4682
*U – Exuding "pure class" in every department, this "perfect pedigree"
Eastsider is "the epitome of elegance" and a "throwback to more gracious
times"; attracting everyone from "statesmen to celebs", it provides "pretty"
antique-filled rooms, "attentive" but "discreet" service, and a "superb"
dining room (food rating, 22); add Bobby Short in The Cafe and you've got
the "best of NYC."*

**Doral Court Hotel**   198R (48S)   | 18 | 19 | 19 | 15 | $146 |
130 E. 39th St. (bet. Park & Lexington Aves.); (800) 22-DORAL; (212) 685-1100;
FAX 889-0287
*U – "Staid but nice", this "small, discreet" Murray Hill hotel satisfies most
surveyors with "pleasant", "comfy" rooms, "friendly" service and "decent"
rates; its Courtyard Cafe is a popular lunch spot, thanks to its good food
and pretty garden; all in all, it's a "quiet" good value; the Doral Fitness
Center is nearby.*

**Doral Inn**   655R (45S)   | 14 | 14 | 13 | 12 | $141 |
541 Lexington Ave. (bet. 49th & 50th Sts.); (800) 22-DORAL; (212) 755-1200;
FAX 319-8344
*M – "Just adequate but reasonable for NYC", this high-volume Midtown
Eastsider delivers a "bed, clean bathroom, and good location" – period;
those who keep their expectations simple are satisfied, but those who don't
call it "no good"; the hectic lobby reminds one surveyor of a "bus terminal."*

**Doral Park Avenue**   188R (14S)   | 17 | 17 | 16 | 15 | $155 |
70 Park Ave. (38th St.); (800) 22-DORAL; (212) 687-7050; FAX 808-9029
*U – "A nice, small NYC hotel", this Murray Hill outpost features rooms that
are "shoe-box" size but "cute", and service that's "warm and friendly";
maybe it's not exciting, but it's a "decent place" and a "good value" as well.*

**Doral Tuscany**   121R (12S)   | 20 | 20 | 19 | 16 | $172 |
120 E. 39th St. (bet. Park & Lexington Aves.); (800) 22-DORAL; (212) 686-1600;
FAX 779-7822
*U – "Outstanding service" is just one reason this "quiet" Murray Hill hotel is
considered a "little gem"; other assets include an "elegant lobby", "nice,
big, old-fashioned rooms", and "superb" French-American food in the Time
& Again restaurant (food rating, 22); fans call it a "best bargain."*

**Dorset**   320R (40S)   | 16 | 16 | 16 | 14 | $170 |
30 W. 54th St. (bet. 5th & 6th Aves.); (800) 227-2348; (212) 247-7300;
FAX 581-0153
*M – Fans of this older Midtown hotel call it "civilized" and "supremely
comfortable", with a warm, wood-paneled lobby and a staff that really
"cares"; critics dub it "shabby" and "just fair", but all agree it has an
"outstanding location" near MoMA and Fifth Avenue shops; its "old-world
dining room" is a breakfast favorite.*

## NEW YORK CITY HOTELS

| | R | S | D | P | $ |
| --- | --- | --- | --- | --- | --- |

**Drake Swissotel New York**   552R (44S)   | 19 | 19 | 20 | 17 | $193 |   *[handwritten: ✗ Club Like]*
440 Park Ave. (56th St.); (800) DRAKE-NY; (212) 421-0900; FAX 688-8053
*M – As you'd expect from a Swiss-run hotel, this Midtowner is*
*"comfortable" and "efficient", if not exactly thrilling; room quality "varies a*
*lot" (largely because of ongoing renovations), but it has a "convenient"*
*location, staffers who "go out of their way" to please and a "fine" restaurant*
*(Lafayette – food rating, 24); critics grouse it's "neither Swiss nor*
*American", just "boring" and pricey.*   *[handwritten: Gov't Rate: ~~$199~~ $198 Midweek Rate: 355-]*

**Dumont Plaza Hotel**   250S   | 19 | 17 | 14 | 15 | $147 |
150 E. 34th St. (bet. Lexington & 3rd Aves.); (800) ME-SUITE; (212) 481-7600;
FAX 889-8856
*U – Roomy suites that feel "like home", and a helpful staff make this*
*recently renovated suites-only south-of-Midtown hotel a good option for*
*both business travelers and families; kitchenettes let you cook your own*
*meals and save a bundle; the well-kept workout room is a plus.*

**Eastgate Tower Suite Hotel**   192S   | 19 | 17 | 13 | 14 | $132 |
222 E. 39th St. (bet. 2nd & 3rd Aves.); (800) ME-SUITE; (212) 687-8000;
FAX 490-2634
*U – "Functional, convenient and a good value", this all-suites Eastsider*
*provides "plain but good" accommodations and a not-unpleasant "small-*
*town feel"; kitchenettes let you save on restaurant bills, making it a "great*
*deal for NYC", especially for families and longer stays.*

**Edison Hotel**   1000R (55S)   | 12 | 12 | 11 | 10 | $102 |
228 W. 47th St. (bet. B'way & 8th Ave.); (800) 637-7070; (212) 840-5000;
FAX 719-9541
*U – It will never be mistaken for a grand hotel, but this recently renovated*
*Theater District oldie now draws mostly positive comments; with "large"*
*rooms, a "great" walk-to-the-theaters location and "cheap" prices, it's called*
*a "budget find" and a top "Times Square bargain"; P.S. the hallways "can*
*be spooky" – ditto the neighborhood late at night.*

**Embassy Suites**   460S   | – | – | – | – | E |
1768 Broadway (47th St. ); (800) EMBASSY; (212) 719-1600; FAX 921-5212
*Located atop the Palace Theater in the heart of Broadway, this brand-new*
*all-suites hotel features spacious, contemporary two-room suites with*
*kitchenettes, at affordable prices; it's especially appealing to families, with*
*two floors featuring "childproof" rooms and a supervised play center; the*
*Embassy Club floors provide a full array of business services, including*
*secretaries, translators and private complimentary breakfast.*

# NEW YORK CITY HOTELS

| R | S | D | P | $ |

**Essex House,**    | 21 | 21 | 20 | 20 | $203 |
**Hotel Nikko New York**    591R (77S)
160 Central Park South (7th Ave.); (800) NIKKO-US; (212) 247-0300;
FAX 315-1839
*U – "Wow" sums up the reaction of most surveyors to the Japanese Nikko chain's "fabulous" $100 million–plus renovation of this Central Park South fixture; what had become a drab businessman's hotel is now a "classy", "elegant" art deco beauty, with "spectacular" public areas, "luxurious rooms" (ask for a park view), "outstanding" service, and a well-equipped business center; its two restaurants, the bargain Cafe Botanica (food rating, 22) and the exquisite Les Celebrites (food rating, 26), are justly celebrated.*

**Fitzpatrick Manhattan Hotel**    92R (52S)    | – | – | – | – | E |
(fka Hotel Dover)
687 Lexington Ave. (bet. 56th & 57th Sts.); (800) 367-7701; (212) 355-0100
*Trading on Midtown convenience, low prices and an Irish chain affiliation, this newly renovated, smaller hotel is quite competitive, price-wise and otherwise.*

**Flatotel International**    104S    | – | – | – | – | E |
135 W. 52nd St. (bet. 6th & 7th Aves.); (800) FLATOTEL; (212) 887-9400;
FAX 887-9442
*The name may sound silly, but it makes sense if you think in terms of flats – the apartmentlike suites that are the stock-in-trade of this new Midtown condo-cum-hotel, the first U.S. property of a successful French company; luxury accommodations feature full gourmet kitchens and whirlpool baths; it's a great value for families and ideal for long stays; N.B. construction delays continue to limit availability and give an unfinished feel to service.*

**Gorham New York, The***    120R (50S)    | 15 | 15 | 14 | 11 | $143 |
(fka Gorham Hotel, The)
136 W. 55th St. (bet. 6th & 7th Aves.); (800) 735-0710; (212) 245-1800;
FAX 582-8332
*M – Its main asset is a "great location" (opposite City Center in Midtown), but after a recent renovation, this old-timer has improved its ratings across the board; families like its large rooms (with refrigerators and microwaves) and low rates; room service is from a nearby diner – but it's a good diner.*

**Gramercy Park Hotel**    360R (120S)    | 12 | 13 | 11 | 11 | $126 |
2 Lexington Ave. (21st St.); (800) 221-4083; (212) 475-4320; FAX 505-0535
*M – Though it has a beautiful facade and borders on "lovely" Gramercy Park, this vintage '20s hotel "hasn't been spruced up for years, and it shows"; the rooms are "shabby", service is "rude" and the "furniture wouldn't sell at a garage sale"; still, it "has a following" for its modest prices, location and air of "divey" elegance.*

**Grand Hyatt New York**   1407R (42S)   | 18 | 17 | 17 | 18 | $181 |
Park Ave. at Grand Central (42nd St.); (800) 233-1234; (212) 883-1234;
FAX 697-3772
*M – This "humongous", "glitzy" "all-purpose" hotel is often as "bustling" and
"noisy" as its neighbor, Grand Central Station; some of the rooms are "too
small for your luggage, never mind you", and service ranges from "super
courteous" to "impersonal", but most find it functional and "convenient";
developer Donald Trump's touch is evident in the "eye-popping" marble-
and-granite lobby, complete with waterfall.*

**Helmsley Palace, The**   963R (104S)   | 22 | 21 | 20 | 22 | $234 |
455 Madison Ave. (bet. 50th & 51st Sts.); (800) 221-4982; (212) 888-7000;
FAX 303-6000
*M – Surveyors either love or loathe this "opulent" Midtown palace:
admirers call it the "epitome of Gotham luxury", with "gorgeous, plush"
decor, "A-1" service and "stunning" public rooms worthy of Versailles;
critics call it a "tacky" example of "wretched excess", with "obsequious"
service, "gaudy" decor ("Elvis's idea of how to decorate") and one royal
quality – the high prices.*

**Helmsley Park Lane Hotel**   640R (40S)   | 20 | 19 | 18 | 18 | $214 |
36 Central Park South (59th St.); (800) 221-4982; (212) 371-4000; FAX 319-9065
*M – Get a room facing Central Park and you're likely to agree with the
majority view that this is a "classy" hotel with "very well appointed rooms",
a "super" location and "wonderful" service; but others call it "too stuffy and
sedate" and find the accommodations "only fair for the price."*

**Holiday Inn Crowne Plaza**   770R   | 19 | 17 | 17 | 18 | $158 |
1605 Broadway (49th St.); (800) 243-NYNY; (212) 977-4000; FAX 333-7393
*U – "New, clean and pleasant" describes everything about this Holiday Inn
flagship, from its cheerful exterior to its "comfortable", well-equipped rooms
(some with "spectacular views"); it also offers "unbelievably friendly"
service, an array of good restaurants, an attractive health club and a handy
location north of Times Square.*

**Holiday Inn Downtown**   223R (8S)   | – | – | – | – | M |
(fka Hotel Maria)
138 Lafayette St. (Canal St.); (800) 282-3933; (212) 966-889; FAX 966-3933
*Appealing to both business and leisure travelers, Holiday Inn's newest
addition to the New York scene is ideally located in SoHo between Little
Italy, Chinatown and TriBeCa; formerly known as the Hotel Maria, this
contemporary hotel delivers an Oriental flair to the otherwise homogenous
Holiday Inn style.*

**Hotel Beverly**   186R (100S)   | 16 | 16 | 12 | 11 | $143 |
125 E. 50th St. (Lexington Ave.); (800) 223-0945; (212) 753-2700; FAX 759-7300
*U – A "good buy in Midtown", this "small, comfy and convenient" Eastsider
may be "old and a little tired", but it has a "great location", nice rooms
(some with kitchenettes) and moderate prices; pluses include a 24-hour
pharmacy adjoining the lobby and "great" upper-floor suites with terraces.*


**Hotel Elysee**   110R (11S)   | 15 | 17 | 15 | 13 | $161 |
60 E. 54th St. (bet. Madison & Park Aves.); (800) 535-9733;
(212) 753-1066;FAX 980-9278
*M – There's "a lot of history" in this quirkily charming Eastsider, once a
haven for privacy-seeking celebs; in recent years its main assets have
been modest prices, a central location, and friendly service ("it's small
enough that they greet you by name"), but now a massive renovation is
aiming to restore its original glory.*


**Hotel Kimberly**   191S   | – | – | – | – | VE |
145 E. 50th St. (bet. Lexington & 3rd Aves.); (800) 683-0400;
(212) 755-0400; FAX 486-6915
*Nice all-suites alternative to pricier East Side International hotels, features
full kitchens in most suites and good Midtown location; elegant European-
style decor, proximity to Madison Avenue shopping and lack of chain
affiliation make this sleeper a well-kept secret.*


**Hotel Lexington**   700R (25S)   | 10 | 11 | 9 | 9 | $136 |
Lexington Ave. & 48th St.; (800) 448-4471; (212) 755-4400; FAX 751-4091
*M – "Only in NYC could you get so little for so much" sigh critics of this
"below-average" Midtowner; it has a "convenient location" – except at night
when the neighborhood is iffy – but that's about all it can brag about;
despite a recent renovation, rooms are "tiny" and "depressing"; on the plus
side, J. Sung Dynasty is a standout Chinese restaurant (food rating, 20).*


**Hotel Macklowe**   638R (11S)   | 20 | 20 | 18 | 20 | $172 |
145 W. 44th St. (bet. B'way & 6th Ave.); (800) MACKLOW; (212) 768-4400;
FAX 789-7688
*M – "Slick, "stylish" and "very NYC", this "sparklingly modern" Midtowner is
considered the "best of the Times Square business hotels", with state-of-
the-art facilities and luxurious corporate bedrooms; guest rooms are
"small" but "elegant", with the latest "high-tech" amenities; "outstanding"
service, its restaurant Charlotte (food rating, 19) and proximity to the B'way
theaters are pluses; critics find it "cold" and overpriced.*

# NEW YORK CITY HOTELS

| R | S | D | P | $ |

**Hotel Millenium, The**  561R (103S)  | – | – | – | – | VE |
55 Church St. (bet. Fulton & Dey Sts.); (800) 835-2220; (212) 693-2001;
FAX 571-2317
*Though it seemed like 1,000 years till it finally opened in 1992, this
futuristic Lower Manhattan tower fills a need for upscale accommodations
in the Wall Street–South Street Seaport area; sleek public spaces, high-
tech fitness and business centers, views of the Lady in the Harbor and
most of Manhattan, and little extras like a staggering choice of in-room
movies may make this newcomer well worth the wait.*

**Hotel Pickwick Arms\***  369R  | 9 | 12 | 11 | 10 | $86 |
230 E. 51st St. (bet. 2nd & 3rd Aves.); (800) PICKWICK; (212) 355-0300;
FAX 755-5029
*U – "Dirt cheap" and conveniently located on the East Side, this is one
hotel where "out-of-town guests can actually afford to stay"; whether they'll
enjoy it or not is iffy, since rooms are the "size of matchboxes" and offer
little in the way of niceties; most raters consider this a "last resort."*

**HOTEL PLAZA ATHENEE**  160R (36S)  | 25 | 25 | 25 | 24 | $282 |
37 E. 64th St. (bet. Madison & Park Aves.); (800) 225-5843;
(212) 734-9100; FAX 772-0958
*U – Possibly the "most elegant small hotel in NYC", this "refined and
intimate" Eastsider is "exquisitely done and run"; it exhibits a "lovely
European attention to detail" in every regard, from its "smallish" but
"beautiful" rooms to its "incredible service" and "superb" restaurant,
Le Regence (food rating, 25); located on a quiet side street, it's a lovely
"escape" – and even lovelier "if someone else pays."*

**Hotel Wales\***  95R (40S)  | 17 | 17 | 19 | 17 | $130 |
1295 Madison Ave. (bet. 92nd & 93rd Sts.); (800) 428-5252;
(212) 876-6000; FAX 860-7000
*M – "Away from the hustle-bustle", this "pleasant" Uptown hotel in
residential Carnegie Hill "feels like London" in its warmth and charm; the
rooms are small but "cute", and though there's not much room service, a
complimentary continental breakfast is served in the "lovely" upstairs
tearoom, and Sarabeth's, downstairs (food rating, 20), is popular for casual
dining and Sunday brunch; it's a "good value" though off the beaten path.*

# NEW YORK CITY HOTELS                    | R | S | D | P | $ |

**Inter-Continental New York**   691R (83S)   | 19 | 18 | 17 | 18 | $188 |
111 E. 48th St. (Park Ave.); (800) 33-AGAIN; (212) 755-5900; FAX 644-0079
*M – With its "old-time classy feel", good central location and generally "courteous and helpful" service, this "European-flavor" Midtowner "can be very charming", but critics object to "small rooms" with "stone-age bathrooms" and say the hotel could use refurbishment; N.B. the lobby bar is a good place to watch the largely international clientele come and go.*

**Journey's End Hotel\***   189R   | 15 | 16 | 8 | 11 | $129 |
3 E. 40th St. (bet. 5th & Madison Aves.); (800) 668-4200; (212) 447-1500;
FAX 683-7839
*U – One of the "best bargains in the Big Apple", this "no-frills" Midtowner is "a gem if all you want is a clean room, good location and a good price"; it's "comfortable" and convenient to everything from Grand Central to the Theater District; let's "hope it doesn't raise its rates and get spoiled."*

**Le Parker Meridien**   697R (202S)   | 20 | 20 | 21 | 20 | $202 |
118 W. 57th St. (bet. 6th & 7th Aves.); (800) 543-4300; (212) 245-5000;
FAX 307-1776
*U – "A bit chilly but very reliable", this "attractive" and "civilized" Midtowner provides "a touch of Paris in NYC"; some think it's time to redo the rooms, but they're nevertheless "comfortable and modern", and service is authentically "French" (i.e. sometimes "cordial", sometimes "brusque"); a "beautiful" lobby, nice health club and rooftop pool are assets.*

**Loews New York Hotel**   726R (53S)   | 14 | 14 | 14 | 13 | $152 |
(fka Loews Summit)
569 Lexington Ave. (51st St.); (800) 23-LOEWS; (212) 752-7000;
FAX 758-6311
*U – It's "nothing fancy", but this recently refurbished Midtowner offers a good location, "small but comfortable" rooms, a "modest health club" and a pleasant restaurant; most call it "basic but solid" – just be sure to request a room away from the firehouse on 51st Street.*

**LOWELL NEW YORK, THE**   61R (48S)   | 25 | 25 | 21 | 21 | $291 |
(fka Lowell Hotel)
28 E. 63rd St. (bet. Madison & Park Aves.); (800) 221-4444;
(212) 838-1400; FAX 319-4230
*U – "Small and perfect", this East Side "jewel" competes with some of the city's larger hotels as "the best NYC has to offer", with its "elegant and quiet" atmosphere, well-appointed rooms, fine restaurants and "personal" service that "makes you feel special"; just steps from Madison Avenue shopping, it still conveys a sense of "splendid isolation."*

| R | S | D | P | $ |
|---|---|---|---|---|

**MARK, THE**   180R (60S)    | 24 | 24 | 23 | 22 | $248 |
25 E. 77th St. (Madison Ave.); (800) 843-6275; (212) 744-4300; FAX 744-2749
U – "Modern elegance" is the hallmark of this sophisticated well-run Upper
Eastsider; "very European" in feel and "very upper crust" in clientele, it
features "comfortable", "luxurious" rooms, "fantastic" service and an
"excellent" restaurant (Mark's); convenient to the Metropolitan Museum
and Central Park, it's a "wonderful NYC escape."

**Marriott Financial Center Hotel**   540R (10S)   | – | – | – | – | VE |
85 West St. (bet. Albany & Carlisle Sts.); (800) 242-8685; (212) 385-4900;
FAX 227-8136
With predictable Marriott efficiency, coupled with outstanding views
overlooking the Hudson River, this recent Marriott addition is conveniently
located in New York's Financial District and near Downtown tourist
attractions and Wall Street offices.

**MAYFAIR HOTEL BAGLIONI**   201R (105S)   | 24 | 25 | 25 | 22 | $277 |
(fka Mayfair Regent)
610 Park Ave. (enter on 65th St.); (800) 223-0542; (212) 288-0800;
FAX 737-0538
U – Now under co-management with Cogeta Palace Hotels, this "quiet and
refined" Eastsider remains an "oasis" of genteel "elegance"; along with
well-appointed rooms and suites, it provides "superb" service and a warm
"European atmosphere", making it a "home away from home" for its
moneyed clientele; the infamous Le Cirque restaurant (food rating, 27) is
"a gourmet's dream", and the lobby lounge is a fashionable meeting place
for breakfast and tea.

**Mayflower Hotel, The**   378R (183S)   | 17 | 17 | 15 | 14 | $151 |
15 Central Park West (bet. 61st & 62nd Sts.); (800) 223-4164; (212) 265-0060;
FAX 265-2026
M – "Location and value" are the highlights of this older West Side hotel
near Lincoln Center and the Great White Way; although it's "comfortable"
and "a pleasure to visit", it's also "showing wear"; if you stay, "get a room
on Central Park" for the view; N.B. because of its location, it gets a
surprising number of celeb guests, from rock bands to opera stars.

**Michelangelo**   178R (52S)   | 23 | 22 | 20 | 20 | $204 | ✗
(fka Parc 51 Hotel)                                                   Club
152 W. 51st St. (7th Ave.); (800) 237-0990; (212) 765-1900; FAX 561-7618   Line
U – Considered "a gem" by those who know it – and that's not many – this
West Midtowner has "gorgeous" decor, "silken service", a chic restaurant
(Bellini by Cipriani) and "lots of amenities"; sure, it's expensive, but our
surveyors say it delivers "luxury at a fair price."

## NEW YORK CITY HOTELS

| R | S | D | P | $ |
|---|---|---|---|---|

**Milford Plaza Hotel** 1300R (29S)  | 9 | 10 | 10 | 9 | $108 |

270 W. 45th St. (8th Ave.); (800) 221-2690; (212) 869-3600; FAX 944-8357

*U – It's "cheap" and close to B'way theaters, but beyond that, this big Times Square–area tourist hotel draws brickbats, e.g., "B-movie flophouse", "wouldn't want my dog to stay here", "a pit"; problems include "tiny", "bare-bones" rooms, "nasty service" and "Eighth Avenue at its worst" out front.*

**Morgans** 113R (29S)  | 21 | 22 | 18 | 18 | $190 |

237 Madison Ave. (bet. 37th & 38th Sts.); (800) 334-3408; (212) 686-0300; FAX 779-8352

*U – The first of the Schrager/Rubell hotels is still a model of "laid-back", "very hip" style and hospitality; the rooms, though mostly "small", are decorated in "ultrachic", minimalist fashion, and the "attractive" staff ("cool in black Armani") offers "polished service"; despite limited facilities, most consider it a "great little understated hotel" that's "very private."*

**Murray Hill East Suite Hotel** 120S  | 19 | 14 | 11 | 12 | $116 |

149 E. 39th St. (bet. Lexington & 3rd Aves.); (800) 221-3037; (212) 661-2100; FAX 818-0722

*U – "It's easy and convenient to have your own apartment and kitchen" in busy Manhattan, and that's basically what this all-suites East Midtowner provides; "comfortable" and well located, it's an especially "good value" for families and longer-term guests who want to cut down on restaurant bills; as ratings show, service and amenities are traded for modest prices.*

**New York Helmsley Hotel, The** 800R (11S)  | 20 | 19 | 18 | 18 | $192 |

212 E. 42nd St. (bet. 2nd & 3rd Aves.); (800) 221-4982; (212) 490-8900; FAX 986-4792

*M – Though "well run" and full of "luxurious" little touches, this "glitzy" Midtowner isn't universally admired; fans say it provides "clean, beautifully decorated rooms" and "polite" service, but detractors find it "sterile and overpriced", with unappealing "nouveau French provincial" decor and service that has its ups and downs.*

**New York Hilton & Towers** 2042R (237S)  | 17 | 16 | 15 | 16 | $174 |

1335 Sixth Ave. (bet. 53rd & 54th Sts.); (800) 445-8667; (212) 586-7000; FAX 315-1374

*M – You haven't experienced "big" until you've stayed at this mammoth "convention factory"; given its size, it's not surprising that it generates different opinions ("enjoyable", "does the job" vs. "the pits"), but there's no question it has an "excellent location" for both Midtown and Broadway theaters; rooms range from "dingy" to "fantastic", with the Towers offering the best quality and respite from the "tumult" below; a recent redesign has upped the quality all around.*

**New York Marriott Eastside**   665R (17S)   | 18 | 18 | 16 | 17 | $162 |
(fka Halloran House)
525 Lexington Ave. (49th St.); (800) 223-0939; (212) 755-4000; FAX 751-3440
*M – It's not exciting, but this conveniently located Midtowner can be
counted on for "comfortable and clean" (if somewhat "small") rooms, "good"
service and more-than-passable food; critics call it the "personification of
indifferent impersonality", but when you're just looking for a pleasant and
reasonable place to park your bags, it may suffice.*

**New York Marriott Marquis Hotel** 1874R (141S)   | 20 | 18 | 17 | 19 | $186 |
1535 Broadway (bet. 45th & 46th Sts.); (800) 843-4898; (212) 398-1900;
FAX 704-8930
*M – Virtually a "city in itself", complete with revolving rooftop restaurant,
in-house Broadway theater and "swarms" of humanity, this "glitzy" Times
Square giant captures all the "hustle-bustle" of Broadway – which pleases
some and dismays others; fans like its "majestic" atrium, "nice, comfortable"
rooms and "efficient" service, but critics grouse that it's "so damn big and
busy" that you could "grow old waiting for an elevator or check-in."*

**New York Vista Hotel**   821R (12S)   | 17 | 16 | 16 | 16 | $183 |
3 World Trade Ctr. (West St.); (800) 258-2505; (212) 938-9100; FAX 321-2237
*M – For years "the only game near Wall Street", this Lower Manhattan
business hotel now has tough new Downtown competition, which may
inspire it to improve what most consider to be merely "acceptable"
accommodations and service; its strong points include "beautiful views"
from some rooms, a nice health club and good restaurants.*

**Novotel New York**   474R (2S)   | 14 | 14 | 13 | 13 | $140 |
226 W. 52nd St. (B'way); (800) 221-4542; (212) 315-0100; FAX 765-5369
*M – "Clean, quiet and reasonably priced" rooms near the Theater District
aren't easy to come by, which is why this "streamlined" French chain hotel
is a basic good value; it's not big on service or amenities, causing critics to
grouse that "it should be called Nohotel"; N.B. children under 16 stay free
in their parents' room.*

**Omni Berkshire Place**   416R (26S)   | 19 | 19 | 17 | 18 | $188 |
21 E. 52nd St. (bet. 5th & Madison Aves.); (800) THE-OMNI; (212) 753-5800;
FAX 355-7646
*M – A "special place of civilized calm" is how admirers view this "intimate"
Eastsider; they praise its "small but classy rooms", lovely atrium lobby,
"superb" location and service that's "responsive to guests' needs"; not
everyone agrees – critics say some rooms are "lovely, others run-down",
and service is similarly inconsistent; but on balance, it's "very pleasant";
and the big square bar is a popular after-work watering hole.*

**Paramount**  600R (10S)                    | 17 | 19 | 19 | 22 | $142 |
235 W. 46th St. (B'way); (800) 225-7474; (212) 764-5900; FAX 354-5237
U – "The lobby is quite a sight", and so is the hip Euro-LA-Rio clientele at
this ultracool model of avant-garde style in the Theater District; it's
"fabulously designed" in every detail, from the "sassy and sleek" lobby and
otherworldly elevators to the "unique", "minute" guestrooms; critics find it
all "too minimalistic" and say "the chicness wears thin", but even they admit
it's a "bargain" for such high design; the Brasserie des Theatres, Mezzanine
Restaurant and Whisky Bar are all hot hangouts.

**Park Central**  1269R (269S)               | 11 | 12 | 12 | 11 | $137 |
(fka Omni Park Central)
870 Seventh Ave. (bet. 55th & 56th Sts.); (800) THE-OMNI; (212) 247-8000;
FAX 757-3374
U – Proof that a "convenient location" and "affordable prices" do not a good
hotel make, this older Westsider located near Carnegie Hall arouses
surveyors' ire with "dank, dark" rooms that "need renovation", and "inept"
customer service; "if you like green shag carpeting, '50s furniture and an
hour-long check-in, this is for you."

**PENINSULA NEW YORK, THE**  250R (30S)   | 24 | 24 | 23 | 23 | $249 |
700 Fifth Ave. (55th St.); (800) 262-9467; (212) 247-2200; FAX 903-3943
U – "Unforgettable" in every way (especially when you get the bill),
this "classy" and convenient Midtowner, part of the Hong Kong–based
Peninsula Group, has "well-thought-out rooms", "fantastic" service and
what many call the "best" pool and spa facilities in town; only the
entrance is awkward.

**PIERRE, THE**  206R (55S)                  | 24 | 25 | 24 | 23 | $266 |
2 E. 61st St. (5th Ave.); (800) 332-3442; (212) 838-8000; FAX 940-8109
U – "One of the greats", this "gracious" and "very classy" Four Seasons–
run hotel is the epitome of "old-world elegance" for many; enjoying a
"superb location" overlooking Central Park, it features "lovely" rooms and
"extraordinary service" that "makes you feel you're their most important
guest"; add "first-class dining" in the Cafe Pierre and you've got "a
treasure"; a few critics find it "stuffy" and say "rooms vary."

**Plaza Fifty Suite Hotel**  206R (130S)     | 19 | 16 | 12 | 13 | $151 |
155 E. 50th St. (Lexington Ave.); (800) ME-SUITE; (212) 751-5710;
FAX 753-1468
U – It's not big on charm, but this Eastsider is a "great buy", thanks to its
"practical", kitchenette-equipped guest rooms and "pleasant location"; what
service exists is "accommodating", and though there are no restaurants or
shops on-site, there are plenty nearby.

**Plaza, The**   814R (96S)                        | 21 | 22 | 22 | 23 | $233 |
Fifth Ave. at Central Park South; (800) 759-3000; (212) 759-3000; FAX 759-3167
*U – "A legend" that "is and always will be the classic NYC hotel", the
Plaza raises high expectations and mostly meets them; restored to its
gilt-edged grandeur by Donald Trump (its face-lift was almost "as good as
Ivana's"), it dazzles with "lovely, well-decorated rooms", "elegant, ritzy"
public spaces and the "perfect location" across from Central Park; yes,
there are complaints, but to natives and tourists alike, this is "the place to
be" in NYC; note, too, the Edwardian Room, Oak Room and Bar, Oyster
Bar and Palm Court supply supreme dining options.*


**Radisson Empire Hotel**   375R (25S)             | 18 | 18 | 17 | 17 | $136 |
(fka Empire Hotel, The)
44 W. 63rd St. (bet. B'way & Columbus Ave.); (800) 545-7400;
(212) 265-7400; FAX 315-0349
*U – Thanks to its redo upon joining the Radisson chain, this once "shabby"
Westsider is now "rather elegant", and though prices rose accordingly, fans
say it's still "one of the best deals" around; rooms are on the "tiny" side, but
they're nicely equipped and "so close to Lincoln Center, one need only roll
over" to see the ballet.*


**Ramada Hotel**   1705R (60S)                     | 12 | 12 | 11 | 11 | $126 |
(fka New York Penta Hotel)
401 Seventh Ave. (bet. 32nd & 33rd Sts.); (800) 223-8585; (212) 736-5000;
FAX 502-8712
*M – Perhaps ongoing renovations by new owner Ramada will improve this
big tourist/convention hotel's dismal ratings; for now it still draws mostly
zingers ("pretty dilapidated", "a hotel factory", "spend some money on
paint"); there's no denying that it's "convenient to Penn Station" and
Madison Square Garden, and cheap as well.*


**Ramada Midtown***   366R (4S)                    | 16 | 14 | 12 | 11 | $118 |
790 Eighth Ave. (bet. 48th & 49th Sts.); (800) 572-6232; (212) 581-7000;
FAX 974-0291
*M – "Surprisingly decent" and a "good value" is how fans assess this
Theater District hotel; though somewhat low on charm, it does have a
"great deli" on the premises and a rooftop pool during summer months;
critics simply say "yuck"; N.B. its location near B'way theaters is also
convenient to Eighth Avenue lowlife.*

## NEW YORK CITY HOTELS

| R | S | D | P | $ |

**Ramada Renaissance**       | 22 | 22 | 20 | 18 | $179 |
**Times Square\***    305R (5S)
2 Times Square (bet. 47th & 48th Sts. on 7th Ave.); (800) 628-5222;
(212) 765-7676; FAX 765-1962
*U – Contributing to the Times Square renaissance, this Theater District
newcomer is making its Broadway debut to positive reviews; along with a
"great location" at the north end of Times Square, it has attractive rooms,
"great personalized service" and "wonderful" valet floors; the area can be
iffy at night, but it couldn't be more convenient for theatergoers.*

**Regency, The**    384R (119S)      | 23 | 23 | 21 | 21 | $245 |
540 Park Ave. (61st St.); (800) 23-LOEWS; (212) 759-4100
*U – This "elegant Park Avenue enclave" is considered a "home away from
home" by well-heeled admirers who appreciate its "classy" and comfortable
accommodations, "top-quality" service and very convenient East Side
location; it's where the city's notables and quotables like to start their deal-
making day over breakfast, but has become a draw for lunch and dinner
too; a nice health club helps combat the effects of all that good eating.*

**RIHGA ROYAL HOTEL**    500S      | 25 | 24 | 22 | 22 | $219 |
151 W. 54th St. (bet. 6th & 7th Aves.); (800) 937-5454; (212) 307-5000;
FAX 765-6530
*U – Almost fit for royalty but priced within reach of commoners, this "very
beautiful" towering Japanese-run Midtowner delivers a "feeling of ultimate
luxury and comfort"; its spacious and "spotless" all-suites accommodations
have a "very rich flavor" and great views from upper floors; efficient service,
fine food in the Halcyon restaurant and a "nice health club" are pluses.*

**Ritz-Carlton, New York**    330R (25S)      | 22 | 23 | 21 | 20 | $235 |
112 Central Park South (6th Ave.); (800) 241-3333; (212) 757-1900;
FAX 757-9620
*M – Admirers say this "clubby" and "elegant" Central Park South hotel
"feels like home", with "luxuriously comfortable" rooms, very good service
and beautiful views from park-facing rooms; detractors call it a "weak link
in the Ritz-Carlton chain", citing variable service and "tiny" rooms in need
of redecorating; the Jockey Club (food rating, 19) has a nice "English
country feel", and Norman the bartender is "a work of art."*

**Roger Smith\***   136R (28S)            | 19 | 18 | 15 | 16 | $139 |
(fka Roger Smith Winthrop)
501 Lexington Ave. (47th St.); (800) 445-0277; (212) 755-1400; FAX 319-9130
*M – This recently renovated Eastsider has improved to the point where
some now consider it "one of NYC's best values"; you get "a decent room
for the price", "smooth" service, a "nice free breakfast" and a "very
convenient" location, but don't go out walking at night.*

**Roosevelt Hotel**   1070R (40S)        | 11 | 11 | 10 | 11 | $131 |
45 E. 45th St. (Madison Ave.); (800) 223-1870; (212) 661-9600; FAX 687-5064
*M – A big, "utilitarian" Midtowner that's rather "dreary but cheap" – "a place
to sleep, nothing more"; its central location puts it within "walking distance
of most attractions", and low prices make it "great for families"; critics
simply say "ugh."*

**Royalton, The**   170R (15S)           | 22 | 21 | 20 | 23 | $198 |
44 W. 44th St. (bet. 5th & 6th Aves.); (800) 635-9013; (212) 869-4400;
FAX 869-8965
*M – A "masterpiece" of futuristic style from the team behind Morgans and
the Paramount, this "sleek", "chic" and "unique" Midtowner features Phillipe
Starke decor that's definitely "not for traditionalists"; all find the rooms
"fantastic"; the staff and clientele are as "cool" as the decor, and 44
restaurant (food rating, 20) draws "superhip movers and shakers",
especially at lunch.*

**Salisbury Hotel**   320R (86S)         | 16 | 15 | 12 | 11 | $115 |
123 W. 57th St. (bet. 6th & 7th Aves.); (800) 223-0680; (212) 246-1300;
FAX 977-7752
*U – "You get what you pay for plus some" at this "small and comfortable"
older hotel across from Carnegie Hall; with "functional" rooms, courteous
service and a "pleasant atmosphere", it's a "terrific value" and a nice
"discovery"; coffeemakers and refrigerators in most rooms are pluses.*

**Shelburne Suite Hotel**   253S         | 18 | 14 | 11 | 11 | $137 |
(fka Shelburne Murray Hill)
303 Lexington Ave. (37th St.); (800) ME-SUITE; (212) 689-5200;
FAX 779-7068
*M – Like its fellows in the Manhattan East chain, this Murray Hill hotel
provides "comfortable", kitchenette-equipped suites at "reasonable" rates;
it's a little "old" but a "find" for those seeking value and the conveniences of
home; an open-air roof garden is an added perk.*

| R | S | D | P | $ |
|---|---|---|---|---|

**Sheraton Manhattan**  659R (28S)    | 15 | 15 | 14 | 13 | $142 |
(fka Sheraton City Squire)
790 Seventh Ave. (51st St.); (800) 325-3535; (212) 581-3300; FAX 541-9219
*M – Though it's not yet fully reflected in the ratings, this Midtowner is
"much improved" after a $47 million renovation; assets now include "nicely
redone" rooms, a "bright", attractive lobby, and "friendly, helpful" staff,
along with a "fabulous" indoor pool and Midtown convenience; the new
Bistro 790 provides "very good casual dining."*

**Sheraton New York**    | 15 | 15 | 13 | 14 | $157 |
**Hotel & Towers**  1750R (75S)
(fka Sheraton Centre Hotel & Towers)
811 Seventh Ave. (bet. 52nd & 53rd Sts.); (800) 233-6550; (212) 581-1000;
FAX 262-4410
*M – A "super" renovation has "made a difference" at this big and "bustling"
convention/tourist hotel; rooms are "new and fresh", and even the staff's
attitude seems to have been made over; not everyone's a convert: critics
say it's still a "madhouse" and claim that "other chains offer similar comfort
and less chaos"; as before, the Towers is preferred; N.B. ratings probably
understate the new conditions.*

**Sheraton Park Avenue**  150R (18S)    | 20 | 19 | 19 | 18 | $178 |
45 Park Ave. (37th St.); (800) 325-3535; (212) 685-7676; FAX 889-3193
*U – Fans say this "classy and sedate" Murray Hill hotel is like a "little
corner of Europe in NYC"; rooms are small but nicely furnished, and
service is "excellent without being obsequious"; Russell's American Grille
(food rating, 18) is a "pleasant" place to dine; given its overall quality and
personal attention, this hotel is a must-try.*

**Sherry-Netherland Hotel**  200R (100S)    | 21 | 22 | 20 | 19 | $287 |
781 Fifth Ave. (59th St.); (800) 247-4377; (212) 355-2800; FAX 319-4306
*U – "Class all the way", this Fifth Avenue grande dame – newly reopened
though still in the final stages of a major renovation – is on its way back to
being a model of "luxury" and "understated elegance"; "beautiful, rich and
warm", it "feels more like a private apartment building than a hotel", with
"huge rooms", efficient, personalized service and a "wonderful location"
across from Central Park; ratings will go up as more people return.*

**Southgate Tower Suite Hotel**  523S    | 16 | 15 | 12 | 13 | $128 |
371 Seventh Ave. (31st St.); (800) 637-8483; (212) 563-1800; FAX 643-8028
*M – Newly renovated kitchen-equipped suites and bargain prices make this
large, older hotel a "good value" and typical of the Manhattan East chain;
it's within walking distance of the Garment District, Macy's and Madison
Square Garden, although the neighborhood is not ideal for a stroll at night.*

**STANHOPE, THE**  140R (90S)  | 23 | 24 | 22 | 21 | $251 |
995 Fifth Ave. (81st St.); (800) 828-1123; (212) 288-5800; FAX 517-0088
*U – "Like staying in an elegant Fifth Avenue home", this "gracious", if
pricey, "European-style" Upper Eastsider provides "comfortable and
well-appointed rooms", "professional service" and a "great location" across
from the Met and Central Park; it's "small enough for the staff to give
personal attention"; "you can't beat the outdoor cafe" in summer, and the
dining room serves a "beautiful high tea" year-round (food rating, 20).*

**St. Moritz on-the-Park**  693R (87S)  | 13 | 14 | 15 | 13 | $147 |
50 Central Park S. (6th Ave.); (800) 221-4774; (212) 755-5800; FAX 751-2952
*U – Those who remember the glory days of this "faded queen" on Central
Park South are hoping that ongoing renovations will bring back "that old
ritzy feeling"; for now it's mostly just "old", with "tired" rooms and lackluster
service, but there are also "panoramic" park views (from some rooms) and
the somewhat dated Rumpelmayer's ice cream parlor.*

**ST. REGIS, THE**  434R (86S)  | 25 | 24 | 24 | 24 | $267 |
2 E. 55th St. (5th Ave.); (800) 759-7500; (212) 753-4500; FAX 787-3447
*U – It would be hard to imagine a more successful renovation than
Sheraton's "sumptuous" rehab of this elegant Louis XV dowager – "one of
the world's finest", "lovely, lovely, lovely", "the best around", are typical
raves; it offers "impeccable" service and "sublime" food in the acclaimed
Lespinasse restaurant (food rating, 25) and drinks in the King Cole Bar; if
the prices "stop your heart", what a way to go.*

**Surrey Hotel**  13S  | 21 | 17 | 15 | 16 | $192 |
20 E. 76th St. (bet. 5th & Madison Aves.); (800) ME-SUITE; (212) 288-3700;
FAX 628-1549
*U – "Very pleasant apartment-style suites" – "huge" and recently renovated –
at very pleasant prices make this Upper Eastsider a "best value",
especially for families and long-term stays; with "friendly" service and good
special packages, it's the kind of place people return to again and again.*

**Sutton**  84R  | – | – | – | – | M |
330 E. 56th St. (bet 1st and 2nd Aves); 752-8888
*This upscale Midtown East Side newcomer aims at the longer-stay trade
with handsome accommodations including up-to-date kitchens and marble
bathrooms that you'd be proud to have at home, plus a pool and exercise
facilities; N.B. it's only available for stays of a month or more.*

# NEW YORK CITY HOTELS

| R | S | D | P | $ |

### U.N. Plaza – Park Hyatt Hotel  428R (35S)  | 22 | 21 | 20 | 21 | $191 |
(fka United Nations Plaza)
1 U.N. Plaza (44th St. at 1st Ave.); (800) 233-1234; (212) 355-3400;
FAX 702-5051
*U – "If not the best overall hotel in NYC, certainly the most underrated",
this "cool and modern" chrome-and-glass tower near the U.N. is a "gem in
the concrete jungle"; assets include "spacious", "contemporary" rooms,
"gorgeous" views, "extraordinarily accommodating service", a "great"
penthouse health club/pool and "deluxe" dining in the Ambassador Grill
(food rating, 20); its weekend packages are a steal.*

### Waldorf-Astoria, The  1410R (191S)  | 20 | 20 | 20 | 22 | $212 |
301 Park Ave. (bet. 49th & 50th Sts.); (800) HILTONS; (212) 355-3000;
FAX 758-9209
*U – A "NYC tradition", this big Midtown "grand dame" is by most accounts
"everything you expect" from one of the city's legendary hotels; its very
name evokes images of old-fashioned glamour and elegance, and though
not every room lives up to them (some are small and "nondescript"), the
"fabulous" art deco public spaces – including what may be "the most
beautiful lobby in America" – certainly do; service is extremely "skilled",
and a recent renovation put a new shine on the hotel's "old-world charm";
"everyone should stay here once."*

### WALDORF TOWERS  (175S)  | 24 | 22 | 20 | 23 | $275 |
301 Park Ave. (bet. 49th & 50th Sts.); (800) 445-8667; (212) 355-3000;
FAX 758-9209
*M – The "place to feel like a sheik" – or a prince, prime minister or simply
someone very privileged – the Towers is an elite enclave worlds apart from
the busy Waldorf-Astoria; "spectacular" suites ("spacious, elegant and well
decorated"), top-notch service and a posh and peaceful atmosphere make
it "truly presidential" (not to mention presidentially priced).*

### Warwick, The  425R (70S)  | 15 | 16 | 15 | 14 | $159 |
65 W. 54th St. (6th Ave.); (800) 223-4099; (212) 247-2700; FAX 957-8915
*M – Fans call this Midtowner an "oldie with great history and style",
praising its "quaint lobby" and "spacious, pretty rooms"; critics call it a
"wrecking-ball special", with "tired and tatty" rooms and "slow service";
recent renovations may account for the discrepancy – get a spruced-up
room and you're better able to appreciate the hotel's undeniable assets: a
"great location" and reasonable rates.*

**Westbury Hotel, The**   231R (52S)          | 22 | 22 | 21 | 20 | $226 |
Madison Ave. at 69th St.; (800) 321-1569; (212) 535-2000; FAX 535-5058
*M – This "quiet, understated" East Side hotel is "warm and wonderful", with "beautiful", chintz-filled rooms and "gracious" staff skilled at making guests feel "like family"; a few find the decor "somewhat faded" and "faux old money", but they're outvoted by those who say it exudes "old-world class and elegance"; the Polo restaurant (food rating, 21) provides good Contemporary French cuisine.*

**Wyndham Hotel**   140R (70S)                | 16 | 17 | 12 | 13 | $143 |
42 W. 58th St. (bet. 5th & 6th Aves.); (212) 753-3500; FAX 754-5638
*M – The furnishings may be "running a bit to seed", and the staff can be "grumpy", but they add to the quirky charm of this "quaint", comfortable older hotel near the Plaza; it has plenty of fans (including show-biz regulars) who appreciate its "huge", "old-fashioned" rooms, "charming European atmosphere" and "great location", not to mention "terrific prices."*

## ● OTHER HOTEL-CHAIN CHOICES
*You will find one or more additional locations of the following hotel chains in the New York City area: Days Inn, Howard Johnson and Travelodge. But this hardly tells the whole story. In the areas surrounding the city – northern New Jersey, Westchester County and nearby Long Island – with a combined population that rivals that of the city itself, you'll find nearly every chain in America represented; for reservations or information, see the toll-free 800 phone listings on page 16.*

# ORANGE COUNTY, CA†

## TOP HOTELS
## (In order of rating)

### BEST OVERALL

27 – Ritz-Carlton, Laguna Niguel
25 – Four Seasons Newport Beach
22 – Le Meridien Newport Beach
21 – Dana Point Resort
20 – Surf & Sand Hotel
    Costa Mesa Marriott Suites
19 – Hyatt Regency Irvine
    Westin South Coast Plaza

### BEST VALUES

Costa Mesa Marriott Suites
Hyatt Regency Irvine
Marriott Suites Newport Beach
Sheraton Newport Beach
Irvine Marriott
Anaheim Marriott
Le Meridien Newport Beach
Hyatt Regency Alicante

\*     \*     \*

### Best Rooms

27 – Ritz-Carlton, Laguna Niguel
26 – Four Seasons Newport Beach
22 – Le Meridien Newport Beach
    Costa Mesa Marriott Suites
    Surf & Sand Hotel
21 – Dana Point Resort
20 – Westin South Coast Plaza
    Hyatt Regency Irvine

### Best Dining

26 – Ritz-Carlton, Laguna Niguel
24 – Four Seasons Newport Beach
    Le Meridien Newport Beach
20 – Surf & Sand Hotel
19 – Dana Point Resort
    Hyatt Regency Irvine
    Doubletree
18 – Anaheim Marriott

### Best Service

26 – Ritz-Carlton, Laguna Niguel
25 – Four Seasons Newport Beach
22 – Le Meridien Newport Beach
21 – Costa Mesa Marriott Suites
20 – Dana Point Resort
    Surf & Sand Hotel
    Westin South Coast Plaza
    Anaheim Marriott

### Best Public Facilities

28 – Ritz-Carlton, Laguna Niguel
25 – Four Seasons Newport Beach
22 – Le Meridien Newport Beach
    Dana Point Resort
20 – Surf & Sand Hotel
19 – Hyatt Newporter
    Marriott Suites Newport Beach
    Costa Mesa Marriott Suites

†For restaurants, see *Zagat Los Angeles/So. California Restaurant Survey.*

## ORANGE COUNTY, CA, HOTELS

| R | S | D | P | $ |

**Anaheim Hilton & Towers**  1600R (100S)  | 18 | 18 | 17 | 19 | $133 |
777 Convention Way, Anaheim; (800) 222-9923; (714) 750-4321; FAX 740-4252
*U – This "top-of-the-line" convention hotel opposite Disneyland and adjacent to the vast Anaheim convention center strikes our raters as "the biggest hotel ever"; some laud its solid accommodations, "nice restaurant variety", "lobby conveniences", state-of-the-art fitness center, free Disneyland shuttle and generally "positive attitude", calling it "nice for a Hilton, typical for Orange County."*

**Anaheim Marriott Hotel**  1033R (54S)  | 19 | 20 | 18 | 19 | $130 |
700 W. Convention Way, Anaheim; (800) 228-9290; (714) 750-8000; FAX 750-9100
*M – "Great if you're going to Disneyland", but you may "feel out of place if you're not wearing mouse ears" at this otherwise "excellent business and convention hotel"; many praise JW's, a "real gem" of a restaurant (food rating, 26); being near Disneyland puts some in "a fantasy state of mind"; P.S. ask about the special family packages.*

**Casa Laguna Inn**  20R (5S)  | – | – | – | – | M |
2510 S. Coast Hwy., Laguna Beach; (800) 233-0449; (714) 494-2996; FAX 494-5009
*This small, "pleasant" Spanish-style inn on a hillside facing the Pacific in the middle of tourist-intensive Laguna has "great Victorian rooms", a cozy library and a "gorgeous floral courtyard"; its breakfasts and afternoon teas are well liked.*

**Costa Mesa Marriott Suites**  253S  | 22 | 21 | 18 | 19 | $115 |
500 Anton Blvd., Costa Mesa; (800) 228-9290; (714) 957-1100; FAX 966-8495
*U – A "good value", this first-class all-suiter does everything well, causing reviewers to describe it as a "refined, pleasant" "business hotel"; it's also near myriad Orange County malls, making it "great for shoppers."*

**Dana Point Resort**  350R (17S)  | 21 | 20 | 19 | 22 | $146 |
25135 Park Lantern, Dana Point; (800) 533-9748; (714) 661-5000; FAX 661-3688
*U – "The marina and ocean lull you to sleep" at this "Easterner's idea of heaven", built in an imposing New England style; it's "reasonably priced", considering the extensive facilities, fine rooms and suites, "great oceanfront" and "beautiful views"; the south-of-Laguna location makes it convenient for day trips to San Diego.*

## ORANGE COUNTY, CA, HOTELS

| R | S | D | P | $ |
|---|---|---|---|---|

**Disneyland Hotel**   1131R (65S)     | 16 | 17 | 15 | 18 | $134 |

1150 W. Cerritos Ave., Anaheim; (714) 778-6600; FAX 956-6582
*M – Our surveyors are of two minds on this "aging giant"; fans say it's a "great hotel in the Disney spirit" (a monorail connects to the nearby Magic Kingdom), but "you have to like kids all over the place"; detractors complain of noise, crowds and "shabby glitz"; P.S. ask about the special Adventure Package.*

**Doubletree Hotel**     | 19 | 18 | 19 | 18 | $112 |

**Orange County\***   454R (19S)
100 The City Dr., Orange; (800) 528-0444; (714) 634-4500; FAX 978-3839
*U – This "clean, comfy" chain hotel, completely refurbished in '91, boasts a "friendly staff" and "good proximity to Disneyland"; it's a "lovely setting" "for a Soroptimist luncheon fashion show" or "perfect for a business trip"; it's also a "very good value."*

**FOUR SEASONS HOTEL**     | 26 | 25 | 24 | 25 | $194 |

**NEWPORT BEACH**   285R (93S)
690 Newport Center Dr., Newport Beach; (800) 332-3442; (714) 759-0808; FAX 759-0568
*U – "Elegance", comfort and service are what this "spacious", "beautiful" resort hotel directly across from Fashion Island shopping center is all about; expect "one of the best", a "superior" hotel that's tastefully decorated in California pastels, with "friendly, courteous personnel", "magnificent rooms", a "good pool area" and a fine restaurant, The Pavilion (food rating, 23) – in sum, "typical Four Seasons attention to detail."*

**Hilton Suites In Orange**   230S     | – | – | – | – | M |

400 N. State College Blvd., Orange; (800) HILTONS; (714) 938-1111; FAX 938-0930
*A "terrific" place to stay when going to Disneyland, with "free buses all day", this "spacious suite" facility with in-room "microwave, refrigerator, coffee-maker, VCR, shower, tub – what else do you need?"; it's a "good value", but apart from Disneyland, there's "nothing to do in the immediate vicinity."*

**Hyatt Newporter**   410R (18S)     | 18 | 19 | 18 | 19 | $138 |

1107 Jamboree Rd., Newport Beach; (800) 233-1234; (714) 729-1234; FAX 644-1552
*U – Though it's gone through owner changes in recent years, this recently "renovated garden hotel" "next to a wildlife sanctuary" and down the road from trendy Balboa Island is "still something special" and "continues to improve since Hyatt took over"; with 16 tennis courts, 3 pools and 3 whirlpools, it's a "lovely place for a family vacation" or a "corporate retreat."*

## ORANGE COUNTY, CA, HOTELS | R | S | D | P | $ |

**Hyatt Regency Alicante**  400R (17S)  | 18 | 19 | 17 | 18 | $128 |
100 Plaza Alicante, Garden Grove; (800) 972-2929; (714) 750-1234;
FAX 741-0465
*M – Despite solid ratings, this Hyatt gets surprisingly negative comments:
"cartoonish" "suburban hotel" with "pink flamingos in front" that's "three
miles from Mickey, Goofy and food"; it's also "passé", with "rooms that
don't have the Hyatt touch" and "desk help who leave a bit to be desired";
N.B. there's a free shuttle to Disneyland.*

**Hyatt Regency Irvine**  556R (41S)  | 20 | 20 | 19 | 19 | $129 |
17900 Jamboree Blvd., Irvine; (800) 233-1234; (714) 863-3111; FAX 852-1574
*M – Most raters call this a "great" business hotel, citing accommodations
and service that are "above and beyond"; some complain that this is "more
a convention hall than a hotel."*

**Inn at the Park\***  509R  | 13 | 15 | 12 | 13 | $98 |
1855 S. Harbor Blvd., Anaheim; (800) 421-6662; (714) 750-1811; FAX 971-3626
*M – A "convenient" property that's near, but not exactly at, Disneyland; this
"ok convention hotel" may offer "good value" and a "nice location", but our
surveyors suggest that it's "showing wear" and "not too great"; their ratings
put this low on the list in all categories other than price, which is modest.*

**Irvine Marriott**  485R (9S)  | 19 | 19 | 17 | 17 | $123 |
18000 Von Karman Ave., Irvine; (800) 228-9290; (714) 553-0100; FAX 250-3957
*U – "Pleasant high-rise motel" that's "just a decent place to stay", a "typical
Marriott" with "clean but small rooms" and a location that's "convenient" to
the airport and the Irvine business complex; otherwise, despite special
meal, golf and Disneyland packages, it's "hopelessly ordinary."*

**Le Meridien Newport Beach**  435R (53S)  | 22 | 22 | 24 | 22 | $156 |
4500 MacArthur Blvd., Newport Beach; (800) 543-4300; (714) 476-2001;
FAX 250-7191
*U – "A slice of the Riviera" convenient to Orange County Airport, this
"expensive but worth it" "oasis in the middle of suburban nowhere" is a
"small gem" with a "European" flair for service and "wonderful" French
food at Antoine (food rating, 27).*

**Marriott Suites Newport Beach**  250S  | 21 | 19 | 17 | 19 | $128 |
500 Bayview Circle, Newport Beach; (800) 228-9290; (714) 854-4500;
FAX 854-3937
*U – "It's sweet to have a suite" for a "wonderful relaxing weekend" at this
"nice family" hotel conveniently situated not far from the Newport Beach/
Balboa Island beaches and shopping areas: indoor and outdoor pools,
"nice service" and "good value" are added benefits.*

| R | S | D | P | $ |

**Newport Beach Marriott Hotel &** | 19 | 19 | 17 | 19 | $143 |
**Tennis Club**   586R (16S)
900 Newport Center Dr., Newport Beach; (800) 228-9290; (714) 640-4000;
FAX 640-5055
*U – "Beautiful grounds", including "pretty gardens" overlooking Newport
Bay, are the salient features of this "pleasant and bright" resort; "good
service" and a "central location" "near Fashion Island shopping" make this
a "fun place" for families or business travelers.*

**Red Lion Orange** | 19 | 16 | 15 | 17 | $121 |
**County Airport**   494R (10S)
3050 Bristol St., Costa Mesa; (800) 547-8010; (714) 540-7000; FAX 540-9176
*U – An "affordable", better-than-expected chain operation convenient to the
Orange County Performing Arts Center, and a half hour from Disneyland;
it's "close to shopping" and offers "easy access to and from appointments",
but critics call it just "a place to sleep."*

**RITZ-CARLTON, LAGUNA NIGUEL** 393R (31S) | 27 | 26 | 26 | 28 | $243 |
33533 Ritz-Carlton Dr., Laguna Niguel; (800) 241-3333; (714) 240-2000;
FAX 240-0829
*U – The "best of the best", this clifftop palace rates not just the "best in
Orange County" but also one of the "best in the world"; an "awesome"
"pinnacle to which all hotels should aspire", this "jewel in the Ritz crown"
"can't be topped for luxury or setting"; our reviewers wax rhapsodic over
the "fabulous grounds" (along with pools, tennis and nearby golf), "the best
ocean view in America", a "great staff" and "excellent food"; "bring designer
clothes and mucho dinero" to this "first-class resort."*

**Sheraton Anaheim Hotel**   491R (26S) | 18 | 17 | 15 | 17 | $116 |
1015 W. Ball Rd., Anaheim; (800) 325-3535; (714) 778-1700; FAX 535-3889
*M – "Good for Sheraton", this "spread-out", recently renovated family hotel
convenient to nearby Disneyland (via a free shuttle) has an unusual
English-manor ambiance in a* "Robin Hood" *setting; though fairly
uninspiring, it's basically a "nice property" in a "good location"; special
packages are available on request.*

**Sheraton Newport Beach Hotel**   338R (5S) | 17 | 17 | 17 | 17 | $114 |
4545 MacArthur Blvd., Newport Beach; (800) 325-3535; (714) 833-0570;
FAX 833-3927
*M – This "very accommodating", "well-maintained" business hotel near the
Irvine Industrial Complex and John Wayne Airport offers sports and fitness
facilities, "great value" and a staff that "tries hard to please"; rates include a
"free buffet in the AM."*

**Surf & Sand Hotel**   157R (4S)          | 22 | 20 | 20 | 20 | $182 |
1555 S. Coast Hwy., Laguna Beach; (800) 524-8621; (714) 497-4477;
FAX 494-7653
*U – "Very romantic", this "quiet" oceanfront "beauty" is considered "the best
on the beach" by many surveyors; the "great view" from this "laid-back,
casual" spot will "blow your mind", and the "rooms feel like you're in the
water" – they're so close "you step out the door right onto the beach."*

**Westin South Coast Plaza, The**   392R (17S)   | 20 | 20 | 18 | 19 | $144 |
666 Anton Blvd., Costa Mesa; (800) 228-3000; (714) 540-2500;
FAX 754-7996
*M – Travelers with a pocketful of credit cards will appreciate this "well-
maintained" "Westin in a shopping center" – in this case, across the street
from the sprawling, "upscale" South Coast Plaza, considered by some to
be the "best mall in America"; it's "well run", with a variety of "weekend
specials" that are "a fine buy."*

● **OTHER HOTEL-CHAIN CHOICES**
*You will find one or more additional locations of the following hotel chains
in the Orange County area: Courtyard by Marriott, Crown Sterling Suites,
Days Inn, Embassy Suites, Hampton Inn, Howard Johnson, La Quinta
Inns, Ramada, Residence Inn, Super 8 and Travelodge/Viscount; for
reservations or information, see the toll-free 800 phone listings on page 16.*

# ORLANDO[†]

## TOP HOTELS
## (In order of rating)

### BEST OVERALL

25 – Disney's Grand Floridian
    Hyatt Regency Grand Cypress
24 – Peabody Orlando
22 – Disney's Village Resort
    Stouffer
21 – Marriott's World Center
    Walt Disney World Swan
20 – Buena Vista Palace
    Disney's Polynesian
    Walt Disney World Dolphin

### BEST VALUES

Disney's Caribbean Beach
Radisson Plaza
Forte Travelodge Hotel
Peabody Orlando
Stouffer
Hyatt Orlando
Sheraton World Resort
Omni Orlando
Grosvenor Resort
Guest Quarters

\*    \*    \*

### Best Rooms

26 – Disney's Grand Floridian
    Hyatt Regency Grand Cypress
24 – Peabody Orlando
23 – Disney's Village Resort
    Guest Quarters
22 – Stouffer
21 – Marriott's World Center
    Walt Disney World Swan
    Disney's Caribbean Beach

### Best Dining

23 – Hyatt Regency Grand Cypress
    Peabody Orlando
22 – Disney's Grand Floridian
21 – Stouffer
20 – Walt Disney World Swan
    Disney's Village Resort
    Marriott's World Center
18 – Walt Disney World Dolphin
    Hyatt Orlando
    Hilton at Walt Disney Village

### Best Service

25 – Disney's Grand Floridian
24 – Hyatt Regency Grand Cypress
    Peabody Orlando
22 – Disney's Village Resort
21 – Walt Disney World Swan
    Disney's Polynesian
    Marriott's World Center
    Walt Disney World Dolphin
    Stouffer
    Disney's Caribbean Beach

### Best Public Facilities

26 – Hyatt Regency Grand Cypress
    Disney's Grand Floridian
24 – Peabody Orlando
23 – Disney's Village Resort
    Disney's Caribbean Beach
    Walt Disney World Swan
22 – Marriott's World Center
    Stouffer
    Disney's Polynesian
21 – Walt Disney World Dolphin

---

[†]For restaurants, see *Zagat Orlando/Central Florida Restaurant Survey.*

**ORLANDO HOTELS**　　　　　　| R | S | D | P | $ |

**Buena Vista Palace**　1028R (200S)　| 20 | 21 | 19 | 21 | $141 |
1900 Buena Vista Dr., Lake Buena Vista; (800) 327-2990; (407) 827-2727;
FAX 827-6034
*M – The Palace's princely rooftop restaurant, Arthur's 27 (food rating, 26),
may be more famous, but most respondents say the hotel downstairs is
"excellent", too, with a "terrific pool" and a friendly staff sporting "Mickey
Mouse smiles"; it's "great for family" and "worth the money" to be "inside
the fence at Disney"; sure, it's "overhyped" and "touristy" – this is D-World.*

**Clarion Plaza Hotel\***　810R (42S)　| 18 | 19 | 19 | 17 | $97 |
9700 International Dr.; (800) 627-VALU; (407) 352-9700; FAX 351-9111
*M – The 800 number says it best: "VALU"; many raters agree, but others
grouse that this "newer facility" is "strictly business"; though it's "convenient
to the convention center" and a mere Shamu's leap from SeaWorld, the
"small rooms" and undistinguished setting make this "serviceable", no better.*

**Courtyard at Lake Lucerne, The**　22R (13S)　| – | – | – | – | M |
(fka Norman Parry Inn)
211 N. Lucerne Circle E.; (800) 444-5289; (407) 648-5188; FAX 246-1368
*A hideaway from the tourist throngs, Orlando's oldest mansion has been
turned into a small Victorian hotel, nestled in a flower-filled courtyard in the
heart of Orlando's booming entertainment district and close to I-4 and the
Worlds beyond; expect personalized service and classical music
everywhere, with limited food but unlimited peace.*

**Disney's Caribbean Beach Resort**　2112R　| 21 | 21 | 16 | 23 | $108 |
900 Cayman Way, Lake Buena Vista; (407) 934-7639
*U – "Best buy in the Park" say bargain hunters of this "jewel" in the WDW
crown; fans say it's a "great family resort" that makes you "feel like you're
in the Caribbean"; "convenience" wins applause, too, along with the "no
problem, mon" service, but the food gets a "mediocre" rating from some.*

**Disney's Contemporary Resort**　1053R (67S)| 19 | 19 | 16 | 21 | $162 |
4600 N. World Dr., Lake Buena Vista; (407) 828-3200; FAX 824-3539
*M – Still "the best for kids at Disney", this venerable grande dame straight
out of The Jetsons is becoming gently frayed, according to its guests, but
"compensates beautifully" with "excellent service", "child-oriented facilities"
and lots of "convenience"; the lobby monorail station gets raves, but the
food could be "Howard Johnson's."*

## ORLANDO HOTELS

| R | S | D | P | $ |

### DISNEY'S GRAND FLORIDIAN
### BEACH RESORT   901R (7S)
| 26 | 25 | 22 | 26 | $215 |

4001 Grand Floridian Way, Lake Buena Vista; (407) 824-3000; FAX 824-3186
*U – "The best of Disney's resorts" has got a lock on "understated luxury",
with an atmosphere that could "out-Victorian any Victorian"; though "grand
at a grander price", it's also called "civilized", "fun" and "fantastic", with
"spacious rooms", three restaurants – Flagler's, Narcoossee's, and Victoria
& Albert, lovely grounds and a monorail to the Magic Kingdom right outside.*

### Disney's Polynesian Resort   855R
| 20 | 21 | 17 | 22 | $164 |

1900 Hotel Plaza Blvd., Lake Buena Vista; (407) 934-7639; FAX 824-3174
*M – The "Poly", like the faithful family pooch, still wins a pat as "old and
trustworthy" from most who stay here; the pool and grounds are favorites,
and "monorail convenience" is a big plus, but whether you think it feels
"like Hawaii" or "South Seas fake" is debatable; it gets "first prize" for kid
appeal but not for its food.*

### Disney's Village Resort Villas
### & Conference Center   585R (11S)
| 23 | 22 | 20 | 23 | $175 |

1900 Hotel Plaza Blvd., Lake Buena Vista; (407) 828-3200; FAX 828-3938
*M – Perch the kids in a tree house at this one-of-a-kind property, where the
efficiency-style rooms are literally built into the trees; it's one of Disney's
older, more laid-back resorts, away from the concrete but still "in the lap of
Mickey"; "be sure to rent a golf cart" to get around the beautiful grounds.*

### Forte Travelodge Hotel
### in Walt Disney World Village*   325R (4S)
| 17 | 17 | 14 | 16 | $99 |

2000 Hotel Plaza Blvd., Lake Buena Vista; (800) 348-3765; (407) 828-2424;
FAX 828-8933
*U – Guests say the "well-fitted and -equipped rooms" are "surprisingly nice"
for a budget hotel, with "super public facilities" and "convenience"; added
attractions include a pool and kiddie pool/playground, minibars and balconies
in all rooms, and lots of package deals; it may not be the equal of other
WDW properties, but it's on the Disney bus route and "the price is right."*

### Grosvenor Resort at
### Walt Disney World   630R (5S)
| 17 | 17 | 17 | 18 | $118 |

1850 Hotel Plaza Blvd., Lake Buena Vista; (800) 624-4109; (407) 828-4444;
FAX 827-6314
*U – So it "needs some renovation" – this "surprisingly pleasant" hotel within
the DW village is "convenient" to all the attractions, is famous for its quirky
but indubitably fun Sherlock Holmes–themed Baskervilles restaurant, and
also offers quiet grounds and a "great pool"; there are better, certainly, but
praisers say "for the price" this place is "reliably good."*

| R | S | D | P | $ |

### Guest Quarters Suite Resort
**Disney Village\*** 229S

| 23 | 17 | 14 | 17 | $124 |

2305 Hotel Plaza Blvd., Lake Buena Vista; (800) 424-2900; (407) 934-1000; FAX 934-1008

*U – "Large" "two-room suites" that are "great for families" get the nod at this otherwise "minimal" place on Disney's outer hotel row; "free breakfast" and a location within "walking distance to WDW Village" are other pluses, but our surveyors were distinctly underwhelmed by the food and service.*

### Harley Hotel of Orlando\* 287R (11S)

| 14 | 13 | 13 | 11 | $92 |

151 E. Washington St.; (800) 321-2323; (407) 841-3220; FAX 849-1839

*M – In Downtown Orlando, this Helmsley-owned "bargain" hotel is an "excellent alternative" if you don't mind "a short ride" to the amusement parks – and there's plenty going on in beautiful Downtown Orlando, with the Church Street entertainment complex and many after-hours jazz and reggae clubs; critics knock the food and service – "they should have sentenced Leona to stay here."*

### Hilton at Walt Disney
**World Village** 897R (84S)

| 19 | 19 | 18 | 19 | $139 |

1751 Hotel Plaza Blvd., Lake Buena Vista; (800) 445-8667; (407) 827-4000; FAX 827-6380

*M – Opinions are mixed on this "standard", "plain old Hilton" "away from the crowds"; fans say it's "pleasant" and "convenient", with a "good pool area" and "some of the best food" around; detractors say it's "very motel-like", with "red carpet everywhere"; it's a "long run from Disney World", but that means it's "not as loaded with noisy children."*

### Hotel Royal Plaza\* 396R (10S)

| 13 | 13 | 11 | 13 | $125 |

1905 Hotel Plaza Blvd., Lake Buena Vista; (800) 248-7890; (407) 828-2828; FAX 827-6338

*M – "Mickey Mouse phones in every room" may make you feel "10 years old again", but the guests aren't the only ones showing their age at this well-located but "run-down" high-rise "vestige of Orlando's early days"; though prices are low, the consensus is that "there are better ways to see Disney."*

### Hyatt Orlando 924R (26S)

| 19 | 19 | 18 | 19 | $122 |

6375 W. Irlo Bronson, Kissimmee; (800) 233-1234; (407) 396-1234; FAX 396-5090

*M – You'd never know our surveyors were talking about the same hotel: one critic's "classy" and "pleasant" is another's "beat-up" "bummer"; unity prevails, however, on the bargain "family" prices and a "great Disney World location"; good ratings across the board support the "classy", "pleasant" view.*

## ORLANDO HOTELS

| R | S | D | P | $ |

### HYATT REGENCY GRAND CYPRESS   750R (74S)

| 24 | 24 | 23 | 26 | $186 |

1 Grand Cypress Blvd.; (800) 233-1234; (407) 239-1234; FAX 239-3800
*U – What many contend is "the best hotel in Orlando" impresses just about everyone with its "extensive facilities" and "beautiful grounds" (including its own nature preserve), plus food at Hemingway's and La Coquina, service, rooms, and tennis and golf facilities that rate the superlative du jour: "great"; true, a few Scrooge McDucks quack that it's nothing more than a "fancy convention factory", but to most, this is "where grown-ups stay in Orlando"; it's so nice, many "never leave the premises" – "sorry, Mickey."*

### Marriott Orlando   1098R (20S)

| 18 | 19 | 17 | 18 | $124 |

8001 Int'l Dr.; (800) 421-8001; (407) 351-2420; FAX 352-8759
*M – Not to be confused with Marriott's Orlando World Center, this "smaller" but still huge and "spread-out" satellite in the middle of International Drive's glut-o-glitz strip is a quick hop from the convention center and another 15-minute drive from WDW; despite decent numbers, most raters say it's "not up to Marriott's usual standards."*

### Marriott's Orlando World Center   1605R (102S)

| 21 | 21 | 20 | 22 | $153 |

1 World Ctr. Dr.; (800) 621-0638; (407) 239-4200; FAX 239-5777
*M – Rising like a glass-and-stone monolith from the prairie east of EPCOT, this "overwhelmingly large" world unto itself "can handle the crowds", providing "surprisingly personal service" and comfortable rooms, decent restaurants, a "beautiful golf course" and the "best swimming pool ever" (slides, grottoes, the works).*

### Omni Orlando   290R (9S)

| 20 | 17 | 16 | 17 | $117 |

400 W. Livingston St.; (800) THE-OMNI; (407) 843-6664; FAX 648-5414
*M – If eating "great Key lime pie" next to a seven-foot basketball player is your idea of a good vacation, this Downtown property – across from the home of the Orlando Magic basketball team and brimming with visiting Goliaths during season – should fill the bill; for the less athletically inclined, the arts center is also adjacent; only mouse meisters complain that it's far from Disney.*

### Orange Lake Country Club   800R

| – | – | – | – | M |

8505 W. Irlo Bronson Memorial Hwy., Kissimmee; (800) 877-6522; (407) 846-0000; FAX 239-1039
*See cows grazing in the fields, so close yet so far, at this condo resort just four miles from the Magic Kingdom; the rooms "aren't plush", but they're "nice", and the fact that there are 27 holes of golf, 16 tennis courts and an 80-acre lake on 400 acres of "beautiful" grounds is a big plus.*

## ORLANDO HOTELS

| | R | S | D | P | $ |
|---|---|---|---|---|---|

**Orlando Heritage Inn**   150R   | – | – | – | – | M |
(fka Golden Tulip Heritage Inn)
9861 Int'l Dr.; (800) 447-1890; (407) 352-0008; FAX 352-5449
*This no-frills lodge caters to families looking for location, not luxury; besides the usual bed-shower-and-TV, this plantation-style hotel sports a wide porch for rocking and a dinner theater.*

**Park Plaza Hotel**   27R (11S)   | – | – | – | – | M |
307 Park Ave. S., Winter Park; (800) 228-7220; (407) 647-1072; FAX 647-4081
*Far (25 miles) from the madding crowd on one of Florida's most distinctive shopping avenues, this tiny, funky, "quaint" hotel hovers between this century and the "mythical past", resisting discovery; guests are more likely to see a movie star than mouse ears in the understated lobby or in its Park Plaza Gardens restaurant (food rating, 26), "one of the best in the city."*

**Peabody Orlando, The**   891R (57S)   | 24 | 24 | 23 | 24 | $151 |
9801 Int'l Dr.; (800) PEABODY; (407) 352-4000; FAX 351-9177
*U – Why did the duck cross the lobby? Because it's a Peabody, that's why; our respondents say the twice-daily mallard march alone is almost enough to make this "beautiful", "classy" hotel worth the expense; besides ducks, there are "well-appointed rooms", a "genuinely nice staff" and "good food" in the top-rated Dux (food rating, 28) Capriccio (22) and the loud but luscious '50s-style B-Line Diner (19).*

**Radisson Inn International Drive***   229R (2S)   | 18 | 15 | 14 | 16 | $97 |
(fka Radisson Inn & Aquatic Center)
8444 Int'l Dr.; (800) 333-3333; (407) 345-0505; FAX 352-5894
*M – Swimmers will love the famous aquatic center next door, where many world records have been set; although its own sports facilities are excellent, the food and service at this "quiet" business hotel won't set any records – but at the modest price, no one expects records.*

**Radisson Plaza Hotel Orlando**   337R (18S)   | 18 | 19 | 17 | 17 | $99 |
60 S. Ivanhoe Blvd.; (800) 333-3333; (407) 425-4455
*M – While liking the rooms and service, and especially the low prices, our raters were otherwise unimpressed by this midrange business and convention hotel located on Lake Ivanhoe in Downtown Orlando; critics call it "boring" and "polyester all the way", though the "good daily breakfast buffet" does get a nod from hungry wakers.*

| R | S | D | P | $ |
|---|---|---|---|---|

**Residence Inn by Marriott –**

| – | – | – | – | VE |
|---|---|---|---|---|

**Lake Buena Vista**    688S (fka Hawthorn Suites Villa Resort)
8800 Meadow Creek Dr. (I-35); (800) 331-3131; (407) 239-7700;
FAX 239-7605
*This comfortable all-suiter, with its own swimming pool and children's playground on 55 landscaped acres, is a short shuttle-bus ride from all area attractions including Disney World; guests also have free use of the health club, 18-hole championship golf course and all other facilities at Marriott's Orlando World Center Resort, next door.*

**Sheraton World Resort**    819R (30S)

| 16 | 17 | 16 | 17 | $109 |
|---|---|---|---|---|

10100 Int'l Dr.; (800) 327-0363; (407) 352-1100; FAX 352-3679
*M – This sprawling, lushly landscaped hotel is more suited than many to the Florida landscape, and while it "needs work", fans say the "great location for sightseeing", "spacious grounds", "nice pool" and "warm staff" make this a "good family hotel"; foes simply note it's "showing its age."*

**Sonesta Villa Resort***    369S

| 23 | 20 | 19 | 19 | $155 |
|---|---|---|---|---|

10000 Turkey Lake Rd.; (800) 766-3782; (407) 352-8051; FAX 345-5384
*U – "Ideal for family vacations", this unusual "village of suites" (actually a series of one- and two-story villas) north of Disney but near Universal Studios strikes our surveyors as a "good hideaway" on a "beautiful setting" of 300 lakefront acres; a few say it's been "run ragged" and is "out too far", but for most people the "casita idea is great."*

**Stouffer Orlando Resort**    780R (62S)

| 22 | 21 | 21 | 22 | $139 |
|---|---|---|---|---|

6677 Sea Harbor Dr.; (800) 468-3571; (407) 351-5555; FAX 351-9991
*U – It's hard to be humble when you have an "incredible" atrium "lobby-as-a-playground" that "takes your breath away"; guests staying at this hotel on Sea World's shoreline heap most praise on the neck-craning atrium but also save raves for a staff "that's super to deal with", the fine dining at Atlantis and Haifeng, and the "large", comfortable rooms.*

**Walt Disney World Dolphin**    1510R (322S)

| 20 | 21 | 18 | 21 | $176 |
|---|---|---|---|---|

1500 Epcot Resorts Blvd., Lake Buena Vista; (800) 227-1500; (407) 934-4000;
FAX 934-4879
*M – If this "whimsically designed" resort/convention hotel is like "living in a cartoon" and an "initial shock", at least it "works well", as strong ratings show; some guests are obsessed with the eclectic decor, which draws comments varying from "art deco chic" and "fantasyland" to "tacky" and "causes seasickness"; most praise that "great Disney service", convenience to EPCOT and the unusual man-made–lagoon pool area; "average" restaurants get less applause.*

| R | S | D | P | $ |

**Walt Disney World Swan**   758R (64S)   | 21 | 21 | 20 | 23 | $182 |
1200 Epcot Resorts Blvd., Lake Buena Vista; (800) 248-SWAN; (407) 934-3000;
FAX 934-4499
*M – Pick your description for this bookend resort, across the lagoon from
the Dolphin and also designed by Michael Graves: "gaudy" or "fantastic",
"spectacularly imaginative" or "in poor taste"; it's only slightly "more
subdued" than its neighbor but gets higher marks for its "pretty rooms" and
"gracious service"; Palio is a "surprisingly decent" Italian restaurant, and
solid scores overall prove that this Swan's no dive.*

## ●OTHER HOTEL-CHAIN CHOICES
*You will find one or more additional locations of the following hotel chains
in the Orlando area: Courtyard by Marriott, Days Inn, Doubletree, Embassy
Suites, Hampton Inn, Hilton, Holiday Inn, Howard Johnson, Hyatt, La Quinta
Inns, Radisson, Ramada and Super 8; for reservations or information, see
the toll-free 800 phone listings on page 16.*

# PALM SPRINGS*†

## TOP HOTELS
### (In order of rating)

**BEST OVERALL**

25 – Ritz-Carlton, Rancho Mirage
23 – Westin Mission Hills
     La Quinta
     Stouffer Esmeralda
     Marriott's Desert Springs
     Hyatt Grand Champions

**BEST VALUES**

Palm Springs Riviera
Wyndham Palm Springs
Palm Springs Hilton
Hyatt Regency Suites
Stouffer Esmeralda
Doubletree Desert Princess

\*      \*      \*

**Best Rooms**

26 – Ritz-Carlton, Rancho Mirage
24 – Hyatt Grand Champions
     La Quinta
23 – Stouffer Esmeralda
     Westin Mission Hills
     Marriott's Desert Springs

**Best Dining**

24 – Ritz-Carlton, Rancho Mirage
22 – Stouffer Esmeralda
21 – Marriott's Desert Springs
     Westin Mission Hills
     La Quinta
     Hyatt Grand Champions

**Best Service**

26 – Ritz-Carlton, Rancho Mirage
24 – Westin Mission Hills
23 – La Quinta
     Stouffer Esmeralda
22 – Hyatt Grand Champions
     Marriott's Desert Springs

**Best Public Facilities**

25 – Ritz-Carlton, Rancho Mirage
     Marriott's Desert Springs
24 – Stouffer Esmeralda
     La Quinta
     Hyatt Grand Champions
23 – Westin Mission Hills

---

*See also: California Resorts.
†For restaurants, see *Zagat Los Angeles/So. California Restaurant Survey*.

## PALM SPRINGS HOTELS

| R | S | D | P | $ |
|---|---|---|---|---|

**Autry Resort Hotel &**        | 15 | 15 | 13 | 15 | $144 |
**Tennis Club, The\***   184R (12S)
4200 E. Palm Canyon Dr.; (800) 443-6328; (619) 328-1171; FAX 324-7280
*M – Though completely revamped in 1991, this tennis resort located some distance out of town still fails to impress some of our surveyors; fans say it's "cowboy heaven in the desert", but grumblers complain that it's a "fancy motel – so what?"; full of "old-world, old-money, old people."*

**Doubletree Resort Palm Springs**  289R (15S)  | 20 | 18 | 16 | 19 | $143 |
67-967 Vista Chino, Cathedral City; (800) 637-0577; (619) 322-7000;
FAX 322-6853
*U – "One of the great deals of the desert", this otherwise "very comfortable" chain hotel has one problem: the "wind is unbelievable", meaning that golfers and tennis players can "get sandblasted"; the good news is that this Doubletree is set "away from busy Palm Springs", with "beautiful grounds", "terrific golf" and "nice brunch on Sundays."*

**HYATT GRAND CHAMPIONS RESORT**  336S  | 24 | 22 | 21 | 24 | $184 |
44-600 Indian Wells Lane, Indian Wells; (800) 233-1234; (619) 341-1000;
FAX 568-2236
*U – "Great golf and tennis" are among the many appealing aspects of this "very elegant", "spectacular" modern resort hotel, which boasts "one of the best golf courses in America" and a pro-tour stadium that makes it "a tennis player's paradise"; the ingenious "bi-level rooms" are "spacious and well decorated", turning this off-the-beaten-path hotel into "the ultimate Hyatt."*

**Hyatt Regency Suites Palm Springs**  192S  | 21 | 19 | 18 | 20 | $144 |
285 N. Palm Canyon Dr.; (800) 233-1234; (619) 322-9000; FAX 325-4027
*M – This centrally located facility is "one of the best suite hotels around", a modernist structure right in the middle of town on busy Palm Canyon Drive, where "you can walk everywhere", lounge by the secluded pool in the rear of the hotel, or enjoy the "state-of-the-art health club"; it's "convenient" and "pleasant", but the one negative, Downtown traffic, may make this "noisy."*

**LA QUINTA HOTEL**        | 24 | 23 | 21 | 24 | $203 |
**GOLF & TENNIS RESORT**  640R (68S)
49-499 Eisenhower Dr., La Quinta; (800) 854-1271; (619) 564-4111;
FAX 564-7656
*U – "Very special", "very romantic", "very peaceful" golf and tennis resort at the east of the Valley, a half hour from Palm Springs, dating back to days when the stars from Hollywood's Golden Age came here for liaisons dangereuse, and to write screenplays in the secluded cottages; for many, the "beautiful" grounds and gardens make this "the best resort in Palm Springs"; a "fireplace in every room" and "swimming pools also help."*

## MARRIOTT'S DESERT SPRINGS     | 23 | 22 | 21 | 25 | $182 |
**RESORT & SPA**   895R (51S)
74-855 Country Club Dr., Palm Desert; (800) 228-9290; (619) 341-2211;
FAX 341-1730
*M – "The next boat to your room leaves in 10 minutes" at this "Disneyland
in the desert" located half an hour outside Palm Springs, complete with a
"lagoon in the lobby" and small ferry boats that carry you from the indoor
atrium to the swimming pool and golf course; it's a "terrific family spot" with
"something for everybody" and all the "bells and whistles" you could ask for.*


### Marriott's Rancho Las Palmas     | 21 | 21 | 20 | 22 | $167 |
**Resort & Country Club**   450R (25S)
41000 Bob Hope Dr., Rancho Mirage; (800) I LUV SUN; (619) 568-2727;
FAX 568-5848
*M – "Not as showy as its sister", Marriott Desert Springs, this "comfortable",
"relaxed" "convention hotel" is nonetheless "delightful", with "beautiful
grounds", "nice public areas" and "great golf and pool", but rooms that a
few of our surveyors think "could be in a motel"; overall, "easy to stay at."*


### Palm Springs Hilton Resort   260R (71S)   | 20 | 18 | 18 | 19 | $126 |
400 E. Tahquitz-Canyon Way; (800) 522-6900; (619) 320-6868; FAX 323-2755
*M – A "very convenient" location makes this Downtown resort one of the
"best places" for weekend shopping and tanning in the heart of town; some
say its "rooms are magnificently luxurious" and cite "great public rooms"
and a "large pool"; others call it "basic", "neat" and "relaxed."*


### Palm Springs Marquis     | 20 | 17 | 16 | 17 | $155 |
**Hotel & Villas**   264R (101S)
150 S. Indian Canyon Dr.; (800) 223-1050; (619) 322-2121; FAX 322-2380
*M – All of Palm Springs is within walking distance of this "lovely Intown
hotel", making it "a good location" for a meeting at the nearby convention
center; the "renovation in progress" should address the only complaint:
"needs a face-lift."*


### Palm Springs Riviera Resort &     | 18 | 18 | 17 | 17 | $114 |
**Racquet Club**   480R (36S)
(fka Radisson Palm Springs)
1600 N. Indian Canyon Dr.; (800) 333-3333; (619) 327-8311; FAX 327-4323
*U – All the normal amenities and comforts plus complete facilities for
"small conventions" and good meeting rooms explain why many consider
booking this functional spot; it has tennis, a health club and a "beautiful golf
course" nearby, and is reasonably priced for the area.*

**Racquet Club Resort of**    | 18 | 17 | 16 | 19 | $143 |
**Palm Springs**    150R (125S)
2743 N. Indian Canyon Dr.; (800) 367-0946; (619) 325-1281; FAX 325-3429
*M – This historic hangout in a quiet location at the out-of-the-way
north end of Palm Springs has "seen better days", according to our
surveyors; however, this taste of "old-time Palm Springs" still attracts a
well-heeled clientele who enjoy it for the sake of nostalgia – and for the
private tennis club, reasonably priced villas (some with private pools)
and other amenities.*

**RITZ-CARLTON,**    | 26 | 26 | 24 | 25 | $220 |
**RANCHO MIRAGE**    240R (21S)
68-900 Frank Sinatra Dr., Rancho Mirage; (800) 241-3333; (619) 321-8282;
FAX 321-8928
*M – "Versailles in the desert", a "best of everything" "grande luxe" hotel
where you'll "think you've gone to heaven"; though for some it's "far too
formal for fun in the sun", this French chateau "on top of a hill" overlooking
the Coachella Valley, where bighorn sheep come down to graze in the
evening, is "first class from top to bottom"; expect all the usual Ritz
amenities, including "spectacular rooms", "elegant service", a fine French
restaurant (food rating, 24) and a full spa.*

**Shadow Mountain Resort**    112R (52S)    | 18 | 18 | 14 | 18 | $146 |
45750 San Luis Rey, Palm Desert; (800) 472-3713; (619) 346-6123;
FAX 346-6518
*M – The freshly renovated SW-style resort offers a "good value" and "lots
and lots of tennis" (the on-site Desert Tennis Academy features no less
than 16 courts – four of them lighted) plus complete exercise and
health-club facilities with swimming and therapy pools; in other ways, the
accommodations and dining are fairly "average."*

**Spa Hotel & Mineral Springs**    230R (20S)    | 17 | 18 | 15 | 19 | $145 |
100 N. Indian Canyon Dr.; (800) 854-1279; (619) 325-1461; FAX 325-3344
*M – This "aging grande dame" with a " '50s feel", just off the main
intersection in PS, is one of the only facilities in town that actually
offers water from the springs, along with "complimentary spa privileges"
that are "one of the last great luxuries" in the world – "and affordable
too"; otherwise, the rooms are "functional" and the setting is "nothing
unusual" – a bit "tacky" but a "really nice" place to go for the "best
massage around."*

## PALM SPRINGS HOTELS  | R | S | D | P | $ |

**STOUFFER ESMERALDA**  560R (44S)  | 23 | 23 | 22 | 24 | $175 |
44-400 Indian Wells Lane, Indian Wells; (800) 468-3571; (619) 773-4444;
FAX 346-9308
*M – "Simply beautiful" neighbor of Grand Champions at the swiftly
expanding east end of the Valley, this "elephantine" golf resort is "great
for sun and pool fans too"; this "impressive" place is very "new and
modern", with "magnificent architecture" and a "great pool" with a "kid's
beach"; the Mediterranean restaurant, Sirocco (food rating, 24), is both
"romantic" and "refined."*

**Two Bunch Palms Resort & Spa**  44S  | – | – | – | – | E |
67-425 Two Bunch Palms Trail, Desert Hot Springs; (800) 472-4334;
(602) 329-8791; FAX 329-1874
*It helps to be a player (in fact the movie of that name was set here), but
even if you're not Tim Robbins, you can be slathered with recuperative
mud and soothed with aromatherapy in the still desert heat of this
oh-so-cool spa/oasis; bungalows, pools, privacy and practically nothing
to do make this the quintessential place to get away from doing lunch.*

**Westin Mission Hills Resort, The**  512R (40S)  | 23 | 24 | 21 | 23 | $182 |
Dinah Shore & Bob Hope Drives, Rancho Mirage; (800) 228-3000;
(619) 328-5955; FAX 321-2955
*U – The "best new resort in Palm Springs" "needs aging" to make it "the
best resort in the area"; it comes complete with "beautiful" Moroccan decor,
a "peaceful setting" and a convenient 18-hole course; everything is "first
rate", including the "wonderful food" and "great staff."*

**Wyndham Palm Springs**  410R (158S)  | 20 | 19 | 16 | 20 | $126 |
888 E. Tahquitz-Canyon Way; (800) 872-4335; (619) 322-6000; FAX 322-5351
*M – Connected to the convention center, this "good facility" has a "fun"
"party atmosphere", "excellent conference facilities" and "large", "clean"
rooms, plus a "great pool" and a "super location"; overall, "perfectly
friendly", but "long corridors make you think you're walking to La Quinta."*

## ●OTHER HOTEL-CHAIN CHOICES
*You will find one or more additional locations of the following hotel chains
in the Palm Springs area: Days Inn, Embassy Suites, Hampton Inn, Hilton,
Holiday Inn, Ramada, Super 8 and Travelodge/Viscount; for reservations
or information, see the toll-free 800 phone listings on page 16.*

# PHILADELPHIA†

## TOP HOTELS
## (In order of rating)

### BEST OVERALL

26 – Four Seasons
25 – Ritz-Carlton
24 – Rittenhouse
23 – Hotel Atop the Bellevue
22 – Omni Independence Park
20 – Sheraton Society Hill
18 – Warwick Hotel
    Latham Hotel

### BEST VALUES

Hyatt Cherry Hill
Omni Independence Park
Sheraton Society Hill
Ritz-Carlton
Latham Hotel
Warwick Hotel
Philadelphia Hilton & Towers
Adam's Mark Philadelphia

\*    \*    \*

### Best Rooms

26 – Four Seasons
    Ritz-Carlton
25 – Rittenhouse
23 – Hotel Atop the Bellevue
    Omni Independence Park
21 – Sheraton Society Hill
19 – Latham Hotel
18 – Warwick Hotel

### Best Dining

26 – Four Seasons
25 – Ritz-Carlton
24 – Rittenhouse
22 – Hotel Atop the Bellevue
21 – Omni Independence Park
18 – Sheraton Society Hill
17 – Warwick Hotel
    Latham Hotel

### Best Service

26 – Ritz-Carlton
    Four Seasons
24 – Rittenhouse
22 – Hotel Atop the Bellevue
    Omni Independence Park
20 – Sheraton Society Hill
    Warwick Hotel
19 – Latham Hotel

### Best Public Facilities

25 – Four Seasons
    Ritz-Carlton
24 – Rittenhouse
23 – Hotel Atop the Bellevue
22 – Omni Independence Park
20 – Sheraton Society Hill
17 – Warwick Hotel
    Latham Hotel

†For restaurants, see *Zagat Philadelphia Restaurant Survey.*

**Adam's Mark Philadelphia**   590R (57S)   | 16 | 16 | 16 | 15 | $115 |
City Ave. & Monument Rd.; (800) 444-2326; (215) 581-5000; FAX 581-5069
*M – The best thing about this "'70s convention hotel" is its "good location as a
central meeting place"; while some praise its "nice rooms and staff" and
"happy-hour buffet", most view it as a "run-of-the-mill commercial" hotel.*

**Barclay Hotel, The***   240R (60S)   | 16 | 17 | 16 | 15 | $136 |
237 S. 18th St.; (800) 421-6662; (215) 545-0300; FAX 545-2896
*M – "Once the grand old lady in Philadelphia", this venerable hotel
overlooking Rittenhouse Square may be "a bit worn" but still has a
"sophisticated", "very comfortable feeling" and "friendly and professional"
service; make sure your room faces the square.*

**Chestnut Hill Hotel***   28R (3S)   | 17 | 18 | 18 | 15 | $105 |
8229 Germantown Ave.; (800) 628-9744; (215) 242-5909; FAX 242-8778
*M – "A little cranky but interesting" sums up the sentiment on this turn-
of-the-century inn in Philadelphia's handsome Chestnut Hill section (25
minutes from Center City); you can't please everyone: one surveyor's
"lots of atmosphere" is another's "seedy."*

**FOUR SEASONS HOTEL**   | 26 | 26 | 26 | 25 | $191 |
**PHILADELPHIA**   371R (99S)
1 Logan Sq., N. 18th St. & Benjamin Franklin Pkwy.; (800) 332-3442;
(215) 963-1500; FAX 963-9506
*U – "The standard by which all others are measured" is this "exceptionally
well run" hotel on "beautiful" Logan Circle; from the "outstanding" Eclectic
food at The Fountain restaurant (food rating, 28) to the "superb" service
and ne plus ultra health club, everything adds up to make this "one of the
best in the U.S.A.", a place that's "always perfect, time after time", where
you "can't miss if you want to impress your honey or your client."*

**Hotel Atop the Bellevue**   170R (13S)   | 23 | 22 | 22 | 23 | $173 |
1415 Chancellor Court; (800) 221-0833; (215) 893-1776; FAX 893-9868
*U – The "elegant grand dame of Philadelphia" offers "fabulous" ambiance
at what is considered "one of the few renovations of a grand historic
property that actually turned out better than the original"; most agree that
it's "a great hotel by any standard", giving it extra points for the "excellent"
Founders restaurant (food rating, 20) and the astonishingly beautiful
Barrymore Room (food rating, 19), where "the most perfect tea" is served.*

## PHILADELPHIA HOTELS

| R | S | D | P | $ |

**Hyatt Cherry Hill**   409R (16S)       | 16 | 16 | 16 | 16 | $105 |
2349 W. Marlton Pike, Cherry Hill, NJ; (800) 233-1234; (609) 662-1234;
FAX 662-3676
*M – "Convenient" is the common refrain about this suburban New Jersey
high rise near the Garden State Race Track, which draws a lot of
businesspeople; though it's reliable and affordable, some surveyors say
the "rooms need renovating" and the "just-folks atmosphere" is somewhere
between "casually nice" and "bland."*

**Independence Park Inn***   36R       | 19 | 20 | 16 | 19 | $120 |
235 Chestnut St.; (800) 624-2988; (215) 922-4443; FAX 922-4487
*U – Located in the oldest part of Philadelphia (Society Hill), within three
blocks of most of the city's historic tourist attractions, this "small but
convenient and charming" inn, built in 1856 and renovated in 1988, gets
high marks for its "historic feel", "perfect location" and "good staff"; it's
small, so reserve ahead – or stop by for tea in the afternoon.*

**Latham Hotel, The**   139R (2S)       | 19 | 19 | 17 | 17 | $130 |
135 S. 17th St.; (800) LATHAM-1; (215) 563-7474; FAX 563-4034
*M – Fans of this "very pleasant", "European-style" "gem of a small hotel"
praise its "elegance and charm", "friendly service" and "central location"
near Rittenhouse Square; outvoted critics say it "lost its charm."*

**Omni Hotel at Independence Park**   149R (7S)   | 23 | 22 | 21 | 22 | $149 |
401 Chestnut St.; (800) THE-OMNI; (215) 925-0000; FAX 925-1263
*U – "Lovely public areas", "beautiful rooms", "quality service" and a "superb
Colonial setting" (one block from Independence Hall and the Liberty Bell)
make this recent addition to Philadelphia's hotel scene a happening
choice; a few dissenters say it's "overpriced for the area" and grumble
about glitches, but most of our travelers call this "luxury hotel" a "gem."*

**Penn's View Inn***   28R (1S)       | 21 | 21 | 23 | 19 | $131 |
Front & Market Sts.; (800) 331-7634; (215) 922-7600; FAX 922-7642
*U – Those few who know it have high praise for this "intimate" and
"charming" new luxury pensione carved from a handsomely restored old
(1828) building in the historic Old City area; it's close to Penn's Landing as
well as Independence Park, and its Northern Italian restaurant, Ristorante
Panorama (food rating, 20), has a spectacular wine bar that's a popular
local hangout.*

**Penn Tower Hotel**   207R (7S)          | 13 | 12 | 11 | 11 | $114 |
Civic Center Blvd. at 34th St.; (800) 356-PENN; (215) 387-8333; FAX 386-8306
*M – Although this high rise has a "great location" vis à vis the Penn
campus and hospital (which owns it), that doesn't save it from being
"nothing spectacular" and merely "functional", with quarters that "need
sprucing up" and front desk staff that's "slow"; still, it's "where you'll find all
the parents."*

**Philadelphia Hilton & Towers**   428R (8S)          | 17 | 17 | 16 | 16 | $122 |
(fka Hershey Philadelphia Hotel)
Broad & Locust Sts.; (800) HILTONS; (215) 893-1600; FAX 893-1663
*M – Its location across from the Academy of Music is one of this "standard
convention" hotel's main attractions; a recent renovation means that
complaints about the "'70s" wallpaper no longer apply; while most like the
"unusual" sawtooth-shaped rooms overlooking Broad Street, some find the
public areas rather "cramped."*

**RITTENHOUSE, THE**   98R (11S)          | 25 | 24 | 24 | 24 | $179 |
210 W. Rittenhouse Square; (800) 635-1042; (215) 546-9000; FAX 546-9858
*U – A "real oasis in a busy city", this high-rise "class act" overlooking
Rittenhouse Square has "gorgeous public areas", "outstanding" service
and "spacious" rooms; though a few say the modern architecture is too
"severe" for the neighborhood, the two restaurants, Treetops (an upscale
bistro – food rating, 21) and Restaurant 210 (upscale gourmet – food
rating, 25), offer "exceptional food" and "lovely" views.*

**RITZ-CARLTON, PHILADELPHIA**   290R (17S)   | 26 | 26 | 25 | 25 | $183 |
17th & Chestnut Sts.; (800) 241-3333; (215) 563-1600; FAX 564-9559
*U – "Sumptuous in every respect", this "dignified" and luxurious newcomer,
located at the tony Liberty Place complex a few blocks west of City Hall,
has been wowing surveyors with its "top-notch restaurants" – The Dining
Room (food rating, 23) and Grill Room (22) – elegant rooms (especially on
the "club floor") and public facilities, and "employees who've been to charm
school" – not to mention "excellent shopping steps from your room"; for "old-
world ambiance in an urban setting, it's hard to beat this "new Philly favorite."*

**Sheraton Society Hill**   365R (17S)          | 21 | 20 | 18 | 20 | $133 |
1 Dock St.; (800) 325-3535; (215) 238-6000; FAX 922-2709
*U – "Even W.C. Fields would rather be happy" at this handsome hotel in
Society Hill, thanks to "nicely furnished rooms", "outstanding service" and
"top-notch" exercise facilities (including a "wonderful" pool), as well as its
convenience to Independence National Park, South Street, Penn's Landing
and several good movie theaters; though a few complain of "noisy" rooms,
most surveyors consider it a "pleasant, quiet retreat" from Center City.*

**PHILADELPHIA HOTELS**                               | R | S | D | P | $ |

**Sheraton University City**   377R (13S)       | 13 | 13 | 11 | 12 | $111 |
36th & Chestnut Sts.; (800) 325-3535; (215) 387-8000; FAX 387-7920
*U – Despite its convenience to Penn and Drexel, most say "Sheraton should be embarrassed to have its name" on this "shabby" and "decrepit" outpost in University City – use "only if all else is booked"; although a few call it a "good value", most say "they don't even seem to try."*

**Society Hill Hotel***   12R (2S)       | 17 | 17 | 18 | 14 | $101 |
301 Chestnut St.; (215) 925-1919; FAX 925-3780
*M – This "tiny", "funky but fun" low-cost hostelry near Independence National Park is "charming" and "European" to some, a little "seedy" to others; even its fans say "don't try to sleep", since the rooms are right over the hotel's popular and "noisy" bar, but then again it's a fine place for a nightcap.*

**Warwick Hotel**   190R (10S)       | 18 | 20 | 17 | 17 | $132 |
17th & Locust Sts.; (800) 523-4210; (215) 735-6000; FAX 790-7766
*M – The verdict is split on this "Philadelphia staple" with a "great location" near Rittenhouse Square; some praise its "quiet elegance" (the lobby was updated recently), "good restaurants" and "personal service"; a lesser number say it's "a little run-down" and complain about the "wake-up call at 5 AM by garbage trucks"; the Capriccio cafe is popular for cappuccino and muffins.*

**Wyndham Franklin Plaza Hotel**   758R (36S)   | 16 | 16 | 15 | 16 | $122 |
17th & Vine Sts.; (800) 822-4200; (215) 448-2000; FAX 448-2864
*M – Expect "lots of conventions and meetings" in this "commercial but pleasant" hotel (the city's largest) off the Benjamin Franklin Parkway; critics complain of "dirty old rooms" and "sterility", but "large rooms for a low price" make this popular with middle-management types; service gets mixed comments, too, from "friendly" to "confused."*

● **OTHER HOTEL-CHAIN CHOICES**
*You will find one or more additional locations of the following hotel chains in the Philadelphia area: Days Inn, Doubletree, Embassy Suites, Guest Quarters, Hampton Inn, Hilton, Holiday Inn, Howard Johnson, Marriott, Radisson, Ramada and Travelodge/Viscount; for reservations or information, see the toll-free 800 phone listings on page 16.*

# PHOENIX/SCOTTSDALE*†

## TOP HOTELS
### (In order of rating)

### BEST OVERALL
26 – Phoenician
25 – Ritz-Carlton
   Scottsdale Princess
24 – Hyatt Regency Scottsdale
   Arizona Biltmore
22 – John Gardiner's
   Marriott's Camelback
   Stouffer Cottonwoods

### BEST VALUES
Crown Sterling Suites
Crescent Hotel
Wyndham Paradise Valley
Scottsdale Plaza
Buttes
Marriott Suites Scottsdale
Red Lion La Posada
Orange Tree Resort

\*    \*    \*

### Best Rooms
26 – Phoenician
   Scottsdale Princess
25 – Ritz-Carlton
24 – Orange Tree
   Stouffer Cottonwoods
23 – John Gardiner's
   Arizona Biltmore
   Hyatt Regency Scottsdale

### Best Dining
25 – Ritz-Carlton
24 – Phoenician
   Scottsdale Princess
23 – Arizona Biltmore
   – Hyatt Regency Scottsdale
22 – Marriott's Camelback
21 – John Gardiner's
20 – Registry

### Best Service
26 – Ritz-Carlton
25 – Phoenician
24 – Scottsdale Princess
   Arizona Biltmore
   Hyatt Regency Scottsdale
23 – John Gardiner's
   Stouffer Cottonwoods
22 – Marriott's Camelback

### Best Public Facilities
27 – Phoenician
26 – Hyatt Regency Scottsdale
   Scottsdale Princess
   Arizona Biltmore
25 – Ritz-Carlton
23 – Scottsdale Plaza
   Marriott's Camelback
22 – Buttes

---

\*See also: Arizona Resorts.
†For restaurants, see *Zagat Southwest Restaurant Survey*.

| R | S | D | P | $ |

## ARIZONA BILTMORE   502R (49S)   | 23 | 24 | 23 | 26 | $197 |
24th St. & Missouri Ave., Phoenix; (800) 950-0086; (602) 955-6600;
FAX 954-2571

*M – Influenced by Frank Lloyd Wright, this "classic resort in a lovely setting" is architecturally "spectacular", with grounds that are equally impressive – be sure to stop and "smell the flowers as you walk around"; though rooms can be "fabulous or meager", most guests are delighted by the aura of "timeless beauty", not to mention "great facilities", "wonderful" food and wine at Gold Room Grille (food rating, 22) and Orangerie (25), and a "spirit of relaxation."*


## Buttes, The   350R (13S)   | 22 | 21 | 20 | 22 | $138 |
(fka Westcourt in the Buttes)
2000 Westcourt Way, Tempe; (800) 843-1986; (602) 225-9000; FAX 431-8433

*U – "A wonderful business resort that is convenient to the airport yet feels far from it all", thanks to a "magnificent pool", "beautiful views" and a "natural environment" that includes a whirlpool carved out of the rocks; this "almost totally self-contained spot" also features three restaurants (special praise for the Top of the Rock), good meeting facilities and public areas, and "excellent service."*


## Camelview Resort   200R (17S)   | 21 | 21 | 20 | 21 | $159 |
(fka Camelview – A Radisson Resort)
7601 E. Indian Bend Rd., Scottsdale; (800) 852-5205; (602) 991-2400;
FAX 998-2261

*U – Despite solid ratings, surveyor comments indicate that this once-preeminent Scottsdale resort has slipped; still, it's no slouch, and nobody can fault the "beautiful grounds"; here's hoping that the complete renovation scheduled for 1993 helps restore this place to its former stature.*


## Crescent Hotel, The   342R (12S)   | 21 | 21 | 19 | 21 | $122 |
2620 W. Dunlap Ave., Phoenix; (800) 423-4126; (602) 943-8200; FAX 371-2856

*U – Reviewers are enthusiastic about this "good business hotel" that "fills a gap on the Westside"; it's judged "an extraordinary value", with "pleasant and clean" rooms, and service that's "sincere and personable"; facilities include a well-equipped health club, lighted tennis courts and the respectable Continental-Southwestern cuisine of Charlie's restaurant.*

### Crown Sterling Suites   232S       | 21 | 18 | 14 | 19 | $106 |
(fka Embassy Suites – Biltmore)
2630 E. Camelback Rd., Phoenix; (800) 433-4600; (602) 955-3992;
FAX 224-9061
*U – "If only all hotels had this suite layout with oversize rooms", not to
mention complimentary breakfast and evening cocktails; the "convenient"
Midtown location on Camelback strip, "interesting lobby with fish ponds
throughout" and "good value" also receive praise; as ratings show, dining is
the weak link, but for conventional American fare it's ok too.*

### Fountains Suite Hotel   316S       | – | – | – | – | ⏐ |
2577 W. Greenway Rd., Phoenix; (800) 527-7715; (602) 375-1777;
FAX 375-1777 x5555
*The suite concept with complimentary breakfast and cocktails goes over
big with our reviewers; they also like this Westsider's "lovely setting" and
"wonderful amenities", though some complain that the hotel is "getting
shabby"; it's cheap enough so no one really gets sore.*

### Hyatt Regency Phoenix   711R (44S)       | 18 | 18 | 17 | 17 | $125 |
122 N. Second St., Phoenix; (800) 233-1234; (602) 252-1234; FAX 252-9472
*M – Some of our critics say this Downtown high rise is "just another Hyatt,
from the revolving restaurant on down" – strictly "for those who would
rather be in Cleveland"; fans of its chain-style dependability laud the
"convenient location", "reasonable" prices and "good service", and report
that a recent redo has brought the rooms up to date.*

### HYATT REGENCY SCOTTSDALE   493R (31S) | 23 | 24 | 23 | 26 | $186 |
7500 E. Doubletree Ranch Rd., Scottsdale; (800) 233-1234;
(602) 991-3388; FAX 483-5550
*U – In contrast to its Intown sibling, this is "not like a Hyatt at all"; it's "a
vacationer's paradise" in a "beautiful setting" with "the best pool in the
world" (cascading water, water slides – the works), not to mention an
excellent restaurant, The Golden Swan (food rating, 26), "professional
service" and all the activities you could hope for; fans call it "Hyatt's best
U.S. property, hands down."*

### John Gardiner's Tennis Ranch   96R (45S)       | 23 | 23 | 21 | 22 | $240 |
5700 E. McDonald Dr., Scottsdale; (800) 245-2051; (602) 948-2100;
FAX 483-7314
*U – This tennis-player's "mecca" offers world-famous clinics along with
"beautiful" grounds, "breathtaking views" and "down-home comfort" in
"nice, rustic accommodations"; a few say the "courts are the thing", with
everything else "second-seeded", but they must have been hit in the head
with a hard serve.*

| R | S | D | P | $ |
|---|---|---|---|---|

### Lexington Hotel & City Square

| – | – | – | – | I |
|---|---|---|---|---|

**Sports Club** 167R (42S) (fka La Mancha Resort Hotel)
100 W. Clarendon Ave., Phoenix; (800) 272-2439; (602) 279-9811; FAX 631-9351
*Few raters know of this '60s-era Downtown high rise, offering extensive athletic facilities including a heated pool, regulation basketball courts, 12 racquetball courts, weight-training equipment and aerobics; it's a good value, especially off-season, and is currently undergoing a complete remodeling.*

### Marriott's Camelback Inn Resort 423R (23S)

| 22 | 22 | 21 | 23 | $174 |
|----|----|----|----|------|

5402 E. Lincoln Dr., Scottsdale; (800) 24-CAMEL; (602) 948-1700; FAX 951-2152
*M – "About as good as they come" say our surveyors; the "desert surroundings are awesome" and food and service are deemed "wonderful", making it "great for a veg-out vacation", but some complain "the resort seems tired" and "rooms need upgrading."*

### Marriott's Mountain Shadows

| 20 | 21 | 19 | 20 | $163 |
|----|----|----|----|------|

**Resort & Golf Club** 338R (38S)
5641 E. Lincoln Dr., Scottsdale; (800) 228-9290; (602) 948-7111; FAX 998-4231
*U – A "classic" old favorite tucked into "beautiful Camelback Mountain"; the "great golf", "lovely grounds and pool" and "large rooms" come in for frequent mentions, but some note that it's kind of "commercial" and "has seen better days"; N.B. a late '92 renovation should take care of at least the latter problem.*

### Marriott Suites Scottsdale 251S

| 22 | 21 | 17 | 19 | $136 |
|----|----|----|----|------|

7325 E. Third Ave., Scottsdale; (800) 228-9290; (602) 945-1550;
FAX 945-2005
*U – Another suite concept located in Downtown Scottsdale, catering primarily to businessfolk; those who've stayed here say it's "quiet", "clean" and a "great value" "in the midst of all the restaurants, boutiques and galleries."*

### Omni Adams Hotel* 534R (86S)

| 16 | 15 | 15 | 14 | $121 |
|----|----|----|----|------|

(fka Sheraton Phoenix)
111 N. Central Ave., Phoenix; (800) 359-7253; (602) 257-1525; FAX 253-9755
*U – "A very convenient location" and rooms that are a "good value" make this Downtown high rise a "comfortable", if "uneventful", favorite for business travelers; the lobby is "bland" – perhaps the renovation now in the works will fix that.*

**Orange Tree Golf & Conference Resort** 160S | 24 | 22 | 20 | 22 | $153 |
10601 N. 56th St., Scottsdale; (800) 228-0386; (602) 948-6100; FAX 483-6074
*U – An "excellent" small all-suites hotel that gets kudos for being "clean and quiet" and loaded with facilities, including 16 tennis courts and an 18-hole PGA golf course; respondents call the rooms "wonderful", with special mention for the "bathrooms with two-person whirlpool tubs."*

**PHOENICIAN, THE** 580R (31S) | 26 | 25 | 24 | 27 | $207 |
6000 E. Camelback Rd., Scottsdale; (800) 888-8234; (602) 941-8200; FAX 947-4311
*U – One of the country's great hotel/resorts is "everything you've heard it is"; despite notoriety growing out of its involvement with the Lincoln Savings Bank debacle, the hotel hasn't missed a beat; our reviewers report it has "superior rooms", "a beautiful setting", a "great restaurant" (Mary Elaine's – food rating, 26), a "wonderful golf course" and "a pool that is a little bit of paradise", in short, "the best money can buy."*

**Pointe Hilton Resort at** | 21 | 20 | 19 | 22 | $146 |
**South Mountain, The** 638S (fka Pointe at South Mountain, The)
7777 S. Pointe Pkwy., Phoenix; (800) 876-4683; (602) 438-9000; FAX 438-8450
*M – "Better than heaven" say fans of this ultra-full-service resort, recently taken over by Hilton; "exceptional grounds" and "family-oriented western comforts" include golf, racquetball, tennis, a "world-class" health club and four restaurants; though some call it a "tacky, baroque, junky palace", they're easily outshouted by fans who find it "first-rate."*

**Pointe Hilton Resort at** | 20 | 19 | 18 | 20 | $140 |
**Squaw Peak, The** 576S (fka Pointe at Squaw Peak)
7677 N. 16th St., Phoenix; (800) 528-0428; (602) 997-2626; FAX 997-2391
*M – Though some of our surveyors think this "Pointe has seen better days", most enjoy its SW style and say it's both "classy" and "fun", with "world-class ambiance and service"; they may have more company soon: under Hilton, all guest rooms and public facilities will be renovated in 1993.*

**Pointe Hilton Resort at** | 21 | 20 | 20 | 21 | $150 |
**Tapatio Cliffs, The** 585S (fka Pointe at Tapatio Cliffs)
11111 N. Seventh St., Phoenix; (800) 528-0428; (602) 866-7500; FAX 993-0276
*M – Some consider this "the best-looking and best-situated of the Pointes", with "a great location in the hills"; "nice facilities", good restaurants and "fine service" help make up for the fact that it may be "in need of refurbishing."*

| R | S | D | P | $ |

**Red Lion La Posada Resort**   264R (10S)   | 20 | 20 | 19 | 21 | $139 |
4949 E. Lincoln Dr., Scottsdale; (800) 547-8010; (602) 952-0420;
FAX 840-8516
*M – Our surveyors break ranks on this Spanish-style valley resort, long a favorite with locals; fans call it "paradise", with "good value", "extra-large rooms" and a "fine" location, but detractors say the place "caters to the bus-and-tour crowd and it shows" at this "step above Holiday Inn"; they reunite in praising the lagoon pool, largest in North America, with a "special rock waterfall" that's "worth the stay."*

**Regal McCormick Ranch\***   125R (54S)   | 20 | 20 | 19 | 21 | $135 |
(fka Inn at McCormick Ranch)
7401 N. Scottsdale Rd., Scottsdale; (800) 243-1332; (602) 948-5050;
FAX 948-9113
*U – This sprawling perennial is charmingly situated on a man-made lake, truly "an oasis in the desert" and a favorite place for an evening boat ride; its "great condo-rental program" is recommended over the regular rooms, which are mostly very good though some are described as "small and lack imagination."*

**Registry Resort of Scottsdale**   318R (35S)   | 21 | 21 | 20 | 21 | $164 |
7171 N. Scottsdale Rd., Scottsdale; (800) 247-9810; (602) 991-3800;
FAX 948-9843
*M – This "huge complex" (75 acres with 2 golf courses, 3 pools, 13 meeting rooms and 21 lighted tennis courts) is deemed "enjoyable" by many surveyors, who appreciate the "tremendous lobby", "wonderful restaurants" and "great bi-level suites"; some report it's a bit "run-down" and the staff needs "serious training", but they're outvoted.*

**RITZ-CARLTON, PHOENIX**   281R (14S)   | 25 | 26 | 25 | 25 | $177 |
2401 E. Camelback Rd., Phoenix; (800) 241-3333; (602) 468-0700;
FAX 957-6076
*U – "They will spoil you rotten" at this "terrific" "touch of civility in the Southwest", with "memorable food" at the Grill (food rating, 25) and The Restaurant (26), "super service", "wonderful rooms" and "lots of atmosphere", all in a convenient location on the tony Camelback strip; curmudgeons grouse that a "city hotel just doesn't work in a resort area" (it lacks sports facilities) and say they don't feel comfortable dressed casually in what feels like a formal London or NYC hotel.*

**Royal Palms Inn**   119R (34S)      | – | – | – | – | I |
5200 E. Camelback Rd., Phoenix; (800) 672-6011; (602) 840-3610; FAX 840-0233
*As the lack of response suggests, this inexpensive old-timer built in the
'40s is pretty much "past its prime"; it's got all the amenities, however,
including golf, tennis and grounds that are lush, overgrown and charming
(with a heart-shaped swimming pool, no less); weekend packages include
meals and sports, but don't be surprised if the rooms and public areas
leave a lot to be desired.*

**Scottsdale Conference Resort**   325R (24S)   | 19 | 21 | 20 | 20 | $156 |
7700 E. McCormick Pkwy., Scottsdale; (800) 528-0293; (602) 991-9000;
FAX 596-7422
*U – The big attraction here is a "very fine convention site with all the
amenities"; as a business facility, it's "top drawer", with "fantastic service"
and all kinds of activities; it's also well located, so "you can slip out and do
some shopping"; the only criticism is that the desert decor may be a little "drab."*

**Scottsdale Hilton Resort & Spa**   232R (45S)   | 17 | 17 | 16 | 17 | $131 |
6333 N. Scottsdale Rd., Scottsdale; (800) 528-3119; (602) 948-7750;
FAX 948-2232
*U – Yes, "the pool is wonderful" and it's near "excellent golf facilities", but
as a whole this older hotel "has seen better days"; however, management
has undertaken a complete 1992 renovation that should address qualms.*

**Scottsdale Plaza Resort, The**   404R (180S)   | 21 | 20 | 19 | 23 | $129 |
7200 N. Scottsdale Rd., Scottsdale; (800) 832-2025; (602) 948-5000;
FAX 998-5971
*M – The "spacious, well-kept grounds" and "good location" in the heart of
town get raves from most respondents, who also shower compliments on
the "stupendous" common areas; generally, the hotel does well across the
board, but a few critics complain of "mediocre" guest rooms at this "very
middle, middle resort."*

**SCOTTSDALE PRINCESS**   600R (75S)   | 26 | 24 | 24 | 26 | $191 |
7575 E. Princess Dr., Scottsdale; (800) 223-1818; (602) 585-4848; FAX 585-0086
*U – "Like being in a dream world" even when you're wide awake, this
"phenomenal resort" boasts "spectacular" rooms and "excellent facilities"
plus "incredible desert landscaping"; though there are some who point out
that the "rooms are a mile from the hotel and the hotel is miles from
civilization", why else would you go to an "oasis in the desert"?; its top-
notch restaurants are also worth noting: Grill at the TPC (food rating, 21),
La Hacienda (25) , and Marquesa (27).*

**Sheraton Mesa Hotel\*** 271R (18S)          | 14 | 14 | 11 | 13 | $99 |
(fka Ramada Renaissance)
200 N. Centennial Way, Mesa; (800) 456-6372; (602) 898-8300; FAX 964-9279
*U – This Downtown Mesa high rise is "adequate", if unexciting; the usual
amenities and very reasonable prices keep its business clientele coming
back; the East Valley location is handy to Tempe, home of ASU.*

**Sheraton San Marcos Golf Resort**          | 18 | 17 | 16 | 18 | $122 |
**& Conference Center\*** 295R (16S)
1 San Marcos Pl., Chandler; (800) 325-3535; (602) 963-6655; FAX 899-5441
*U – Offering "a bit of yesteryear", this "renewed" historic resort in Chandler
may be "out of the way", but the "great golf" and "accommodating service",
not to mention solid value, make it an ideal getaway.*

**Stouffer Cottonwoods Resort** 278R (106S)          | 24 | 23 | 19 | 22 | $154 |
6160 N. Scottsdale Rd., Scottsdale; (800) 468-3571; (602) 991-1414;
FAX 951-3350
*M – Our correspondents adore the "super rooms with lanai and hot tubs" at
this "romantic" central Scottsdale resort – "within walking distance of
shopping and dining" when the hearts and flowers wane; it's considered
"great for golfers, honeymooners or travelers who like well-appointed
spaces to live in away from home."*

**Sunburst Hotel &**          | 16 | 16 | 15 | 17 | $99 |
**Conference Center\*** 209R (9S)
4925 N. Scottsdale Rd., Scottsdale; (800) 528-7867; (602) 945-7666;
FAX 946-4056
*U – "Modest" is about the kindest thing our reviewers have to say about
this central Scottsdale old-timer; though the "lobby is light and airy" and
the location is "convenient", there's "much better nearby."*

**Wyndham Paradise Valley Resort** 404R (17S)          | 21 | 19 | 19 | 20 | $123 |
5401 N. Scottsdale Rd., Scottsdale; (800) 822-4200; (602) 947-5400;
FAX 946-1524
*U – A "very convenient" central Scottsdale location makes this "a good
business choice"; the "grounds are gorgeous", while rooms, service and
dining facilities are all "very good"; best of all, "rates are reasonable."*

## ●OTHER HOTEL-CHAIN CHOICES
*You will find one or more additional locations of the following hotel chains
in the Phoenix/Scottsdale area: Days Inn, Embassy Suites, Holiday Inn,
Howard Johnson, La Quinta Inns, Preferred Hotels, Ramada and Travelodge/
Viscount; for reservations or information, see the toll-free 800 phone listings
on page 16.*

# PITTSBURGH

## TOP HOTELS
### (In order of rating)

**BEST OVERALL**

19 – Westin William Penn
     Pittsburgh Vista
17 – Hyatt Regency

**BEST VALUES**

Pittsburgh Green Tree Marriott
Pittsburgh Vista
Sheraton Station Square

\*        \*        \*

**Best Rooms**

21 – Pittsburgh Vista
20 – Westin William Penn
17 – Hyatt Regency

**Best Dining**

18 – Westin William Penn
17 – Pittsburgh Vista
16 – Hyatt Regency

**Best Service**

19 – Westin William Penn
     Pittsburgh Vista
18 – Hyatt Regency

**Best Public Facilities**

19 – Westin William Penn
18 – Pittsburgh Vista
17 – Sheraton Station Square

| R | S | D | P | $ |
|---|---|---|---|---|

**Hyatt Regency Pittsburgh**  400R (19S)

| 17 | 18 | 16 | 16 | $131 |
|---|---|---|---|---|

112 Washington Place; (800) 233-1234; (412) 471-1234; FAX 355-0315
*M – Despite a somewhat "off-the-main-track" location, this "pretty" high rise
situated atop an office building across from the Civic Center is considered a
"good, safe" bet for business stays; though no world-beater, it provides
reasonable quality at reasonable rates, with some "lovely views" to boot;
ratings suggest both food and facilities need a shot in the arm.*

| R | S | D | P | $ |

**Pittsburgh Green Tree Marriott**   467R (5S)   | 16 | 17 | 14 | 15 | $100 |
101 Marriott Dr.; (800) 525-5902; (412) 922-8400; FAX 922-8981
*M – Fans say this Southwest Side hotel is a good value for the money,
offering "nice rooms" and "very dependable" service; but critics call it "most
impersonal" and "full of salespeople", advising: "only stay here if you must,
for business."*

**Pittsburgh Hilton & Towers, The**  714R (31S)  | 17 | 17 | 15 | 16 | $125 |
Gateway Center, 600 Commonwealth Dr.; (800) HILTONS; (412) 391-4600;
FAX 594-5161
*M – It boasts "beautiful views" of Three Rivers and an easy walk to
the stadium, but beyond those assets this '50s riverfront high rise isn't
much more than an "adequate" business hotel – "for salesmen as
opposed to executives."*

**Pittsburgh Vista Hotel**   616R (47S)      | 21 | 19 | 17 | 18 | $123 |
1000 Penn Ave.; (800) 367-8478; (412) 281-3700; FAX 281-2687
*U – A "modern and efficient" Downtown high rise that guests call a "class
act", with "nice rooms", "great views" and good facilities, including an
excellent health club; the executive floors are also singled out for praise;
it's among the "best locations for large meetings" in town.*

**Priory – A City Inn, The***   24R (3S)      | 28 | 23 | 22 | 25 | $101 |
614 Pressley St.; (412) 231-3338; FAX 231-4838
*U – "Peace and old-time elegance" reign at this small, lovely Victorian inn
in Deutschtown; originally a haven for Benedictine priests, it's "comfortable"
and attractive, with period furnishings and a "genuine homestyle-welcome
atmosphere"; near Downtown, it's a "nice change for travelers tired of
large, modern hotels" – or anyone seeking a restful hideaway.*

**Ramada Suite Hotel**   300S      | – | – | – | – | M |
1 Bigelow Square; (800) 225-5858; (412) 281-5800; FAX 281-8467
*"Well located for Downtown business", this all-suites Golden Triangle
mid-rise provides "pleasant" rooms and dependable service at reasonable
prices; the food isn't much more than "ok."*

**Sheraton Hotel Station Square**   296R (3S)   | 17 | 17 | 15 | 17 | $115 |
7 Station Square Dr.; (800) 255-7488; (412) 261-2000; FAX 261-2932
*M – "Wonderful" views of the Pittsburgh skyline and river and proximity to
the adjoining Station Square mall are the main assets of this mid-rise
Downtown business and convention hotel; despite its respectable ratings,
some say it "needs redecorating" and is "expensive for what you get."*

**Westin William Penn**   595R (47S)          | 20 | 19 | 18 | 19 | $136 |
530 William Penn Place; (800) 228-3000; (412) 281-7100; FAX 281-5252
*U – The "grand old lady" of Pittsburgh hotels, this "stately" and "elegant"
Downtown dowager has admirers who prefer it to all others for its spacious
and "very pleasant" rooms, "wonderful" service and from-another-era
atmosphere; the "beautiful lobby" is a perfect setting for afternoon tea.*

## ●OTHER HOTEL-CHAIN CHOICES
*You will find one or more additional locations of the following hotel chains
in the Pittsburgh area: Days Inn, Embassy Suites, Hampton Inn, Hilton,
Holiday Inn, Howard Johnson, La Quinta Inns, Radisson, Ramada and
Super 8; for reservations or information, see the toll-free 800 phone listings
on page 16.*

# SAN ANTONIO

## TOP HOTELS
### (In order of rating)

**BEST OVERALL**
23 – Fairmount Hotel
21 – Marriott Rivercenter
     Plaza San Antonio
20 – La Mansion del Rio

**BEST VALUES**
Sheraton Gunter Hotel
Menger Hotel
Marriott Rivercenter
Saint Anthony Hotel

\*      \*      \*

**Best Rooms**
24 – Fairmount Hotel
22 – Marriott Rivercenter
21 – Plaza San Antonio
20 – La Mansion del Rio

**Best Dining**
23 – Fairmount Hotel
20 – Plaza San Antonio
     La Mansion del Rio
19 – Marriott Rivercenter

**Best Service**
23 – Fairmount Hotel
22 – Marriott Rivercenter
20 – Plaza San Antonio
     La Mansion del Rio

**Best Public Facilities**
22 – Fairmount Hotel
     Marriott Rivercenter
20 – Plaza San Antonio
     La Mansion del Rio

| R | S | D | P | $ |
|---|---|---|---|---|

**Best Western Historical**

| R | S | D | P | $ |
|---|---|---|---|---|
| 19 | 20 | 17 | 18 | $117 |

**Crockett Hotel\***   206R (11S) (fka Crockett Hotel)
320 Bonham St.; (800) 292-1050; (512) 225-6500; FAX 225-7418
*U – With the Alamo in its backyard and in "walking distance of the Riverwalk", this 1909-vintage "winner" has a prime location, well-rated staff and "old-world charm" at the right price; you can "sit in the hot tub on the roof" and peer down at the Alamo.*

## SAN ANTONIO HOTELS | R | S | D | P | $ |

**Emily Morgan\*** 177R (24S)            | 20 | 20 | 20 | 18 | $104 |
705 E. Houston St.; (800) 824-6674; (512) 225-8486; FAX 225-7227
*M – This converted office building bespeaks "old elegance", but detractors
say it's "just plain old and funky"; opinions on the rooms range from "nice"
to "basic, basic", but most agree that the adjacent Alamo and nearby
Riverwalk make for a "good location", despite infamous parking problems,
and the price is right.*

**Fairmount Hotel, The** 36R (17S)           | 24 | 23 | 23 | 22 | $160 |
401 S. Alamo St.; (800) 642-3363; (512) 224-8800; FAX 224-2767
*U – Victorian style wins this "boutique hotel" accolades as "first-class" and
"truly outstanding"; although its edge-of-Downtown locale is "a bit out of the
way", Polo's restaurant and "professional service" make this "very pleasant
in every way"; yes, this is the hotel that was moved to its present location.*

**Hilton Palacio del Rio** 484R (26S)          | 18 | 18 | 18 | 18 | $132 |
200 S. Alamo St.; (800) HILTONS; (512) 222-1400; FAX 270-0761
*M – "Convenient for conventioneers" and often full, this basic, basic
on-the-Riverwalk Hilton has "charming appointments", "great bars" and
"many personal amenities" in a "lovely setting" across from the convention
center; the down side is rooms that are "too small" and "in need of
modernization" N.B. ask for a room with a river view.*

**Hyatt Regency San Antonio** 631R (27S)        | 20 | 20 | 18 | 20 | $135 |
123 Losoya St.; (800) 233-1234; (512) 222-1234; FAX 227-4925
*M – This well-run large hotel is located "right where the action is", with the
river running through its lobby; the "Southwestern-style, large rooms" are
"amazingly quiet" for a convention hotel, but some think it's beginning to
"rest on its laurels" and that service is "inconsistent."*

**La Mansion del Rio** 337R (11S)           | 20 | 20 | 20 | 20 | $144 |
112 College St.; (800) 292-7300; (512) 225-2581; FAX 226-1365
*U – Away from the bustle, this romantic "grande dame of the Riverwalk"
is "a wonderful retreat from the tourist hoopla" on the quiet end of San
Antonio's signature waterway; "excellent food", "perfect grounds" and
"wonderful service" make this a favorite for those who don't mind paying
more for "old-world charm" in a historic setting; ask for a river view.*

## SAN ANTONIO HOTELS

**Marriott Rivercenter**   1002R (82S)   | 22 | 22 | 19 | 22 | $132 |
101 Bowie St.; (800) 228-9290; (512) 223-1000; FAX 223-4092
*U – Those who like to shop till they drop have found a "beautiful new hotel"
with "gold-medal service and hospitality" right in "shopper's paradise"
(it's attached to a mall); a "cut above the usual Marriott", it's a mega-location
for meetings, also popular with tourists looking for a weekend base to
tour the Riverwalk.*

**Menger Hotel, The**   319R (15S)   | 18 | 18 | 17 | 19 | $111 |
204 Alamo Plaza; (800) 345-9285; (512) 223-4361; FAX 228-0022
*U – A sense of history – it's "right next to the Alamo and on an old cattle
route" – evokes "wild West fantasies" in a "charming" Victorian-style
setting; some prefer the new wing that some prefer over the original
building, with its big but less-spiffy rooms.*

**Plaza San Antonio Hotel**   252R (10S)   | 21 | 20 | 20 | 20 | $150 |
555 S. Alamo St.; (800) 421-1172; (512) 229-1000; FAX 229-1418
*U – With "European elegance" and a "SW spirit", this collection of hacienda-
style buildings includes three 19th-century cottages used as meeting
facilities, which makes you feel "like you're in another country"; it's just a
five-minute stroll from the Riverwalk and shopping, but the hotel's six-acre
grounds and "pretty garden" are so pleasant you may never go out.*

**Saint Anthony Hotel**   350R (42S)   | 18 | 20 | 18 | 19 | $122 |
300 E. Travis St.; (800) 338-1338; (512) 227-4392; FAX 227-0915
*M – No, "they don't build them like this anymore"; our surveyors mostly
compliment the "beautiful public areas" and solid service, but some find the
antique-filled rooms in need of updating; privacy and "old-world styling"
make it a "honeymoon haven", and it's a bargain to boot; Pola Negri spent
her final years here.*

**San Antonio Riverwalk Marriott**   500R (12S)   | 20 | 20 | 18 | 19 | $126 |
711 E. Riverwalk; (800) 228-9290; (512) 224-4555; FAX 228-0548
*U – Like a kiss from your sister, this busy convention hotel is "nice", but it
doesn't make your toes curl; business types say it's "ideally organized for
large meetings", but the place loses points on "disappointing" food;
"location is its best point."*

**Sheraton Gunter Hotel**   323R (17S)   | 17 | 18 | 17 | 17 | $106 |
205 E. Houston St.; (800) 222-4276; (512) 227-3241; FAX 227-FAXX
*M – Another refurbished, landmark older hotel; though detractors say that it
still seems "shabby", with a "dark lobby and overdecorated rooms", its "old
West flavor" satisfies most visitors; a current renovation project offers the
promise of better days.*

## SAN ANTONIO HOTELS

| R | S | D | P | $ |
|---|---|---|---|---|

**Wyndham San Antonio**   326R (3S)

| 18 | 17 | 16 | 18 | $119 |
|---|---|---|---|---|

9821 Colonnade Blvd.; (800) 822-4200; (512) 691-8888; FAX 691-1128
*U – "Off the beaten path", this is a place "for those who need solitude in the city"; proximity to Sea World and Fiesta Texas amusement park lures the family trade, making it necessary to book a room well in advance, but typical modern high-rise architecture makes it forgettable; all in all, it's "ok" but no more.*

## ● OTHER HOTEL-CHAIN CHOICES
*You will find one or more additional locations of the following hotel chains in the San Antonio area: Days Inn, Embassy Suites, Hampton Inn, Holiday Inn, Howard Johnson, Hyatt, La Quinta Inns, Marriott, Radisson, Super 8 and Travelodge/Viscount; for reservations or information, see the toll-free 800 phone listings on page 16.*

# SAN DIEGO†

## TOP HOTELS
## (In order of rating)

### BEST OVERALL
**24** – Loews Coronado Bay
   Le Merldien
**23** – Sheraton Grande Torrey Pines
**22** – Westgate Hotel
   La Valencia
   Hyatt Regency La Jolla
   Rancho Bernardo
**21** – Hotel del Coronado

### BEST VALUES
Horton Grand
Pan Pacific
Doubletree Horton Plaza
Catamaran Resort
Embassy Suites
Sheraton Grande Torrey Pines
Hyatt Regency La Jolla
U.S. Grant Hotel

\*　　　\*　　　\*

### Best Rooms
**25** – Loews Coronado Bay
**24** – Le Meridien
   Sheraton Grande Torrey Pines
**23** – Westgate Hotel
**22** – Pan Pacific
   Hyatt Regency La Jolla
   Horton Grand
   La Valencia

### Best Dining
**23** – Le Meridien
   Loews Coronado Bay
**22** – Rancho Bernardo
   Sheraton Grande Torrey Pines
   Westgate Hotel
   La Valencia
**21** – Hyatt Regency La Jolla
   Hotel del Coronado

### Best Service
**24** – Le Meridien
   Sheraton Grande Torrey Pines
**23** – Loews Coronado Bay
   La Valencia
**22** – Hyatt Regency La Jolla
   Westgate Hotel
   U.S. Grant
   Rancho Bernardo

### Best Public Facilities
**25** – Loews Coronado Bay
**24** – Sheraton Grande Torrey Pines
   Le Meridien
   Hotel del Coronado
**23** – Hyatt Regency La Jolla
**22** – Westgate Hotel
   La Valencia
   Rancho Bernardo

†For restaurants, see *Zagat Los Angeles/So. California Restaurant Survey.*

## SAN DIEGO HOTELS

| | R | S | D | P | $ |
|---|---|---|---|---|---|

**Bahia Hotel**   325R (75S)  | 15 | 14 | 13 | 15 | $117 |
(fka Bahia Resort Hotel)
998 W. Mission Bay Dr.; (800) 288-0770; (619) 488-0551; FAX 490-3328
*U – It may be "tacky" and "tired", but this spot is "good for families" who want to stay on Mission Bay, near Sea World and the San Diego Zoo; despite a "lovely" "bay location" and "helpful" staff, this "beach bargain" is "threadbare"; "great location, poor rooms" may sum it up.*

**Catamaran Resort Hotel**   312R (50S)  | 19 | 18 | 17 | 19 | $117 |
3999 Mission Blvd.; (800) 288-0770; (619) 488-1081; FAX 490-3328
*U – A "well-run" resort hotel in popular Mission Bay, featuring a "parrot in the lobby" and "water beds" in some of the rooms; as with many of the Mission Bay properties, "gorgeous surroundings", complete with lush tropical plantings, often outshine the "gussied-up" rooms.*

**Colonial Inn***   75R (8S)  | 19 | 20 | 18 | 19 | $117 |
910 Prospect St., La Jolla; (800) 832-5525; (619) 454-2181; FAX 454-5679
*U – The convenient Downtown La Jolla location means you can "walk to the beach, shops, restaurants, museums, etc." from this "funky", "quaint" hotel that's very popular with tourists; expect "small rooms" (ask for "ocean views") at this landmark that's "fun for the kids."*

**Doubletree Hotel at Horton Plaza**   450R (14S)  | 20 | 20 | 18 | 19 | $124 |
(fka Omni San Diego)
· 910 Broadway Circle; (800) 828-7447; (619) 239-2200; FAX 239-3216
*U – "Older", "good-value" hotel attached to a sprawling mall, featuring "a legit theater in the basement" and a "mega movie/shopping complex up above"; it's a "clean, businesslike" hotel right "in the center of things", but all told, it lacks character.*

**Embassy Suites San Diego Downtown**   337S  | 21 | 18 | 16 | 18 | $121 |
601 Pacific Hwy.; (800) EMBASSY; (619) 239-2400; FAX 239-1520
*U – Expect "great location" and "quality" at this "functional" all-suiter located in the middle of San Diego's redeveloped Downtown, hard by the convention center; as with all Embassy Suites, it's "good for families with young children", with a "free breakfast and happy hour."*

**Gaslamp Plaza Suites**   65R (40S)  | – | – | – | – | M |
(fka Horton Park Plaza)
520 E St.; (800) 443-8012; (619) 232-9500; FAX 238-9945
*"Just another hotel" to some, though for others this "gingerbread palace" in the "center of San Diego", with "large", plushly decorated rooms, is a "fine place to stay" as long as you're "careful walking at night."*

| R | S | D | P | $ |

**Hanalei Hotel**   436R (16S)   | 16 | 15 | 13 | 15 | $104 |
2270 Hotel Circle N.; (800) 822-0858; (619) 297-1101; FAX 297-6049
*M – "A good value for little money", if you don't mind the "tacky plastic
flora" and "ersatz Polynesian decor" at this rather "run-down" conference
hotel; though detractors say it's got "no redeeming features", its devotees
find it "friendly" and even "charming."*

**Horton Grand, The**   132R (26S)   | 22 | 21 | 20 | 21 | $122 |
311 Island Ave.; (800) 542-1886; (619) 544-1886; FAX 239-3823
*U – A "real sleeper", this "historic" Victorian located near "exciting" Horton
Plaza offers "dark, frilly and romantic" ambiance and "funky Victorian fun"
for a "total escape to another era"; on the other hand, it's also "close to the
convention center", with a "comfortable bar."*

**Hotel del Coronado**   691R (35S)   | 20 | 21 | 21 | 24 | $174 |
1500 Orange Ave., Coronado; (800) HOTEL-DEL; (619) 435-6611;
FAX 522-8491
*M – The queen mother of San Diego hotels, this "elegant dowager" has
"lots of old-world charm" and "lovely Victorian style", plus plenty to do for
the sedentary or athletic; the 'Del' is located on a peninsula reached by a
toll bridge, 15 minutes from San Diego, and staying there is "like being in
another world and another time"; however, some rooms are small and old,
and critics say "the old girl really needs a face-lift" and has become touristy.*

**Humphrey's Half Moon Inn\***   182R (54S)   | 17 | 17 | 17 | 17 | $113 |
2303 Shelter Island Dr.; (800) 542-7400; (619) 224-3411; FAX 224-3478
*U – San Diego Chargers supposedly spend their preseason nights at this
"pseudo Polynesian" that's a "sentimental favorite" and "a lot of hotel for
the money"; there's a "great view – with or without the moon" of "boats in
the harbor"; don't miss the "marvelous" Polynesian restaurant, one of the
best on Shelter Island, making it "worth the stay just to eat here."*

**Hyatt Islandia**   423R (95S)   | 19 | 19 | 17 | 19 | $143 |
1441 Quivira Rd.; (800) 233-1234; (619) 224-1234; FAX 224-0348
*M – This "better-than-expected" "family-style" hotel boasts a "good location"
in Mission Bay; some say it's got the "feel of Hawaii", especially in the new
building that's "practically on the wharf"; others think it's just a "basic
Hyatt", but, as ratings show, that's just fine for most surveyors.*

## SAN DIEGO HOTELS

| | R | S | D | P | $ |
|---|---|---|---|---|---|

**Hyatt Regency La Jolla**   400R (25S)        | 22 | 22 | 21 | 23 | $148 |
3777 La Jolla Village Dr., La Jolla; (800) 233-1234; (619) 552-1234;
FAX 552-6066
*U – "Architecturally entertaining", this Robert Graves–designed "modern"
Hyatt in the middle of La Jolla (convenient to UCSD) sports a "gorgeous"
"Italianate lobby", "great workout area" and "beautiful pool" that remind
many of the "new Disney World hotels"; even Hyatt doubters admit this
one is "spiffy."*


**Hyatt Regency San Diego**   875R (56S)        | – | – | – | – | E |
One Market Place; (800) 233-1234; (619) 232-1234; FAX 239-5678
*Opened in 1992, this 39-story, pyramid-topped hotel with a palm-filled
lobby has splendid views of San Diego Bay from the rooms and rooftop
lounge, and a convenient location next to the convention center and
Seaport Village; huge meeting areas and superb facilities make it
particularly popular with business travelers.*


**Kona Kai Resort***   178R (40S)        | 19 | 16 | 16 | 15 | $130 |
1551 Shelter Island Dr.; (800) 325-2218; (619) 222-1191; FAX 222-9738
*U – "Nice-size rooms" and a "magnificent" location on the harbor (including
a private beach) make this older resort a "best value" on Shelter Island;
it's also got a fully equipped business center and plenty of meeting rooms,
making it popular with business execs.*


**La Jolla Marriott**   367R (16S)        | 19 | 19 | 17 | 18 | $128 |
4240 La Jolla Village Dr., La Jolla; (800) 228-9290; (619) 587-1414;
FAX 546-8518
*M – This "solid, basic Marriott" is considered "ok for an overnight stay" and
"good for business and groups", but the fact that it's "too far from the town
center", with "no ocean nearby", leaves vacationers unimpressed.*


**La Valencia Hotel**   100R (10S)        | 22 | 23 | 22 | 22 | $182 |
1132 Prospect St., La Jolla; (800) 451-0772; (619) 454-0771; FAX 456-3921
*M – You'll "feel like a silent movie star" at this "heavenly" 1926 legend
that puts the resort town of La Jolla "at your feet", offering "old Spanish
charm" and "superior views" of the cove; maybe it's "falling apart in
places", but this "grand hotel" has a loyal following for whom that's just part
of its "great character."*

**Le Meridien San Diego**   | 24 | 24 | 23 | 24 | $177 |
**at Coronado**   300R (7S)
2000 Second St., Coronado; (800) 543-4300; (619) 435-3000;
FAX 435-3032
*U – "Wonderfully romantic", this "gem on the bay" has "beautiful, spacious rooms", a "great breakfast buffet" and a "stunning view of SD"; just 10 minutes from Downtown, this "very California" newer hotel outruns the fabled Del Coronado with a "fantastic spa", "great food" at Marius (food rating, 27), "grand luxury" and the "best bathrooms."*

**LOEWS CORONADO**   | 25 | 23 | 23 | 25 | $166 |
**BAY RESORT**   440R (37S)
4000 Coronado Bay Rd.; (800) 23-LOEWS; (619) 424-4000; FAX 424-4400
*U – The newest property opened by the detail-obsessed Loews chain, this "jewel box of a resort" has a "manager who oversees perfection", including "proper napkin folding" and service mandating that "every guest is treated like a king"; fans say it's "magnificent", with "beautiful" rooms, "great food" at Azzura Point (food rating, 21) and "lots of fun" activities for a "family weekend in SD": on-site amenities include boat rentals, a marina, tennis, fishing and a health club.*

**Marriott Mission Valley**   350R (5S)   | 21 | 19 | 17 | 19 | $132 |
8757 Rio San Diego Dr.; (800) 228-9290; (619) 692-3800; FAX 692-0769
*U – Located 20 minutes north and east of town in a rapidly expanding suburban area, this "good property" has comfortable rooms, a "popular nightclub" and dependable service; in the final analysis, however, it may be "better than most Marriotts, but it's still a Marriott."*

**Pan Pacific**   436R (20S)   | 22 | 21 | 20 | 21 | $123 |
400 W. Broadway; (800) 327-8585; (619) 239-4500; FAX 239-3274
*U – This "futuristic" hotel within "walking distance of the convention center" boasts "great harbor views" and "fabulous rooms" that are just a "notch below" the "sparkling" lobby; it's good for "upscale restaurants", though the cognoscenti say it "doesn't compare with other Pan Pacifics"; N.B. watch out for homeless problems on the street.*

**Radisson La Jolla**   200R (2S)   | 14 | 14 | 13 | 13 | $120 |
(fka La Jolla Village Inn)
3299 Holiday Court, La Jolla; (800) 333-3333; (619) 453-5500;
FAX 453-9909
*U – Our surveyors are unimpressed by this "over-the-hill" "motel reached through a shopping center"; though a "good bargain" in an "expensive resort area", it's "pretty grim", with "beat-up rooms" and "nonexistent service"; there's "too much competition" to make this an option.*

| R | S | D | P | $ |

### Rancho Bernardo Inn   287R (58S)

| 21 | 22 | 22 | 22 | $172 |

17550 Bernardo Oaks Dr.; (800) 542-6096; (619) 487-1161; FAX 673-0311
*U – This "relaxing", "classic" tennis and golf resort north of San Diego may "need modernizing", but it's still a "great place to nest", with "great warmth", a civilized "afternoon tea" and "fabulous" Belgian food at El Bizcocho restaurant (food rating, 27); dissenters say it's just "a fancy motel with golf."*


### Rancho Valencia*   43S

| 25 | 24 | 24 | 25 | $232 |

(fka John Gardiner's Rancho Valencia)
5921 Valencia Circle, Rancho Santa Fe; (800) 548-3664; (619) 756-1123; FAX 756-0165
*U – "Oh, is this place great!" say those few lovers of luxury who know of, and can afford, this "gorgeous" resort; if you can stand to leave your suite ("the best of anyplace in the USA", each with fireplace and private terrace), you'll find tennis, a health club, an outdoor pool and two nearby golf courses, plus a winning restaurant.*


### San Diego Hilton
### Beach & Tennis Ranch   354R (17S)

| 20 | 18 | 17 | 19 | $137 |

1775 E. Mission Bay Dr.; (800) HILTONS; (619) 276-4010; FAX 275-7991
*U – A "relaxing oasis" with "wonderful Mission Bay views", where you'll "wish you could have stayed longer", this "newly renovated" "family" hotel near Sea World is "great fun for kids"; it's one of San Diego's prime hotels – reserve a "picturesque minisuite facing the bay."*


### San Diego Marriott
### Hotel & Marina   1355R (67S)

| 21 | 21 | 19 | 21 | $151 |

333 W. Harbor Dr.; (800) 228-9290; (619) 234-1500; FAX 234-8678
*U – "Watch submarines" go by while "ducking low-flying planes" at this "flashy" convention hotel with a "beautiful" bay view, praised for "fine convention facilities" and "the best personal service", including an "iron and ironing board in each room"; you may get tired walking around the place – you'll either "need a guide" or "roller skates to get through the long lobby" – and bring a book to read while awaiting the elevator.*


### San Diego Princess Resort   462R (103S)

| 19 | 19 | 18 | 22 | $138 |

1404 W. Vacation Rd.; (800) 344-2626; (619) 274-4630; FAX 581-5929
*M – "Beautiful grounds on Mission Bay" are the big draw at this "family vacation retreat" with "first-rate outdoor facilities" spread over "45 acres", complete with "water sports, tennis and a putting green" that satisfy both parents and kids; "if you never go inside your room, you've got it made."*

## SAN DIEGO HOTELS

**Sea Lodge**   128R (8S)   | 19 | 18 | 16 | 18 | $163 |
8110 Camino del Oro, La Jolla; (800) 237-5211; (619) 459-8271;
FAX 456-9346
*M – "The Pacific makes the difference" at this "casual", "rustic Spanish" inn
"far from the La Jolla hype"; expect "small", but comfortable rooms at this
"true beachfront property", where you can "walk out of your room and into
the water"; critics call it "just a motel", but if that's the case, this is motel
heaven with prices to match.*


**SHERATON GRANDE**   | 24 | 24 | 22 | 24 | $156 |
**AT TORREY PINES**   400R
10950 N. Torrey Pines Rd., La Jolla; (800) 325-3535; (619) 558-1500;
FAX 450-4584
*U – Golf nuts and sun worshipers love the "superb golf course" and
"fabulous setting" on the beach just south of Del Mar, adjacent to a popular
state park; "golf-course rooms are better than par", as are the "very
attentive service" and "beautiful landscaping" at this "resort in the city" a
bit north of San Diego.*


**Sheraton Grande on**   | 19 | 18 | 17 | 18 | $145 |
**Harbor Island**   359R (30S)
1590 Harbor Island Dr.; (800) 325-3535; (619) 291-6400; FAX 294-9627
*U – In terms of ratings, it's the identical sibling of the nearby Sheraton
Harbor, but "less crowded"; in many ways a "typical Sheraton", but with a
"great view of the harbor", "helpful service" and an appealing "island
atmosphere"; the fact that it's "very close to the airport" makes it "pleasant
and convenient" for business, but also very noisy.*


**Sheraton – Harbor Island East**   712R (47S)   | 19 | 18 | 17 | 18 | $132 |
1380 Harbor Island Dr.; (800) 325-3535; (619) 291-2900; FAX 543-0643
*U – Expect "great views of the marina and harbor" from the larger, but
slightly less expensive, of the two Sheraton convention hotels on Harbor
Island; this "stunning place" also has "beautiful grounds" and an "excellent
staff"; for some, "proximity to the airport" makes it more a "nice commercial
hotel" than a true resort.*


**Town & Country Hotel**   1062R (58S)   | 13 | 14 | 13 | 14 | $108 |
500 Hotel Circle N.; (800) 854-2608; (619) 297-7131; FAX 291-3584
*M – Going "downhill" fast, this "motel-type" "convention hotel" is judged
"mediocre" by our respondents; though a few say it's "conveniently situated
off the freeway" and "ok for the money", most think it's "time to retire" or
retread this place that's "desperately in need of additional refurbishing."*

## SAN DIEGO HOTELS

| R | S | D | P | $ |

**U.S. Grant Hotel**   283R (60S)     | 21 | 22 | 20 | 20 | $141 |
326 Broadway; (800) 237-5029; (619) 232-3121; FAX 232-3626
*U – You "step back in time" at this "historic" and "charming" "landmark",
with its "beautiful" public areas, "small" but "nicely redone" rooms and
"manly dining room"; "old-world elegance" is the word at what fans call
"San Diego's best hotel"; just be careful where you walk at night, and
don't trip over sleeping bodies.*

**Westgate Hotel**   223R (11S)     | 23 | 22 | 22 | 22 | $167 |
1055 Second Ave.; (800) 221-3802; (619) 238-1818; FAX 232-4526
*U – A "very European", elegant hotel in the heart of Downtown, whose
"large, large rooms" "full of antiques" convey a "luxurious feeling"; though a
few surveyors suggest it's "showing wear and tear", even they admit it's a
"great old-timer."*

### ● OTHER HOTEL-CHAIN CHOICES
*You will find one or more additional locations of the following hotel chains
in the San Diego area: Courtyard by Marriott, Days Inn, Doubletree,
Embassy Suites, Holiday Inn, Howard Johnson, La Quinta Inns, Ramada,
Residence Inn, Travelodge/Viscount and Wyndham; for reservations or
information, see the toll-free 800 phone listings on page 16.*

# SAN FRANCISCO[†]

## TOP HOTELS
## (In order of rating)

### BEST OVERALL
27 – Sherman House
26 – Ritz-Carlton
25 – Mandarin Oriental
24 – Campton Place Kempinski
    Four Seasons Clift
    Park Hyatt
    Pan Pacific Hotel
23 – Petite Auberge

### BEST VALUES
Hotel Bedford
Hotel Vintage Court
Villa Florence Hotel
Beresford Arms
Prescott Hotel
Petite Auberge
Chancellor Hotel
Majestic

\*     \*     \*

### Best Rooms
28 – Sherman House
27 – Mandarin Oriental
26 – Ritz-Carlton
25 – Park Hyatt
24 – Pan Pacific Hotel
    Huntington
    Four Seasons Clift
    Petite Auberge

### Best Dining
27 – Prescott
26 – Campton Place Kempinski
    Sherman House
25 – Ritz-Carlton
24 – Mandarin Oriental
    Four Seasons Clift
23 – Stouffer Stanford Court
    Donatello

### Best Service
28 – Sherman House
27 – Mandarin Oriental
26 – Ritz-Carlton
25 – Four Seasons Clift
    Campton Place Kempinski
    Petite Auberge
24 – Park Hyatt
    Pan Pacific Hotel

### Best Public Facilities
26 – Sherman House
    Ritz-Carlton
24 – Sheraton Palace
    Pan Pacific Hotel
23 – Park Hyatt
    Four Seasons Clift
    Mandarin Oriental
22 – Campton Place Kempinski

[†]For restaurants, see *Zagat San Francisco Bay Area Restaurant Survey*.

## SAN FRANCISCO HOTELS

| R | S | D | P | $ |

**ANA Hotel San Francisco**  670R (26S)  | 20 | 19 | 19 | 18 | $159 |
(fka Le Meridien San Francisco)
50 Third St.; (800) ANA-HOTELS; (415) 974-6400; FAX 543-8268
*U – The just-renovated ANA is a "high-quality" facility offering "spectacular
views" and "good service" in a "great location for Moscone Convention
Center"; some call the lobby and public area "sparkling", others say "cold",
but most consider the rooms "compact" but "beautiful."*

**Andrews Hotel**  48R (5S)  | 15 | 17 | 12 | 13 | $110 |
624 Post St.; (800) 926-3739; (415) 563-6877; FAX 928-6919
*M – "Good value, small rooms" is the consensus; whether you'll like this
"modest" little Downtown place probably depends on your mind-set: one
man's "tiny refuge in a sophisticated city" is another's "noisy" "disappointment."*

**Archbishops Mansion Inn**  15R (5S)  | 23 | 20 | 14 | 19 | $162 |
1000 Fulton St.; (800) 543-5820; (415) 563-7872; FAX 885-3193
*M – Most surveyors forgive the "lousy" Alamo Square locale in light of the
"intimate and homey" accommodations at this "wonderful" renovated
circa-1904 Victorian manse; there's no restaurant, but breakfast is
delivered to your room in a French picnic basket, and wine and piano
music in the "beautiful common areas" are special evening touches; if
you like your hotels small and "unique", this is worth a try.*

**Beresford Arms**  148R (54S)  | 16 | 17 | 12 | 13 | $98 |
701 Post St.; (800) 533-6533; (415) 673-2600; FAX 474-0449
*U – An "old-timer" with "modest rates"; the location is "handy", service
"attentive", every room "clean" and "nicely furnished", and the
complimentary continental breakfast "more than adequate"; "nothing
exceptional", but a good buy.*

**Best Western Canterbury Hotel**  | 13 | 14 | 14 | 15 | $127 |
**& Whitehall Inn***  250R (13S)
750 Sutter St.; (800) 227-4788; (415) 474-6464; FAX 474-5856
*U – A "walking location" is about the only amenity at this hotel; rooms are
"predictable", but the adjoining restaurant (Lehr's Greenhouse) is "a real
plus"; this is popular for airline-crew layovers, which should tell you
something, for better or worse.*

**CAMPTON PLACE KEMPINSKI**  121R (10S)  | 23 | 25 | 26 | 22 | $223 |
(fka Campton Place Hotel)
340 Stockton St.; (800) 647-4007; (415) 781-5555; FAX 955-8536
*U – Except for qualifiers about prices and diminutive rooms, this San
Francisco outpost of the international Kempinski chain gets unanimous raves:
"exquisite in every way", "classy small hotel in a great Union Square
location" and "fabulous service"; the restaurant (food rating, 26) continues
to receive superior ratings; tip: "corner rooms are best."*

**Cartwright Hotel**  114R (5S)  | 16 | 18 | 13 | 15 | $139 |
524 Sutter St.; (800) 227-3844; (415) 421-2865; FAX 421-2865
*U – A "very European atmosphere" is the hallmark of this "small, intimate"
and "exceedingly comfortable" hotel near Union Square, "close to everything";
the rooms are "tiny" but a "bargain"; the restaurant serves only breakfast,
though a "fine" complimentary high tea is served in the "small" lobby; notes
one reviewer, "I've stayed there for 25 years", but ratings suggest not much has
changed in that time.*

**Cathedral Hill**  411R (11S)  | 14 | 16 | 13 | 14 | $123 |
1101 Van Ness Ave.; (800) 227-4730; (415) 776-8200; FAX 441-2841
*M – An unexciting but "affordable budget hotel" with a "helpful staff", this
"slightly elderly convention hotel offers "spacious" rooms and "notable"
views; it's "away from Downtown", but there's free parking.*

**Chancellor Hotel**  140R (6S)  | 16 | 18 | 16 | 15 | $110 |
433 Powell St.; (800) 428-4748; (415) 362-2004; FAX 362-1403
*M – More surveyors remarked on the "cable-car noise" than anything else
about this moderately priced circa-1913 hotel, but that means "Union
Square without the high prices" to those who choose to see the bright side;
it's a "best bargain" despite "small" rooms, so "stay in a rear room" and
save your money for the neighborhood's other pleasures.*

**Donatello**  90R (6S)  | 22 | 22 | 23 | 20 | $175 |
501 Post St.; (800) 227-3184; (415) 441-7100; FAX 885-8842
*U – "Exclusive", "dignified" and "elegant", with "beautiful, spacious rooms"
and "a great Italian restaurant", Donatello (food rating, 22); the service has a
"European" polish at this "special place in Downtown SF", and you'll find "thick
bathrobes on your bed."*

**SAN FRANCISCO HOTELS**　　　　　| R | S | D | P | $ |

**Fairmont Hotel**　600R (60S)　　| 22 | 22 | 21 | 22 | $190 |
Atop Nob Hill; (800) 527-4727; (415) 772-5000; FAX 781-3929
*M – The dowager of Nob Hill is an "excellent large city hotel" that's "aging
nicely" (though at least a few think the rooms "need refurbishing"); "no
one should miss" the "grand" lobby, which evokes "another era" with its
chandeliers and "wonderful piano lounge"; some say the place is "too
impersonal", though fans claim they are "treated like royalty"; as for the
views, "what a place to watch the fog roll in."*

**FOUR SEASONS CLIFT HOTEL**　330R (25S)　| 24 | 25 | 24 | 23 | $204 |
495 Geary St.; (800) 332-3442; (415) 775-4700; FAX 776-9238
*U – "Classy with a capital C", this standout hotel garners unanimous
accolades for its Redwood Room (the "most beautiful hotel lounge in the
U.S.") and its "lovely" guest rooms; service is "exceptional", and the lobby
"warm" and "impressive"; its location just blocks off Union Square is central
but quiet, and the "small-hotel atmosphere" makes it "a real gem in a city
of jewels."*

**Galleria Park Hotel**　177R (15S)　　| 17 | 19 | 20 | 17 | $126 |
191 Sutter St.; (800) 792-9639; (415) 781-3060; FAX 433-4409
*U – A "boutique" with "tiny, tasteful" rooms, this "quaint" small Kimco hotel
offers "very good food", "excellent service" and a rooftop jogging track;
"nothing fancy", but it's "a real gem for price and location" that's "run like a
bed-and-breakfast."*

**Grand Hyatt San Francisco**　693R (32S)　| 21 | 20 | 19 | 20 | $176 |
(fka Hyatt on Union Square)
345 Stockton St.; (800) 233-1234; (415) 398-1234; FAX 391-1780
*U – A "shopper's-paradise" location "in the center of everything"
accompanies solid grades across the board, especially for the
"outstanding" concierge floors; food at the Plaza (one of those "rotating
restaurants") is "surprisingly good", but expect problems when there
are "too many conventions at one time."*

**Harbor Court Hotel**　130R　　| – | – | – | – | E |
165 Stuart St.; (800) 346-0555; (415) 882-1300; FAX 882-1313
*The earthquake brought down the Embarcadero freeway, providing
spectacular water views for many of the small, luxurious rooms at this
1907 charmer redone by the trendy Kimco group; amenities include a
fireplace, wine and cheese in the lobby and an on-site health club and pool
(after all, this is a revamped Y); Harry Denton's Bar & Grill (food rating, 18)
is a place to be seen – and to see the lights on the Bay Bridge.*

## SAN FRANCISCO HOTELS

| R | S | D | P | $ |

**Hotel Bedford**   143R (7S)           | 16 | 18 | 16 | 14 | $96 |
761 Post St.; (800) 227-5642; (415) 673-6040; FAX 563-6739
*U – You'll find good value and a location "convenient to Downtown" at this "charming, efficient little hotel"; though the "good, clean rooms" can be "tiny", this recently renovated Kimco property is "reasonable and quaint", best for "times you don't need a fancy hotel."*

**Hotel Diva**   108R (1S)           | 17 | 18 | 13 | 14 | $111 |
440 Geary St.; (800) 553-1900; (415) 885-0200; FAX 346-6613
*U – "Hip but not affected", this "very modern", "very arty" mid-priced boutique/business hotel offers all kinds of high-priced amenities, including "VCRs in every room", free continental breakfast, a business center and morning limo service to the Financial District; rooms may be "small" and somewhat "noisy", but prices are "modest" for a "neat place to stay."*

**Hotel Nikko San Francisco**   522R (22S)      | 22 | 23 | 21 | 21 | $161 |
222 Mason St.; (800) NIKKO-US; (415) 394-1111; FAX 421-0455
*U – "Clean and sleek", the ultramodern Nikko offers "Japanese elegance" with "precision service" and "great food"; rooms, available in both Western and Japanese styles, are "small" but "well appointed", and the suites are "fabulous, huge and homey", with "beautiful" bathrooms to boot; the glass-enclosed pool/hot tub in "a soothing Japanese garden" atrium is a knockout.*

**Hotel Vintage Court**   107R (1S)      | 18 | 18 | 22 | 16 | $117 |
650 Bush St.; (800) 654-1100; (415) 392-4666; FAX 392-4666
*U – "A wonderful small hotel for people on a budget"; the rooms are named after California vineyards and "individually decorated à la Laura Ashley", and there's complimentary evening wine in the "cozy salon"; the Downtown location is "pretty central", and, lest we forget, Masa's contemporary French restaurant is one of SF's best (food rating, 28) – for people not on a budget.*

**HUNTINGTON HOTEL –**           | 24 | 24 | 22 | 21 | $209 |
**NOB HILL**   140R (40S)
1075 California St.; (800) 227-4683; (415) 474-5400; FAX 474-6227
*U – Recently renovated (and featured in* Architectural Digest*), this small hotel is "almost like having an apartment on Nob Hill"; reviewers commend its "wonderful" rooms, "superb" service and "very good food"; it's "the best of old San Francisco" – "not just a hotel, but a way of life."*

**Hyatt at Fisherman's Wharf**   313R (8S)      | 20 | 20 | 18 | 20 | $151 |
555 N. Point St.; (800) 233-1234; (415) 563-1234; FAX 749-6122
*U – "An oasis in the midst of tourist tacky"; the location, "convenient to pier restaurants and shops" and "close to the water", takes top honors, but this "excellent small business hotel" is also "friendly and comfortable."*

## SAN FRANCISCO HOTELS                    | R | S | D | P | $ |

**Hyatt Regency San Francisco**   803R (44S)   | 20 | 20 | 18 | 20 | $167 |
5 Embarcadero Center; (800) 233-1234; (415) 788-1234; FAX 398-2567
*U – Within "walking distance of everything", this "typical business traveler's
hotel" is best known for its trademark atrium lobby, which some consider
"showy" and "passé"; rooms are "boxy" but efficient, and the staff is
"properly accommodating."*

**Hyde Park Suites***   24S   | 23 | 24 | – | 20 | $181 |
2655 Hyde St.; (415) 771-0200; FAX 346-8058
*U – Few surveyors know of this small all-suiter (week-or-more stay only)
conveniently located at Fisherman's Wharf; the rooftop patio features
panoramic views of the throngs and harbor beyond; there's no restaurant
in house, but there are plenty nearby, and you can cook for yourself thanks
to in-room kitchenettes.*

**Inn at the Opera**   48R (18S)   | 20 | 21 | 21 | 17 | $158 |
333 Fulton St.; (800) 325-2708; (415) 863-8400; FAX 861-0281
*M – This "fine small hotel" is "nice for staying in town after the opera", but
it's a little "far from any other action in town"; the rooms are "small" but
freshly renovated, and it has a "great bar and restaurant": Act IV; all in all,
"charming and different", if a little inconvenient.*

**Inn at Union Square**   30R (6S)   | 21 | 22 | 18 | 18 | $159 |
440 Post St.; (800) 288-4346; (415) 397-3510; FAX 989-0529
*U – "For antiques buffs", this "quaint" hotel has "lots of character"; like so
many SF hotels, it has "very small" ("albeit charming") rooms and "tiny"
bathrooms, but you'll get "personal attention" and a good dose of
"European style"; "a great escape."*

**Juliana Hotel, The**   106R (22S)   | 17 | 18 | 14 | 15 | $113 |
590 Bush St.; (800) 382-8800; (415) 392-2540; FAX 391-8447
*U – A "reasonable and convenient", "inexpensive and clean" hotel for the
"value-conscious business traveler"; the rooms can be "a little too cozy" or
even "small and claustrophobic", depending on your mood.*

**Kensington Park**   86R (2S)   | 17 | 18 | – | 15 | $112 |
450 Post St.; (800) 553-1900; (415) 788-6400; FAX 399-9484
*U – "Small and inexpensive" "civilized" hotel in the heart of Downtown;
there's "no dining or room service", and the rooms are "small", but people
love such personal touches as "lemon cookies and sherry at 4 PM."*

**Lombard Hotel\*** 100R                    | 16 | 17 | – | 13 | $96 |
1015 Geary St.; (800) 227-3608; (415) 673-5232; FAX 885-2802
*M – Some reviewers like the "European atmosphere" and the short walk to
Union Square from this inexpensive Geary Street hotel, although the
neighborhood's a little iffy and the lack of a restaurant elicits gripes;
popular with European tourists, this hotel features a rooftop sun deck.*

**Majestic, The** 59R (9S)                  | 21 | 20 | 23 | 18 | $141 |
1500 Sutter St.; (800) 869-8966; (415) 441-1100; FAX 673-7331
*M – "Victorian San Francisco at its best", with a "beautiful antique lobby
and rooms" and a "wonderful" restaurant: Cafe Majestic (food rating, 20);
the Pacific Heights location can be "great" or "out of the way", depending
on your interests; fans claim it's a "supreme restoration."*

**MANDARIN ORIENTAL**                       | 27 | 27 | 24 | 23 | $221 |
**SAN FRANCISCO** 156R (4S)
222 Sansome St.; (800) 622-0404; (415) 885-0999; FAX 433-0289
*U – "Wow! bubble bath and the Golden Gate"; windows in the bathrooms
make for "views to die for", and the "beautifully appointed rooms" aren't
bad either – nor is Silks restaurant (food rating, 24); this "classy and elegant"
"hidden treasure" offers a "serene atmosphere" and service that "can't be
beat"; a lot of our surveyors "wouldn't stay anywhere else."*

**Mansions Hotel, The** 21R (3S)            | 23 | 23 | 22 | 22 | $177 |
2220 Sacramento St.; (800) 826-9398; (415) 929-9444; FAX 567-9391
*U – "Lovers and dreamers" who want "Victorian at its best" appreciate the
"great hospitality" at this "unusual and kooky bed-and-breakfast" in Pacific
Heights; it's "overpriced but interesting", and the "magic show" and dinner
package on Friday and Saturday nights add to a "fun weekend."*

**Mark Hopkins Inter-Continental** 391R (30S)  | 21 | 21 | 20 | 20 | $188 |
1 Nob Hill; (800) 327-0200; (415) 392-3434; FAX 421-3302
*M – With its famous No. 1 Nob Hill address, this "SF classic" is still a
"lovely hotel", offering "views, views, views" and "plenty of style and
old-world charm"; critics say it "must have been a stunner in 1945" but
"needs to be refurbished", and only caters to tourists; "joggers beware – all
routes are uphill."*

**Marriott Fisherman's Wharf** 255R (10S)   | 18 | 19 | 17 | 17 | $150 |
1250 Columbus Ave.; (800) 525-0956; (415) 775-7555; FAX 474-2099
*U – Reviewers rave about the "terrific" location, but basically this is nothing
more than a reliable standard, a comfortable but "undistinguished" hotel
that happens to be in the Fisherman's Wharf area; the "friendly" staff gets
an extra nod.*

**Miyako Hotel**   218R (14S)    | 21 | 21 | 18 | 18 | $141 |
Japan Center, 1625 Post St.; (800) 533-4567; (415) 922-3200;
FAX 921-0417
*U – "A nice change from the typical Western-style hotel"; "Japanese rooms
with furo tubs are a treat" at this "old favorite" with "cool style" in Japan
Town; though "somewhat out of the way", it's "refined, elegant and
unusual"; N.B. not all the rooms are Japanese-style, so be sure to specify.*

**Orchard Hotel, The\***   94R (2S)    | 13 | 15 | 13 | 14 | $113 |
562 Sutter St.; (800) 433-4434; (415) 433-4434; FAX 433-3695
*U – "Efficient" "small European-style" hotel that's the SF outpost of an
Australian chain; though affordable, "quiet and conveniently located",
"the place needs updating."*

**PAN PACIFIC HOTEL**    | 24 | 24 | 22 | 24 | $176 |
**SAN FRANCISCO, THE**   330R (19S)
500 Post St.; (800) 533-6465; (415) 771-8600; FAX 398-0267
*U – "Luxury and location" are tops at this "well-run" and "very lovely"
Downtowner; "anyone who relishes plushness and pampering" will
appreciate the "attractive rooms", "beautiful bathrooms" and staff that
"seems to anticipate your needs"; in sum, a "perfect business hotel."*

**Parc 55**   1006R (23S)    | 21 | 19 | 18 | 19 | $142 |
55 Cyril Magnin St.; (800) 338-1338; (415) 392-8000; FAX 296-8054
*U – Besides being "good for shopping", this very big, very busy convention
hotel near Moscone Center and Union Square is "clean", "modern",
"pleasant" and, as these things go, reasonably priced; it may be "average"
in other respects, but the "views from the upper floors are great."*

**PARK HYATT**   360R (60S)    | 25 | 24 | 23 | 23 | $186 |
333 Battery St.; (800) 323-7275; (415) 392-1234; FAX 421-2433
*U – In the "understated elegance" of this Financial District "jewel box", rooms
are "small but superbly laid out", service is "outstanding" and the Park Grill
(food rating, 23) is known for "the best power breakfast in town"; "a bit of
Europe in SF", it's "all that a good business hotel should be."*

**PETITE AUBERGE**   26R (1S)    | 24 | 25 | 23 | 22 | $157 |
863 Bush St.; (415) 928-6000; FAX 775-1755
*U – Whether you find it "charming" or "too cutesy" with "too many teddy
bears", this "country inn" "smack dab in the middle of SF" is certainly
"unique"; maybe "it's not for men", but it's "very romantic" and "great for a
getaway"; "wonderful hosts" and "little extras" like "push-button fireplaces"
make guests "quickly forget" that some of the rooms are "tiny."*

## SAN FRANCISCO HOTELS

| R | S | D | P | $ |

**PRESCOTT HOTEL, THE**  167R (37S)    | 22 | 23 | 27 | 20 | $156 |
545 Post St.; (800) 283-7322; (415) 563-0303; FAX 563-6831
*U – Best known as the home of Postrio restaurant (food rating, 25),
Wolfgang Puck's famed SF outpost, this "busy" but "intimate" Union
Square–area hostelry is "nice if you are in love"; rooms and bathrooms are
"beautifully decorated", though "small", and service can be exceptional.*

**Queen Anne, The**  49R (4S)    | 18 | 18 | 14 | 17 | $136 |
1590 Sutter St.; (800) 227-3970; (415) 441-2828; FAX 775-5212
*M – A "beautiful Victorian" decorated with "lovely antiques", this "small"
converted girls' school with "bed-and-breakfast charm" and "friendly
service" is "a good find away from busy Downtown" to one reviewer, "dark
and depressing" and in a "bad location" to another; there's no restaurant,
but breakfast and afternoon tea are on the house.*

**Raphael Hotel, The**  152R (2S)    | 17 | 18 | 15 | 14 | $124 |
386 Geary St.; (800) 821-5343; (415) 986-2000; FAX 397-2447
*M – A "quaint" but "middle-of-the-road" hotel "one block off Union Square"
that is "charming" and "intimate" to some, but is visibly "aging" to others;
make sure to "get the larger rooms."*

**RITZ-CARLTON,**    | 26 | 26 | 25 | 26 | $213 |
**SAN FRANCISCO**  378R (42S)
600 Stockton St.; (800) 241-3333; (415) 296-7465; FAX 296-8559
*U – A "classy sanctuary" with "first-class everything": "beautiful public areas",
"very attentive service", "excellent sports facilities" and "terrific amenities";
fans call the 1991 conversion of the old Metropolitan Life headquarters a
"brilliant" job that "shows what imagination can do"; the result is an
"architectural gem" with "gorgeous interiors", good food in the Restaurant
(food rating, 21) and the Dining Room (24), and "small but luxurious" rooms.*

**San Francisco**    | 21 | 20 | 19 | 21 | $155 |
**Downtown Marriott**  1500R (134S)
55 Fourth St.; (800) 228-9290; (415) 896-1600; FAX 777-2799
*U – "Huge and efficient", this "very busy" "basic business hotel" adjoining
the Moscone Convention Center is "comfortable", "reliable" and
"reasonable" but has "no personality"; locals and cabbies call it "the
jukebox hotel" because of its design.*

## SAN FRANCISCO HOTELS

| R | S | D | P | $ |
|---|---|---|---|---|

**San Francisco Hilton**   1914R (183S)    | 18 | 17 | 17 | 18 | $151 |
333 O'Farrell St.; (800) HILTONS; (415) 771-1400; FAX 771-6807
*M – You may "need a compass" to navigate this "very large", "very typical chain hotel" that underwent major renovation in 1988; "rooms vary", with those in the Tower offering some "spectacular" views, and the service is "very organized", but several reviewers comment that "the location is dicey" and the lines for checkout are "long, long, long."*

**Seal Rock Inn**   27R    | – | – | – | – | I |
545 Point Lobos Ave.; (415) 752-8000; FAX 752-6034
*Sure, "it's a little out of the way", but you "can't get any closer to the seal rocks" than this "children-friendly" low-budget inn at the end of Point Lobos Avenue; it's basic but "nice" – at least go for the view.*

**Sheraton at Fisherman's Wharf**   525R (7S)    | 17 | 16 | 14 | 14 | $138 |
2500 Mason St.; (800) 325-3535; (415) 362-5500; FAX 956-5275
*M – A "good location for tourists" is the best feature of this "somewhat shopworn" but "very functional" hotel; it's "great for families", with staff that seems "eager to help", but "SF has much better values."*

**Sheraton Palace**   550R (30S)    | 22 | 21 | 21 | 24 | $168 |
2 New Montgomery St.; (800) 325-3535; (415) 392-8600; FAX 543-0671
*U – "A classic restored" after the 1989 earthquake, this "beautiful old hotel" is one of the "prettiest around", and the famed Garden Court restaurant is "still wonderful", especially "nice for brunch"; the "lobby is sensational", like "being in a time machine to the '30s", and our surveyors exult that this "grand old lady has returned after millions of $$$$"; P.S. it's still a Sheraton.*

**SHERMAN HOUSE, THE**   14R (7S)    | 28 | 28 | 26 | 26 | $300 |
2160 Green St.; (800) 424-5777; (415) 563-3600; FAX 563-1882
*U – "For the most special of occasions", this restored 19th-century mansion atop Pacific Heights is "great for privacy and/or lovers" – or "celebs"; the rooms are "glorious", with "great big comfy beds" and fireplaces, and the French cuisine is "legendary" at the restaurant (food rating, 25); for "Victorian charm" at up-to-date prices, this is the place.*

**Sir Francis Drake**   415R (10S)    | 17 | 18 | 17 | 17 | $146 |
450 Powell St.; (800) 227-5480; (415) 392-7755; FAX 392-8719
*M – The "prime" location on Union Square gets high praise, but this "old favorite" has become a "faded classic" (though renovations are under way); some say it's "old and sedate like an English gentleman", but others just "go for a drink" on the famous Starlight Roof and stay elsewhere.*

# SAN FRANCISCO HOTELS

| R | S | D | P | $ |
|---|---|---|---|---|

**Stanyan Park Hotel\*** 36R (6S)　　　| 19 | 21 | 21 | 17 | $98 |
750 Stanyan St.; (415) 751-1000; FAX 668-5454
*U – "Good bargain" is an understatement for this Haight-Ashbury "favorite"*
*with "charming rooms and bathrooms", adjacent to the UC Medical Center;*
*a "delicious" continental breakfast is included; it reminds surveyors of*
*"small hotels in France and Italy."*

**Stouffer Stanford Court Hotel** 402R (34S)　| 22 | 24 | 23 | 22 | $208 |
(fka Stanford Court Hotel)
905 California St.; (800) 227-4736; (415) 989-3500; FAX 391-0513
*M – Stouffer spent $10 million on a renovation but couldn't do a thing about*
*the "closet-size rooms"; still, it's a "gracious" place in a "prime" Nob Hill*
*location, with a "superior" staff and "the fastest room service in town"; "don't*
*miss" Fournou's Ovens (food rating, 22) or the "bar overlooking the cable*
*crossing"; former guests don't like this place becoming part of a chain.*

**Tuscan Inn\*** 220R (13S)　　　| 18 | 20 | 19 | 19 | $125 |
425 Northpoint St.; (800) 648-4626; (415) 561-1100; FAX 561-1199
*U – The Fisherman's Wharf location is "great for sightseers" and people*
*doing business with the government; rooms are "small" but "quaint", and*
*the fact that this newcomer is managed by Kimco means service is "good."*

**Victorian Inn on the Park** 12R (1S)　| – | – | – | – | M |
301 Lyon St.; (800) 435-1967; (415) 931-1830; FAX (415) 931-1830
*This small bed-and-breakfast on the edge of Haight-Ashbury and Golden*
*Gate Park has a romantic, old-world charm that appeals to honeymooners;*
*though the rooms are "small", it's a great change of pace.*

**Villa Florence Hotel, The** 177R (36S)　| 19 | 19 | 21 | 17 | $121 |
225 Powell St.; (800) 553-4411; (415) 397-7700; FAX 397-1006
*U – The location of this "comfortably restored" hotel right on Union*
*Square "can't be beat", especially "for a low-cost stay"; rooms are "nice for*
*the price" but "small", and there's a "friendly, accommodating" staff and a*
*ticket-service desk; Kuleto's, the resident restaurant (food rating, 20)*
*gets extra kudos.*

**Washington Square Inn, The\*** 15R　| 19 | 22 | 18 | 21 | $143 |
1660 Stockton St.; (800) 388-0220; (415) 981-4220; (415) 397-7242
*U – "San Francisco quaintness at its best" is the hallmark of this "charming*
*bed-and-breakfast in the heart of North Beach"; our surveyors call it a*
*"perfect tourist hotel" and a "lovely place for the wedding guests to stay."*

**Westin St. Francis**   1200R (85S)     | 21 | 21 | 20 | 22 | $178 |
335 Powell St.; (800) 228-3000; (415) 397-7000; FAX 774-0124
*M – To some, this Downtown spot is just "too big and busy", with "too many people running around"; but if you like "lots going on all the time" and want a "great Union Square location" plus "nice-size" rooms, "elegant views" from the tower and a "fabulous" just-renovated lobby, this "grand old classic" may be for you; however, many rooms "need sprucing up."*

## ●OTHER HOTEL-CHAIN CHOICES
*You will find one or more additional locations of the following hotel chains in the San Francisco Bay area: Courtyard by Marriott, Crown Sterling Suites, Days Inn, Doubletree, Embassy Suites, Hilton, Holiday Inn, Howard Johnson, Hyatt, La Quinta Inns, Marriott, Radisson, Ramada and Super 8; for reservations or information, see the toll-free 800 phone listings on page 16.*

## TOP HOTELS
### (In order of rating)

### BEST OVERALL

25 – Four Seasons Olympic
22 – Sorrento Hotel
    Alexis Hotel
    Inn at the Market
21 – Sheraton Seattle
20 – Westin Hotel

### BEST VALUES

Inn at the Market
Edgewater
Sheraton Seattle
Red Lion Hotel Bellevue
Hyatt Regency Bellevue
Holiday Inn Crowne Plaza

\*      \*      \*

### Best Rooms

25 – Four Seasons Olympic
23 – Inn at the Market
    Alexis Hotel
22 – Sorrento Hotel
21 – Sheraton Seattle
20 – Westin Hotel

### Best Dining

24 – Four Seasons Olympic
23 – Sorrento Hotel
22 – Alexis Hotel
21 – Sheraton Seattle
20 – Inn at the Market
19 – Westin Hotel

### Best Service

25 – Four Seasons Olympic
23 – Alexis Hotel
    Inn at the Market
    Sorrento Hotel
21 – Sheraton Seattle
20   Stouffer Madison

### Best Public Facilities

25 – Four Seasons Olympic
22 – Sorrento Hotel
21 – Inn at the Market
20 – Sheraton Seattle
    Alexis Hotel
19 – Westin Hotel

| R | S | D | P | $ |

**Alexis Hotel – Seattle**   54R (15S)    | 23 | 23 | 22 | 20 | $161 |
1007 First Ave.; (800) 426-7033; (206) 624-4844; FAX 621-9009
*U – In a town that thinks Eddie Bauer is a fashion designer, an elegant "European-style hotel" might seem out of place, but "gorgeous antique- filled rooms", a "no-tipping policy" and staff that "learns your name" are enough to make this "art deco gem" located near the waterfront, Pioneer Square and the new Seattle Art Museum a "favorite"; its restaurants – Cafe Alexis (food rating, 24), Cajun Corner (16) and 92 Madison (18) are also popular.*

†For restaurants, see *Zagat Pacific Northwest Restaurant Survey.*

## SEATTLE HOTELS | R | S | D | P | $ |

**Doubletree Seattle Inn\*** 198R (5S)    | 15 | 16 | 13 | 14 | $114 |
205 Strander Blvd.; (800) 528-0444; (206) 246-8220; FAX 575-4743
*U – "Reasonable" and "decent" are the words that first come to mind for our reviewers, who also find "airport convenience" and Southcenter Mall proximity pluses; "good service" helps explain why this chain is such a popular one with business travelers who crave reliability.*

**Doubletree Suites Seattle\*** 221S    | 19 | 19 | 16 | 17 | $126 |
16500 Southcenter Pkwy.; (800) 528-0444; (206) 575-8220; FAX 575-4743
*U – Slightly-more-stylish sister property of the Doubletree Inn and only a few blocks away; the draw here is all-suites at a price below regular rooms Downtown – a good choice for budget-minded businesspeople.*

**Edgewater, The** 238R (5S)    | 18 | 18 | 18 | 18 | $121 |
2411 Alaskan Way; (800) 624-0670; (206) 728-7000; FAX 441-4119
*U – It's been a while since the Beatles fished from their room in this "motel-like" waterfront inn; a recent renovation combines with "novel design", "wonderful food" and a "beautiful view of the Sound" to keep the place popular; ask for a "room over the water and feed the gulls" from your window – they're still here, although fishing poles are no longer offered.*

**FOUR SEASONS OLYMPIC** 450R (12S)    | 25 | 25 | 24 | 25 | $179 |
411 University St.; (800) 223-8772; (206) 621-1700; FAX 682-9633
*U – As far as our surveyors are concerned, this is "the hotel in Seattle"; typical comments include: "the best Downtown hotel anywhere" and "my favorite hotel in America"; "gorgeous public areas", "an old-world feel", "superb, thoughtful service" and "great restaurants" combine to make Washington State's only AAA Five Diamond "reason enough to go to Seattle"; on a bad day you'll realize "the swimming pool is too small for laps."*

**Holiday Inn Crowne Plaza** 415R (62S)    | 19 | 17 | 16 | 17 | $123 |
1113 Sixth Ave.; (800) 521-2762; (206) 464-1980; FAX 340-1617
*U – Though it "could be anywhere", the fact that this "very nice urban hotel" is an "easy walk to all of Downtown Seattle" makes it a "good value"; "comfortable rooms", some with "some good views", and modest prices keep this chain hotel "bustling with tour groups" and "business travelers"; truly a "pleasant surprise."*

**Hyatt Regency Bellevue** 382R (23S)    | 20 | 20 | 18 | 19 | $134 |
900 Bellevue Way NE, Bellevue; (800) 233-1234; (206) 462-1234; FAX 646-7567
*U – "Friendly staff", "above-average rooms" and "quiet" make this a "gem of a hotel"; though "similar to other Hyatts – yet on a smaller scale – it's "easy to stay" in such "fresh and warm surroundings"; in sum, "a wonderful hotel in all respects save for food, but with Seattle's restaurants..."*

**Inn at the Market**   65R (9S) | 23 | 23 | – | 21 | $139 |
86 Pine St.; (800) 446-4484; (206) 443-3600; FAX 448-0631
*U – Perhaps the "best place for the first-time Seattle visitor", thanks to its location "right in the heart of Pike Place Market"; there's a "rooftop-deck view", "French country charm" and "outstanding nearby dining", but some find the "crowds, odors and noise" of the Market distracting; N.B. though there's no on-site restaurant, the adjacent Campagne (food rating, 23) might as well be.*

**Mayflower Park Hotel***   176R (15S) | 20 | 21 | 17 | 18 | $113 |
405 Olive Way; (800) 426-5100; (206) 623-8700; FAX 382-6997
*U – For 65 years this "pleasant older hotel with a pretty lobby", located "in the heart of the shopping district", has been cultivating its clientele with pleasant accommodations, service and old-fashioned prices that make it "a real value for Seattle."*

**Red Lion Hotel Bellevue**   353R (5S) | 17 | 17 | 16 | 17 | $113 |
300 112th Ave., SE, Bellevue; (800) 547-8010; (206) 455-1300; FAX 455-0466
*U – "You can count on them" for "serviceable" accommodations and "efficient" service – nothing more, nothing less; it's a "decent alternative away from Downtown", but some say "it's difficult to find" and "a bit tired."*

**Seattle Hilton**   237R (6S) | 17 | 17 | 16 | 16 | $124 |
Sixth Ave. & University St.; (800) 426-0535; (206) 624-0500; FAX 682-9029
*M – "Convenient" and "ordinary" but "good for business"; "complimentary apples" and proximity to the convention center and Pike Place Market make up for "no lobby to speak of" and a "weird" location "atop a multistory garage"; "serviceable" only because it's "in the center of town."*

**Sheraton Seattle Hotel & Towers**   958R (78S) | 21 | 21 | 21 | 20 | $141 |
1400 Sixth Ave.; (800) 325-3535; (206) 621-3446; FAX 447-5534
*U – A million-dollar collection of Northwest glass art, convenience to the convention center, a "great health club", "excellent concierge floor" and the top-rated Fullers restaurant combine to make this bustling chain outlet a favorite of many surveyors; rooms are "excellent in the tower" but "in need of redecoration" and merely "ok" in the main hotel.*

**Sorrento Hotel**   76R (42S) | 22 | 23 | 23 | 22 | $158 |
900 Madison St.; (800) 426-1265; (206) 622-6400; FAX 625-1059
*M – "A little out of the way but worth it", this "beautiful" "European-style" hotel sports limo service, an "excellent restaurant", the Hunt Club (food rating, 23), a "cozy lobby bar" and "hot water bottles in every bed" on chilly nights; fans say it's an "exquisite old hotel" – "don't let the hilltop location stop you"; however, a growing number of critics say its reputation is better than the reality.*

**Stouffer Madison**   554R (90S)     | 20 | 20 | 18 | 19 | $139 |
515 Madison St.; (800) 468-3571; (206) 583-0300; FAX 447-0992
*U – A sleeper on the Seattle scene; the "enclosed rooftop pool", "good public areas" and "many rooms with views" have created a discreet following; if you avoid the "noisy rooms on the highway" side and don't mind being fairly "far from everything up a steep hill", then this chain outlet is "luxurious and attentive for a great price."*

**Warwick Hotel, The\***   233R (4S)     | 19 | 19 | 17 | 16 | $113 |
401 Lenora St.; (800) 426-9280; (206) 443-4300; FAX 448-1662
*U – Recent remodeling has created a "charming smaller hotel" whose "quiet and comfy rooms" have "great bathrooms" and wet bars; some find that being a few blocks from Downtown is a drag, but complimentary transport is provided.*

**Westin Hotel Seattle**   865R (47S)     | 20 | 20 | 19 | 19 | $145 |
1900 Fifth Ave.; (800) 228-3000; (206) 728-1000; FAX 728-2259
*U – A "central location" within "walking distance of Pike Place Market and the pier" distinguishes this above-average "convention hotel" – you're so close to the water that "sea gulls peck at your windows"; the "double towers can be confusing", but "excellent amenities" and the "spectacular Japanese restaurant" Nikko spell "a warm, pleasant hotel."*

### ● OTHER HOTEL-CHAIN CHOICES
*You will find one or more additional locations of the following hotel chains in the Seattle area: Courtyard by Marriott, Days Inn, Embassy Suites, Hampton Inn, Howard Johnson, La Quinta Inns, Marriott, Radisson, Residence Inn, Super 8 and Travelodge/Viscount; for reservations or information, see the toll-free 800 phone listings on page 16.*

# ST. LOUIS†

## TOP HOTELS
## (In order of rating)

### BEST OVERALL
25 – Ritz-Carlton
24 – Majestic
21 – Seven Gables Inn
 Hyatt Regency

### BEST VALUES
Drury Inn Union Station
Holiday Inn - Clayton Plaza
Hyatt Regency
Seven Gables Inn

\*    \*    \*

### Best Rooms
26 – Majestic
 Ritz-Carlton
21 – Hyatt Regency
 Seven Gables Inn

### Best Dining
25 – Ritz-Carlton
23 – Seven Gables Inn
22 – Majestic
20 – Hyatt Regency

### Best Service
26 – Ritz-Carlton
24 – Majestic
22 – Seven Gables Inn
20 – Hyatt Regency

### Best Public Facilities
25 – Ritz-Carlton
24 – Majestic
 Hyatt Regency
21 – Drury Inn Union Station

| R | S | D | P | $ |

**Adam's Mark St. Louis**  910R (96S)  | 20 | 20 | 19 | 20 | $132 |
315 Chestnut St.; (800) 444-ADAM; (314) 241-7400; FAX 241-9839
*M – A prime convention site, this large, ornate Downtown hotel overlooks
Gateway Arch and the Mississippi, so "try to get a room with a view"; public
areas, the lobby and restaurants, especially Faust's (food rating, 25) get
solid scores, but some respondents are unhappy with "musty" rooms.*

---

†For restaurants, see *Zagat St. Louis Restaurant Survey.*

## ST. LOUIS HOTELS

| R | S | D | P | $ |

**Cheshire Inn Motor Hotel**   107R (10S)   | 20 | 19 | 19 | 18 | $119 |
6300 Clayton Rd.; (800) 325-7378; (314) 647-7300; FAX 647-0442
*M – Small and out of the mainstream, but close to Washington University
and Forest Park's various attractions (zoo, art and history museums,
planetarium), this midsize Tudor-style hotel is praised by some for its
"interesting theme rooms" and "very unique, old English setting", but
knocked by others for being "dark, dingy and very noisy."*

**Clarion Hotel St. Louis**   797R (29S)   | 14 | 16 | 14 | 13 | $98 |
200 S. Fourth St.; (800) 325-7353; (314) 241-9500; FAX 241-6171
*M – This "large and impersonal" round riverfront tower with a revolving
restaurant (Top of the Riverfront) offers "great views of St. Louis" and
proximity to Downtown and Busch Stadium, but even a "great location"
that's "clean and cheap" fails to offset a general feeling that it's "just a
place to sleep"; N.B. "don't miss" the Sunday brunch.*

**Daniele Hotel**   90R (6S)   | 17 | 17 | 17 | 15 | $130 |
(fka Daniele Hilton Hotel)
216 N. Meramec St.; (800) 325-8302; (314) 721-0101; FAX 721-0609
*U – A recent ownership change makes this small Clayton property, close to
St. Louis County political and business offices and to Washington U, hard
to rate, but the experienced new management offers some optimism for
the future; meanwhile, expect the usual amenities from this European-style
small hotel, known for quiet elegance and friendly staff.*

**Doubletree Hotel &**   | – | – | – | – | E |
**Conference Center**   223R (8S)
16625 Swingley Ridge Dr.; (800) 528-0444; (314) 532-5000; FAX 532-9984
*Designed to suit the needs of the busy executive, every room is equipped
with video links to the conference center; located in Chesterfield, a western
suburb of St. Louis, the Doubletree is convenient to the Chesterfield Mall,
the Gateway Arch, the St. Louis Zoo and the Anheuser Busch Brewery.*

**Doubletree Mayfair***   184S   | 20 | 21 | 19 | 19 | $113 |
806 St. Charles St.; (800) 528-0444; (314) 421-2500; FAX 421-6254
*U – Long a Downtown landmark and now sporting a new Doubletree
affiliation plus considerable remodeling, this veteran is within a few
blocks of Busch Stadium and St. Louis's expanded convention center
(which should help dispel complaints of a "terrible location"); live elevator
operators add a touch of old-fashioned style, while the recently renovated
rooms are large and well appointed; the Doubletree affiliation ensures
that it'll be well run.*

**Drury Inn Union Station**   176R (2S)   | 21 | 19 | 18 | 21 | $109 |
20th & Eugenia Sts. (across from west side of Union Station)
(800) 325-8300; (314) 231-3900; FAX 231-3900
*U – Once a YMCA that catered to workers from Union Station across the
street, this is now a remodeled, one-of-a-kind spot praised for "nicer rooms
than at the Hyatt" and a "fun location" adjacent to a popular shopping and
entertainment area; "you could end up walking halfway to Chicago to find
your room", but the "special station rooms" can be a treat; ditto the old St.
Louis Italian-style Lombardo's Trattoria (food rating, 21).*

**Embassy Suites –**   | 20 | 19 | 17 | 19 | $108 |
**St. Louis Riverfront Hotel\***   297S
901 N. First St.; (800) 241-5151; (314) 241-4200; FAX 241-6513
*M – A block north of the Laclede's Landing entertainment area but still
close to Downtown, the new convention center and Busch Stadium, this
affordable courtyard-style all-suiter draws praise for being "well planned";
some complain of "ho-hum rooms" and say "good location but something
missing"; the dining gets less-than-excellent comments.*

**Holiday Inn – Clayton Plaza**   253R (29S)   | 16 | 16 | 13 | 15 | $88 |
7730 Bonhomme Ave.; (800) HOLIDAY; (314) 863-0400; FAX 863-8513
*M – A location "convenient to Clayton businesses" and Washington U is
the highest praise for this high-rise hotel that's otherwise rated "basic" and
"your average Holiday Inn in the Midwest"; if you need a "good location"
and the usual amenities and not much else, at a modest price, this place
fills the bill.*

**Holiday Inn Downtown/**   | 16 | 16 | 15 | 16 | $85 |
**Convention Center\***   296R (6S)
Ninth St. at Convention Plaza; (800) 289-8338; (314) 421-4000; FAX 421-5974
*M – An ideal location – across the street from the convention center and a
few blocks from Busch Stadium and Downtown – should position this
affordable atrium-style building for a booming sports business; otherwise,
the facilities elicit "ok" responses but no raves.*

**Holiday Inn Downtown/Riverfront** 456R (95S) | 16 | 16 | 13 | 14 | $90 |
200 N. Fourth St.; (800) 325-1395; (314) 621-8200; FAX 621-8073
*M – Convenient to Busch Stadium and the newly expanded convention
center, this former high-rise apartment house overlooking the river is
touted as "comfortable, with a good location"; however, our surveyors
generally downplay its other features, calling it "adequate", "mediocre but
cheap", "old and tired."*

| R | S | D | P | $ |

### HOTEL MAJESTIC, THE   91R (3S)

| 26 | 24 | 22 | 24 | $131 |

1019 Pine St.; (800) 451-2355; (314) 436-2355; FAX 436-2355
*U – This remodeled Downtown gem, with its European-style high service and outstanding rooms, draws praise as an "excellent small business hotel" with "old-world charm"; concierge service and a convenient location also get good marks, and the Just Jazz restaurant brings in top jazz groups for an old St. Louis feel.*

### Hyatt Regency   538R (12S)

| 21 | 20 | 20 | 24 | $124 |

1 St. Louis Union Station; (800) 233-1234; (314) 231-1234; FAX 436-6827
*U – Located right inside the remodeled former railroad terminal, this Hyatt is adjacent to shopping, restaurants and entertainment; its "historic" lobby is "breathtaking", and the more "spacious" rooms in the older part of the hotel convey a "beautiful, turn-of-the-century" feel; that it's "touristy" should come as no surprise.*

### Marriott Pavilion Hotel   670R (32S)

| 19 | 19 | 17 | 18 | $114 |

1 Broadway; (800) 228-9290; (314) 421-1776; FAX 331-9029
*M – Across the street from Busch Stadium, this Downtown veteran is a natural for baseball fans and conventioneers, though some say it's "just another Marriott" that happens to be in the "shadow of a stadium";* N.B. *the city's top restaurant, Tony's (food rating, 28), recently moved to a new location across the street from the hotel.*

### Radisson Hotel Clayton   228R (24S)

| 16 | 15 | 14 | 14 | $103 |

7750 Carondelet Ave., Clayton; (800) 333-3333; (314) 726-5400;
FAX 726-6105
*M – Convenience to the Clayton Business District and Washington U is the strong point for this otherwise "nothing special" midsize hotel; fans note "good value, good location", but critics say "they favor banquet business over business travelers"; the new restaurants have earned good marks, especially Max's Bar & Grill.*

### RITZ-CARLTON, ST. LOUIS   301R (33S)

| 26 | 26 | 25 | 25 | $157 |

100 Carondelet Plaza; (800) 241-3333; (314) 863-6300; FAX 863-7486
*U – The area's newest hotel gets accolades in all categories, with consensus reviews as "the best in St. Louis", thanks to its wonderful rooms, "impeccable service", "superior" food at The Dining Room and The Grill, and "beautiful" public spaces; it has "that great Ritz style" – enough said.*

## ST. LOUIS HOTELS | R | S | D | P | $ |

**Seven Gables Inn** 32R (4S) | 21 | 22 | 23 | 18 | $128 |
26 N. Meramec St.; (800) 433-6590; (314) 863-8400; FAX 863-8846
*U – This tiny, European-style hotel is "a charming place" where the "service never stops"; it gets compliments for "wonderful food" and for rooms that, though "small", are nicely furnished; all in all, a "great hideaway, especially for lovers and gourmets", but not centrally located.*

**St. Louis Marriott West** 301R (1S) | – | – | – | – | M |
660 Maryville Center Dr.; (800) 352-1175; (314) 878-2747; FAX 878-3005
*Opened in 1992, this Marriott, located in West County, is convenient to Monsanto, AT&T, Southwestern Bell and IBM; expect the usual features of a chain hotel appealing to business travellers, but also functional for families.*

## ● OTHER HOTEL-CHAIN CHOICES
*You will find one or more additional locations of the following hotel chains in the St. Louis area: Courtyard by Marriott, Days Inn, Doubletree, Hampton Inn, Hilton, Holiday Inn, Howard Johnson, La Quinta Inns, Marriott, Preferred Hotels, Radisson, Ramada, Residence Inn, Stouffer and Super 8; for reservations or information, see the toll-free 800 phone listings on page 16.*

# TAMPA BAY†

## TOP HOTELS
## (In order of rating)

### BEST OVERALL

**22** – Wyndham Harbour Island
    Don Ce-Sar Registry
**21** – Innisbrook Resort
    Hyatt Regency Westshore
    Saddlebrook

### BEST VALUES

Tampa Marriott Westshore
Wyndham Harbour Island
Embassy Suites Tampa Airport
Hyatt Regency Westshore
St. Petersburg Beach Hilton

\*    \*    \*

### Best Rooms

**23** – Wyndham Harbour Island
    Innisbrook Resort
**22** – Saddlebrook
    Hyatt Regency Westshore
**21** – Embassy Suites

### Best Dining

**21** – Don Ce-Sar Registry
    Wyndham Harbour Island
    Hyatt Regency Westshore
**20** – Innisbrook Resort
**19** – Saddlebrook

### Best Service

**23** – Wyndham Harbour Island
**22** – Don Ce-Sar Registry
    Hyatt Regency Westshore
**21** – Saddlebrook
**20** – Innisbrook Resort

### Best Public Facilities

**23** – Innisbrook Resort
    Don Ce-Sar Registry
    Saddlebrook
**22** – Wyndham Harbour Island
**21** – Hyatt Regency Westshore

---

†For restaurants, see *Zagat Orlando/Central Florida Restaurant Survey*.

## TAMPA BAY HOTELS

|  | R | S | D | P | $ |
|---|---|---|---|---|---|

### Adam's Mark Caribbean Gulf Resort*  211R (5S)

| 15 | 15 | 14 | 16 | $99 |
|---|---|---|---|---|

430 S. Gulfview Blvd., Clearwater Beach; (800) 444-ADAM;
(813) 443-5714; (813) 442-8389

*M – If you love "magnificent" Clearwater Beach as much as some of our surveyors do, then this tourist hotel may suit you; fans say "it's the place to be on Clearwater Beach", with lots of water sports and a nightclub that hops; critics say the only thing it's got going for it is "location."*

### Belleview Mido Resort Hotel  365R (40S)

| – | – | – | – | M |
|---|---|---|---|---|

(fka Belleview Biltmore Resort Hotel)
25 Belleview Blvd., Clearwater; (800) 237-8947; (813) 442-6171;
FAX 443-6361

*The purchase by Japanese investors of this former queen of West Coast resorts has not been well received: "the Japanese have no idea how to run one of these great old Victorian family resorts"; however, it still offers a stately setting that includes all the modern amenities plus "incredible golf."*

### Courtyard by Marriott – Westshore  156R (11S)

| 20 | 20 | 17 | 18 | $114 |
|---|---|---|---|---|

3805 W. Cypress St., Tampa; (800) 228-9290; (813) 874-0555; FAX 870-0685

*U – A good value that lives up to its reputation for solid comfort at a good price, this suburban hotel is judged "fine" for a business stay (it's only three miles from the airport and has a pool and workout facility) and a "nice place to live long-term."*

### Crown Sterling Suites  129S

| – | – | – | – | I |
|---|---|---|---|---|

(fka Embassy Suites – Busch Gardens)
11310 N. 30th St., Tampa; (800) 433-4600; (813) 971-7690; FAX 972-5525

*Embassy Suites traded in its Busch Gardens location for Crown Sterling, and while most folks won't say it's sterling, they do agree that this "good family hotel" is "homey" and a reasonably priced place to stay near the wildlife-and-amusement park and the airport.*

### Don Ce-Sar Registry Resort  328R (51S)

| 21 | 22 | 21 | 23 | $163 |
|---|---|---|---|---|

3400 Gulf Blvd., St. Petersburg Beach; (800) 247-9810; (813) 360-1881;
FAX 367-7597

*U – They don't make 'em like this anymore; "the grand old pink lady" still looks lovely after 65 "elegant" years on the "wonderful beach", and she's still turning guests' heads: "gorgeous", "beautiful"; this "throwback to the '20s" offers "old-fashioned" "luxury", "excellent service" and "sunset meals on the patio"; the Continental fare at King Charles restaurant (food rating, 23) is also well-regarded; however, rooms may be "small and awkward."*

| R | S | D | P | $ |
|---|---|---|---|---|

### Embassy Suites Tampa Airport   200S

| 21 | 18 | 14 | 19 | $111 |
|----|----|----|----|------|

(fka Guest Quarters Suite Hotel on Tampa Bay)
3050 N. Rocky Point Dr., Tampa; (800) 424-2900; (813) 888-8800; FAX 888-8743
*M – "Standard chain style but good value" sums up the sentiment on this well-priced, well-placed contemporary-style all-suiter right on Tampa Bay; business travelers like the "good services", comfortable rooms and free breakfast and cocktail hour, making this a "solid value."*

### Heritage Hotel, The   70R (10S)

| – | – | – | – | M |
|---|---|---|---|---|

234 Third Ave. N., St. Petersburg; (800) 283-7829; (813) 822-4814;
FAX 823-1644
*To many who stay here, this landmark in Downtown St. Pete is a lot like its name; guests praise the old-world atmosphere and the food, especially the complimentary continental breakfast; the staff wins high marks, and certainly no one complains about the old-world prices.*

### Holiday Inn Ashley Plaza
### Convention Center*   311R (8S)

| 17 | 18 | 17 | 15 | $88 |
|----|----|----|----|-----|

111. W. Fortune St., Tampa; (800) ASK-VALUE; (813) 223-1351;
FAX 221-2000
*M – Location, location...well, you get the idea; this Downtown high rise may "need help" in the eyes of some guests, but despite "standard rooms" and standard everything else, fans choose it for its setting near the Performing Arts Center, Harbor Island, Tampa Stadium and Busch Gardens.*

### Hyatt Regency Westshore   468R (23S)

| 22 | 22 | 21 | 21 | $139 |
|----|----|----|----|------|

6200 Courtney Campbell Causeway, Tampa; (800) 233-1234;
(813) 874-1234; FAX 286-9864
*M – A "stylish", "lovely" hotel in the heart of the city, this one has "friendly" service, a "tropical feel" and "comfort", though some detractors think it also has a "convention atmosphere"; Armani's, the hotel's signature top-floor restaurant (food rating, 27), wins raves.*

### Innisbrook Resort   1000S

| 23 | 20 | 20 | 23 | $150 |
|----|----|----|----|------|

U.S. Hwy. 19 S., Tarpon Springs; (800) 456-2000; (813) 942-2000;
FAX 942-2000
*U – Tarpon may be famous for its sponges, but conventioneers and duffers alike can soak up "fabulous golf", "great service" and "good but expensive" food in this resort that's "remote" but worth the trip; rooms are "large and comfortable", the grounds are "beautiful", and a tour of the nearby fishing village is a trip back in time.*

## TAMPA BAY HOTELS    | R | S | D | P | $ |

**Radisson Bay Harbor Inn\***   257R (11S)   | 20 | 20 | 16 | 17 | $108 |
7700 Courtney Campbell Causeway, Tampa; (800) 333-3333; (813) 281-8900;
FAX 281-0189
*U – This chain hotel binds visitors with a few extras, like private balconies
with "a nice view of the water" in all rooms, a "beautiful" pool and bargain
packages; besides all that, look for a king-size bed, continental breakfast
for two and thoughtful complimentary amenities.*

**Saddlebrook Golf &**   | 22 | 21 | 19 | 23 | $155 |
**Tennis Resort**   770R (635S)
100 Saddlebrook Way, Wesley Chapel; (800) 729-8383; (813) 973-1111;
FAX 973-4504
*M – At this "attractive resort in an area cut from a swamp", "wildlife
abounds on the grounds"; there's also golf (36 holes), tennis (45 courts),
swimming in the half-million-gallon Superpool and plenty of walking on 480
acres of natural countryside; however, critics say that while the condo-style
lodging is "comfortable", "unless you play golf, you will die of boredom."*

**Sheraton Grand Hotel\***   325R (22S)   | 20 | 20 | 19 | 18 | $120 |
4860 W. Kennedy Blvd., Tampa; (800) 325-3535; (813) 286-4400;
FAX 286-4053
*M – Though vacationers may find it a bit "out of the way", this hotel has a
solid reputation among business travelers, enhanced by a location just two
miles from the airport; "nice rooms" complement a convivial lobby bar,
three restaurants, and nearby shopping and nightlife.*

**Sheraton Sand Key Resort\***   405R (15S)   | 19 | 18 | 18 | 18 | $118 |
1160 Gulf Blvd., Clearwater Beach; (800) 325-3535; (813) 595-1611;
FAX 596-8488
*M – "Casual Florida atmosphere" and a "wonderful beach" are the draws
at this beachside hotel that also offers the full complement of recreational
activities; some find it "disappointing", but a recent renovation should
address any lingering complaints, and the poolside bar and cookouts
attract a crowd of sun-and-funners.*

**Stouffer Vinoy Resort**   360R (43S)   | – | – | – | – | M |
(fka Vinoy Park Hotel)
501 Fifth Ave. NE, St. Petersburg; (800) 468-3571; (813) 894-1000;
FAX 822-2785
*Too new to rate, this luxuriously restored 1925 Mediterranean-revival resort
sports a wide range of activities and amenities, from a fine location on the
beach to golf, 16 tennis courts, 4 restaurants, a 74-slip marina and 20,000
square feet of outdoor function space; early indications are that it's
attracting throngs of well-heeled vacationers and corporate-meeting types.*

## TAMPA BAY HOTELS

| R | S | D | P | $ |

**St. Petersburg Beach** | 17 | 16 | 16 | 16 | $108 |
**Hilton Resort**   151R (16S)
5250 Gulf Blvd., St. Petersburg Beach; (800) 448-0901; (813) 360-1811;
FAX 360-6919
*M – Salvador Dali may not have slept here, but his not-to-be-missed
museum is nearby – and the free views of the Gulf right outside your
window defy description, too; while the quality of the accommodations,
service and food rate a mere "pleasant", you can't beat the location and
the "affordable rates."*

**Tampa Marriott Westshore**   312R (2S) | 18 | 20 | 19 | 19 | $108 |
1001 N. Westshore Blvd., Tampa; (800) 228-9290; (813) 287-2555;
FAX 289-5464
*M – A shipshape shoreside hotel catering to cruise-takers and landlubbers
with briefcases alike, handy to the airport and Busch Gardens; Champions
restaurant is a contender and so is the service, but critics complain that
this "convention mill" is "very busy" and just "ok", though moderately priced.*

**Trade Winds on St. Petersburg Beach\*** 373R | 18 | 19 | 16 | 19 | $129 |
5500 Gulf Blvd., St. Petersburg Beach; (800) 237-0707; (813) 367-6461;
FAX 360-3848
*U – Though out of the way, this reasonably priced, laid-back resort
provides "beautiful grounds", "nice" rooms, a pool, "reasonable" prices and
a "great setting" on the beach that few care to leave; to quote Cole Porter,
"who could ask for anything more?"*

**Wyndham Harbour Island Hotel** 300R (20S) | 23 | 23 | 21 | 22 | $132 |
725 S. Harbour Island Blvd., Tampa; (800) 822-4200; (813) 229-5000;
FAX 229-5022
*U – This "wonderful" Downtown Tampa hotel has it all: a "pretty setting"
with "gorgeous views" of the bay, "beautiful rooms", excellent sports
facilities ("great for joggers"), heads-up service and dining, plus an
"attractive location" attached to a civilized shopping center full of boutiques
and restaurants; "great for Tampa."*

### ● OTHER HOTEL-CHAIN CHOICES
*You will find one or more additional locations of the following hotel chains
in the Tampa Bay area: Crown Sterling Suites, Days Inn, Doubletree, Guest
Quarters, Hampton Inn, Hilton, Holiday Inn, Howard Johnson, Omni, Ramada,
Residence Inn, Ritz-Carlton, Super 8 and Travelodge/ Viscount; for
reservations or information, see the toll-free 800 phone listings on page 16.*

# WASHINGTON, D.C.†

## TOP HOTELS
## (In order of rating)

### BEST OVERALL

25 – Four Seasons
    Ritz-Carlton, Pentagon City
24 – Willard Inter-Continental
    Ritz-Carlton, Tysons Corner
    Park Hyatt
    Ritz-Carlton, Washington
23 – Jefferson Hotel
    Hay-Adams Hotel
22 – ANA Hotel
    Madison Hotel

### BEST VALUES

Tabard Inn
Wyndham Briston Hotel
Ritz-Carlton, Pentagon City
Embassy Suites Chevy Chase
Omni Georgetown
One Washington Circle
ANA Hotel
Embassy Row Hotel
Ritz-Carlton, Tysons Corner
Morrison-Clark Inn

\*    \*    \*

### Best Rooms

25 – Ritz-Carlton, Pentagon City
    Four Seasons
    Willard Inter-Continental
24 – Ritz-Carlton, Tysons Corner
    Park Hyatt
    Jefferson Hotel
    Ritz-Carlton, Washington
23 – Watergate Hotel
    ANA Hotel
    Hay-Adams Hotel

### Best Dining

25 – Four Seasons
24 – Ritz-Carlton, Tysons Corner
    Ritz-Carlton, Pentagon City
    Ritz-Carlton, Washington
    Willard Inter-Continental
23 – Morrison-Clark Inn
    Park Hyatt
22 – Jefferson Hotel
    Watergate Hotel
    Hay-Adams Hotel

### Best Service

25 – Four Seasons
    Ritz-Carlton, Pentagon City
    Ritz-Carlton, Tysons Corner
24 – Park Hyatt
    Jefferson Hotel
    Willard Inter-Continental
    Ritz-Carlton, Washington
23 – Hay-Adams Hotel
    Madison Hotel
22 – Watergate Hotel

### Best Public Facilities

25 – Willard Inter-Continental
    Four Seasons
24 – Ritz-Carlton, Pentagon City
23 – Ritz-Carlton, Tysons Corner
    ANA Hotel
    Jefferson Hotel
    Park Hyatt
    Ritz-Carlton, Washington
21 – Grand Hyatt
    Grand Hotel

†For restaurants, see *Zagat Washington, D.C./Baltimore Restaurant Survey.*

**ANA Hotel**   415R (8S)                        | 23 | 22 | 21 | 23 | $167 |
(fka Westin Hotel, The)
2401 M St., NW; (800) 228-3000; (202) 429-2400; FAX 457-5010
*U – Surveyors laud this "classy" West End hostelry as a "perfect example
of a top-notch hotel", citing its "beautiful, open, floral" lobby, "good-size
rooms", "superb" staff, "great meeting facilities" and "wonderful" dining, not
to mention an "outdoor garden" and health club; only its sale to ANA gets
mixed reviews: "much better run now" vs. "lost its charm."*


**Canterbury Hotel, The**   99S          | 18 | 19 | 17 | 15 | $132 |
1733 N St., NW; (800) 424-2950; (202) 393-3000; FAX 785-9581
*U – Travelers "who like small hotels" seek out this all-suiter just off Dupont
Circle; it's "neat, clean, obliging and reasonable", with "great beer" (and
recently upgraded food) in the olde English pub, an "interesting clientele"
and plenty of "discreet" charm; critics fault "old rooms off halls that need
upgrading" and service that "leaves much to be desired", but that's not
enough to diminish its popularity "with weekend bargain hunters."*


**Capital Hilton, The**   541R (28S)        | 18 | 18 | 16 | 18 | $158 |
16th & K Sts., NW; (800) HILTONS; (202) 393-1000; FAX 639-5742
*U – This Downtown "workhorse" just "on the edge of the desirable section
of town" is favored "for a sightseeing trip" (it's near the White House and
the Mall), for conferencing ("does a good job with meetings") and for
business overnights ("the concierge floor works").*


**Carlton, The**   200R (15S)             | 21 | 21 | 20 | 20 | $186 |
(fka Sheraton Carlton Hotel)
923 16th St., NW (K St.); (800) 325-3535; (202) 638-2626; FAX 638-4231
*U – A "lovely old classic" with a great Downtown location – it's "small
enough to be intimate", yet "close to the politicians"; while the rooms can't
match the quiet grandeur of its beautifully restored Italianate lobby,
restaurant and public rooms (few places do), they are "very nice" indeed,
and enhanced by friendly service and pleasant dining.*


**Dupont Plaza Hotel**   314R            | – | – | – | – | E |
1500 New Hampshire Ave. N.W. (Dupont Circle); (800) 841-0003;
(202) 483-6000; FAX 328-3265
*Located right on Dupont Circle, its guests are within walking distance of
Embassy Row, Georgetown, Adams Morgan, the White House and DC's
Downtown business district; it's good for the price.*

**Embassy Row Hotel, The**  196R (28S)  | 20 | 20 | 20 | 18 | $148 |
2015 Massachusetts Ave., NW; (800) 424-2400; (202) 265-1600; FAX 328-7526
*M – Consider this "quiet", "European-style" hotel if you think it sounds
appealing to be treated "like a dignitary" or to have "outstanding dining"
and a rooftop pool and bar near Dupont Circle; these attractions
compensate for small and "slightly worn rooms" and meeting facilities that
are "not up to par", causing most to call it a "trusty DC choice."*

**Embassy Suites**  | 23 | 21 | 19 | 20 | $148 |
**Chevy Chase Pavilion**  (198S)
4300 Military Rd., NW; (800) EMBASSY; (202) 362-9300; FAX 686-3405
*M – Because it's handy for shopping or suburban business and has easy
Metro access for sightseeing, most visitors give this smart-looking all-suiter
good marks (though some find the rooms too "small"); the atrium terrace
and conference space are popular for special events.*

**FOUR SEASONS WASHINGTON**  197R (30S)  | 25 | 25 | 25 | 25 | $215 |
2800 Pennsylvania Ave., NW (800) 332-3442; (202) 342-0444; FAX 944-2076
*U – Acclaimed as the "best in Washington", thanks to a feeling of seclusion
that attracts celebrities, a lush Georgetown setting and "perfect attention to
detail"; it also has rooms "decorated like a private home", award-winning
dining at Aux Beaux Champs (food rating, 24), an "outstanding" tea and a
luxurious fitness center; apart from a few small rooms (request a canal
view), this is an all-around winner.*

**Georgetown Inn, The**  95R (10S)  | 18 | 17 | 15 | 15 | $149 |
1310 Wisconsin Ave., NW; (800) 424-2979; (202) 333-8900; FAX 625-1744
*U – In the heart of bustling Georgetown's nightlife and shops; last spring's
multimillion-dollar renovation by new owners has improved this formerly
"decent" lodging; the guest rooms are "big" and tastefully decorated, the
staff tries hard and the handsome bar and grill is a civilized retreat, but
"beware": rooms on the Wisconsin Avenue side can be noisy.*

**Grand Hotel, The**  262R (31S)  | 22 | 22 | 20 | 21 | $181 |
2350 M St., NW; (800) 848-0016; (202) 429-0100; FAX 429-9759
*M – Grand in terms of "palatial" marble bathrooms, "pampering" service,
"stunning" public spaces and a price tag to match; yet this West End spot
is not always so grand when it comes to maintenance and some "cramped"
rooms; the English pub draws a lively crowd, and the new chef may put the
Promenade dining room on the map.*

**Grand Hyatt Washington**   891R (60S)   | 21 | 20 | 19 | 21 | $165 |
1000 H St., NW; (800) 228-9000; (202) 582-1234; FAX 637-4797
*U – An "easy-to-stay-at" convention center hotel where you "feel anonymous yet taken care of" (especially on the "club floor"), this "surprising" business spot doubles as a "nice weekend getaway"; the "well-designed" atrium lobby/ concourse, with its dramatic waterfall and varied dining facilities, really hums at cocktail time; it's "convenient to the Metro" – but don't walk too far at night.*

**Guest Quarters**   123S   | – | – | – | – | M |
2500 Pennsylvania Ave. N.W. (25th St.); (800) 424-2900; (202) 333-8060; FAX 338-3818
**Guest Quarters**   101S
801 New Hampshire Ave. N.W. (24th & H Sts.); (800) 424-2900; (202) 785-2000; FAX 785-9485
*These two all-suiters may be showing their age, but families and weekenders enjoy the fully equipped kitchens and quiet residential location, near the Kennedy Center and Georgetown; if you don't wish to eat out all the time, this duo's for you.*

**HAY-ADAMS HOTEL, THE**   142R (21S)   | 23 | 23 | 22 | 23 | $214 |
800 16th St., NW; (800) 424-5054; (202) 638-6600; FAX 638-2716
*U – "Better than staying in the White House" (across Lafayette Square) – well, not quite, but Bill and Hillary chose this venerable Downtowner over Blair House for their transition visit with the Bushes; on a day-to-day basis it's integral to the Washington political scene; guests praise its gentility, "superb service" and "marvelous brunch", but warn: "get the right room" (specify the front of the hotel), since "one side is history, the other garbage cans."*

**Henley Park Hotel***   96R (15S)   | 24 | 24 | 23 | 22 | $138 |
926 Massachusetts Ave., NW; (800) 222-8474; (202) 638-5200; FAX 638-6740
*U – "One of DC's better-kept secrets" is this cozy old English hotel near the convention center and not much else; however, its "romantic" air, "quiet" guest rooms, antique-filled public rooms, "unobtrusive" hospitality, stellar dining and a "great jazz trio" keep guests happy on premises.*

**Holiday Inn Crowne Plaza**   468R (12S)   | 18 | 17 | 16 | 16 | $130 |
775 12th St., NW; (800) 465-4329; (202) 737-2200; FAX 347-5886
*M – Getting "what you pay for" at this "commercial setting" means a handy daytime location (across from the convention center and near the Metro and the Mall) that becomes "a bit eerie" at night; there's also "pretty good" comfort, but a few surveyors expect more service and less noise.*

**Hotel Washington**   350R (16S)      | 16 | 16 | 16 | 16 | $131 |
15th St. & Pennsylvania Ave., NW; (800) 424-9540; (202) 638-5900;
FAX 638-4275
*M – A few feel that this "aging" dowager "has the potential to be charming"
again; good points include an "unparalleled" view of the White House from
the rooftop terrace, "walking to many attractions" and the relatively modest
price tag; but "regular rooms are cramped", the staff is "not strong" and
there are "other values around town."*

**Hyatt Arlington at Key Bridge**   303R (9S)      | 17 | 17 | 15 | 15 | $128 |
1325 Wilson Blvd., Arlington, VA; (800) 233-1234; (703) 525-1234; FAX 875-3393
*M – A notch below "Hyatt standards", this "older" version offers a relatively
inexpensive stay for Rosslyn business trips and for tourists willing to take
the Metro (15 minutes to Downtown DC); once you get past a "far-from-
appealing" exterior and public spaces, service is "competent", and recently
renovated rooms are "ok."*

**Hyatt Fair Lakes\***   316S      | 21 | 19 | 17 | 17 | $89 |
12777 Fair Lakes Circle, Fairfax, VA; (800) 233-1234; (703) 818-1234;
FAX 818-3140
*U – Only a few respondents doing business in Fairfax have discovered this
Hyatt "prototype" that offers "exactly what you want for a business stay":
"privacy", "big rooms", "friendly" service, "good" food, exercise and
conference facilities, and a convenient "shuttle to the airport"; what's more,
your office manager will smile at the bill; but remember it's "in the boonies."*

**Hyatt Regency Bethesda**   381R (13S)      | 18 | 18 | 16 | 17 | $134 |
1 Bethesda Metro Ctr., Bethesda, MD; (800) 233-1234; (410) 657-1234;
FAX 657-6453
*M – Some rank this "very Hyatt"-looking place as the "best of the Uptown
hotels", giving it extra points for an in-house Metro stop and Downtown
Bethesda convenience; the rest carp that it's "quite a distance from the
airport" and that the staff must have "learned service in NYC"; meeting
facilities are "good, not great", while the food "needs help."*

**Hyatt Regency Washington**      | 19 | 17 | 17 | 18 | $148 |
**on Capitol Hill**   834R (31S)
400 New Jersey Ave., NW; (800) 233-1234; (202) 737-1234; FAX 393-7927
*M – By day "the best of locations for Capitol doings" (near Union Station,
Congress and the Mall) keeps this older Hyatt's "knockout" lobby "busy"
with lobbyists, tourists and conference-goers; while its atrium and rooftop
restaurant are its most notable features, good things are said about recent
room renovations and meeting facilities; not-so-good things are said about
the neighborhood at night.*

| R | S | D | P | $ |

**Inn at Foggy Bottom**   95S            | 17 | 17 | 15 | 15 | $125 |
824 New Hampshire Ave., NW; (800) 426-4455; (202) 337-6620; FAX 298-7499
*M – Useful "for longer stays" when kitchenettes and the "homelike" feeling
and personalized service of a small hotel matter; this all-suiter offers "great
value close to the Kennedy Center" but is marred by "poor execution" and
rooms in need of "an overhaul"; Fiore's cafe is a plus.*

**JEFFERSON HOTEL, THE**   100R (32S)       | 24 | 24 | 22 | 23 | $204 |
16th & M Sts., NW; (800) 368-5966; (202) 347-2200; FAX 223-9039
*U – Unless your address is the nearby White House, chances are good
that you'll find this elegant period piece "better than home" (it's used by the
President's guests); "intimate" common rooms, "comfortable" sleeping
rooms (some with four-poster beds), a caring management and a "wonder"
of a kitchen leave most respondents saying it's "hard to fault in any way."*

**J.W. Marriott Hotel**   772R (52S)         | 20 | 20 | 19 | 21 | $166 |
1331 Pennsylvania Ave., NW; (800) 228-9290; (202) 393-2000; FAX 626-6995
*M – Business travelers and tourists flag this Marriott for its "easy access from
the airport", "excellent" parking and a location with links to a shopping mall, food
court and the Metro and "within walking distance" of Downtown agencies and
"many attractions"; consider a "splurge for the concierge level", otherwise
it's "impersonal" and "a little too convention-oriented for family vacations."*

**Key Bridge Marriott Hotel**   585R (30S)   | 17 | 17 | 15 | 15 | $124 |
1401 Lee Hwy., Arlington, VA; (800) 642-3234; (202) 524-6400; FAX 524-8964
*U – A good launching pad for an "early flight" from National Airport or
"touring Washington" en famille – you can "walk across the bridge to
Georgetown" or take the nearby Metro everywhere else; it's "an original
Marriott" – "clean" and "well run" – but despite "many face-lifts", it shows
its age; don't miss the view from the rooftop restaurant.*

**Latham Hotel Georgetown, The**   143R (9S)   | – | – | – | – | M |
(fka Georgetown Marbury Hotel)
3000 M St., NW; (800) 368-5922; (202) 726-5000; FAX 337-4250
*This newly renovated, moderately priced Georgetowner offers spiffy rooms
("great ... or teeny tiny", depending on the floor), a small rooftop pool,
business facilities and parking (a Georgetown necessity); the big attraction,
an outpost of LA's trendy restaurant Citron, opened in late 1992.*

**Loews L'Enfant Plaza Hotel**  370R (14S)      | 20 | 19 | 17 | 19 | $161 |
408 L'Enfant Plaza, SW; (800) 243-1166; (202) 484-1000; FAX 646-4456
*U – "Highly recommended" for a stylish business or family stay" because of
its "perfect location" near the mall, shopping and Metro, this "upscale hotel"
has a "pretty lobby" and "pleasant" rooms; however, its setting is "lonely" at
night and a few critics point to "alienated" staff and "sterile" decor.*

**Madison Hotel, The**  353R (35S)      | 23 | 23 | 22 | 21 | $206 |
15th & M Sts., NW; (800) 424-8577; (202) 862-1600; FAX 785-1255
*M – Well-heeled international businesspeople and diplomats get the "royal
treatment" at this elegant old-liner; the antique-filled lobby and formal
Continental dining are synonymous with "Washington refinement"
(surveyors compare it to NYC's St. Regis or SF's Fairmont); the 1992
renovation provided a needed "refurbishing" but left small rooms.*

**Morrison-Clark Inn**  54R (25S)      | 21 | 20 | 23 | 19 | $158 |
1015 L St., NW; (800) 332-7898; (202) 898-1200; FAX 289-8576
*U – This "charmingly restored" Victorian is a little-known in-town retreat,
not far from the convention center; it combines individual attention ("they
greeted me by name!") with "quaint" decor (get a balcony room in the
original house) and some of the best Contemporary American dining in DC
(food rating, 25), courtesy of the Dining Room and Grill Room.*

**Morrison House\***  45R (3S)      | 24 | 22 | 21 | 23 | $170 |
116 S. Alfred St., Alexandria, VA; (800) 367-0800; (703) 838-8000;
FAX 684-6283
*U – Staying in historic old-town Alexandria at this posh hotel is a delightful
way to combine tourism and quiet comfort; the elegant parlor or library and
the clubby grill provide a sophisticated backdrop for business meetings or
visiting with friends – and there are nearby shops plus the Morrison House
Grill (food rating, 21).*

**Omni Georgetown**  300R (64S)      | 19 | 18 | 16 | 15 | $121 |
2121 P St., NW; (800) THE-OMNI; (202) 293-3100; FAX 857-0134
*U – "Close to fun" in Dupont Circle (but a half-mile hike to Georgetown),
the "large, cheap rooms" in this former apartment house can be among the
best deals in DC; while a "dingy, commercial" appearance, "unimpressive
lobby" and "disorganized" front desk discourage business travelers, this
hotel is fine for families and groups looking for basics and bargains.*

# WASHINGTON, D.C., HOTELS

| R | S | D | P | $ |
|---|---|---|---|---|

**Omni Shoreham**  770R (55S)   | 17 | 16 | 15 | 16 | $141 |
2500 Calvert St., NW; (800) THE-OMNI; (202) 234-0700; FAX 234-2500
*M – An art deco classic set on lovely grounds sloping down to Rock Creek Park, with an outdoor swimming pool and tennis courts, yet only steps away from the Metro; it's a "solid choice" if you're assured one of the "beautifully refurbished" rooms in the main building; otherwise, "forget it if you're not conventioneering", since food and service are "average."*

**One Washington Circle Hotel**  151S   | 19 | 18 | 18 | 14 | $125 |
1 Washington Circle, NW; (800) 424-9671; (202) 872-1680; FAX 223-3961
*U – This low-profile converted apartment house is one of the "best buys in DC"; its West End location is "great for Downtown business meetings" at the California-style restaurant West End Cafe (food rating, 20), or for socializing by the jazz piano in the bar, but we hear complaints about noisy rooms overlooking Washington Circle.*

**PARK HYATT WASHINGTON**  224R (125S)   | 24 | 24 | 23 | 23 | $189 |
24th & M Sts., NW; (800) 233-1234; (202) 789-1234; FAX 457-8823
*U – Surveyors "smile from start to finish" at this "serene" West End "getaway", offering "generously sized rooms" with "super baths" and "great room service", excellent conference facilities and Melrose (food rating, 24) is "more than just a hotel restaurant"; "pricey", perhaps, but you get what you pay for.*

**Phoenix Park Hotel**  87R (9S)   | – | – | – | – | M |
520 N. Capitol St., NW; (800) 824-5417; (202) 638-6900; FAX 393-3236
*Despite its prime Senate-side location and Edwardian elegance, this Capitol Hill hotel is better known for its power dining – at Powerscourt (food rating, 22) – and the suds and legislative scuttlebutt in the Irish pub than for its overnight accommodations "run by the Keystone Kops."*

**Pullman-Highland Hotel, The**  145R (40S)   | – | – | – | – | M |
1914 Connecticut Ave., NW; (800) 424-2464; (202) 797-2000; FAX 462-0944
*A charming contrast to the nearby Connecticut Avenue convention specialists, this "nicely renovated", Parisian-feeling property provides "nice rooms" that are "really suites", with a separate office area, "excellent service" and good dining at a "fair price"; it's not well known, but should be.*

**Radisson Park Terrace Hotel***  260R (40S)   | 18 | 17 | 18 | 16 | $122 |
1515 Rhode Island Ave., NW; (800) 333-3333; (202) 232-7000; FAX 332-7152
*U – Surveyors "enjoy" this New York Regency facsimile for its elegant public rooms, comfortable guest rooms, gracious attitude, fine Contemporary American dining in the Chardonnay restaurant (food rating, 19), and a delightful courtyard; affordable luxury, especially on weekends, sums it up.*

## WASHINGTON, D.C., HOTELS

| R | S | D | P | $ |

**Radisson Plaza Hotel**
**at Mark Center\*** 500R (13S)

| 19 | 18 | 18 | 18 | $142 |

5000 Seminary Rd., Alexandria, VA; (800) 333-3333; (703) 845-1010;
FAX 820-6425

*M – "Wonderful views from penthouse rooms" earn good marks for this
sophisticated-looking "suburban property"; it offers solid value – "nice
rooms", "great service", plenty of meeting space and sports facilities;
Yannick's, one of the top-rated restaurants in the area, is an added plus.*

**Ramada Renaissance**
**Hotel – Techworld** 800R (60S)

| 18 | 16 | 15 | 19 | $132 |

999 9th St., NW; (800) 2-RAMADA; (202) 898-9000; FAX 789-4213

*M – Conflicting reports on this high-tech-looking convention facility indicate
inconsistency; one surveyor swears that "does-it-right" performance
matches the "supermodern" facade; others complain of "small rooms",
"horrible staff" and "poor management"; late-night strolls are contraindicated.*

**Residence Inn Bethesda** 187R

| – | – | – | – | E |

7335 Wisconsin Ave. (Waverly St.); (800) 718-0679; (301) 718-0200;
FAX 961-6459

*More like a friendly neighborhood apartment building than a hotel, this new
Marriott, located in Bethesda, is just minutes from Downtown D.C. and
area's finest attractions via the Metro; for reasonable prices, guests enjoy
the unique features of a well-run all-suites hotel.*

**RITZ-CARLTON,**
**PENTAGON CITY** 345R (43S)

| 25 | 25 | 24 | 24 | $178 |

1250 S. Hayes St., Arlington, VA; (800) 241-3333; (703) 415-5000;
FAX 415-5060

*U – Getting "what you expect from the Ritz" in the case of this Pentagon
Center paragon means a "miraculous" room with a "huge marble bath",
"great staff", "incredible" restaurants – The Dining Room (food rating, 26)
and The Grill (23), and a champagne-and-caviar brunch; even its location
in a close-to-the-airport shopping mall can be advantageous.*

**RITZ-CARLTON,**
**TYSONS CORNER** 339R (31S)

| 24 | 25 | 24 | 23 | $183 |

1700 Tysons Blvd., McLean, VA; (800) 241-3333; (703) 506-4300; FAX 506-4305

*U – "A spa atmosphere", "lovely accommodations", the "best service
anywhere", a "great bar (The Grill – food rating, 24) and restaurant (The
Restaurant – food rating, 23)" and "Saks, Neiman's" and "two huge
shopping malls within walking distance" make this a suburban destination
par excellence; a shopper's paradise, it's also "suited to businesspeople."*

**RITZ-CARLTON,**                                | 24 | 24 | 24 | 23 | $198 |
**WASHINGTON** (Pr)    230R (21S)
2100 Massachusetts Ave., NW; (800) 241-3333; (202) 293-2100; FAX 293-0641
*U – This elegant Embassy Row haunt of the diplomatic and smart set has "cozy" period rooms and an elegant wood-paneled lobby and bar, which help create a "lovely" country house ambiance enhanced by a staff of pros; few other places provide its caliber of care, total comfort and first-rate food at the Jockey Club restaurant (food rating, 23), all under one roof.*


**River Inn, The**   97S                         | – | – | – | – | M |
924 25th St.; (202) 337-7600; FAX 337-6520
*Hard by the Potomac, this little-known Foggy Bottom all-suites hotel is also handy to Georgetown shops and restaurants and to the Kennedy Center; newly renovated suites feature fully equipped kitchens, right down to coffee grinders with fresh beans, making this ideal for longer stays.*


**Sheraton City Centre Hotel**   351R (16S)      | 16 | 16 | 14 | 14 | $138 |
1143 New Hampshire Ave., NW; (800) 325-3535; (202) 775-0800; FAX 331-9491
*U – "Better than it looks", this "well-maintained" former hospital, within striking distance of the Business District and Georgetown, is a "good choice for small conventions" or overnight stays but is otherwise undistinguished, and the price tag is friendlier than the concierge.*


**Sheraton Premiere at**                         | 21 | 20 | 18 | 19 | $116 |
**Tysons Corner\***   452R (20S)
8661 Leesburg Pike, Vienna, VA; (800) 572-ROOM; (703) 448-1234;
FAX 893-8193
*U – Towering above Tysons Corner, this suburban high rise wins applause for corporate amenities that extend from business ("fax machines, IBM PCs" and a conference center) to pleasure (attractive rooms, dining options, vaulted public spaces and sports facilities), all at modest prices.*


**Sheraton Washington Hotel**   1505R (129S)     | 18 | 17 | 16 | 17 | $144 |
2660 Woodley Rd., NW; (800) 325-3535; (202) 328-2000; FAX 234-0015
*M – Convention City – this aging behemoth suffers from the sprawls; it handles masses of people efficiently, but the single traveler may find "nightmare registration", "mazelike" halls and service that "evaporates after a large conference leaves"; N.B. Wardman Towers section is still "charming."*

| R | S | D | P | $ |
|---|---|---|---|---|

**Stouffer Mayflower Hotel**   724R (78S)       | 20 | 20 | 20 | 21 | $166 |

1127 Connecticut Ave., NW; (800) HOTELS-1; (202) 347-3000; FAX 466-9082
*M – This grande dame features an "old-world" lobby and a wedding-perfect
ballroom that keep her booked with events; a recent major remodeling
brought this landmark into the 20th century and ended gripes about "dingy"
rooms – though some are still odd-shaped or small; Nicholas (food rating, 25),
is one of DC's best-kept secretes and the coffee shop is a "power place."*

**Tabard Inn**   40R       | 17 | 18 | 21 | 18 | $124 |

1739 N St., NW; (202) 785-1277; FAX 785-6173
*M – The charms of this endearing "hideaway off Dupont Circle" include
"period decorated" guest rooms (some say the period is "early Salvation
Army"), "brandy by the fireplace" in the lounge, a "wonderful garden" and
a dining room serving outstanding "organic and healthy" food.*

**Washington Court Hotel, The**   268R (14S)       | 20 | 17 | 16 | 18 | $141 |

525 New Jersey Ave., NW; (800) 321-3010; (202) 628-2100; FAX 879-7918
*U – "Optimally" situated for "a quick business trip to the Hill", "tourist
attractions" and getting around town, this attractive spot offers "spacious,
well-decorated" rooms, the usual business amenities and a skylit lobby to
see and be seen in; neither dining nor service is notable.*

**Washington Hilton & Towers, The** 1150R (82S)  | 17 | 17 | 15 | 16 | $152 |

1919 Connecticut Ave., NW; (800) HILTONS; (202) 483-3000; FAX 265-8221
*U – Most know this Connecticut Avenue "convention hotel" for its ability to
handle mega-events (there's a special entrance for the President) or as a
base "for sightseeing"; it features "lovely" tower "minisuites" and "resort"-
like sports facilities, but complaints about long hikes to "closet"-size rooms,
combined with varied reactions to food and service ("staff tries, but is too
busy"), indicate that it's "not one of the better Hiltons."*

**Washington Marriott**   418R (4S)       | 18 | 17 | 16 | 17 | $138 |

1221 22nd St., NW; (800) 344-4445; (202) 872-1500; FAX 872-1424
*U – "Nothing spectacular", just a "functional" business-class chain hotel in
the West End, not far from Georgetown; surveyors single out a "nice suite
setup" and attentive staff for special mention; check out Lulu's, the lively
New Orleans bistro around the corner.*

**Washington Vista Hotel**   399R (12S)       | 20 | 19 | 17 | 17 | $162 |

1400 M St., NW; (800) 847-8232; (202) 429-1700; FAX 785-0786
*U – Despite mostly favorable comments from its clientele (and the publicity
generated by ex-mayor Barry's arrest in one of its guest rooms), this "very
nice" Center City property "often seems deserted"; its problem is its mall –
it's "not convenient", and "needs sprucing up."*

### Watergate Hotel, The   235R (84S)          | 23 | 22 | 22 | 21 | $197 |
2650 Virginia Ave., NW; (800) 424-2736; (202) 965-2300; FAX 965-1173
*U – Kennedy Center performers and other familiar faces in the lobby vie
with "gorgeous river views" from the suites as attractions at the hotel
"where history was made"; "nicely decorated" rooms "with many extras",
"professional" staff and a "wonderful spa" draw praise, while surveyors run
out of superlatives to describe dining at Jean-Louis (food rating, 27); only a
few gripe about "sterile architecture" and some small rooms.*

### Westfield's International          | 25 | 24 | 21 | 25 | $170 |
### Conference Center*   360R (20S)
14750 Conf. Ctr. Dr., Chantilly, VA; (800) 635-5666; (703) 818-0300;
FAX 818-3655
*U – Business tops the agenda at this "elegant" and "pricey" conference
center/hotel with its "excellent" meeting rooms, services and banquet/
reception facilities; critics point out that on-site diversions like the spa,
tennis, health club and several restaurants are essential, since it's "way
out in the boonies" near nothing "except Dulles Airport."*

### WILLARD          | 25 | 24 | 24 | 25 | $205 |
### INTER-CONTINENTAL, THE   340R (35S)
1401 Pennsylvania Ave., NW; (800) 327-0200; (202) 628-9100; FAX 637-7326
*U – A beautifully "revived" "Victorian hotel" whose "history as the home of
Presidents makes it special"; a splendid lobby, "stately" guest rooms with
the "little extras that make a great hotel", "outstanding service" and fine
dining in the Willard Room (food rating, 24) "leave even NYC chauvinists
impressed" by "DC's answer to The Plaza"; if only the "staff would turn
down their noses" and top-floor rooms weren't so small.*

### Wyndham Bristol Hotel   239R (137S)          | 22 | 21 | 20 | 20 | $143 |
2430 Pennsylvania Ave., NW; (800) 822-4200; (202) 955-6400; FAX 775-8489
*M – Stylish understatement is the keynote of this Continental-feeling hotel
that's on the way to the Kennedy Center, Georgetown and Downtown;
praise for "large rooms, many with kitchenettes", a "decent restaurant"
(Bristol Grill – food rating, 18) and the "best ever" concierge are mixed with
enough negatives to suggest an uneven performer; however, strong ratings
put naysayers out in the cold.*

### ● OTHER HOTEL-CHAIN CHOICES
*You will find one or more additional locations of the following hotel chains
in the Washington, D.C. area: Courtyard by Marriott, Days Inn, Embassy
Suites, Guest Quarters, Hampton Inn, Hilton, Holiday Inn, Howard Johnson,
Hyatt, Ramada and Super 8; for reservations or information, see the
toll-free 800 phone listings on page 16.*

# TOP HOTELS
# IN OTHER CITIES

# Albuquerque, NM

**Doubletree Albuquerque** (Pr)   307R (13S)     | 20 | 19 | 18 | 19 | $80 |
201 Marquette NW, Albuquerque; (800) 528-0444; (505) 247-3344;
FAX 247-7025
*U – A "good Downtown location" next to the convention center combined
with moderate prices make this an outstanding value in Albuquerque;
"reasonably imaginative food" at La Cascada SW restaurant, including a
"good breakfast", is an extra plus.*

**Hyatt Regency Albuquerque**   395R (14S)     | – | – | – | – | M |
330 Tijeras NW, Albuquerque; (800) 233-1234; (505) 842-1234;
FAX 842-1184
*A modern, convention-oriented hotel with good-size rooms that are all
decorated in SW style; amenities include an outdoor pool, health club, two
lounges and McGrath's restaurant; the regency club level (19th and 20th
floors) provides extra perks.*

**Marriott Albuquerque** (Pr)   411R (11S)     | 21 | 20 | 18 | 19 | $90 |
2101 Louisiana Blvd. NE, Albuquerque; (800) 228-9290; (505) 881-6800;
FAX 881-1780
*U – This high rise business hotel,"well located" in the Uptown area near
regional shopping malls and I-40, offers "beautiful rooms", "great views" of
the mountains and valley, a "wonderful" indoor/outdoor pool and a "helpful,
friendly staff", plus excellent meeting rooms and generally good food.*

# Anchorage, AK

**Captain Cook Hotel**   677R (77S)     | 19 | 19 | 20 | 19 | $147 |
939 W. Fifth Ave., Anchorage; (800) 843-1950; (907) 276-6000; FAX 278-5366
*M – An elegant, unique hotel on the edge of "the last frontier"; be ready for
tourist bustle all summer – they bus 'em in and they bus 'em out; great
views of the Chugach Mountains and Cook Inlet, plus the predictable
"stuffed polar bear in the lobby"; though some say it's just "so-so", others
call this the "best hotel in Anchorage" and "surprisingly good for Alaska."*

# Austin, TX

**FOUR SEASONS HOTEL –** | 25 | 24 | 24 | 25 | $146 |
**AUSTIN**   292R (27S)
98 San Jacinto Blvd., Austin; (800) 332-3442; (512) 478-4500;
FAX 478-3117
*U – Our surveyors bestow "best-in-Austin" honors on this "very enjoyable" hotel on Town Lake, giving it kudos for "beautiful SW decor", "elegant service" and "great food" – like so many Four Seasons, "fabulous in all respects"; this "lakeside luxury" seems like "a terrific bargain" just a few blocks from the Capitol and the UT-Austin campus; besides, there's "great golf" and "running or biking on Town Lake Path."*

# Birmingham, AL

**Tutwiler, The\***   147R (51S) | 23 | 23 | 21 | 23 | $123 |
2100 Sixth Ave. N., Birmingham; (800) 866-ROOM; (205) 322-2100;
FAX 325-1183
*U – "A class act", this elegant old hotel (once a private residence) conveniently located in the heart of Downtown Birmingham is "one of the city's – and Alabama's – best"; from its atmospheric lobby to its spacious, tastefully appointed rooms, it exhibits "real style" and warmth; service and food are also high-caliber.*

**Wynfrey Hotel, The\***   339R (10S) | 24 | 24 | 21 | 23 | $127 |
1000 Riverchase Galleria, Birmingham; (800) 476-7006; (205) 987-1600;
FAX 988-4597
*U – This luxurious, "old-world" hotel is located in the soaring and "very modern" Riverchase Galleria shopping complex; the opulent marble lobby sets a lavish tone, which is carried through in the plush rooms and spacious conference/meeting facilities; well equipped for business and ideally situated for shoppers, it's a solid performer in all categories.*

# Charlotte, NC

**Dunhill Hotel, The**   60R (1S) | – | – | – | – | M |
237 N. Tryon St., Charlotte; (800) 354-4141; (704) 332-4141; FAX 376-4117
*"Cozy and elegant", this lovely old stone inn features "impeccable decor", fine service and excellent Californian-style cuisine in its Monticello restaurant; all in all, it's a "well-done small hotel"; "stay in the main house if possible."*

**TOP HOTELS/OTHER CITIES**    | R | S | D | P | $ |

# Columbus, OH

**Worthington Inn\***   26R (7S)    | 21 | 23 | 23 | 19 | $101 |
649 High St., Columbus; (614) 885-2600; FAX 885-2600
*U – Restored to its original 1830s grandeur, this "lovely" inn is now one of the "best in the Columbus area", offering spacious rooms, top-notch service and "excellent" classic Continental cuisine; "champagne and homemade cookies at bedtime are a typically nice touch."*

# Corpus Christi, TX

**Corpus Christi Marriott**    | 20 | 19 | 20 | 20 | $109 |
**Bayfront Hotel**   474R (28S) (fka Corpus Christi Wyndham)
900 N. Shoreline Blvd., Corpus Christi; (800) 874-4585; (512) 887-1600; FAX 883-8084
*M – High-rising quarters and an "on-the-coast" location provide "nice views", but an early-1992 renovation hasn't had time to make much of an impression – "it's ok, but it could be much better"; fans say it's a "lovely place" and suggest you request a "room overlooking the bay."*

# Florham Park, NJ

**Hamilton Park Executive**    | 18 | 23 | 20 | 20 | $144 |
**Conference Center\***   219R (13S)
175 Park Ave., Florham Park; (800) 321-6000; (201) 377-2424; FAX 514-1670
*U – Looking for all the world like a suburban office complex, this "quiet" corporate retreat adjacent to the Fairleigh Dickinson campus sports a well-equipped health club and a dedicated conference wing; pretty straightforward, but one guest suggests that you "might see some New York Giants", and the Sunday brunch is a "real treat."*

# Fort Worth, TX

**Stockyards Hotel\***   52R (4S)    | 22 | 21 | 17 | 21 | $106 |
109 E. Exchange Ave., Fort Worth; (800) 423-8471; (817) 625-6427; FAX 624-2571
*U – Saddle-topped bar stools, stamped-tin ceilings and guest rooms "individually appointed" in Victorian, Indian, cowboy and mountain-man themes make this the place for the "most fun in the city where the West begins"; it's "old-west charm" at a "good price" in the heart of the Fort Worth Stockyards Historic District – Billy Bob's and the rodeo are right in the neighborhood – so "don't miss it", y'all hear?*

**Worthington, The**   507R (70S)   | 20 | 21 | 21 | 20 | $128 |
200 Main St., Fort Worth; (800) 433-5677; (817) 870-1000; FAX 332-5679
*M – Downtown in Cowtown, this "modern" hotel eschews the wild-west theme in favor of Spartan simplicity; though a few grumble that it has "little charm", most feel that it's "working hard to be special"; "friendly employees make you feel at home" and "excellent food", plus a recent spruce-up and an "excellent" exercise program, all score well.*

# Hartford, CT

**Goodwin Hotel, The\***   124R (11S)   | 21 | 20 | 23 | 22 | $121 |
(fka J.P. Morgan)
1 Haynes St., Hartford; (800) 922-5006; (203) 246-7500; FAX 247-4576
*U – This historic Queen Anne–style building built in 1891 was renovated in 1991, and is now an interesting alternative to modern Downtown chains; some rooms have fireplaces, and there's a health club, an outstanding restaurant (Pierpont's) and weekend packages too.*

# Little Rock, AR

**Capital Hotel, The**   118R (5S)   | – | – | – | – | M |
111 W. Markham St.; (800) 766-7666; (501) 374-7474; FAX 370-7091
*This landmark hotel, built in 1877, is located in the heart of Downtown, across from the Statehouse Convention Center and convenient to the business and historic districts; a restored Victorian with old-world charm, it's overshadowed by the modern Excelsior Hotel, but a good second bet now that rooms are hard to get in Bill and Hillary's town.*

**Arkansas' Excelsior Hotel**   418R (32S)   | – | – | – | – | M |
3 Statehouse Plaza; (800) 527-1745; (501) 375-5000;
FAX 375-4721
*The largest luxury hotel in Arkansas has recently undergone extensive renovation, including the Grand Ballroom, renamed the President Bill Clinton Ballroom, plus the redesigning and naming of two suites to honor the President and Vice President; this flagship hotel for Little Rock's convention trade shares its premises with the Statehouse Convention Center and its 130,000-square-foot meeting facilities; it's said to be first daughter Chelsea's first choice for dining.*

# Louisville, KY

**Seelbach Hotel, The** 321R (31S)　　| 20 | 21 | 21 | 21 | $125 |
500 Fourth Ave., Louisville; (800) 333-3399; (502) 585-3200; FAX 587-6564
*U – A "beautifully restored" grande dame in the heart of Louisville, near the
Galleria shopping mall and convention center; guests rave about the Old
Seelbach Bar in the elegant lobby and the Rathskellar, with its Rookwood
pottery walls and tiled floor; "any other hotel in Louisville is a letdown"; a
concierge club with lots of amenities has recently been added, along with a
well-equipped business center.*

# Memphis, TN

**Peabody Memphis** 454R (16S)　　| 22 | 24 | 24 | 24 | $132 |
149 Union Ave., Memphis; (800) 732-2639; (901) 529-4000; FAX 529-4184
*U – If ducks are your thing, the Peabody's a "must visit", if only to see the
twice-daily parade of quackers from the roof to the lobby fountain; if you
decide to stay, expect a lively lobby and a classy Sunday brunch at this
grande dame that's " the meeting place in Memphis."*

# Oklahoma City, OK

**Waterford Hotel\*** 197R (31S)　　| 23 | 21 | 20 | 19 | $136 |
6300 Waterford Blvd., Oklahoma City; (800) 992-2009; (405) 848-4782;
FAX 843-9161
*U – "An oasis", this classy, European-style mid-rise is judged "outstanding"
in all categories, from its "large, beautiful rooms" and impressive public
areas to its gracious service and good food; though somewhat pricey, it's
more elegant than most people expect of Oklahoma City.*

# Portland, OR

**Heathman Hotel, The** 152R (16S)　　| 21 | 24 | 23 | 20 | $144 |
SW Broadway at Salmon, Portland; (800) 551-0011; (503) 241-4100;
FAX 790-7110
*U – A "winner on all counts": "one of the best new discoveries" in the area;
from "nice rooms with Oriental touches" to high tea in the lounge, this
"well-run hotel" with "state-of-the-art service" offers "plenty of character"
and a "good Downtown location"; a "grand piano bar", well-rated restaurant
and a popular bakery make this "one of the most pleasant hotels ever."*

**Hotel Vintage Plaza**   107R (21S)   | – | – | – | – | M |
422 SW Broadway, Portland; (800) 243-0555; (503) 228-1212; FAX 228-3598
*"Wow!" – as only a hotel built in 1894 and "rehabbed to a gorgeous state"
in 1991 can elicit; if you find the two-story townhouse suites with spiral
staircases too indulgent (or expensive), try the "starlight rooms with floor-
to-ceiling windows that slope over your bed"; the hotel's Pazza Ristorante
(food rating, 22) plus a "terrific staff" make it all as good as it looks.*

**RIVER PLACE ALEXIS HOTEL**   84R (45S)   | 25 | 25 | 23 | 23 | $159 |
1510 SW Harbor Way, Portland; (800) 227-1333; (503) 228-3233;
FAX 295-6161
*M – Its location on the Willamette River, with a "gorgeous view of the marina"
and "wonderful service", leads many to conclude that a stay in this Downtown
hotel constitutes "a vacation in itself"; the "beautiful lobby and common
areas" and fireplaces in some of the suites add to a feeling of luxury at this
European-style hotel that caters to execs and well-heeled pleasure
travelers; the Esplanade restaurant (food rating, 23) is a local favorite.*

# Raleigh-Durham, NC

**Carolina Inn, The**   140R (15S)   | 16 | 19 | 18 | 19 | $100 |
211 Pittsboro St., Chapel Hill; (800) 962-3400; (919) 933-2001
*U – It may be a "throwback to the '50s" in terms of ambiance,
sophistication and cuisine, but this Colonial-style landmark enjoys a prime
location on the edge of the lovely UNC campus and is just a block from the
heart of Chapel Hill; owned and operated by the university, it's "the only
place to be besides Dean Dome for UNC fans" on sports weekends.*

**Siena Hotel***   | 23 | 23 | 24 | 22 | $112 |
1505 E. Franklin St., Chapel Hill; (800) 223-7379; (919) 929-4000; FAX 968-8527
*M – "Elegant old-world charm and service" are the themes of this
Italian-style hotel located near UNC; fans consider it a "special" place with
attractive rooms, "pleasant" service and "five-star" cuisine in the tony
Il Palio restaurant, but some find it a "little too gimmicky."*

**Washington Duke Inn & Golf Club**   171R (7S)  | – | – | – | – | M |
3001 Cameron Blvd., Durham; (800) 443-3853; (919) 490-0999; FAX 688-0105
*Duke-family heirlooms fill the lobby and hallways of this on-campus luxury
hotel that's also on an 18-hole Robert Trent Jones Jr. golf course; the ambiance
is classic and low-key; full business facilities entice corporate types, who
vie with visiting parents.*

# Richmond, VA

**Commonwealth Park Suites Hotel\***   59S   ⎹ 25 ⎹ 24 ⎹ 22 ⎹ 17 ⎹ $125 ⎹
901 Bank St., Richmond; (800) 343-7302; (804) 343-7300; FAX 343-1025
*U – Though it may be "old", our surveyors say "the rooms are large and the service is great" at this historic Downtown hotel, certainly "one of the nicest" around; it gets additional praise for its central location overlooking the Capitol, and near Shokoe Slip and shopping; N.B. its restaurant, The Assembly, has drawn favorable reviews from the local press.*

# San Jose, CA

**Fairmont Hotel**   541R (41S)   ⎹ 23 ⎹ 22 ⎹ 22 ⎹ 23 ⎹ $140 ⎹
170 S. Market St., San Jose; (800) 527-4727; (408) 998-1900;
FAX 280-0394
*U – A "touch of class in convention city", this "very new" "luxury hotel" with "all the amenities" strikes surveyors as a "first-class hotel in a second-tier city", but about as good as things get south of San Fran; "makes you forget you're in Downtown San Jose."*

# Teaneck, NJ

**Marriott Glenpointe**   354R   ⎹ 19 ⎹ 18 ⎹ 18 ⎹ 18 ⎹ $138 ⎹
(fka Loews Glenpointe Hotel)
100 Frank W. Burr Blvd., Teaneck; (800) 228-9290; (201) 836-0600;
FAX 836-0638
*M – A well-equipped health club and reasonable proximity to New York City and the Meadowlands distinguish this otherwise-anonymous "commercial hotel" "in the middle of nowhere"; local businesspeople don't seem to mind the "uninteresting rooms", but it's too bad about Bronzini, the first-rate Italian restaurant that closed when Marriott took over.*

# Wilmington, DE

**Hotel du Pont**   216R (10S)   ⎹ 20 ⎹ 23 ⎹ 23 ⎹ 21 ⎹ $144 ⎹
11th & Market Sts., Wilmington; (800) 441-9019; (302) 594-3100;
FAX 594-1421
*U – Dramatic public spaces, "stately and unruffled" ambiance and "unsurpassed" dining convince big-city types that "class isn't limited to major metropolises", while weekend rates put "du Pont elegance" in reach of the Smiths; this dowager was completely renovated in 1992, making her "comfortable rooms" and "beautiful public areas" even more so.*

# ALPHABETICAL
# DIRECTORY OF RESORTS
# AND INNS BY STATE

# TOP 50 RESORTS AND INNS*

## (In order of rating)

| | | |
|---|---|---|
| **27 –** | The Point | New York |
| | Inn at Little Washington | Virginia |
| | Lodge at Koele | Hawaii |
| | Four Seasons, Wailea | Hawaii |
| | Boulders Resort | Arizona |
| | Ritz-Carlton, Naples | Florida |
| **26 –** | Ritz-Carlton, Amelia Island | Florida |
| | Little Palm Island | Florida |
| | Mauna Lani Bay Hotel | Hawaii |
| | Blantyre | Massachusetts |
| | Stonepine Estate Resort | California |
| | Auberge du Soleil | California |
| | Little Nell | Colorado |
| | Ritz-Carlton, Palm Beach | Florida |
| | Stein Eriksen Lodge | Utah |
| **25 –** | Ritz-Carlton, Mauna Lani | Hawaii |
| | Grand Hyatt Wailea | Hawaii |
| | Greenbrier | West Virginia |
| | Inn at Spanish Bay | California |
| | Hotel Hana-Maui | Hawaii |
| | Hyatt Regency Beaver Creek | Colorado |
| | Cloister | Georgia |
| | Hyatt Regency Kauai | Hawaii |
| | Ocean Grand Hotel | Florida |
| | Ventana – Big Sur | California |
| | Mauna Kea Beach Hotel | Hawaii |
| | Timberhill Ranch | California |
| | Charlotte Inn | Massachusetts |
| | Lodge at Pebble Beach | California |
| | John Gardiner's Tennis Ranch | California |
| | Princeville Hotel | Hawaii |
| **24 –** | Westin La Paloma | Arizona |
| | Tremont House | Texas |
| | Manele Bay Hotel | Hawaii |
| | Four Seasons Biltmore | California |
| | Carmel Valley Ranch | California |
| | American Club | Wisconsin |
| | Registry Resort | Florida |
| | Kapalua Bay Hotel | Hawaii |
| | Mayflower Inn | Connecticut |
| | Loews Ventana Canyon | Arizona |
| | Salishan Lodge | Oregon |
| | Inn of the Anasazi | New Mexico |
| | Salish Lodge | Washington |
| | Wauwinet | Massachusetts |
| | Hyatt Regency Maui | Hawaii |
| | Inn at Sawmill Farm | Vermont |
| | Kona Village Resort | Hawaii |
| | Wheatleigh | Massachusetts |
| | Homestead | Virginia |

*Based on overall ratings derived by averaging ratings for rooms, service, dining and public facilities, this list excludes places with voting too low to be reliable.

# California

## TOP RESORTS AND INNS
## (In order of rating)

**BEST OVERALL**

26 – Stonepine Estate Resort
   Auberge du Soleil
25 – Inn at Spanish Bay
   Ventana – Big Sur
   Timberhill Ranch
   Lodge at Pebble Beach
   John Gardiner's Tennis Ranch
24 – Four Seasons Biltmore

**BEST VALUES**

Little River Inn
Vintage Inn
Inn at Morro Bay
Deetjen's Big Sur Inn
St. Orres
Benbow Inn
Madrona Manor
Wine Country Inn


# Florida

## TOP RESORTS AND INNS
## (In order of rating)

**BEST OVERALL**

27 – Ritz-Carlton, Naples
26 – Ritz-Carlton, Amelia Island
   Little Palm Island
   Ritz-Carlton, Palm Beach
25 – Ocean Grand Hotel
24 – Registry Resort
23 – Lodge at Ponte Vedra
   Boca Raton Resort
   Marriott's Bay Point Resort
   Resort at Longboat Key

**BEST VALUES**

Marriott's Bay Point Resort
'Tween Waters
Grenelefe Resort
Chalet Suzanne
Marriott at Sawgrass
Ponte Vedra Inn
Indian River Plantation
Sonesta Sanibel Harbour
Sheraton Key Largo
Ritz-Carlton, Amelia Island

# Hawaiian Islands

## TOP RESORTS AND INNS
## (In order of rating)

### BEST OVERALL

**27** – Lodge at Koele
    Four Seasons Wailea
**26** – Mauna Lani Bay Hotel
**25** – Ritz-Carlton, Mauna Lani
    Grand Hyatt Wailea
    Hotel Hana-Maui
    Hyatt Regency Kauai
    Mauna Kea Beach Hotel
    Princeville Hotel
**24** – Manele Bay Hotel

### BEST VALUES

Kona Hilton Resort
Royal Waikoloan
Maui Marriott
Volcano House
Royal Lahaina Resort
Hyatt Regency Kauai
Stouffer Waiohai Beach
Maui Inter-Continental
Kaanapali Beach Hotel
Hyatt Regency Maui

# Midwest

## (Illinois, Indiana, Iowa, Michigan, Minnesota, Missouri, Ohio, South Dakota, Wisconsin)

## TOP RESORTS AND INNS
## (In order of rating)

### BEST OVERALL

**24** – American Club (WI)
    Grand Hotel (MI)
**23** – Grand Traverse Resort (MI)
**21** – Eagle Ridge Inn (IL)
**18** – Heidel House Resort (WI)
    Clock Tower Resort (IL)
    Lincolnshire Marriott (IL)
    Abbey Resort (WI)
    Lake Lawn Lodge (WI)
**17** – Indian Lakes Resort (IL)

### BEST VALUES

Clock Tower Resort (IL)
Indian Lakes Resort (IL)
Heidel House Resort (WI)
Olympia Resort (WI)
Eagle Ridge Inn (IL)
Grand Traverse Resort (MI)
Lodge of Four Seasons (MO)
Lake Lawn Lodge (WI)
Marriott's Tan-Tar-A (MO)
Lincolnshire Marriott (IL)

# New England

## (Connecticut, Maine, Massachusetts, New Hampshire, Rhode Island, Vermont)

### TOP RESORTS AND INNS
### (In order of rating)

**BEST OVERALL**

26 – Blantyre (MA)
25 – Charlotte Inn (MA)
24 – Mayflower Inn (CT)
    Wauwinet (MA)
    Wheatleigh (MA)
    Inn at Sawmill Farm (VT)
23 – Shelburne House (VT)
    White Barn Inn (ME)
    Orchards (MA)
22 – Captain Lord Mansion (ME)

**BEST VALUES**

Publick House (MA)
Orchards (MA)
Griswold Inn (CT)
Coonamessett Inn (MA)
Cortina Inn (VT)
Tara Hyannis (MA)
Captain Lord Mansion (ME)
Middlebury Inn (VT)
Homestead Inn (CT)
Trapp Family Lodge (VT)

# New York and Mid-Atlantic

## (Delaware, Maryland, New Jersey, New York, Pennsylvania)

### TOP RESORTS AND INNS
### (In order of rating)

**BEST OVERALL**

28 – The Point (NY)
24 – Atlantic Hotel (MD)
    Imperial Hotel (MD)
23 – Inn at Perry Cabin (MD)
    Mainstay Inn (NJ)
    Troutbeck (NY)
    Sweetwater Farm (PA)
22 – Evermay on Delaware (PA)
    Omni Sagamore (PA)
21 – Virginia (NJ)

**BEST VALUES**

Atlantic Hotel (MD)
Imperial Hotel (MD)
Mainstay Inn (NJ)
Strasburg Inn (PA)
Loews Annapolis (MD)
Inn at Millrace Pond (NJ)
Sterling Inn (PA)
Evermay on Delaware (PA)
Abbey (NJ)
Queen Victoria (NJ)

# Pacific Northwest

## (Alaska, Oregon, Washington)

### TOP RESORTS AND INNS
### (In order of rating)

**BEST OVERALL**

24 – Salishan Lodge (OR)
    Salish Lodge (WA)
22 – Sunriver Lodge (OR)
    Columbia Gorge Hotel (OR)
21 – Timberline Lodge (OR)
20 – Captain Whidby Inn (WA)

**BEST VALUES**

Captain Whidby Inn (WA)
Lake Quinault Lodge (WA)
Timberline Lodge (OR)
Sun Mountain Lodge (WA)
Kalalock Lodge (WA)
Columbia Gorge Hotel (OR)

# Rocky Mountains

## (Colorado, Idaho, Montana, Nevada, Utah, Wyoming)

### TOP RESORTS AND INNS
### (In order of rating)

**BEST OVERALL**

26 – Little Nell (CO)
    Stein Eriksen Lodge (UT)
25 – Hyatt Reg. Beaver Creek (CO)
23 – Broadmoor (CO)
    Hotel Jerome
    Coeur d'Alene Resort (ID)
    Jenny Lake Lodge (WY)
22 – Sun Valley Lodge (ID)
    Keystone Lodge (CO)
21 – Lodge at Vail (CO)

**BEST VALUES**

Bryce Canyon Lodge (UT)
Boulderado (CO)
Many Glacier Hotel (MT)
Lake McDonald Lodge (MT)
Glacier Park Lodge (MT)
Old Faithful Inn (WY)
Harrah's Lake Tahoe (NV)
Coeur d'Alene Resort (ID)
Caesars Lake Tahoe (NV)
Hyatt Regency Resort (NV)

# South

## (Alabama, Arkansas, Georgia, Kentucky, Louisiana, Mississippi, North and South Carolina, Tennessee, Virginia, West Virginia)

### TOP RESORTS AND INNS
### (In order of rating)

**BEST OVERALL**
27 – Inn at Little Washington (VA)
26 – Greenbriar (WV)
25 – Cloister (GA)
24 – Homestead (VA)
    Westin Hilton Head (SC)
    Ferrington House (NC)
23 – Williamsburg Inn (VA)
22 – Pinehurst Res./Country Cl. (NC)
    Marriott's Grand (AL)
    Kingsmill Resort (VA)

**BEST VALUES**
Carolina Inn (NC)
Natchez Eola Hotel (MS)
Jekyll Island Club (GA)
Callaway Gardens Inn (GA)
Grover Park Inn (NC)
Williamsburg Hospitality House (VA)
Nottoway Plantation (LA)
Ferrington House (NC)
Marriott's Grand (AL)
Mill's House/Charleston (SC)

# Southwest

## (Arizona, New Mexico, Oklahoma, Texas)

### TOP RESORTS AND INNS
### (In order of rating)

**BEST OVERALL**
27 – Boulders (AZ)
24 – Westin La Paloma (AZ)
    Loews Ventana Canyon (AZ)
    Inn of the Anasazi (NM)
23 – Ventana Canyon Club (AZ)
    Wigwam Resort (AZ)
    L'Auberge de Sedona (AZ)
22 – Barton Creek Resort (TX)
    Sheraton Conquistador (AZ)
    Los Abrigados (AZ)

**BEST VALUES**
Tremont House (TX)
Grand Canyon Lodge (AZ)
Arizona (AZ)
Barton Creek Resort (TX)
Lakeway Inn/Austin (TX)
Historic Taos Inn (NM)
Westward Look (AZ)
El Tovar Grand Canyon Village (AZ)
Inn of the Mountain Gods (NM)
Poco Diablo Resort (AZ)

# ALABAMA

---

| R | S | D | P | $ |

**MARRIOTT'S**                                      | 22 | 23 | 20 | 24 | $153 |
**GRAND HOTEL**   306R (21S); (800)
U.S. Hwy. 98, Point Clear; (800) 544-9938; (205) 928-9201; FAX 928-1149
*U – A "favorite for years" of well-heeled Southerners, this "classy" resort
overlooking Mobile Bay is both "the epitome of the old South" and a fine
modern vacation/business facility; assets include an "outstanding"
waterside setting, "beautiful" tree-filled grounds, "great" golf, tennis and
boating facilities, and the "best personal service anywhere"; supervised
children's programs help make it the "perfect family resort."*

| R | S | D | P | $ |
|---|---|---|---|---|

**Brooks Lodge**   16S            | – | – | – | – | E |
Katmai National Park; (800) 544-0551; (907) 243-5448; FAX 243-0649
*Being in this "majestic setting" in Katmai National Park justifies the price of this "rustic" Alaska lodge, the only place in the world where you're virtually certain to see the elusive Alaskan brown bear; besides bear viewing, there are float trips, camping and sportfishing (all additional) at this "well-run" "wilderness camp"; food is not included in the price, nor is the requisite pickup in a seaplane.*

**Camp Denali\***   16S            | 19 | 19 | 20 | 20 | $251 |
Denali National Park; (603) 675-2248 (winter); (907) 683-2290 (summer); FAX 675-9125 (winter); 683-2290 (summer)
*U – A class act in the middle of six million acres at Denali National Park – quite possibly the most "breathtaking", remote location in North America accessible by road; "rustic" accommodations in individual cabins (without electricity or plumbing) are offset by magnificent views of Mt. McKinley and "access to hiking and wildlife that can't be beat."*

**Denali National Park Hotel**   100R      | 15 | 16 | 16 | 17 | $113 |
Denali National Park; (907) 683-2215; FAX 683-2398
*M – "The heart of the wilderness is at your doorstep" at this "utilitarian" hotel (a "prefab" structure) right in Denali National Park; prices are subject to Park Service approval so rates are lower than those at surrounding hotels; naturalists give evening presentations and several hiking trails originate at the hotel; though it's "very crowded" and "caters toward groups", our surveyors say "so what?" – you're "sitting on top of the world"; if you'd prefer not to drive, note the Alaska Railroad stops across the road daily in summer.*

**Glacier Bay Lodge\***   55S          | 19 | 18 | 18 | 22 | $138 |
Glacier Bay National Park; (800) 451-5952; (907) 697-2226; FAX 697-2227
*M – A rustic lodge in a "beautiful" location "on the shores of Glacier Bay"; "comfortable", reasonably priced rooms and "overpriced" food are not nearly so important as the "great fishing", whale-watching, kayaking or exploring; many packages are available, including a glacier cruise.*

## ALASKA RESORTS

| R | S | D | P | $ |

**Gustavus Inn at Glacier Bay**  14R   | – | – | – | – | E |
Glacier Bay; (913) 649-5220 (winter); (907) 697-2254 (summer);
FAX 649-5220 (winter); 697-2291 (summer)
*A homey, full-service inn, featuring fishing, whale-watching trips and*
*kayaking on Glacier Bay – 13 tidewater glaciers can be seen on the*
*package boat tours; three meals a day ("wonderful, unpretentious food")*
*and transportation are included at this "great place to fish or relax."*

**Harper Lodge Princess**  192R (8S)   | – | – | – | – | M |
Denali National Park; (800) 426-0500; (907) 683-2282; FAX 683-2545
*A handsome, contemporary-rustic hotel perched high above the Nenana*
*River just outside the entrance to Denali National Park; food in the*
*restaurant and bar is good, but service is spotty; owned by Princess cruise*
*lines, the hotel caters to tour groups; you can go white-water rafting, riding*
*or hiking right nearby; ask for a room with a river view.*

**King Salmon Lodge**  17R   | – | – | – | – | VE |
Naknek River, King Salmon; (800) 437-2464; (907) 277-3033; FAX 246-7486
*A weekly rate, $4,900 per person, includes everything, from three meals*
*a day and an open bar to incomparable fishing fly-outs throughout the*
*extraordinary wilderness of the Katmai area; a remote location on the*
*Naknek River and beautifully rustic accommodations attract an*
*international clientele who don't care what it costs.*

**Red Quill Lodge**  24R   | – | – | – | – | VE |
Lake Iliamna; (907) 571-1215
*This mecca for avid fishermen is nestled near the tiny village of Iliamna,*
*with an outstanding view of Alaska's largest lake and surrounding*
*mountains; skilled guides bring anglers to areas abundant with salmon*
*and trout; catch your limit, then repair to the lodge for a hot tub and sauna*
*and a hearty meal, but remember if you have to ask the price, you're in*
*the wrong place.*

**Tikchik Narrows Lodge**  12S   | – | – | – | – | VE |
P.O. Box 690, Dillingham; (907) 842-5464; FAX 243-8450
*Accessible only by floatplane, this isolated, deluxe lodge in the Wood-*
*Tikchik State Park caters to corporate retreaters and other affluent anglers*
*who can afford to pay $4,300 a week (all inclusive) for world-class fishing;*
*rates include daily fly-outs, fine meals and accommodations in individual*
*cabins with spectacular mountain and lake views.*

## ALASKA RESORTS

| R | S | D | P | $ |
| --- | --- | --- | --- | --- |

**Waterfall Resort**   40R (30S)      | – | – | – | – | VE |
Prince of Wales Island, Ketchikan; (800) 544-5125; (907) 225-9461;
FAX 225-8530
*Take a floatplane to this fisherman's paradise on Prince of Wales Island, 63*
*miles from Ketchikan, to enjoy luxurious accommodations and superb guided*
*fishing from the lodge's own cabin cruisers; $2,275 packages (three nights*
*and four days) include everything you need to enjoy fabulous wilderness*
*fishing and exploring – a favorite of the wealthy and well-rewarded.*

**Yes Bay Lodge**   16R      | – | – | – | – | VE |
Ketchikan; (800) 999-0784; (907) 225-3875; FAX 247-3835
*Spectacular wildlife and scenery abound at this fresh and saltwater fly-in*
*fishing resort located 50 miles northwest of Ketchikan; upscale rates of*
*$1,695 per person for 3 nights, $3,795 for a week, include all gear, guides,*
*boats, meals and round-trip transportation to Ketchikan; expect basic*
*accommodations, fabulous fishing.*

# ARIZONA*

| R | S | D | P | $ |

**Arizona Inn**  80R (14S)     | 21 | 22 | 20 | 23 | $137 |
2200 E. Elm St., Tucson; (800) 933-1093; (602) 325-1541; FAX 881-5830
*U – This "homey", circa-1930 inn in the desert is "a throwback to another
era" – and "please don't ever let it change"; the "beautiful grounds" and
"library lounge with comfy furniture and a huge fireplace" make this a
"perfect place to relax alone or with a partner"; though some find it "a little
musty", for most it's "ideal for someone avoiding the glitz."*

**BOULDERS RESORT, THE**  136R (3S)     | 28 | 27 | 25 | 27 | $272 |
34631 N. Tom Darlington Dr., Carefree; (800) 553-1717; (602) 488-9009;
FAX 488-4118
*U – "This place has it all", starting with a magnificent high-Sonoran desert
setting and continuing on to the "most beautiful rooms", "top dining",
"warm, accommodating staff" and "terrific golf"; it's "a bit out of the way",
but hey, you won't hear "coyotes howling at night" in Downtown Scottsdale;
overall, it's one of America's great resorts.*

**EL CONQUISTADOR**  434R (100S)     | 22 | 22 | 20 | 23 | $158 |
(fka Sheraton El Conquistador)
10000 N. Oracle Rd., Tucson; (800) 325-7832; (602) 544-5000; FAX 544-1224
*M – Still under Sheraton management, this "quite beautiful" resort is in the
process of a major renovation, perhaps not reflected in surveyor comments
of "aging rooms" and "average otherwise"; it's got a "nice setting" and
"great view", plus "very good food" and "friendly service", but it still
underwhelms many of our voters.*

**El Tovar Hotel – Grand Canyon**     | 18 | 19 | 20 | 21 | $137 |
**National Park Lodges**  78R (12S)
Grand Canyon South Rim; (602) 638-2401; FAX 638-9247
*M – "Can't beat the view"; well, guess not, since it's on the edge of the
Grand Canyon; but while a room with a balcony is "a naturalist's dream",
you have to book a lifetime ahead or endure "ordinary rooms" that "need
modernizing"; still, it oozes "rustic charm" and "history", and the "beautiful
dining room" compensates for an aura of "decrepitude."*

---

*See also: Phoenix/Scottsdale Hotels.

## ARIZONA RESORTS

| R | S | D | P | $ |

**Enchantment Resort**  168S

| – | – | – | – | E |

(fka John Gardiner's Tennis Resort)
525 Boynton Canyon, Sedona; (800) 826-4180; (602) 282-2900;
FAX 282-9249
*Casitas, casas and haciendas with balconies and fireplaces dot the 70
acres of this elegant and rugged resort, set in the spectacular Red Rock
Canyon of northern Arizona's mountains; stunning views, great sports
facilities, candlelight dinners and nearby artsy Sedona help prove the
name correct for both vacationers and small business groups.*

**Grand Canyon Lodge**  200R

| 16 | 16 | 16 | 18 | $106 |

Grand Canyon North Rim; (801) 586-7686; FAX 586-3157
*U – When you can't get a room at El Tovar, this "basic park hotel – no
frills!" offers "a bed, a room" and an "awesome location", with "sweeping
views of the Canyon", just "a short walk" away; and remember, "you are
not there for the accommodations."*

**Hassayampa Inn***  67R (10S)

| 17 | 17 | 16 | 17 | $94 |

122 E. Gurley St., Prescott; (800) 322-1927; (602) 778-9434; FAX 778-9434
*U – Though few of our surveyors know of it, this "nicely restored" old hotel
(it dates from the 1920s) in the charming frontier town of Prescott offers
a simple, moderately priced base from which to explore the local sites,
including the Governor's Mansion, Old Fort Misery and the Smoki
Museum, with its Native American artifacts.*

**L'AUBERGE DE SEDONA HOTEL**  96R (34S)

| 24 | 22 | 24 | 22 | $197 |

301 L'Auberge Lane, Sedona; (800) 272-6777; (602) 282-1661; FAX 282-1064
*U – "A hidden surprise in Red Rock Country", this "bit of France in Arizona"
delights surveyors with its splendid restaurant (food rating, 25), "charming"
Pierre Deux–decorated log cottages, "breathtaking vistas" and "romantic"
rooms; some mind the prices, but most call it "a perfect refuge."*

**LOEWS VENTANA
CANYON RESORT**  398R (27S)

| 25 | 24 | 23 | 25 | $189 |

7000 N. Resort Dr., Tucson; (800) 234-5117; (602) 299-2020; FAX 299-6832
*U – For "luxury in a native setting", it's hard to top this "spectacular resort";
"the view is unbeatable", the "service couldn't be better", and there's golf,
tennis, a "great" pool and a health club if you can stand to leave your
"outstanding" room – or don't: "bring a friend and enjoy the great bathtub."*

## ARIZONA RESORTS

| R | S | D | P | $ |
|---|---|---|---|---|

### Los Abrigados   175S

| 23 | 21 | 21 | 21 | $157 |
|----|----|----|----|------|

160 Portal Lane, Sedona; (800) 521-3131; (602) 282-1777; FAX 282-2614
*M – Our surveyors are of two minds on this well-located "strategic base to explore Sedona": most love the "huge rooms", "amazing food and wine list" and "picture-perfect manicured Hollywood Mexican setting", but despite all this, there are a few who call it "boring" and "nothing special"; go figure.*

### Poco Diablo Resort   110R (3S)

| 18 | 17 | 16 | 17 | $123 |
|----|----|----|----|------|

1752 S. Hwy. 179, Sedona; (800) 352-5710; (602) 282-7333; FAX 282-2090
*M – Though it's "rather Spartan", this "charming place" in a pretty town boasts "beautiful grounds", a "nice view of the Red Hills", a "lovely creek in the back for rock hopping" and an "all-night hot tub" for watching the stars; though a few detractors say "head for the Auberge" instead and call the restaurant "overrated", this "pleasant" mainstay is a lot cheaper.*

### Rancho de los Caballeros   74R (11S)

| – | – | – | – | VE |
|---|---|---|---|----|

1551 S. Vulture Mine Rd., Wickenburg; (602) 684-5484; FAX 684-2267
*Don't let the cost scare you – Rancho guests are on the American plan; with golf, tennis, horseback riding, skeet and trap, and a pool, it's "great for families" or anyone who just wants to get away from it all; no credit cards.*

### Tanque Verde Ranch*   60R (10S)

| 22 | 22 | 19 | 21 | $187 |
|----|----|----|----|------|

14301 E. Speedway Blvd., Tucson; (800) 234-DUDE; (602) 296-6275; FAX 721-9426
*U – "City slickers" looking for "rustic fun" will love the "down-home cooking and accommodations" and "hand-shaking" "friendly service" at this real live Arizona dude ranch; built in 1868, it's been a guest ranch since the '50s and boasts 640 acres and 110 horses; here's a "great family spot", with "lots of activities for the kids" and plenty of "good relaxing" for grown-ups.*

### VENTANA CANYON GOLF & RACQUET CLUB   48S

| 24 | 23 | 21 | 25 | $187 |
|----|----|----|----|------|

6200 N. Clubhouse Lane, Tucson; (800) 828-5701; (602) 577-1400; FAX 299-0256
*M – "A wonderful smaller property" that has "beautiful rooms" and "great golf" (36 holes) and tennis, plus a "terrific" setting near the Sabino Canyon Recreation Area; the "extremely accommodating staff" gets extra mentions.*

## ARIZONA RESORTS

| R | S | D | P | $ |

**Wahweap Lodge & Marina**   350R (4S)   | 16 | 15 | 12 | 15 | $103 |
100 Lake Shore Dr., Page; (800) 528-6154; (602) 645-2433; FAX 645-1031
*M – "Really a glorified motel, but the rooms have an unbelievable view of Lake Powell" – and that's the reason our raters like this large, comfortable, if "a little institutional", lodge on the Arizona side of the lake; to fans it's a "great vacation spot", with "so much to do", including the only guided boat tours – perhaps the reason "tourist buses flock here."*

**WESTIN LA PALOMA, THE**   487R (31S)   | 25 | 24 | 23 | 26 | $182 |
3800 E. Sunrise Dr., Tucson; (800) 876-3683; (602) 742-6000;
FAX 577-5887
*U – The "spectacular" "natural" setting of this large resort and business hotel (it's got 42,000 square feet of meeting space) is matched by a dramatic lobby, "lovely rooms", highly rated dining in any of the four restaurants and "superior service", not to mention a beautiful free-form pool with a swim-up bar and all the activities you could think of; for "glitz and golf", this is "one of the finest in Arizona."*

**Westward Look Resort**   244R (10S)   | 20 | 21 | 19 | 20 | $139 |
245 E. Ina Rd., Tucson; (800) 722-2500; (602) 297-1151; FAX 297-9023
*M – "Sunsets, saguaro and the Santa Catalinas" are what you'll see from this "bit tired but still romantic" "old hotel" (it was built in the 1940s, all "Spanish architecture and tiles"); it may be "in the middle of nowhere", but it's "great if you are into relaxing", offering "attractive grounds" and "superb service"; a current renovation will no doubt cure complaints of "shabby" rooms.*

**Wickenburg Inn Tennis**   | 21 | 22 | 20 | 21 | $170 |
**& Guest Ranch**   46R (41S)
Hwy. 89, Wickenburg; (800) 528-4227; (602) 684-7811; FAX 684-2981
*U – "The quintessential dude ranch" offers that "casual, laid-back feel"; it's "hokey and fun", with cookouts, tennis, horseback riding and even an arts-and-crafts center; rustic lodging is in casitas with fireplaces; "a must for families."*

**WIGWAM, THE**   331R (70S)   | 24 | 23 | 21 | 23 | $183 |
300 E. Indian School Lane, Litchfield Park; (800) SAY-PATT;
(602) 935-3811; FAX 935-3737
*U – This place "has everything", including "golf, tennis and more golf"; it's in a remote location, a "magnificent ranch" about 20 miles from Phoenix-Scottsdale, but the "low-key" atmosphere, "nice rooms", "excellent service" and, yes, that golf (three championship courses) make it a "great resort for the price."*

# ARKANSAS

|  | R | S | D | P | $ |
|--|---|---|---|---|---|

**Arlington Resort Hotel & Spa***   486R (39S)   | 16 | 19 | 20 | 20 | $109 |
Central Ave. & Fountain St., Hot Springs; (800) 643-1502; (501) 623-7771;
FAX 623-6191
*M – There's "lots of history" here in Bill Clinton's hometown and in this
"grand old" Downtown dowager; partisans suggest you "slow down and
relax" to enjoy the "charming", old-fashioned ambiance, "excellent"
restaurant and "almost medicinal" spa treatments, but critics call it
"Spartan" and "out-of-date" and say it "needs a massive rehab" to return
it to former glory; "good service" is a plus and so is proximity to the Hot
Springs Country Club.*

**Gaston's White River Resort**   73S   | – | – | – | – | M |
1 River Rd., Lakeview; (501) 431-5202
*Fishermen, nature lovers and those just out for a relaxing, affordable
getaway head to this heart-of-the-Ozarks resort; with homey cottages,
good food and friendly service, it's a pleasant base from which to explore
the lovely countryside, which offers hiking, trout fishing, river-float trips and
much more; there's a private airstrip – if your plane's not in the shop.*

**Palace Hotel & Bath House**   8S   | – | – | – | – | M |
135 Spring St., Eureka Springs,; (501) 253-7474; (501) 253-8280
*You'll experience Victorian-style pampering at this carefully restored,
turn-of-the-century bath house, which is now a National Historic Register
property; it features eight comfortable, antique-filled suites (each with a
king-size bed and spa tub) plus a full range of spa treatments ranging from
mineral baths to massage; it's old-fashioned but "a nice find", conveniently
close to shops, galleries and restaurants.*

# CALIFORNIA*

| R | S | D | P | $ |
|---|---|---|---|---|

**Ahwahnee Hotel**   123R (4S)                    | 20 | 20 | 21 | 24 | $175 |
Yosemite Valley; (209) 372-1407; FAX 372-1463
*M – A "majestic" "grand lodge" that has hosted "presidents, kings and queens" in the midst of "an incredible setting"; this "old-style" hotel with "strict rules" (jacket and tie for dinner – Herbert Hoover was asked to leave because he wasn't properly dressed) offers "magnificent public rooms" for tea, reading and meals, but "ordinary" guest rooms – unless you stay in the "romantic" cabins; reserve a year ahead of time.*

**Alisal Ranch, The**   75R (37S)                 | 19 | 22 | 19 | 22 | $199 |
1054 Alisal Rd., Solvang; (805) 688-6411; FAX 688-2510
*U – This "relaxing" "Santa Barbara rustic" dude ranch north of LA in affluent Santa Ynez Valley, near ranches owned by Ronald Reagan and Michael Jackson, has a "beautiful natural setting" and "its own fishing lake"; "great fun" if you like to ride – just don't mind the "rooms out of the '50s"; it's a "fabulous family resort", and great if you want to get away from the phones.*

**Alta Mira**   29R (13S)                         | 17 | 20 | 19 | 18 | $151 |
125 Bulkley Ave., Sausalito; (415) 332-1350; FAX 331-3862
*M – Venerable Sausalito hillside landmark that's best if you "get a bay view room", with a staff that's "very pleasant" and an "excellent brunch" noted by many reviewers; though the rooms are just "so-so", it's fun to be able to walk to Bridgeway in Sausalito and take the ferry around SF Bay.*

**AUBERGE DU SOLEIL**   48R (19S)                 | 27 | 25 | 26 | 25 | $264 |
180 Rutherford Hill Rd., Rutherford; (800) 348-5406; (707) 963-1211;
FAX 963-8456
*U – "The South of France incarnate" is what you'll find at this "heavenly" resort overlooking the vineyards of the Napa Valley, where there's also a "fabulous" restaurant; "if you've got the bucks", you're in store for a "romantic", "pampered experience" – "you can't stay here and not enjoy yourself."*

---

*See also: Los Angeles, Orange County, Palm Springs, San Diego and San Francisco Hotels.

**Benbow Inn**  55R          | 21 | 21 | 21 | 22 | $140 |
445 Lake Benbow Dr., Garberville; (707) 923-2124
*U – A grand old hotel "near the great trees", offering a "turn-of-the-century"*
*"feeling of leisure as you walk the grounds"; this "rustic", old inn is like*
*something out of* Twin Peaks*; the place is "anything but modern", but that's*
*precisely what makes it so appealing.*

**Big Sur Lodge**  61R (15S)          | 18 | 17 | 16 | 19 | $124 |
Pfeiffer Big Sur State Park, Big Sur; (408) 667-2171; FAX 667-3110
*U – "Rustic", "rustic", "rustic", this "lodge in the state park" has a "wonderful*
*location" at Big Sur and "walking paths" reminiscent of "camping in Maine";*
*it's ideal "for family and kids" and "communing with nature"; otherwise, it's*
*a "Motel 6 in the forest."*

**CARMEL VALLEY RANCH RESORT**  100S     | 25 | 24 | 23 | 24 | $205 |
1 Old Ranch Rd., Carmel; (800) 422-7635;
(408) 625-9500; FAX 624-2858
*U – A "spectacular" "all-suites resort" with "fireplaces in every bedroom"*
*and "beautifully landscaped grounds with deer and flowers", this "romantic*
*getaway" in secluded Carmel Valley is the "nicest in the area" for those*
*who yearn for "space and privacy"; after playing on the "cardiac-arrest golf*
*course", you'll appreciate relaxing in the hot tubs.*

**Casa Madrona Hotel**  34R          | 23 | 22 | 23 | 21 | $156 |
801 Bridgeway, Sausalito; (800) 288-0502; (415) 332-0502;
FAX 332-2537
*M – You feel transported to Provence at this Sausalito "hideaway" "nestled*
*into a hillside", with its "spectacular Golden Gate view" and "most romantic*
*dining room"; the rooms, each different, are "honeymoonish" – though*
*some could have been "decorated by the Flintstones."*

**Casa Sirena Marina Resort***  273R (30S)     | 17 | 17 | 16 | 16 | $117 |
23605 Peninsula Rd., Oxnard; (800) 228-6026; (805) 985-6311;
FAX 985-4329
*M – "Escape for the weekend" to this marina hotel with "magnificent views" of*
*the Channel Islands Harbor; this "real sleeper" offers "fair prices" for*
*"ordinary rooms in a good setting" that includes complete sports facilities*
*as well as a number of meeting rooms; detractors say it's "ok if you like*
*vacationing in the suburbs."*

**Claremont Resort, Spa &** | 18 | 19 | 19 | 21 | $152 |
**Tennis Club, The**   239R (34S)
Ashby & Domingo Aves., Oakland; (800) 551-7266; (415) 843-3000;
FAX 843-6239
*M – A "Victorian beauty" that "survived the fire" in the Oakland hills, this
"nostalgic" "architectural relic" is often compared to San Diego's Hotel del
Coronado; it's a "comfortable old resort" that boasts a marvelous "Olympic
pool", spa and views, and is also convenient to UC – Berkeley, and such
notable restaurants as Chez Panisse.*

**Deetjen's Big Sur Inn**   19R | 15 | 14 | 18 | 16 | $103 |
Hwy. 1, Big Sur; (408) 667-2377
*M – For some, this "shabby", "funky" "very rustic" "cabin under the
redwoods" is the "heart of Big Sur", with "lots of cats" and a coed hot tub
where bathing suits are optional; it's not for everybody, but fans say "even
a tent would be fine in this location"; "unusual food", local wines and
"friendly" people make it "worth the trip."*

**El Encanto Hotel & Garden Villas**   84R | 19 | 20 | 21 | 20 | $176 |
1900 Lasuen Rd., Santa Barbara; (800) 346-7039; (805) 687-5000;
FAX 687-3903
*M – A "little tired" and "very untrendy", this "hideaway" high in the hills above
Santa Barbara still strikes reviewers as a "wonderful place" for "old-time
comfort" and a "gorgeous view"; the "cottagelike rooms" are good for a
"romantic getaway", the "villa suites have wonderful kitchenettes", and the
"gardens are pretty."*

**Eureka Inn***   105R (15S) | 18 | 17 | 18 | 18 | $116 |
518 Seventh St., Eureka; (800) 862-4906; (707) 442-6441; FAX 442-0637
*U – This "charming" Northern California inn is the nicest place around for
miles, despite some "rough edges"; most of our travelers think it's "top of
the line", especially given its modest prices.*

**Fess Parker's Red Lion**   385R (25S) | 19 | 18 | 17 | 19 | $151 |
633 E. Cabrillo Blvd., Santa Barbara; (800) 879-2929; (805) 564-4333;
FAX 564-4964
*M – A "very big" "upscale motel" owned by TV's "Davy Crockett"; described
by some as "Las Vegas by the sea", it's known for "large, modern rooms"
and popular for conventions and meetings, especially because of its
beach-adjacent location in lovely Santa Barbara; service seems to be a
problem – "Fess should hunt down better help."*

## CALIFORNIA RESORTS

| R | S | D | P | $ |

**FOUR SEASONS BILTMORE**   236R (12S)   | 24 | 24 | 24 | 25 | $220 |
1260 Channel Dr., Santa Barbara; (800) 332-3442; (805) 969-2261;
FAX 969-4682
*U – This "world-class" grand old resort, near old-money Montecito, has
been brought back to its former glory thanks to "deluxe Four Seasons"
treatment; if you have a taste for the elegance of yesteryear, you'll enjoy
the "beautiful grounds" and "tranquil lobby" that "reek of history"; stay, if
you can, in the "stately cottages", and go for a "sunset stroll on the beach"
at this neighbor to nirvana.*


**Furnace Creek Inn &**   | 18 | 19 | 17 | 20 | $174 |
**Ranch Resort**   292R (2S)
Hwy. 190, Death Valley; (800) 528-6367; (619) 786-2345; FAX 786-2307
*M – "Almost a mirage", this "cool oasis in the desert" surprises our
surveyors with "very high standards even though there's no competition";
whether you choose the inn (only open mid-October to mid-May) or the
more relaxed ranch, you're in for a "unique experience" "within a national
monument"; the spring-fed pool is "amazing."*


**Harvest Inn**   54R (3S)   | 20 | 18 | 15 | 18 | $150 |
1 Main Street, St. Helena; (800) 950-8466; (707) 963-9463; FAX 963-4402
*U – This "romantic country haven" ("fireplace in every room") reminds
some of "England"; the decor at this "step back in time" falls somewhere
between "rustic and luxurious", with a lot of "charm"; it's so quiet and close
to the vineyards, you can "listen to the grapes grow."*


**HERITAGE HOUSE**   74R (17S)   | 23 | 22 | 22 | 23 | $196 |
5200 N. Hwy. 1, Little River; (800) 235-5885; (707) 937-5885
*U – "The perfect place to sit by the fire and watch the fog roll in", this
"romantic" spot overlooking the "rugged Mendocino coastline" and the
waves crashing below is also "perfect for a honeymoon", especially in the
"homey" cabins with their fireplaces and down comforters; one visit and
"you'll say 'same time next year'" (the movie was filmed here); closed
December and January.*


**HIGHLANDS INN**   142R (105S)   | 24 | 22 | 24 | 23 | $218 |
Hwy. 1, Carmel; (800) 682-4811; (408) 624-3801; FAX 626-1574
*U – This "fantastic" cliffside resort in the pines north of Big Sur features
"breathtaking views", "whirlpools, fireplaces and decks" in every room, and
"excellent, inventive" Californian cuisine in the Pacific's Edge restaurant
(food rating, 26); how wonderful "to be awakened by the sound of barking
sea lions" – the "setting is to die for, and the inn does it justice."*

### Hill House Inn*  44R  | 22 | 21 | 19 | 18 | $147 |
10701 Palette Dr., Mendocino; (707) 937-0554; (707) 937-1123
*U – "A neat getaway place" for a "moderate price" is this "lovely",
"antique-filled" Mendocino country inn with lots of "charm" and "pretty, airy
rooms" where "everything matches"; the "genteel" neo-Gothic ambiance
makes this "an unsurpassed setting" for relaxing – "take several books."*

### Inn at Morro Bay  96R (1S)  | 19 | 18 | 20 | 19 | $124 |
Morro Bay State Park, Morro Bay; (800) 321-9566; (805) 772-5651;
FAX 772-4779
*U – A "tranquil" "golfer's haven" (the course is right across the street)
that's "the only decent place to stay in town"; this oceanfront inn "at the
edge of a state park" has a "beautiful view" of Morro Rock and the tidal
pools below; N.B. don't miss Mille Fleur, the French restaurant located
nearby (food rating, 27).*

### Inn at Rancho Santa Fe  80R (15S)  | 19 | 22 | 20 | 20 | $173 |
5951 Linea Del Cielo, Rancho Santa Fe; (800) 654-2928; (619) 756-1131;
FAX 759-1604
*M – This "pastoral" "sleeper" located in a secluded spot in an old-money,
"old California" suburb north of San Diego and east of Del Mar feels like
"the Italian countryside"; it's got "that patina that comes with age", along
with "comfort", "charm" and "one of the best golf courses in California";
though the numbers don't reflect it, some surveyors "wish they'd hired a
better chef."*

### INN AT SPANISH BAY  270R (16S)  | 26 | 25 | 24 | 26 | $235 |
2700 17 Mile Dr., Pebble Beach; (800) 654-9300; (408) 647-7500; FAX 624-6357
*U – "Everything is just right" at this "outstanding" luxury resort amid the many
golf courses of Pebble Beach, just outside Carmel; considered by many to
be the "best newcomer California has had in years", this "first-rate" hotel
offers "magnificent vistas" and prices to match; "the Scottish pipes played
at sundown bring lumps to the throats of those putting on the 18th green."*

### Inn at the Tides*  86R  | 19 | 18 | 17 | 17 | $134 |
800 Coast Hwy. 1, Bodega Bay; (800) 541-7788; (707) 875-2751; FAX 875-3023
*M – North of San Francisco, this "hideaway" in a "magnificent location" has
a "great pool" and "local-winemaker dinners"; those who don't mind "small
rooms" find it pleasantly "isolated" and "tasteful."*

**JOHN GARDINER'S TENNIS RANCH**   14R   | 26 | 25 | 24 | 23 | $267 |
Carmel Valley & Ford Rds., Carmel Valley; (408) 659-2207; FAX 659-2492
*U – "Heaven on earth in all categories", this open-to-the-public "private
club" is what tennis buffs "dream of" with a tennis tour for each room,
unbelievable grounds, "spacious, well-stocked rooms", "wonderful food"
and "excellent tennis instruction"; it's "not cheap", but fans come here
year after year.*

**La Casa del Zorro Desert Resort***   77R (73S)   | 18 | 18 | 16 | 18 | $165 |
3845 Yaqui Paso Rd., Borrego Springs; (800) 824-1884; (619) 767-5323;
FAX 767-4782
*U – This romantic small resort, built in the 1930s and completely renovated
in 1990, is a luxurious oasis near Anza Borrego Desert; lodging is in suites
or casitas, most with fireplaces and some with private pools; facilities
include tennis, hiking and golf plus complete meeting services, making it
as popular for a corporate retreat as for a honeymoon.*

**La Playa Hotel**   80R (6S)   | 20 | 20 | 19 | 20 | $172 |
Eighth Ave. & Camino Real, Carmel by the Sea; (800) 582-8900;
(408) 624-6476; FAX 624-7966
*U – In a "historic setting" that's "the best of Carmel by the Sea", this
"old-world" inn boasts a "great location", "close yet far" from the nearby
shopping streets, plus a "splendid garden setting" and "bright, cheery
rooms" with true Carmel feeling; watch out for the "noisy" streetside rooms.*

**Little River Inn**   55R (4S)   | 20 | 21 | 21 | 20 | $122 |
Hwy. 1, Little River; (707) 937-5942; FAX 937-3944
*U – Take a "great escape" along the North Coast via this "charming", funky
but fine little spot with its antique-filled rooms and beautiful views from
virtually every window; "attractive grounds" are complemented by complete
sports facilities at this lovely Mendocino spot that's "tops for weekends away."*

**LODGE AT PEBBLE BEACH**   161R (6S)   | 25 | 25 | 23 | 25 | $256 |
17 Mile Dr., Pebble Beach; (800) 654-9300; (408) 624-3811; FAX 624-6357
*U – "Absolutely idyllic", this "golfer's heaven" "overlooking the bay" and
the greens on Carmel's dramatic 17–Mile Drive features "perfect
service", "great golf" and "romantic rooms with fireplaces" and "luxurious
bathrooms" in a "spectacular" setting that's the "1930s all over again";
"bring money" to see "how West Coast blue bloods vacation"; lunch on
the terrace in the sun can be a joy.*

| R | S | D | P | $ |

**Los Olivos Grand Hotel**   21R (1S)          | 24 | 22 | 23 | 20 | $160 |
2860 Grand Ave., Los Olivos; (800) 446-2455; (805) 688-7788; FAX 688-1942
*M – An "undiscovered jewel" "in the middle of nowhere", this "elaborate
B&B" reminds some of a "beautiful" French Provincial inn, and others of
the "fine inns of New England"; in either case, it's a "nice getaway", with
"gracious", "old-fashioned" service and "attention to detail."*

**Madonna Inn**   109R (40S)          | 20 | 17 | 15 | 17 | $132 |
100 Madonna Rd., San Luis Obispo; (800) 543-9666 (CA only); (805) 543-3000;
FAX 543-1800
*M – Unquestionably the most unusual hotel on the West Coast, this
homage to "kitsch squared" is designed to be "the height of bad taste",
with guest rooms decorated in varied "Holiday Inn on acid" themes with
imitation boulders, lace or you-name-it; it's "outrageously exotic" and
"the tops in glitz and gauche."*

**MADRONA MANOR**   21R (3S)          | 21 | 21 | 25 | 20 | $148 |
1001 Westside Rd., Healdsburg; (800) 258-4003; (707) 433-4231; FAX 433-0703
*U – A "beautiful Victorian" complete with "friendly ghosts", this is "what a
B&B should be", with "fresh flowers" and "herbs and vegetables from the
garden"; "first-class all the way", this romantic getaway is considered "a
must in the Sonoma Wine Country", but those seeking privacy should
"watch out for frequent wedding parties."*

**MEADOWOOD RESORT**   98R (43S)          | 24 | 23 | 23 | 24 | $229 |
900 Meadowood Lane, St. Helena; (800) 458-8080; (707) 963-3646;
FAX 963-3532
*U – This "absolutely wonderful", "very private" resort on the "secluded"
eastern edge of Napa Valley is a "golfer's paradise" and, believe it or not, a
"mecca for croquet"; "cozy hideaway cottages" and rustic rooms complete
this "tony little oasis" known for staff that "treats you like a king" and one of
the valley's best restaurants.*

**Mendocino Hotel**   51R (6S)          | 17 | 18 | 18 | 17 | $130 |
45080 Main St., Mendocino; (800) 548-0513; (707) 937-0511; FAX 937-0513
*U – A "well-preserved" "historic" hotel in "idyllic surroundings", with
"beautiful interiors" and a "fine bar" and restaurant; this "charming",
"romantic" inn in an "old-world" setting is a good place to while away a few
days on the rugged North Coast.*

## CALIFORNIA RESORTS

| R | S | D | P | $ |

**Monterey Plaza Hotel**   290R (15S)      | 23 | 23 | 21 | 22 | $157 |
400 Cannery Row, Monterey; (800) 631-1339; (408) 646-1700; FAX 646-5937
*M – A "gorgeous setting on the Pacific" and "beautiful ocean vistas" are
the big draws at this "pretty hotel" just a short stroll from the Monterey
Aquarium; spring for one of the "balcony rooms overlooking the water"
and then "go sightseeing", the "most exciting activity in town."*

**Northstar-at-Tahoe**   230R      | 20 | 17 | 15 | 20 | $138 |
Hwy. 267 & Northstar Dr., Truckee, Lake Tahoe; (800) 533-6787;
(916) 562-1010; FAX 587-0215
*U – This "well-kept-up" condo resort at North Lake Tahoe is "wonderful for
the skiing family", thanks to its setting at the foot of the slopes, as well as a
"special treat in the off-season"; one restaurant features unusual Basque
cuisine; being on the California side means no gambling.*

**Ojai Valley Inn**   212R (14S)      | 22 | 22 | 20 | 23 | $191 |
Country Club Rd., Ojai; (800) 422-6524; (805) 646-5511; FAX 646-7969
*U – "Beautifully restored" "all-around" golf and tennis resort in a
"spectacular" valley location that was the setting for the movie* Lost Horizon
*back in the '30s, and thankfully, it hasn't changed much since; it's also a
"superb conference center" and has "amazing service."*

**Petersen Village Inn**   40R (1S)      | – | – | – | – | M |
1576 Mission Dr., Solvang; (800) 321-8985; (805) 688-3121; FAX 688-5732
*Admirers say this little "family-owned" Four Diamond inn features "great
service" and a "romantic" Scandinavian tone in keeping with the ambiance
of its tourist-intensive town founded by Danish settlers in 1911; the Danish
Inn restaurant offers a typical smorgasbord meal, and there's a
"wine-and-cheese happy hour."*

**Portofino Hotel & Yacht Club***   165R (3S)      | 18 | 18 | 15 | 19 | $146 |
(fka Portofino Inn)
260 Portofino Way, Redondo Beach; (800) 835-8668; (310) 379-8481;
FAX 798-2766
*U – A "good place to view the sunset and sip cool drinks", this "small but
pretty" "beachfront" hotel has "laid-back service" and easy access to the
beach towns of LA's South Bay; it's a good hideaway just south of LAX.*

294

## CALIFORNIA RESORTS

| R | S | D | P | $ |
|---|---|---|---|---|

**Post Ranch Inn**   30R (24S)

| – | – | – | – | VE |
|---|---|---|---|---|

Hwy. 1, Big Sur; (800) 527-2000; (408) 667-2200; FAX 669-2824
*Very expensive, but highly esteemed new resort in Big Sur; those few who have been here so far rave about the "wonderful food", "great views" from 1,100 feet above the Pacific (ocean views are even more expensive), and luxurious facilities (24 of the 30 rooms are private cottages) at this "sophisticated" newcomer.*

**QUAIL LODGE RESORT &**
**GOLF CLUB**   100R (14S)

| 24 | 23 | 23 | 23 | $211 |
|---|---|---|---|---|

8205 Valley Greens Dr., Carmel; (800) 538-9516; (408) 624-1581; FAX 624-3726
*U – "Grown-up", "secluded" "convention resort" at the Carmel Valley Golf and Country Club, with "large comfortable rooms" and "lovely grounds" right on a "golf course and pond"; expect a "country-club feel" and "personalized service", along with "noisy seals" down by the shore.*

**Santa Barbara Miramar**   200R (9S)

| 16 | 18 | 15 | 17 | $130 |
|---|---|---|---|---|

1555 S. Jameson Lane, Santa Barbara; (800) 322-6983; (805) 969-2263; FAX 969-3163
*M – "Seedy" "oceanfront" resort just south of Santa Barbara, where "the only good thing is that it's right on the beach"; old-fashioned style makes this a bit "like stepping back 40 years", but the fun fades when you try to sit in the "cheap furniture" and discover that "the customer comes second"; note, an Amtrak line runs through the middle of the property.*

**SAN YSIDRO RANCH**   43R (27S)

| 24 | 24 | 24 | 22 | $255 |
|---|---|---|---|---|

900 San Ysidro Lane, Santa Barbara; (800) 368-6788; (805) 969-5046; FAX 565-1995
*M – A "deluxe dude ranch", popular with Hollywood glitterati who like the fact that it's "rustic and secluded", and happily overlook the "seedy Astroturf around the pool" and slightly "strange rooms"; this "private mountain getaway" is a "great place to be missing in action" if you want to be "treated like a queen" and "feel like a '30s movie star"; fans, a clear majority, call it "sedate and civilized" and "pure bliss."*

**Silverado Country Club & Resort**   275S

| 21 | 21 | 20 | 22 | $193 |
|---|---|---|---|---|

1600 Atlas Peak Rd., Napa; (800) 532-0500; (707) 257-0200; FAX 257-2867
*M – Wine country "rustic", "old but reliable" resort that's "great for golf" it's a "convention place" that's "too much club, not enough hotel" for those who don't spend their days on the links or on the tennis courts; critics say it's "very dated" and "you pay for the location", "close to the wineries."*

**Squaw Valley Inn**  60R (3S)          | 20 | 19 | 18 | 21 | $145 |
1120 Squaw Valley Rd., Olympic Valley; (800) 323-1666; (916) 583-1576;
FAX 583-5619
*U – If you're coming to Tahoe to ski, this site of the 1960 Winter Olympics
is the place; it's "convenient to the mountain", with all levels of slopes for
skiers, but as one reviewer complains, "nothing, absolutely nothing, is
happening après ski here"; a recent renovation brought an English-manor
look to already-luxurious accommodations.*

**STONEPINE ESTATE RESORT**  13S          | 26 | 26 | 25 | 26 | $277 |
150 Carmel Valley Rd., Carmel Valley; (408) 659-2245; FAX 659-5160
*U – Guests call this "unique" "country estate" the "best private hideaway in
America", a "secluded secret" that "you'll hate to leave – it's "exquisite from
the lawn to the rooftop"; a weekend at this "lovely oasis" is "like staying in a
rich friend's country home", complete with a "first-class stable."*

**ST. ORRES**  19R (11S)          | 20 | 21 | 25 | 21 | $144 |
36601 S. Hwy. 1, Gualala; (707) 884-3303
*U – "Another world", this is a bit of California history, dating back from a
time when there were Russian hunting outposts on the Pacific Coast; the
Russian-domed architecture is "very unusual", even "magnificent", and
balconies from the "quaint cottages" offer "glorious views" (watch out for
"dormitorylike" lack of privacy in the "main building"); the Dining Room gets
extra points for its "great" Californian fare.*

**TIMBERHILL RANCH**  15R          | 25 | 25 | 25 | 24 | $267 |
35755 Hauser Bridge Rd., Cazadero; (707) 847-3258; (707) 847-3342
*U – "Sit back and relax" at this "romantic", "isolated" Central Coast retreat,
the "ultimate getaway from everything" with "no television and no phones",
just "beautiful views and complete solitude"; "a must for those seeking
wind-down time", with a "fine restaurant" and "great warmth."*

**VENTANA – BIG SUR**  62R (6S)          | 26 | 25 | 24 | 25 | $235 |
Hwy. 1, Big Sur; (800) 628-6500; (408) 677-2331; FAX 667-2419
*U – "A place to either be in love or fall in love", this "sybaritic", "très
romantic" resort in the hills above Big Sur is often fog-shrouded much of
the year, keeping guests happily sequestered in warm, woodsy yet
"luxurious" cabins with fireplaces and hot tubs; there's wine and cheese in
the lobby all day long, a "fantastic" open-air restaurant and a "clothing-
optional" pool; this is the place "where God goes on vacation."*

**CALIFORNIA RESORTS**                    | R | S | D | P | $ |

**Villa Royale, The**   2R (32S)          | – | – | – | – | E |
1620 Indian Trail, Palm Springs; (800) 245-2314; (619) 327-2314;
FAX 322-4151
*This European-style country inn is a desert oasis with two swimming pools,
a spa, fountains and lush gardens; each guest room is decorated to
represent a different European country, and themed gourmet dinners at the
Europa Restaurant spotlight a different country nightly; located just beyond
the bustle of Downtown, this spot's pleasant for a romantic rendezvous or
just plain solitude.*


**VINTAGE INN – NAPA VALLEY**  80R (8S)   | 25 | 22 | 20 | 21 | $142 |
6541 Washington St., Yountville; (800) 351-1133; (707) 944-1112; FAX 944-1617
*U – "A very romantic place to combine thou and wine" is this "superior"
wine country hotel, conveniently located off the freeway and near wineries
and good restaurants; a "fireplace in every room", "whirlpools", free "buffet
breakfast" and "complimentary wine" make this one of the "best in Napa
Valley", a "luxurious" hostelry at a "decent price."*


**Vintners Inn**   39R (5S)               | – | – | – | – | M |
4350 Barnes Rd., Santa Rosa; (800) 421-2584; (707) 575-7350;
FAX 575-1426
*The superb John Ash & Co. restaurant sets the tone for this charming
Provence-meets-California inn located in a 45-acre Sonoma County
vineyard; Country French ambiance abounds, with airy, antique-filled
rooms (those on the second floor are especially striking); it's best known
as a corporate retreat, but opportunities for relaxing abound in the area –
spas, winery tours, hot-air ballooning and, oh, that food!*


**Wawona Hotel**   104R                   | 12 | 16 | 15 | 18 | $115 |
Yosemite National Park; (209) 252-4848
*M – When you can't stay at the Ahwahnee, consider this more affordable,
"venerable", "turn-of-the-century" grand hotel that conveys the "ambiance
of a bygone era"; "far from Yosemite Village", it's a "spectacular" spot with
"small but adequate bedrooms" and some "shared bathrooms."*


**Wine Country Inn**   25R (1S)           | 22 | 21 | 19 | 19 | $140 |
1152 Lodi Lane, St. Helena; (800) 473-3463; (707) 963-7077; FAX 963-9018
*U – Enjoy "good value" and "views of the vineyards" from this "lovely B&B"
with a "good location" in the "heart of Napa wine country"; it's got all those
nice little touches, like "fireplaces and hot tubs", "handmade quilts" and a
breakfast ("great muffins and breads") that are "worth the room rate."*

# COLORADO

**Antlers Doubletree Hotel**   290R (6S)        | 19 | 19 | 18 | 17 | $132 |
4 S. Cascade Ave., Colorado Springs; (800) 528-0444; (719) 473-5600;
FAX 389-0259
*U – This "centrally located" business hotel features "a great view of Pike's Peak"; reviewers find it "a cut above your standard Doubletree, with prices to match"; "everything is first-rate", from rooms and food to meeting space and the fitness center.*


**Aspen Club Lodge**   90R (7S)        | 18 | 20 | 16 | 18 | $180 |
709 E. Durant St., Aspen; (800) 882-2582; (303) 925-6760; FAX 925-6778
*U – Renovations under new ownership aren't reflected in the ratings; guest rooms, public areas and a tony gourmet restaurant now match the contemporary hotel's "great location" at the base of Aspen Mountain.*


**Breckenridge Hilton**   208R (7S)        | – | – | – | – |  M  |
550 Village Rd., Breckenridge; (800) 321-8444; (303) 453-4500; FAX 453-0212
*A modern mountain hotel with an "excellent location" just steps from the ski slopes and close to the center of town; all rooms have a refrigerator, coffeemaker and wet bar; come summer, duffers delight in the Jack Nicklaus–designed Breckenridge Golf Course just a chip shot away.*


**Broadmoor, The**   551R (65S)        | 23 | 24 | 23 | 25 | $188 |
1 Lake Ave., Colorado Springs; (800) 634-7711; (719) 577-5765; FAX 577-5779
*U – An expansive, "classic resort" that "has everything going for it": "beautiful location", "wonderful facilities", "grand restaurants", "friendly service" – what more could you ask?; some "older rooms still need help", but renovations are ongoing; unmatched amenities include an on-site ice skating rink, three championship golf courses, 16 tennis courts and a movie theater.*

## COLORADO RESORTS

| R | S | D | P | $ |

**Charter at Beaver Creek\***   244R (100S)   | 21 | 19 | 18 | 19 | $184 |
120 Offerson Rd., Beaver Creek; (800) 525-6660; (303) 949-6660; FAX 949-4667
*M – Reviews are mixed on this "exclusive enclave" in the "European"
tradition: some consider it an "exquisite" condo lodge, while others say it's
"nice but too big" or even "run-down, with too many groups"; style varies
according to the condo owner's taste, but most rooms have kitchens and
wood-burning fireplaces; the "great staff" is praised and the new Tra Monti
Restaurant looks promising.*

**Cheyenne Mountain**   | 23 | 21 | 21 | 22 | $152 |
**Conference Resort\***   278R (9S)
3225 Broadmoor Valley Rd., Colorado Springs; (800) 428-8886;
(719) 576-4600; FAX 576-4711
*U – Considered one of the best meeting facilities in the state, this
sprawling property covers almost 12 acres; "great views" of Pike's Peak
and Cheyenne Mountain are a plus, as are nicely appointed rooms and
"outstanding" food; it's "close to the Broadmoor at half the price."*

**C Lazy U Ranch\***   38R (19S)   | 23 | 26 | 25 | 24 | $265 |
3640 Colorado Hwy. 125, Granby; (303) 887-3344
*M – A "perfect vacation spot for families" with deep pockets, this dude
ranch is for those who enjoy roughing it in comfort; rooms are "comfortable",
and the grounds are downright "gorgeous"; summers are devoted to
horseback riding, winters to cross-country skiing, and extensive children's
programs leave parents free to do what they like; open June to mid-
September and Christmas through March.*

**Club Med, Copper Mountain**   225R   | 13 | 18 | 19 | 19 | $155 |
50 Beeler Place, Copper Mountain; (800) CLUB-MED; (303) 968-2161;
FAX 968-2166
*M – A "typical Club Med" property with "small", "Spartan" rooms and "no
amenities"; still, nice public spaces, "fine food" and "fabulous" atmosphere
"all add up to a wonderful vacation for skiers"; special packages include
lodging, lift tickets, equipment, ski instruction and meals; winter season only.*

**Doral Telluride Resort & Spa\***   177R (22S)   | 22 | 25 | 22 | 26 | $223 |
Country Club Dr., Telluride; (800) 22-DORAL; (303) 728-6800;
FAX 728-6175
*U – Destined to become a classic, this "beautiful" new hotel already awes,
with "breathtaking" panoramic views of the San Juan Mountains; it has
spacious, comfortable rooms, excellent food in the Alpenglow restaurant, a
championship golf course and tennis courts, and a four-level, full-service
spa featuring personalized treatments, a fitness center, three heated
swimming pools and a beauty salon.*

## COLORADO RESORTS

| R | S | D | P | $ |

**Grande Butte Hotel**   262R (51S)    | 21 | 20 | 17 | 21 | $132 |
500 Gothic, Mt. Crested Butte; (800) 544-8448; (303) 349-7561; FAX 349-6332
*U – Crested Butte's finest is favored by skiers, who adore the "ski-in/ ski-out" access; spacious guest rooms come with refrigerator, coffeemaker, wet bar, whirlpool tub and private balcony – try for a fireplace as well; summertime packages for golfers are an added benefit; open June to mid-October, and late November through mid-April.*

**Home Ranch**   13R (7S)    | – | – | – | – | VE |
RCR 129, Clark; (800) 223-7094; (303) 879-1780; FAX 879-1795
*"Expensive but worth it" for an idyllic all-inclusive getaway near Steamboat Springs; "great cabins, great food" rave those who immerse themselves in ranch offerings: horseback riding, biking, hiking, fishing and cross-country skiing; after all that activity, guests can relax in a soothing private whirlpool;* N.B. *only week-long packages are available in summer.*

**Hotel Boulderado**   160R (16S)    | 19 | 20 | 19 | 21 | $116 |
2115 13th St., Boulder; (800) 433-4344; (303) 442-4344; FAX 442-4344
*U – A historic landmark considered by most to be "absolutely the place to stay in Boulder"; a "wild west feel" pervades the "charming" rooms, restaurants and bars at this "funky classic" "right in the middle of things", and modestly priced to boot;* N.B. *Q's restaurant is one of Colorado's best.*

**HOTEL JEROME**   94R (16S)    | 24 | 23 | 22 | 24 | $227 |
330 E. Main St., Aspen; (800) 331-7213; (303) 920-1000; FAX 920-1040
*U – Nothing "personifies Aspen" like the Hotel Jerome, "a gorgeous place to see and be seen"; fans tout the restored 1889 landmark for its "great decor", fine dining and "fantastic service"; "fun and charming", with lots of "eccentric types" milling about; at sunset, enjoy "chamber music in the lobby" or head for the hottest spot in town – the infamous Jerome Bar.*

**Hotel Lenado***   19R    | 23 | 24 | 21 | 23 | $176 |
200 S. Aspen St., Aspen; (800) 321-3457; (303) 925-6246; FAX 925-3540
*U – Aspen's "best-kept secret" "defines charm"; a "wonderful, comfy, homey" bed-and-breakfast within walking distance of Aspen's shops and restaurants; rooms come with handmade log beds, Laura Ashley comforters, wood-burning stoves and whirlpool baths.*

**Hot Springs Lodge**   107R    | – | – | – | – | I |
415 6th St., Glenwood Spgs.; (800) 537-SWIM; (303) 945-6571; FAX 945-3540
*This older, but also less expensive, tourist hotel is famous for having the largest natural hot springs pool in the world; simple rooms, some with refrigerator, and an on-site athletic club suit a sporty clientele; it's a short walk from Downtown, and next door to the newly restored Yampah Spa & Vapor Caves.*

## HYATT REGENCY
**BEAVER CREEK**   295R (5S)

| 26 | 25 | 23 | 26 | $239 |

Beaver Creek Resort, Avon; (800) 233-1234; (303) 949-1234; FAX 949-4164
*U – It's "hard to find any criticism" of this "excellent hotel" with ski-in/ski-out access to Beaver Creek Mountain; our surveyors gush over the "warm, friendly lobby", "accommodating service", "spectacular rooms" and "perfect location"; almost self-contained, the resort boasts a luxurious health spa, Italian restaurant and indoor/outdoor swimming pool plus access to championship golf.*

**Inn at Aspen\***   119R (14S) (fka Holiday Inn)

| 21 | 20 | 18 | 21 | $146 |

38750 Hwy. 82, Aspen; (800) 952-1515; (303) 925-9037; FAX 925-9037
*U – Not as posh as some Aspen properties – then again, you don't have to mortgage your home to stay here; surveyors like the "spacious accommodations" and "private, beautiful setting" at the base of Buttermilk Mountain; indoor/outdoor whirlpool bath, outdoor pool, Barrington's restaurant and nearby Aspen Golf Course add to its value.*

**Inn at Beaver Creek\***   45R (8S)

| 22 | 20 | 19 | 20 | $192 |

10 Elk Track, Beaver Creek; (303) 845-7800; FAX 949-2308
*U – "Beautiful, upper-class" small hotel, ideal for a romantic getaway; the "formal" rooms have a minibar and snack basket; complimentary breakfast, easy lift access and an indoor garage are nice extras; and, of course, there's no charge for the "breathtaking" views of the Gore Range.*

**Iron Horse Resort Retreat, The**   130R (15S)

| – | – | – | – | M |

257 Winter Park Dr., Winter Park; (800) 621-8190; (303) 726-8851;
FAX 726-8851 x6023
*Skiers have discovered this relaxing roost just a short schuss from the base of Winter Park – it's quite comfortable, though detractors say "nothing special"; "tasteful" condominium suites feature a full kitchen, fireplace and private deck or balcony; it also makes a good base camp for touring Rocky Mountain National Park in summer.*

**Keystone Lodge**   152R (14S)

| 22 | 22 | 20 | 23 | $158 |

Hwy. 6, Keystone; (800) 222-0188; (303) 468-2316; FAX 468-4105
*M – This sprawling hotel/condo complex suits guests year-round: families like the all-inclusive ski-season packages, but "off-season is also terrific" and Keystone is "a great summer experience"; reviewers agree on the "lovely" accommodations and scenery, but food and service get mixed reactions.*

**COLORADO RESORTS**                              | R | S | D | P | $ |

**Limelite Lodge\***   63R (4S)                    | 18 | 17 | – | 16 | $139 |
228 E. Cooper St., Aspen; (800) 433-0832; (303) 925-3025; FAX 925-5120
*U – A good place if you're "conserving dollars", thanks to an "excellent
location" in the heart of Aspen across from Wagner Park; the modern,
clean rooms won't dazzle or disgust, but the outdoor pool, whirlpool and
sauna are pluses; N.B. there's no on-site restaurant.*


**LITTLE NELL, THE**   92R (13S)                   | 26 | 26 | 26 | 26 | $261 |
675 E. Durant St., Aspen; (800) 525-6200; (303) 920-4600; FAX 920-4670
*U – An "outstanding" hotel that remains the "best in Aspen"; "beautiful,
contemporary rooms", "superb service", and "delightful dining" and
"creative food" make our surveyors wish they "could live here"; a location
right at the foot of Aspen Mountain next to the Silver Queen Gondola, and
unexpected extras like afternoon tea and a ski concierge keep it "first-class
all the way", including prices.*


**Lodge at Cordillera\***   28R (3S)               | 24 | 24 | 24 | 25 | $284 |
Cordillera Way, Edwards; (800) 548-2721; (303) 926-2200; FAX 926-2486
*M – "Pretty but isolated" hotel and spa about 30 minutes from Vail; the
complimentary breakfast, "excellent" Picasso restaurant and "great spa
facilities" have a large contingent of fans who cite this as "the ultimate in
luxury", but considering the cost, "tiny" rooms make one reviewer cry
"this is a joke."*


**Lodge at Vail**   100R (40S)                     | 22 | 21 | 22 | 21 | $225 |
174 E. Gore Creek Dr., Vail; (800) 331-5634; (303) 476-5011; FAX 476-7425
*U – "Classic Vail": "very nice, but very expensive"; our surveyors deem this
resort "almost like a fairy tale", noting "excellent rooms", two "fabulous"
restaurants, "caring staff" and "great location" "in the heart of Vail"; it's a
"lively" ski spot where "amenities abound", including a heated outdoor pool
and service vans at your beck and call, but popular in summer too.*


**Mountain Haus at Vail\***   79R                  | 22 | 18 | 17 | 17 | $211 |
292 E. Meadow Dr., Vail; (800) 237-0922; (303) 476-2434; FAX 476-3007
*M – It may have the "best location in Vail", but guests take "potluck" with
individually owned rooms and condos, some of which are "falling apart"; for
the price, many customers think it's "rip-off city", especially with what many
consider the "worst service in town."*

**Pines Lodge at Beaver Creek Resort** 60R (12S) | – | – | – | – | VE |
(fka Camberley Club Hotel, The)
Beaver Creek Resort, 141 Scott Hill Rd., Avon; (800) 688-2411;
(303) 845-7900; FAX 845-7809
*"Ski-in/ski-out" convenience is but one lure of this luxurious resort hotel
on Beaver Creek Mountain; the "wonderful" rooms, outstanding French
restaurant and personalized service reflect the heady rates; there's also a
fitness center, outdoor pool, whirlpool, game room and conference suites.*

**Radisson Resort Vail**   350R (50S)          | 18 | 19 | 18 | 18 | $170 |
(fka Marriott's Mark Resort)
715 W. Lionshead Circle, Vail; (800) 648-0720; (303) 476-4444; FAX 479-6996
*M – Ratings are solid already and recent guest room renovation should
improve reviews, but we still hear complaints of "no lobby", "mediocre food"
and "poor service"; no one's complaining about the close proximity to the
mountain's gondola, however, and Radisson's recent takeover of
management is probably good news.*

**Ritz-Carlton, Aspen**  257R (28S)          | – | – | – | – | VE |
315 Dean St., Aspen; (800) 241-3333; (303) 920-3300; FAX 920-9555
*Opened in late 1992 and too new to rate, this elegant neo-classic Ritz
nonetheless promises great things, thanks to its first-rate lineage and
glorious location right at the base of Aspen Mountain and near the town's
shops, restaurants and thriving nightlife.*

**Sardy House\***  20R (6S)                    | – | – | – | – | VE |
128 E. Main St., Aspen; (800) 321-3457; (303) 920-2525; FAX 920-4478
*This lovely country inn is made for those seeking romance in the Rockies;
a complimentary full breakfast is served in the lovely Victorian dining room
or in bed, and Colorado spruce trees shade the lush grounds, heated pool,
spa and sauna; the only complaints are "small" rooms and "no closets."*

**Sheraton Steamboat Resort**                | 19 | 20 | 18 | 20 | $146 |
**& Conference Center**   273R (8S)
Mt. Werner Circle & Village Inn Court, Steamboat Springs; (800) 848-8878;
(303) 879-2220; FAX 879-7686
*U – A youthful, "friendly staff" and an unbeatable ski location steps away
from the Silver Bullet Gondola make up for "average food" and rooms with
"furnishings that need to be replaced"; value packages and the 18-hole
Robert Trent Jones Jr. golf course attract summer guests.*

**Silver Tree Hotel\***   277R (15S)        | 19 | 19 | 18 | 18 | $186 |
100 Elbert Lane, Snowmass Village; (800) 525-9402; (303) 923-3520;
FAX 923-5192
U – "Right on the Snowmass slopes", this contemporary resort offers
handsome rooms, an attractive atrium lobby, "friendly staff" and "good desk
help"; nightly specials, including an all-you-can-eat BBQ rib dinner at the
Brother's Grille, make this a locals' favorite, while the intimate health club
keeps fitness types happy as well.


**Sitzmark Lodge\***   35R        | 21 | 20 | 21 | 17 | $129 |
183 Gore Creek Dr., Vail; (303) 476-5001; FAX 476-8702
U – "Quaint" Bavarian-style hotel with a "great location" in the center of
town; the cozy rooms are nicely decorated, some with fireplaces, and
a complimentary continental breakfast is served during ski season;
conscientious staff go out of their way to make guests feel at home; other
amenities include an outdoor pool and the extra-fine Left Bank restaurant.


**Snowmass Lodge & Club, The**   136R (60S)   | 22 | 22 | 20 | 22 | $186 |
239 Snowmass Club Circle, Snowmass Village; (800) 525-6200;
(303) 923-5600; FAX 923-6944
U – Altitude isn't the only thing to take your breath away at this "luxurious"
mountain resort with lift tickets included in winter room rates; the "lodge
has a cozy, warm feel, with fireplaces and overstuffed furniture
throughout"; "large rooms" sport "postcard views", and you "can't beat the
on-site health-club facilities"; a new chef should help future food reviews;
in summer there's championship golf.


**Sonnenalp Resort**   207R (67S)        | 20 | 22 | 20 | 21 | $208 |
20 Vail Rd., Vail; (800) 654-8312; (303) 476-5656; FAX 476-1639
M – This "European-style hotel" spans three separate buildings; most call
it "fun" and "homey", but some complain that it "caters to large groups";
hand-carved beds, down comforters and alpine furnishings create "cute"
rooms, and there's a full-treatment spa on-site; take a free shuttle to the
hotel-owned country club, offering a PGA golf course and tennis courts.


**Stanley Hotel\***   92R (3S)        | 16 | 18 | 18 | 21 | $129 |
333 Wonderview Ave., Estes Park; (800) ROCKIES; (303) 586-3371;
(303) 586-3673
M – Stephen King's model for The Shining, this historic hotel (built by F.O.
Stanley of Stanley Steamer fame) is "convenient to Rocky Mountain National
Park"; modest rates and "spectacular" scenery don't necessarily make up
for what some call "small" rooms and "surly service."

**COLORADO RESORTS**                        | R | S | D | P | $ |

**Tall Timber\***  10R                      | 24 | 24 | 20 | 24 | $293 |
Silverton Star Rte., San Juan Forest, Durango; (303) 259-4813
*U – This "truly isolated" lodge surrounded by the San Juan National Forest
is reached only by narrow-gauge train or private helicopter; it's ideal "for
serious naturalists" with deep pockets and an affinity for the outdoors;
guests can try their hand at cross-country skiing, horseback riding, fishing,
tennis, golf or hiking; the "great staff lines up to greet new arrivals";
naturally, there are no phones, TVs or radios.*

**Tamarron Resort**  350R (50S)            | 22 | 21 | 19 | 23 | $157 |
40292 Hwy. 550 N., Durango; (800) 678-1000; (303) 259-2000; FAX 259-0745
*U – Golf, golf and more golf attracts serious players to this "rustic", "western-
style resort" where the food and "comfortable", "large" rooms may be
"nothing to rave about", but trail rides, tennis clinics, jeep tours, white-water
rafting and the Zoo Crew children's program are bound to impress those
seeking a "wonderful family place."*

**Vail Athletic Club**  38R                | 21 | 22 | 20 | 20 | $174 |
(fka Vail Hotel & Athletic Club)
352 E. Meadow Dr., Vail; (800) 822-4754; (303) 838-5981; (303) 476-0700;
FAX 476-6451
*M – "Excellent exercise and spa facilities" compensate for an otherwise
"ho-hum" modern hotel in the center of Vail Village; its "large, well-
decorated rooms" overlook Gore Creek; rates include continental buffet
breakfast and use of the fitness-center facilities; don't miss the club's
indoor climbing wall.*

**Vista Verde Guest Ranch**  8S            | – | – | – | – | VE |
Steamboat Springs,; (800) 526-RIDE; (303) 879-3858; (303) 879-1413
*Few of our surveyors know about this picturesque ski-touring ranch, with
its log cabins and cozy fireplaces; summer packages feature plenty of time
in the saddle plus mountain biking, float trips, cookouts, hayrides, even
gold-panning expeditions; come winter, activities turn to snowshoeing,
sleigh rides and ski-in lunches; rates are all-inclusive.*

**Westin Resort Vail, The**  300R (28S)    | 22 | 20 | 18 | 21 | $186 |
1300 Westhaven Dr., Vail; (800) 228-3000; (303) 476-7111; (303) 479-7050
*M – Isolation from Vail Village dismays some surveyors – a private chair lift
makes this convention-oriented hotel "convenient for skiing, but it's
otherwise out-of-the-way"; reaction is mixed to other things as well:
"excellent services" and "good health club" vs. "smaller-than-average
rooms" and "lots of people with attitudes."*

305

# CONNECTICUT

| R | S | D | P | $ |

**Boulders, The**   17R (2S)                     | 19 | 20 | 20 | 18 | $150 |
E. Shore Rd. (Rte. 45), New Preston (203) 868-0541; FAX 868-1925
*U – A "great spot to contemplate life while digesting great views", this
"romantic", antique-filled country inn on a lake near Litchfield provides
swimming, bicycling, boating, fishing, tennis and ice skating; fans say it's
the "best inn in the area" and recommend it for brunch especially.*

**Griswold Inn, The**   25R(8S)                  | 18 | 19 | 19 | 18 | $128 |
36 Main St., Essex; (203) 767-1776; FAX 767-0481
*U – The British burned the fleet in 1812 but, praise be, not the "romantic,
hokey" Gris; it's "seen better days" but retains "a creaky charm" – "small
rooms", "narrow steps, slanting floors and all"; nightly entertainment,
maritime art on the walls and a nearby historic area are bonuses.*

**Homestead Inn, The**   23R (7S)                | 22 | 22 | 25 | 20 | $157 |
420 Field Point Rd., Greenwich; (203) 869-7500
*U – "Comfortable and classy", this inn close to NYC was built as a
farmhouse in 1799 but is now best known for its "wonderful" Classic
French cuisine; "Laura Ashley comes to life" in "charming rooms" that are
best in the Main House; lovely lawns, big trees and a wraparound porch
add to the atmosphere, as does "excellent service."*

**Interlaken Inn**   79R (7S)                    | 16 | 18 | 16 | 16 | $135 |
74 Interlaken Rd., Lakeville; (800) 222-2909; (203) 435-9878; FAX 435-2980
*U – Set between two lakes across from the Hotchkiss School in Northwestern
Connecticut, this "pleasant, clean" "sleepaway camp for adults – without
counselors" has the "most active bar in the area"; recently renovated
rooms remind some of "an upscale motel with good service."*

**MAYFLOWER INN**   25R (9S)                     | 24 | 24 | 23 | 25 | $235 |
Rte. 47, Washington; (203) 868-9466; FAX 868-1497
*U – Your forebears didn't have to come over on the ship in order for you to
stay at this "elegant" country inn, which has been renovated with loving
care and megabucks; an "outstanding chef", a huge wine cellar, charming
rooms with canopied four-poster beds and luxury linens, and a pool set on
"manicured lawns" are pampering details; some say it's the "best in the
NE", a few feel it's "gone over the top."*

## CONNECTICUT RESORTS

| R | S | D | P | $ |

### Riverwind Inn, The  8R

| – | – | – | – | M |

209 Main St., Deep River; (203) 526-2014
*In quiet, historic Deep River, this farmhouse B&B on the town green is a "romantic hideaway"; stenciled, antique-filled rooms have names like "Hearts and Flowers"; there's a wicker-intensive sun porch, a 12-foot stone fireplace, and a gratis Southern buffet breakfast – plus great antiquing nearby.*

### Stonehenge  16R (2S)

| 20 | 21 | 23 | 20 | $153 |

Rte. 7, Ridgefield; (203) 438-6511; FAX 438-2478
*U – Beside a stream with swans, this "quiet and comfortable" country house is set on 19 acres and gives a "dose of country for city folk", about an hour from NYC; an "excellent dining room" and "traditional bedrooms" "round out the experience" in "beautiful, old New England style."*

### Under Mountain Inn*  7R

| 19 | 18 | 19 | 17 | $132 |

482 Under Mountain Rd.; (Rte. 41), Salisbury (203) 435-0242
*U – A British-born chef-owner imparts England's flavor to this "small and friendly", tree-shaded inn "with English fare"; red, white and blue – patriotic for both countries – decorates the guest rooms, and the intimate dining rooms are warmed by burning logs and old floorboards.*

### Water's Edge Inn & Resort*  31R

| 21 | 20 | 21 | 20 | $146 |

1525 Boston Post Rd., P.O. Box 938, Westbrook; (800) 222-5901; (203) 399-5901; FAX 399-6172
*U – Four-story windows in a dining room serving "excellent" food open onto a "beautiful view of Long Island Sound" at this "crisp-clean" resort; villas overlook a "small beach", and there's a "good spa and exercise program."*

# FLORIDA*

|   | R | S | D | P | $ |
|---|---|---|---|---|---|

**Amelia Island Plantation**   1100R (420S)   | 23 | 20 | 19 | 23 | $173 |
Hwy. A1A S., Amelia Island; (800) 874-6878; (904) 261-6161; FAX 277-5950
*U – "The serenity" of this place and its "outstanding" golf and tennis help
make it "one of the finest resorts in the world", where "convenience to the
beach", "lots to do" and "constant supervision for the kids" add up to a
great family getaway;* N.B. *ask to see the rental condos, which vary in
design and quality.*

**BOCA RATON RESORT & CLUB**   963R (41S)   | 23 | 23 | 22 | 24 | $218 |
501 E. Camino Real, Boca Raton; (800) 327-0101; (407) 395-3000;
FAX 391-3183
*U – "If you like being among the beautiful people", you'll love this "fine
European-style resort"; "magnificent grounds", "great food" in "four different
restaurants", "impeccable service" and "accommodations in the new tower
and beachfront" are all winners; what some call "old-world charm in the
main hotel" building, others call "shabby."*

**Brazilian Court**   526R (40S)   | 20 | 20 | 19 | 21 | $176 |
301 Australian Ave., Palm Beach; (800) 833-3141; (407) 655-7740;
FAX 659-8403
*M – Known for "great food and service" since 1920 by "those who prefer a
more reasonable taste of elegance", the "best hotel in Palm Beach needs
to upgrade its rooms"; though there are those who still call it a "terrific small
out-of-the-way hotel", others say "too bad" this "romantic, fabulous taste of
old Florida" off Worth Avenue is "getting run-down."*

**Breakers, The**   528R (40S)   | 21 | 22 | 21 | 24 | $219 |
1 S. County Rd., Palm Beach; (800) 833-3141; (407) 655-6611; FAX 659-8403
*M – This "gracious dowager" with her "beautiful rooms", spectacular
facilities and oceanfront setting evokes "old Palm Beach" when it was the
"croquet capital of the world"; to critics she's "pompous", with "double-
breasted suits at the pool", and some feel "the spirit of the old Breakers is
missing in what is now a big corporate and convention resort", but for the
vast majority of our surveyors, she's still the "crème de la crème" – "you
must stay at this great, glorious place at least once in your life."*

---

*See also: Miami/Miami Beach and Tampa Bay Hotels.

**FLORIDA RESORTS**                                    | R | S | D | P | $ |

**Captiva Beach Resort** 19R (fka Captiva Hotel) | 22 | 20 | 20 | 22 | $174 |
6772 Sara Sea Circle, Siesta Key; (813) 349-4131
*U – Swim, sun, snorkel, sail and fish off the white-sand beach of a "quiet"
"South Seas plantation" on the Gulf of Mexico three miles from Downtown
Sarasota; all rooms and apartments provide cooking facilities and good
value for families – better yet, ask for weekly and monthly rates at this
"lovely location with all the activities and seashells, too."*


**Chalet Suzanne**  30R (4S)                    | 20 | 23 | 24 | 18 | $145 |
3800 Chalet Suzanne Dr., off U.S. Hwy. 27, Lake Wales; (800) 288-6011;
(813) 676-6011; FAX 671-1814
*M – "If you've never been to Lake Wales", this "funky and fun" "unique
country Inn" known for its soup cannery and "absolutely wonderful food"
is "worth the experience – once" – for its "wild, wacky and eclectic"
hodgepodge of rooms, each one different and "amusing"; the private
airstrip "makes for a great overnighter" or "murder-mystery weekend."*


**Cheeca Lodge**  203R (63S)                    | 21 | 21 | 21 | 21 | $184 |
Mile Marker 82, Islamorada; (800) 327-2888; (305) 664-4651; FAX 664-2083
*U – "The pride of the Keys" has "the best lodgings between Miami and Key
West"; "beautiful grounds" and "sparkling waters" make this "a sportsman's
and fisherman's paradise", but even duffers will enjoy the rooms, service
and "delicious food" at this "classy", albeit pricey, getaway.*


**Club Med Sandpiper**  330R                    | 19 | 18 | 18 | 19 | $160 |
(fka Village Hotel of St. Piper)
3500 SE Morningside Blvd., Port St. Lucie; (800) 258-2633; (407) 335-4400;
FAX 335-9497
*M – A circus workshop for children puts this Club Med just north of Stuart
"one notch above most Meds"; "big old rooms", a "fabulous golf course",
and baby and children's clubs make it "good for families and activity-
seeking vacationers" who don't mind being "away from the beach."*


**Colony Beach & Tennis Resort**  235S          | 21 | 21 | 22 | 20 | $189 |
1620 Gulf of Mexico Dr., Longboat Key; (800) 4-COLONY; (813) 383-6464;
FAX 383-7549
*U – The 21 available courts keep "serious tennis players" happy here,
while a "great kids' program", "spacious" rooms, "super staff" and an
"excellent though expensive restaurant" bring folks off the courts and
"back for return visits."*

**Grenelefe Resort & Conf. Center** 950R (574S)| 21 | 19 | 18 | 21 | $132 |
3200 State Rd. 546, Haines City; (800) 237-9549; (813) 422-7511; FAX 421-5000
*M – Howie Barrow's golf school and Rick Macci's tennis program offer
"personalized instruction" at this "isolated" "complete resort" with "elegant
suites" on nearly 1,000 acres of grounds, and newly "upgraded facilities";
summer brings "deadly heat" and mosquitoes.*

**Hawk's Cay Resort & Marina** 176R (16S) | 19 | 20 | 19 | 20 | $163 |
Mile Marker 61, Duck Key; (800) 432-2242; (305) 743-7000; FAX 743-5215
*M – There's "no need to leave" this hotel with "excellent water sports"
on a private island between the Atlantic and the Gulf, with its fishing,
"dolphin show" and "little beach lagoon"; "pretty and relaxing", it's a
"great place to take the kids"; dissenters call it "a bit pricey" and complain
about all the children.*

**Hyatt Key West** 120R (4S) | 23 | 22 | 21 | 22 | $178 |
601 Front St., Key West; (800) 233-1234; (305) 296-9900; FAX 292-1038
*U – "The best chain hotel in Key West" gets "praise all around" for
"excellent service", "lovely, airy public areas" and a "good location" in the
heart of Old Town; the "great suites with beautiful views" overlooking the
Gulf of Mexico outrank the ordinary rooms.*

**Indian River Plantation** | 22 | 22 | 19 | 21 | $159 |
**Resort & Marina** 323R (100S)
555 NE Ocean Blvd., Stuart; (800) 444-3389; (407) 225-3700; FAX 225-0003
*U – The quiet of Stuart's beach is interrupted by this resort that's got more
activities than you can shake a fishing pole at; new oceanfront rooms and
suites with kitchenettes are "luxurious yet comfortable", and besides golf,
tennis and swimming, there's plenty to do, including cruising on the hotel's
own 150-passenger boat; it's "great for families", who say that everything
here is "very special."*

**Inn at Fisher Island** 58S | – | – | – | – | VE |
1 Fisher Island Dr., Fisher Island; (800) 537-3708; (305) 535-6020;
FAX 535-6003
*Formerly the winter home of William Vanderbilt II, this Mediterranean-style
resort located on a private 206-acre island off of Miami Beach is accessible
only by water or air; its amenities include a championship golf course,
European-style spa, world-class tennis center, two deep-water marinas, six
gourmet restaurants and a mile-long private beach; guests are pampered
like royalty – for a princely price.*

**Lakeside Inn**   87R (17S)   | – | – | – | – | M |
100 N. Alexander St., Mount Dora; (904) 383-4101; (904) 735-2642
*Afternoon tea, served from a silver service on the galleried front porch of*
*the main building, sets the clock back to 1883, when this picturesque*
*landmark was built; its 19th-century feeling has been preserved in four*
*newly refurbished separate buildings circled around the lake; the interesting*
*boutiques and antiques shops of Mount Dora make walking fun.*

**LITTLE PALM ISLAND**   30S   | 27 | 26 | 26 | 26 | $291 |
Overseas Hwy. 1, Little Torch Key; (800) 343-8567; (305) 872-2524;
FAX 872-4843
*M – A 20-minute ferry ride to this five-acre island near Key West will "put a*
*little romance back in your life", without phones, TVs or cars; private*
*thatch-roofed villas with Mombasa-netted king-size beds, a lagoon-style*
*pool and fancy French food add up to an "expensive" place that's "like*
*being in the South Pacific."*

**LODGE AT**   | 24 | 23 | 22 | 24 | $201 |
**PONTE VEDRA BEACH**   66R (24S)
607 Ponte Vedra Blvd., Ponte Vedra Beach; (800) 243-4304; (904) 273-9500;
FAX 273-0210
*U – "If you can find it", this is a "lovely retreat" near St. Augustine; "new*
*and richly appointed", it has "beautiful oceanfront rooms" "made for*
*romance" (fireplaces, 24-hour room service – the works); a health club with*
*spa and exercise facilities, and the well-rated food of the Mediterranean*
*Restaurant entice some to leave their rooms.*

**Marquesa Hotel**   15R (6S)   | – | – | – | – | E |
600 Fleming St., Key West; (800) 869-4631; (305) 292-1919; FAX 294-2121
*The "impeccable restoration" of this "century-old" replica of a New England*
*rooming house created 15 different rooms and suites with period furniture*
*and antiques for "a bit of sanity amid the tawdriness of Key West"; "great*
*service" and "the best restaurant in Key West" (Cafe Marquesa) make this*
*"charming" "historic landmark" a very different place to stay.*

**Marriott at Sawgrass Resort**   538R (223S)   | 22 | 22 | 21 | 23 | $161 |
1000 TPC Blvd., Ponte Vedra Beach; (800) 228-9290; (904) 285-7777;
FAX 285-0906
*M – "Your standard waterfall-inspired resort" is also a "golfer's paradise"*
*thanks to its "famous PGA course"; fans call it a "wonderful, relaxing" place*
*with "friendly, helpful staff", "delicious Sunday brunch" and a "beautiful*
*atrium setting"; critics, on the other hand, say it's "nothing special", perhaps*
*because of "sometimes-noisy" accommodations judged "not up to the golf."*

## FLORIDA RESORTS

| R | S | D | P | $ |

### MARRIOTT'S BAY
### POINT RESORT  385R (82S)

| 23 | 23 | 22 | 24 | $132 |

100 Delwood Beach Rd., Panama City Beach; (800) 874-7105; (904) 234-3307;
FAX 233-1308

*U – "Superior service" and "gorgeous" public facilities mark this "undiscovered family resort" halfway between Tallahassee and Pensacola; it's off the traditional Florida route, but golf and tennis packages, newly renovated rooms, a health club and a paddle-wheel cruise make it worth seeking out.*

### Marriott's Casa Marina Resort  381R (67S)

| 20 | 20 | 20 | 22 | $178 |

1500 Reynolds St., Key West; (800) 228-9290; (305) 296-3535;
FAX 296-4633

*M – On "the best beach in Key West" and in the "old-world elegant setting" of the "historic Flagler mansion", most guests are more than satisfied; however, "despite the grand architecture and beautiful grounds", some say the old rooms are "musty and dark", "the new rooms lack the romance they advertise", and the location is "away from what's happening."*

### Marriott's Marco Island
### Resort & Golf Club  735R (86S)

| 21 | 21 | 19 | 21 | $165 |

400 S. Collier Blvd., Marco Island; (800) GET-HERE; (813) 394-2511;
FAX 394-4645

*U – A "wonderful way to combine business and pleasure", this "big and sprawling" resort–cum–convention facility is suspended off the SW tip of Florida "with more seashells than most of us see in a lifetime"; white sand, 16 tennis courts and John Jacobs's restaurant make for "great fun" and "appeal to couples and families"; critics say it's more "convention than vacation", with "a commercial feel."*

### Mission Inn*  187R (44S)

| 21 | 21 | 18 | 21 | $120 |

10400 County Rd. 48, Howey-in-the-Hills; (800) 874-9053; (904) 324-3101;
FAX 324-3101 x7443

*M – Rising out of nowhere on a back highway 45 minutes northwest of Orlando is a Spanish-style hacienda, "one of Florida's hidden treasures"; complete with a marina on Lake Harris, it's also "one of the nicest golf [and tennis] resorts in the U.S."; if you can bring yourself to leave, it's also 10 minutes away from Mount Dora, which is a dream town for an the antique collector.*

**FLORIDA RESORTS**                    | R | S | D | P | $ |

**OCEAN GRAND HOTEL**   210R (14S)      | 25 | 24 | 25 | 26 | $215 |
2800 S. Ocean Blvd., Palm Beach; (800) 432-2335; (407) 582-2800;
FAX 547-1557
*U – Palm Beach's "best new hotel" on the ocean draws accolades for
"informal luxury" and "upscale service"; "small and very elegant", it offers a
"quiet and intimate" atmosphere, "lovely rooms with amenities", "a fine
fitness center" and "beautiful dining", contemporary-style, for those who
can afford to pay a bit more for their bed and board.*

**Ocean Key House**   95S              | – | – | – | – | M |
(fka Zero Duval Street)
Zero Duval St., Key West; (800) 328-9815; (305) 296-7701; FAX 292-7685
*With a rare view of both Atlantic and Gulf waters at the foot of Downtown's
Duval Street, each apartment in this onetime-condominium offers a
romantic, oversize whirlpool bath in the master bedroom; request rooms
on the street, not in back where catwalk spotlights glare.*

**Ocean Reef Club**   203R (9S)        | 21 | 21 | 20 | 22 | $211 |
31 Ocean Reef Dr., Key Largo; (800) 741-REEF; (305) 367-2611; FAX 367-2224
*M – "Wear your blue Oxford shirt and khaki pants" at this Upper Key "escape
from Miami", a "sport resort" known for its "yacht watching" and private
airstrip for the rich; "you get your own golf cart to zip about" the beautiful
"secluded grounds", where "the dolphin show alone is worth the price."*

**Palm Beach Polo**                    | 23 | 22 | 20 | 22 | $226 |
**& Country Club***   100R (60S)
13198 Forest Hill Blvd., Palm Beach; (800) 327-4204; (407) 798-7000;
FAX 798-7052
*M – Posh villas amid "magnificent manicured grounds" provide condo-style
lodging with complete hotel services at this "playground for the horsey
set"; during the Winter Equestrian Festival, international teams battle it out
on 10 polo fields while clubhouse viewers sip champagne; it's also an
"excellent choice" if "you're a tennis or golfing buff"; yes, it's expensive.*

**PGA National**   420R (57S)          | 20 | 21 | 20 | 23 | $163 |
400 Ave. of the Champions, Palm Beach Gardens; (800) 633-9150;
(407) 627-2000; FAX 622-0261
*M – "Sports lovers" love this "very attractive resort" on the white-sand
beach of Lake Lytal 25 miles north of Palm Beach, for its "great variety of
courses" and courts, not to mention "moderate prices"; though it's a "golf
and tennis player's paradise", a few detractors find it "very sterile."*

**Pier House Resort & Caribbean Spa**   120R   | 20 | 20 | 21 | 20 | $176 |
1 Duval St., Key West; (800) 327-8340; (305) 276-4600; FAX 296-7568
*M – "There's no better location in crowded, overrun Key West" than this
smaller resort "within walking distance of everything"; "top-notch dining on
the deck" gives the "best view of the fantastic sunset in all Key West",
where "island atmosphere" is everything; insiders suggest you stay in the
"elegant Caribbean spa rooms" rather than the "outdated regular rooms";
the nearby topless beach is a definite attraction.*

**Plantation Inn & Golf Resort***   142R (10S)   | 19 | 23 | 19 | 20 | $98 |
9301 W. Fort Island Trail, Crystal River; (800) 632-6262; (904) 795-4211;
FAX 795-1368
*U – A wide range of hotel-related activities win praise from surveyors, as
do the "big rooms" and "great dining" with a "down-home atmosphere";
bonefish enthusiasts fall hook, line and sinker for this Crystal River place,
especially when they take note of its modest price.*

**Ponce de Leon Resort***   194R (8S)   | 18 | 19 | 17 | 18 | $107 |
4000 U.S. Hwy. 1 N., St. Augustine; (800) 228-2821; (904) 824-2821;
FAX 829-6108
*U – In a unique setting under oak trees by the Intracoastal Waterway is the
only 18-hole championship putting course in the U.S.; Spanish architecture
"takes you back in time to the early '50s", and the casual atmosphere is
"very comfortable"; you can take the sightseeing train from the front door
two miles to St. Augustine's historic district.*

**Ponte Vedra Inn & Club**   202R (20S)   | 22 | 22 | 20 | 22 | $158 |
200 Ponte Vedra Blvd., Ponte Vedra Beach; (800) 234-7842;
(904) 285-1111; FAX 285-2111
*M – An "old-world feeling" prevails at this "golfer's paradise", established in
1928 as a luxury oceanfront resort and private country club; "low-rise units
right on the beach" offer a "great escape for an active family vacation" with
"good accommodations" and a "fully staffed children's nursery"; critics say
it's "nice but not special" and "only worth the golf."*

**Reach Resort, The**   149R (70S)   | 20 | 19 | 19 | 20 | $182 |
1435 Simonton St. at the Ocean, Key West; (800) 874-4118;
(305) 296-5000; FAX 296-2830
*M – All "Victorian and gingerbread", this "perfect Key West confection" is
on the island's only natural beach; the "very nice" suites with views (all
rooms have private balconies) were modernized in 1991; it's got a "quiet
location away from the tumult" but is still well within walking distance of
Duval Street and all that's happening in this fanciful town.*

**REGISTRY RESORT**  474R (29S)  | 25 | 24 | 24 | 25 | $191 |
475 Seagate Dr., Naples; (800) 247-9810; (813) 597-3232; FAX 597-3147
*U – Not one adverse comment came from our respondents, who call this gulffront "luxurious California-style hotel" "great in all areas"; there's plenty to do, from tennis and water skiing to golf and fishing; "personalized service", "relaxed atmosphere" and nifty facilities keep clients devoted to "one of the best around."*

**RESORT AT LONGBOAT**  | 24 | 22 | 21 | 23 | $202 |
**KEY CLUB, THE**  231R (211S)
301 Gulf of Mexico Dr., Longboat Key; (800) 237-8821; (813) 383-8821; FAX 383-0359
*U – "The place to go in Sarasota" has "the best beach in Florida", "great golf and tennis" and an "attentive staff"; "impressive" newly renovated condos have "spacious", well-furnished rooms complete with washers and dryers, but there's no public area to speak of; "gracious and comfortable", it's "a first-class experience" for "families" or "the over-60 crowd."*

**RITZ-CARLTON, AMELIA ISLAND** 449R (45S) | 27 | 27 | 25 | 27 | $205 |
4750 Amelia Island Pkwy., Amelia Island; (800) 241-3333; (904) 277-1100; FAX 277-1145
*U – "Luxurious beyond compare", this "beautiful" new resort hotel is an "island of calm and gentility" in a "drop-dead location"; it's got a wonderful "on-site health club", "exceptional grounds", a "nice dining room" and service that's sometimes "too good" – the "staff insists on escorting you everywhere"; all that plus the full complement of activities and amenities that you expect from a Ritz make this a "world-class" "getaway."*

**RITZ-CARLTON, NAPLES**  449R (45S)  | 27 | 27 | 26 | 27 | $226 |
280 Vanderbilt Beach Rd., Naples; (800) 241-3333; (813) 277-1100; FAX 277-1145
*U – "Paradise lost is found" at this "absolutely wonderful" resort, which is definitely "the place you want to be in Naples" – if you can afford it; "truly a Ritzy place", it provides a fine beach location, "beautiful" grounds, "elegant" accommodations, and stellar service and dining to set "the standard all others strive for", including "snob appeal"; a few find its formal elegance out of place in a beach town.*

**RITZ-CARLTON, PALM BEACH**   270R (58S)   | 27 | 26 | 25 | 26 | $228 |
100 S. Ocean Blvd., Manalapan; (800) 241-3333; (407) 533-6000; FAX 588-4202
*U – "Not the Taj Mahal, but a close second" 20 minutes south of Palm
Beach; it "stands up to all the rest" of its ritzy-Ritz family by making sure
that "fabulous food", "great service", "pristine" rooms and "anything you
want is always available" – why, they even "comb the fringe on the lobby
rugs"; if you think all this luxury is "too stiff for Florida", look elsewhere, but
for people who want "new elegance", it's "the place to stay."*

**Sheraton Key Largo**   200R (10S)   | 19 | 18 | 17 | 18 | $141 |
97000 S. Overseas Hwy., Key Largo; (800) 826-1006; (305) 852-5553;
FAX 852-8056
*M – "Acceptable accommodations" at a "better value" than some of its local
competitors make this "laid-back" Upper Key Sheraton, with "fantastic
seafood" and "great Sunday brunch", a good "stop on the way" to Key
West, though "not a destination in itself."*

**Sonesta Sanibel Harbour Resort**   342R (47S)   | 23 | 23 | 21 | 23 | $171 |
17260 Harbour Pointe Dr., Fort Myers; (800) 767-7777; (813) 466-4000;
FAX 466-6050
*U – "A beautiful hotel at the foot of the bridge to Sanibel Island", this
Victorian reproduction offers "spacious, spotless rooms", "genuinely caring
service", "great spa and tennis", and "wonderful conference facilities" that
are "a good buy on- and off-season."*

**South Seas Plantation**   | 21 | 19 | 19 | 22 | $183 |
**Resort & Yacht Harbour**   600R (500S)
13000 South Seas Plantation Rd., Captiva Island; (800) 237-3102;
(813) 472-5111; FAX 472-7541
*M – "Go with a group of six and stay in the beach cottages", where three
bedrooms and three baths make this "ideal family resort" a good buy; "the
private beach is wonderful", and the "extensive facilities" "have everything
you could imagine"; a few complaints about "housekeeping" and summer
"bugs" drop an otherwise "great place" down a notch.*

**Sundial Beach & Tennis Resort**   265S   | 20 | 18 | 17 | 19 | $162 |
1451 Middle Gulf Rd., Sanibel Island; (800) 237-4184; (813) 472-4151;
FAX 472-1809
*M – "Lovely accommodations", "lots of kids' activities" and an "excellent
location on a mile of Gulf beach" make these condo units good for families;
there's golf, tennis, bicycling, boating and jogging on-site; insiders suggest
you ask for an updated apartment on the beach.*

**'Tween Waters Inn**   126R (20S)     | 17 | 19 | 18 | 19 | $119 |
15951 Captiva Rd., Captiva Island; (800) 223-5865; (813) 472-5161;
FAX 472-0249
*M – With the bay on one side and the ocean on the other, this "excellent low-budget vacation spot" sits on the narrowest part of the island; most of the rustic cottages were remodeled in '91 and '92, along with the water- view rooms in the motel; respondents say "Captiva's second-best", "quiet but small" resort is a good "alternative to the high rise rat race."*

**Windjammer Resort and Beach Club**   33R     | – | – | – | – | M |
4244 El Mar Dr., Lauderdale-by-the-Sea; (800) 356-1220; (305) 776-4232;
FAX 351-9153
*There's "lots of fun" plus "bright, airy rooms" here on this tiny stretch of well-kept beach, where casual Keys-style attitude prevails; there's no restaurant on the premises, but just walk out the door for lots of oceanfront options, outdoors or in.*

# GEORGIA

|   | R | S | D | P | $ |
|---|---|---|---|---|---|

**Callaway Gardens Resort**  800R (350S)  | 20 | 21 | 20 | 23 | $137 |
U.S. Hwy. 27, Pine Mountain; (800) 282-8181; (404) 663-2281; FAX 663-5080
*U – "Rooms aren't spectacular, but the azaleas are" at this "lush" family resort in the foothills just south of Atlanta; waterskiing, fishing, butterfly-filled gardens, three 18-hole golf courses for adults and "circus activities" for kids are some of the delights; the breakfast buffet is a "1937 cholesterol trip"; N.B. townhouses or cottages are preferred over the main house.*

**CLOISTER, THE**  264R (24S)  | 25 | 26 | 24 | 26 | $232 |
Sea Island; (800) SEA-ISLAND; (912) 638-3611; FAX 638-5159
*U – "Sleep with sounds of the ocean" at this Spanish-style "gracious family resort" loaded with "classic Southern charm"; some call it "stuffy" – i.e. Ivory soap, jackets at breakfast, bingo – but the "absolutely beautiful" landscaped surroundings and the beach, spa and activities, including golf school, help make it an "elegant retreat" "in a class by itself."*

**Eliza Thompson** (Pr)  25R  | 18 | 18 | – | 18 | $102 |
5 W. Jones St., Savannah; (800) 348-9378; (912) 236-3620; FAX 238-1920
*M – A "charming", "wonderful place to stay", report visitors to this historic Savannah residence that offers free newspapers and a deluxe continental breakfast; despite a beautiful courtyard and period furnishings, some are "disappointed" that guest rooms are "not quaint"; no on-site restaurant.*

**Foley House Inn**  20R  | – | – | – | – | M |
14 W. Hull St., Savannah; (800) 647-3708; (912) 232-6622; FAX 231-1218
*Another of Savannah's graciously restored manses, this historic B&B is located on the lovely park at Chippewa Square; it's very romantic, with an old-fashioned courtyard, fireplaces and antique furnishings; a continental-plus breakfast and an afternoon tea with cordials and wine are bonuses.*

**Gastonian, The**  13R (3S)  | – | – | – | – | E |
220 E. Gaston St., Savannah; (800) 322-6603; (912) 232-2869; FAX 232-0710
*Set in a historic district, this "small, lovely" 1868 Italianate inn reflects the charms of this special city; "elegant but homey", "each room is a treat"; reviewers note the antiques, whirlpool tubs, gardens and "greatest breakfasts in Savannah"; "don't look any further" if you're heading this way.*

**GEORGIA RESORTS**                    | R | S | D | P | $ |

**Greyfield Inn**  9R                    | – | – | – | – | VE |
Cumberland Island; (904) 261-6408
*"Off the coast and offbeat", this "unique" turn-of-the-century mansion is on
Georgia's southernmost barrier island, accessible only by boat or plane; it's
an "isolated" nature-lover's dream – 17 miles of deserted beach filled with
wildlife – "one of America's best-kept secrets"; there's good food, but no
air-conditioning, so "avoid midsummer."*

**Jekyll Island Club Hotel**  134R (17S)   | 21 | 21 | 21 | 21 | $135 |
371 Riverview Dr., Jekyll Island; (800) 333-3333; (912) 635-2600; FAX 635-2818
*U – This "historic" Victorian hotel (run by Radisson) on one of Georgia's
barrier islands may "need some TLC", but it's "still great" – like being back
in 1886 – with "carriage rides around the grounds" and "Spanish moss
galore"; 63 holes of golf, whirlpool tubs and "good-plus" dining.*

**King & Prince Beach Resort***  168R (46S)  | 19 | 18 | 17 | 20 | $139 |
201 Arnold Rd., St. Simons Island; (800) 342-0212; (912) 638-3631;
FAX 634-1720
*M – Always "fun", this traditional terra cotta–filled resort has an atrium
lobby, "fine" rooms in the (higher priced) villas and "top-notch food at
moderate prices"; a white-sand beach helps make it "outstanding in
summer"; a children's program rates well with families, but dissenters
say it's "too polyestery" and "commercial."*

**Mulberry Inn** (Pr)  119R (20S)          | 21 | 20 | 21 | 20 | $96 |
601 E. Bay St., Savannah; (800) 688-91298; (912) 238-1200; FAX 236-2184
*M – Our surveyors find much to like about this midsize hotel in the Historic
District – "charming", "out-of-this-world food", "gracious atmosphere",
excellent meeting facilities and pool, and a "very good value"; a recent
room renovation should address prior complaints.*

**Planter's Inn**  56R (4S)               | – | – | – | – | I |
29 Abercorn St., Savannah; (800) 554-1187; (912) 232-5678; FAX 232-8893
*Though few of our surveyors have tried this "tasteful" restoration, those
who have report "comfortable" quarters and a staff eager to please; it's
also less expensive than most of its competitors.*

**President's Quarters**  16R             | – | – | – | – | M |
225 E. Presidents St., Savannah; (800) 233-1776; (912) 233-1600;
FAX 238-0849
*A "beautiful" period bed-and-breakfast inn in the Historic District, with
fireplaces and refrigerators in all rooms, full afternoon tea, turndown
service in the evening and continental breakfast in the morning.*

**Sea Palms Golf & Tennis Resort\*** 200R (30S) | 24 | 21 | 18 | 20 | $167 |
5445 Frederica Rd., St. Simons Island; (800) 841-6268; (912) 638-3351;
FAX 634-8029
*M – A "megadecompression chamber", with 3 golf courses, good tennis
and a health club, this casual oceanside resort gets mixed reviews; critics
cite the "garden apartment" buildings and "uninspired service"; fans point
to the new clubhouse, kitchenettes and conference facilities.*

**Sheraton Savannah Resort\*** 202R (29S) | 18 | 17 | 16 | 17 | $119 |
612 Wilmington Island Rd., Wilmington Island, Savannah; (800) 325-3535;
(912) 897-1612; FAX 897-1612
*U – This "relaxing" Mediterranean-style Wilmington Island retreat, built in
1927, is minutes from historic Savannah; extensive tennis facilities, a huge
pool and small beach, plus an 18-hole golf course give it a country-club
feeling, while sunsets over the Intracoastal Waterway draw crowds.*

**Stouffer Pineisle Resort** 250R (9S) | 19 | 20 | 18 | 21 | $156 |
9000 Holiday Rd., Lake Lanier Islands; (800) 468-3571; (404) 945-8921;
FAX 945-1024
*M – Proximity to landlocked Atlanta helps keep this Lake Lanier resort
afloat; it has lots of activities to keep guests going, including golf, tennis,
a health club, boating and fishing, two pools and three restaurants.*

# HAWAIIAN ISLANDS*

| R | S | D | P | $ |
|---|---|---|---|---|

**EMBASSY SUITES RESORT**　　　| 25 | 22 | 20 | 23 | $204 |
**MAUI – KAANAPALI BEACH**　413S
104 Kaanapali Shores Place, Lahaina, Maui; (800) 462-6284;
(808) 661-2000; FAX 667-5821
*U – "True paradise" on Maui is this newish all-suites hotel, which our
surveyors say is "gorgeous" and "very tropical", with waterfalls and birds in
the "open-air lobby"; "incredibly huge" suites and the "beach and pool are
the main reasons to stay here"; a year-round children's program and "lots
of inexpensive food" make it also "very popular with families."*

**FOUR SEASONS**　　　　| 27 | 27 | 26 | 27 | $258 |
**RESORT WAILEA**　374R (55S)
3900 Wailea Alanui, Wailea, Maui; (800) 332-3442; (808) 874-8000;
FAX 874-6449
*U – "I want to be here when I die, and as often as possible in the
meantime", says one surveyor; better yet, think of this "spectacular"
beachfront "luxury hotel" on Maui as "a place to renew yourself", to be
"spoiled silly" and eat "the best meals ever"; "everything is excellent":
"enormous rooms", "great service", "beautiful" public areas, a world-class
"health spa" – "wow!"*

**GRAND HYATT WAILEA**　　　| 26 | 25 | 24 | 27 | $272 |
**RESORT & SPA**　787R (53S)
3850 Wailea Alanui Dr., Wailea, Maui; (800) 233-1234; (808) 875-1234;
FAX 874-5143
*M – "Yowza wowza, nothing can compare" to this "brand-new", "most
luxurious resort of the year" – unless you find it "overblown", as a number
of our travelers do, "lacking focus on the individual guest"; like the name,
everything's on a grand scale: "unbelievable" "tropical-paradise grounds", a
"phenomenal spa", but you "need a map" to find your way around this "real
playground for adults."*

---

*See also: Honolulu Hotels.

## HAWAIIAN ISLANDS RESORTS | R | S | D | P | $ |

**HOTEL HANA – MAUI**  96R (38S) | 27 | 25 | 23 | 26 | $292 |
Hana Hwy., Hana, Maui; (800) 321-HANA; (808) 248-8211; FAX 248-7202
*U – "This is the Hawaii you dream about" according to surveyors who
obviously don't mind the "horrendous trip" down the Hana Highway (you
can also fly) to this "great escape", where "your blood pressure drops" the
minute you check in; this "modern-day Eden" is "very romantic", with
"gracious" service, "wonderful dining", "very comfortable" rooms and
"unspoiled beauty" in a "corner of paradise" – "why leave?"; P.S. people
worry whether the new Sheraton management will maintain the former
owner's high standards.*

**HYATT REGENCY KAUAI**  | 25 | 25 | 23 | 27 | $209 |
**RESORT & SPA**  600R (41S)
1571 Poipu Rd., Koloa, Kauai; (800) 228-9000; (808) 742-1234; FAX 742-1557
*U – "It feels like territorial Hawaii" at this "excellent central location" on
beautiful Poipu Beach; the hotel itself is "spanking new and wonderful",
with "breathtaking" grounds (including five acres of beach-rimmed
lagoons and two pools complete with waterfalls), "exquisite" rooms and
"friendly staff"; the downside of its "beautiful" convention facilities is
"too many conventioneers."*

**HYATT REGENCY MAUI**  815R (32S) | 23 | 23 | 23 | 26 | $210 |
200 Nohea Kai Dr., Lahaina, Maui; (800) 233-1234; (808) 661-1234;
FAX 667-4499
*M – Recently renovated and "still gorgeous after all these years", Hyatt's
jumbo "fantasyland" delights surveyors with its "great water slides and live
penguins" (in an on-site wildlife preserve), "lovely outdoor gardens" and fine
food in the Swan Court (food rating, 23); fans call it "the best playground"
on Kaanapali Beach, with a "breathtaking view" and "superb service";
detractors say rooms are "small", and it's "overcrowded" and "too big."*

**HYATT REGENCY WAIKOLOA**  1241R (57S) | 23 | 22 | 22 | 26 | $229 |
1 Waikoloa Beach Dr., Kamuela, Hawaii; (800) 228-9000; (808) 885-1234;
FAX 885-5737
*M – The word "Disneyland" keeps cropping up – a positive comment for
some, decidedly negative for others, who don't like the artificial beach or
taking trams, boats or long walks between facilities; still, for many, it's a
"spectacular", "fun-filled resort", complete with an outdoor luau area, "lush
decor", nine restaurants and a multimillion-dollar art collection – "the next
best thing to a cruise ship."*

**Kaanapali Beach Hotel**   430R (8S)   | 20 | 19 | 18 | 20 | $163 |
2525 Kaanapali Pkwy., Lahaina, Maui; (800) 262- 8450; (808) 661-0111;
FAX 667-5978
*U – Vastly improved in recent years, this "older resort that has retained its
well-kept and well-managed charm" strikes our surveyors as the "most
friendly" place on the island; certainly it's "not as classy as its neighbors"
(Westin, Hyatt, Marriott), but it's "well situated", offering a "beautiful beach",
"more casual" ambiance and "great value for the location."*

**Kanaloa at Kona\***   166S   | 26 | 22 | 18 | 24 | $164 |
78-261 Manukai St., Kailua-Kona, Hawaii; (808) 322-9625; FAX 322-3818
*U – "The rooms are tremendous" at this oceanfront all-suites establishment
operated by Radisson's Colony Hotels & Resorts group; a pool, whirlpool,
sauna, outdoor barbecue facilities, and access to golf and tennis make this
a good value for families; only the food falls short.*

**KAPALUA BAY HOTEL & VILLAS**   329R (3S) | 24 | 23 | 23 | 25 | $242 |
1 Bay Dr., Lahaina, Maui; (800) 367-8000; (808) 669-5656; FAX 669-4694
*U – "Secluded and pretty", this older tropical resort set in a seaside
pineapple plantation offers "courteous quiet" away from the crowds at
Lahaina and Kaanapali; with 54 holes of golf, it's "a golfer's paradise", but
there are also "terrific views", a "beautiful beach" and lovely grounds.*

**KONA HILTON RESORT**   445R (10S)   | 19 | 20 | 18 | 21 | $156 |
75-5852 Alii Dr., Kailua-Kona, Hawaii; (800) HILTONS; (808) 329-3111;
FAX 329-9532
*M – A convenient five-minute walk to village shops and restaurants, this
rocky-shoreline resort gets mixed reviews: "one of the best", "very
relaxing", "great water sports" and "large", comfortable rooms vs. "tired"
and just "passable."*

**Kona Village Resort**   125R   | 24 | 24 | 23 | 24 | $289 |
Kailua-Kona, Hawaii; (800) 367-5290; (808) 325-5555; FAX 325-5124
*U – This unique collection of plush (some say "tired") Polynesian huts is
capable of providing "the most restful vacation ever"; its full American plan
means there are "no major decisions to be made", though some say "the
food could be better"; the "ultimate escape" includes a "black-sand beach",
excellent snorkeling" and "royal treatment in a casual way"; expect lots of
kids at school vacation times and no phones or TV.*

**LODGE AT KOELE, THE**   102R (10S)          | 28 | 26 | 27 | 28 | $264 |
Lanai City, Island of Lanai; (800) 321-4666; (808) 565-7300; FAX 565-3868
*U – "It doesn't get any better than this" small, "romantic hideaway"
"secluded" in the cool center highland of Lanai, the tiny "heaven on earth"
that feels like the best of New England or Northern California; the "sheer
perfection and elegance" here provide "the standard against which other
resorts have to be measured", including "outstanding service", "rooms (with
fireplaces) to snuggle up in", "fabulous dining" and "incredible attention to
detail" – "one of the very best on the islands."*

**MANELE BAY HOTEL, THE**   250R (26S)          | 26 | 23 | 22 | 26 | $247 |
Lanai City, Island of Lanai; (800) 321-4666; (808) 565-7700; FAX 565-2483
*U – Brand-new and still gaining a following, this Mediterranean-style
beachfront sister to the Lodge at Koele provides "a luxurious refuge on the
shore" of an isolated island that's strictly for quiet getaways; our surveyors
say the "ocean rooms are the prettiest in Hawaii" and it's got every
conceivable amenity and activity, but the staff's "aloha attitude" indicates
that service still needs some polishing.*

**Maui Inter-Continental Resort**   516R (43S)          | 21 | 21 | 20 | 26 | $182 |
3700 Wailea Alanui Rd., Kihei, Maui; (800) 367-2960; (808) 879-1922;
FAX 874-8331
*M – "In the same great area as the Four Seasons and Grand Hyatt but less
expensive", this "wonderful" resort provides "breathtaking views", "spacious
manicured grounds", "beds as big as airports" and "incredible sunsets and
whale-watching"; comparatively speaking, "it's not extraordinary", but
ordinary on Maui is extraordinary anywhere else.*

**Maui Marriott**   720R (19S)          | 21 | 22 | 20 | 22 | $174 |
100 Nohea Kai Dr., Lahania, Maui; (800) 228-9290; (808) 667-1200;
FAX 667-0692
*U – "For the budget-minded on Maui" (everything's relative, of course), this
"comfortable", family-oriented resort "in the middle of everything" offers
"spacious rooms" and pleasing "open-air" architecture that's "not grand, but
very acceptable"; for "value" and "unpretentious" ambiance, this one's got
them all beat.*

## HAWAIIAN ISLANDS RESORTS | R | S | D | P | $ |

**MAUI PRINCE HOTEL**   310R (20S)   | 23 | 23 | 23 | 24 | $216 |
5400 Makena Alanui, Makena, Maui; (800) 321-MAUI; (808) 874-1111;
FAX 879-8763
*M – The centerpiece of the "isolated" Makena resort area, beyond Wailea,
this "marble palace" has a "beautiful" golf course and extensive tropical
grounds (including a beach and private islet offshore), along with unusual,
"beautifully appointed" facilities, and service that can be "excellent";
surveyors who find it "long in the tooth" and "shabby" are a distinct minority.*

**MAUNA KEA BEACH HOTEL**   310R (10S)   | 25 | 25 | 24 | 26 | $279 |
1 Mauna Kea Beach Dr., Kohala Coast, Hawaii; (800) 882-6060;
(808) 882-7222; FAX 882-7657
*U – Though one of the oldest resorts on Hawaii, this original Rockresort is
still "one of the world's most beautiful", with a "magnificent" beach setting,
"spectacular views", "superb golf" and "excellent service"; despite
complaints that this "old favorite" is "tired", its fans believe that "if you're
really good, you'll have a choice between heaven and the Mauna Kea
when you die" – of course, "it will take your entire estate to pay for it."*

**MAUNA LANI BAY HOTEL**   | 27 | 26 | 25 | 27 | $269 |
**& BUNGALOWS**   350R (17S)
1 Mauna Lani Dr., Kohala Coast, Hawaii; (800) 367-2323; (808) 885-6622;
FAX 885-4556
*U – "Physically fabulous", this platonic ideal of "tropical paradise" is "top
drawer in every way", from its "gorgeous" grounds and "incredible service"
to the "fabulous golf" and Canoe House restaurant, with its highly rated
Pacific Rim cuisine; only its beach could be better.*

**PRINCEVILLE HOTEL**   252R (10S)   | 25 | 25 | 23 | 26 | $216 |
(fka Sheraton Mirage Princeville Hotel)
5520 Ka Haku Rd., Princeville, Kauai; (800) 826-4400; (808) 826-9644;
FAX 826-1166
*U – The Sheraton name is downplayed at this "astonishingly beautiful"
North Shore resort in a "surreal setting" on the "prettiest part of Kauai"
overlooking Hanalei Bay where "they serve rainbows at breakfast"; guests
also praise the "outstanding" food, rooms and service, along with two
"top-rated golf courses" and "everything you could want"; N.B. though
damaged by Hurricane Iniki, the hotel is expected to reopen shortly.*

**RITZ-CARLTON, MAUNA LANI** 542R (52S) | 26 | 26 | 24 | 26 | $254 |
1 N. Kaniku Dr., Kohala Coast, Hawaii; (800) 845-9905; (808) 885-2000;
FAX 885-1064
*M – Oddly enough, the "luxurious" Ritz-Carlton formula doesn't work as
well in this "classy" new resort, deemed "too stuffy for Hawaii" by some
surveyors; that said, for the majority this is "just right", with "gorgeous
scenery", "very nice rooms" (the "club level" is like staying "in your own
private home"), "the best" (if rather "formal") service and lots of activities.*

**Ritz-Carlton Kapalua** 550R (65S) | – | – | – | – | VE |
1 Ritz-Carlton Dr., Kapalua, Maui; (800) 241-3333; (808) 669-6200;
FAX 669-3908
*Located 10 miles north of Lahaina, this recently opened deluxe destination
has 10 tennis courts, three 18-hole championship golf courses, a three-
level swimming pool and a fitness center; guests have four dining choices
plus 24-hour room service, and there is afternoon tea; conference facilities
plus a conference concierge are pluses.*

**Royal Lahaina Resort** 521R (26S) | 18 | 18 | 16 | 18 | $145 |
2780 Kekaa Dr., Lahaina, Maui; (800) 733-7777; (808) 661-3611; FAX 661-6150
*M – "For those who want a great beach location but don't want to spend
every last dollar" to get it, this "laid-back" older hotel is "still dependable
after all these years"; besides the beach, it has "friendly service" and a
"great bar and patio area to have cocktails and watch the sunset"; critics
say it "attracts tourists in polyester" and "needs more than fresh paint."*

**Royal Waikoloan** 545R (35S) | 22 | 21 | 20 | 22 | $170 |
Waikoloa Beach Dr., Waikoloa, Hawaii; (800) 537-9800; (808) 885-6789;
FAX 885-7852
*U – The "most affordable on the Waikoloa strip", this "comfortable" hotel,
with an "open feeling" and "great views", gets more favorable comments
for its "moderate prices", "pretty beach" and "friendly service" than for its
"so-so" rooms and "ordinary food"; the bottom line is you "can't get more
for your money."*

**STOUFFER WAILEA** | 23 | 23 | 22 | 23 | $203 |
**BEACH RESORT** 347R (12S)
3550 Wailea Alanui Dr., Wailea, Maui; (800) HOTELS1; (808) 879-4900;
FAX 879-6128
*M – Though outshone by flamboyant new neighbors, this "peaceful",
"comfortable old friend" strikes fans as "one of the prettiest places" on Maui
and "more down-to-earth than a Maui Prince or a Ritz-Carlton"; it's praised
for "beautiful grounds", beach and service, along with the "nice luau" and
"terrific food" at Raffles restaurant; N.B. some rooms may be "small."*

## HAWAIIAN ISLANDS RESORTS | R | S | D | P | $ |

**Stouffer Waiohai Beach Resort**   426R (21S)  | 22 | 22 | 22 | 22 | $185 |
2249 Poipu Rd., Poipu Beach, Kauai; (800) HOTELS1; (808) 742-9511;
FAX 741-7214
*U – Being a "laid-back older hotel" on the "sunny south side of the island"*
*makes up for such tropical hazards as mosquitoes and power failures;*
*though it has "beautiful, lush grounds", "excellent service", "large rooms"*
*and a "great beach", detractors say its rooms "need brightening up" and*
*too few have "ocean views"; after heavy damage from Hurricane Iniki, it*
*may not reopen until fall 1993.*


**Volcano House**   42R  | 12 | 15 | 13 | 16 | $115 |
Volcanoes National Park, Hawaii; (808) 967-7321; FAX 967-8429
*M – Perched on the rim of Kilauea Crater, this "hot spot for lava lovers" is*
*a place that people either love or hate; luxurious it's not, but fans call it*
*"rustic and rewarding", a touch of " '40s funky Hawaii" that everyone should*
*see "at least once"; the unconverted say it's "old" and "run-down", but even*
*they agree, "being right on the crater rim" is an "unbelievable" experience.*


**WESTIN KAUAI**   843R (29S)  | 23 | 23 | 23 | 26 | $207 |
Kalapaki Beach, Lihue, Kauai; (800) 228-3000; (808) 245-5050; FAX 246-5097
*M – The most controversial hotel in Hawaii, this "glitzy" "Dolly Parton of*
*resorts" is either "a tacky dump", "Caesars Palace after bad acid" or "the*
*most luxurious place in the islands"; everything's on a "grand scale" –*
*"magnificent sprawling" grounds, a "spectacular pool", "majestic fountains",*
*"live parrots" – except for the "typical Westin" (read: "small") rooms.*


**WESTIN MAUI**   761R (28S)  | 22 | 23 | 22 | 24 | $207 |
2365 Kaanapali Pkwy., Lahaina, Maui; (800) 228-3000; (808) 667-2525;
FAX 661-5831
*U – "Wowie" on Maui, this "beautiful hotel with exquisite grounds" is "a*
*favorite" with many of our surveyors; "breathtaking views", "great"*
*restaurants", "lush grounds", "terrific staff" and "waterfall pools" that are*
*"way cool" more than make up for what some call "small rooms"; overall,*
*it's "visually stunning" "without going overboard."*

# IDAHO

| R | S | D | P | $ |
|---|---|---|---|---|

**COEUR D'ALENE RESORT**   353R (15S)   | 23 | 22 | 22 | 24 | $152 |
First & Sherman Sts., Coeur d'Alene; (800) 688-5253; (208) 765-4000;
FAX 667-2707
*U – "Tremendous views and unbelievable golf" are just two reasons our
surveyors suggest you "go before the crowds discover it"; besides "lots of
activity" (fishing, tennis, bicycling, boating, et al), expect "great atmosphere
and service" at this "top-quality" mountain resort.*

**Idaho Rocky Mountain Ranch**   4R (1S)   | – | – | – | – | I |
HC 64, Box 9934, Stanley; (208) 774-3544
*Located in the spectacular Sawtooth and White Cloud mountains of
Central Idaho, this guest lodge offers the west at its coziest and most
elegant, in authentic log cabins; wonderful rock fireplaces, a natural hot-
springs pool, standout American food and a beautiful rugged backdrop
make this low-price sleeper a well-kept secret.*

**Middle Fork Lodge**   15R (1S)   | – | – | – | – | VE |
3815 Rickenbacker, Boise; (208) 342-7888
*"You'll never want to leave" this remote luxury resort, accessible only by
plane or horseback, in the heart of the* River of No Return *wilderness area;
rib-stickin' ranch-style meals can be worked off on horseback, playing
tennis or in the hot-springs bathhouse.*

**Sun Valley Lodge**   265R   | 21 | 23 | 21 | 23 | $170 |
Sun Valley Rd., Sun Valley; (800) 635-8261; (208) 622-4111; FAX 622-3700
*M – Though "very busy during the ski season", this legendary lodge remains
"the 'in' place to stay when there's snow" according to reviewers; it attracts
a lively crowd with ice skating, heated pools, fine dining and, of course,
skiing; even those who find the place "a bit tired" concur that "it's still
holding its own, without the Aspen snobbery."*

| R | S | D | P | $ |
|---|---|---|---|---|

**Clock Tower Resort &** | 19 | 19 | 17 | 19 | $96 |
**Conference Center**   253R (28S)
7801 E. State St., Rockford; (800) 358-7666; (815) 398-6000; FAX 398-8062
*M – The Time Museum, a "fascinating" clock museum, may be worth a visit
all by itself – never mind that Survey participants say this "quiet", '60s-era
resort is a "nice place for a weekend getaway"; ratings moved up after the
1992 renovation, but some still fault the ho-hum rooms.*

**Eagle Ridge Inn**   80R (20S) | 21 | 20 | 20 | 22 | $137 |
U.S. Rte. 20, Galen; (800) 892-2269; (815) 777-2444; FAX 777-0445
*U – Set in the rolling bluffs just west of historic Galena and not far from
Mississippi Riverboat gambling, this New England–style lodge offers a
"wonderful" "homey" atmosphere and two "well-kept" golf courses; a 1992
renovation added 20 rooms and a conference center; the resort also offers
rental homes (one to five bedrooms) that are "much better than the inn"
according to some, "especially with kids."*

**Indian Lakes Resort**   308R (18S) | 17 | 17 | 16 | 17 | $104 |
250 W. Schick Rd., Bloomingdale; (800) 334-3417; (708) 529-0200;
FAX 529-9271
*M – Golf-course improvements, new volleyball and horseshoe plts, and
softball diamonds make this an athlete's paradise; rustic decor, a
"beautiful" indoor atrium and "good views" also help make this a "popular"
spot for "family getaways"; others wonder why anyone would build a resort
in "the middle of suburbia" and dismiss this big complex as "nothing great."*

**Marriott's Lincolnshire Resort**   390R (6S) | 18 | 18 | 17 | 19 | $124 |
10 Marriott Dr., Lincolnshire; (800) 228-9290; (708) 634-0100; FAX 634-1278
*M – A live theater on the premises is "the highlight" of this "polyester
heaven in a truly tacky suburb"; the consensus is that it's "ok for the
location", but "Holiday Inn rooms" in a "resort setting" leave much to be
desired; don't miss Le Français, one of the nation's best French
restaurants, just down the road.*

**Nordic Hills Resort & Conf. Ctr.**   220R (8S)   | 16 | 16 | 15 | 17 | $112 |
Nordic Rd., Itasca; (800) 334-3417; (708) 773-2750; FAX 773-3622
*U – A "nice walking path" and "good golfing" cannot mask the fact that
this 106-acre spread near O'Hare Airport "needs refurbishing"; "so-so"
food, a "plain exterior" and "average" facilities make it less than exciting.*

**Pheasant Run Resort**   474R (49S)          | 14 | 15 | 14 | 16 | $105 |
4051 E. Main St., St. Charles; (800) 999-3319; (708) 584-6300; FAX 584-4693
*M – A complete renovation in 1992 is not yet reflected by the ratings or the
comments of our reviewers; it's good for conventions and business
meetings, perhaps, but it "lacks charm" despite "pleasant grounds"; most
like the "good shows" at the theater and comedy club.*

| R | S | D | P | $ |

**Fourwinds Clarion\***   126R (3S)     | 18 | 18 | 16 | 17 | $108 |
Lake Monroe, Bloomington; (800) 252-7466; (812) 824-9904; FAX 824-9816
*M – This little resort and conference center near Bloomington "feels too
much like a motel"; however, a 1992 room remodeling should help those
who find the decor "boring"; "good value", "outstanding lake views" and
on-site miniature golf for the kids recommend this place.*

**French Lick Springs**         | 15 | 17 | 17 | 18 | $115 |
**Golf & Tennis Resort**   485R (17S)
Hwys. 56 & 45, French Lick; (800) 457-4042; (812) 936-9300; FAX 936-2100
*U – A multimillion-dollar renovation completed in 1992 may improve the
ratings of this once "top-notch hotel" that's been "hanging on from the glory
days when roulette wheels and dice tables paid the freight"; rooms are
"small", but "beautiful grounds", two 18-hole golf courses, "wonderful" mineral
baths and a variety of children's programs keep visitors happy without
leaving the complex – but then, there's "nowhere else in the area" to go if
you did.*

# IOWA

| R | S | D | P | $ |
|---|---|---|---|---|

**Redstone Inn, The**  15R (6S)

| – | – | – | – | M |
|---|---|---|---|---|

504 Bluff St., Dubuque; (319) 582-1894
*Despite sketchy response, this "beautifully furnished, lovely old home" is
a Midwestern winner; in addition to "charming" rooms, it has high-caliber
food and service; all in all, it's one of the most "civilized" inns in the
Midwest and a great base of operations for visiting the Dubuque area.*

# KENTUCKY

| R | S | D | P | $ |
|---|---|---|---|---|

**Beaumont Inn\***   33R
638 Beaumont Dr., Harrodsburg; (606) 734-3381; FAX 734-6879

| 23 | 23 | 22 | 22 | $100 |
|---|---|---|---|---|

*U – Built in 1845 as a women's college, this "comfortable" inn has been owned by the same family for four generations; 30 acres of trees and flora surround the main building, plus three smaller buildings, tennis courts and a swimming pool; the restaurant is known locally for its regional cooking, including country ham and fried chicken; be advised that you're in a "dry county", and reservations are an absolute necessity; closed mid-December to mid-March.*

**Inn at Shaker Village
of Pleasant Hill\***   80R (5S)
3500 Lexington Rd., Harrodsburg; (606) 734-5411

| 24 | 22 | 24 | 24 | $94 |
|---|---|---|---|---|

*U – Visitors delight in this restored 19th-century, 2,700-acre Shaker village – "a grand American-heritage adventure" whose rooms are decorated with Shaker furniture and hand-woven rugs and curtains; you learn about the Shakers through tours of 33 buildings where weavers, broommakers, coopers, quilters and singers show their talents; surveyors say the modestly priced inn is "perfect in every way" and the Trustees' Office restaurant serves "wholesome", Kentucky-style country food – but no alcohol.*

# LOUISIANA

---

**Asphodel Plantation Inn\*** 18R    | 15 | 19 | 21 | 19 | $115 |
Rte. 2, Jackson; (504) 654-6868
*U – A "platonic plantation", this "comfy" colony of cottages is located 30
miles south of Baton Rouge in an area dotted with beautiful homes – Paul
Newman's* The Long Hot Summer *was filmed here; "quiet and relaxing",
it boasts a pool, whirlpool, even a bird sanctuary and nature trail, plus
delicious Southern meals;* N.B. *not all rooms have private baths.*

**Madewood Plantation\*** 9R    | 21 | 22 | 19 | 21 | $109 |
4250 Hwy. 308, Napoleonville; (504) 369-7151
*U – Built in 1846, this "beautiful" Greek Revival mansion rests quietly on
Bayou Lafourche, joined by two smaller houses on 20 acres of oak trees
and beautiful riverine countryside; guests are treated to wide porches,
feather pillows and canopied beds in rooms filled with antiques and fresh
flowers; all rates include Southern-style breakfast and dinner.*

**Nottoway Plantation** 13R (1S)    | 21 | 20 | 19 | 22 | $137 |
River Rd., White Castle; (504) 545-2409; FAX 545-8632
*M – "A* Gone With the Wind *fantasy in the Deep South", this 1859 National
Historic Landmark, located two hours from New Orleans, offers "beautiful
surroundings", rooms with fireplaces and private baths, and the Randolph
Hall Restaurant, serving excellent Creole cuisine; though some surveyors
warn of "tour groups walking through", most say this is a "delightful return"
to the 19th century.*

| R | S | D | P | $ |

**Asticou Inn – Cranberry Lodge**   50R (17S)   | 19 | 22 | 21 | 20 | $184 |
Northeast Harbor; (207) 276-3344; FAX 276-3373
*U – The "elegant old" inn overlooking the harbor on Mount Desert Island
is open only in summer, while the smaller lodge does business most winter
months as well; although it's "not luxurious", the formal "dinner dress code
adds a certain air"; aside from nearby golf, "sports" entail watching birds,
seals, porpoises and whales; a few note that rooms are "threadbare – stay
in detached units" if you can.*

**Bayview Hotel & Inn\***   38R (7S)   | 22 | 22 | 21 | 20 | $134 |
111 Eden St., Bar Harbor; (800) 356-3585; (207) 288-5861; FAX 288-3173
*U – "Soothing is the best way to describe" this "European-style" inn,
located down a winding drive on eight wooded acres surrounded by the
Schoodic Mountains; "terrific rooms", a "friendly, attentive staff" and
"romantic" candlelight dining please our surveyors; the large rooms are
furnished with antiques, and the suites have full kitchens.*

**Bethel Inn & Country Club\***   120R (9S)   | 21 | 20 | 20 | 18 | $131 |
Broad St. on the Common, Bethel; (800) 654-0125; (207) 824-2175;
FAX 824-2233
*M – A year-round dining veranda overlooks the White Mountains at this
Federal-style inn on 200 acres; besides "character", there are townhouses,
a conference center, covered bridges, waterfalls and 26 miles of trails,
"excellent" cross-country skiing, golf and heated outdoor pool; naysayers
complain of "ordinary facilities" and a "ski-dorm" atmosphere.*

**Black Point Inn Resort**   | 19 | 21 | 19 | 21 | $195 |
**Scarborough**   80R (10S)
510 Black Pt. Rd., Prouts Neck; (800) 258-0003; (207) 883-4311; FAX 883-9976
*M – This 1876 hotel at a "super location" on the Maine coast "shines with
Yankee individuality" to most surveyors, who report being "overwhelmed"
by the service and meals – especially the poolside lunch; a few say it's
"starchy", "dated" and "inbred"; open May through October.*

## MAINE RESORTS

| R | S | D | P | $ |
|---|---|---|---|---|

### Captain Lord Mansion  22R

| 24 | 22 | 21 | 22 | $155 |
|---|---|---|---|---|

Kennebunkport; (800) 522-3141; (207) 967-3141; FAX 967-3172
*U – It's "like living in a museum" at this "beautiful", "romantic" mansion-with-a-cupola, filled with "four-posters and antiques" – but not children; it's praised for being "immaculately clean", and for "delicious breakfasts" served family-style in the kitchen; fans rave "good old New England at its finest", and there's "no better place to stay in Maine."*

### Cliff House  162R (2S)

| 19 | 19 | 19 | 18 | $147 |
|---|---|---|---|---|

Shore Rd., Bald Head Cliff, Ogunquit; (207) 361-1000; FAX 361-2122
*M – With the "sound of waves" and "memorable" views from balconied rooms on a 90-foot cliff, you couldn't hope for better "Down East atmosphere"; two large pools, exercise facilities, tennis courts, walking paths on 70 acres and golf nearby are diversions; "improved accommodations" are still "motel- type", but "the nicest in the area"; closed in winter.*

### Colony Resort*  135R

| 17 | 17 | 17 | 18 | $181 |
|---|---|---|---|---|

140 Ocean Ave., Kennebunkport; (207) 967-3331; FAX 967-8738
*U – "A little frayed around the edges", this "great New England institution", filled with 1920s charm, is "like coming home" to its devoted regulars; "for the older set", it's a "wonderful place to relax and forget about the world" – insiders say "splurge" on one of the large, oceanside rooms; open June to September.*

### Harraseeket Inn*  54R (6S)

| 24 | 23 | 22 | 22 | $162 |
|---|---|---|---|---|

162 Main St., Freeport; (800) 342-6423; (207) 865-9377; (207) 865-9377
*U – This complex of Colonial buildings on five acres is in a sea-tanged, pine-scented area that's like "a visit to long ago"; a "top-notch restaurant", "accommodating staff" and rooms with fireplaces, canopied beds and antique furnishings add up to a "lovely inn"; being only a short walk from Freeport Village, L.L.Bean and 100 factory-outlet stores should keep any bargain-hunter happy.*

### High Tide Inn on the Ocean  30R

| – | – | – | – | M |
|---|---|---|---|---|

Rte. 1, Camden; (207) 236-3724
*Between a mountain and the sea, this recently renovated inn with cottages and motel is on seven acres of landscaped lawn with a tranquil view of lobster boats and the sea off a private beach; swimming, sailing, hiking, antiquing and shopping in charming Camden are diversions; a good home-baked breakfast is served on the glass-enclosed porch.*

### Nonantum Resort   125R     | – | – | – | – | M |
Ocean Ave., Kennebunkport; (800) 552-5621; (207) 967-4050;
FAX 967-8451
*A mile from the Bushes' home and a few hundred yards from the ocean,
this "delightful" resort's 19th-century main building was recently renovated
(another building was built in 1987); a heated pool, some fireplaces and
kitchenettes, "good" food and an "excellent" staff make for a pleasant stay,
especially if you get a room with an ocean view; open May through October.*

### Pilgrim's Inn*   14R     | 21 | 25 | 26 | 21 | $145 |
Deer Isle; (207) 348-6615
*U – This rambling, rooster-red house, built in 1793, provides what Pilgrims
never dreamed of: "wonderful, warm" ambiance and great food; "small but
pretty rooms" are decorated in pastels; the barn houses a "charming dining
room"; sailing instruction, bicycling, tennis, nearby golf, bird-watching,
clamming and swimming are all available at this "champion" inn.*

### Poland Spring Inn*   200R (25S)     | 11 | 11 | 11 | 12 | $105 |
Rte. 26, Poland Spring; (207) 998-4351; FAX 998-2811
*M – Guests bring their own towels and soap (but not the famous water) to
this "cheap, fun place"; the four old buildings afford a unique vacation
bargain, including summer theater, tennis on grass courts, live bands and
golf on the country's second-oldest course; although some call it a "flea
bag" and its ratings are embarrassing, regulars book a year in advance.*

### Samoset Resort   150R (18S)     | 19 | 19 | 19 | 20 | $148 |
Warrenton St., Rockport; (800) 341-1650; (207) 594-2511; FAX 594-0722
*U – A "good combo of Maine coast and golf", this family resort offers
"excellent" ocean views, "a friendly staff" and a championship golf course
that hugs the ocean; add a "great indoor swimming-and-exercise center"
and "plenty of activities", and despite a layout that critics compare to "an
army terminal", it's a fine "getaway spot."*

### WHITE BARN INN, THE   24R (7S)     | 22 | 23 | 24 | 22 | $164 |
Beach St., Kennebunkport; (207) 967-2321; FAX 967-1100
*U – A "civilized inn with pretty rooms", this member of the elite Relais &
Chateaux has often hosted the VIPs visiting George Bush; it's "a class act",
with "wonderful service", guest rooms full of antiques and fresh flowers,
and luxurious suites with whirlpool baths; two "charming" restored barns
and "wonderful" service provide the setting for award-winning dining that
can be magical; put this one on your second-honeymoon list.*

**Whitehall Inn**   50R (5S)           | 15 | 17 | 17 | 14 | $129 |
52 High St., Camden; (207) 236-3391; FAX 236-4427
*M – Sprawling porches, patios and parlors recall a time when Edna St. Vincent Millay read her poems here; now they're part of a "charming" inn, with "good food and service"; some guests complain the guest rooms are "too small and noisy, with uncomfortable beds", and although the beautiful setting is "true New England", the place "needs some perking up."*

# MARYLAND

| R | S | D | P | $ |
|---|---|---|---|---|

**Atlantic Hotel, The\*** 16R   | 23 | 25 | 24 | 24 | $115 |
2 N. Main St., Berlin; (410) 641-3589; FAX 641-4928
*U – "So lovely, so Victorian" coo the fortunate few who have discovered this
beautifully restored Eastern Shore hotel, where dining on "food for royalty",
being coddled by a superb staff and soaking up the historic small-town
atmosphere may be all you need to unwind; if not, there's nearby golf and
tennis, with the beach and Ocean City just a few miles away.*

**Imperial Hotel\*** 13R (2S)   | 25 | 20 | 27 | 23 | $118 |
200 High St., Chestertown; (410) 778-5000; FAX 778-9662
*U – This Victorian hotel has interiors so "elegant", hosts so "charming"
and regional American dining so "very special" that people drive from
Wilmington and Philadelphia just for lunch; it's also a "great weekend
getaway" in a well-preserved Colonial-era Chesapeake Bay port town.*

**Inn at Mitchell House** 6R (2S)   | – | – | – | – | E |
8796 Maryland Pkwy., Chestertown; (301) 778-6500
*Though this welcoming B&B is "off the beaten track", it's still handy for
exploring Colonial Chestertown and the nearby wildlife preserve;
"beautifully appointed" rooms with roaring fires, helpful hosts and one of
the "best breakfasts ever" make it a good choice for a relaxing sojourn.*

**INN AT PERRY CABIN** 41R (3S)   | 24 | 22 | 23 | 24 | $197 |
308 Watkins Lane, St. Michaels; (800) 722-2949; (410) 745-2200; FAX 745-3348
*U – Cross Chesapeake Bay by boat or drive to this "dream" retreat with
"all the charm, beauty and warmth of an English country inn"; it has "Laura
Ashley looks but so much more" – first-rate food, "beautiful public areas"
and what some consider the "best staff in the industry"; and there's
picturesque St. Michael's to explore.*

**Loews Annapolis** 217R (25S)   | 21 | 19 | 19 | 20 | $121 |
126 West St., Annapolis; (800) 23-LOEWS; (410) 263-7777; FAX 263-0084
*U – This classy contemporary is a "good bet" when business brings you to
Annapolis; it's "close to the courts" and the Capitol, with "average" rooms,
well-intentioned staff and decent bottom-line business dining; when the
legislature's in session, you can practically pass a bill in the bar.*

## MARYLAND RESORTS

| R | S | D | P | $ |
|---|---|---|---|---|

**Maryland Inn**   43R     | 19 | 19 | 20 | 18 | $129 |
16 Church Circle, Annapolis; (800) 847-8882; (301) 263-2641;
FAX 268-3813
*U – Known for its "great basement bar" and the "best evening restaurant"
in town, this historic Annapolis inn "near the State House" served the
Founding Fathers and waits to serve you; the "antiquey" bedrooms "reek
history" (i.e. "charm") to some but are "damp and stuffy" to others;
"don't miss Charlie Byrd's jazz guitar (most weekends) or the "best-in-
Maryland" brunch.*

**Robert Morris Inn**   35R (10S)     | 20 | 19 | 20 | 20 | $136 |
Morris St. & The Strand, Oxford; (410) 226-5111; FAX 226-5744
*U – Countless intimacies have been exchanged over romantic dinners at
this legendary Chesapeake Bay Colonial inn (built in 1710); the guest
rooms in the inn are "comfortably quaint", if a "little shabby", but there's
also a "delightful" annex "on the water" with a private beach; N.B. "staying
at the inn doesn't guarantee a dinner reservation."*

**Tidewater Inn, The**   114R (7S)     | 19 | 19 | 19 | 18 | $131 |
101 E. Dover St., Easton; (800) 237-8775; (410) 822-1300; FAX 820-8847
*M – An aura of "more elegant times" pervades this Eastern Shore hotel
with its "old-fashioned" rooms and an "old-world" respect for "value";
sportsmen like it best in duck-hunting season; its location is also "great for
boaters and golfers" and corporate retreaters; critics wish it would brighten
up some "drab" rooms and "reach a little more on the menu."*

# MASSACHUSETTS

| R | S | D | P | $ |

**Beach Plum Inn & Restaurant**  12R (1S)   | 18 | 18 | 20 | 19 | $179 |
North Rd., Menemsha, Martha's Vineyard; (508) 645-9454
*M – Overlooking the sea and sunset and next to "lovely woods", the inn could not be more "splendid"; tennis, fishing, biking, a "great beach" and "great food" also please surveyors, but some claim the service is "haughty" and, because of ownership changes, "you don't know what to expect."*

**BLANTYRE**  23R (4S)   | 27 | 26 | 26 | 26 | $248 |
Rte. 20, Lenox; (413) 637-3556; FAX 637-4282
*U – Guests are "treated like royalty in this castle", set on 85 acres in the Berkshires; add tennis courts, pool, sauna, hot tub, a croquet lawn and "unbelievable French food" and you have "a lovely fairy tale", "spectacular in all things" and "worth the price"; its worst critic says "expensive – one day is enough", but the consensus is that this Relais & Chateaux member is "simply world-class"; open May 15 through November 1.*

**CHARLOTTE INN, THE**  23R (2S)   | 25 | 24 | 26 | 25 | $206 |
27 S. Summer St., Edgartown, Martha's Vineyard; (508) 627-4751
*U – Staying in this whaling captain's mansion is like "living in a museum of New England history"; guest rooms with fireplaces are "exceptional", the art gallery and public rooms "lovely", and baroque music adds to the "best dinner on the island"; in sum, this place is "expensive but worth it."*

**Chatham Bars Inn**  152R (20S)   | – | – | – | – | E |
Shore Rd., Chatham; (508) 945-0096; FAX 945-5491
*This lovely old Queen Anne–style resort of brick and weather-beaten shingles on the elbow of the Cape is an all-season charmer, with a laid-back spirit in the day and a coat-and-tie policy at dinner; swimming, biking, boating and a putting green are all on-site, and there's a golf course adjacent; rooms are cozy, with fireplaces in some cottages; there's a private beach too.*

## MASSACHUSETTS RESORTS | R | S | D | P | $ |

**Coonamessett Inn**  26R (25S) | 19 | 20 | 20 | 20 | $136 |
Jones & Giffords Sts., Falmouth; (508) 548-2300; (508) 540-9831
*U – Rooms decorated in pine and paisley create a "quaint, homespun
atmosphere" in this mostly all-suites inn at the south end of the Cape; fresh
flowers every other day, memorable clam bisque and "excellent facilities"
rate general praise at this "lovely resort."*

**Daggett House\***  26R (4S) | 20 | 21 | 18 | 18 | $145 |
59 N. Water St., Edgartown, Martha's Vineyard; (508) 627-4600
*M – "Tranquil and peaceful", with a "beautiful view of the water" and a
"good location for walking", these three centuries-old shingled buildings on
the harbor have been here almost as long as Edgartown; fireside dinners
are always "special"; regulars suggest you "stay in the main house."*

**Harbor View Hotel**  130R (8S) | 20 | 19 | 19 | 19 | $176 |
131 N. Water St., Edgartown, Martha's Vineyard; (800) 225-6005;
(508) 627-4333; FAX 627-8417
*M – After 100 years, a $6 million renovation has turned this traditional hotel
and adjacent cottages in the midst of historic Edgartown into a place of
real "New England charm"; its meeting capacity of 235 appeals to small
corporate groups, but all agree that its sensational waterfront "location is
the bottom line."*

**Jared Coffin House**  60R | 20 | 20 | 21 | 20 | $159 |
29 Broad St., Nantucket; (800) 248-2405; (508) 228-2400; FAX 228-8549
*M – "The name sounds morbid, but it's a beautiful inn"; these six "old
homes" fairly "reek Colonial New England"; the food is "good", the staff
"friendly", and fans say the place is "everything an inn should be"; if "a little
run-down", it's "charming" and "picturesque" nonetheless.*

**Kelley House\***  60R (8S) | 16 | 17 | 15 | 17 | $157 |
Kelley St., Edgartown, Martha's Vineyard; (800) 225-6005; (508) 627-4394;
FAX 627-8142
*M – Some reviewers "love" this recently renovated inn with "nice staff" in
"central" Edgartown a block from the harbor, and find it a "perfect place to
stay on the Vineyard"; the Garden House is the newest and most popular,
and suites are best, but at a minimum, the assorted rooms are "modest
and clean"; open May through October.*

## MASSACHUSETTS RESORTS

| R | S | D | P | $ |

**Nantucket Inn &**      | 21 | 20 | 20 | 20 | $154 |
**Conference Center***   100R (6S)
27 Macy's Lane, Nantucket (800) 321-8484; (508) 228-6900; FAX 228-9861
*U – "It's almost like being in another century" at this "ideally located" inn,
where "beautiful, classic" rooms have refrigerators, and each suite has a
fireplace; bay views are "lovely", the staff is "friendly", the food "good", and
overall, it's a "great place for seclusion."*

**New Seabury Cape Cod**   165S   | 22 | 18 | 15 | 19 | $171 |
New Seabury; (800) 999-9033; (508) 477-9111; FAX 477-9790
*U – New England's largest waterfront resort is set on 2,000 landscaped
acres on the Cape, with more than three miles of private beach, two
well-rated golf courses, 16 tennis courts, miles of secluded paths and
comfortable cottages, villas and suites; children's programs and "maybe
the best family restaurant" around also make it "great" for kids.*

**Ocean Edge Resort & Conf. Center** 90R (2S)   | 21 | 19 | 19 | 21 | $147 |
185 Main St., Brewster; (800) 343-6074; (508) 896-2781; FAX 896-9123
*M – The "beachfront apartments are best" at this "sprawling", "functional"
"condo resort with hotel rooms"; championship golf, tennis, track, big pools,
whirlpools, sauna, "good food", "excellent conference facilities" and a
private beach add up to a good bet for conferees and families.*

**ORCHARDS, THE**   49R (2S)   | 23 | 22 | 22 | 22 | $152 |
222 Adams Rd., Williamstown; (800) 225-1517; (413) 458-9611; FAX 458-3273
*U – A "pearl in a deserted area", Williamstown's "only good hotel" selects
antiques, goose-down pillows and fresh flowers to create a "favorite
weekend getaway" near Williams College, art museums and a summer
theater; "huge rooms", "wonderful atmosphere", "excellent food" and "best
service" are praised, but a few say that "dining can be uneven."*

**Publick House, The**   130R (5S)   | 19 | 19 | 20 | 19 | $121 |
Rte. 131, Sturbridge; (800) 782-5425; (508) 347-3313; FAX 347-7073
*M – This "family favorite" near Old Sturbridge Village "tries too hard to be
Ye Olde Inn"; however, most agree it's "reasonable", the "service is good"
and the "authentic" early American cuisine an enjoyable change of taste.*

**Queen Anne Inn\*** 30R | 18 | 17 | 19 | 15 | $137 |
70 Queen Anne Rd., Chatham; (800) 545-4667; (508) 945-0394;
FAX 945-4884
*M – "Everything is quaint and cozy" at this "lovely, traditional Cape Cod inn" a few minutes' walk to Main Street, Chatham, and "close to shops and the beach"; "each room is decorated with antiques", and "the food is superb"; dissenters say "the inn is becoming shabby", and as one poet sums it up, "bikes are rusty, tennis courts dusty, closets musty."*


**Red Lion Inn** 91R (17S) | – | – | – | – | M |
Main Street, Stockbridge; (413) 298-5545; FAX 298-5130
*One of the few remaining American inns in continuous use since the 18th century, the Red Lion epitomizes New England hospitality; filled with antiques, it offers comfortable lodging and fine food in the New England tradition – 19th-century atmosphere plus 20th-century efficiency; located in the Berkshire Hills, the inn is just minutes from ski areas, Tanglewood Music Festival, Berkshire Theatre Festival and the Norman Rockwell Museum.*


**Seacrest Manor\*** 8R | 17 | 18 | 18 | 18 | $125 |
131 Marmion Way, Rockport; (508) 546-2211
*M – The upstairs porch of this Cape Ann former private home provides beautiful views of Sandy Bay and Rockport, the site of an art colony, woods and granite quarries; full breakfast is served overlooking the gardens; some say the "rooms are poor", but most of them have been recently renovated, and the owners' "enthusiasm is contagious"; open April through November.*


**Ship's Knees Inn** 19R (1S) | – | – | – | – | I |
Beach Rd., East Orleans; (508) 255-1312; FAX 240-1351
*This "great inn" "close to Nauset Beach" was an 18th-century sea captain's house; some of the cottages, suites and guest rooms have ocean views, while others overlook the lovely gardens and pool; a few baths are shared, so specify; no children under 12 allowed.*


**Summer House\*** 10R (5S) | – | – | – | – | E |
17 Ocean Ave., Siasconset, Nantucket; (508) 257-9976; FAX 257-4590
*"Pretty, pretty, pretty" describes this secluded retreat with ocean views from atop a "superb location on a bluff"; its flower-covered whalers' cottages are "Laura Ashley style", with whirlpool baths; the pool is nestled in the dunes behind the beach, and candlelight dining with piano music is an "event"; grand, indeed, but "you pay for the privilege."*

**Village Inn, The**  32R (1S)                     | – | – | – | – | E |
16 Church St., Lenox; (800) 253-0917; (413) 637-0020; FAX 637-9756
*Built in 1771 and completely renovated in 1992, this inn near the center
of town is particularly handy to Tanglewood; guest rooms – many with
fireplaces – are furnished with antiques, and high tea and chamber
music are served in the parlor; all that plus champagne breakfasts and
candlelight dinners make for a cultured weekend getaway.*

**WAUWINET**  35R                     | 25 | 24 | 23 | 24 | $245 |
Wauwinet Rd., Nantucket; (800) 426-8718; (508) 228-0145; FAX 228-6712
*U – "Romance" is captured in this "peaceful, low-key" resort, with a big
porch and wicker chairs, flowers in every antique-furnished room, and
afternoon cheese and port; there's also a private beach, croquet, tennis
and the "upscale" Topper's restaurant; although breakfast and activities
are included, critics call it "too expensive."*

**Wequassett Inn**  104R (7S)                     | 20 | 21 | 19 | 20 | $190 |
Pleasant Bay, Chatham; (800) 225-7125; (508) 432-5400; FAX 432-5032
*U – Beautiful seasonal flower beds surround the 18 buildings of this classic
Cape Cod inn, all with "spectacular views" of water or woods; in this "great
setting", activities include sailing school, and the "staff can organize any
kind of sport", resulting in what one surveyor calls a "summer-camp
atmosphere"; it also has "one of the best dining rooms on the Cape."*

**Westmoor Inn**  14R (3S)                     | – | – | – | – | E |
Cliff Rd., Nantucket; (508) 228-0877
*Built after the turn of the century, this Federal-style inn, all pine floorboards
and lots of wicker, is a change of pace from the shingle-sided cottages
more common to this low-key island; the "friendly hosts introduce guests
over gratis cocktails" in "spotless public rooms" with water views; there's no
air-conditioning, but some rooms have fireplaces; breakfasts are "luscious",
and dining and service splendid; open May through October.*

**WHEATLEIGH**  17R                     | 23 | 23 | 25 | 24 | $236 |
Hawthorne Rd., Lenox; (800) 321-0610; (413) 637-0610; FAX 637-4507
*M – "You feel like you're staying at a friend's mansion" at this "romantic"
"dream chateau" built 100 years ago, with pool and tennis on grounds
by Frederick Law Olmsted overlooking the Berkshires and lakes near
Tanglewood (be sure to "get a balcony"); the "best place I have ever
stayed" and "one of the best dinners we've had" are typical raves; a few
feel it's "pompous", "overpriced and overrated."*

**Whistler's Inn**  14R                    | – | – | – | – | E |
5 Greenwood St., Lenox; (413) 637-0975
*A railroad tycoon built this Tudor-style estate in 1870; antiques and
fireplaces are in some rooms, and there also are rambling gardens, a
croquet lawn and a badminton court that lure both corporate clientele
and romantics; it's a short walk to Tanglewood or Downtown Lenox;
tea, sherry and port in the library are a few of its civilized pleasures.*

**White Elephant**  80R (30S)           | 19 | 19 | 18 | 19 | $206 |
Nantucket; (800) 475-2637; (508) 228-2500; FAX 325-1195
*M – With "beautiful, spacious rooms" right on the harbor, "the main hotel is
lovely" (and recommended by some over the cottages); the atmosphere
here "feels more like a country club than a hotel"; "food and service are
excellent", but for some, this "relaxed and lovely" place is "fine for the beach,
but could use a little updating"; open mid-May through mid-November.*

**Yankee Clipper Inn**  27R (7S)        | 19 | 17 | 18 | 20 | $130 |
96 Granite St., Rockport; (800) 545-3699; (508) 546-3407; FAX 546-9730
*U – "You can't beat watching the sun rise as waves lap outside your room";
a remarkable natural setting with "lovely flowers", "stunning views and
stillness", canopied beds, glass-enclosed porches and open sundecks
make this "pretty", "quiet" place "a favorite" "to enjoy year-round"; the
"romantic restaurant" (Glass Veranda) provides "an excellent breakfast."*

| R | S | D | P | $ |

**Botsford Inn**   63R (3S)   | – | – | – | – | I |
28000 Grand River Ave., Farmington Hills; (313) 474-4800; FAX 474-7669
*Originally built in the 1830s as a stagecoach stop and "lovingly restored" by Henry Ford in the 1920s, this "unique country inn" is "historical", "slanting wooden floors" and all; "stunning public areas" include extensive gardens; some of our surveyors say service and food are "not good", but at the modest price criticism is muted.*

**Boyne Highlands Inn***   361R (126S)   | 20 | 21 | 19 | 20 | $113 |
Highlands Dr., Harbor Springs; (800) GO BOYNE; (616) 526-2171;
FAX 526-5636
*U – This "ideal getaway" 10 miles north of Petoskey offers year-round fun, including "great skiing" on 27 runs in winter and three top golf courses; it has "wonderful" American food in the two dining rooms, plus well-rated service and lots of special packages; insiders prefer the "quiet months of May and September."*

**Boyne Mountain Hotel***   244R   | 15 | 16 | 16 | 17 | $124 |
Boyne Mountain Dr., Boyne Falls; (800) GO-BOYNE; (616) 549-2441;
FAX 549-2912
*U – Boyne Highland's older sibling is a "rustic vacation site" that prides itself on all kinds of activities "for winter and summer", including skiing, golf, bicycling, boating, fishing, ice skating and a complete health club; unrepentently unrestored since the 1940s, it nonetheless offers a variety of comfortable villas overlooking Deer Lake and a number of condos.*

**GRAND HOTEL**   317R (4S)   | 22 | 24 | 23 | 25 | $201 |
Mackinac Island; (800) 33-GRAND; (906) 847-3331 (summer);
(906) 349-4600 (winter); FAX 847-3259
*U – "If you're staying on the island, you must stay" at this "throwback to another era" when "old elegance" mixes with "excellent service" and "great views of the beautiful grounds" to create a "memorable experience"; though some mind dress codes ("jacket and tie for dinner – this is the 1990s!"), and "small" rooms "still in the 1890s", all in all, it's a "grand old place."*

**GRAND TRAVERSE RESORT**　750R　　| 23 | 23 | 21 | 24 | $150 |
6300 U.S. 31 N., Acme; (800) 748-0303; (616) 938-2100; FAX 938-5495
*M – "Outstanding facilities", "a real Olympic pool" and 36 holes of
championship golf (including Jack Nicklaus's The Bear) make this
"classy summer-vacation stopover" a "gem" of a "hotel and condo resort";
"good food" and a "range of restaurants" offset what some consider
"cramped" rooms.*

**Shanty Creek –**　　　　　　| 18 | 18 | 18 | 20 | $131 |
**Schuss Mountain Resort***　600R (240S)
Schuss Mountain Rd, RR3, Bellaire; (800) 678-4111; (616) 533-8621;
FAX 533-7001
*U – You can vacation year-round at this "superfriendly" golf and ski resort
with 54 holes of golf, 28 downhill runs and miles of groomed cross-country
trails on more than 3,000 acres northeast of Traverse City; you have a
choice of "comfortable" villas, condos and suites plus rooms in the rustic
lodge with its wood-beamed lobby and giant fieldstone fireplaces
overlooking the lake below.*

**Stafford's Bay View Inn***　34R (7S)　| 20 | 23 | 20 | 19 | $117 |
Hwy. 31 N., Petoskey; (616) 347-2771
*U – "Like snuggling into Grandma's down comforter", you can tuck into this
"homey" "old" Victorian-style B&B on the shores of Little Traverse Bay of
Lake Michigan for a bit of old-fashioned R&R; "comfortable", newly
renovated rooms (all with private baths), "good food" and rocking chairs on
the wraparound "porch with a view" add to the pleasures of this country inn.*

**Sugar Loaf Resort**　270R (68S)　| – | – | – | – | M |
Rte. 1, Cedar; (800) 748-0117; (616) 228-5461; FAX 228-6545
*Cross-country and downhill skiing in the winter and plenty of golf in the
summer keep this "small" but "convenient" resort popular all year; the
availability of condos and suites makes this place "great for reunions";
there's also a private airstrip on-site for fly-in vacationers.*

**Treetops Sylvan Resort**　173R (20S)　| – | – | – | – | M |
3962 Wilkinson Rd., Gaylord; (800) 444-6711; (517) 732-6711; FAX 732-6595
*This Bavarian-style resort started out as a small destination spot for skiers,
but over the years it's expanded to include three golf courses, indoor and
outdoor pools and complete exercise facilities; meeting rooms and
secretarial services make it popular for corporate retreats, while moderate
prices and the kitchenettes in some rooms appeal to families.*

| R | S | D | P | $ |

### Arrowwood, A Radisson Resort  170R    | – | – | – | – | M |
2100 Arrowwood Lane, Alexandria; (800) 333-3333; (612) 762-1124;
FAX 762-1124 x488
*A "beautiful lake and hiking paths" aren't even the half of it at this big,
rambling, rustic Northwoods lodge, located about two hours north of
Minneapolis; boating, swimming, skiing, golf, fishing and horseback riding,
not to mention good meeting facilities and rooms, make this an all-season
destination for conferencing or vacationing; the Camp Arrowwood program
will watch the kids when you're busy.*

### Breezy Point Resort  200R    | – | – | – | – | M |
County Rd., Breezy Point; (800) 328-2284; (218) 562-7811; FAX 562-4510
*With 3,000 acres on Big Pelican Lake in central Minnesota, this
four-season family vacation spot offers something for everybody, from
cross-country skiing, ice skating and snowmobiling in winter to swimming,
boating, fishing, tennis and golf in summer; accommodations range from
rustic cabins in the woods to beach houses and condos with fireplaces; a
supervised kids' program is an added benefit.*

### Fitgers Inn  48R (6S)    | – | – | – | – | I |
600 E. Superior St., Duluth; (800) 726-2982; (218) 722-8826; FAX 727-8871
*Beautiful views of Lake Superior are part and parcel of the Victorian-style
accommodations offered in this small hotel, crafted from a 150-year-old
former brewery located on the lakeshore; renovated in 1992, it offers all the
modern comforts, including three on-site restaurants, as well as easy
access to lots of local activities.*

### Grand View Lodge  100R (60S)    | – | – | – | – | E |
134 Nokomis, Nisswa; (800) 432-3788; (218) 963-2234; FAX 963-2269
*The name says it all about this rustic resort, built in 1918 on Gull Lake
about 150 miles north of the Twin Cities, and renovated in 1992; in addition
to a lovely beach, it offers tennis, golf, horseback riding and hiking, as well
as fishing for the incomparable walleye (a specialty of the Pine Room
American restaurant); lakeside townhouses and cottages are good for
families, while meeting rooms and secretarial services also make it popular
as a corporate retreat; open late April to mid-October.*

## MINNESOTA RESORTS

| R | S | D | P | $ |
|---|---|---|---|---|

### Lutsen Resort   100R (2S)

| – | – | – | – | M |
|---|---|---|---|---|

Hwy. 61, Lutsen; (800) 346-1467; (218) 663-7212
*Built in the 1950s in Scandinavian style, this rustic resort on Lake Superior is "the best in the area"; for the hardy, "the frigid winter is a beautiful time to visit" for snowmobiling, and cross-country and alpine skiing, but the warmer months have their tennis and fishing, boating and golf, even hunting; there are comfortable pine-paneled condos and two charming lodges; hearty meals, starring homemade bread and pies, are well worth an extra workout.*

### Madden's on Gull Lake*   285R (30S)

| 19 | 19 | 16 | 21 | $125 |
|---|---|---|---|---|

8001 Pine Beach Peninsula, Brainerd; (800) 242-1040; (218) 829-2811; FAX 829-2811
*U – This capacious Colonial-style resort on Gull Lake 130 miles northwest of Minneapolis is a popular destination for corporate and family retreats; though the rustic accommodations are pretty straightforward, it has no fewer than 6 pools, 45 holes of golf, 2 marinas, 3 serviceable restaurants and a brand-new Tennis & Croquet Club; its relatively low rates make it popular with large business groups and families.*

### Schumacher's New Prague   (11S)

| – | – | – | – | M |
|---|---|---|---|---|

212 W. Main St., New Prague; (612) 758-2133; FAX 758-2400
*"Absolutely charming", this small inn offers "typical Minnesota" style in the small country town of New Prague; each of the 11 suites has been individually decorated with an in-room fireplace and an aura of romance that makes it ideal for honeymooners; the eponymous restaurant is popular for its Czech-German fare.*

### St. James Hotel*   60R

| 18 | 19 | 19 | 17 | $117 |
|---|---|---|---|---|

406 Main St., Red Wing; (800) 252-1875; (612) 388-2846; FAX 388-5226
*U – Just a block from the Mississippi in historic Red Wing (home of Red Wing Pottery, and a great area for antiquing and shopping), this small Victorian-style hotel (built as a boarding house in 1875 and restored in 1979) is a restful and romantic weekend getaway for stressed-out Twin Citians; however, "get a riverfront room in the new section to avoid the noisy trains" that rumble by from time to time.*

# MISSISSIPPI

| | R | S | D | P | $ |
|---|---|---|---|---|---|

**Burn, The\*** 7R (2S)   | 23 | 24 | 22 | 23 | $113 |
712 N. Union St., Natchez; (800) 654-8859; (601) 442-1344; FAX 445-0606
*U – One of Natchez's most historic homes, this 1832 Greek Revival–style
mansion is now an intimate inn bursting with Victoriana; hard to beat for
atmosphere and authenticity, the place "has real charm" and no small
measure of "Southern gentility and hospitality"; a plantation breakfast, pool
and private tour of the premises are added benefits.*

**Monmouth Plantation\*** 19R   | 26 | 24 | 23 | 25 | $126 |
36 Melrose, Natchez; (800) 828-4531; (601) 442-5852; FAX 446-7762
*U – Live out your Gone With the Wind fantasies at this beautifully restored
19th-century plantation, which perfectly captures "the charm of the South";
set on 26 oak-studded acres, it's "one of the largest and loveliest mansions
in Natchez", with attractive, antique-filled rooms, "proprietors who couldn't
be nicer" and a staff that defines "Southern hospitality"; an outdoor pool
adds to the charm; N.B. no children under 14.*

**Natchez Eola Hotel** 131R (6S)   | 19 | 20 | 19 | 20 | $110 |
110 N. Pearl St., Natchez; (800) 888-9140; (601) 445-6000; FAX 446-5310
*U – Like "stepping back 100 years" in time, this old plantation house is
considered by partisans to be "an absolute must when you're in Natchez";
the atmospheric rooms "each tell a different story", and the staff exhibits
"true Southern hospitality"; formal sit-down dinners provide both "good
food" and the chance to get to know your fellow guests.*

# MISSOURI

**Lodge of Four Seasons, The**   414R    | 20 | 20 | 20 | 21 | $135 |
State Rd. HH, Lake of the Ozarks; (800) THE-LAKE; (314) 365-3000;
FAX 365-8525
*M – This rustic, 30-year-old lakeside resort is praised for its fishing, tennis
and myriad other activities, but draws mixed reactions overall; fans note
"good restaurants", a "variety of accommodations (including condos) and
"so much to see", but critics say it's "on the decline" and "had its heyday";
some see problems of a more basic sort, as in "forget the Ozarks."*

**Marriott's TanTarA**    | 20 | 20 | 19 | 21 | $135 |
**Resort & Golf Club**   930R (176S)
State Rd. KK, Lake of the Ozarks, Osage Beach; (800) 826-8272;
(314) 348-3131; FAX 348-3206
*M – There's a slew of activities (golf, tennis, sailing, ice skating) at this
huge and popular Lake of the Ozarks resort, causing fans to exclaim "you
never have to leave"; the other side of the coin is that it's "very, very spread
out"; despite a "great location" on a "beautiful" lake, some say the rooms
and service are only "fair" and the place is "stuck in the '50s"; it seems to
function best as a "super" conference facility and "nice family place."*

# MONTANA

**Chico Hot Springs Lodge\*** 74R (11S)      | 13 | 17 | 21 | 19 | $86 |
Chico Rd., Pray; (800) 468-9232; (406) 333-4933; FAX 333-4694
*U – A "fun funky place", located in Paradise Valley at the base of the
Absaroka Mountains just north of Yellowstone; this local legend features
a "combination of cowboys and movie stars", plus riding, fishing, biking,
cross-country skiing, slot machines, meetings facilities and "a great hot
springs pool open 24 hours a day", 365 days a year; "the best restaurant
in Montana" and "kitsch personified" are yours at this reasonably priced,
"crazy resort in the wilderness."*

**Flathead Lake Lodge** 40R      | – | – | – | – | E |
Flathead Lake Lodge Rd., Big Fork; (406) 837-4391; FAX 837-6977
*A "rustic" dude ranch on the shores of Flathead Lake; canoeing, sailing,
horseback riding and family-style meals are included; parents appreciate
the cozy family cottages and children's program with counselors, plus
proximity to summer-stock theater and the Eagle Bend golf course; for "a
great family vacation" with "good, hearty, not gourmet, food" in a "beautiful"
locale, this place is hard to beat; open May to September only.*

**Gallatin Gateway Inn** 25R (3S)      | – | – | – | – | I |
U.S. Rte. 191, Bozeman; (406) 763-4672; FAX 763-4672 x313
*An original Milwaukee Railroad hotel, restored in the mid-1980's to western-
style "luxury" with small, but quite comfortable rooms – some with
individual baths – plus a heated pool, hot tub, a good restaurant and
tennis; the real attraction, though, is fly-fishing.*

**Glacier Park Lodge** 143R (4S)      | 15 | 16 | 14 | 18 | $95 |
Montana 49, E. Glacier Park; (800) 332- 9351; (406) 226-5551;
FAX 226-4404
*M – One of three "wonderful, old, unique" hotels built by the Great
Northern Railway in the 'teens to attract visitors to Glacier National Park;
the location and the "spectacular" log-timbered lobby rate raves, but the
rooms and the food get mixed reviews; a large pool, golf course and riding
stable are on the premises; open May through October.*

## MONTANA RESORTS

|   | R | S | D | P | $ |
|---|---|---|---|---|---|

**Grouse Mountain Lodge\*** 145R (12S)  | 23 | 22 | 22 | 25 | $116 |
1205 Hwy. 93 W., Whitefish; (800) 321-8822; (406) 862-3000; FAX 862-0326
*U – A modern version of the big-timbered hotels from the early part of the
century; the etched-glass windows depicting scenes from nearby Glacier
National Park make it worth a visit; the ambitious restaurant lives up to its
aspirations, and there's a great bar with a big fireplace for relaxing after
golf, tennis or cross-country skiing in season – Big Mountain Ski Area is
six miles away; all in all, a "fabulous escape."*

**Holland Lake Lodge** 14R (5S)  | – | – | – | – | I |
Holland Lake Rd., Condon; (800) 648-8859; (406) 754-2282; FAX 754-2208
*This small, rustic log lodge adjacent to the Bob Marshall Wilderness was
built in 1921 and is well known locally as an affordable getaway for
vacationers, family reunions and hunters in the fall; its hiking, riding, skiing
and ice skating appeal to sports enthusiasts and families.*

**Huntley Lodge/Big Sky Resort\*** 298R (94S)  | 20 | 22 | 20 | 22 | $131 |
Big Sky; (800) 548-4486; (406) 995-4211; FAX 995-4860
*U – Our surveyors agree – the skiing's great, and the hotel's ok, too;
though the rooms are "small", they're comfortable, and the fact that you
can ski "incredible" Big Sky right from your door is a definite plus,
especially for ski clubs; the three dining rooms are judged "beautiful with
good food";* N.B. *starting this season, children under 10 ski free.*

**Izaak Walton Inn** 31R (3S)  | – | – | – | – | I |
123 Izaak Walton Rd., Essex; (406) 888-5700; FAX 888-5200
*"Not fancy, but one of the greatest places to stay in the U.S." sums up
the sentiment on this old-fashioned (1939) alpine-lodge railroad
hotel in a spectacular setting near Glacier Park; cozy rooms include
three authentic cabooses that have been turned into cabins for four,
with kitchenettes and private bath; guided ski tours into Glacier are an
added benefit.*

**Kandahar Lodge** 50R (16S)  | – | – | – | – | M |
Big Mountain Rd., Whitefish; (406) 862-6098; FAX 862-6095
*Built at the base of Big Mountain Ski Area by a local couple fulfilling their
dream, "this small hotel with a European feel" sports a "cozy" lobby
dominated by a huge fireplace – unfortunately, the all-wood construction
doesn't always lend itself to quiet rooms; the restaurant has a great local
reputation, but the real attraction is that you can walk to the slopes; our
surveyors enthusiastically recommend it for both "winter and summer."*

# MONTANA RESORTS

| | R | S | D | P | $ |
|---|---|---|---|---|---|

### Lake McDonald Lodge   100R

| | 15 | 17 | 17 | 22 | $102 |
|---|---|---|---|---|---|

Going-to-the-Sun Rd., W. Glacier Park; ((800) 332-9351; 406) 226- 5551;
FAX 888-5681
*M – This "quiet and woodsy" old hotel in a "beautiful remote location" on
the shores of Lake McDonald on the west side of Glacier National Park
defines the word "tranquillity"; our surveyors applaud the setting, but
downplay the facilities – "views are breathtaking", and the "scenery makes
up for lackluster", "very simple rooms" and food that can be spotty; open
May through October.*

### Lone Mountain Ranch   23R

| | – | – | – | – | E |
|---|---|---|---|---|---|

Lone Mountain Ranch Rd., Big Sky; (406) 995-4645; FAX 995-4670
*The definitive cross-country skiing resort, originally built in 1915 and last
renovated in 1989, Lone Mountain is "rustic – very", but it boasts
"comfortable cabins", a "great small bar" and a masseuse and whirlpool;
rates range from $800 to $1,700 per person per week, meals included,
depending on cabin and extras; book early.*

### Many Glacier Hotel   208R (2S)

| | 15 | 18 | 16 | 21 | $102 |
|---|---|---|---|---|---|

U.S. Rte. 89, E. Glacier Park; (800) 332-9351; (406) 226-5551;
FAX 732-5522
*M – Pretend you're at "sleepaway camp" at this "trip to the past" with
"fabulous Rocky Mountain views" in the center of Glacier National Park;
the hiking trails are as spectacular as any in the U.S., and if you score a
room facing Swiftcurrent Lake, you'll enjoy the same view the Wilderness
Society uses in its ads; food is "mediocre" and rooms are modest, but so
are the Park Service–controlled prices; open June through September.*

### Mountain Sky Guest Ranch   27R (6S)

| | – | – | – | – | E |
|---|---|---|---|---|---|

Big Creek Rd., Bozeman; (800) 548-3392
*Sign up for the "best family vacation yet" in a spectacular mountain valley
("maybe the most beautiful sky of all") along the Yellowstone River less
than an hour north of Yellowstone National Park; a "great children's
program" plus fishing, horseback riding and hiking will whet everyone's
appetite for "humongous" portions of well-"above-average" food;
accommodations include comfortable cabins.*

### 9 Quarter Circle Ranch   20S

| | – | – | – | – | M |
|---|---|---|---|---|---|

5000 Taylor Fork Rd., Gallatin Gateway; (406) 995-4276
*"Not fancy but a great family vacation"; since 1946, it's been one of the
best-known dude ranches in Montana, within an hour's drive of
Yellowstone National Park; families enjoy the rustic cabins with fireplaces,
and activities including fly-fishing, horseback riding, cookouts and pack
trips into the wilderness; open June through September.*

**Triple Creek Mountain Hideaway**   32R (14S) | – | – | – | – | VE |
551 W. Fork Stage Rte., Darby; (406) 821-4664; FAX 821-4666
*The motto at this isolated mountain hideaway is "you'll feel like the owner" –*
*and since the hefty tab includes all meals, activities, unlimited libations*
*and a filled cookie jar in every cabin, you very well may; all cabins have*
*fireplaces, and some have king-size log beds and hot tubs; outdoor activities*
*include fishing, cross-country skiing and river rafting; a one-to-one guest-staff*
*ratio will make you feel special; N.B. no children.*

# NEVADA

| R | S | D | P | $ |

**Caesars Lake Tahoe**   409R (37S)   | 20 | 19 | 18 | 18 | $124 |
Hwy. 50, South Lake Tahoe; (702) 588-3515; (800) 648-3353;
(406) 587-1244; FAX 586-2102
*M – In this "fabulous part of the United States", Caesars offers its own
"special glitter", with "beautiful scenery overlooking the golf course" and
the "best casino in Tahoe"; comments indicate some problems: the public
areas – "gaudy", rooms – "worn" and service – "New York–rude"; still,
ratings show most guests are more than satisfied.*

**Harrah's Lake Tahoe**   535R (80S)   | 22 | 20 | 19 | 20 | $129 |
Hwy. 50, South Lake Tahoe; (800) 648-3773; (702) 588-6611; FAX 586-6601
*U – Despite the prevailing wisdom that Nevada visitors are either "skiing,
hiking, or gambling", Harrah's gets highest marks for its "tremendous"
rooms with "breathtaking views of the lake", including (believe it or not) "his
and hers bathrooms" in all rooms and "three phones and TVs per person";
service is "good", and the "friendly" casino almost "makes it fun to lose."*

**Hyatt Regency Lake Tahoe**   | 21 | 21 | 20 | 20 | $145 |
**Resort & Casino**   458R (24S)
Country Club Dr. at Lakeshore, Incline Village; (800) 233-1234;
(702) 832-1234; FAX 831-7508
*U – Located on the north shore, away from the gambling strip, in a
"comfortable, rustic setting" that offers "a new view every half-hour as the
mountains change color"; in addition to a "great location for skiing" and a
"beautiful" private beach, this "comfortable" hotel provides "attractive"
rooms and "wonderful" service; amid all this splendor, however, some
reviewers find the lobby "pretty garish."*

# NEW HAMPSHIRE

| R | S | D | P | $ |

**Balsams, The**   232R (4S)                      | 20 | 22 | 21 | 22 | $159 |
Dixville Notch; (800) 255-0600; (603) 255-3400; FAX 255-4221
*U – On the list of "Historic Hotels of America" and in the White Mountains
on 15,000 lakeside acres, this "piney", rustic 19th-century family resort with
"camp furniture" (as in summer camp) is real Americana; award-winning
cuisine – with meals included in the rate – personal service and an
"incomparable" setting filled with unlimited recreation make it "world-class."*

**Christmas Farm Inn\***   37R (4S)              | 19 | 21 | 19 | 18 | $131 |
Rte. 16B, Jackson; (800) 443-5837; (603) 383-4313; FAX 383-6495
*U – This country inn set in the White Mountains is a "delightful retreat" for
hikers and skiers; rooms named after Santa's elves may be terminally
cute, and desserts like Christmas Farm Sundae are comfort food to the
max (all meals are included), but a "memorable staff" and "great ambiance"
make tough critics feel "perfectly at home."*

**Mount Washington**                             | 17 | 18 | 17 | 21 | $147 |
**Hotel & Resort, The**   250R (8S)
Rte. 302, Bretton Woods; (800) 258-0330; (603) 278-1000; FAX 278-1010
*M – "A charming relic" with "breathtaking" views of Mount Washington, this
"grand old lady" has "great grounds and facilities", but "there may not be
enough money to do this landmark up right"; complaints include basics like
mundane food and "almost no electricity."*

**Snowy Owl Inn\***   82R (2S)                    | – | – | – | – | I |
Village Rd., Waterville Valley; (800) 766-9969; (603) 236-8383; FAX 236-4890
*Quaint charm, it's not – but modern facilities set in the White Mountain
National Forest provide "comfortable country atmosphere", with whirlpools
in many rooms and free breakfast and snacks; four-season recreation
abounds, including horseback riding, fishing and golf.*

## NEW HAMPSHIRE RESORTS

| R | S | D | P | $ |

### Stonehurst Manor*  24R (7S)

| 18 | 17 | 21 | 17 | $117 |

Rte. 16, North Conway; (800) 525-9100; (603) 356-3113
*M – A turn-of-the-century mansion set on 33 acres in the White Mountains,
this "quiet", romantic inn has "lovely rooms", "excellent food" and "interesting"
decor, including stained-glass windows; "a few minor maintenance problems"
are cited, but hey, you can always jump in the hot tub, go canoeing or swim
in the pool to forget the glitches.*

### Whitney's Inn Jackson

| 19 | 19 | 21 | 15 | $99 |

(fka Whitney's Village Inn)
Rte. 16B, Jackson; (800) 252-5622; (603) 383-8916
*U – "A wonderful family place with adult food", this "pleasant" converted
farmhouse at the foot of Black Mountain offers "a charming setting" plus
"good service", great skiing, a swimming pond and "kids, kids and more
kids" for holidays and summers that are informally fun.*

# NEW JERSEY

| R | S | D | P | $ |
|---|---|---|---|---|

**Abbey, The\***  14R (2S)       | 22 | 21 | 20 | 20 | $140 |
34 Gurney St., Cape May; (609) 884-4506
*U – The "romantic, authentic" Victorian appointments throughout this
charming bed-and-breakfast send guests a "step back in time" to the
"really old Cape May"; the large main house is a "unique" Gothic Revival
former summer home, while the smaller cottage nearby is in the Second
Empire style; hosts Jay and Marian Schatz are "quirky and fun."*

**Chalfonte Hotel, The**  100R       | 13 | 16 | 17 | 15 | $113 |
301 Howard St., Cape May; (609) 884-8409
*M – "Old-fashioned" is a polite way to describe this rambling 19th-century
wooden Victorian (all breezy porches and plenty of rocking chairs), now
undergoing a piecemeal restoration; you must expect plainly furnished
rooms without air-conditioning, TV or phones, and communal bathrooms
down creaky halls; the generous "Southern-style" breakfast and suppers,
included in the price of the room, help deliver "cheap" "summer fun" at this
"campy" slice of shore history.*

**Inn at Millrace Pond, The**  17R       | 21 | 20 | 22 | 19 | $126 |
Rte. 519, Hope; (908) 459-4884
*U – "There's not much to do" in this scenic Delaware Valley farming
community, but that's part of the charm of this "very relaxing" little country
inn "in the sticks"; hewn from a group of structures built around a 1769 grist
mill, the rooms feature "Spartan" furnishings and "soaring ceilings", but
"thin walls that are definitely pre-Revolutionary" can put a damper on
romance; the food in the beautiful restaurant is "quite good", and the staff
is "helpful."*

**MAINSTAY INN & COTTAGE**  12R (3S)       | 24 | 24 | 21 | 24 | $138 |
635 Columbia Ave., Cape May; (609) 884-8690
*U – Universally praised as the best bed-and-breakfast in Cape May for its
"old-world charm", "high-Victorian" accommodations and "service plus";
both the large main inn (a former 19th-century men's gambling club) and
the nearby cottage are booked months ahead for the summer – so you
may have to "wait until September or the spring."*

## NEW JERSEY RESORTS | R | S | D | P | $ |

### Queen Victoria, The*   23R (7S)   | 20 | 21 | 19 | 19 | $135 |
182 Ocean St., Cape May; (609) 884-8702
*U – "Bed-and-breakfast as it ought to be"; Victoriana buffs find it "utterly
charming", warmed by antiques and a "brick fireplace in the front parlor",
and rave about "great breakfasts and teas" and a "terrific" location within a
block of Cape May's Washington Mall shopping area; only a curmudgeon
(or a modernist) could dislike this place.*

### Virginia, The*   24R   | 22 | 21 | 21 | 21 | $162 |
25 Jackson St., Cape May; (609) 884-5700; FAX 884-1236
*U – If you're not into the B&B scene, this smaller restored hotel is a good
alternative, with a conference room, private baths, cable TV, in-room VCRs
and other modern features behind its ornate and "charming" 19th-century
gingerbread exterior; expect "great service", "small" but "deluxe" rooms
and "consistently good" Contemporary American food in the beautiful Ebbit
Room restaurant.*

# NEW MEXICO

**Bishop's Lodge**   74R (21S)          | 20 | 21 | 20 | 21 | $192 |
Bishop's Lodge Rd., Santa Fe; (505) 983-6377; FAX 989-8739
*U – "Old-world charm" prevails at this "superior resort" five minutes north of Santa Fe; "steeped in history", the 1,000-acre rancho is a "wonderful family place", "very convenient to town" but "away from tourists"; an extensive children's program and "hearty breakfasts" draw raves; the only drawbacks are "so-so rooms" and food that doesn't measure up to other local options.*

**Casa Benevides***   22R (1S)          | 26 | 26 | 23 | 23 | $125 |
137 Kit Carson Rd., Taos; (505) 758-1772
*U – "Too bad you've discovered this gem" cry our surveyors; every room within this "well-run" B&B is "lovely and unique", with kiva fireplaces and unusual antiques; family-style breakfasts featuring "the world's best granola" receive high marks, as does the "great location near the Plaza."*

**Dos Casas Viejas**   3R (1S)          | – | – | – | – | M |
610 Agua Fria St., Santa Fe; (505) 983-1636
*An intimate bed-and-breakfast just blocks from central Santa Fe, catering to those who seek privacy; rooms are resplendently decorated with SW antiques and feature Mexican tile floors, original art, kiva fireplaces, down comforters and large private patios; plus, there's a heated lap pool.*

**Eldorado Hotel** (Pr)   218R (8S)          | 22 | 21 | 19 | 21 | $145 |
309 W. San Francisco St., Santa Fe; (800) 955-4455; (505) 988-4455;
FAX 983-9136
*M – A sensible choice for business, this hotel is in the heart of Santa Fe's artistic community and just three blocks from the central Plaza; it has "small" but "pleasant rooms", "large, comfortable public areas", "excellent service" and first-rate SW food at the Old House restaurant.*

**Historic Taos Inn, The**   39R (1S)          | 18 | 19 | 19 | 19 | $129 |
125 Paseo del Pueblo Norte, Taos; (800) TAOS-INN; (505) 758-2233;
FAX 758-5776
*M – Reports that this once-venerable Taos property "needs a refurbishing throughout" probably predate the recent renovation; still, some say it "doesn't live up to the hype"; on a positive note, its "good location" is praised, and Doc Martin's Restaurant (food rating, 23) still serves "the best food."*

# NEW MEXICO RESORTS

| R | S | D | P | $ |
| --- | --- | --- | --- | --- |

## Hotel Edelweiss, The   14R (7S)

| – | – | – | – | E |
| --- | --- | --- | --- | --- |

P.O. Box 83, Taos Ski Valley; (505) 776-2301; FAX 776-5540
*Very European chalet that appeals to an upscale family crowd with delicious French food served family-style and a location right off the base of the mountain; it's modifed American plan, but you'll be happy to eat here; ski classes are included and even the experts take lessons; no phones in the rooms.*

## Hotel Plaza Real*   56R (44S)

| 17 | 17 | 16 | 17 | $130 |
| --- | --- | --- | --- | --- |

125 Washington Ave., Santa Fe; (800) 279-7325; (505) 988-4900; FAX 988-4000
*U – At this "very comfortable", well-located hotel half a block off Santa Fe's historic Plaza, the rooms are "cramped" but "nice" – though beware, since "some have steep stairs"; rates include "extensive breakfast", and the underground garage means no scrambling to find an elusive parking space.*

## Hotel Santa Fe   222R (91S)

| – | – | – | – | M |
| --- | --- | --- | --- | --- |

1501 Paseo de Peralta, Santa Fe; (800) 825-9876; (505) 982-1200; FAX 984-2211
*Popular with the California crowd, this year-old pueblo-style hotel in the Guadalupe Historic District offers quiet, comfortable accommodations in a handy location; the suites with microwaves and minibars facilitate an extended stay, and while there's no restaurant on-site, a buffet breakfast is available daily.*

## Hotel St. Francis   82R (4S)

| – | – | – | – | M |
| --- | --- | --- | --- | --- |

210 Don Gaspar Ave., Santa Fe; (800) 666-5700; (505) 983-5700; FAX 989-7690
*This charming, intimate hotel is noted for its traditional afternoon teas in the lobby; the cozy rooms have brass beds and cherrywood furnishings, and the ideal Downtown locale makes for great people-watching, either from the open-air veranda or in the award-winning Francisco's restaurant.*

## INN OF THE ANASAZI   59R (8S)

| 25 | 24 | 25 | 23 | $195 |
| --- | --- | --- | --- | --- |

113 Washington Ave., Santa Fe; (800) 688-8100; (505) 988-3030; FAX 988-3277
*U – Santa Fe's hippest, this "elegant small hotel" in Downtown Santa Fe is "like walking into a kiva"; reviewers gush over "beautiful appointments", "authentic artifacts", "good food" and "attractive rooms"; "extremely courteous" staff and a location "within walking distance of everything" – a "fabulous find."*

**Inn of the Mountain Gods**   250R (20S)    | 20 | 18 | 18 | 21 | $140 |
Carrizo Canyon Rd., Mescalero; (800) 257-6173; (505) 257-5141; FAX 257-6173
*M – This "magical place" on Mescalero Apache Indian Reservation is
"lovely", but "service seems to have an "I-don't-care attitude"; rooms and
food are more than satisfactory, but still nothing to write home about;
however, most agree "it's a great spot for a vacation" and the "golf course
is spectacular."*

**Inn on the Alameda**   47R (6S)    | – | – | – | – | E |
303 E. Alameda St., Santa Fe; (800) 289-2122; (505) 984-2121;
FAX 986-8325
*Next door to the Santa Fe River, this small hotel has traditional
wormwood-and-adobe decor; though a bit drab, it's a comfortable place to
stop for business or pleasure, made more so by the free morning paper,
concierge service, complimentary gourmet breakfast and the use of
facilities at a local spa.*

**La Fonda Hotel on the Plaza** (Pr)   159R (40S) | – | – | – | – | M |
100 E. San Francisco St., Santa Fe; (800) 523-5002; (505) 982-5511;
FAX 988-2952
*Dating back to 1610 when it marked "the end of the Santa Fe trail", this
bustling hotel attracts visitors seeking the hub of activity; every room is
different, but all have a Southwest touch, with hand-decorated wooden
furniture and original Indian paintings; the enclosed skylit La Pazuela
restaurant delights with its New Mexican specialties.*

**La Posada de Albuquerque** (Pr)   114R (3S)   | – | – | – | – | I |
125 Second St. NW, Albuquerque; (800) 777-5732; (505) 242-9090;
FAX 242-8664
*Built by Conrad Hilton in 1939, this historic Downtown hotel epitomizes
"new Mexico" with its Spanish tile, handcrafted furniture and SW art; the
lobby bar offers live jazz Friday and Saturday nights; a convenient location
and modest prices are added fillips.*

**La Posada de Santa Fe** (Pr)   119R (31S)    | 18 | 17 | 17 | 19 | $120 |
330 E. Palace Ave., Santa Fe; (800) 727-LAPO; (505) 986-0000;
FAX 982-6850
*U – Nestled among fountains and rose gardens, this rambling hotel
complex of Victorian houses and Southwestern casitas is "very charming"
and "loaded with Santa Fe character" (pinion-wood-burning fireplaces in
many rooms); for a special stay, request the Staab House main bedroom.*

**Lodge at Cloudcroft\*** 58R (10S) | 19 | 20 | 22 | 20 | $124 |
U.S. 82, Cloudcroft; (800) 395-6343; (505) 682-2566; FAX 682-2715
*U – "A little jewel that's not too well known", featuring "beautiful
views", "wonderful ambiance" and nicely appointed rooms; enjoy the
"wonderfully secluded feeling", "great golf" and "very good restaurant"
featuring nightly entertainment.*

**Quail Ridge Inn\*** 110R | 20 | 18 | 17 | 19 | $155 |
Ski Valley Rd., Taos; (800) 624-4448; (505) 776-2211; FAX 776-2949
*U – "Well situated between town and the ski area", this resort boasts
rooms with fireplaces, a giant swimming pool, hot tubs and saunas; it's
ideal for the sports-minded: you can ski, raft, mountain-bike, golf or fly-fish
nearby; squash, racquetball, tennis and aerobics classes are available at
the on-site fitness center.*

**Rancho Encantado Resort** 22R (10S) | 22 | 21 | 20 | 23 | $201 |
State Rd. 592, Tesuque; (800) 722-9339; (505) 982-3537; FAX 983-8269
*M – Like "something out of a John Wayne western", "this tremendous place
is full of New Mexican high-desert spirituality"; some surveyors find the
resort "starting to show wear and tear", and say "the food could be
improved on", but based on the "great setting" and "gorgeous views", most
conclude "out-of-the-way but sublime."*

**Sagebrush Inn\*** 80R (35S) | 15 | 17 | 14 | 17 | $102 |
S. Santa Fe Rd., Taos; (800) 428-3626; (505) 758-2254; FAX 758-9009
*M – Visitors choose between the original rustic (circa-1929) hotel rooms
and the elegant newer suites; some think the hotel is "kind of tacky" with
"rooms like the Bates Motel" – but fireplaces, tennis, hot tubs and an
outdoor pool are pluses.*

**Sheraton Old Town** (Pr) 190R (20S) | – | – | – | – | I |
800 Rio Grande Blvd. NW, Albuquerque; (800) 237-2133; (505) 843-6300;
FAX 842-9863
*This comfortable hotel has the three keys to success: location, location
location – it's just one block from historic Old Town and its shops,
restaurants and galleries; rooms are nothing fancy, but the nice swimming
pool is ideal for cooling off after a long day's touring, and the price is right.*

**St. Bernard Hotel & Condominium** 27R (13S) | – | – | – | – | E |
P.O. Box 88, Taos Ski Valley; (505) 776-2251
*Ski-in/ski-out Swiss chalet at the base of Taos Mountain where lingering
over the wonderful French food is a favorite pastime; it's a sibling of
Edelweiss and appeals to an equally tony family crowd for its thorough
comfort as well as access to the outdoors.*

# NEW YORK STATE

| R | S | D | P | $ |

**Beekman Arms Hotel**  59R (2S)  | 20 | 19 | 21 | 19 | $127 |
4 Mill St.; (Rte. 9), Rhinebeck (914) 876-7077; FAX 846-7077 x367
*M – The oldest hotel in America in continuous operation is a Dutchess County "traveler's dream" to some, "not worth the visit" to others; "cozy" and set in a "lovely", "historic" town, the inn has 10 buildings from Colonial to modern, "nice antiques" and "romantic fireplaces"; the new suites are tops, and the new star chef (Larry Forgione, at the 1766 Tavern) is, too.*

**Clarion Inn at Saratoga**  38R (4S)  | 20 | 21 | 20 | 19 | $161 |
231 Broadway, Saratoga Springs; (800) 252-7466; (518) 583-1890;
FAX 583-2543
*M – This restored, gabled historic inn in the heart of Saratoga has English gardens, a conference center and a "great location" close to the State Park; most think it's a "top-notch place" with "good service" and "a touch of class", but others complain it's "dark" and "a little too commercial."*

**Concord Resort Hotel**  1200R (100S)  | 15 | 15 | 15 | 17 | $159 |
Kiamesha Lake; (800) 431-3850; (914) 794-4000; FAX 794-7471
*M – "Quantity over quality" is the rule at this "giant" Catskills "queen of the Borscht Belt"; "the emphasis is on food" – three meals a day are included – "dirty dancing" sort of entertainment and singles activities, but great golf, sports and children's facilities are "thoroughly enjoyable", and the meeting space is huge; some love the meal plan that "guarantees weight gain", others call it "indigestion city."*

**Doral Arrowwood**  272R (28S)  | 19 | 19 | 19 | 20 | $165 |
(fka Arrowwood)
Anderson Hill Rd., Rye Brook; (800) 22-DORAL; (914) 939-5500; FAX 939-1877
*U – "A blue-blazer-and-golf-slacks kind of place", this Westchester County conference center in a "country-club setting" offers "awesome" sports facilities (especially a "killer" golf course) and "terrific" buffet breakfasts, but some say the businesslike rooms feel like you're "sleeping in the office."*

# NEW YORK STATE RESORTS

| R | S | D | P | $ |

**Elk Lake Lodge**  18R (12S)

| – | – | – | – | M |

Blue Ridge Rd., North Hudson; (518) 532-7616
*On a 12,000-acre private preserve with two beautiful lakes (Clear Pond
and Elk Lake) surrounded by Adirondack high peaks, this May-through-
November resort is one of the loveliest in the Eastern U.S. – and a certified
"best buy"; it's a nature-lover's and fisherman's haven that's both rustic and
relaxing; the 1904 main lodge has a huge stone fireplace and a few rooms,
but the cottages (some with kitchens) are best for families; hearty but
otherwise undistinguished Country American food – included in the price –
is served in a wing of the lodge viewing Elk Lake; book well in advance.*


**Geneva on the Lake***  29S

| 18 | 20 | 19 | 19 | $154 |

1001 Lochland Rd.; (Rte. 145), Geneva (800) 3GENEVA; (315) 789-7190;
FAX 789-0322
*M – "Overlooking Seneca Lake", this "beautiful", villa-like small resort is a
top destination for executive retreats; formal gardens, antique-filled rooms,
candlelight dining and complimentary breakfast are pluses; fans laud the
"pleasant rooms" and "wonderful views", but critics claim it's "overrated"
and "needs remodeling."*


**Gideon Putnam Hotel**  132R

| 18 | 19 | 17 | 20 | $149 |

Saratoga Spa State Park, Saratoga Springs; (800) 732-1560;
(518) 584-3000; FAX 584-1354
*M – This "stately" and "reserved" Georgian-style resort has a wonderful
location near the racetrack and Saratoga Arts Center, in the middle of a
2,000-acre park with mineral baths and outdoor recreation; though some
love the "old-world charm" and say "it has a lot going for it", others feel it's
"dowdy" and say "if it's not racing or concert season, don't bother."*


**Guest House, The**  7R (1S)

| – | – | – | – | M |

223 DeBruce Rd., Livingston Manor; (914) 439-4000; FAX 439-3344
*The real Lifestyles of the Rich and Famous is here in the heart of the
Catskills trout-fishing area, located on 40 acres on the banks of the
Willowemoc, with stocked fishing and a natural swimming pond; the
owners (he an English lord-to-be, she a semifamous society lady) are
charming hosts; guests choose a custom breakfast and cocktail, then book
a superb dinner for Saturday night; rooms are a rustic luxury, and the
feeling is pure escape.*

## NEW YORK STATE RESORTS | R | S | D | P | $ |

**Harrison Conference Center**   199R (4S)   | 20 | 20 | 20 | 20 | $153 |
580 White Plains Rd., Glen Cove; (800) HCC-MEET; (516) 671-6400;
FAX 759-2669
*U – "Big-hair" wedding guests and business types frequent this Long Island
mansion with a "rich feel", set on "magnificent grounds" and overlooking the
Sound; rooms are considered only "fair", but "excellent food", good sports
facilities and "wonderful, caring service" come in for high praise.*

**Mohonk Mountain House**   276R   | 17 | 19 | 16 | 22 | $170 |
Lake Mohonk, New Paltz; (800) 772-6646 (NY only); (914) 255-1000;
FAX 256-2161
*M – Our surveyors split on this sprawling 19th-century lodge, "the last of
the old mountain resorts", with its splended views of Mohonk Lake and
Mohonk Mountain; fans call it a "wonderful family resort", with "quaint
common areas" and a "magnificent setting"; foes call it a "drafty"
"anachronism"; mostly, though, it's a "historic experience extraordinaire",
so "forget the food" and the "small, hot rooms with old bathrooms", and
enjoy "5,000 acres of wilderness two hours from Manhattan."*

**Montauk Yacht Club & Inn**   107R (3S)   | 19 | 18 | 18 | 19 | $195 |
Star Island, Montauk; (800) 832-4200; (516) 668-3100; FAX 668-3303
*M – A "lovely setting" at the tip of Long Island is the place to "sit on the
terrace and watch the sunset"; once a posh private club, this pricey
waterfront getaway with pools, a small beach, spa and marina is "lovely"
and "well run" to most, with a popular restaurant; to some, however, it's "a
bit far out" – geographically or culturally, we can't guess.*

**Old Drovers Inn**   4R   | – | – | – | – | M |
Old Rte. 22 (East Duncan St.), Dover Plains; (914) 832-9311; FAX 832-6356
*The newest and smallest member of the Relais & Chateaux group has
operated continuously since 1750 when it served Dutchess County drovers
(i.e. men who drove cattle, sheep and pigs to market); almost every room
has a fireplace, and the inn as a whole is nonstop early American charm –
with first-class American cooking to match.*

**Omni Sagamore**   350R (176S)   | 22 | 21 | 20 | 23 | $186 |
110 Sagamore Rd., Bolton Landing, Lake George; (800) THE-OMNI;
(518) 644-9400; FAX 644-2626
*U – "On a little island on Lake George", this "elegant turn-of-the-century
resort" has "an absolutely spectacular view", great golf, an indoor sports
center, cross-country skiing and "beautiful, rolling grounds"; reviewers
recommend the "moonlight dinner sail" and the "lovely" rooms in the main
lodge; "Lake George in all its glory makes this incomparable"; it's popular
for group meetings.*

## NEW YORK STATE RESORTS | R | S | D | P | $ |

**Otesaga Hotel**   124R (6S)   | 18 | 20 | 19 | 22 | $157 |
Lake St., Cooperstown; (607) 547-9931; FAX 547-9675
*U – In this renovated school, "your room could be a former classroom or a broom closet", but "the great porch – overlooking the lake and valley – makes it worth it"; "not in many guidebooks", this "stately" hotel nonetheless boasts lots of sports facilities, a "quiet atmosphere" and a "splendid location" – aside from the Baseball Hall of Fame, it's "the other reason to visit" this "picturesque" town; open May through October.*

**POINT, THE**   11R   | 28 | 28 | 27 | 27 | $406 |
Saranac Lake; (800) 255-3530; (518) 891-5674; FAX 891-1152
*U – The top resort in our Survey was formerly the lodge of the Rockefellers; according to charmed reviewers, "there are not enough superlatives" to describe this "fantastic hideaway" located on Saranac Lake in the Adirondacks, a "serene" wilderness lodge offering uncommon luxury "for the nonoutdoors type", with "outstanding" service and a "superb setting and food"; it's a "very special, one-of-a-kind retreat", but you may have to be a Rockefeller to afford it.*

**Three Village Inn**   27R   | 17 | 18 | 18 | 17 | $124 |
150 Main St., Stony Brook, Long Island; (516) 751-0555; FAX 751-0593
*M – "Quaint and cutesy", this 1751 inn with cottages, only a few hours east of Manhattan, is a "nicely maintained" "grand old lady"; food gets mixed reviews, and surveyors say the "public rooms are more charming than the guest rooms", but nearby beach and golf and the university-town setting are pluses.*

**TROUTBECK INN**   34R (8S)   | 22 | 23 | 24 | 23 | $223 |
Leedsville Rd., Amenia; (914) 373-9681; FAX 373-7080
*U – Like an English country estate, this highly praised inn and conference center just two hours from NYC, in lovely Dutchess County, is "a small gem"; its "superb service", "gourmet food", "beautiful English gardens" and "lovely pool" are some of the reasons it's a "fantasy" weekend getaway; it also functions as a conference center and the site of business retreats.*

# NORTH CAROLINA

|   | R | S | D | P | $ |
|---|---|---|---|---|---|

**FEARRINGTON HOUSE INN, THE** 20R (10S)  | 24 | 22 | 26 | 22 | $159 |
2000 Fearrington Village Ctr., Pittsboro; (919) 542-2121;
FAX 542-4202
*U – Set against a backdrop of rolling farmland amid a picturesque complex
of homes and shops eight miles south of Chapel Hill, this "lovely" English
country–style inn has "beautiful" rooms and excellent service plus a well
regarded restaurant, featuring "outstanding" gourmet Southern cuisine.*

**Green Park Inn*** 83R (7S)  | – | – | – | – | M |
Hwy. 321 S., Blowing Rock; (800) 852-2462; (704) 295-3141;
FAX 295-3141 x116
*Authentic 19th-century atmosphere is both the charm and pitfall of this
sprawling Victorian inn; partisans like its wraparound porch, views of the
Blue Ridge Mountains and relaxing, from-another-era ambiance; critics
blast it for unair-conditioned rooms that need refurbishing; tennis and golf
privileges at the nearby Blowing Rock Country Club are a plus.*

**Greystone Inn*** 33R (1S)  | 24 | 24 | 23 | 25 | $172 |
Greystone Lane, Lake Toxaway; (800) 824-5766; (704) 966-4700;
FAX 862-5689
*U – It may be pricey, but this lovely Swiss chalet–style inn offers superior
quality across the board; tucked away "up in the hills", it offers a full range
of recreational activities (tennis, boating, fishing, golf), as well as fine
Contemporary American and Continental cuisine in its Lakeside Dining Room.*

**Grove Park Inn Resort** 510R (12S)  | 21 | 21 | 21 | 23 | $144 |
290 Macon Ave., Asheville; (800) 438-5800; (704) 252-2711;
FAX 253-7053
*U – "So big it can take 10 minutes to walk to breakfast", this sprawling
resort, built in 1913, is known for its mountain views, "lovely old lobby with
huge stone fireplaces" and "grand and glorious" arts-and-crafts furnishings;
activities include "anything and everything you have in mind"; "stay in the
old section" for the most charm.*

**High Hampton Inn & Country Club** 130R (6S)  | 15 | 17 | 15 | 18 | $130 |
Hwy. 107 S., Cashiers; (800) 334-2551; (704) 743-2411; FAX 743-5991
*M – The rooms are "Spartan" at best ("no TV, no AC", no phones and "very
thin walls") and the food's "homely", but this rustic 19th-century lodge set
on a 2,300-acre mountain estate offers plenty to keep you out of your
room: swimming, boating, tennis, golf, hiking, horseback riding and rafting
are just some of the activities; it's an affordable option for a fresh-air family
vacation; individual guest cottages are also available.*

**Pinehurst Hotel & Country Club** 500R (12S)  | 21 | 23 | 22 | 24 | $165 |
Carolina Vista Dr., Pinehurst; (800) 927-4653; (919) 295-6811;
FAX 295-1339
*U – "Pack the plaid pants" and head for this turn-of-the-century Colonial-
style inn, a "golfer's paradise" thanks to its seven "great" 18-hole courses
(it's also a hacker's heaven, with 24 tennis courts); "rooms and meals are
acceptable but secondary" – ditto the "first-class service" and "lovely"
gardens; what counts here is "getting on the course or on a court."*

**Richmond Hill Inn**   21R (2S)                | – | – | – | – | M |
87 Richmond Hill Dr., Asheville; (800) 545-9238; (704) 252-7313;
FAX 252-8726
*Built in 1889, this impressive Queen Anne–style hilltop mansion is today a
"beautiful" inn featuring 12 "wonderful, antique-filled" rooms in the main
building and nine more in the "charming" new Victorian-style cottages
that surround the croquet courtyard; besides croquet, the only on-site
recreational activity is "rocking on the porch"; Gabrielle's restaurant also
gets high marks.*

**Sanderling Inn Resort\***   61R (5S)          | 27 | 24 | 23 | 27 | $161 |
1461 Duck Rd., Duck; (919) 261-4111; FAX 261-4111 x121
*U – A "perfect retreat" situated on North Carolina's majestic Outer Banks,
this "self-contained" resort "invites relaxation" with its large, lovely rooms,
"great" water views and excellent service; "good taste abounds" in both the
sprawling main building, patterned after 19th-century resorts, and the
adjacent Sanderling restaurant, housed in an old Coast Guard station and
featuring Southern Regional cuisine; there's also a full range of sports facilities.*

# OHIO

| R | S | D | P | $ |
|---|---|---|---|---|

**Quail Hollow Resort\***   169R (3S)   | 20 | 21 | 21 | 20 | $115 |
11080 Concord-Hambden Rd., Concord; (800) 792-0258; (216) 352-6201;
FAX 792-0258 x3586
*U – "Solid all around", this contemporary low-rise in the Cleveland suburbs
is spiffier-looking, thanks to a recent $4.5 million renovation, and as always
offers an appealing range of activities, from golf and tennis in warm
weather to cross-country skiing and murder-mystery weekends off-season;
"pretty grounds", "friendly" service and reasonable prices win fans.*

**Sawmill Creek Resort\***   240R (20S)   | 18 | 20 | 17 | 18 | $111 |
2401 Cleveland Rd., W., Huron; (800) SAWMILL; (419) 433-3800;
FAX 433-7610
*A popular hotel/resort on the shores of Lake Erie, this "pleasant Ohio
kind of place" offers something for all ages, from golf, swimming and
all-weather tennis to poolside BBQs, hiking, volleyball and more; it's
nothing fancy, but neither are the prices.*

**Worthington Inn\***   26R (7S)   | 21 | 23 | 23 | 19 | $101 |
649 High St., Columbus; (614) 885-2600; FAX 885-2600
*U – Restored to its original 1830s grandeur, this "lovely" inn is now one
of the "best in the Columbus area", offering spacious rooms, top-notch
service and "excellent" classic Continental cuisine; "champagne and
homemade cookies at bedtime is a typically nice touch."*

| R | S | D | P | $ |
|---|---|---|---|---|

**Lake Texoma Resort**   167R (8S)     | – | – | – | – | M |

Hwy. 70, Kingston; (800) 654-8240; (405) 564-2311; FAX 564-9322
*For avid anglers and other sports and nature nuts, this lakeside resort near the Texas border provides first-rate fishing no matter the weather thanks to – we kid you not – a heated enclosed dock with a fishing hole in the middle; other activities include golf, tennis, swimming, riding and, for indoor types, fireplace-lounging and good dining; with a "friendly staff" and "nice grounds", it gives you "more than what you pay for."*

**Shangri-La Resort***   423R (120S)     | 19 | 18 | 17 | 19 | $116 |

Rte. 3, Afton; (800) 331-4060; (918) 257-4204; FAX 257-5619
*U – It may not quite live up to its name, but fans call this recently renovated resort on Grand Lake o' the Cherokees a "winner" thanks to its spiffed-up rooms and public areas and array of facilities, including superb golf courses, tennis, volleyball, biking, a pool and neat beach; it's worth a return by anyone who hasn't visited in a while.*

# OREGON

**Columbia Gorge Hotel**                    | 20 | 22 | 24 | 21 | $143 |
4000 Westcliff Dr., Hood River; (800) 345-1921; (503) 386-5566;
FAX 386-3359
*U – This "charming" historic Spanish stucco inn has been renovated with
great success; besides a "beautiful, unique setting" above the Columbia
River Gorge – windsurfing capital of the world – and under the shadow of
Mt. Hood, it offers "outstanding food" ("stupendous breakfast"), "exceptional
service" and "antiqued rooms."*

**Embarcadero Resort**                       | – | – | – | – | I |
**Hotel & Marina**   100R (50S)
1000 SE Bay Blvd., Newport; (800) 547-4779; (503) 265-8521; FAX 265-7844
*A "beautiful location" on a quiet bay just off the Pacific Coast Highway",
"lovely suites" (many with full kitchen and fireplace) and very reasonable
prices make this condo-ish resort a good base from which to explore the
pristine beauty of the Oregon coast; N.B. there are two decent restaurants
in the hotel for those who don't want to cook.*

**Inn at Spanish Head, The**   142R (30S)   | 20 | 20 | 21 | 19 | $105 |
4009 S. Hwy. 101, Lincoln City; (800) 452-8127; (503) 996-2161;
FAX 996-4089
*U – All rooms face the Pacific in this condominium resort hotel, popular for
its getaway weeks and weekends, honeymoons and winter-storm-watching
packages; local shopping and art galleries, the Oregon Coast Aquarium
and fishing provide a range of diversion – and you can cook what you
catch in the in-room kitchenette; a beach is adjacent.*

**Kah-Nee-Ta Resort\***   164R (25S)        | 20 | 19 | 18 | 20 | $129 |
Hwy. 3, Warm Springs; (800) 831- 0100; (503) 553-1112; FAX 553-1071
*U – For those who think the Northwest is just evergreens and rain,
discover the rugged high-plateau landscape here on the Warm Springs
Indian Reservation, located in a part of eastern Oregon where the sun
shines more than 300 days a year; white-water rafting, tennis, golf and
hiking-and-biking trails will put you in the mood for a hot mineral bath or a
swim in the spring-fed pool, capped by a Native American dinner.*

## OREGON RESORTS

| R | S | D | P | $ |
|---|---|---|---|---|

**Rock Springs Guest Ranch**  26R (14S)

| – | – | – | – | M |
|---|---|---|---|---|

64201 Tyler Rd., Bend; (800) 225-DUDE; (503) 382-1957; FAX 382-7774
*A working dude ranch located in a high, remote valley in the lovely Central Oregon Cascade Mountains, this unique 2,500-acre property offers complete recreational facilities, plus room and board on an American plan, for families and couples during the summer; in the winter, it's a full-service conference center, never taking more than one group at a time.*

**SALISHAN LODGE**  208R (3S)

| 24 | 24 | 24 | 24 | $177 |
|---|---|---|---|---|

Hwy. 101, Gleneden Beach; (800) 452-2300; (503) 764-2371; FAX 764-3510
*U – "Outstanding rooms with fireplaces", "service, food and wine that's about the best there is", and "a lovely golf course on the unsurpassable Oregon coast" have established this as "one of the finest resorts in the world" in the minds of many; though it's pretty "remote", its fans find it "worth the trip" out to the coast to enjoy the "gorgeous" 700-acre grounds and dramatic beach on Siletz Bay.*

**Sunriver Lodge & Resort**  397S

| 23 | 22 | 22 | 23 | $153 |
|---|---|---|---|---|

Sunriver; (800) 547-3922; (503) 593-1221; FAX 593-5458
*U – For those who want to "rent an A-frame and spend a week" just "relaxing", or for sports buffs who enjoy golf, boating, fishing, tennis, skiing, ice skating, etc., this is an ideal year-round "family getaway" place with a "good pool and health-spa facilities" and "beautiful outdoor-activity areas"; you have the choice of a gourmet restaurant or just fixing your own in the in-room kitchenette.*

**Sylvia Beach Hotel**  20R

| – | – | – | – | M |
|---|---|---|---|---|

267 NW Cliff St., Newport; (503) 265-5428
*Named for the legendary owner of a Paris bookstore of the '20s and '30s, and featuring rooms individually decorated and named for literary figures, this "most interesting" historic hotel was once the honeymoon capital of Oregon; now beach-walking or lounging in the oceanfront library are precursors to "great food" in the Tables of Content restaurant; N.B. the entire building is nonsmoking.*

**Timberline Lodge**  70R (8S)

| 20 | 20 | 19 | 23 | $125 |
|---|---|---|---|---|

South slope of Mt. Hood, Timberline; (800) 547-1406; (503) 272-3311; FAX 272-3710
*U – Built in 1937 by WPA master craftsmen and updated in 1991, this lodge of "huge timbers and rocks" on the slopes of Mt. Hood is "a place you could stay at forever" even if you don't ski; it's "a piece of history", with accommodations "not luxurious but appropriate to the setting" and manned by an "exceptionally helpful and pleasant" staff.*

## OREGON RESORTS

**Tu Tu' Tun Lodge\***   18R (2S)         | 20 | 23 | 24 | 22 | $161 |
96550 N. Bank Rogue, Gold Beach; (503) 247-6664; FAX 247-6664
*U – Near the mouth of the Rogue River on the Oregon coast, "wonderful owners" have created a "special place" where guests are treated "like family"; "great rooms" and the "best dinners anywhere" make for a "whole that's greater than the sum of its parts"; "friendly and fun" – "a real find."*

# PENNSYLVANIA

| R | S | D | P | $ |
|---|---|---|---|---|

**Black Bass Hotel**   9R (2S)
| 16 | 18 | 20 | 17 | $129 |

374 River Rd., Lumberville; (215) 297-5770; FAX 297-0262
*M – "Peaceful and lovely", this old inn on the Delaware River north of New
Hope gets mostly good marks for its "charming rooms" and "beautiful,
quiet, riverside setting", as well as its "excellent" American cuisine; critics
say the rooms are more ramshackle than rustic and the food is "overrated",
but most agree that it's great for a "romantic weekend escape."*

**Bridgeton House**   11R (3S)
| – | – | – | – | M |

River Rd., Upper Black Eddy; (215) 982-5856
*As if "beautiful rooms", "lovely breakfasts" and "terrific amenities" weren't
enough, this homey, romantic inn also offers great views and plenty of
opportunities for outdoor sports, including boating, fishing, hiking and skiing;
not surprisingly, guests "can't praise this bed-and-breakfast highly enough."*

**Evermay on-the-Delaware**   16R
| 22 | 21 | 25 | 20 | $142 |

River Rd., Erwinna; (215) 294-9100; FAX 294-8249
*U – A "charming setting" on the river, "exquisite" French-American food
and the "lovely garden and parlor" – not to mention the four-poster beds,
fireplaces and antiques – make this "elegant", "romantic" 18th-century inn a
favorite; a handful complain about "creaky" beds and "aloof" hosts, but
most agree that it's a "wonderful getaway."*

**Historic Strasburg Inn***   102R (6S)
| 20 | 19 | 18 | 17 | $112 |

Penna. Rte. 896, Strasburg; (800) 872-0201; (717) 687-7691; FAX 687-6098
*M – Not what you'd expect "in Amish country", this rural, Williamsburg-style
inn is deemed "interesting" by fans who appreciate its rustic setting and
comfortable, very reasonably priced accommodations; detractors, on the
other hand, describe it as "prefab" and advise "hop on the train and go right by."*

**Hotel Hershey, The**   240R (18S)        | 19 | 20 | 19 | 20 | $141 |
Hotel Rd., Hershey; (800) HERSHEY; (717) 533-2171; FAX 534-8887
*M – "Old and slightly worn but still elegant", this "wonderful step back into
an earlier, gracious time" strikes fans as a "grand hotel in the land of
chocolate"; despite an engaging blend of traditional European and Spanish
decor – or perhaps because of it – dissenters dismiss it as an "average
tourist spot" and an "overpriced conference hotel in a boring town"; lovely
gardens and service that aims to please are sweet notes.*


**Mount Airy Lodge**   585R (85S)          | 14 | 14 | 13 | 15 | $130 |
42 Woodland Rd., Mt. Pocono; (800) 441-4410; (717) 839-8811;
FAX 839-8811 x7000
*U – This "hokey" resort in the Poconos "caters to the lowest denominator"
in the view of most of our respondents, who say it's "ok if you're a
newlywed" but complain of a "seedy", "run-down" atmosphere and
"mediocre" food to boot; while a few tout the "great activities" and "romantic
rooms", they're in the minority.*


**Nemacolin Woodlands**   175R (10S)       | 22 | 19 | 20 | 22 | $155 |
Rte. 40, Farmington; (800)422-2736; (412) 329-8555; FAX 329-6198
*U – Those few who know it sing the praises of this "luxurious" resort and
spa/conference center near Frank Lloyd Wright's 'Fallingwater' house in
the Laurel Mountains; in addition to the "unique" English-tudor decor,
"friendly" staff and "super food", there's golf, horseback riding and a host
of other activities.*


**Pocono Manor Inn & Golf Resort**   255R (5S)  | 16 | 17 | 15 | 16 | $124 |
Mt. Pocono; (800) 233-8150; (717) 839-7111; FAX 839-0708
*M – This "comfortable", "old-fashioned", turn-of-the-century resort in a
woodsy setting may have "lots of potential", but more than a few say it's "run-
down" and the food tastes "out of a can"; there's no arguing with the sports
facilities, though, which include stables, two golf courses, tennis courts and
a complete health club, making it great for affordable family vacations.*


**Seven Springs Mountain Resort**   385R (12S) | – | – | – | – | E |
Champion; (800) 452-2223; (814) 352-7777; FAX 352-7911
*About an hour from Pittsburgh, this huge, all-seasons round-the-clock
'30s-era mountain resort offers varied accommodations in condos and
cabins; golf, good skiing – for the area – white-water rafting, a full spa,
child-care programs and endless activities appeal to families; 25 meeting
rooms, 8 restaurants and 6 lounges also attract groups.*

## PENNSYLVANIA RESORTS

| | R | S | D | P | $ |
|---|---|---|---|---|---|

**Skytop Lodge**   178R (3S)    | 17 | 18 | 17 | 19 | $154 |
One Skytop, Skytop; (800) 345-7SKY; (717) 595-7401; FAX 595-9618
*M – The "lovely setting" of this sprawling, "genteel" and "low-key" "pick of the Poconos" is praised by all, and everyone agrees "there's lots to do", including "great golf", but some say "the indoors do not match the outdoors" and grumble about "bland food"; it's a "throwback to a bygone era."*

**Split Rock Resort**   350R (150S)    | 18 | 17 | 16 | 18 | $131 |
Lake Dr., Lake Harmony; (800) 255-7625; (717) 722-9111; FAX 722-8831
*M – Partisans say this Pocono resort on Lake Harmony is "what a lodge in the mountains should be", with "nonstop fun", "great sports facilities and staff", and good skiing in winter; others say it's a "bit tawdry" and complain of "terrible meals" and "dark", uncomfortable rooms – choose a cabin, lodge or condo if you can.*

**Sweetwater Farm\***   13R (4S)    | 25 | 23 | 23 | 21 | $156 |
Sweetwater Rd., Glen Mills; (215) 459-4711; FAX 358-4945
*U – This "absolutely charming" Colonial inn in western Delaware County is "all the things a bed-and-breakfast should be", with "lovely decor and beautiful, spacious, farmlike grounds"; it's "the perfect refuge from metropolitan strife", and even "great with a young family."*

# RHODE ISLAND

| R | S | D | P | $ |
|---|---|---|---|---|

**Atlantic Inn**  31R
| – | – | – | – | E |
|---|---|---|---|---|

High St., Block Island; (401) 466-5883; FAX 466-5678
*"Wind and salt air seem part of the decor" at this seasonal, "storybook" place overlooking Old Harbor, 20 minutes from the beach; a "majestic old inn" with croquet, tennis, a small farm and a porch to sip cocktails on at sunset, it inspires reviewers' raves: "truly wonderful."*

**Doubletree Hotel**  253R (17S)
| 17 | 17 | 16 | 18 | $133 |
|----|----|----|----|------|

(fka Sheraton Islander Inn)
Goat Island, Newport; (800) 528-0444; (401) 849-2600; FAX 846-7210
*M – Two minutes across the causeway to Newport, this high-rise island hotel "on the water" seems as though it should be peaceful, but some complain of a somewhat "rowdy" bar atmosphere; good recreational facilities, superb sunsets and "decent" renovated rooms are noteworthy.*

**Hotel Manisses\***  18R
| 20 | 19 | 20 | 19 | $144 |
|----|----|----|----|------|

Spring St., Block Island; (401) 466-2063; FAX 466-2858
*U – This island jewel, built in 1872, has a good restaurant, charming rooms and "casual elegance"; the romantic ambiance is heightened by stained glass, staff in period dress, and outdoor dining complete with vegetables picked from the garden and home-baked bread; reviewers say it's "top-notch" and "well worth a visit": everyone should see Block Island!*

**Inn at Castle Hill**  20R (2S)
| 21 | 21 | 22 | 22 | $163 |
|----|----|----|----|------|

Ocean Ave., Newport; (401) 849-3800
*M – The "sprawling lawn" down to Narragansett Bay and "the view, the view!" of the harbor are praised at this Victorian "mansion on a bluff" with its own private beach; some find it "memorable", others say "overrated"; rooms are "adequate" at best, and oddly, although the inn is open year-round, the restaurant isn't; P.S. don't miss the jazz brunch.*

**Inntowne Inn\***  26R (8S)
| 20 | 20 | 16 | 20 | $159 |
|----|----|----|----|------|

6 Mary St., Newport; (800) 457-7803; (401) 846-9200; FAX 846-1534
*M – The name says it all, because if you like being in the center of things, this "great" Colonial-style B&B is within "walking distance of town"; "pretty" rooms suffer from "raucous" street noise, but a rooftop deck, complimentary high tea and convenience are trade-offs that satisfy a loyal following.*

## RHODE ISLAND RESORTS | R | S | D | P | $ |

**Newport Harbor Hotel & Marina**   133R (1S)   | 17 | 17 | 15 | 16 | $140 |
(fka Treadway Newport Resort & Marina)
49 America's Cup Ave., Newport; (800) 955-2558; (401) 847-9000;
FAX 849-6380
*M – A comedy club, live jazz and "good harbor views" ("above the first
floor") are pluses at this motel-style Downtowner "in the thick of the
Newport scene", but most surveyors say that, in general, it's "nothing to
write home about."*

**1661 Inn, The**   39R                      | – | – | – | – | M |
1 Spring St., Block Island; (401) 466-2421; FAX 466-2858
*Authentic New England decor with antiques and paintings are what make
this 1870 inn "quaint" and "homey", but being on this rustic island, rife with
ponds and meadows, is "like being a million miles from the stresses and
strains of city life"; most rooms have ocean views; rates include buffet
breakfast plus "wine and nibbles."*

# SOUTH CAROLINA

**Hilton Head Island Hilton Resort** 324R (28S)  | 22 | 20 | 18 | 22 | $147 |
(fka Mariner's Inn)
23 Ocean Lane, Hilton Head Island; (800) 845-8001; (803) 842-8010;
FAX 842-4988
*U – We hear no complaints about this oceanfront resort on Hilton Head;
surveyors like everything from its "beautiful grounds" and "large,
comfortable rooms" to its "good low-country cooking", served by a "cordial"
young staff; with golf, tennis, a private beach and "great kids' activities", it
offers something for everyone, all at a fair price.*

**Hyatt Regency Hilton Head**  505R (31S)   | 22 | 21 | 20 | 22 | $167 |
Palmetto Dunes, Hilton Head Island; (800) 233-1234; (803) 785-1234;
FAX 842-4695
*U – "One of the best beaches" on Hilton Head is enough to make this
oceanfront resort popular, but it also has "great golf and fishing", "plush
interiors", "efficient service" and "beautiful views"; the hotel can be a "bit
noisy", but overall, most rate it "A-1."*

**Indigo Inn\*** 40R                        | 22 | 23 | 22 | 22 | $133 |
1 Maiden Lane, Charleston; (800) 845-7639; (803) 577-5900; FAX 577-0378
*U – This "well-kept" small hotel near Market Place – parts of which
date back to the 1850s – has a pretty lobby, "lovely period furniture",
"helpful" service and a "great" courtyard that's a pleasant setting for
breakfast and afternoon tea; despite solid ratings, some critics complain
of "dark, small rooms."*

**Jasmine House Inn**  8R (2S)              | – | – | – | – | M |
64 Hasell St., Charleston; (800) 845-7639; (803) 577-5900; FAX 577-0378
*The "real Southern McCoy", this antebellum mansion and carriage house
has just six rooms and two suites, but they're "huge and beautifully
decorated", not to mention dripping with romance and history; complimentary
breakfast and afternoon wine with hors d'oeuvres add to a pampering
ambiance that provides a restful getaway.*

## SOUTH CAROLINA RESORTS       | R | S | D | P | $ |

**John Rutledge House Inn**   19R (3S)       | – | – | – | – | E |
116 Broad St., Charleston; (800) 476-9741; (803) 723-7999;
FAX 720-2515
*This beautifully restored, pre-Revolutionary landmark in the heart of the
Historic District features 19 rooms, each furnished with antiques and period
reproductions that capture the elegance and grace of earlier times;
breakfast is the only meal served, but it's done in style, brought in on silver
trays with fresh flowers.*


**Kiawah Island Resort**   450R (300S)       | 22 | 21 | 19 | 23 | $164 |
Kiawah Beach Dr., Kiawah Island; (800) 845-2471; (803) 768-2121;
FAX 768-9339
*M – "Super golf" and tennis, "secluded beaches" and "beautifully natural"
surroundings (don't be surprised if "alligators snap at your door") are
highlights of this "lush tropical haven" near Charleston; with accommodations,
service and food equal to the scenery, it's a "great family resort."*


**Lodge Alley Inn**   93R (59S)       | 21 | 18 | 14 | 16 | $115 |
195 E. Bay St., Charleston,; (800) 845-1004; (803) 722-1611;
FAX 722-1611 x7777
*U – A "best value in the Historic District", this well-liked inn, carved out of
19th-century warehouse buildings, offers spacious rooms and suites (the
latter with full kitchens) that offer all the warmth and convenience of home;
and, there's all-American cuisine at the French Quarter restaurant.*


**Marriott's Hilton Head Resort**   338R (25S)       | 20 | 21 | 19 | 20 | $152 |
130 Shipyard Dr., Hilton Head Island; (800) 334-1881; (803) 842-2400;
FAX 842-9975
*U – "Not elegant but very comfortable", this convention-type hotel wins
mostly praise for its "lush grounds", "nice beach and pool" and other
facilities that offer "lots to see and do"; it's often overflowing with "groups
on package deals", but most say "join the crowd" and have "fun."*


**Mills House Hotel**   215R (21S)       | 21 | 21 | 20 | 20 | $142 |
115 Meeting St., Charleston; (800) 874-9600; (803) 577-2400;
FAX 722-2112
*U – Combining the "old-time elegance" of a renovated historic building with
modern amenities that meet the needs of tourist and business groups, this
centrally located midsize hotel is an example of "the Southland at its best";
fans consider it the reigning "Charleston queen"; though under Holiday Inn
management it bears no resemblance to that chain.*

383

## SOUTH CAROLINA RESORTS

| R | S | D | P | $ |

**Planters Inn***  41R (5S)   | 24 | 23 | 22 | 19 | $118 |
112 N. Market St., Charleston; (800) 845-7082; (803) 722-2345;
FAX 577-2125
*U – Nineteenth-century Southern charm mixes with European style and
elegance at this centrally located inn; fans consider it the "best in every
regard", from its "darling", period-style decor to its "attentive" service;
Roberts restaurant, a local fixture, also gets pretty high marks.*


**Seabrook Island Resort**  140S   | 22 | 20 | 17 | 20 | $169 |
1002 Landfall Way, Seabrook Island; (800) 845-2475; (803) 768-1000;
FAX 768-4922
*U – The "island itself is a treat", and most say this well-equipped resort is,
too; besides good golf, tennis and other sports facilities, it offers "endless
beaches" and plenty of "quiet"; only the kitchen is not up to snuff.*


**Sea Pines**  600S   | 23 | 21 | 20 | 22 | $167 |
Sea Pines, Hilton Head Island; (800) 845-6131; (803) 785-3333;
FAX 686-3325
*U – A "golfer's heaven" and pretty blissful for lovers of tennis, biking,
beachgoing and more, this sprawling granddaddy of Hilton Head resorts
offers "many different options" in terms of activities and accommodations;
even the smallest suite (a two-bedroom villa) has a full kitchen; though the
decor is only "standard" according to some, there's no denying that the
scenery's "gorgeous" and there's "plenty to do", which makes it a "great
family resort" in most people's books.*


**Vendue Inn**  26R (7S)   | – | – | – | – | M |
19 Vendue Range, Charleston; (800) 922-7900; (803) 577-7970
*Near the confluence of the Cooper and Ashley rivers in Charleston's lovely
Historic District, this former ugly-duckling warehouse is now a swan of an
inn; Oriental rugs, fresh flowers, breakfast on a silver tray, wine and
cheese in the afternoon, and a rooftop bar overlooking the harbor are
some of its pleasures; nearby shops and restaurants are pluses.*


**WESTIN RESORT, THE**  412R (29S)   | 24 | 23 | 23 | 25 | $175 |
(fka Inter-Continental Hilton Head)
Port Royal Plantation, 2 Grasslawn Ave., Hilton Head Island; (800) 228-3000;
(803) 681-4000; FAX 681-1087
*M – "Tops" on the island, this "luxurious" high rise – a modern take on a
1900s seaside resort – provides rooms overlooking the ocean or island,
"very good" golf, tennis and other sports facilities, and "excellent" food in
the Barony Grill; a few consider it "a little too big" to give personal service,
but most consider it "outstanding" and "worth" the high tab.*

## SOUTH CAROLINA RESORTS

| R | S | D | P | $ |

**Wild Dunes Resort**   250S

| 22 | 20 | 19 | 23 | $161 |

5757 Palm Blvd., Isle of Palms; (800) 845-8880; (803) 886-6000;
FAX 886-2916

*U – A "beautiful" location – oceanfront on a barrier island just 15 miles from historic Charleston – plus "great" golf and tennis facilities make this a "let's-repeat" kind of resort; the all-suites accommodations offer all the conveniences of home, including kitchen and laundry facilities; supervised programs for children add to its family appeal.*

# SOUTH DAKOTA

|  | R | S | D | P | $ |
|---|---|---|---|---|---|

**Franklin Hotel**   27R (15S)           | – | – | – | – | I |
700 Main St., Deadwood; (800) 688-1876; (605) 578-2241; FAX 578-3452
*"It's historic, all right", but some wish this turn-of-the-century Victorian*
*would speed up its ongoing and "long-overdue" renovation; for now, it's*
*"ok if quaint rusticity is your preference" or if you want to avail yourself of*
*the blackjack, poker and slot machines in the lobby.*

**Hotel Alex Johnson\***   137R (62S)      | 15 | 17 | 14 | 13 | $104 |
523 Sixth St., Rapid City; (800) 888-2539; (605) 342-1210; FAX 342-1210
*M – No doubt this 1920s Tudor-style hotel has "lots of character", but*
*opinion on its quality differs, with some praising the rooms, views and*
*"caring staff", and others warning "you'll be roughing it" in "depressing*
*and dark" surroundings; still, there aren't many options in Rapid City.*

**Palmer Gulch Lodge**   26S           | – | – | – | – | I |
Hwy. 244, Hill City; (800) 233-4331; (605) 574-2525; (605) 574-2574
*Only five miles from Mount Rushmore, this affordable lodge and motor*
*camp offers rustic cabins and activities including hiking, riding, swimming,*
*fishing, campfire programs and Native American dancing; the food's basic*
*at best, but it's nice eating by the stone fireplace or on the deck.*

# TENNESSEE

**Buckhorn Inn**   12R (6S)   | – | – | – | – | M |
2140 Tudor Mountain Rd., Gatlinburg; (615) 436-4668
*Guests find serenity and seclusion at this "beautiful and unique" inn, with magnificent views of the Great Smokies and Mt. LeConte; the main lodge is homey and romantic, with a massive stone fireplace, grand piano and big picture windows overlooking 35 acres of lovely grounds that include a fishing pond and rolling meadows; insiders say the individual cottages with fireplaces are "worth the money."*

**Fairfield Glade Resort**   200R (8S)   | – | – | – | – | I |
101 Peavine Rd., Fairfield Glade; (615) 484-7521; FAX 484-3788
*This large, quiet family resort with all the amenities nestles in the Cumberland Plateau near Lake St. George, two hours' drive from both Knoxville and Nashville; plain food and what a few surveyors call "run-down" facilities are offset by 12,000 acres of beautiful countryside; four golf courses, tennis, horseback riding, boating, and indoor and outdoor pools at budget rates.*

**Inn at Blackberry Farm**   25R   | – | – | – | – | E |
1471 W. Millers Cove Rd., Walland; (800) 862-7610; (615) 984-8166; FAX 983-5708
*Luxury and relaxation are yours at this 1940s country house adjoining Great Smoky Mountains National Park; it's furnished with fine art and antiques, cozy feather mattresses and comforters; full meeting facilities appeal to corporate types, but it's also popular for its tennis, swimming, bicycling, croquet, fishing or just relaxing on the veranda; room rates include meals with a Southern flair (jackets requested at dinner); BYO.*

# TEXAS

| R | S | D | P | $ |
|---|---|---|---|---|

**Barton Creek**  147R (3S)   | 23 | 21 | 21 | 24 | $150 |

8212 Barton Club Dr., Austin; (800) 77-CREEK; (512) 329-4000;
FAX 329-4597
*M – With its "great golf course" and a "pretty" setting that may be too good
("how can you keep your mind on your conference?"), this 4,000-acre
spread located in the Hill Country just outside the state capital gets better
marks as a conference center than a vacation destination; "nice with a
group", it's got a "cold feeling" as a resort – for "golf and conferences only."*

**Flying L Guest Ranch**  (36S)   | – | – | – | – | E |

HCR 1, Bandera; (800) 292-5134; (512) 796-3001; FAX 796-8455
*Urban cowpokes don't have to rough it at this resort 40 miles from San
Antonio – there are TVs and kitchens in all rooms, hot tubs and fireplaces
in some; meals, horseback riding, greens fees and the use of all facilities
are included in the price: don't forget the hayrides and old-west shows
each evening; yippee-yi-o.*

**Horseshoe Bay Resort &**   | 18 | 17 | 17 | 20 | $151 |
**Conference Center***  114R (4S)

1 Horseshoe Bay Blvd., Austin; (800) 531-5105; (512) 598-2511;
FAX 598-5338
*U – A serious golf resort (it has three 18-hole Robert Trent Jones Jr. courses,
no less); what our surveyors call "a world-class, cosmopolitan resort
hidden in Texas" also features 12 tennis courts, a huge spa, water gardens
and "beautiful grounds" that make it "perfect for business meetings" –
jet-setting execs are welcome to use the resort's private airport.*

**Lakeway Inn &**   | 19 | 18 | 17 | 20 | $127 |
**Conference Center**  253R (115S)

101 Lakeway Dr., Austin; (800) 525-3929; (512) 261-6600; FAX 261-7322
*U – "The views from this hotel are so beautiful you won't believe you're in
Texas", but in fact you're just 20 miles from Downtown Austin; all that plus
a "beautiful lake", "well-kept grounds", and noteworthy golf, tennis and
swimming make this "a good place for a conference"; however, our raters
are more impressed with the facilities than with the "so-so food."*

| R | S | D | P | $ |

**Mayan Dude Ranch\***   65R (2S)   | 20 | 21 | 15 | 18 | $102 |
Bandera; (512) 796-3312; (512) 796-8025
*U – Cowboy basics – horseback ridin', swimmin' and two-steppin' – on 400
acres at Bandera, the "Cowboy Capital of the World" in the Texas Hill
Country 50 miles from Old San Antone, make this the "best dude ranch in
Texas"; apparently the campfire chow doesn't make a big impression on
our respondents, but the western hospitality ("you're part of the family")
and "comfortable rooms and fun" put this ranch on the map.*

**Radisson South Padre Island\***   178R (50S)   | 19 | 17 | 17 | 19 | $140 |
500 Padre Blvd., South Padre Island; (800) 333-3333; (512) 761-6511;
FAX 761-1602
*U – "OK for a beach hotel" sums up the reaction to this "glitzy" hotel that
one surveyor says is "definitely for the disco crowd"; families and
sun-worshipers like the beach and "fun stuff for kids" ("crab races with
prizes"), but more staid types may find it "a weekend in purgatory."*

**Sheraton South Padre Island**   | 17 | 16 | 16 | 15 | $107 |
**Beach Resort\***   256R (56S)
310 S. Padre Blvd., South Padre Island; (800) 222-4010; (512) 761-6551;
FAX 761-6570
*U – In "a quiet spot" near the end of an often-boisterous island, this resort
boasts "good beach facilities" and "lots to do", including "para-sailing at the
beach cabana"; the staff is "friendly" and the food "surprisingly good", with
the "Friday seafood buffet" and Sunday brunch "overlooking the beach"
winning extra praise.*

**TREMONT HOUSE**   117R (6S)   | 26 | 24 | 23 | 24 | $131 |
2300 Ship's Mechanic Rd., Galveston; (800) 874-2300; (409) 763-0300;
FAX 763-1539
*U – The consensus favorite in Galveston, Tremont House is a "prime spot"
for the city's Mardi Gras social whirl, and by far the best hotel in the area;
this "great remodel of an old warehouse with high ceilings and windows" is
"quiet despite being in the heart of the Strand"; "elegant" decor and big
rooms with "nice extras" make it "great for a romantic getaway"; it's "not by
the beach, but who cares"; check out the "exquisite" condos.*

# UTAH

| R | S | D | P | $ |

**Brigham Street Inn***   9R (1S)     | 25 | 22 | 21 | 21 | $103 |
1135 E. South Temple, Salt Lake City; (801) 364-4461; FAX 532-3201
*U – "An exquisite small inn, if a bit impersonal"; nevertheless, reviewers
call this restored Victorian bed-and-breakfast "quite lovely and relaxing"
and "the best in Utah"; others add that "designer-showcase decorating
makes each room special, but there's not a real innkeeper."*

**Bryce Canyon Lodge**   114R (4S)     | 17 | 17 | 15 | 18 | $96 |
Bryce Canyon National Park; (801) 586-7686; FAX 586-3157
*U – Situated among the splendors of Bryce Canyon National Park, the
lodge's suites, cabins and motel rooms are deemed "adequate" though
"never intended to rival the Waldorf"; the rustic-style cabins, with gas
fireplaces and porches, are especially popular; at day's end, refuel with
hearty meals in the lodge's dining room.*

**Cliff Lodge, The**   532R (48S)     | 20 | 19 | 19 | 23 | $163 |
Entry 4, Snowbird Ski & Summer Resort, Little Cottonwood Canyon,
Snowbird; (800) 453-3000; (801) 521-6040; FAX 742-2211
*U – Snowbird's flagship hostelry is "a gourmet skier's delight", with
"location and service that can't be beat"; except for "small rooms", critics
find few drawbacks at this "remarkable hotel" housing four restaurants, a
superb full-service health spa and an in-house ski shop; summertime
programs – biking, hiking, fishing and tennis – equally impress.*

**Shadow Ridge Hotel**   153R     | – | – | – | – | M |
50 Shadow Ridge St., Park City; (800) 451-3031; (801) 649-4300; FAX 649-5951
*"Convenience to the lifts at Park City" and "good service" make up for
lackluster rooms at this condominium hotel; besides "the best, hottest
outdoor pool in the city", amenities include an indoor spa, billiard room,
entertainment center and underground parking.*

| R | S | D | P | $ |

**STEIN ERIKSEN LODGE**   115R (43S)   | 26 | 25 | 26 | 26 | $261 |
7700 Stein Way, Park City; (800) 453-1302; (801) 649-3700; FAX 649-5825
*U – "You don't even have to like skiing" to enjoy "a hotel as great as Utah*
*powder" (though the ski-in/ski-out access can't be beat); "beautiful rooms",*
*"excellent food" and "caring staff" make it "a resort to return to year after*
*year"; the price tag matches its "upscale" reputation: to avoid sticker-shock,*
*"go in the summer, when it's affordable."*

**Washington School Inn**   12R (3S)   | – | – | – | – | E |
543 Park Ave., Park City; (800) 824-1672; (801) 649-3800; FAX 649-3802
*Attention to detail distinguishes this beautifully restored 1889 B&B country*
*inn; guests revel in the "exquisite furnishings" and extra pampering on*
*which the inn prides itself; plush robes, full complimentary breakfast,*
*afternoon wine and cheese, piping hot whirlpool and relaxing sauna add*
*to the gracious atmosphere.*

# VERMONT

|  | R | S | D | P | $ |
|---|---|---|---|---|---|

**Basin Harbor Club**   136R (77S)   | 19 | 20 | 18 | 21 | $196 |
Basin Harbor Rd., Vergennes; (800) 622-4000; (802) 475-2311
*U – "Old-fashioned warmth and charm" abound at this "wonderful", "rustic"
family resort on Lake Champlain; rooms may be basic, but the activities,
grounds and setting of this seasonal spot – "like the places of our youth" –
make up for deficiencies, and then some; open mid-May through
mid-October.*

**Cortina Inn**   97R (6S)   | 18 | 19 | 20 | 18 | $130 |
HCR-34, U.S. Rte. 4, Killington; (800) 451-6108; (802) 773-3333; FAX 773-6948
*M – Convenient to Killington and Pico, this "pleasant, small" ski resort
draws a mixed clientele and mixed comments; on the downside are
"Spartan rooms" and, on weekends, skiers packed in "like sardines"; on the
upside are "exceptional food", "super tennis", "great service", sleigh rides
and a "beautiful setting" (though some claim it's "too far from the slopes.")*

**Equinox, The**   163R (17S)   | 20 | 20 | 19 | 21 | $159 |
Rte. 7A, Manchester Village; (800) 362-4747; (802) 362-4700;
FAX 362-1595
*M – A $13 million face-lift given this "grande dame" hasn't erased "an
attitude problem"; opinions vary widely, from "everything you want in a
charming resort" to "disappointing", "noisy" and "uncomfortable"; the
"stupendous" view, top golf and stocked pond are undeniable assets.*

**Hawk Inn & Mountain Resort\***   50R (6S)   | 23 | 22 | 21 | 22 | $164 |
Rte. 100, Plymouth; (800) 451-HAWK; (802) 672-3811; FAX 672-5067
*U – "Mountain and brook views", "gourmet dining" and a children's camp
are a few of the enticements at this "quiet" all-season resort on a lake near
Okemo and Killington ski areas; reviewers suggest renting a private house
or condo, although "the rooms at the inn" are also "beautifully decorated."*

**Hermitage Inn\***   29R   | 19 | 20 | 21 | 21 | $153 |
Coldbrook Rd., Wilmington; (802) 464-3511; FAX 464-2688
*U – A hunting preserve, "good" food and an award-winning wine cellar are
highlights at this "quaint and picturesque" inn complex near Mount Snow;
rooms vary – many are "small" and "simple" – but the "secluded location in
the woods" makes for a "quiet" getaway that's "lovely any time of the year."*

**Inn at Essex, The\***  97R (2S)  | 25 | 25 | 27 | 22 | $136 |
70 Essex Way, Essex Junction; (800) 727-4295; (802) 878-1100;
FAX 878-0063
*U – The fact that the New England Culinary Institute is based here means
that "perfect" food is yours at this three-year-old country inn, and that the
special packages include cooking classes; although the atmosphere is still
rather "new", many of the "huge", "delightful" Colonial-style rooms have
fireplaces;* N.B. *it may be overkill, but Ben & Jerry's factory is nearby.*

**Inn at Manchester, The\***  20R (2S)  | 22 | 21 | 20 | 19 | $122 |
Rte. 7A, Manchester Village; (802) 362-1793
*U – Near Bromley and Stratton skiing and great discount shopping, this
historic inn, built in 1880, is "small" but has "lots of country charm"; recent
renovations and new gardens add to the restful atmosphere, and the
included breakfast is "great for people who like waffles and ice cream."*

**INN AT SAWMILL FARM, THE**  21R (15S)  | 24 | 24 | 25 | 23 | $221 |
Mt. Snow Valley, W. Dover; (802) 464-8131; FAX 464-1130
*U – "Ah, romance" (and no children allowed); "plush and special", this
"quintessential" Relais & Chateaux inn set in an upscale barn in southern
Vermont remains "the ultimate in every respect": "great accommodations",
"congenial hosts", all-season activities and "food to die for" never fail to
please our surveyors, even though all these good things come at a price.*

**Middlebury Inn, The**  75R (4S)  | 18 | 18 | 18 | 18 | $127 |
14 Courthouse Sq., Middlebury; (800) 842-4666; (802) 388-4961; FAX 388-4563
*U – Built in 1827, this "charming old country inn" in the "perfect college
town" is "well appointed" and "quaint", with a porch overlooking the village
green; of the three buildings on the property, one is contemporary and less
interesting – so stick with the two originals.*

**Mountain Top Inn**  55R (20S)  | 18 | 19 | 18 | 21 | $165 |
Mountain Top Rd., Chittenden; (800) 445-2100; (802) 483-2311; FAX 483-6373
*M – "A rustic health camp for grown-ups", this cross between an inn and a
resort near Killington "focuses on the holistic approach to living"; a huge
lake with beach and boats, a "beautiful setting", "comfortable" rooms and
"superb" facilities – including a golf school – are praised; some feel the
food is "disappointing", others call it "excellent."*

## VERMONT RESORTS

| R | S | D | P | $ |
|---|---|---|---|---|

**Rabbit Hill Inn**   16R (4S)

| – | – | – | – | E |
|---|---|---|---|---|

Lower Waterford; (800) 76-BUNNY; (802) 748-5168
*Romance is everywhere, from the fainting couches, canopied beds and
fireplaces in the guest rooms to the lacy heart-shaped pillow (a gift) at this
exquisitely detailed, elegant inn in a tiny Vermont town; other pleasures
include a swimming pond, theme weekends, gazebos and porches, walks
along the Connecticut River, and gourmet dining and high tea.*

**SHELBURNE HOUSE, THE INN**
**AT SHELBURNE FARMS**   24R

| 23 | 23 | 24 | 23 | $195 |
|---|---|---|---|---|

Shelburne Farms, Shelburne; (802) 985-8498
*U – "On a 1,000-acre farm with dairy cows" and an "unbelievable setting on
Lake Champlain" near Burlington, as well as the Shelburne Museum, this
"lovely" 1899 inn will enchant anyone seeking serenity; the decor is "beautiful",
and the food is fresh and regional – "try their own extra-sharp cheddar."*

**Stratton Mountain Inn**
**& Village Lodge**   216R (4S)

| 17 | 17 | 15 | 18 | $150 |
|---|---|---|---|---|

Middle Ridge Rd., Stratton Mountain; (800) 777-1700; (802) 297-2500;
FAX 297-1778
*M – Enjoy slopeside ski-in/ski-out convenience from this "fun" inn and
newer lodge; the setting is a "wonderful Austrian-flavored village", and
although the rooms may be "college-dorm" level, thanks to a fine sports
center and interesting activities, most agree it's a "year-round winner."*

**Sugarbush Inn, The**   356R (310S)

| 20 | 21 | 20 | 20 | $161 |
|---|---|---|---|---|

Mountain Rd., Warren; (800) 451-4213; (802) 583-2301; FAX 583-3209
*U – This somewhat "isolated" all-season resort has invested $60 million
since 1988, producing "pleasant" accommodations in the main building and
in townhouses with fireplaces; great golf, horseback riding, a health club and
tennis school are available; tea, apples and cookies are "always waiting."*

**Topnotch at Stowe Resort & Spa** 107R (25S)

| 22 | 22 | 20 | 22 | $175 |
|---|---|---|---|---|

4000 Mountain Rd., Stowe; (800) 451-8686; (802) 253-8585; FAX 253-9263
*M – This "chic", award-winning, northern Vermont all-season resort is
"great any time of year"; the tennis center, spa, facilities and food are
indeed tops, but some take it down a notch because the exceptional
conference center makes it seem too "group-oriented."*

**Trapp Family Lodge**   93R (5S)        | 21 | 21 | 21 | 22 | $152 |
42 Trapp Hill Rd., Stowe; (800) 826-7000; (802) 253-8511; FAX 253-7864
*U – "The hills really are alive" at this "little Austria in northern Vermont", of*
The Sound of Music *fame; our reviewers' favorite things include "wonderful
family events", "an attentive staff", great tennis and trails, and "excellent"
food; most feel it's nice to be trapped here.*

**Woods at Killington Resort & Spa\***   108S   | 16 | 16 | 14 | 16 | $137 |
R.R. 1, Killington; (800) 633-0127; (802) 422-3100; FAX 422-4070
*M – Scores have slipped badly at this once-praised resort complex,
although all-condominium lodging, moderate prices and lots of packages
still keep it busy with skiers in season; it's convenient to Killington and has
fishing, golf, tennis, swimming and other warm-weather activities as well,
but our surveyors tend to be disappointed.*

**Woodstock Inn & Resort, The**   146R (7S)        | 21 | 22 | 20 | 22 | $170 |
14 The Green, Woodstock; (800) 448-7900; (802) 457-1100; FAX 457-3824
*U – Extensive renovations and a new tavern wing with fireplaced rooms
have kept up the quality at this "elegant" Rockefeller-built resort "straight
out of a calendar"; rocking chairs overlooking the green, hot-buttered rum
and a toll-house-cookie tea are small delights – larger ones include the
"special" town, the big sports center down the road, "great" golf and
"outstanding" food; seasonal crowds can be a negative.*

# VIRGINIA

**Ashby Inn\*** 10R          | 20 | 24 | 24 | 21 | $122 |
Rtes. 701 & 759, Paris; (703) 592-3900; FAX 592-3781
*U – A rural location near Virginia's Hunt Country makes this historic little inn "great for a romantic getaway"; with its "cozy dining room", "fabulous food" and "great hosts", it's also good for small business retreats; one fan calls it a "Little Washington cum value, sans hype."*


**Boar's Head Inn** 173R (10S)     | 20 | 20 | 19 | 21 | $146 |
Rte. 250, Charlottesville; (800) 476-1988; (804) 296-2181; FAX 977-1306
*M – "Southern hospitality" in a "beautiful setting" are the claims to fame of this "charming" country inn, which fans cite as a "chintz-lover's paradise" and for its "lovely Southern cooking" and sports facilities; unconvinced reviewers say that the "help could be friendlier" and the premises are "somewhat dreary"; pluses include a tennis complex, workout facility and suites with fireplaces.*


**HOMESTEAD, THE** 600R (75S)    | 22 | 25 | 22 | 25 | $217 |
U.S. Rte. 220, Hot Springs; (800) 468-7747; (703) 839-5500; FAX 839-7656
*M – An examplar of the grand hotels of "an era past", this "gorgeous" "formal" mountainside spa and retreat (for both families and executives) indulges visitors with a "luxurious" array of activities, including its famous hot springs, horseback riding, tennis, skiing and swimming in pools both indoors and out; one surveyor's "elegant", however, is another's "frumpy" – "rooms can be Spartan", and "everything (golf, riding, spas) costs extra"; in sum, this "old-world tradition resort deserves to be experienced", before deciding whether it's your homestead.*

**INN AT LITTLE WASHINGTON** 12R (3S) | 27 | 28 | 29 | 25 | $269 |
Middle & Main Sts., Washington; (703) 675-3800;FAX 675-3100
*U – For "an experience of a lifetime", this "elegant, welcoming" little English
country house of a hotel bewitches our surveyors with its "poetic beauty"
and "restorative pampering"; superlatives abound: the "best food in the
U.S.A.", "stunning romantic rooms", a "pretty country setting" and "perfect
service" make it "worth every penny"; "a place fit for a king", "sheer bliss",
"a great way to celebrate a special occasion" (but do book well in advance); it
ranks No. 2 among all resorts and inns in this Survey and No. 1 for food in
our Washington, D.C. Restaurant Survey – you can't do better than this.*

**Kingsmill Resort &** | 22 | 22 | 21 | 24 | $163 |
**Conference Center** 350R (120S)
1010 Kingsmill Rd., Williamsburg; (800) 832-5665; (804) 253-1703;
FAX 253-8246
*M – Nearby Busch Gardens and likewise owned by Anheuser Busch, this
"quite nice" resort and luxury community enjoys a "beautiful" setting on the
James River, with a world-class golf course and proximity to Colonial
Williamsburg; our surveyors can't decide, however, whether it's "Southern
gentility" personified or a "time warp, and the past wasn't good"; solid
ratings suggest it's worth a try.*

**Lansdowne Conference Resort\*** 319R (17S) | 23 | 24 | 21 | 24 | $142 |
44050 Woodridge Pkwy., Leesburg; (800) 541-4801; (703) 729-8400;
FAX 729-4096
*U – "Lovely grounds", a "superb staff" and a "well-equipped health club"
are a big boon to this "top-notch if rather barren" conference center and
resort; good food (desserts are "phenomenal") and "excellent" golf earn
bonus points.*

**Manor House at Ford's Colony** 110R (25S) | – | – | – | – | M |
King Carter Dr., Irvington; (800) 843-3746; (804) 438-5000; FAX 438-5222
*In the pine woods on the northerly outskirts of Williamsburg, this Oz-like
resort and conference center offers exemplary condos and recreational
facilities including fireplaces and kitchenettes that are good for families,
plus a pair of 18-hole golf courses, exercise facilities, tennis courts and a
pool; the restaurant is also excellent.*

**Tides Inn, The**   111R (6S)                          | 20 | 22 | 20 | 21 | $174 |
King Carter Dr., Irvington; (800) 843-3746; (804) 438-5000; FAX 438-5222
*U – On Chesapeake Bay at the tip of Virginia's remote and romantic
Northern Neck, this "lovely" family-run and family-oriented resort has
inspired a loyal, lifetime clientele, who return year after year to golf, swim
and sail; rooms are "pretty" but "could use some refurbishing"; with "great"
"Southern cooking", some feel that "eating is the main activity" at the
proverbial "good place to do nothing."*

**Williamsburg Hospitality House**   309R (9S)   | 21 | 21 | 20 | 20 | $135 |
415 Richmond Rd., Williamsburg; (800) 932-9192; (804) 229-4020;
FAX 220-1560
*M – A slightly offbeat setting closer to William and Mary than to Colonial
Williamsburg renders this "not the best location, but it's close enough to
"walk"; the wisdom on the rooms and food, overall, is "good."*

**WILLIAMSBURG INN**   232R (26S)               | 23 | 23 | 23 | 24 | $179 |
S. Francis St., Williamsburg; (800) HISTORY; (804) 229-1000
*M – "Graciousness lives" in this magnificent yet unpretentious Georgian
mansion which, though located in the heart of Colonial Williamsburg (and
run by the foundation), evinces Continental grandeur and Southern
gentility second to none; "you couldn't ask for a better base" for exploring
Williamsburg, Jamestown and Yorktown; bonus points go to the "plantation
breakfast" on Sunday, and it's "a must-see at Christmas."*

# WASHINGTON

**Captain Whidbey Inn**  32R (9S)       | 18 | 21 | 20 | 21 | $118 |
2072 W. Captain Whidbey Inn Rd., Coupeville; (800) 366-4097;
(206) 678-4097; FAX 678-4110
*U – A "very rustic" madrona-log and knotty pine lodge that has been a*
*welcome "stopover for boaters" since 1907; situated on Penn Cove, source*
*of the Northwest's most famous mussels, this "pleasant", "relaxing",*
*"romantic" retreat has new owners, who pose no threat to its "low-key"*
*atmosphere.*

**Inn at Semiahmoo, The***  198R (12S)       | 23 | 20 | 20 | 23 | $147 |
9565 Semiahmoo Pkwy., Blaine; (800) 854-2608; (206) 371-2000;
FAX 371-5490
*U – Situated on a sand spit virtually astride the Canadian border, this*
*destination resort and corporate retreat (on the site of an old salmon*
*cannery) "is surrounded on all sides by salt water and snowcapped*
*mountains"; the lodge-style rooms are "spacious"; besides boating, there's*
*golf, tennis, swimming, etc.*

**Kalaloch Lodge***  58R (40S)       | 15 | 17 | 16 | 20 | $106 |
Olympic National Park, Hwy. 101, Forks; (206) 962-2271
*U – The rocky Pacific shore of the Olympic Peninsula will never be*
*mistaken for Maui or Bermuda, but for those seeking a unique experience,*
*the "comfortable, rustic, modern cabins" offer "beautiful views"; an*
*"attentive staff" takes care of basics; the first rule of real estate is fulfilled*
*here: "location! location! location!"*

**Lake Quinault Lodge**  89R (2S)       | 18 | 18 | 19 | 22 | $114 |
South Shore Rd., Olympic National Forest, Lake Quinault; (206) 288-2571;
FAX 288-2415
*U – This "historical old inn" is in the fabled middle of nowhere; like most*
*such "rustic" places, the "comfortable and cozy", if "basic", "rooms could be*
*improved, but not the views"; "gorgeous surroundings", "surprisingly good*
*food" and "wonderful trails" also contribute to a "great place to relax."*

| R | S | D | P | $ |

**Rosario Resort*** 179R (30S)  | 17 | 17 | 18 | 20 | $144 |
1 Rosario Way, Eastsound, Orcas Island; (800) 562-8820; (206) 376-2222;
FAX 376-3680
*M – In the lee of the San Juan Islands, this "remote", private estate-cum-resort inspires mixed reviews: though the view is "incredible", the rooms are filled with "mobile-home–style furniture"; lots of activities and the newer, larger dormitory-style rooms make this a "great family resort", but that the service and food may be less than stellar.*

**SALISH LODGE** 92R (4S)  | 25 | 24 | 24 | 23 | $173 |
37807 SE Snoqualmie - Fall City Rd., Snoqualmie; (800) 826-6124;
(206) 888-2556; FAX 888-9634
*U – Clinging to the edge of the falls, this legendary retreat was completely renovated by new owners in 1988, then reborn as the haunting centerpiece of* Twin Peaks; *the "stupendous breakfast" and "breathtaking views" are joined by "wonderful service" and the opportunity to "drink champagne in your private whirlpool by the fireplace overlooking the waterfall"; the result: a "charming place", "excellent, outstanding in every respect."*

**Sun Mountain Lodge*** 50R (8S)  | 21 | 22 | 20 | 23 | $132 |
Peterson Lake Rd., Winthrop; (800) 572-0493; (509) 996-2211; FAX 996-3133
*U – In summer, drive one of America's most scenic mountain roads (the North Cascades Highway) to the lodge, then head off into the scenery either on foot or horseback; in winter, when the highway is closed, the "excellent cross-country ski trails" will provide you with more views than you can absorb; atop a 360-degree-view perch, this cross between country modern and peeled-log "rustic" provides access to all the pleasures of the northern Cascades.*

| R | S | D | P | $ |

**GREENBRIER, THE**   695R (47S)   | 25 | 26 | 24 | 27 | $238 |
White Sulphur Springs; (800) 624-6070; (304) 536-1110; FAX 536-7834
*M – "Romantic" and "charming", "elegant" and "expensive", this grande dame
of country resorts is famed for its quintessential Southern ambiance and
hospitality and "luxury you don't see anymore"; a location lovely enough to
be "a national park" provides the setting for service "so good it's almost
embarrassing"; activities range from hiking and horseback riding to ice
skating and fishing, and include "great golfing" and the famous spa; though a
few complain that it's "stuffy" and "showing its age", for most surveyors, they
"don't get better than this"; ergo, many corporations and trade associations
use it as a top execs' retreat.*

# WISCONSIN

**Abbey, The**   358R (24S)                  | 17 | 18 | 17 | 19 | $131 |
Fontana Blvd., Fontana; (800) 558-2405; (414) 275-6811; FAX 275-3264
*U – Just outside of Lake Geneva, this rustic hotel is currently under
renovation – a good thing, too, because while* Survey *participants praise
the "first-class spa", "gigantic fireplaces" and "relaxing" atmosphere of this
sprawling facility, they complain that it's as "dark as a cave", with "small",
"tacky" rooms and "friendly but inept" service – definitely "past its prime."*

**Americana Lake Geneva Resort**   200R (5S)   | 16 | 15 | 15 | 17 | $110 |
Hwy. 50 E., Lake Geneva; (800) 558-3417; (414) 248-8811; FAX 248-3192
*M – Lovely grounds, good golf courses and pleasant surroundings could
make this former Playboy Club a winner, and some call it a "great family
place", especially for skiing; but others find it a "run-down" "disaster" in
need of "renovation or demolition"; the resort has great potential if a major
upgrade takes place.*

**AMERICAN CLUB, THE**   237R (2S)          | 25 | 24 | 23 | 24 | $171 |
Highland Dr., Kohler; (800) 344-2838; (414) 457-8000; FAX 457-0299
*U – Few hotels or resorts are destinations for their plumbing, but plumbing
manufacturer Kohler owns this "oasis of luxury" in "nowhere Wisconsin",
and not surprisingly, the "state-of-the-art" bathroom/minispas are "to die
for"; the careful staff provides an "almost perfect" "European" experience;
this is a good spot to relax "for a day or two by yourself", but you don't
need to be inactive, since there's an indoor sports complex plus a
championship golf course and cross-country ski trails.*

**Gordon Lodge***   40R (6S)               | 19 | 19 | 19 | 21 | $138 |
1420 Pine Dr., Bailey's Harbor; (414) 839-2331
*U – You almost feel as if you're "back in summer camp" at this "quiet and
relaxing" little Door County resort on Lake Michigan, complete with villas at
the water's edge and cottages set in pine forests; to some it feels too much
like a camp, given the price, but ratings show most people are more than
satisfied; a recent renovation upped the comfort level.*

## WISCONSIN RESORTS                    | R | S | D | P | $ |

**Heidel House Resort, The\***   200R (80S)      | 19 | 18 | 19 | 18 | $116 |
643 Illinois Ave., Green Lake; (800) 472-2812; (414) 294-3344; FAX 294-6128
*U – A new five-story main lodge opened in June 1992 on this 20-acre
estate set on the shore of "beautiful" Green Lake, the deepest body of
water in Wisconsin; the "countrylike grounds", "professional staff", "good
food" and location 90 miles northwest of Milwaukee make this an attractive
weekend-getaway destination, with or without the kids.*

**Lake Lawn Lodge**   284R (20S)      | 17 | 17 | 17 | 19 | $118 |
Hwy. 50, Delevan; (800) 338-5253; (414) 728-5511; FAX 728-2347
*U – "Good value" and "lots of activities", especially for the little ones, make
this rustic lakefront lodge popular with families; "genuine Indian graves"
are nearby, and there's a toboggan slide that's "fun for kids" in the winter,
but despite ongoing renovations, some say there's still room for "major
improvements", because the resort is definitely showing its age.*

**Lakewoods Resort & Lodge**   91R (64S)      | – | – | – | – | E |
H.C. 60, Cable; (800) 255-5937; (715) 794-2561; FAX 794-2553
*This out-of-the-way historic lodge was built in 1907, then rebuilt in 1985;
situated on 3,200-acre Lake Namakagon in the Chequenugon National
Forest, it is a nature lover's delight, with fishing, boating, hiking and
bicycling in summer, and ice skating, cross-country and downhill skiing,
and snowmobiling in winter; condos and cottages are also available.*

**Olympia Resort**   413R (136S)      | 16 | 15 | 14 | 16 | $100 |
1350 Royale Mile Rd., Oconomowoc; (800) 558-9573; (414) 567-0311;
FAX 567-5934
*M – A "long way from Mt. Olympus", this aging modern resort near the
beautiful Kettle Moraine State Forest "needs an update", but prices are
"reasonable"; "many activities" are provided, including two cinemas and "ski
facilities for beginners"; our correspondents report that, after some financial
difficulties, the place is "trying hard to make a comeback"; stay tuned.*

# WYOMING

| R | S | D | P | $ |

**Colter Bay Village\*** 209R    | 17 | 18 | 16 | 19 | $82 |
Grand Teton National Park, Moran; (307) 543-2811
*U – Families enjoy this "beautiful" mountain retreat near the shores of
Jackson Lake, featuring cabins that are "charming", "comfortable" and "well
equipped"; facilities include the Chuckwagon restaurant, a general store,
post office and laundry; open mid-May through September.*

**Jackson Hole Racquet Club\*** 125R    | 22 | 21 | 20 | 24 | $156 |
Star Rte. 3647, Jackson Hole; (800) 443-8616; (307) 733-3990;
FAX 733-5551
*M – Our surveyors mostly find the fully equipped (kitchen, TV,
washer/dryer, fireplace) units at this condo resort near Yellowstone
Park "classy", but a few retort "cold and overrated"; sporting types
appreciate the "good" 18-hole golf course, tennis and racquetball
courts, heated pool and health club.*

**Jackson Lake Lodge** 385R (10S)    | 20 | 20 | 19 | 22 | $142 |
Hwy. 89, Grand Teton National Park, Moran; (307) 543-2811; FAX 543-2869
*M – "Deer and moose greet you" and there are "magnificent views of the
Tetons", especially sunsets watched from the Mural Room restaurant; a
recent guest room renovation should quell many mutters about Spartan
accommodations; open June through September.*

**Jenny Lake Lodge** 30R (5S)    | 22 | 23 | 23 | 22 | $232 |
Hwy. 89, Grand Teton National Park, Moran; (307) 733-4647
*U – "Almost heaven" in "gorgeous wooded surroundings" near Grand
Teton and Yellowstone National Parks; "reserve early" to enjoy "a civilized
way to camp"; "food is homey and delicious"; "attractive cabins" sport
"western elegance"; the ultimate in privacy makes it "the kind of place to
spend a honeymoon or anniversary"; open June through September.*

| R | S | D | P | $ |

**Moose Head Ranch**   (14S)          | – | – | – | – | M |
Jackson Hole; (307) 733-3141
*"Good horses and good people" make this "rustic" ranch resort "a glorious
place to cowboy"; completely surrounded by Grand Teton National Park,
the ranch caters to families eager for lots of time in the saddle; come
dinnertime, the cook serves up gourmet grub in the lodge dining room;
open mid-June through August; no plastic.*

**Old Faithful Inn**   325R (2S)          | 17 | 18 | 17 | 21 | $116 |
Yellowstone National Park; (307) 344-7311
*M – It's "always crowded in anticipation of the next geyser", but visitors find
the inn "something of a disappointment"; rooms are merely "adequate" and
"overpriced", while the food "should be better"; still, many enjoy this place
for the "wonderful" 1904 log architecture with its soaring central lobby and
"amazing location"; open May through mid-October.*

**Paradise Guest Ranch**   (18S)          | – | – | – | – | M |
Buffalo; (307) 684-7876
*Horseback riding, fishing, swimming, chuckwagon BBQs and overnight
pack trips keep guests busy at this first-class dude ranch near the Big Horn
Mountains; younger buckaroos have their own specialized programs and
private playground; log cabins feature fireplace and patio, and family-style
meals are served in the rustic dining room; open June through September.*

**Ranch at Ucross, The**   33R          | – | – | – | – | M |
2673 U.S. Hwy. 14E, Clearmont; (800) 447-0194; (307) 737-2281; FAX 737-2211
*Rustic meets modern to create "city-slicker tacky" at this "glitzy" resort and
conference center southeast of Sheridan; outdoor enthusiasts can try their
hand at big-game hunting, skeet, horseback riding, snowmobiling and
fishing, then chow down with a gourmet meal in the ranch dining room, and
hit the sack in either the historic ranch house or more modern annex.*

**R Lazy S Ranch**   12R          | – | – | – | – | M |
Teton Village; (307) 733-2655
*You won't be bored at this family-owned dude ranch bordered by the
Snake River; a central lodge is surrounded by log cabins; there's a
complete riding program plus trout fishing, white-water rafting, water skiing
and swing dancing; open mid-June through September; weekly rates only.*

## WYOMING RESORTS

| R | S | D | P | $ |
|---|---|---|---|---|

**Roosevelt Lodge**   80R

| – | – | – | – | VI |

Yellowstone National Park; (307) 344-7311
*Once a favorite campsite for Teddy Roosevelt, the log cabins are now among the simplest (and cheapest) within Yellowstone Park; there are few frills save a dining room, a lounge and a gift shop; horseback and stagecoach rides, plus chuckwagon dinner cookouts, score points.*

**Snow King Resort\***   235R (31S)

| 16 | 16 | 16 | 17 | $118 |

400 E. Snow King Ave., Jackson Hole; (800) 522-5464; (307) 733-5200; FAX 733-4086
*U – Skiers find it hard to resist a "ski mountain at your door", and Snow King is no exception; the mountain rivals big peaks elsewhere but is "always empty", and rooms provide views of the towering Tetons; amenities include two restaurants, a heated pool, sauna and game room.*

**SPRING CREEK RANCH**   116R (80S)

| 25 | 20 | 23 | 23 | $190 |

1800 Spirit Dance Rd., Jackson Hole; (800) 443-6139; (307) 733-8833; FAX 733-1524
*U – Only "mediocre service" mars this otherwise-luxurious resort; "huge rooms" include lodgepole furniture, stone fireplaces, cable TV and refrigerators; visitors rave over the "spectacular view of the Jackson Hole valley" and applaud the Contemporary Western cuisine of The Granary restaurant; open year-round for horseback riding, skiing, fishing and tennis.*

**Teton Pines Resort**   20R (16S)

| – | – | – | – | E |

3450 Clubhouse, Jackson Hole; (800) 238-2223; (307) 733-1005; FAX 733-2860
*A "beautiful setting and good golf" make this a favorite mountain getaway, intimate and "homey"; tennis, summer hiking and fishing (in a stocked pond), plus a fine Italian restaurant, outdoor pool and whirlpool add to the pleasure.*

**Wort Hotel\***   60R (5S)

| 17 | 18 | 16 | 18 | $119 |

50 N. Glenwood, Jackson; (800) 322-2727; (307) 733-2190; FAX 733-2067
*U – "Don't let the name fool you – in Jackson Hole it's the place to stay"; surveyors agree that this "lovely" hotel in the heart of Jackson boasts "beautiful, large rooms", "excellent service" and "good value"; the location "near great shopping" is tops, and the Silver Dollar Bar (inlaid with 2,032 uncirculated 1921 silver dollars) is "one-of-a-kind – don't miss it"; free airport transportation will help you get there.*

# ALPHABETICAL
# DIRECTORY OF SPAS

# TOP 10 U.S. SPAS*

## (In order of rating)

| | |
|---|---|
| 27 – Doral Saturnia | Florida |
| Golden Door | California |
| 24 – Canyon Ranch in Berkshires | Massachusetts |
| Canyon Ranch | Arizona |
| 23 – La Costa | California |
| Rancho La Puerta | California |
| 22 – Sonoma Mission Inn | California |
| 20 – Bonaventure Resort & Spa | Florida |
| Safety Harbor Spa | Florida |
| Norwich Inn | Connecticut |

**BEST OVERALL**

Doral Saturnia
Golden Door
Canyon Ranch in Berkshires
Canyon Ranch, AZ
La Costa
Rancho La Puerta
Sonoma Mission Inn
Bonaventure Resort & Spa
Safety Harbor Spa
Norwich Inn

**BEST VALUES**

New Age Health Spa
Murrieta Hot Springs
Rancho La Puerta
Bonaventure Resort & Spa
Sonoma Mission Inn
Oaks at Ojai
Norwich Inn
La Costa
Safety Harbor Spa
Harbor Island Spa

\*      \*      \*

**Best Rooms**

28 – Doral Saturnia
26 – Golden Door
23 – La Costa
Canyon Ranch in Berkshires
22 – Canyon Ranch, AZ
Rancho La Puerta
21 – Sonoma Mission Inn
20 – Gurney's Inn
Norwich Inn
19 – Bonaventure Resort & Spa

**Best Dining**

26 – Doral Saturnia
Golden Door
24 – Canyon Ranch in Berkshires
Canyon Ranch
23 – Sonoma Mission Inn
Rancho La Puerta
22 – La Costa
21 – Safety Harbor Spa
20 – Bonaventure Resort & Spa
Norwich Inn

---

\* Based on overall ratings derived by averaging ratings for rooms, service, dining and public facilities, this list excludes places with voting too low to be reliable.

# SPAS

## Best Service

**28** – Golden Door
**27** – Doral Saturnia
**25** – Canyon Ranch
Canyon Ranch in Berkshires
**23** – Rancho La Puerta
La Costa
**22** – Sonoma Mission Inn
**21** – Safety Harbor Spa
**20** – Bonaventure Resort & Spa
Norwich Inn

## Best Public Facilities

**28** – Doral Saturnia
**27** – Golden Door
**26** – Canyon Ranch in Berkshires
**25** – Canyon Ranch
**24** – La Costa
**23** – Rancho La Puerta
**22** – Sonoma Mission Inn
**20** – Bonaventure Resort & Spa
Safety Harbor Spa
Norwich Inn

| R | S | D | P | $ |

**Ashram Retreat, The\*** 5R   | 16 | 23 | 20 | 18 | $302 |
PO Box 8009, Calabasas, CA; (818) 222-6900; FAX 310-455-2572
*M – Accommodations are "rustic and casual" at this intimate retreat in California's Santa Barbara Mountains above Malibu, complete with springs and rolling hills for long meditative hikes; it's "a cross between boot camp and a New Age family" place – they really work your butt off, from 6 AM till supper; you're bound to lose weight and shape up with all the exercise and sticking to a tasty raw-food diet (not haute cuisine); a caring staff headed by Drs. Anne Marie Bennstrom and Catharine Hedeberg help ensure your well-being; one-week minimum stay.*

**Bonaventure Resort & Spa** 378R (96S)   | 19 | 20 | 20 | 20 | $183 |
250 Racquet Club Rd., Fort Lauderdale, FL; (800) 327-8090;
(305) 389-3300; FAX 384-0063
*M – Particularly popular with convention-goers, this "beautiful spot" is an all-around resort plus a spa, with great golf and an equestrian center, among other "gorgeous facilities"; fans laud the "lovely accommodations", "friendly staff" and fine "spa cuisine"; detractors say it "needs a redo – but with an herbal wrap you can't see anything anyway", and current renovations may address that problem.*

**Bon Reussite Resort** 40R (fka Bermuda Inn)　| – | – | – | – | E |
43019 N. Sierra Hwy., Lancaster, CA; (800) HEALTHR; (805) 942-1493;
FAX 942-7115
*With a name that means "good results" in French, this informal spa offers
resort-style sports and physical activities – there's an additional charge for
all spa pampering services; it's known as a nonregimented, recreational
reducing spa for those who aren't looking for luxury; the location in the high
Mohave Desert is definitely a treat for city-stressed nerves.*

**Cal-A-Vie, the Ultimate Spa\*** 24R　　| 24 | 26 | 23 | 23 | $422 |
2249 Somerset Rd., Vista, CA; (619) 945-2055; FAX 630-0074
*U – A European country-villa setting of "rustic elegance" in the Southern
California desert that caters to an exclusive clientele who call it "the best
way to reduce stress" and "totally self-indulgent"; rooms and service are
"brilliant but a little sedate"; the one-week minimum stay will make up for
months of overworking, but remember – you need to work hard to afford
this place.*

**CANYON RANCH**　151R (41S)　　| 22 | 25 | 24 | 25 | $310 |
8600 E. Rockcliff Rd., Tucson, AZ; (800) 742-9000; (602) 749-9000;
FAX 749-1646
*U – "Pampering with an iron fist" is the specialty of this "awesome" high-
desert destination spa known to "cater to fitness more than beauty";
compliments are given to the "wonderful facilities, classes and services"
and to a "great staff"; the cognoscenti suggest it's for "serious athletes and
dieters", but you may get the feeling that some guests are more into deals
than exercise.*

**CANYON RANCH**　　　　　　　| 23 | 25 | 24 | 26 | $277 |
**IN THE BERKSHIRES**　120R (24S)
91 Kemble St., Lenox, MA; (800) 742-9000; (413) 637-4100; FAX 637-0057
*M – "Expensive but well worth it because of the great workout", "wonderful"
facilities and "exceptionally good" food; the attractive premises were
designed by the same architect who did the Doral Saturnia; detractors,
who liken the operation to a grown-up summer camp, say the "instructors
are not as talented as Tucson's and a little more stuck up"; given the
paucity of spas in the Northeast, however, who's complaining?*

**Deerfield Manor Spa\*** 22R | 16 | 17 | 17 | 15 | $143 |
RD 1, Rte. 402, East Stroudsburg, PA; (800) 852-4494; (717) 223-0160
*M – The mountainous northeastern Pennsylvania countryside can do as much to help you relax from daily stress as the spa program at this relatively inexpensive summer-only facility; fans find this "homey and unpretentious" place "marvelous", though "sans sex appeal"; the country walks, outdoor pool and "proximity to NYC make this a good bet", but the fact is "there are much better spas."*

**DORAL SATURNIA** | 28 | 27 | 26 | 28 | $308 |
**INTERNATIONAL SPA RESORT** 48S
8755 NW 36th St., Miami, FL; (800) 331-7768; (305) 593-6030;
FAX 591-9266
*U – "A spa like none other", this "heaven on earth" is a full-service resort, not just a destination spa; the bottom line is its "great food" – "you'll never know you're dieting" – a "staff that excels at service", "incredible rooms" and a beautiful setting that even makes exercise bearable; "excellent in every respect" and "fabulous if you can afford it" – that's why it copped the honors as No. 1 spa in our* Survey; *P.S. the option of using the adjacent golf course and Doral Ocean Beach Resort facilities adds appeal for non-spa participations and a variation on a theme for spa-goers.*

**GOLDEN DOOR** 39R | 26 | 28 | 26 | 27 | $415 |
777 Deer Springs Rd., San Marcos, CA; (619) 744-5777; FAX 471-2393
*U – A close second to the Doral Saturnia, it's "first-class in every area", according to our surveyors, with "the best thought-out programs and services", very personal attention and fabulous rooms and food; most of the year, the programs are for women only, but men are welcome for a few hard-to-reserve weeks every quarter; one-week minimum stay; sure, it's expensive, but the* Who's Who *clientele consider their time and money spent here, spent well.*

**Greenhouse, The\*** 37R (21S) | 27 | 27 | 25 | 25 | $268 |
1171 107th St., Grand Prairie, TX; (817) 640-4000; FAX 649-0422
*U – The "very best in comfort and luxury" is offered at this women-only oasis incongruously set in a suburban Dallas office park; however, "great food", "wonderful treatment and fabulous attention" await, and more than half the rooms are suites; with a choice of three weight-loss regimens, you're not forced into a starvation program during your one-week minimum stay.*

# SPAS

**Green Mountain at Fox Run**   25R   | – | – | – | – | E |
Fox Lane, Ludlow, VT; (800) 448-8106; (802) 228-8885
*Not for pampering, this women-only dormitory-style facility offers an
educational experience in weight and health management, with workshops
on compulsive overeating, recovering from a liquid diet and managing food
cravings – and how to take the program home; one-week minimum stay.*

**Gurney's Inn Resort & Spa**   125R (17S)   | 20 | 19 | 18 | 20 | $217 |
(aka International Health & Beauty Spa)
Old Montauk Hwy., Montauk, NY; (800) 8GURNEYS; 516) 668-2345;
FAX 668-3576
*M – The only spa on Long Island, Gurney's for many years has been a
near-monopoly favored for its location, its views of the Atlantic Ocean and
its indoor saltwater pool; however, comments include "rooms are large, but
the food is so bad that you don't need the spa cuisine", and "it's very
disturbing to get a massage and hear the water pipes banging in the wall";
still, for NYers used to being abused, "this is the place to be rubbed,
scrubbed, peeled and pampered."*

**Harbor Island Spa Resort**   172R (107S)   | – | – | – | – | E |
7900 Larry Paskow Way, North Bay Village, FL; (800) 772-7546;
(305) 751-7561; FAX 754-6244
*Destroyed by Hurricane Andrew, this "sleeper" of a spa located on a
private island in Biscayne Bay is currently being rebuilt and, with luck,
should reopen in time for the 1993-94 winter season.*

**Heartland Retreat***   14R (1S)   | 19 | 24 | 19 | 18 | $165 |
Rte. 1, Gilman, IL; (800) 545-4853; (815) 683-2182; FAX 683-2144
*M – In the heartland south of Chicago, this converted farm offers a respite
from busy city life; some find the "rustic" quality appealing, the vegetarian
food "innovative" and the staff, as ratings reflect, top-notch, but some just
find the place "dull", with exercises that are better than the body
pampering;* N.B. *a 1993 renovation is scheduled.*

**Hilton Head Island Health Institute**   20S   | – | – | – | – | E |
14 Valencia Rd., Hilton Head Island, SC; (800) 292-2420; (803) 785-7292;
(803) 686-5659
*Not a spa for pampering, this residential facility on Hilton Head Island
specializes in serious health education, including exercise and weight-loss
programs; swimming, water-skiing, windsurfing, fishing, boating, golf and
tennis facilities are also available; accommodations are in fully equipped
individual villas; one-week minimum stay.*

# SPAS

| R | S | D | P | $ |

## Jimmy LeSage's New Life
| – | – | – | – | E |
**Fitness Vacations**  103S (fka New Life Spa)
Inn of the Six Mountains, Killington, VT; (800) 228-4676; (802) 422-4302;
FAX 422-4321
*Recently moved from Stratton Mountain to a corner of the Inn at Six
Mountains ski resort, the ever-enthusiastic Jimmy LeSage still offers "a
unique and magical experience" where the atmosphere is "homey, simple
and restful, like adult camp"; it's great for yoga, massage and lots of gorgeous
hiking, but it's definitely "not for manicures"; open May through November.*

## Kerr House, The  5S
| – | – | – | – | VE |
17777 Beaver St., Grand Rapids, OH; (419) 832-1733
*Small and intimate Victorian home converted to a retreat specializing in the
care and cosseting of those going through a lifestyle transition; weekend
and five-day diet/exercise programs focus on attitude, stress management
and improving self-esteem; "great views in a rustic atmosphere" and
delicious, elegant food make you feel like a special guest in the home of an
understanding friend – who just happens to serve breakfast in bed; the
atmosphere is slightly New Age.*

## Kripalu Center for Yoga and Health*  98R
| 14 | 18 | 16 | 17 | $71 |
Rte. 183, Lenox, MA; (800) 967-3577; (413) 637-3280; FAX 637-3101
*U – "More an ashram or yoga center than a glamour spa", the affordable
Kripalu gets the nod for its "silent meals and vegetarian menu"; most call
this holistic-healing place in the Berkshires a "fabulous retreat" and an
"extremely restful milieu"; "no cynics allowed", comments one believer, but
low room ratings suggest that some cynics managed to get in anyway.*

## LA COSTA HOTEL & SPA  478R (82S)
| 23 | 23 | 22 | 24 | $245 |
Costa del Mar Rd., Carlsbad, CA; (619) 438-9111
*M – A Mediterranean-style country club for Hollywood's ailing, this "shrine
of the nouveau riche" is noted by its many admirers as a "classic" and "a
great place to unwind and relax", with "pampering to the extreme"; others
complain that it's "overrated", with service that's "marginal at best"; new
management is equally blamed (a "change for the worse") and praised
("has restored new luster to a fine place"); N.B. spa supplies and clothing
are available plus golf, tennis and a full range of sun sports.*

413

# SPAS                                           | R | S | D | P | $ |

**Lake Austin Resort\*** 40R                    | 18 | 21 | 21 | 17 | $173 |
1705 Quinlan Park Rd., Austin, TX; (800) 847-5637; (512) 266-2444;
FAX 266-1572
*U – A "great place for the price", cheer fans of this comfortable, down-to-earth Texas Hill Country spa for rest, relaxation, recreation and insight, with culinary emphasis on tasty SW salsa flavors and spa-program emphasis on group problem-solving in areas such as stress management, lifestyle changes and behavior modification.*

**Maine Chance\*** 46R                          | 26 | 28 | 27 | 27 | $374 |
5830 E. Jean Ave., Phoenix, AZ; (602) 947-6365; FAX 481-9654
*U – The handful of our surveyors who can afford it "can't find any fault" with this famous, Elizabeth Arden-run, women-only facility; "more of a beauty spa than a health spa, it appeals to a crème-de-la-crème audience of female execs, socialites and power wives who check in for six full days of pampering – facials, massages, hair and nail treatments, the works; service, food and facilities are all top-of-the-line, but unless you've been there before or have a friend who has, there may be a line to face before you get in.*

**Mario's International Hotel &**               | – | – | – | – | E |
**Aurora House Spa** 14R (1S) (fka Aurora House Spa)
35 E. Garfield Rd., Aurora, OH; (216) 562-9171; FAX 562-2386
*This northern Ohio Victorian-era country retreat gives equal emphasis to health and beauty, and has a male following that nearly equals the size of its female clientele; there's casual as well as calorie-control dining plus supervised fitness programs that include biking and walking treks.*

**Murrieta Hot Springs Resort** 152R (4S)      | 15 | 17 | 15 | 17 | $137 |
Snow Canyon National Park, 39405 Murrieta Hot Springs Rd., Murrieta, CA;
(800) 238-6357; (714) 677-7451; FAX 677-7451
*M – A "tranquil" old-fashioned hot springs with mud and mineral baths and other water "cures" plus some New Age and Zen perspectives; it's a spot that's been around since 1906, but some folks say it's "seen better days";*
N.B. *this place is very handy to Temecula Valley wineries.*

**National Institute of Fitness** 56R (20S)    | – | – | – | – | I |
202 N. Snow Canyon Rd., Ivins, UT; (801) 673-4905; FAX 673-1363
*A major health club located in Snow Canyon National Park specializes in health maintenance and weight reduction, with little to no pampering of the body – just the mind and spirit; though modestly priced, this may be a case of you-get-what-you-pay-for; one-week minimum stay.*

414

**New Age Health Spa**  40R          | 12 | 17 | 17 | 18 | $138 |
Rte. 55, Neversink, NY; (800) 682-4348; (914) 985-7600; FAX 986-2467
*M – This "rustic, no-modern-amenities" place, set in the Catskills, attracts*
*"motivated spa-goers" who "make their own experience"; it has "great*
*exercise classes", particularly "yoga and swimming", plenty of "individualized*
*attention" plus "beauty treatments" and a well-praised all-vegetarian menu;*
*in sum, it's a "quiet place to check out of reality."*

**Northern Pines**  25R          | – | – | – | – | M |
559 Rte. 85, Raymond, ME; (207) 655-7624
*Roughing it is a good way to describe this woodsy, log-cabin place that's now*
*open year-round, with special diet and exercise programs available in the*
*summer and at key times in the winter; lake swimming and skiing are*
*enticements to those who remember vacations in the Maine woods, but one*
*of our surveyors complains of "blasé service and Boy/Girl Scout facilities"; a*
*new conference center is scheduled for completion early in 1993.*

**Norwich Inn, Spa & Villas**  140R (75S)          | 20 | 20 | 20 | 20 | $200 |
607 W. Thames St., Norwich, CT; (800) ASK-4-SPA; (203) 886-2401;
FAX 886-9483
*M – Most reviewers like the "quaint" facilities – particularly the "tastefully*
*furnished" and "charming" rooms and the "very quiet and peaceful" setting –*
*that make this "one of the better" East Coast spas, but the fact that this*
*"lovely place off the beaten track" is trying to be all things to all people –*
*spa, inn and conference center – leaves guests a little confused: "a great*
*experience" vs. "no attempt to introduce people to healthy living"; it's*
*definitely not a regimented program.*

**Oaks at Ojai**  46R          | 14 | 19 | 18 | 17 | $166 |
122 E. Ojai Ave., Ojai, CA; (805) 646-5573; FAX 640-1504
*M – For the reasonable prices charged here, it's more spa than you could*
*expect; still, while many appreciate this "poor man's spa in tranquil Ojai"*
*for its "fine classes and services" and "back-to-basics" philosophy, not to*
*mention "fabulous nature walks" and "scenic surroundings", the "small",*
*"older" rooms and "physical facilities leave something to be desired."*

**Palm-Aire Hotel & Spa**  191R (34S)          | 18 | 18 | 16 | 17 | $237 |
2501 Palm-Aire Dr. N., Pompano Beach, FL; (800) PALM-AIR;
(305) 972-3300; FAX 968-2744
*M – Called "beauty and the best" by its partisans, this "convenient" spa is*
*appreciated most by the local condo owners and tenants who are regulars;*
*other spa guests say the facilities need to be updated and the rooms could*
*be better, but the fact that there are 37 tennis courts and 5 golf courses*
*makes this good for sports enthusiasts, not just spa-goers.*

**Palms at Palm Springs, The**   43R      | 15 | 20 | 18 | 17 | $191 |
572 N. Indian Canyon Dr., Palm Springs, CA; (800) 753-6250;
(619) 325-1111; FAX 327-0867
*M – You could hardly be closer to the pulse of glamorous Palm Springs
than you are here, and the possibility of rubbing elbows with the well-
known and well-heeled adds an exciting cachet to the experience;
complaints about "Spartan" rooms in this "revamped old motel" and service
that ranges from "friendly" to "almost nonexistent" are offset by a sense of
"very good value" augmented by plenty of value packages.*

**Phoenix Health Spa, The**   20R      | – | – | – | – | E |
111 N. Post Oak Lane, Houston, TX; (800) 548-4700; (713) 680-2626;
FAX 680-1657
*The physical program is deemed "very good" at this secluded and tranquil
spa located in an art deco mansion; the evening lectures on fitness,
nutrition, stress management, fashion, make-overs and low-calorie cooking
are interesting; it's a "good value for your money" considering the quality of
the spa program, and an à la carte beauty/pampering program is available;
one-week minimum stay.*

**RANCHO LA PUERTA**   75R (12S)      | 22 | 23 | 23 | 23 | $201 |
777 Deer Springs Rd., Tecate, Baja, CA; (800) 443-7565; (619) 744-4222;
FAX 744-5007
*U – For those who can't afford its sister spa, Golden Door, or who prefer
a simpler environment, this is an "understated, serious spa" offering
almost-comparable treatments, services, classes and philosophy plus
good food that's mostly vegetarian; it's a great place "to refuel and clear
your head", where your fellow guests are really interesting and where you
can be "pampered or pushed to the limit – your choice"; one-week
minimum stay, but many stay longer.*

**Russell House**   21R      | – | – | – | – | E |
611 Truman Ave., Key West, FL; (800) 851-4111; (305) 294-8787; FAX 296-7354
*Vegetarian meals and juices or fasting are prime components of the health
program offered at this tropical spa located in a former hotel; surrounded
by lush plantings and trees, this laid-back place feels secluded from the
bustle of Key West, but all the nightlife is right there in town if you feel like
undoing at night the good effects of your day.*

**Safety Harbor Spa**   182R (16S)                   | 17 | 21 | 21 | 20 | $210 |
105 N. Bayshore Dr., Safety Harbor, FL; (800) 237-0155; (813) 726-1161;
FAX 726-4268
*M – One of the first spas in the country, if not the first, and much of its
following has aged with the spa; among the efforts being made to attract a
younger, sportier clientele are cooking demonstrations, new equipment, a
revamped menu and newly renovated rooms and facilities; still, the "well-
run spa facilities" are judged "very good", the staff is "quite wonderful" and
the "food is too good to believe."*

**Sans Souci Resort**   3S                          | – | – | – | – | VE |
3145 Rte. 725, Bellbrook, OH; (513) 848-4851
*A vegetarian diet regimen and strong, loving guidance from director Susie
Kircher provide the backbone of the 18-point slim plan and the healthy
meals for fitness and weight control offered at this tiny, individualized spa
set in a Colonial-style home; despite serving just six guests at a time, it
offers all spa amenities plus a pool, hiking, horseback riding and other
sports facilities.*

**Shangri-La Health Spa**   62R (12S)               | – | – | – | – | M |
27580 Old 41 Rd., Bonita Springs, FL; (813) 992-3811
*A well-worn tropical retreat with vegetarian meals and health consultations
(fasting instructions are also available) for the health-conscious vacationer;
exercise programs are more or less do-it-yourself, with swimming, tennis and
a walk along the beach among the options that you might find at any resort.*

**Sonoma Mission Inn & Spa**   170R (3S)            | 21 | 22 | 23 | 22 | $207 |
18140 Sonoma Hwy. 12, Sonoma, CA; (800) 358-9022; (707) 938-9000;
FAX 938-4250
*M – "If there have to be spas, they should all be as lovely as this"
"excellent" resort in Sonoma, the historic town "in the heart of Wine
Country"; however, compliments about "tasty food", a "luxurious" "sylvan"
setting and "pampering" staff are offset by a few grumbles about "snotty"
service and "teeny rooms."*

**Vista Clara Spa & Health Retreat**   14R          | – | – | – | – | VE |
Galisteo 111 HC-75, Lamy, NM; (800) 247-0301; (505) 988-8865;
FAX 983-8109
*A very exclusive New Age spa set in beautiful New Mexico hinterlands,
with pueblo-style architecture and mountain views; an experience of inner
healing is complemented by what fans call "excellent food" and a "great
staff"; one-week minimum stay.*

# INDEXES

---

# SPECIAL FEATURES
# AND APPEALS

# AIRPORT BEST

## Albuquerque
Marriott Albuquerque

## Atlantic City
Bally's Grand Hotel & Casino
Bally's Park Place
Claridge Casino Hotel
Holiday Inn Diplomat
Trump Plaza Hotel & Casino
Trump Regency Hotel

## Atlanta
Atlanta Airport Hilton*
Embassy Suites Hotel*
Hyatt Atlanta Airport*

## Baltimore
Courtyard by Marriott*
BWI Airport Marriott*

## Chicago
Chicago Marriott O'Hare
Chicago Marriott Suites O'Hare
Courtyard by Marriott*
Hotel Sofitel
Hyatt Regency O'Hare
Quality Inn & Clarion Hotel
Radisson Suite Hotel
Westin Hotel O'Hare

## Cincinnati
Embassy Stes. Cincinnati*

## Cleveland
Pierre Radisson Inn - Airport*
Residence Inn - Cleveland Airport*

## Dallas
DFW Hilton Executive Conf. Ctr.*
Doubletree Hotel at Park West
Embassy Suites*
Four Seasons Hotel
Hyatt Regency DFW*
Omni Mandalay Hotel
Sheraton Grand*
Wyndham Garden Las Colinas*

## Denver
Courtyard by Marriott Airport*
Embassy Suites Denver Airport*
Red Lion
Stouffer Concourse Hotel

## Detroit
Courtyard by Marriott*
Guest Quarters Suite*

Marriott Romulus*
Radisson Hotel*

## Fort Lauderdale
Sheraton Design Center

## Honolulu
Ritz-Carlton Kapalua

## Houston
Hotel Sofitel
Sheraton Crown Hotel*
Wyndham Greenspoint

## Indianapolis
Adam's Mark
Courtyard by Marriott*

## Kansas City
Courtyard by Marriott*
Embassy Suites Hotel KCI*

## Little Rock
Arkansas' Excelsior Hotel

## Los Angeles
Barnabey's Hotel
Compri Hotel*
Courtyard by Marriott*
Embassy Suites LAX*
Hyatt at Los Angeles Airport
Loews Santa Monica Beach Hotel
Los Angeles Airport Hilton
Marriott LAX
Radisson Plaza Hotel & Golf Course
Sheraton Los Angeles Airport
Stouffer Los Angeles Concourse

## Miami/Miami Beach
Biltmore Hotel
Embassy Suites Hotel - Miami Airport*
Hyatt Regency Coral Gables
Miami Marriott Dadeland*
Residence Inn by Marriott*
Sheraton River House Hotel
Sofitel Miami Airport Hotel*

## Milwaukee
Courtyard by Marriott*
Grand Milwaukee Hotel*
Manchester Suites - Airport

## Minneapolis/St. Paul
Hotel Sofitel
Registry Hotel
Residence Inn by Marriott*

*Not in *Survey*

**Nashville**
Embassy Suites
Nashville Airport Marriott
Sheraton Music City Hotel
Wyndham Garden Hotel*

**New York City**
Holiday Inn Crowne Plaza -
  LaGuardia*
Hotel Kimberly
Marriott Financial Center Hotel

**Orange County, CA**
Irvine Marriott
Le Meridien Newport
Red Lion Orange County Airport
Sheraton Newport Beach Hotel
Westin South Coast Plaza

**Orlando**
Courtyard by Marriott*
Hyatt Hotel Orlando Int'l Airport*
Radisson Hotel Orlando Airport*
Residence Inn by Marriott

**Palm Springs**
Autry Resort
Hyatt Regency Suites
Palm Springs Hilton Resort
Spa Hotel & Mineral Springs
Wyndham Palm Springs

**Philadelphia**
Embassy Suites*
Radisson Hotel Philadelphia*

**Phoenix/Scottsdale**
Buttes
Courtyard by Marriott - Phoenix Airport*
Doubletree Suites at Phoenix Ctr.*
Embassy Suites Camelhead*
Hyatt Regency Phoenix
Omni Adams Hotel
Phoenix Airport Hilton*

**Pittsburgh**
Embassy Suites*
Pittsburgh Airport Marriott*

**San Antonio**
Courtyard by Marriott*
Embassy Suites - San Antonio Airport*

**San Diego**
Doubletree Hotel at Horton Plaza
Horton Grand

Humphrey's Half Moon Inn
Marriott Mission Valley
Pan Pacific
Sheraton Grande Harbor Island
Sheraton - Harbor Island East

**San Francisco**
Courtyard by Marriott*
Embassy Suites Burlingame*
Ibis Hotel*
Radisson Inn*
Hyatt Regency S.F. Airport*
San Francisco Airport Marriott*
Westin Hotel*

**Seattle**
Courtyard Seattle Southcenter*
Doubletree Seattle Inn
Doubletree Suites Seattle
Embassy Suites*

**St. Louis**
Compri Hotel Riverport*
Doubletree Hotel & Conference
  Center
Embassy Suites - St. Louis Airport*
Radisson Plaza Hotel*
St. Louis Marriott West
Stouffer Concourse Hotel*

**Tampa Bay**
Courtyard by Marriott
Embassy Suites Tampa Airport
Hyatt Regency Westshore
Radisson Bay Harbor Inn
Sheraton Grand Hotel
Tampa Marriott Westshore

**Washington, D.C.**
Courtyard by Marriott*
Embassy Suites*
Hyatt Dulles*
Hyatt Regency Reston
Marriott Suites Washington Dulles*

**California**
Villa Royale

**Florida**
Inn at Fisher Island

**New Mexico**
La Posada de Albuquerque

# ALL-SUITES

**Atlanta**
Biltmore Suites
Embassy Suites Perim. Ctr.
French Quarter Suites
Marriott Suites Atlanta Midtown
Marriott Suites Perimeter
Summerfield Suites Hotel

**Baltimore**
Brookshire Hotel
Tremont Plaza Hotel

**Boston**
Eliot Hotel
Guest Quarters Suite Hotel

**Chicago**
Barclay Chicago
Chicago Marriott Suites O'Hare
Hyatt Regency Suites
Lenox House Suites
Radisson Suite Hotel

**Cleveland**
Radisson Plaza Hotel

**Dallas**
Embassy Suites
Hotel St. Germain
Sheraton Suites

**Denver**
Burnsley Hotel
Cambridge Hotel
Embassy Suites Denver Dtwn.
Residence Inn

**Detroit**
Atheneum Suites
Townsend Hotel

**Fort Lauderdale**
Crown Sterling Suites Cypress

**Honolulu**
Colony Surf Hotel

**Houston**
Guest Quarters
La Colombe d'Or

**Indianapolis**
Embassy Suites Hotel

**Kansas City**
Hotel Savoy
Radisson Suite Hotel
Sheraton Suites

**Las Vegas**
Alexis Park Resort
St. Tropez

**Los Angeles**
BelAge Hotel
Le Dufy
Le Parc Hotel
L'Ermitage Hotel
Mondrian Hotel
Sunset Marquis Hotel
Westwood Marquis Hotel

**Miami/Miami Beach**
Alexander All-Suite Luxury Hotel
Mayfair House Hotel Grand Luxe

**Milwaukee**
Embassy Suites, West
Manchester Suites - Airport

**Minneapolis/St. Paul**
Crown Sterling (Minn/St. Paul)
Hotel Luxeford Suites
Northland Inn

**Nashville**
Embassy Suites
Hermitage Hotel

**New Orleans**
Avenue Plaza Suite & Eurovita
Radisson Suite Hotel

**New York City**
Beekman Tower Hotel
Dumont Plaza Hotel
Eastgate Tower Suite Hotel
Embassy Suites Hotel
Flatotel International
Hotel Kimberly
Murray Hill East Suite Hotel
Plaza Fifty Suite Hotel
Rihga Royal
Shelburne Suite Hotel
Southgate Tower Suite Hotel
Surrey Hotel

**Orange County, CA**
Costa Mesa Marriott Suites
Hilton Suites In Orange
Marriott Suites Newport Beach

**Orlando**
Guest Quarters Disney Village
Residence Inn by Marriott
Sonesta Villa Resort

**Palm Springs**
Hyatt Grand Champions Resort
Hyatt Regency Suites
Two Bunch Palms Resort

**Phoenix/Scottsdale**
Crown Sterling Suites
Fountains Suite Hotel
Marriott Suites Scottsdale
Orange Tree Golf & Conf. Resort
Pointe at South Mountain
Pointe at Squaw Peak
Pointe at Tapatio Cliffs

**Pittsburgh**
Ramada

**Richmond**
Commonwealth Park Suites Hotel

**San Diego**
Embassy Suites
Rancho Valencia

**San Francisco**
Hyde Park Suites

**Seattle**
Doubletree Suites Seattle

**St. Louis**
Doubletree Mayfair
Embassy Suites

**Tampa Bay**
Crown Sterling Suites
Embassy Suites Tampa Airport
Innisbrook Resort

**Washington, DC**
Canterbury Hotel
Embassy Suites Chevy Chase
Guest Quarters
Hyatt Fair Lakes
Inn at Foggy Bottom
One Washington Circle Hotel
Residence Inn Bethesda
River Inn

**Arizona**
Enchantment Resort
Los Abrigados
Ventana Canyon

**Arkansas**
Palace Hotel & Bath House

**California**
Carmel Valley Ranch Resort
Silverado Country Club & Resort
Stonepine Estate Resort
Villa Royale

**Colorado**
Tall Timber

**Florida**
Colony Beach & Tennis Resort
Little Palm Island
Ocean Key House
Resort at Longboat Key Club
Sundial Beach & Tennis Resort

**Hawaii**
Embassy Suites Resort Maui
Kanaloa at Kona

**Massachusetts**
Coonamessett Inn
New Seabury Cape Cod

**Montana**
Triple Creek Mountain Hideaway

**New York State**
Geneva on the Lake

**Pennsylvania**
Hotel Hershey

**South Carolina**
Seabrook Island Resort
Wild Dunes Resort

**Wyoming**
Jackson Hole Racquet Club

**Spas**
Doral Saturnia

# AMUSEMENT PARK CONVENIENCE

**Atlanta**
Atlanta Marriott Marquis
Atlanta Marriott Perim. Ctr.
Courtyard by Marriott
Embassy Suites Perim. Ctr.
French Quarter Suites
Holiday Inn Buckhead
Holiday Inn Crowne Plaza
Hyatt Regency
Marque of Atlanta
Marriott Suites Atlanta Midtown
Marriott Suites Perimeter
Ramada Hotel Dunwoody
Sheraton Colony Square Hotel
Stouffer Waverly Hotel
Wyndham Garden Hotel - Vinings
Wyndham Garden - Midtown

**Cincinnati**
Cincinnati Marriott
Cincinnati Terrace Hilton
Clarion Hotel Cincinnati
Holiday Inn I-275
Hyatt Regency Cincinnati
Omni Netherland Plaza
Vernon Manor Hotel

**Charlotte**
Dunhill Hotel

**Cleveland**
Cleveland Marriott East
Cleveland Marriott Society Center
Cleveland South Hilton Inn
Stouffer Tower City Plaza Hotel

**Dallas**
Four Seasons Resort & Club

**Denver**
Loews Giorgio Hotel

**Detroit**
Dearborn Inn Marriott

**Houston**
Guest Quarters
Harvey Suites
Holiday Inn Crowne Plaza
Holiday Inn Houston West
Holiday Inn West Loop
Houstonian Hotel & Conf. Ctr.
Houston Marriott Astrodome
Hyatt Regency Houston
La Colombe d'Or
Marriott Medical Center

Plaza Hilton
Ritz-Carlton, Houston
Sheraton Astrodome Hotel
Sheraton Grand Hotel
Stouffer Presidente Hotel
Wyndham Warwick Hotel

**Kansas City**
Adam's Mark
Hotel Savoy
Radisson Suite Hotel

**Nashville**
Doubletree Hotel Nashville
Embassy Suites
Hermitage Hotel
Opryland Hotel
Regal Maxwell House
Sheraton Music City Hotel
Stouffer Nashville Hotel

**Orange County, CA**
Anaheim Hilton & Towers
Anaheim Marriott Hotel
Dana Point Resort
Disneyland Hotel
Doubletree Hotel Orange County
Hilton Suites In Orange
Hyatt Regency Alicante
Inn at the Park
Irvine Marriott
Le Meridien Newport
Sheraton Anaheim Hotel
Westin South Coast Plaza

**Orlando**
Buena Vista Palace
Clarion Plaza Hotel
Disney's Caribbean Beach Resort
Disney's Contemporary Resort
Disney's Grand Floridian
Disney's Polynesian Resort
Disney's Village Resort
Forte Travelodge Hotel
Grosvenor Resort at WDW
Guest Quarters Disney Village
Hilton at WDW Village
Hotel Royal Plaza
Hyatt Orlando
Hyatt Regency Grand Cypress
Marriott
Marriott's Orlando World Center
Orange Lake Country Club
Peabody Orlando
Radisson Inn International Dr.

Residence Inn by Marriott
Sheraton World Resort
Sonesta Villa Resort
Stouffer Orlando Resort
Walt Disney World Dolphin
Walt Disney World Swan

**Richmond**
Commonwealth Park Suites Hotel

**San Antonio**
Wyndham San Antonio

**San Diego**
Bahia Hotel
Catamaran Resort Hotel
Embassy Suites
Gaslamp Plaza Suites
Hanalei Hotel
Hyatt Islandia
Hyatt Regency San Diego
Sheraton - Harbor Island East

**San Jose, CA**
Fairmont Hotel

**Seattle**
Edgewater
Four Seasons Olympic
Inn at the Market
Mayflower Park Hotel
Seattle Hilton
Sheraton Seattle Hotel & Towers
Sorrento Hotel
Stouffer Madison
Warwick Hotel
Westin Hotel Seattle

**St. Louis**
Doubletree Hotel & Conf. Center

**Tampa Bay**
Adam's Mark Caribbean Gulf
Courtyard by Marriott
Crown Sterling Suites
Embassy Suites Tampa Airport
Holiday Inn Ashley Plaza
Hyatt Regency Westshore
Innisbrook Resort
Sheraton Grand Hotel
Trade Winds
Wyndham Harbour Island Hotel

**California**
Ojai Valley Inn
Sheraton Universal Hotel

**Georgia**
Evergreen Conference Center

**Illinois**
Clock Tower Resort & Conf. Ctr.
Marriott's Lincolnshire Resort

**New Jersey**
Abbey
Virginia

**North Carolina**
High Hampton Inn & Country Club

**Ohio**
Kings Island Inn & Conf. Ctr.

**Vermont**
Woods at Killington

**Virginia**
Kingsmill Resort & Conf. Ctr.

**Spas**
Mario's International Hotel

# BEACH SETTING

## Atlantic City
Bally's Grand Hotel & Casino
Bally's Park Place
Caesars Atlantic City
Claridge Casino Hotel
Holiday Inn Diplomat
Merv Griffin's Resorts
Sands Hotel & Casino
Showboat Hotel
TropWorld
Trump Plaza Hotel & Casino
Trump Regency Hotel
Trump Taj Mahal

## Chicago
Drake Hotel

## Fort Lauderdale
Bahia Mar Resort
Lago Mar Resort & Club
Marriott's Harbor Beach Resort
Ocean Manor Resort Hotel
Sheraton Yankee Clipper

## Honolulu
Colony Surf Hotel
Halekulani
Hawaiian Regent
Hawaiian Waikiki Beach Hotel
Hilton Hawaiian Village
Hyatt Regency Waikiki
Kahala Hilton
New Otani Kaimana Beach Hotel
Outrigger Waikiki
Pacific Beach Hotel
Ritz-Carlton Kapalua
Royal Hawaiian Hotel
Sheraton Moana Surfrider
Sheraton Princess Kaiulani
Sheraton Waikiki Hotel
Turtle Bay Hilton

## Los Angeles
Barnabey's Hotel
Loews Santa Monica Beach Hotel
Malibu Beach Inn
Shangri-La

## Miami/Miami Beach
Alexander All-Suite Luxury Hotel
Doral Ocean Beach Resort
Eden Roc Hotel & Marina
Fontainebleau Hilton
Grove Isle Yacht & Tennis Club
Sheraton Bal Harbour Hotel

Sonesta Beach Hotel
Turnberry Isle Club

## Orange County, CA
Casa Laguna Inn
Dana Point Resort
Four Seasons Hotel
Hyatt Newporter
Ritz-Carlton, Laguna Niguel
Surf & Sand Hotel

## Orlando
Disney's Caribbean Beach Resort
Disney's Grand Floridian
Hyatt Regency Grand Cypress
Sonesta Villa Resort
Walt Disney World Dolphin
Walt Disney World Swan

## Palm Springs
Marriott's Desert Springs Resort
Stouffer Esmeralda

## Phoenix/Scottsdale
Hyatt Regency Scottsdale

## San Diego
Bahia Hotel
Catamaran Resort Hotel
Hotel del Coronado
Kona Kai Resort
La Valencia Hotel
Le Meridien San Diego
Loews Coronado Bay Resort
San Diego Hilton
San Diego Princess Resort
Sea Lodge
Sheraton Grande Harbor Island
Sheraton - Harbor Island East

## Tampa Bay
Adam's Mark Caribbean Gulf
Courtyard by Marriott
Don Ce-Sar Registry Resort
Radisson Bay Harbor Inn
Sheraton Sand Key Resort
St. Petersburg Beach Hilton
Trade Winds

## Alabama
Marriott's Grand Hotel

## Alaska
Glacier Bay Lodge

## Arizona

Wahweap Lodge & Marina

## California

Fess Parker's Red Lion Resort
Four Seasons Biltmore
Inn at Morro Bay
Inn at Spanish Bay
Little River Inn
Lodge at Pebble Beach
Mendocino Hotel
Monterey Plaza Hotel
Portofino Hotel & Yacht Club
Santa Barbara Miramar
St. Orres

## Connecticut

Boulders
Water's Edge Inn & Resort

## Florida

Amelia Island Plantation
Boca Raton Resort & Club
Breakers
Cheeca Lodge
Colony Beach & Tennis Resort
Hawk's Cay Resort & Marina
Hyatt Key West
Indian River Plantation Resort
Inn at Fisher Island
Little Palm Island
Lodge at Ponte Vedra Beach
Marriott at Sawgrass Resort
Marriott's Bay Point Resort
Marriott's Casa Marina Resort
Marriott's Marco Island Resort
Ocean Grand Hotel
Ocean Reef Club
Pier House Resort
Ponte Vedra Inn & Club
Reach Resort
Resort at Longboat Key Club
Ritz-Carlton, Amelia Island
Ritz-Carlton, Naples
Ritz-Carlton, Palm Beach
Sheraton Key Largo Resort
Sonesta Sanibel Harbour
South Seas Plantation Resort
Sundial Beach & Tennis Resort
'Tween Waters Inn
Windjammer Resort

## Georgia

Callaway Gardens Resort
Cloister
Greyfield Inn
Jekyll Island Club Hotel
King & Prince Beach Resort
Sheraton Savannah Resort
Stouffer Pineisle Resort

## Hawaii

Embassy Suites Resort Maui
Four Seasons Resort Wailea
Grand Hyatt Wailea
Hotel Hana-Maui
Hyatt Regency Kauai
Hyatt Regency Maui
Hyatt Regency Waikoloa
Kaanapali Beach Hotel
Kapalua Bay Hotel & Villas
Kona Hilton Resort
Kona Village Resort
Manele Bay Hotel
Maui Inter-Continental Resort
Maui Marriott
Maui Prince Hotel
Mauna Kea Beach Hotel
Mauna Lani Bay Hotel
Princeville Hotel
Ritz-Carlton, Mauna Lani
Royal Lahaina Resort
Royal Waikoloan
Stouffer Wailea Beach Resort
Stouffer Waiohai Beach Resort
Westin Kauai
Westin Maui

## Idaho

Coeur d'Alene Resort
Robert Morris Inn

## Maine

Bayview Hotel & Inn
Black Point Inn Resort
Colony Resort
High Tide Inn on the Ocean

## Maryland

Inn at Mitchell House

## Massachusetts

Chatham Bars Inn
Daggett House

# BEACH SETTING

Harbor View Hotel
New Seabury Cape Cod
Ocean Edge Resort & Conf. Ctr.
Wauwinet
Wequassett Inn
White Elephant Inn

## Michigan

Boyne Mountain Hotel
Grand Traverse Resort
Shanty Creek - Schuss Mountain

## Minnesota

Arrowwood, A Radisson Resort
Fitgers Inn
Grand View Lodge
Lutsen Resort
Madden's on Gull Lake

## Missouri

Lodge of Four Seasons
Marriott's TanTarA Resort

## Nevada

Harrah's Lake Tahoe
Hyatt Regency Lake Tahoe

## New Jersey

Virginia

## New Mexico

Inn of the Mountain Gods

## New York State

Mohonk Mountain House
Montauk Yacht Club

## North Carolina

Sanderling Inn Resort

## Oklahoma

Shangri-La Resort

## Oregon

Inn at Spanish Head
Salishan Lodge
Sylvia Beach Hotel

## Pennsylvania

Split Rock Resort

## Rhode Island

Hotel Manisses
Inn at Castle Hill
1661 Inn

## South Carolina

Hilton Head Island Hilton Resort
Hyatt Regency Hilton Head
Kiawah Island Resort
Marriott's Hilton Head Resort
Seabrook Island Resort
Sea Pines
Westin Resort
Wild Dunes Resort

## Texas

Horseshoe Bay Resort
Radisson South Padre Island
Sheraton South Padre Island

## Vermont

Basin Harbor Club
Hawk Inn & Mountain Resort
Mountain Top Inn
Shelburne House

## Virginia

Tides Inn

## Washington

Captain Whidbey Inn
Inn at Semiahmoo
Rosario Resort & Spa

## Wisconsin

Abbey
Colter Bay Village
Heidel House Resort
Jenny Lake Lodge
Lake Lawn Lodge
Lakewoods Resort & Lodge

## Spas

Gurney's Inn Resort & Spa
Hilton Head Health Institute
Lake Austin Resort

# BODY CARE
**(B** = Barber; **H** = Hairdresser; **J** = Jacuzzi;
**M** = Massage; **S** = Sauna/Steam)
All spas, plus the following:

## Albuquerque
Marriott Albuquerque (J,S)
Hyatt Reg. Albuquerque (H,M,S)

## Anchorage
Captain Cook Hotel (B,H,J,M,S)

## Atlanta
Ansley Inn (J)
Atlanta Hilton & Towers (J,S)
Atlanta Marriott Marquis (B,H,J,M,S)
Atlanta Marriott Perim. Ctr. (J,S)
Courtyard by Marriott (J)
Doubletree Concourse (B,H,J,M,S)
Embassy Suites Perim. Ctr. (J,S)
French Quarter Suites (J,S)
Holiday Inn Crowne Plaza (H,J,M,S)
Hotel Nikko (J,M,S)
Hyatt Regency (S)
J.W. Marriott at Lenox (M,S)
Lanier Plaza (H,M)
Marque of Atlanta (J,S)
Marriott Suites Atlanta Midtown (J)
Marriott Suites Perimeter (J,M,S)
Omni CNN Ctr. (B,H,J,M,S)
Peachtree Executive Conf. Ctr. (J,S)
Radisson Hotel (H,J,M,S)
Ritz-Carlton, Atlanta (M,S)
Ritz-Carlton, Buckhead (B,H,J,M,S)
Sheraton Colony Square Hotel (B,H)
Stouffer Waverly Hotel (B,H,J,M,S)
Summerfield Suites Hotel (J)
Swissotel Atlanta (H,J,M,S)
Terrace Garden Inn - Buckhead (J,S)
Westin Peachtree Plaza (M,S)
Wyndham Garden Hotel - Vinings (J)
Wyndham Garden - Midtown (J,S)
Wyndham Perimeter Center (J)

## Atlantic City
Bally's Grand (B,H,M,S)
Bally's Park Place (H,J,M,S)
Caesars Atlantic City (B,H,J,M,S)
Claridge Casino Hotel (B,H,J,M,S)
Harrah's Marina (B,H,J,M,S)
Marriott's Seaview Resort (S)
Merv Griffin's Resorts (B,H,J,M,S)
Sands Hotel & Casino (J,M,S)
Showboat Hotel (B,H,J,M,S)
TropWorld (B,H,J,M,S)

Trump Castle Resort (B,H,J,M,S)
Trump Plaza (B,H,J,M,S)
Trump Regency Hotel (J,M,S)
Trump Taj Mahal (B,H,J,M,S)

## Austin
Four Seasons Hotel (J,M,S)

## Baltimore
Admiral Fell Inn (J)
Clarion Hotel - Inner Harbor (J)
Cross Keys Inn (M)
Doubletree Inn Colonnade (H)
Harbor Court Hotel (H,J,M,S)
Hyatt Regency Baltimore (M,S)
Marriott's Hunt Valley Inn (J,M)
Peabody Court Hotel (J)
Sheraton Baltimore North (J,S)
Sheraton Inner Harbor Hotel (S)
Tremont Hotel (S)
Tremont Plaza Hotel (S)

## Birmingham
Tutwiler (B)
Wynfrey Hotel (S)

## Boston
Boston Harbor Hotel (J,M,S)
Bostonian Hotel (M)
Boston Marriott Peabody (J,S)
Boston Park Plaza (B,H)
Cambridge Center Marriott (J,S)
Charles Hotel (B,H,J,M,S)
Colonnade Hotel (B,H)
Copley Plaza Hotel (B,H)
Four Seasons Hotel (J,M,S)
Guest Quarters (J,M,S)
Hyatt Regency Cambridge (J,M,S)
Le Meridien Boston (S)
Lenox Hotel (B)
Marriott Copley Place (J,M,S)
Marriott Hotel Long Wharf (J,S)
Midtown Hotel (J)
Omni Parker House (B,H)
Ritz-Carlton, Boston (B,H,J,M,S)
Royal Sonesta (J,M,S)
Sheraton Boston Hotel (J,M)
Swissotel Boston (S)
Westin Copley Place (J,M,S)

# BODY CARE

## Charlotte
Dunhill Hotel (J)

## Chicago
Allerton Hotel (B,H,M)
Barclay Chicago (H)
Bismarck Hotel (B)
Chicago Hilton & Towers (H,M,S)
Chicago Marriott Dtwn. (B,H,J,M,S)
Chicago Marriott O'Hare (B,H,J,S)
Chicago Marr. O'Hare (B,H,J,S)
Drake Hotel (B)
Four Seasons Hotel (M,S)
Holiday Inn City Centre (H,J,M,S)
Hotel Inter-Continental (M,S)
Hotel Nikko (M,S)
Hotel Sofitel (M,S)
Hyatt Regency O'Hare (B,H,M,S)
Hyatt Regency Suites (J,S)
Mayfair (B,H,M)
McCormick Center Hotel (J,M,S)
Midland Hotel (B,H)
Palmer House Hilton (B,H,J,M,S)
Quality Inn & Clarion Hotel (S)
Radisson Plaza Ambass. West (B)
Radisson Suite Hotel (J,M,S)
Ritz-Carlton, Chicago (M,S)
Sheraton Chicago Hotel (M,S)
Stouffer Riviere (J,M,S)
Swissotel Chicago (J,M,S)
Westin Hotel, Chicago (M,S)
Westin Hotel O'Hare (J,M,S)

## Cincinnati
Cincinnatian Hotel (S)
Cincinnati Marriott (H,J)
Cincinnati Terrace Hilton (J,S)
Clarion Hotel Cincinnati (B,H,S)
Holiday Inn I-275 (S)
Hyatt Regency Cincinnati (B,J,S)
Kings Island Inn & Conf. Ctr. (J,S)
Omni Netherland Plaza (B,H,J,M,S)
Vernon Manor Hotel (B)
Westin Hotel (J,M,S)

## Cleveland
Cleveland Marriott East (J,M,S)
Cleveland Marriott Society Ctr. (J,S)
Cleveland South Hilton Inn (J,S)
Glidden House (M)
Holiday Inn Lakeside City Ctr. (S)
Omni International Hotel (H)
Pierre Radisson Inn (J,S)

Radisson Plaza Hotel (S)
Ritz-Carlton, Cleveland (J,M,S)
Sheraton City Centre (B,H,M)
Stouffer Tower City (B,H,S)

## Corpus Christi
Corpus Christi Marriott (B,H,J,M,S)

## Dallas
Adolphus (B,H)
Dallas Grand (B,H,J)
Dallas Marriott Park Central (J)
Dallas Marriott Quorum (J,S)
Dallas Parkway Hilton (J,S)
Doubletree Campbell Ctr. (J)
Doubletree Hotel at Park West (J)
Doubletree Hotel Lincoln Ctr. (J)
Embassy Suites (J,S)
Fairmont Hotel (H)
Four Seasons (H,J,M,S)
Grand Kempinski Dallas (B,H,J,M,S)
Hotel Crescent Court (H,J,M,S)
Hyatt Regency Reunion (J,S)
Loews Anatole Hotel (H,J,M,S)
Mansion on Turtle Creek (B,H,M)
Omni Mandalay Hotel (J,M,S)
Plaza of the Americas Hotel (J,S)
Sheraton Park Central (J)
Stoneleigh Hotel (H,M)
Stouffer Dallas Hotel (S)
Westin Galleria (B,H)
Wyndham Garden Hotel (J,S)

## Denver
Brown Palace Hotel (B)
Denver Marriott City Center (J,S)
Doubletree Hotel Denver (J)
Embassy Stes. Denver Dtwn. (J,S)
Hyatt Regency Tech Center (J,S)
Marriott Southeast (B,H,J)
Radisson Hotel (B,J,S)
Red Lion (J,S)
Residence Inn (J)
Scanticon (J,S)
Sheraton Tech Ctr. (B,H,J,S)
Stouffer Concourse Hotel (J,S)
Westin Hotel Tabor Center (J,S)

## Detroit
Atheneum Suites (J)
Hyatt Regency Dearborn (J,S)
Novi Hilton (J,S)
Omni (B,H,J,M,S)
Radisson Pontchartrain (B,H,J,S)

Radisson Plaza Hotel (J,S)
Ritz-Carlton (B,H,J,M,S)
River Place Inn (J,S)
Townsend Hotel (H,M)
Westin Hotel (B,H,M,S)

**Florham Park**
Hamilton Park (J,M,S)

**Fort Lauderdale**
Bahia Mar Resort (B,H)
Crown Sterling Suites Cypress (J,S)
Fort Laud. Marina Marriott (J,S)
Fort Lauderdale Marriott North (J,S)
Marriott's Harbor Beach (B,H,J,M,S)
Ocean Manor Resort Hotel (B,H)
Pier 66 Resort & Marina (B,H,J,M,S)
Sheraton Design Center (J,M,S)
Westin Cypress Creek (J,M,S)

**Fort Worth**
Worthington (J,M,S)

**Hartford**
Goodwin Hotel (B,H,M)

**Honolulu**
Ala Moana Hotel (J,M)
Colony Surf Hotel (B,H,M)
Halekulani (H,M)
Hawaiian Regent (H,M)
Hawaii Prince Waikiki (B,H,J,M)
Hilton Hawaiian Village (B,H,J,M,S)
Hyatt Regency Waikiki (J,M)
Ilikai Hotel Nikko Waikiki (B,H)
Kahala Hilton (B,H,M,S)
New Otani Kaimana Beach (H)
Outrigger Waikiki (J)
Pacific Beach Hotel (J)
Park Plaza Waikiki (M,S)
Ritz-Carlton Kapalua (B,H,J,M,S)
Royal Hawaiian Hotel (B,H,M)
Sheraton Makaha Resort (B,H)
Sheraton Moana Surfrider (B,H,M)
Sheraton Princess Kaiulani (B)
Turtle Bay Hilton (B,H,J,M)
Waikiki Beachcomber Hotel (M)
Waikiki Joy Hotel (S)

**Houston**
Adam's Mark (J,M,S)
Allen Park Inn (B,J,S)
Doubletree at Post Oak (H,S)
Fit Inn Charlie Club (J,S)
Four Seasons Hotel (B,H,J,M,S)

Guest Quarters (J)
Holiday Inn Crowne Plaza (J,S)
Holiday Inn Houston West (J,S)
Holiday Inn West Loop (J)
Hotel Sofitel (J,M,S)
Houstonian Hotel (B,H,J,M,S)
Houston Marriott Astrodome (B)
Houston Marriott West Loop (J,S)
Houston Marriott Westside (J,S)
Hyatt Regency Houston (B,H)
J.W. Marriott Hotel (H,J,M)
Marriott Medical Center (J)
Nassau Bay Hilton & Marina (H,J)
Omni (J,S)
Plaza Hilton (J,M,S)
Ramada Kings Inn (H)
Sheraton Astrodome (B,H,S)
Sheraton Grand Hotel (J,S)
Stouffer Presidente Hotel (J,S)
Woodlands (B,H,J,M,S)
Wyndham Greenspoint (J)
Wyndham Warwick Hotel (H,S)

**Indianapolis**
Adam's Mark (J,S)
Embassy Suites Hotel (J,S)
Holiday Inn Union Station (J,S)
Hyatt Regency (B,H,J,M,S)
Indianapolis Marriott (J)
Radisson Plaza & Suites Hotel (J)
Westin Hotel Indianapolis (J)
Wyndam Garden Hotel (J)

**Kansas City**
Adam's Mark (J,S)
Allis Plaza Hotel (M,S)
Doubletree Hotel (J,S)
Hilton Plaza Inn (B,H)
Holiday Inn Crowne Plaza (J)
Hyatt Regency Crown Ctr. (J,S)
Marriott Overland Park (J)
Quarterage Hotel (J,S)
Ritz-Carlton, Kansas City (M,S)
Sheraton Suites (J)
Westin Crown Center (J,S)

**Las Vegas**
Aladdin Hotel (H)
Alexis Park Resort (B,H,J,M,S)
Bally's (B,H,J,M,S)
Caesars Palace (B,H,J,M,S)
Desert Inn (B,H,J,M,S)
Dunes Hotel & Country Club (B,H)

# BODY CARE

Excalibur Hotel (B,H,J)
Fitzgerald's Casino Hotel (J,S)
Flamingo Hotel (B,H,M,S)
Frontier Hotel (H,J)
Golden Nugget (H,J,M,S)
Hacienda Hotel & Casino (B,H)
Imperial Palace (B,H,J,M,S)
Las Vegas Hilton (B,H,J,M,S)
Maxim Hotel (B,H)
Mirage (B,H,J,M,S)
Plaza Hotel (B,H)
Riviera Hotel & Casino (B,H,J,M,S)
Sahara Hotel & Casino (B,H)
Sands Hotel & Casino (H,J,M,S)
Showboat Hotel (B)
Stardust Resort & Casino (B,H,J,M)
St. Tropez (B,H,J)
Tropicana (B,H,J,M,S)
Vegas World Hotel & Casino (B,H)

## Little Rock
Arkansas' Excelsior Hotel (J,M)

## Los Angeles
Barnabey's Hotel (J)
BelAge Hotel (H,J,M)
Beverly Hills Hotel (B,H,J,M)
Beverly Hilton (B,H)
Biltmore Los Angeles (B,H,J,M,S)
Century Plaza Hotel (B,H,J)
Checkers Hotel Kempinski (J,M,S)
Four Seasons Hotel (B,H,J,M)
Hollywood Roosevelt Hotel (J,M)
Hotel Bel-Air (H,J,M)
Hotel Inter-Continental (S)
Hotel Nikko (M,S)
Hyatt at LAX (B,H,J,S)
Industry Hills Sheraton Resort (J)
J.W. Marriott at Century City (J,M,S)
Le Dufy (J)
Le Parc Hotel (J,M,S)
L'Ermitage Hotel (B,H,J,M,S)
Loews Santa Monica (B,H,J,M,S)
Los Angeles Airport Hilton (J,S)
L.A. Hilton & Towers (B,H,M)
Malibu Beach Inn (J)
Ma Maison Sofitel (B,H,M,S)
Marriott LAX (B,H,J,S)
Mondrian Hotel (J,M,S)
New Otani (B,H,J,M,S)
Peninsula Beverly Hills (J,M,S)
Radisson Bel-Air Summit (B,H,M)
Radisson Plaza (J,S)

Regent Beverly Wilshire (J,M,S)
Ritz-Carlton, Huntington (B,H,J,M,S)
Ritz-Carlton, Marina (J,M,S)
Sheraton Los Angeles Airport (J)
Sportsmen's Lodge Hotel (B,H,J)
St. James's Club & Hotel (S)
Stouffer L.A. Concourse (J,S)
Sunset Marquis Hotel (J,S)
Tower at Century Plaza (B,H,J)
Warner Center Marriott (J,S)
Westwood Marquis (B,H,J,M,S)
Wilshire Plaza Hotel (B)

## Memphis
Peabody Memphis (B,H,J,M,S)

## Miami/Miami Beach
Alexander (B,H,J,S)
Biltmore Hotel (M,S)
Biscayne Bay Marriott (H,J)
Colonnade Hotel (B,H,J,M,S)
Doral Ocean (B,H,J,M,S)
Doral Resort (B,H,J,M,S)
Eden Roc Hotel & Marina (B,H)
Fontainebleau Hilton (B,H,J,M,S)
Grand Bay Hotel (B,H,J,M,S)
Grove Isle (B,H)
Hotel Inter-Continental (B,H)
Hyatt Regency Coral Gables (J,S)
Mayfair House (H,J,M,S)
Occidental Parc Hotel (J)
Omni International Hotel (B,H)
Radisson Mart Plaza (H,S)
Sheraton River House Hotel (S)
Sonesta Beach Hotel (B,H,J,M,S)
Turnberry Isle Club (B,H,J,M,S)

## Milwaukee
Astor Hotel (H)
Embassy Suites, West (J,S)
Marc Plaza Hotel (B,H,S)
Milwaukee Marriott (J,S)
Pfister Hotel (B,H,M)
Wyndham Milwaukee Center (J,S)

## Minneapolis/St. Paul
Crown Sterling (Minn/St. Paul) (J,S)
Hotel Luxeford Suites (J,S)
Hotel Sofitel (M,S)
Hyatt Reg. Minneapolis (B,H,J,S)
Minneapolis Marriott (J,M,S)
Radisson Hotel & Conf. Ctr. (J,M,S)
Radisson Hotel Metrodome (B,H)
Radisson Hotel St. Paul (B,H)

Radisson Plaza Hotel (J,S)
Registry Hotel (J,S)
Sheraton Park Place (J,S)

## Nashville
Doubletree Hotel Nashville (S)
Embassy Suites (J,S)
Loews Vanderbilt Plaza Hotel (H,M)
Nashville Airport Marriott (J,S)
Opryland Hotel (B,H,M)
Regal Maxwell House (J,S)
Sheraton Music City Hotel (J,S)
Stouffer Nashville Hotel (J,S)

## New Orleans
Avenue Plaza Suite (B,H,J,M,S)
Fairmont Hotel (H)
Hotel Inter-Continental (B,H,J)
Hyatt Reg. New Orleans (B,H,M)
Le Meridien Hotel (H,J,M,S)
Maison Dupuy Hotel (M)
Monteleone Hotel (B,H)
New Orleans Hilton Riverside (M,S)
New Orleans Marriott (S)
Omni Royal Orleans (B,H)
Radisson Suite Hotel (J)
Westin Canal Place (B,H,M,S)
Windsor Court Hotel (J,M,S)

## New York City
Beekman Tower Hotel (S)
Carlyle Hotel (B,H,J,M,S)
Doral Court Hotel (M)
Doral Park Avenue (M)
Dorset (H)
Drake Swissotel (B,H)
Dumont Plaza Hotel (S)
Edison Hotel (H)
Essex House, Hotel Nikko (M,S)
Flatotel International (J,M)
Gramercy Park Hotel (B,H)
Helmsley Palace (B,H)
Helmsley Park Lane Hotel (H)
Holiday Inn Crowne Plaza (M,S)
Hotel Beverly (B,H)
Hotel Lexington (B)
Hotel Macklowe (M,S)
Inter-Continental (M,S)
Le Parker Meridien (J,M,S)
Loews New York Hotel (J,S)
Lowell New York (H,M)
Mark (M)
Marriott Financial Center Hotel (S)

Milford Plaza Hotel (H)
Morgans (M)
New York Hilton (B,H,M,S)
New York Marriott Marquis (H,J,S)
New York Vista (B,H,M,S)
Park Central (B,H)
Peninsula New York (H,J,M,S)
Pierre (B,H)
Plaza Hotel (B,H,J,M)
Ramada Hotel (B,H)
Regency (B,H,J,S)
Rihga Royal (M,S)
Roosevelt Hotel (H)
Royalton (M)
Shelburne Suite Hotel (S)
Sheraton Manhattan (S)
Sherry-Netherland Hotel (B,H)
Southgate Tower (B,H)
St. Regis (B,H,M,S)
U.N. Plaza - Park Hyatt (M,S)
Waldorf-Astoria/Towers (H,M,S)
Westbury Hotel (S)
Wyndham Hotel (B,H)

## Oklahoma City
Waterford Hotel (M,S)

## Orange County, CA
Anaheim Hilton (B,H,J,M,S)
Anaheim Marriott Hotel (B,H,J,S)
Costa Mesa Marriott Suites (J)
Dana Point Resort (J,M,S)
Disneyland Hotel (B,H,J,M)
Doubletree Orange County (J)
Four Seasons Hotel (J,M,S)
Hilton Suites In Orange (S)
Hyatt Newporter (H,J)
Hyatt Regency Alicante (J,M)
Hyatt Regency Irvine (J,S)
Inn at the Park (J)
Irvine Marriott (B,H,J,M,S)
Le Meridien Newport (J,M,S)
Marriott Suites Newport Beach (J,S)
Newport Beach Marriott (B,H,J,M,S)
Red Lion Orange County (B,H,J,S)
Ritz-Carlton, Laguna (B,H,J,M,S)
Sheraton Newport Beach Hotel (J)
Surf & Sand Hotel (B,H,M)

## Orlando
Buena Vista Palace (B,H,J,M)
Clarion Plaza Hotel (J)
Courtyard at Lake Lucerne (J,S)

## BODY CARE

Disney's Caribbean (B,H,J,M,S)
Disney's Contemporary (B,H,M,S)
Disney's Gr. Floridian (B,H,J,M,S)
Disney's Polynesian (B,H,J,M,S)
Disney's Village Resort (B,H,J)
Grosvenor Resort at WDW (J)
Guest Quarters Disney Village (J,S)
Hilton at WDW Village (B,H,J,M,S)
Hotel Royal Plaza (B,H,J,S)
Hyatt Orlando (J)
Hyatt Grand Cypress (B,H,J,M,S)
Marriott (B,H,J)
Marriott's World Ctr. (B,H,J,M,S)
Omni (J)
Orange Lake Country Club (B,H)
Park Plaza Hotel (M)
Peabody Orlando (B,H,J,M,S)
Radisson Plaza Hotel (J,S)
Sheraton World Resort (H,J)
Sonesta Villa Resort (J,S)
Stouffer Orlando Resort (B,H,J,M,S)
Walt Disney Dolphin (B,H,J,M,S)
Walt Disney World Swan (H,J,S)

### Palm Springs

Autry Resort (B,H,J,M,S)
Doubletree (B,H,J,M,S)
Hyatt Grand Champions (B,H,J,M,S)
Hyatt Regency Suites (H,J,M)
La Quinta Hotel (H,J,M)
Marriott's Desert Spgs. (B,H,J,M,S)
Marriott's Rancho (B,H,J,M)
Palm Springs Hilton (B,H,J,M,S)
Palm Springs Marquis (B,H,J,M)
Palm Springs Riviera Resort (H,J)
Racquet Club Resort (J,M,S)
Ritz-Carlton (J,M,S)
Shadow Mountain Resort (J,M,S)
Spa Hotel (B,H,J,M,S)
Stouffer Esmeralda (J,M,S)
Two Bunch Palms Resort (J,M,S)
Westin Mission Hills (H,J,M,S)
Wyndham Palm Springs (H,J,M,S)

### Philadelphia

Adam's Mark (H,J,S)
Four Seasons Hotel (B,H,J,M,S)
Omni Independence Park (J,M,S)
Philadelphia Hilton & Towers (S)
Rittenhouse (H,M,S)
Ritz-Carlton, Philadelphia (M,S)
Sheraton Society Hill (J,M,S)

Warwick Hotel (B)
Wyndham Franklin (B,H,J,M,S)

### Phoenix/Scottsdale

Arizona Biltmore (H,J,M,S)
Buttes (J,M,S)
Camelview Resort (J)
Crescent Hotel (J,S)
Crown Sterling Suites (J)
Fountains Suite Hotel (J,S)
Hyatt Regency Phoenix (H,J,M)
Hyatt Reg. Scottsdale (B,H,J,M,S)
John Gardiner's (J,M,S)
Lexington Hotel (B,H,J,M,S)
Marriott's Camelback (H,J,M,S)
Marriott's Mtn. Shadows (H,J,M,S)
Marriott Suites Scottsdale (J,S)
Omni Adams Hotel (H,M,S)
Orange Tree (B,H,J,M,S)
Phoenician (B,H,J,M,S)
Pointe at S. Mtn. (B,H,J,M,S)
Pointe at Squaw Peak (J,M,S)
Pointe at Tapatio Cliffs (H,J,M,S)
Red Lion La Posada (B,H,J,M,S)
Regal McCormick Ranch (J,M)
Registry Resort (B,H,J,M,S)
Ritz-Carlton, Phoenix (B,H,M,S)
Royal Palms Inn (B,H,J)
Scottsdale Conf. Resort (B,H,J,M,S)
Scottsdale Hilton (B,H,J,M,S)
Scottsdale Plaza Resort (B,H,J,M,S)
Scottsdale Princess (B,H,J,M,S)
Sheraton Mesa Hotel (J)
Sheraton San Marcos (B,H,J)
Stouffer Cottonwoods Resort (H,J)
Sunburst Hotel & Conf. Ctr. (J)
Wyndham Paradise (B,H,H,J,M,S)

### Pittsburgh

Hyatt Regency Pittsburgh (J,M,S)
Pittsburgh Green Tree (B,H,J,S)
Pittsburgh Hilton & Towers (S)
Pittsburgh Vista (J,M,S)
Ramada (H,S)
Sheraton Station Square (J,M,S)
Westin William Penn (H)

### Portland, OR

River Place Alexis Hotel (J,S)

### Richmond

Commonwealth Park Suites (J,M,S)

## San Antonio
Best Western Historical Crockett (J)
Emily Morgan (J,S)
Hyatt Regency San Antonio (J)
Marriott Rivercenter (J,M,S)
Menger Hotel (J,M,S)
Plaza San Antonio (J,S)
San Antonio Riverwalk Marriott (J,S)
Sheraton Gunter Hotel (B,J)
Wyndham San Antonio (J,S)

## San Diego
Bahia Hotel (J)
Catamaran Resort Hotel (J)
Doubletree Horton Plaza (J,M,S)
Embassy Suites (B,H,J,S)
Gaslamp Plaza Suites (M)
Hanalei Hotel (J)
Hotel del Coronado (H,J,M,S)
Humphrey's Half Moon Inn (J)
Hyatt Islandia (J)
Hyatt Regency La Jolla (J,M,S)
Hyatt Regency S.D. (B,H,J,M,S)
Kona Kai Resort (H,J,M,S)
La Jolla Marriott (J,S)
La Valencia Hotel (J,M,S)
Le Meridien (B,H,J,M,S)
Loews Coronado (H,J,M,S)
Marriott Mission Valley (J,S)
Pan Pacific (J,M,S)
Radisson La Jolla (J)
Rancho Bernardo Inn (J,M,S)
Rancho Valencia (J,M,S)
San Diego Hilton (B,H,J,M,S)
San Diego Marriott (B,H,J,M,S)
San Diego Princess (J,M,S)
Sea Lodge (J,S)
Sheraton Grande Torrey (J,S)
Sheraton Grande Hrbr. Isl. (J,S)
Sheraton - Hrbr. Isl. E. (J,M,S)
Town & Country Hotel (B,H,J)
U.S. Grant Hotel (M)
Westgate Hotel (B,H)

## San Francisco
ANA Hotel (M)
Cathedral Hill (B,H)
Fairmont Hotel (B,H,J,M)
Grand Hyatt (B,H,M)
Harbor Court Hotel (J,M,S)
Hotel Nikko (H,J,M)
Hyatt Fisherman's Whf. (J,M,S)
Hyatt Regency (B,H)

Mandarin Oriental (J)
Mansions Hotel (J,M)
Marriott Fisherman's Wharf (S)
Miyako Hotel (M)
Parc 55 (M,S)
Rancho Valencia (J,M,S)
Ritz-Carlton, San Francisco (J,M,S)
San Francisco Marriott (J,M,S)
San Francisco Hilton (B,H,M,S)
Sheraton Fisherman's Whf. (B,H,M)
Sheraton Palace (J,M,S)
Villa Florence Hotel (H)
Westin St. Francis (B,H)

## San Jose, CA
Fairmont Hotel (M,S)

## Seattle
Alexis Hotel (S)
Doubletree Suites Seattle (J,S)
Four Seasons Olympic (H,J,M,S)
Holiday Inn Crowne Plaza (J,S)
Inn at the Market (H,J,M)
Red Lion Hotel Bellevue (B,H)
Sheraton Seattle (B,J,M,S)
Sorrento Hotel (M)
Stouffer Madison (B,H,J)
Warwick Hotel (J,S)
Westin Hotel Seattle (B,H)

## St. Louis
Adam's Mark (H,J,S)
Cheshire Inn Motor Hotel (J,S)
Clarion Hotel St. Louis (B,H,J)
Doubletree Hotel & Conf. (J,M,S)
Doubletree Mayfair (J,M)
Drury Inn Union Station (J)
Embassy Suites (J,S)
Holiday Inn Clayton Plaza (B,H,J,S)
Holiday Inn Conv. Ctr. (J,S)
Hyatt Regency St. Louis (S)
Marriott Pavilion Hotel (J,S)
Radisson Hotel Clayton (J,S)
Ritz-Carlton, St. Louis (J,M,S)
Seven Gables Inn (J,S)
St. Louis Marriott West (J,S)

## Tampa Bay
Belleview Mido Resort Hotel (J,M,S)
Courtyard by Marriott (J)
Crown Sterling Suites (J)
Don Ce-Sar (B,H,J,M,S)
Embassy Suites Tampa Airport (J,S)
Holiday Inn Ashley Plaza (J)

## BODY CARE

Hyatt Reg. Westshore (B,H,J,M,S)
Innisbrook Resort (B,H,M)
Radisson Bay Harbor Inn (B,H)
Saddlebrook (B,H,J,M,S)
Sheraton Grand Hotel (H)
Sheraton Sand Key Resort (J)
Stouffer Vinoy Resort (J)
Tampa Marriott Westshore (J,S)
Trade Winds (H,J,S)
Wyndham Harbour Island (J,S)

### Teaneck
Marriott Glenpointe (H,J,M,S)

### Washington, DC
ANA Hotel (J,M,S)
Capital Hilton (B,H,S)
Carlton (B,J,M)
Embassy Stes. Chevy Chase (J,S)
Four Seasons Hotel (H,J,M,S)
Grand Hyatt Washington (J,M,S)
Holiday Inn Crowne Plaza (J,S)
Hyatt Fair Lakes (J,S)
Hyatt Regency Reston (J,M,S)
Hyatt Reg. Washington (B,H,M,S)
J.W. Marriott Hotel (J,M,S)
Key Bridge Marriott (H,J,S)
Loews L'Enfant Plaza (M)
Madison Hotel (S)
Morrison House (S)
Omni Georgetown (S)
Park Hyatt (H,J,M,S)
Radisson Plaza Hotel (B,H,J,S)
Ramada Renaissance (J,S)
Ritz-Carlton, Pent. Cty. (J,M,S)
Ritz-Carlton, Tysons (J,M,S)
Sheraton Premiere (B,H,J,M,S)
Sheraton Washington (B,H,S)
Stouffer Mayflower Hotel (B,H)
Washington Court Hotel (S)
Washington Hilton (J,M,S)
Washington Marriott (J,S)
Washington Vista Hotel (H,S)
Watergate Hotel (H,J,M,S)
Westfield's (B,H,J,M,S)
Willard Inter-Continental (M)

### Wilmington
Hotel du Pont (B,H,M)

### Alabama
Marriott's Grand Hotel (B,H,J,M)

### Alaska
Harper Lodge Princess (B,H,J)
King Salmon Lodge (S)
Red Quill Lodge (J,S)
Tikchik Narrows Lodge (S)
Waterfall Resort (J,M)
Yes Bay Lodge (J)

### Arizona
Boulders Resort (B,H,J,M,S)
El Conquistador (B,H,J,M,S)
Enchantment Resort (B,H,J,M,S)
L'Auberge de Sedona (J)
Los Abrigados (J,M,S)
Poco Diablo Resort (J)
Sheraton San Marcos (B,H,J)
Tanque Verde Ranch (J,S)
Ventana Canyon (B,H,J,M,S)
Wahweap Lodge & Marina (J)
Westin La Paloma (H,J,M,S)
Westward Look Resort (J,M)
Wickenburg Inn (J)
Wigwam (J,M,S)

### Arkansas
Arlington Resort (H,J,M,S)
Palace Hotel & Bath House (J,M,S)

### California
Alisal Ranch (J)
Auberge du Soleil (B,H,J,M,S)
Benbow Inn (J)
Carmel Valley Ranch Resort (J,M,S)
Casa Madrona Hotel (J)
Casa Sirena (B,H,J,M,S)
Claremont Resort (B,H,J,M,S)
Eureka Inn (J,S)
Fess Parker's Red Lion (H,J,S)
Four Seasons Biltmore (B,H,J,M,S)
Furnace Creek Inn (H,M,S)
Harvest Inn (J)
Highlands Inn (J)
Inn at Morro Bay (M)
Inn at Rancho Santa Fe (M)
Inn at the Tides (J,M,S)
John Gardiner's (J,M,S)
La Casa del Zorro (H,J,M)
Lodge Pebble Bch. (B,H,J,M,S)
Los Olivos Grand Hotel (H,J,M)
Meadowood Resort (M,S)
Northstar-at-Tahoe (J,S)
Ojai Valley Inn (J,M,S)

Portofino Hotel & Yacht Club (J,M)
Post Ranch Inn (J,M,S)
Quail Lodge (J,M)
Santa Barbara Miramar (H,M,S)
San Ysidro Ranch (J,M)
Sheraton Universal Hotel (J)
Silverado Country Club (J,S)
Squaw Valley Inn (J)
Stonepine Estate Resort (J,M)
St. Orres (J,M,S)
Timberhill Ranch (J)
Ventana - Big Sur (H,J,M,S)
Villa Royale (J,M)
Vintage Inn (M)
Vintners Inn (J,M)
Wine Country Inn (J)

## Colorado

Antlers Doubletree (B,H,J,M)
Aspen Club Lodge (J,M,S)
Breckenridge Hilton (J,M,S)
Broadmoor (B,H,J,M,S)
Charter Beaver Crk. (H,J,M,S)
Cheyenne Mountain (J,M,S)
C Lazy U Ranch (J)
Club Med, Copper Mountain (J,S)
Doral Telluride (B,H,J,M,S)
Grande Butte Hotel (J,S)
Home Ranch (J,M,S)
Hotel Jerome (J)
Hotel Lenado (J,M)
Hot Springs Lodge (J)
Hyatt Reg. Beaver Creek (J,M,S)
Inn at Aspen (J,M,S)
Inn at Beaver Creek (J,S)
Iron Horse Resort Retreat (J,S)
Keystone Lodge (J,M,S)
Limelite Lodge (J,S)
Little Nell (J,M,S)
Lodge at Cordillera (B,H,J,M,S)
Lodge at Vail (J,M,S)
Mountain Haus at Vail (J,M,S)
Pines Lodge (J,M,S)
Radisson Resort Vail (H,J,M,S)
Ritz-Carlton, Aspen (B,H,J,M,S)
Sardy House (J,M,S)
Sheraton Steamboat Resort (J,M,S)
Silver Tree Hotel (J,M,S)
Snowmass Lodge & Club (J,M,S)
Sonnenalp Resort (J,M,S)
Stanley Hotel (J)
Tall Timber (J,S)

Tamarron Resort (J,M,S)
Vail Athletic Club (H,J,M,S)
Vista Verde Guest Ranch (J,S)
Westin Resort Vail (J,M,S)

## Connecticut

Interlaken Inn (M,S)
Mayflower Inn (M,S)
Water's Edge Inn & Resort (J,S)

## Florida

Amelia Island Plantation (B,H,J,M,S)
Boca Raton Resort (B,H,J,M,S)
Breakers (B,H,M)
Chalet Suzanne (J,M)
Cheeca Lodge (J,M)
Colony Beach Resort (J,M,S)
Don Shula's (J,M,S)
Grenelefe Resort (B,H,J,S)
Hawk's Cay Resort & Marina (J,M)
Hyatt Key West (J,M)
Indian River Plantation Resort (J,M)
Inn at Flsher Island (H,J,M,S)
Lakeside Inn (B,H,M)
Little Palm Island (J,M,S)
Lodge at Ponte Vedra (J,M,S)
Marriott at Sawgrass Resort (J,M,S)
Marriott's Bay Point (B,H,J,M,S)
Marriott's Casa Marina (B,H,J,M,S)
Marriott's Marco Island (B,H,J,M)
Ocean Grand Hotel (B,H,J,M,S)
Ocean Key House (J)
Ocean Reef Club (B,H,J,M)
Palm Beach Polo (J,M)
PGA National (B,H,J,M,S)
Pier House Resort (H,J,M,S)
Ponte Vedra Inn (B,H,J,M,S)
Reach Resort (S)
Registry Resort (H,J,M,S)
Resort at Longboat (B,H,J,M,S)
Ritz-Carlton, Am. Isl. (B,H,J,M,S)
Ritz-Carlton, Naples (B,H,J,M,S)
Ritz-Carlton, P.B. (B,H,J,M,S)
Sheraton Key Largo (B,H,J)
Sonesta Sanibel Harbour (H,M)
South Seas Plantation (H,M)
Sundial Beach Resort (H,J)

## Georgia

Callaway Gardens Resort (B,H)
Cloister (B,H,J,M,S)
Evergreen Conf. Ctr. (J,M,S)

# BODY CARE

Gastonian (J)
Greyfield Inn (M)
Jekyll Island Club Hotel (M)
King & Prince Beach Resort (J,S)
Sea Palms Resort (J,S)
Sheraton Savannah Resort (S)
Stouffer Pineisle Resort (J,S)

## Hawaii

Embassy Suites Resort Maui (J,S)
Four Seasons Wailea (H,J,M,S)
Grand Hyatt Wailea (H,H,J,M,S)
Hotel Hana-Maui (B,H,J,M)
Hyatt Regency Kauai (H,J,M,S)
Hyatt Regency Maui (B,H,J,M,S)
Hyatt Reg. Waikoloa (B,H,J,M,S)
Kaanapali Beach Hotel (H)
Kanaloa at Kona (J,S)
Kapalua Bay Hotel & Villas (H,M)
Kona Hilton Resort (H)
Kona Village Resort (M)
Lodge at Koele (B,H,J,M,S)
Manele Bay Hotel (B,H,J,M,S)
Maui Inter-Continental (B,H,J,M)
Maui Marriott (B,H,J,M)
Maui Prince Hotel (M)
Mauna Kea Hotel (B,H,J,M,S)
Mauna Lani Bay Hotel (H,J,M,S)
Princeville Hotel (B,H,J,M,S)
Ritz-Carlton, Mauna Lani (B,H,J,M,S)
Royal Lahaina Resort (B,H,J,M)
Royal Waikoloan (J,M)
Stouffer Wailea (H,J,M)
Stouffer Waiohai Beach (H,J,M,S)
Westin Kauai (B,H,J,M,S)
Westin Maui (B,H,J,M,S)

## Idaho

Coeur d'Alene Resort (B,H,J,M,S)
Sun Valley Lodge (H,J,M,S)

## Illinois

Clock Tower (B,H,J,M,S)
Eagle Ridge Inn & Resort (J,M)
Indian Lakes Resort (B,H,J,M,S)
Marriott's Lincolnshire (J,M,S)
Nordic Hills Resort & Conf. Ctr. (J,S)
Pheasant Run Resort (H,J,M,S)

## Indiana

Four Winds Clarion (J,S)
French Lick (B,H,J,M,S)

## Iowa

Redstone Inn (M)

## Louisiana

Asphodel Plantation Inn (J)

## Maine

Bayview Hotel & Inn (J,M)
Bethel Inn & Country Club (J,S)
Black Point Inn Resort (B,H,J,M,S)
Cliff House (J,M,S)
Harraseeket Inn (J)
Samoset Resort (J,M,S)
White Barn Inn (M)

## Maryland

Imperial Hotel (M)
Inn at Perry Cabin (J,S)
Loews Annapolis (H)

## Massachusetts

Blantyre (J,M,S)
Daggett House (J)
Nantucket Inn & Conf. Ctr. (J)
Ocean Edge Resort (J,M,S)
Orchards (J,M,S)
Red Lion Inn (M)
Summer House (J,M)
Village Inn (J)
Wequassett Inn (M)
Wheatleigh (M)

## Michigan

Boyne Highlands Inn (S)
Boyne Mountain Hotel (H,J,M,S)
Grand Hotel (B,H,J,S)
Grand Traverse Resort (H,J,M,S)
Shanty Creek (B,H,J,M,S)
Sugar Loaf Resort (J)
Treetops Sylvan Resort (J,M,S)

## Minnesota

Arrowwood (J,S)
Breezy Point Resort (J,S)
Grand View Lodge (J)
Lutsen Resort (J,S)
Madden's on Gull Lake (H,J,M,S)
St. James Hotel (H,J,M)

## Missouri

Lodge of Four Seasons (H,J,M,S)
Marriott's TanTarA (B,H,J,M,S)

## Montana

Chico Hot Springs Lodge (J,M)
Gallatin Gateway Inn (J)
Grouse Mountain Lodge (H,J,M,S)
Huntley Lodge (J,M,S)
Izaak Walton Inn (S)
Kandahar Lodge (J,M,S)
Lone Mountain Ranch (J,M)
Mountain Sky Guest Ranch (J,S)
Triple Creek (J,M,S)

### Nevada

Caesars Lake Tahoe  (J,S)
Harrah's Lake Tahoe (B,H,J,M,S)
Hyatt Regency Lake Tahoe (M,S)

### New Hampshire

Balsams (H)
Christmas Farm Inn (S)
Mount Washington Hotel (S)
Snowy Owl Inn (M,S)
Stonehurst Manor (J)

### New Mexico

Bishop's Lodge (J,M,S)
Casa Benevides (J)
Dos Casas Viejas (M)
Eldorado Hotel (J,S)
Historic Taos Inn (S)
Hotel Edelweiss (J,M,S)
Hotel Plaza Real (J,M)
Hotel Santa Fe (J,M)
Inn of the Anasazi (M)
Inn of the Mountain Gods (J,S)
Inn on the Alameda (H,J)
La Fonda Hotel on the Plaza (H,J)
La Posada de Albuquerque (H,M)
La Posada de Santa Fe (H)
Lodge at Cloudcroft (J,M,S)
Quail Ridge Inn (J,S)
Rancho Encantado Resort (J,M)
Sagebrush Inn (J)
Sheraton Old Town (H,J,M,S)
St. Bernard Hotel (S)

### New York State

Concord Resort Hotel (B,H,M,S)
Doral Arrowwood (J,M,S)
Gideon Putnam Hotel (M)
Guest House (J,M)
Harrison Conference Center (J,M,S)
Mohonk Mountain House (M,S)

Montauk Yacht Club (M,S)
Omni Sagamore (B,H,J,M,S)
Point (M)
Troutbeck Inn (S)

### North Carolina

Greystone Inn (J)
Grove Park Inn Resort (J,M,S)
High Hampton Inn (M)
Pinehurst Hotel (M)
Sanderling Inn Resort (J,S)

### Ohio

Quail Hollow Resort (J,M,S)
Sawmill Creek Resort (J,S)

### Oklahoma

Lake Texoma Resort (S)
Shangri-La Resort (B,H,J,S)

### Oregon

Embarcadero Resort Hotel (J,S)
Inn at Spanish Head (J,S)
Kah-Nee-Ta Resort (J,M,S)
Rock Springs Guest Ranch (J,M)
Salishan Lodge (B,H,J,M,S)
Sunriver Lodge & Resort (J,S)
Timberline Lodge (J,M,S)

### Pennsylvania

Bridgeton House (M)
Hotel Hershey (J,S)
Mount Airy Lodge (J,M,S)
Nemacolin (B,H,J,M,S)
Pocono Manor Inn (M,S)
Seven Springs (B,H,J,M,S)
Skytop Lodge (J,S)
Split Rock Resort (H,J,M,S)

### Rhode Island

Doubletree Hotel (B,H,M,S)
Hotel Manisses (J)
Newport Harbor Hotel (S)

### South Carolina

Hilton Head Hilton (J,S)
Hyatt Reg. Hilton Head (H,J,M,S)
Jasmine House Inn (J)
Marriott's Hilton Head (B,H,J,M,S)
Seabrook Island Resort (J)
Sea Pines (B,H,S)
Vendue Inn (J)
Westin Resort (B,H,J,M,S)

## BODY CARE

### South Dakota

Franklin Hotel (B,H)
Hotel Alex Johnson (S)
Palmer Gulch Lodge (J)

### Tennessee

Fairfield Glade Resort (S)

### Texas

Barton Creek (B,H,J,M,S)
Flying L Guest Ranch (J)
Horseshoe Bay Resort (J,M,S)
Lakeway Inn & Conf. Ctr. (J,M,S)
Radisson South Padre Island (J)
Sheraton South Padre Island (J)

### Utah

Cliff Lodge (B,H,J,M,S)
Shadow Ridge Hotel (J,M,S)
Stein Eriksen Lodge (J,M,S)
Washington School Inn (J,S)

### Vermont

Basin Harbor Club (M)
Cortina Inn (J,M,S)
Equinox (M,S)
Hawk Inn & Mountain (J,M,S)
Hermitage Inn (S)
Mountain Top Inn (S)
Rabbit Hill Inn (J,M)
Stratton Mountain Inn (H,J,M,S)
Sugarbush Inn (J,M,S)
Topnotch at Stowe (B,H,J,M,S)
Trapp Family Lodge (M,S)
Woods at Killington (J,M,S)
Woodstock Inn & Resort (J,M,S)

### Virginia

Boar's Head Inn (M,S)
Homestead (B,H,M,S)
Inn at Little Washington (M)
Kingsmill Resort & Conf. Ctr. (J,S)
Lansdowne Conf. Resort (J,M,S)
Williamsburg Inn (B,H,J,M,S)

### Washington

Inn at Semiahmoo (H,J,M,S)
Rosario Resort & Spa (H,J,M,S)
Salish Lodge (J,S)
Sun Mountain Lodge (J,M)

### West Virginia

Greenbrier (B,H,J,M,S)

### Wisconsin

Abbey (B,H,J,M,S)
Americana Lake Geneva (J,M,S)
American Club (H,J,M,S)
Heidel House Resort (J,S)
Lake Lawn Lodge (B,H,M,S)
Lakewoods Resort & Lodge (J,S)
Olympia Resort (J,M,S)

### Wyoming

Jackson Hole R.C. (B,H,J,M,S)
Jackson Lake Lodge (B,H)
Old Faithful Inn (H)
Paradise Guest Ranch (J)
Snow King Resort (B,H,J,M,S)
Spring Creek Ranch (J,M)
Teton Pines Resort (J)
Wort Hotel (H,J)

# BUSINESS EXECUTIVES

## Albuquerque
Doubletree Albuquerque
Hyatt Regency Albuquerque
Marriott Albuquerque

## Anchorage
Captain Cook Hotel

## Atlanta
Aberdeen Woods Conf. Ctr.
Atlanta Marriott Marquis
Courtyard by Marriott
Doubletree Hotel at Concourse
Embassy Suites Perim. Ctr.
French Quarter Suites
Holiday Inn Crowne Plaza
Hotel Nikko
Hyatt Regency
J.W. Marriott at Lenox
Marriott Suites Perimeter
Peachtree Executive Conf. Ctr.
Ritz-Carlton, Atlanta
Ritz-Carlton, Buckhead
Stouffer Waverly Hotel
Swissotel Atlanta
Westin Peachtree Plaza
Wyndham Garden Hotel - Vinings
Wyndham Garden - Midtown

## Austin
Four Seasons Hotel

## Baltimore
Baltimore Marriott Inner Harbor
Clarion Hotel - Inner Harbor
Cross Keys Inn
Doubletree Inn at the Colonnade
Harbor Court Hotel
Hyatt Regency Baltimore
Peabody Court Hotel
Sheraton Baltimore North
Stouffer Harborplace

## Birmingham
Tutwiler
Wynfrey Hotel

## Boston
Boston Harbor Hotel
Bostonian Hotel
Boston Marriott Peabody
Cambridge Center Marriott
Charles Hotel in Harvard Square
Copley Plaza Hotel
Eliot Hotel

Four Seasons Hotel
Hyatt Regency Cambridge
Le Meridien Boston
Marriott Copley Place
Marriott Hotel Long Wharf
Ritz-Carlton, Boston
Sheraton Boston Hotel & Towers
Sheraton Commander Hotel
Swissotel Boston
Westin Hotel Copley Place

## Charlotte
Dunhill Hotel

## Chicago
Chicago Hilton & Towers
Chicago Marriott Downtown
Chicago Marriott O'Hare
Chicago Marriott Suites O'Hare
Drake Hotel
Fairmont Hotel
Forum Hotel
Four Seasons Hotel
Hotel Inter-Continental
Hotel Nikko
Hotel Sofitel
Hyatt Printers Row
Hyatt Regency Chicago
Hyatt Regency O'Hare
Hyatt Regency Suites
Le Meridien Hotel Chicago
Mayfair
Midland Hotel
Omni Ambassador East
Palmer House Hilton
Park Hyatt
Quality Inn & Clarion Hotel
Radisson Plaza Ambass. West
Radisson Suite Hotel
Raphael Hotel
Ritz-Carlton, Chicago
Sheraton Chicago Hotel & Towers
Stouffer Riviere
Swissotel Chicago
Tremont Hotel
Westin Hotel, Chicago
Westin Hotel O'Hare

## Cincinnati
Cincinnatian Hotel
Hyatt Regency Cincinnati
Omni Netherland Plaza
Westin Hotel

# BUSINESS EXECUTIVES

## Cleveland
Cleveland Marriott East
Cleveland Marriott Society Center
Cleveland South Hilton Inn
Omni International Hotel
Pierre Radisson Inn
Ritz-Carlton, Cleveland
Stouffer Tower City Plaza Hotel

## Columbus
Worthington Inn

## Corpus Christi
Corpus Christi Marriott Bayfront

## Dallas
Adolphus
Dallas Marriott Quorum
Doubletree Hotel at Park West
Doubletree Hotel Campbell Ctr.
Doubletree Hotel Lincoln Ctr.
Fairmont Hotel
Four Seasons Resort & Club
Grand Kempinski Dallas
Hotel Crescent Court
Hyatt Regency Dallas at Reunion
Loews Anatole Hotel
Mansion on Turtle Creek
Melrose Hotel
Omni Mandalay Hotel
Plaza of the Americas Hotel
Sheraton Park Central
Sheraton Suites
Stouffer Dallas Hotel
Westin Galleria
Wyndham Garden Hotel

## Denver
Brown Palace Hotel
Burnsley Hotel
Cambridge Hotel
Denver Marriott City Center
Doubletree Hotel Denver
Hyatt Regency Denver
Hyatt Regency Tech Center
Loews Giorgio Hotel
Marriott Southeast
Oxford Hotel
Red Lion
Residence Inn
Scanticon
Sheraton Denver Tech Center
Stouffer Concourse Hotel

Warwick Hotel
Westin Hotel Tabor Center

## Detroit
Atheneum Suites
Dearborn Inn Marriott
Hotel St. Regis
Hyatt Regency Dearborn
Omni
Radisson Hotel Pontchartrain
Radisson Plaza Hotel
Ritz-Carlton, Dearborn
River Place Inn
Westin Hotel

## Florham Park
Hamilton Park

## Fort Lauderdale
Crown Sterling Suites Cypress
Fort Lauderdale Marriott North
Marriott's Harbor Beach Resort
Pier 66 Resort & Marina
Sheraton Design Center
Westin Hotel, Cypress Creek

## Fort Worth
Worthington

## Hartford
Goodwin Hotel

## Honolulu
Halekulani
Hawaii Prince Hotel Waikiki
Hyatt Regency Waikiki
Kahala Hilton
Sheraton Moana Surfrider

## Houston
Adam's Mark
Doubletree at Post Oak
Doubletree Hotel at Allen Center
Four Seasons Hotel
Hotel Sofitel
Houstonian Hotel & Conf. Ctr.
Houston Marriott Westside
Hyatt Regency Houston
J.W. Marriott Hotel
La Colombe d'Or
Lancaster
Omni
Plaza Hilton
Ritz-Carlton, Houston

Sheraton Grand Hotel
Stouffer Presidente Hotel
Westin Oaks
Wyndham Greenspoint
Wyndham Warwick Hotel

**Indianapolis**
Canterbury Hotel
Embassy Suites Hotel
Hyatt Regency Indianapolis
Omni Severin
Radisson Plaza & Suites Hotel
University Place
Westin Hotel Indianapolis

**Kansas City**
Allis Plaza Hotel
Doubletree Hotel
Holiday Inn Crowne Plaza
Hyatt Regency Crown Center
Marriott Overland Park
Radisson Suite Hotel
Raphael Hotel
Ritz-Carlton, Kansas City
Sheraton Suites
Westin Crown Center

**Las Vegas**
Alexis Park Resort
Caesars Palace

**Los Angeles**
BelAge Hotel
Beverly Hills Hotel
Biltmore Los Angeles
Century Plaza Hotel
Checkers Hotel Kempinski
Four Seasons Hotel
Hotel Bel-Air
Hotel Inter-Continental
Hotel Nikko
Hyatt Regency Los Angeles
J.W. Marriott at Century City
Le Dufy
Le Parc Hotel
L'Ermitage Hotel
Loews Santa Monica Beach Hotel
Los Angeles Airport Hilton
Los Angeles Hilton & Towers
Ma Maison Sofitel
Marriott LAX
Mondrian Hotel
New Otani Hotel & Garden
Peninsula Beverly Hills
Radisson Plaza Hotel & Golf Course

Regent Beverly Wilshire
Ritz-Carlton, Huntington Hotel
Ritz-Carlton, Marina del Rey
Sheraton Grande Hotel
Sheraton Los Angeles Airport
St. James's Club & Hotel
Stouffer Los Angeles Concourse
Tower at Century Plaza
Warner Center Marriott
Westwood Marquis Hotel

**Louisville**
Seelbach Hotel

**Memphis**
Peabody Memphis

**Miami/Miami Beach**
Alexander All-Suite Luxury Hotel
Biltmore Hotel
Colonnade Hotel
Grand Bay Hotel
Grove Isle Yacht & Tennis Club
Hotel Inter-Continental
Hyatt Regency Coral Gables
Hyatt Regency Miami
Mayfair House Hotel Grand Luxe
Sonesta Beach Hotel

**Milwaukee**
Embassy Suites, West
Hyatt Regency Milwaukee
Marc Plaza Hotel
Milwaukee Marriott - Brookfield
Park East Hotel
Pfister Hotel
Wyndham Milwaukee Center

**Minneapolis/St. Paul**
Crown Sterling (Minn/St. Paul)
Hotel Sofitel
Marquette
Minneapolis Marriott City Center
Northland Inn
Omni Northstar Hotel
Radisson Hotel & Conf. Ctr.
Radisson Hotel Metrodome
Radisson Plaza Hotel
Registry Hotel
Saint Paul Hotel
Whitney

**Nashville**
Doubletree Hotel Nashville
Embassy Suites

## BUSINESS EXECUTIVES

Holiday Inn Crowne Plaza
Loews Vanderbilt Plaza Hotel
Opryland Hotel
Regal Maxwell House
Sheraton Music City Hotel
Stouffer Nashville Hotel
Union Station Hotel

### New Orleans
Fairmont Hotel
Hotel Inter-Continental
Le Meridien Hotel
New Orleans Hilton Riverside
Omni Royal Orleans
Pontchartrain Hotel
Saint Louis Hotel
Sheraton New Orleans Hotel
Westin Canal Place
Windsor Court Hotel

### New York City
Box Tree
Carlyle Hotel
Doral Court Hotel
Doral Tuscany
Dorset
Drake Swissotel
Essex House, Hotel Nikko
Flatotel International
Grand Hyatt
Helmsley Palace
Helmsley Park Lane Hotel
Hotel Macklowe
Hotel Millenium
Hotel Plaza Athenee
Inter-Continental
Le Parker Meridien
Loews New York Hotel
Lowell New York
Mark
Mayfair Hotel Baglioni
Michelangelo
Morgans
New York Helmsley Hotel
New York Hilton & Towers
New York Marriott Eastside
New York Marriott Marquis
New York Vista
Novotel New York
Omni Berkshire Place
Peninsula New York
Pierre
Plaza Hotel

Ramada Renaissance
Regency
Rihga Royal
Ritz-Carlton, New York
Sheraton Manhattan
Sheraton New York
Stanhope
St. Regis
Surrey Hotel
U.N. Plaza - Park Hyatt
Waldorf-Astoria/Towers
Warwick
Westbury Hotel

### Oklahoma City
Waterford Hotel

### Orange County, CA
Costa Mesa Marriott Suites
Doubletree Hotel Orange County
Four Seasons Hotel
Hyatt Newporter
Hyatt Regency Irvine
Irvine Marriott
Le Meridien Newport
Marriott Suites Newport Beach
Newport Beach Marriott Hotel
Red Lion Orange County Airport
Ritz-Carlton, Laguna Niguel
Sheraton Newport Beach Hotel
Westin South Coast Plaza

### Orlando
Courtyard at Lake Lucerne
Omni

### Palm Springs
Hyatt Grand Champions Resort
Ritz-Carlton, Rancho Mirage

### Philadelphia
Adam's Mark
Barclay Hotel
Four Seasons Hotel
Hotel Atop the Bellevue
Hyatt Cherry Hill
Independence Park Inn
Latham Hotel
Omni Hotel at Independence Park
Penn's View Inn
Philadelphia Hilton & Towers
Rittenhouse
Ritz-Carlton, Philadelphia
Sheraton Society Hill

Sheraton University City
Wyndham Franklin Plaza Hotel

**Phoenix/Scottsdale**
Arizona Biltmore
Buttes
Crown Sterling Suites
Hyatt Regency Phoenix
Hyatt Regency Scottsdale
Marriott's Camelback Inn
Marriott Suites Scottsdale
Phoenician
Pointe at South Mountain
Pointe at Squaw Peak
Pointe at Tapatio Cliffs
Ritz-Carlton, Phoenix
Scottsdale Conference Resort
Scottsdale Princess
Sheraton San Marcos Golf Resort
Wyndham Paradise Valley Resort

**Pittsburgh**
Hyatt Regency Pittsburgh
Pittsburgh Vista
Westin William Penn

**Portland, OR**
Heathman Hotel
Hotel Vintage Plaza
River Place Alexis Hotel

**Raleigh-Durham**
Carolina Inn
Siena Hotel
Washington Duke Inn

**Richmond**
Commonwealth Park Suites Hotel

**San Antonio**
Fairmount Hotel
Hyatt Regency San Antonio
La Mansion del Rio
Marriott Rivercenter
Plaza San Antonio
Saint Anthony Hotel
Wyndham San Antonio

**San Diego**
Doubletree Hotel at Horton Plaza
Hyatt Regency La Jolla
Hyatt Regency San Diego
La Jolla Marriott
Le Meridien San Diego
Loews Coronado Bay Resort
Pan Pacific

San Diego Marriott
Sheraton Grande at Torrey Pines
U.S. Grant Hotel
Westgate Hotel

**San Francisco**
ANA Hotel
Campton Place Kempinski
Donatello
Fairmont Hotel
Four Seasons Clift Hotel
Grand Hyatt
Hotel Diva
Hotel Nikko
Huntington Hotel Nob Hill
Hyatt Regency San Francisco
Juliana Hotel
Kensington Park
Mandarin Oriental
Mark Hopkins Inter-Continental
Miyako Hotel
Pan Pacific
Parc 55
Park Hyatt
Prescott Hotel
Ritz-Carlton, San Francisco
San Francisco Downtown Marriott
San Francisco Hilton
Sheraton Palace
Sherman House
Stouffer Stanford Court Hotel
Villa Florence Hotel
Westin St. Francis

**San Jose, CA**
Fairmont Hotel

**Seattle**
Alexis Hotel
Edgewater
Four Seasons Olympic
Holiday Inn Crowne Plaza
Hyatt Regency Bellevue
Inn at the Market
Mayflower Park Hotel
Sheraton Seattle Hotel & Towers
Sorrento Hotel
Stouffer Madison
Warwick Hotel
Westin Hotel Seattle

**St. Louis**
Adam's Mark
Cheshire Inn Motor Hotel

# BUSINESS EXECUTIVES

Daniele Hotel
Embassy Suites
Hotel Majestic
Hyatt Regency St. Louis
Marriott Pavilion Hotel
Radisson Hotel Clayton
Ritz-Carlton, St. Louis
Seven Gables Inn

## Tampa Bay
Courtyard by Marriott
Crown Sterling Suites
Heritage Hotel
Hyatt Regency Westshore
Sheraton Grand Hotel
Tampa Marriott Westshore
Wyndham Harbour Island Hotel

## Teaneck
Marriott Glenpointe

## Washington, DC
ANA Hotel
Capital Hilton
Carlton
Embassy Row Hotel
Embassy Suites Chevy Chase
Four Seasons Hotel
Georgetown Inn
Grand Hotel
Grand Hyatt Washington
Hay-Adams Hotel
Henley Park Hotel
Hyatt Arlington at Key Bridge
Hyatt Fair Lakes
Hyatt Regency Bethesda
Hyatt Regency Reston
Hyatt Regency Washington
J.W. Marriott Hotel
Jefferson Hotel
Key Bridge Marriott
Latham Hotel
Loews L'Enfant Plaza
Madison Hotel
Morrison-Clark Inn
Morrison House
Omni Georgetown
Park Hyatt
Phoenix Park Hotel
Pullman-Highland Hotel
Radisson Park Terrace Hotel
Radisson Plaza Hotel
Ritz-Carlton, Pentagon City

Ritz-Carlton, Tysons Corner
Ritz-Carlton, Washington DC
Sheraton Premiere
Stouffer Mayflower Hotel
Washington Court Hotel
Washington Hilton & Towers
Washington Marriott
Washington Vista Hotel
Watergate Hotel
Westfield's Intl. Conf. Ctr.
Willard Inter-Continental
Wyndham Bristol Hotel

## Wilmington
Hotel du Pont

## Arizona
Poco Diablo Resort
Sheraton San Marcos Golf Resort
Westin La Paloma

## California
Four Seasons Biltmore
Portofino Hotel & Yacht Club

## Colorado
Antlers Doubletree
Cheyenne Mountain Conf. Resort
Hotel Boulderado
Ritz-Carlton, Aspen

## Florida
Boca Raton Resort & Club
Brazilian Court
Indian River Plantation Resort
Ocean Grand Hotel
PGA National
Registry Resort
Ritz-Carlton, Palm Beach

## Georgia
Eliza Thompson
Evergreen Conference Center
Foley House Inn
Gastonian
Mulberry Inn
Planter's Inn
President's Quarters

## Illinois
Clock Tower Resort & Conf. Ctr.
Indian Lakes Resort

Marriott's Lincolnshire Resort
Nordic Hills Resort & Conf. Ctr.

## Maryland

Loews Annapolis
Maryland Inn

## Minnesota

Fitgers Inn

## New York State

Doral Arrowwood
Harrison Conference Center

## Ohio

Quail Hollow Resort

## South Carolina

Lodge Alley Inn
Mills House Hotel

## Tennessee

Inn at Blackberry Farm

## Texas

Barton Creek
Lakeway Inn & Conf. Ctr.

## Utah

Brigham Street Inn

## Vermont

Inn at Essex

## Virginia

Kingsmill Resort & Conf. Ctr.
Lansdowne Conf. Resort

## Spas

Loews Ventana Canyon Resort

# CONFERENCE CENTERS

**Albuquerque**
Hyatt Regency Albuquerque

**Atlanta**
Aberdeen Woods Conf. Ctr.
Lanier Plaza Hotel & Conf. Ctr.
Peachtree Executive Conf. Ctr.

**Atlantic City**
Holiday Inn Diplomat

**Chicago**
Palmer House Hilton

**Cincinnati**
Kings Island Inn & Conf. Ctr.

**Dallas**
Four Seasons Resort & Club

**Denver**
Scanticon

**Florham Park**
Hamilton Park

**Houston**
Houstonian Hotel & Conf. Ctr.

**Indianapolis**
University Place

**Little Rock**
Arkansas' Excelsior Hotel

**Minneapolis/St. Paul**
Northland Inn
Radisson Hotel & Conf. Ctr.

**New Orleans**
Hotel Inter-Continental

**New York City**
Hotel Kimberly
Hotel Macklowe

**Phoenix/Scottsdale**
Scottsdale Conference Resort
Sheraton San Marcos Golf Resort
Sunburst Hotel & Conf. Ctr.

**St. Louis**
Doubletree Hotel
St. Louis Marriott

**Washington, DC**
DuPont Plaza Hotel
Residence Inn Bethesda
Westfield's Intl. Conf. Ctr.

**California**
Silverado Country Club & Resort
Squaw Valley Inn

**Colorado**
Cheyenne Mountain Conf. Resort
Sheraton Steamboat Resort

**Florida**
Amelia Island Plantation
Grenelefe Resort
Inn at Fisher Island
Lakeside Inn
Ponce de Leon Resort
South Seas Plantation Resort

**Georgia**
Evergreen Conference Center

**Illinois**
Clock Tower Resort & Conf. Ctr.
Eagle Ridge Inn & Resort
Nordic Hills Resort & Conf. Ctr.
Pheasant Run Resort

**Massachusetts**
Chatham Bars Inn
Nantucket Inn & Conf. Ctr.
Ocean Edge Resort & Conf. Ctr.

**Michigan**
Boyne Mountain Hotel

**New Mexico**
Eldorado Hotel

**New York State**
Doral Arrowwood
Gideon Putnam Hotel
Harrison Conference Center

**Oklahoma**
Shangri-La Resort

**Pennsylvania**
Nemacolin Woodlands
Seven Springs Mountain Resort
Split Rock Resort

**Texas**
Barton Creek
Horseshoe Bay Resort
Lakeway Inn & Conf. Ctr.
Woodlands Executive Conf. Ctr.

**Virginia**
Kingsmill Resort & Conf. Ctr.
Lansdowne Conf. Resort

**Wisconsin**
American Club
Olympia Resort

# CONVENTION CENTER CONVENIENCE

**Albuquerque**
Doubletree Albuquerque
Hyatt Regency Albuquerque

**Anchorage**
Captain Cook Hotel

**Atlanta**
Ansley Inn
Atlanta Hilton & Towers
Atlanta Marriott Marquis
Atlanta Penta Hotel
Hyatt Regency
Omni Hotel at CNN Center
Radisson Hotel
Ritz-Carlton, Atlanta
Sheraton Colony Square Hotel
Westin Peachtree Plaza

**Atlantic City**
Bally's Grand Hotel & Casino
Bally's Park Place
Caesars Atlantic City
Claridge Casino Hotel
Holiday Inn Diplomat
Merv Griffin's Resorts
Sands Hotel & Casino
Showboat Hotel
TropWorld
Trump Plaza Hotel & Casino
Trump Regency Hotel
Trump Taj Mahal

**Baltimore**
Baltimore Marriott Inner Harbor
Brookshire Hotel
Clarion Hotel - Inner Harbor
Harbor Court Hotel
Hyatt Regency Baltimore
Omni Inner Harbor Hotel
Sheraton Inner Harbor Hotel
Society Hill Hotel
Stouffer Harborplace
Tremont Hotel
Tremont Plaza Hotel

**Birmingham**
Tutwiler

**Boston**
Back Bay Hilton
Boston Park Plaza
Colonnade Hotel
Copley Plaza Hotel
Copley Square Hotel

Eliot Hotel
Four Seasons Hotel
Lenox Hotel
Marriott Copley Place
Ritz-Carlton, Boston
Sheraton Boston Hotel & Towers
Swissotel Boston
Westin Hotel Copley Place

**Charlotte**
Dunhill Hotel

**Chicago**
Allerton Hotel
Best Western Inn
Bismarck Hotel
Blackstone Hotel
Chicago Hilton & Towers
Chicago Marriott Downtown
Congress Hotel
Drake Hotel
Executive Plaza
Fairmont Hotel
Forum Hotel
Four Seasons Hotel
Holiday Inn City Centre
Hotel Inter-Continental
Hotel Nikko
Hyatt Printers Row
Hyatt Regency Chicago
Hyatt Regency Suites
Knickerbocker Chicago Hotel
Le Meridien Hotel Chicago
Mayfair
McCormick Center Hotel
Omni Ambassador East
Palmer House Hilton
Park Hyatt
Radisson Plaza Ambass. West
Raphael Hotel
Richmont Hotel
Ritz-Carlton, Chicago
Sheraton Chicago Hotel & Towers
Sheraton Plaza Hotel
Stouffer Riviere
Swissotel Chicago
Talbott Hotel
Tremont Hotel
Westin Hotel, Chicago

**Cincinnati**
Cincinnatian Hotel
Cincinnati Terrace Hilton
Clarion Hotel Cincinnati

# CONVENTION CENTER CONVENIENCE

Hyatt Regency Cincinnati
Omni Netherland Plaza
Westin Hotel

## Cleveland
Cleveland Marriott Society Center
Holiday Inn Lakeside City Center
Radisson Plaza Hotel
Ritz-Carlton, Cleveland
Sheraton City Centre
Stouffer Tower City Plaza Hotel

## Dallas
Adolphus
Aristocrat Hotel
Dallas Grand
Fairmont Hotel
Hotel St. Germain
Hyatt Regency Dallas at Reunion
Plaza of the Americas Hotel
Sheraton Suites
Southland Center Hotel
Stoneleigh Hotel

## Denver
Brown Palace Hotel
Burnsley Hotel
Cambridge Hotel
Denver Marriott City Center
Embassy Suites Denver Dtwn.
Hyatt Regency Denver
Oxford Hotel
Radisson Hotel
Residence Inn
Warwick Hotel
Westin Hotel Tabor Center

## Detroit
Atheneum Suites
Hotel St. Regis
Omni
Radisson Hotel Pontchartrain
River Place Inn
Westin Hotel

## Fort Lauderdale
Crown Sterling Suites Cypress
Fort Lauderdale Marina Marriott
Lago Mar Resort & Club
Marriott's Harbor Beach Resort
Ocean Manor Resort Hotel
Pier 66 Resort & Marina
Riverside Hotel
Sheraton Yankee Clipper

## Fort Worth
Worthington

## Hartford
Goodwin Hotel

## Honolulu
Ritz-Carlton Kapalua

## Houston
Doubletree Hotel at Allen Center
Four Seasons Hotel
Houstonian Hotel & Conf. Ctr.
Houston Marriott Astrodome
Hyatt Regency Houston
La Colombe d'Or
Lancaster

## Indianapolis
Canterbury Hotel
Embassy Suites Hotel
Holiday Inn Union Station
Hyatt Regency Indianapolis
Indianapolis Hilton Downtown
Omni Severin
Westin Hotel Indianapolis

## Kansas City
Allis Plaza Hotel
Americana Hotel on Convention
Hilton Plaza Inn
Hotel Savoy
Hyatt Regency Crown Center
Radisson Suite Hotel
Sheraton Suites
Westin Crown Center

## Las Vegas
Aladdin Hotel
Alexis Park Resort
Bally's
Caesars Palace
Circus Circus Hotel
Desert Inn Hotel & Country Club
Dunes Hotel & Country Club
Excalibur Hotel
Flamingo Hotel
Frontier Hotel
Hacienda Hotel & Casino
Imperial Palace Hotel & Casino
Las Vegas Hilton
Maxim Hotel
Mirage
Riviera Hotel & Casino
Sahara Hotel & Casino

## CONVENTION CENTER CONVENIENCE

Sands Hotel & Casino
Stardust Resort & Casino

**Little Rock**
Arkansas' Excelsior Hotel
Capital Hotel

**Los Angeles**
Biltmore Los Angeles
Checkers Hotel Kempinski
Hotel Inter-Continental
Hyatt Regency Los Angeles
Los Angeles Hilton & Towers
New Otani Hotel & Garden
Sheraton Grande Hotel
Sportsmen's Lodge Hotel
Westin Bonaventure

**Memphis**
Peabody Memphis

**Miami/Miami Beach**
Alexander All-Suite Luxury Hotel
Biscayne Bay Marriott
Doral Ocean Beach Resort
Doubletree Hotel Coconut Grove
Eden Roc Hotel & Marina
Fontainebleau Hilton
Grand Bay Hotel
Grove Isle Yacht & Tennis Club
Hotel Inter-Continental
Hyatt Regency Coral Gables
Hyatt Regency Miami
Mayfair House Hotel Grand Luxe
Occidental Parc Hotel
Omni International Hotel
Sheraton Bal Harbour Hotel
Sonesta Beach Hotel

**Milwaukee**
Astor Hotel
Hyatt Regency Milwaukee
Marc Plaza Hotel
Park East Hotel
Pfister Hotel
Wyndham Milwaukee Center

**Minneapolis/St. Paul**
Crown Sterling (Minn/St. Paul)
Hotel Luxeford Suites
Hyatt Regency Minneapolis
Marquette
Minneapolis Marriott City Center
Northland Inn

Omni Northstar Hotel
Radisson Hotel Metrodome
Radisson Hotel St. Paul
Radisson Plaza Hotel
Saint Paul Hotel
Whitney

**Nashville**
Doubletree Hotel Nashville
Hermitage Hotel
Holiday Inn Crowne Plaza
Loews Vanderbilt Plaza Hotel
Regal Maxwell House
Sheraton Music City Hotel
Stouffer Nashville Hotel
Union Station Hotel

**New Orleans**
Clarion Hotel New Orleans
Cornstalk Hotel
Dauphine Orleans Hotel
Doubletree Hotel New Orleans
Fairmont Hotel
Holiday Inn Crowne Plaza
Hotel Inter-Continental
Hotel Maison de Ville
Hotel Ste. Helene
Hotel St. Marie
LaMothe House
Le Meridien Hotel
Le Pavillon Hotel
Le Richelieu
Monteleone Hotel
New Orleans Hilton Riverside
New Orleans Marriott
Omni Royal Orleans
Place d'Armes Hotel
Radisson Suite Hotel
Royal Sonesta
Saint Louis Hotel
Sheraton New Orleans Hotel
Soniat House
St. Pierre
Westin Canal Place
Windsor Court Hotel

**New York City**
Edison Hotel
Embassy Suites Hotel
Holiday Inn Crowne Plaza
Hotel Macklowe
Mayflower Hotel

451

## CONVENTION CENTER CONVENIENCE

Michelangelo
Milford Plaza Hotel
New York Hilton & Towers
New York Marriott Marquis
Novotel New York
Paramount
Park Central
Radisson Empire Hotel
Ramada Midtown
Ramada Hotel
Ramada Renaissance
Rihga Royal
Sheraton Manhattan
Sheraton New York
Southgate Tower Suite Hotel
Warwick
Wyndham Hotel

### Orange County, CA

Anaheim Hilton & Towers
Anaheim Marriott Hotel
Dana Point Resort
Disneyland Hotel
Doubletree Hotel Orange County
Hyatt Regency Alicante
Inn at the Park
Sheraton Anaheim Hotel

### Orlando

Clarion Plaza Hotel
Courtyard at Lake Lucerne
Disney's Contemporary Resort
Hilton at WDW Village
Marriott
Omni
Orange Lake Country Club
Peabody Orlando
Residence Inn by Marriott
Sheraton World Resort
Sonesta Villa Resort
Stouffer Orlando Resort

### Palm Springs

Autry Resort
Hyatt Regency Suites
Palm Springs Hilton Resort
Palm Springs Marquis
Palm Springs Riviera Resort
Ritz-Carlton, Rancho Mirage
Spa Hotel & Mineral Springs
Westin Mission Hills Resort
Wyndham Palm Springs

### Philadelphia

Four Seasons Hotel
Latham Hotel
Penn's View Inn
Penn Tower Hotel
Philadelphia Hilton & Towers
Rittenhouse
Ritz-Carlton, Philadelphia
Sheraton University City
Society Hill Hotel
Wyndham Franklin Plaza Hotel

### Phoenix/Scottsdale

Hyatt Regency Phoenix
Omni Adams Hotel
Ritz-Carlton, Phoenix

### Pittsburgh

Hyatt Regency Pittsburgh
Pittsburgh Hilton & Towers
Pittsburgh Vista
Ramada
Westin William Penn

### Raleigh-Durham

Siena Hotel

### San Antonio

Best Western Historical Crockett
Emily Morgan
Fairmount Hotel
Hilton Palacio del Rio
Hyatt Regency San Antonio
La Mansion del Rio
Marriott Rivercenter
Menger Hotel
Plaza San Antonio
Saint Anthony Hotel
San Antonio Riverwalk Marriott
Sheraton Gunter Hotel

### San Diego

Doubletree Hotel at Horton Plaza
Embassy Suites
Gaslamp Plaza Suites
Horton Grand
Hyatt Regency San Diego
Kona Kai Resort
Pan Pacific
San Diego Marriott
Sheraton Grande Harbor Island
Sheraton - Harbor Island East
U.S. Grant Hotel
Westgate Hotel

## San Francisco
ANA Hotel
Andrews Hotel
Beresford Arms
Best Western Canterbury
Campton Place Kempinski
Cartwright Hotel
Cathedral Hill
Chancellor Hotel
Donatello
Four Seasons Clift Hotel
Galleria Park Hotel
Grand Hyatt
Harbor Court Hotel
Hotel Bedford
Hotel Diva
Hotel Nikko
Hotel Vintage Court
Hyatt Regency San Francisco
Inn at Union Square
Juliana Hotel
Kensington Park
Mandarin Oriental
Mark Hopkins Inter-Continental
Orchard Hotel
Pan Pacific
Parc 55
Park Hyatt
Prescott Hotel
Raphael Hotel
Ritz-Carlton, San Francisco
San Francisco Downtown Marriott
San Francisco Hilton
Sheraton Palace
Sir Francis Drake
Stouffer Stanford Court Hotel
Villa Florence Hotel
Westin St. Francis
York Hotel

## San Jose, CA
Fairmont Hotel

## Seattle
Edgewater
Four Seasons Olympic
Holiday Inn Crowne Plaza
Inn at the Market
Mayflower Park Hotel
Seattle Hilton
Sheraton Seattle Hotel & Towers
Sorrento Hotel
Stouffer Madison

Warwick Hotel
Westin Hotel Seattle

## St. Louis
Adam's Mark
Clarion Hotel St. Louis
Doubletree Hotel & Conf. Center
Doubletree Mayfair
Embassy Suites
Holiday Inn
Holiday Inn Downtown/Conv. Ctr.
Holiday Inn Downtown/Riverfront
Hotel Majestic
Hyatt Regency St. Louis
Marriott Pavilion Hotel
St. Louis Marriott West

## Tampa Bay
Adam's Mark Caribbean Gulf
Heritage Hotel
Holiday Inn Ashley Plaza
Hyatt Regency Westshore
Wyndham Harbour Island Hotel

## Washington, DC
ANA Hotel
Capital Hilton
Carlton
Grand Hyatt Washington
Guest Quarters
Hay-Adams Hotel
Henley Park Hotel
Holiday Inn Crowne Plaza
Hotel Washington
Hyatt Regency Washington
Jefferson Hotel
J.W. Marriott Hotel
Loews L'Enfant Plaza
Madison Hotel
Morrison-Clark Inn
Phoenix Park Hotel
Radisson Park Terrace Hotel
Ramada Renaissance
Ritz-Carlton, Washington DC
Tabard Inn
Washington Court Hotel
Washington Marriott
Washington Vista Hotel
Willard Inter-Continental

## Arkansas
Arlington Resort

# CONVENTION CENTER CONVENIENCE

## Colorado

Ritz-Carlton, Aspen

## Florida

Inn at Fisher Island

## Georgia

Eliza Thompson
Foley House Inn
Gastonian
Mulberry Inn
Planter's Inn
President's Quarters

## Mississippi

Natchez Eola Hotel

## New Mexico

Eldorado Hotel
Hotel St. Francis
Inn on the Alameda
La Fonda Hotel on the Plaza

## Oklahoma

Shangri-La Resort

## South Carolina

Indigo Inn
Jasmine House Inn
Mills House Hotel
Vendue Inn

## Texas

Tremont House

# CORPORATE RETREATS

**Atlanta**
Peachtree Executive Conf. Ctr.

**Atlantic City**
Marriott's Seaview Resort

**Baltimore**
Cross Keys Inn

**Cleveland**
Glidden House

**Columbus**
Worthington Inn

**Dallas**
Doubletree Hotel at Park West
Four Seasons Resort & Club
Omni Mandalay Hotel

**Denver**
Scanticon

**Detroit**
Dearborn Inn Marriott

**Florham Park**
Hamilton Park

**Honolulu**
Kahala Hilton
Sheraton Makaha Resort
Turtle Bay Hilton

**Houston**
Houstonian Hotel & Conf. Ctr.

**Indianapolis**
University Place

**Little Rock**
Arkansas' Excelsior Hotel

**Los Angeles**
Barnabey's Hotel
Hotel Bel-Air
Malibu Beach Inn
Ritz-Carlton, Huntington Hotel

**Miami/Miami Beach**
Biltmore Hotel
Doral Resort & Country Club
Grove Isle Yacht & Tennis Club
Turnberry Isle Club

**Minneapolis/St. Paul**
Northland Inn

**Nashville**
Opryland Hotel

**Orange County, CA**
Dana Point Resort
Four Seasons Hotel
Newport Beach Marriott Hotel
Ritz-Carlton, Laguna Niguel

**Orlando**
Orange Lake Country Club

**Palm Springs**
Autry Resort
Doubletree Resort Palm Springs
Hyatt Grand Champions Resort
La Quinta Hotel
Marriott's Desert Springs Resort
Marriott's Rancho Las Palmas
Palm Springs Hilton Resort
Palm Springs Riviera Resort
Ritz-Carlton, Rancho Mirage
Shadow Mountain Resort
Stouffer Esmeralda
Two Bunch Palms Resort

**Phoenix/Scottsdale**
Arizona Biltmore
Buttes
Hyatt Regency Scottsdale
John Gardiner's Tennis Ranch
Marriott's Camelback Inn
Marriott's Mountain Shadows
Orange Tree Golf & Conf. Resort
Phoenician
Pointe at South Mountain
Pointe at Squaw Peak
Pointe at Tapatio Cliffs
Red Lion La Posada Resort
Registry Resort
Scottsdale Conference Resort
Scottsdale Hilton
Scottsdale Princess
Sheraton San Marcos Golf Resort
Stouffer Cottonwoods Resort

**Raleigh-Durham**
Washington Duke Inn

**San Diego**
Hotel del Coronado
Hyatt Regency San Diego
Le Meridien San Diego
Loews Coronado Bay Resort
Rancho Bernardo Inn
Rancho Valencia

**San Jose, CA**
Marriott Glenpointe

455

# CORPORATE RETREATS

## Tampa Bay
Belleview Mido Resort Hotel
Don Ce-Sar Registry Resort
Innisbrook Resort
Saddlebrook

## Washington, DC
Morrison House
Ritz-Carlton, Tysons Corner
Westfield's Intl. Conf. Ctr.

## Alabama
Marriott's Grand Hotel

## Alaska
Glacier Bay Lodge
King Salmon Lodge
Tikchik Narrows Lodge
Waterfall Resort
Yes Bay Lodge

## Arizona
Arizona Inn
Boulders Resort
El Conquistador
Enchantment Resort
Hassayampa Inn
L'Auberge de Sedona
Los Abrigados
Poco Diablo Resort
Rancho de los Caballeros
Tanque Verde Ranch
Ventana Canyon
Westin La Paloma
Wickenburg Inn
Wigwam

## Arkansas
Gaston's White River Resort

## California
Alisal Ranch
Auberge du Soleil
Big Sur Lodge
Carmel Valley Ranch Resort
Casa Madrona Hotel
Claremont Resort
El Encanto Hotel
Eureka Inn
Four Seasons Biltmore
Furnace Creek Inn
Highlands Inn
Hill House Inn
Inn at Morro Bay

Inn at Rancho Santa Fe
Inn at the Tides
La Casa del Zorro
Little River Inn
Lodge at Pebble Beach
Los Olivos Grand Hotel
Madrona Manor
Meadowood Resort
Northstar-at-Tahoe
Ojai Valley Inn
Petersen Village Inn
Portofino Hotel & Yacht Club
Quail Lodge Resort & Golf Club
San Ysidro Ranch
Silverado Country Club & Resort
Squaw Valley Inn
Timberhill Ranch
Villa Royale
Vintage Inn
Vintners Inn

## Colorado
Aspen Club Lodge
Breckenridge Hilton
Broadmoor
Cheyenne Mountain Conf. Resort
C Lazy U Ranch
Doral Telluride
Home Ranch
Hotel Jerome
Hotel Lenado
Hyatt Regency Beaver Creek
Inn at Aspen
Iron Horse Resort Retreat
Keystone Lodge
Little Nell
Lodge at Cordillera
Lodge at Vail
Pines Lodge at Beaver Creek
Radisson Resort Vail
Ritz-Carlton, Aspen
Sardy House
Sheraton Steamboat Resort
Snowmass Lodge & Club
Tall Timber
Tamarron Resort
Vail Athletic Club
Vista Verde Guest Ranch
Westin Resort Vail

## Connecticut
Boulders
Griswold Inn
Homestead Inn

Interlaken Inn
Mayflower Inn
Stonehenge
Water's Edge Inn & Resort

## Florida

Amelia Island Plantation
Boca Raton Resort & Club
Breakers
Chalet Suzanne
Cheeca Lodge
Colony Beach & Tennis Resort
Don Shula's Hotel & Golf Club
Grenelefe Resort
Hawk's Cay Resort & Marina
Hyatt Key West
Indian River Plantation Resort
Inn at Fisher Island
Lakeside Inn
Lodge at Ponte Vedra Beach
Marriott at Sawgrass Resort
Marriott's Bay Point Resort
Marriott's Casa Marina Resort
Marriott's Marco Island Resort
Mission Inn Golf & Tennis Resort
Ocean Grand Hotel
Ocean Reef Club
PGA National
Ponce de Leon Resort
Ponte Vedra Inn & Club
Reach Resort
Registry Resort
Resort at Longboat Key Club
Ritz-Carlton, Amelia Island
Ritz-Carlton, Naples
Ritz-Carlton, Palm Beach
Sheraton Key Largo Resort
Sonesta Sanibel Harbour
South Seas Plantation Resort
Sundial Beach & Tennis Resort

## Georgia

Callaway Gardens Resort
Cloister
Evergreen Conference Center
Gastonian
Jekyll Island Club Hotel
Sea Palms Golf & Tennis Resort
Stouffer Pineisle Resort

## Hawaii

Four Seasons Resort Wailea
Grand Hyatt Wailea
Hotel Hana-Maui

Hyatt Regency Maui
Hyatt Regency Waikoloa
Kapalua Bay Hotel & Villas
Lodge at Koele
Manele Bay Hotel
Maui Marriott
Maui Prince Hotel
Mauna Kea Beach Hotel
Mauna Lani Bay Hotel
Princeville Hotel
Ritz-Carlton, Mauna Lani
Stouffer Waiohai Beach Resort
Volcano House
Westin Kauai
Westin Maui

## Idaho

Coeur d'Alene Resort
Middle Fork Lodge

## Illinois

Clock Tower Resort & Conf. Ctr.
Eagle Ridge Inn & Resort
Indian Lakes Resort
Marriott's Lincolnshire Resort
Nordic Hills Resort & Conf. Ctr.
Pheasant Run Resort

## Indiana

Four Winds Clarion
French Lick Springs Resort

## Kentucky

Inn at Shaker Village

## Maine

Bayview Hotel & Inn
Bethel Inn & Country Club
Black Point Inn Resort
Captain Lord Mansion
Cliff House
Harraseeket Inn
Samoset Resort
White Barn Inn
Whitehall Inn

## Maryland

Imperial Hotel
Inn at Perry Cabin
Tidewater Inn

## Massachusetts

Blantyre
Chatham Bars Inn

# CORPORATE RETREATS

Coonamessett Inn
Nantucket Inn & Conf. Ctr.
New Seabury Cape Cod
Ocean Edge Resort & Conf. Ctr.
Orchards
Red Lion Inn
Village Inn
Wauwinet
Wequassett Inn
Wheatleigh

## Michigan

Boyne Mountain Hotel
Grand Traverse Resort
Shanty Creek - Schuss Mountain
Stafford's Bay View Inn
Sugar Loaf Resort
Treetops Sylvan Resort

## Minnesota

Arrowwood, A Radisson Resort
Breezy Point Resort
Fitgers Inn
Grand View Lodge
Lutsen Resort
Madden's on Gull Lake
Schumacher's New Prague

## Missouri

Lodge of Four Seasons
Marriott's TanTarA Resort

## Montana

Chico Hot Springs Lodge
Grouse Mountain Lodge
Holland Lake Lodge
Huntley Lodge
Kandahar Lodge
Triple Creek Mountain Hideaway

## Nevada

Harrah's Lake Tahoe
Hyatt Regency Lake Tahoe

## New Hampshire

Balsams
Snowy Owl Inn
Stonehurst Manor

## New Jersey

Inn at Millrace Pond
Mainstay Inn & Cottage
Virginia

## New Mexico

Bishop's Lodge
Inn of the Anasazi
Inn of the Mountain Gods
Lodge at Cloudcroft
Rancho Encantado Resort

## New York State

Clarion Inn at Saratoga
Concord Resort Hotel
Doral Arrowwood
Geneva on the Lake
Gideon Putnam Hotel
Harrison Conference Center
Mohonk Mountain House
Montauk Yacht Club
Omni Sagamore
Otesaga Hotel
Point
Three Village Inn
Troutbeck Inn

## North Carolina

Fearrington House Inn
Green Park Inn
Greystone Inn
Grove Park Inn Resort
High Hampton Inn & Country Club
Pinehurst Hotel & Country Club
Richmond Hill Inn
Sanderling Inn Resort

## Ohio

Kings Island Inn & Conf. Ctr.
Quail Hollow Resort

## Oklahoma

Lake Texoma Resort

## Oregon

Columbia Gorge Hotel
Kah-Nee-Ta Resort
Rock Springs Guest Ranch
Salishan Lodge
Sylvia Beach Hotel
Timberline Lodge

## Pennsylvania

Bridgeton House
Evermay on-the-Delaware
Hotel Hershey
Nemacolin Woodlands
Pocono Manor Inn & Golf Resort

Seven Springs Mountain Resort
Split Rock Resort
Sweetwater Farm

## Rhode Island

Doubletree Hotel
Newport Harbor Hotel & Marina
1661 Inn

## South Carolina

Hilton Head Island Hilton Resort
Hyatt Regency Hilton Head
Kiawah Island Resort
Marriott's Hilton Head Resort
Seabrook Island Resort
Sea Pines
Vendue Inn
Westin Resort
Wild Dunes Resort

## Tennessee

Fairfield Glade Resort
Inn at Blackberry Farm

## Texas

Barton Creek
Flying L Guest Ranch
Horseshoe Bay Resort
Lakeway Inn & Conf. Ctr.
Radisson South Padre Island
Sheraton South Padre Island
Woodlands Executive Conf. Ctr.

## Utah

Cliff Lodge
Shadow Ridge Hotel
Stein Eriksen Lodge
Washington School Inn

## Vermont

Basin Harbor Club
Cortina Inn
Equinox
Hawk Inn & Mountain Resort
Hermitage Inn
Inn at Essex
Inn at Sawmill Farm
Mountain Top Inn
Stratton Mountain Inn
Sugarbush Inn
Topnotch at Stowe
Trapp Family Lodge
Woodstock Inn & Resort

## Virginia

Ashby Inn
Boar's Head Inn
Homestead
Inn at Little Washington
Lansdowne Conf. Resort
Tides Inn
Williamsburg Inn

## Washington

Captain Whidbey Inn
Inn at Semiahmoo
Rosario Resort & Spa
Salish Lodge
Sun Mountain Lodge

## West Virginia

Greenbrier

## Wisconsin

Abbey
Americana Lake Geneva Resort
American Club
Heidel House Resort
Lake Lawn Lodge
Lakewoods Resort & Lodge
Olympia Resort

## Wyoming

Jackson Hole Racquet Club
Jackson Lake Lodge
Jenny Lake Lodge
Ranch at Ucross
Snow King Resort
Spring Creek Ranch
Teton Pines Resort

## Spas

Canyon Ranch in the Berkshires
Doral Saturnia
Heartland Retreat
Kerr House
La Costa Hotel & Spa
Lake Austin Resort
Loews Ventana Canyon Resort
Mario's International Hotel
Murrieta Hot Springs Resort
National Institute of Fitness
New Age Health Spa
Northern Pines
Norwich Inn, Spa & Villas
Palm-Aire Hotel & Spa
Sonoma Mission Inn & Spa

# DANCING/NIGHTCLUBS

## Atlanta
Atlanta Hilton & Towers
Atlanta Marriott Marquis
French Quarter Suites
Peachtree Executive Conf. Ctr.
Radisson Hotel
Ramada Hotel Dunwoody
Ritz-Carlton, Buckhead
Stouffer Waverly Hotel

## Atlantic City
Caesars Atlantic City
Marriott's Seaview Resort
Merv Griffin's Resorts
TropWorld
Trump Castle Resort

## Baltimore
Baltimore Marriott Inner Harbor
Hyatt Regency Baltimore
Marriott's Hunt Valley Inn
Sheraton Baltimore North

## Boston
Back Bay Hilton
Best Western Boston
Charles Hotel in Harvard Square
Guest Quarters Suite Hotel
Marriott Hotel Long Wharf
Omni Parker House
Sheraton Boston Hotel & Towers

## Chicago
Bismarck Hotel
Chicago Marriott Downtown
Executive Plaza
Fairmont Hotel
Hyatt Regency O'Hare
Ritz-Carlton, Chicago
Westin Hotel O'Hare

## Cincinnati
Hyatt Regency Cincinnati
Kings Island Inn & Conf. Ctr.
Quail Hollow Resort

## Cleveland
Cleveland Marriott East
Radisson Plaza Hotel

## Corpus Christi
Corpus Christi Marriott Bayfront

## Dallas
Dallas Marriott Park Central
Grand Kempinski Dallas

Hyatt Regency Dallas at Reunion
Loews Anatole Hotel
Sheraton Park Central
Westin Galleria

## Denver
Doubletree Hotel Denver
Scanticon
Sheraton Denver Tech Center

## Detroit
Dearborn Inn Marriott
Hyatt Regency Dearborn
Novi Hilton
Radisson Plaza Hotel

## Fort Lauderdale
Fort Lauderdale Marina Marriott
Fort Lauderdale Marriott North
Lago Mar Resort & Club
Ocean Manor Resort Hotel
Pier 66 Resort & Marina
Sheraton Design Center
Sheraton Yankee Clipper

## Fort Worth
Stockyards Hotel
Worthington

## Honolulu
Ala Moana Hotel
Colony Surf Hotel
Hawaiian Regent
Hawaiian Waikiki Beach Hotel
Hilton Hawaiian Village
Hyatt Regency Waikiki
Ilikai Hotel Nikko Waikiki
Kahala Hilton
Turtle Bay Hilton
Waikiki Beachcomber Hotel

## Houston
Adam's Mark
Holiday Inn Houston West
Nassau Bay Hilton & Marina
Omni
Ramada Kings Inn
Ritz-Carlton, Houston
Sheraton Astrodome Hotel
Stouffer Presidente Hotel
Westin Galleria
Westin Oaks

## Indianapolis
Adam's Mark
Radisson Plaza & Suites Hotel

## Kansas City
Adam's Mark
Holiday Inn Crowne Plaza
Hyatt Regency Crown Center
Radisson Suite Hotel
Ritz-Carlton, Kansas City

## Las Vegas
Caesars Palace
Desert Inn Hotel & Country Club
Four Queens Hotel & Casino
Las Vegas Hilton
Riviera Hotel & Casino
Sands Hotel & Casino

## Little Rock
Arkansas' Excelsior Hotel

## Los Angeles
Barnabey's Hotel
Beverly Hilton
Hollywood Roosevelt Hotel
Industry Hills Sheraton Resort
Los Angeles Airport Hilton
Mondrian Hotel
New Otani Hotel & Garden
Ritz-Carlton, Marina del Rey
Warner Center Marriott
Westin Bonaventure

## Miami/Miami Beach
Doral Ocean Beach Resort
Doral Resort & Country Club
Doubletree Hotel Coconut Grove
Grand Bay Hotel
Hyatt Regency Coral Gables
Sheraton Bal Harbour Hotel
Sheraton River House Hotel
Sonesta Beach Hotel

## Milwaukee
Milwaukee Marriott - Brookfield
Pfister Hotel

## Minneapolis/St. Paul
Registry Hotel

## Nashville
Opryland Hotel
Sheraton Music City Hotel

## New Orleans
New Orleans Hilton Riverside
Pontchartrain Hotel
Sheraton New Orleans Hotel
Windsor Court Hotel

## New York City
Carlyle Hotel
Hotel Kimberly
New York Hilton & Towers
New York Marriott Marquis
Paramount

## Oklahoma City
Waterford Hotel

## Orange County, CA
Anaheim Hilton & Towers
Anaheim Marriott Hotel
Dana Point Resort
Disneyland Hotel
Hyatt Newporter
Hyatt Regency Irvine
Irvine Marriott
Newport Beach Marriott Hotel
Ritz-Carlton, Laguna Niguel

## Orlando
Buena Vista Palace
Clarion Plaza Hotel
Disney's Caribbean Beach Resort
Disney's Contemporary Resort
Disney's Polynesian Resort
Forte Travelodge Hotel
Grosvenor Resort at WDW
Harley Hotel
Hotel Royal Plaza
Marriott
Stouffer Orlando Resort
Walt Disney World Dolphin

## Palm Springs
Autry Resort
Doubletree Resort Palm Springs
Hyatt Regency Suites
La Quinta Hotel
Marriott's Desert Springs Resort
Marriott's Rancho Las Palmas
Palm Springs Riviera Resort
Racquet Club Resort

## Philadelphia
Adam's Mark
Rittenhouse
Warwick Hotel

## Phoenix/Scottsdale
Buttes
Camelview Resort
Crown Sterling Suites
Fountains Suite Hotel
John Gardiner's Tennis Ranch

## DANCING/NIGHTCLUBS

Lexington Hotel & City Square
Marriott's Mountain Shadows
Phoenician
Pointe at South Mountain
Pointe at Squaw Peak
Pointe at Tapatio Cliffs
Red Lion La Posada Resort
Registry Resort
Ritz-Carlton, Phoenix
Royal Palms Inn
Scottsdale Hilton
Scottsdale Plaza Resort
Scottsdale Princess
Sheraton San Marcos Golf Resort
Sunburst Hotel & Conf. Ctr.

### Pittsburgh
Pittsburgh Green Tree Marriott
Pittsburgh Vista
Westin William Penn

### San Antonio
Saint Anthony Hotel
San Antonio Riverwalk Marriott

### San Diego
Bahia Hotel
Catamaran Resort Hotel
Doubletree Hotel at Horton Plaza
Gaslamp Plaza Suites
Hanalei Hotel
Hotel del Coronado
Hyatt Regency La Jolla
La Jolla Marriott
Loews Coronado Bay Resort
Marriott Mission Valley
Rancho Bernardo Inn
San Diego Hilton
San Diego Marriott
San Diego Princess Resort
Town & Country Hotel
U.S. Grant Hotel

### San Francisco
Fairmont Hotel
Harbor Court Hotel
Pan Pacific
San Francisco Hilton
Sir Francis Drake
Westin St. Francis
York Hotel

### Seattle
Doubletree Seattle Inn
Doubletree Suites Seattle

Red Lion Hotel Bellevue
Seattle Hilton
Sheraton Seattle Hotel & Towers
Westin Hotel Seattle

### St. Louis
Adam's Mark
Doubletree Hotel & Conf. Center
Hyatt Regency St. Louis
Ritz-Carlton, St. Louis
St. Louis Marriott West

### Tampa Bay
Adam's Mark Caribbean Gulf
Innisbrook Resort
Saddlebrook
Sheraton Grand Hotel
St. Petersburg Beach Hilton

### Washington, DC
Four Seasons Hotel
J.W. Marriott Hotel
Omni Shoreham
One Washington Circle Hotel
Sheraton Premiere
Stouffer Mayflower Hotel
Washington Hilton & Towers

### Alabama
Marriott's Grand Hotel

### Arizona
Boulders Resort
El Conquistador
Enchantment Resort
Los Abrigados
Sheraton San Marcos Golf Resort
Wahweap Lodge & Marina
Westward Look Resort
Wigwam

### Arkansas
Arlington Resort

### California
Alisal Ranch
Casa Sirena Marina Resort
Claremont Resort
Four Seasons Biltmore
Furnace Creek Inn
La Casa del Zorro
Madonna Inn
San Ysidro Ranch
Silverado Country Club & Resort

## Colorado

Breckenridge Hilton
Broadmoor
Grande Butte Hotel
Keystone Lodge
Little Nell
Sheraton Steamboat Resort

## Connecticut

Interlaken Inn
Mayflower Inn

## Florida

Amelia Island Plantation
Brazilian Court
Breakers
Club Med Sandpiper
Colony Beach & Tennis Resort
Grenelefe Resort
Hawk's Cay Resort & Marina
Indian River Plantation Resort
Inn at Fisher Island
Marriott at Sawgrass Resort
Marriott's Bay Point Resort
Marriott's Casa Marina Resort
Marriott's Marco Island Resort
Ocean Reef Club
Pier House Resort
Ponce de Leon Resort
Ponte Vedra Inn & Club
Registry Resort
Resort at Longboat Key Club
Ritz-Carlton, Naples
Sheraton Key Largo Resort
Sonesta Sanibel Harbour
South Seas Plantation Resort
Sundial Beach & Tennis Resort
'Tween Waters Inn

## Georgia

Callaway Gardens Resort
Cloister
Sheraton Savannah Resort

## Hawaii

Four Seasons Resort Wailea
Grand Hyatt Wailea
Hotel Hana-Maui
Hyatt Regency Maui
Hyatt Regency Waikoloa
Kona Hilton Resort
Maui Inter-Continental Resort
Maui Marriott

Maui Prince Hotel
Mauna Kea Beach Hotel
Mauna Lani Bay Hotel
Royal Lahaina Resort
Royal Waikoloan
Westin Maui

## Idaho

Coeur d'Alene Resort

## Illinois

Clock Tower Resort & Conf. Ctr.
Indian Lakes Resort
Marriott's Lincolnshire Resort
Nordic Hills Resort & Conf. Ctr.
Pheasant Run Resort

## Indiana

Four Winds Clarion

## Maine

Black Point Inn Resort
Colony Resort
Poland Spring Inn
Samoset Resort

## Maryland

Maryland Inn

## Massachusetts

Chatham Bars Inn
Coonamessett Inn
New Seabury Cape Cod

## Michigan

Boyne Highlands Inn
Grand Hotel
Grand Traverse Resort
Shanty Creek - Schuss Mountain
Sugar Loaf Resort
Treetops Sylvan Resort

## Minnesota

Arrowwood, A Radisson Resort
Grand View Lodge
Madden's on Gull Lake

## Missouri

Lodge of Four Seasons
Marriott's TanTarA Resort

## Montana

Chico Hot Springs Lodge
Huntley Lodge

## DANCING/NIGHTCLUBS

Many Glacier Hotel
Mountain Sky Guest Ranch

### New Hampshire

Balsams

### New Mexico

Inn of the Mountain Gods
Lodge at Cloudcroft
Sagebrush Inn

### New York State

Concord Resort Hotel
Doral Arrowwood
Mohonk Mountain House
Montauk Yacht Club
Omni Sagamore
Otesaga Hotel

### North Carolina

Grove Park Inn Resort
High Hampton Inn & Country Club
Pinehurst Hotel & Country Club

### Oregon

Kah-Nee-Ta Resort
Sunriver Lodge & Resort

### Pennsylvania

Hotel Hershey
Mount Airy Lodge
Nemacolin Woodlands
Pocono Manor Inn & Golf Resort
Seven Springs Mountain Resort
Skytop Lodge
Split Rock Resort

### Rhode Island

Newport Harbor Hotel & Marina

### South Carolina

Hilton Head Island Hilton Resort
Marriott's Hilton Head Resort
Sea Pines
Westin Resort
Wild Dunes Resort

### Tennessee

Fairfield Glade Resort

### Texas

Horseshoe Bay Resort
Radisson South Padre Island
Sheraton South Padre Island

### Vermont

Basin Harbor Club
Cortina Inn
Equinox
Stratton Mountain Inn
Topnotch at Stowe

### Virginia

Boar's Head Inn
Homestead
Tides Inn

### Washington

Inn at Semiahmoo
Sun Mountain Lodge

### West Virginia

Greenbrier

### Wisconsin

Abbey
Americana Lake Geneva Resort
American Club
Gordon Lodge
Heidel House Resort
Lake Lawn Lodge
Lakewoods Resort & Lodge

### Wyoming

Paradise Guest Ranch
R Lazy S Ranch
Snow King Resort

### Spas

Bonaventure Resort & Spa
Harbor Island Spa Resort
La Costa Hotel & Spa
Loews Ventana Canyon Resort
Murrieta Hot Springs Resort

# DOWNTOWN CONVENIENCE

## Albuquerque
Doubletree Albuquerque
Hyatt Regency Albuquerque

## Anchorage
Captain Cook Hotel

## Atlanta
Ansley Inn
Atlanta Hilton & Towers
Atlanta Marriott Marquis
Atlanta Penta Hotel
Biltmore Suites
Hyatt Regency
Omni Hotel at CNN Center
Radisson Hotel
Ritz-Carlton, Atlanta
Sheraton Colony Square Hotel
Westin Peachtree Plaza
Wyndham Garden - Midtown

## Atlantic City
Bally's Grand Hotel & Casino
Bally's Park Place
Caesars Atlantic City
Claridge Casino Hotel
Holiday Inn Diplomat
Merv Griffin's Resorts
Sands Hotel & Casino
Showboat Hotel
TropWorld
Trump Plaza Hotel & Casino
Trump Regency Hotel
Trump Taj Mahal

## Baltimore
Admiral Fell Inn
Baltimore Marriott Inner Harbor
Brookshire Hotel
Clarion Hotel - Inner Harbor
Harbor Court Hotel
Hyatt Regency Baltimore
Omni Inner Harbor Hotel
Peabody Court Hotel
Sheraton Inner Harbor Hotel
Society Hill Hotel
Stouffer Harborplace
Tremont Hotel
Tremont Plaza Hotel

## Birmingham
Tutwiler

## Boston
Back Bay Hilton
Boston Harbor Hotel
Bostonian Hotel
Boston Park Plaza
Colonnade Hotel
Copley Plaza Hotel
Copley Square Hotel
Four Seasons Hotel
Le Meridien Boston
Lenox Hotel
Marriott Copley Place
Marriott Hotel Long Wharf
Midtown Hotel
Omni Parker House
Ritz-Carlton, Boston
Sheraton Boston Hotel & Towers
Swissotel Boston
Westin Hotel Copley Place

## Charlotte
Dunhill Hotel

## Chicago
Allerton Hotel
Barclay Chicago
Best Western Inn
Bismarck Hotel
Blackstone Hotel
Chicago Hilton & Towers
Chicago Marriott Downtown
Congress Hotel
Drake Hotel
Executive Plaza
Fairmont Hotel
Forum Hotel
Four Seasons Hotel
Holiday Inn City Centre
Hotel Inter-Continental
Hotel Nikko
Hyatt Printers Row
Hyatt Regency Chicago
Hyatt Regency Suites
Knickerbocker Chicago Hotel
Le Meridien Hotel Chicago
Lenox House Suites
Mayfair
McCormick Center Hotel
Midland Hotel
Omni Ambassador East
Palmer House Hilton
Park Hyatt
Radisson Plaza Ambass. West
Raphael Hotel
Richmont Hotel
Ritz-Carlton, Chicago
Sheraton Chicago Hotel & Towers

## DOWNTOWN CONVENIENCE

Sheraton Plaza Hotel
Stouffer Riviere
Swissotel Chicago
Talbott Hotel
Tremont Hotel
Westin Hotel, Chicago

### Cincinnati
Cincinnatian Hotel
Cincinnati Terrace Hilton
Clarion Hotel Cincinnati
Hyatt Regency Cincinnati
Omni Netherland Plaza
Westin Hotel

### Cleveland
Cleveland Marriott Society Center
Holiday Inn Lakeside City Center
Omni International Hotel
Radisson Plaza Hotel
Ritz-Carlton, Cleveland
Sheraton City Centre
Stouffer Tower City Plaza Hotel

### Dallas
Adolphus
Aristocrat Hotel
Dallas Grand
Fairmont Hotel
Hotel Crescent Court
Hotel St. Germain
Hyatt Regency Dallas at Reunion
Mansion on Turtle Creek
Plaza of the Americas Hotel
Sheraton Suites
Southland Center Hotel
Stoneleigh Hotel

### Denver
Brown Palace Hotel
Burnsley Hotel
Cambridge Hotel
Denver Marriott City Center
Embassy Suites Denver Dtwn.
Hyatt Regency Denver
Oxford Hotel
Radisson Hotel
Residence Inn
Warwick Hotel
Westin Hotel Tabor Center

### Detroit
Atheneum Suites
Hotel St. Regis

Omni
Radisson Hotel Pontchartrain
River Place Inn
Westin Hotel

### Fort Lauderdale
Bahia Mar Resort
Fort Lauderdale Marina Marriott
Marriott's Harbor Beach Resort
Ocean Manor Resort Hotel
Pier 66 Resort & Marina
Riverside Hotel
Sheraton Yankee Clipper
Westin Hotel, Cypress Creek

### Fort Worth
Worthington

### Hartford
Goodwin Hotel

### Honolulu
Ritz-Carlton Kapalua

### Houston
Allen Park Inn
Doubletree Hotel at Allen Center
Four Seasons Hotel
Houstonian Hotel & Conf. Ctr.
Houston Marriott Astrodome
Hyatt Regency Houston
La Colombe d'Or
Lancaster

### Indianapolis
Canterbury Hotel
Embassy Suites Hotel
Holiday Inn Union Station
Hyatt Regency Indianapolis
Indianapolis Hilton Downtown
Omni Severin
University Place
Westin Hotel Indianapolis

### Kansas City
Allis Plaza Hotel
Americana Hotel on Convention
Hilton Plaza Inn
Hotel Savoy
Hyatt Regency Crown Center
Radisson Suite Hotel
Ritz-Carlton, Kansas City
Sheraton Suites
Westin Crown Center

## Las Vegas
Binion's Horseshoe
Fitzgerald's Casino Hotel
Four Queens Hotel & Casino
Golden Nugget Hotel & Casino
Lady Luck Casino Hotel
Plaza Hotel
Sam Boyd's Fremont Hotel

## Little Rock
Arkansas' Excelsior Hotel
Capital Hotel

## Los Angeles
Barnabey's Hotel
Biltmore Los Angeles
Checkers Hotel Kempinski
Hotel Inter-Continental
Hyatt Regency Los Angeles
Los Angeles Hilton & Towers
New Otani Hotel & Garden
Sheraton Grande Hotel
Westin Bonaventure

## Memphis
Peabody Memphis

## Miami/Miami Beach
Biscayne Bay Marriott
Colonnade Hotel
Eden Roc Hotel & Marina
Grand Bay Hotel
Grove Isle Yacht & Tennis Club
Hotel Inter-Continental
Hyatt Regency Coral Gables
Hyatt Regency Miami
Occidental Parc Hotel
Omni International Hotel
Sonesta Beach Hotel

## Milwaukee
Astor Hotel
Hyatt Regency Milwaukee
Marc Plaza Hotel
Park East Hotel
Pfister Hotel
Wyndham Milwaukee Center

## Minneapolis/St. Paul
Crown Sterling (Minn/St. Paul)
Hotel Luxeford Suites
Hyatt Regency Minneapolis
Marquette
Minneapolis Marriott City Center
Omni Northstar Hotel

Radisson Hotel Metrodome
Radisson Plaza Hotel
Whitney

## Nashville
Doubletree Hotel Nashville
Hermitage Hotel
Holiday Inn Crowne Plaza
Loews Vanderbilt Plaza Hotel
Regal Maxwell House
Stouffer Nashville Hotel
Union Station Hotel

## New Orleans
Bourbon Orleans Hotel
Clarion Hotel New Orleans
Cornstalk Hotel
Dauphine Orleans Hotel
Doubletree Hotel New Orleans
Fairmont Hotel
Holiday Inn Crowne Plaza
Hotel Inter-Continental
Hotel Maison de Ville
Hotel Ste. Helene
Hotel St. Marie
Hyatt Regency New Orleans
LaMothe House
Le Meridien Hotel
Le Pavillon Hotel
Le Richelieu
Maison Dupuy Hotel
Monteleone Hotel
New Orleans Hilton Riverside
New Orleans Marriott
Omni Royal Orleans
Place d'Armes Hotel
Radisson Suite Hotel
Royal Sonesta
Saint Louis Hotel
Sheraton New Orleans Hotel
Soniat House
St. Pierre
Westin Canal Place
Windsor Court Hotel

## New York City
Algonquin Hotel
Barbizon
Beekman Tower Hotel
Box Tree
Doral Court Hotel
Doral Inn
Doral Park Avenue

# DOWNTOWN CONVENIENCE

Doral Tuscany
Dorset
Drake Swissotel
Dumont Plaza Hotel
Eastgate Tower Suite Hotel
Edison Hotel
Essex House, Hotel Nikko
Flatotel International
Gorham New York
Gramercy Park Hotel
Grand Hyatt
Helmsley Palace
Helmsley Park Lane Hotel
Holiday Inn Crowne Plaza
Holiday Inn Downtown
Hotel Beverly
Hotel Elysee
Hotel Kimberly
Hotel Lexington
Hotel Macklowe
Hotel Millenium
Hotel Pickwick Arms
Hotel Plaza Athenee
Inter-Continental
Journey's End Hotel
Le Parker Meridien
Loews New York Hotel
Lowell New York
Mark
Marriott Financial Center Hotel
Mayfair Hotel Baglioni
Michelangelo
Milford Plaza Hotel
Morgans
New York Helmsley Hotel
New York Hilton & Towers
New York Marriott Eastside
New York Marriott Marquis
New York Vista
Novotel New York
Omni Berkshire Place
Paramount
Park Central
Peninsula New York
Pierre
Plaza Fifty Suite Hotel
Plaza Hotel
Radisson Empire Hotel
Ramada Midtown
Ramada Hotel
Ramada Renaissance
Regency

Rihga Royal
Ritz-Carlton, New York
Roger Smith
Roosevelt Hotel
Royalton
Salisbury Hotel
Shelburne Suite Hotel
Sheraton Manhattan
Sheraton New York
Sheraton Park Avenue
Sherry-Netherland Hotel
Southgate Tower Suite Hotel
Stanhope
St. Moritz on-the-Park
St. Regis
Surrey Hotel
U.N. Plaza - Park Hyatt
Warwick
Wyndham Hotel

## Orange County, CA
Costa Mesa Marriott Suites
Disneyland Hotel
Doubletree Hotel Orange County
Le Meridien Newport
Marriott Suites Newport Beach
Sheraton Anaheim Hotel
Surf & Sand Hotel
Westin South Coast Plaza

## Orlando
Harley Hotel
Omni
Park Plaza Hotel
Peabody Orlando
Radisson Plaza Hotel

## Palm Springs
Autry Resort
Doubletree Resort Palm Springs
Hyatt Grand Champions Resort
Hyatt Regency Suites
La Quinta Hotel
Palm Springs Hilton Resort
Palm Springs Marquis
Palm Springs Riviera Resort
Ritz-Carlton, Rancho Mirage
Shadow Mountain Resort
Spa Hotel & Mineral Springs
Wyndham Palm Springs

## Philadelphia
Barclay Hotel
Chestnut Hill Hotel

Four Seasons Hotel
Hotel Atop the Bellevue
Independence Park Inn
Latham Hotel
Penn's View Inn
Penn Tower Hotel
Philadelphia Hilton & Towers
Rittenhouse
Ritz-Carlton, Philadelphia
Sheraton Society Hill
Sheraton University City
Society Hill Hotel
Warwick Hotel
Wyndham Franklin Plaza Hotel

## Phoenix/Scottsdale
Arizona Biltmore
Crown Sterling Suites
Hyatt Regency Phoenix
John Gardiner's Tennis Ranch
Lexington Hotel & City Square
Marriott's Mountain Shadows
Marriott Suites Scottsdale
Omni Adams Hotel
Regal McCormick Ranch
Ritz-Carlton, Phoenix
Sheraton San Marcos Golf Resort
Sunburst Hotel & Conf. Ctr.
Wyndham Paradise Valley Resort

## Pittsburgh
Hyatt Regency Pittsburgh
Pittsburgh Hilton & Towers
Pittsburgh Vista
Priory - A City Inn
Ramada
Sheraton Hotel Station Square
Westin William Penn

## Portland, OR
River Place Alexis Hotel

## Raleigh-Durham
Siena Hotel
Washington Duke Inn

## San Antonio
Best Western Historical Crockett
Emily Morgan
Fairmount Hotel
Hilton Palacio del Rio
Hyatt Regency San Antonio
La Mansion del Rio
Marriott Rivercenter

Menger Hotel
Plaza San Antonio
Saint Anthony Hotel
San Antonio Riverwalk Marriott
Sheraton Gunter Hotel

## San Diego
Doubletree Hotel at Horton Plaza
Embassy Suites
Gaslamp Plaza Suites
Horton Grand
Hyatt Regency San Diego
Kona Kai Resort
Pan Pacific
San Diego Marriott
U.S. Grant Hotel
Westgate Hotel

## San Francisco
ANA Hotel
Andrews Hotel
Beresford Arms
Best Western Canterbury
Campton Place Kempinski
Cartwright Hotel
Cathedral Hill
Chancellor Hotel
Donatello
Fairmont Hotel
Four Seasons Clift Hotel
Galleria Park Hotel
Grand Hyatt
Harbor Court Hotel
Hotel Bedford
Hotel Diva
Hotel Nikko
Hotel Vintage Court
Huntington Hotel Nob Hill
Hyatt at Fisherman's Wharf
Hyatt Regency San Francisco
Inn at the Opera
Inn at Union Square
Juliana Hotel
Kensington Park
Lombard Hotel
Mandarin Oriental
Mark Hopkins Inter-Continental
Marriott Fisherman's Wharf
Orchard Hotel
Pan Pacific
Parc 55
Park Hyatt
Petite Auberge

## DOWNTOWN CONVENIENCE

Prescott Hotel
Raphael Hotel
Ritz-Carlton, San Francisco
San Francisco Downtown Marriott
San Francisco Hilton
Sheraton at Fisherman's Wharf
Sheraton Palace
Sir Francis Drake
Stouffer Stanford Court Hotel
Tuscan Inn
Villa Florence Hotel
Westin St. Francis
York Hotel

### San Jose, CA
Fairmont Hotel

### Seattle
Alexis Hotel
Edgewater
Four Seasons Olympic
Holiday Inn Crowne Plaza
Inn at the Market
Mayflower Park Hotel
Seattle Hilton
Sheraton Seattle Hotel & Towers
Sorrento Hotel
Stouffer Madison
Warwick Hotel
Westin Hotel Seattle

### St. Louis
Adam's Mark
Clarion Hotel St. Louis
Doubletree Mayfair
Drury Inn Union Station
Embassy Suites
Holiday Inn Downtown/Conv. Ctr.
Holiday Inn Downtown/Riverfront
Hotel Majestic
Hyatt Regency St. Louis
Marriott Pavilion Hotel
St. Louis Marriott West

### Tampa Bay
Adam's Mark Caribbean Gulf
Belleview Mido Resort Hotel
Courtyard by Marriott
Heritage Hotel
Holiday Inn Ashley Plaza
Hyatt Regency Westshore
Tampa Marriott Westshore
Wyndham Harbour Island Hotel

### Washington, DC
ANA Hotel
Canterbury Hotel
Capital Hilton
Carlton
DuPont Plaza Hotel
Embassy Row Hotel
Four Seasons Hotel
Georgetown Inn
Grand Hotel
Grand Hyatt Washington
Guest Quarters
Hay-Adams Hotel
Henley Park Hotel
Holiday Inn Crowne Plaza
Hotel Washington
Hyatt Regency Washington
Inn at Foggy Bottom
Jefferson Hotel
J.W. Marriott Hotel
Latham Hotel
Loews L'Enfant Plaza
Madison Hotel
Morrison-Clark Inn
Omni Georgetown
One Washington Circle Hotel
Park Hyatt
Phoenix Park Hotel
Pullman-Highland Hotel
Radisson Park Terrace Hotel
Ramada Renaissance
Residence Inn Bethesda
Ritz-Carlton, Pentagon City
Ritz-Carlton, Washington DC
River Inn
Sheraton City Centre Hotel
Sheraton Washington Hotel
Stouffer Mayflower Hotel
Tabard Inn
Washington Court Hotel
Washington Hilton & Towers
Washington Marriott
Washington Vista Hotel
Watergate Hotel
Willard Inter-Continental
Wyndham Bristol Hotel

### Wilmington
Hotel du Pont

### Arizona
Hassayampa Inn
L'Auberge de Sedona
Poco Diablo Resort

### Arkansas

Arlington Resort
Palace Hotel & Bath House

### California

Carmel Valley Ranch Resort
Fess Parker's Red Lion Resort
Four Seasons Biltmore
Villa Royale

### Colorado

Antlers Doubletree
Hotel Boulderado
Hot Springs Lodge

### Florida

Inn at Fisher Island

### Georgia

Eliza Thompson
Foley House Inn
Gastonian
Mulberry Inn

Planter's Inn
President's Quarters

### New Mexico

Eldorado Hotel
Hotel Santa Fe
Hotel St. Francis
Inn on the Alameda
La Fonda Hotel on the Plaza
La Posada de Albuquerque
La Posada de Santa Fe
Sheraton Old Town

### North Carolina

High Hampton Inn & Country Club

### South Carolina

Indigo Inn
Jasmine House Inn
Mills House Hotel
Vendue Inn

### Texas

Tremont House

# DRAMATIC PUBLIC SPACES

## Atlanta
Atlanta Marriott Marquis
Holiday Inn Crowne Plaza
Hotel Nikko
Hyatt Regency
J.W. Marriott at Lenox
Omni Hotel at CNN Center
Stouffer Waverly Hotel
Swissotel Atlanta
Westin Peachtree Plaza

## Atlantic City
Bally's Grand Hotel & Casino
Bally's Park Place
Marriott's Seaview Resort
Trump Castle Resort
Trump Plaza Hotel & Casino
Trump Taj Mahal

## Austin
Four Seasons Hotel

## Baltimore
Harbor Court Hotel
Hyatt Regency Baltimore
Omni Inner Harbor Hotel
Peabody Court Hotel
Stouffer Harborplace

## Birmingham
Wynfrey Hotel

## Boston
Boston Harbor Hotel
Boston Park Plaza
Copley Plaza Hotel
Hyatt Regency Cambridge
Marriott Copley Place
Marriott Hotel Long Wharf
Omni Parker House
Swissotel Boston
Westin Hotel Copley Place

## Chicago
Chicago Hilton & Towers
Congress Hotel
Drake Hotel
Fairmont Hotel
Four Seasons Hotel
Hotel Inter-Continental
Hotel Nikko
Hyatt Regency Chicago
Hyatt Regency O'Hare
Knickerbocker Chicago Hotel
Le Meridien Hotel Chicago

Palmer House Hilton
Ritz-Carlton, Chicago
Sheraton Chicago Hotel & Towers

## Cincinnati
Cincinnatian Hotel
Hyatt Regency Cincinnati
Omni Netherland Plaza

## Cleveland
Cleveland Marriott Society Center
Ritz-Carlton, Cleveland

## Dallas
Adolphus
Doubletree Hotel at Park West
Four Seasons Resort & Club
Grand Kempinski Dallas
Hotel Crescent Court
Hyatt Regency Dallas at Reunion
Loews Anatole Hotel
Omni Mandalay Hotel
Plaza of the Americas Hotel
Sheraton Park Central
Stouffer Dallas Hotel

## Denver
Brown Palace Hotel
Hyatt Regency Tech Center
Loews Giorgio Hotel
Stouffer Concourse Hotel

## Detroit
Dearborn Inn Marriott
Omni
Radisson Plaza Hotel
River Place Inn
Westin Hotel

## Fort Lauderdale
Westin Hotel, Cypress Creek

## Fort Worth
Worthington

## Hartford
Goodwin Hotel

## Honolulu
Hawaii Prince Hotel Waikiki
Hyatt Regency Waikiki
Royal Hawaiian Hotel
Sheraton Moana Surfrider

## Houston
Adam's Mark
La Colombe d'Or

Omni
Ritz-Carlton, Houston
Wyndham Greenspoint

**Indianapolis**
Omni Severin

**Kansas City**
Hyatt Regency Crown Center
Radisson Suite Hotel
Ritz-Carlton, Kansas City
Westin Crown Center

**Las Vegas**
Aladdin Hotel
Bally's
Caesars Palace
Excalibur Hotel
Golden Nugget Hotel & Casino
Mirage
Tropicana Hotel & Country Club

**Little Rock**
Arkansas' Excelsior Hotel
Capital Hotel

**Los Angeles**
BelAge Hotel
Beverly Hills Hotel
Biltmore Los Angeles
Century Plaza Hotel
Chateau Marmont
Four Seasons Hotel
Hotel Bel-Air
Hotel Inter-Continental
Hotel Nikko
J.W. Marriott at Century City
Loews Santa Monica Beach Hotel
Ma Maison Sofitel
New Otani Hotel & Garden
Peninsula Beverly Hills
Regent Beverly Wilshire
Sheraton Grande Hotel
St. James's Club & Hotel
Tower at Century Plaza
Westin Bonaventure

**Louisville**
Seelbach Hotel

**Memphis**
Peabody Memphis

**Miami/Miami Beach**
Biltmore Hotel
Colonnade Hotel

Fontainebleau Hilton
Grand Bay Hotel
Grove Isle Yacht & Tennis Club
Hotel Inter-Continental
Hyatt Regency Coral Gables
Hyatt Regency Miami
Turnberry Isle Club

**Milwaukee**
Hyatt Regency Milwaukee
Pfister Hotel
Wyndham Milwaukee Center

**Minneapolis/St. Paul**
Crown Sterling Suites (Minn/St. Paul)
Hyatt Regency Minneapolis
Minneapolis Marriott City Center
Radisson Plaza Hotel
Saint Paul Hotel

**Nashville**
Hermitage Hotel
Loews Vanderbilt Plaza Hotel
Opryland Hotel
Union Station Hotel

**New Orleans**
Fairmont Hotel
Hotel Inter-Continental
New Orleans Hilton Riverside
Windsor Court Hotel

**New York City**
Essex House, Hotel Nikko
Grand Hyatt
Helmsley Palace
Holiday Inn Crowne Plaza
Hotel Macklowe
Hotel Millenium
Hotel Plaza Athenee
Inter-Continental
Le Parker Meridien
Mayfair Hotel Baglioni
Morgans
New York Marriott Marquis
Paramount
Peninsula New York
Pierre
Plaza Hotel
Rihga Royal
Royalton
St. Regis
U.N. Plaza - Park Hyatt
Waldorf-Astoria/Towers

# DRAMATIC PUBLIC SPACES

## Oklahoma City
Waterford Hotel

## Orange County, CA
Anaheim Hilton & Towers
Dana Point Resort
Disneyland Hotel
Four Seasons Hotel
Hyatt Newporter
Le Meridien Newport
Ritz-Carlton, Laguna Niguel

## Orlando
Disney's Grand Floridian
Hyatt Regency Grand Cypress
Orange Lake Country Club
Peabody Orlando
Stouffer Orlando Resort
Walt Disney World Dolphin
Walt Disney World Swan

## Palm Springs
Hyatt Grand Champions Resort
Marriott's Desert Springs Resort
Ritz-Carlton, Rancho Mirage
Stouffer Esmeralda
Westin Mission Hills Resort

## Philadelphia
Four Seasons Hotel
Hotel Atop the Bellevue
Rittenhouse

## Phoenix/Scottsdale
Arizona Biltmore
Buttes
Crown Sterling Suites
Hyatt Regency Scottsdale
Phoenician
Red Lion La Posada Resort
Ritz-Carlton, Phoenix
Scottsdale Conference Resort
Scottsdale Princess
Sheraton San Marcos Golf Resort

## Pittsburgh
Pittsburgh Vista
Westin William Penn

## Portland, OR
Heathman Hotel
Hotel Vintage Plaza

## San Antonio
Marriott Rivercenter
Menger Hotel

## San Diego
Doubletree Hotel at Horton Plaza
Hotel del Coronado
Hyatt Regency La Jolla
Hyatt Regency San Diego
La Valencia Hotel
Loews Coronado Bay Resort
Pan Pacific
Rancho Bernardo Inn
Rancho Valencia
U.S. Grant Hotel
Westgate Hotel

## San Francisco
ANA Hotel
Fairmont Hotel
Grand Hyatt
Harbor Court Hotel
Hotel Diva
Hotel Nikko
Huntington Hotel Nob Hill
Hyatt Regency San Francisco
Mark Hopkins Inter-Continental
Miyako Hotel
Pan Pacific
Park Hyatt
Ritz-Carlton, San Francisco
San Francisco Downtown Marriott
Sheraton Palace
Sherman House
Stouffer Stanford Court Hotel
Westin St. Francis

## Seattle
Four Seasons Olympic
Hyatt Regency Bellevue
Sorrento Hotel

## St. Louis
Adam's Mark
Hotel Majestic
Hyatt Regency St. Louis
Ritz-Carlton, St. Louis

## Tampa Bay
Belleview Mido Resort Hotel
Wyndham Harbour Island Hotel

## Washington, DC
Capital Hilton
Carlton
Embassy Suites Chevy Chase
Four Seasons Hotel
Grand Hyatt Washington

474

Hay-Adams Hotel
Hyatt Regency Washington
Madison Hotel
Radisson Park Terrace Hotel
Radisson Plaza Hotel
Ritz-Carlton, Tysons Corner
Ritz-Carlton, Washington DC
Stouffer Mayflower Hotel
Washington Court Hotel
Washington Vista Hotel
Willard Inter-Continental

## Wilmington
Hotel du Pont

## Alabama
Marriott's Grand Hotel

## Arizona
Arizona Inn
Boulders Resort
El Conquistador
Westin La Paloma

## California
Ahwahnee Hotel
Carmel Valley Ranch Resort
Claremont Resort
Four Seasons Biltmore
Highlands Inn
Inn at Spanish Bay
Lodge at Pebble Beach
Monterey Plaza Hotel
Portofino Hotel & Yacht Club
Ventana - Big Sur
Villa Royale

## Colorado
Antlers Doubletree
Broadmoor
Doral Telluride
Hyatt Regency Beaver Creek
Ritz-Carlton, Aspen

## Connecticut
Mayflower Inn

## Florida
Boca Raton Resort & Club
Breakers
Inn at Fisher Island
Marriott at Sawgrass Resort
Marriott's Bay Point Resort

Mission Inn Golf & Tennis Resort
Ocean Grand Hotel
Registry Resort
Ritz-Carlton, Amelia Island
Ritz-Carlton, Naples
Ritz-Carlton, Palm Beach

## Hawaii
Four Seasons Resort Wailea
Grand Hyatt Wailea
Hotel Hana-Maui
Hyatt Regency Maui
Hyatt Regency Waikoloa
Kapalua Bay Hotel & Villas
Manele Bay Hotel
Maui Inter-Continental Resort
Maui Marriott
Mauna Kea Beach Hotel
Mauna Lani Bay Hotel
Princeville Hotel
Ritz-Carlton, Mauna Lani
Stouffer Wailea Beach Resort
Westin Kauai
Westin Maui

## Idaho
Coeur d'Alene Resort

## Indiana
French Lick Springs Resort

## Louisiana
Nottoway Plantation

## Maine
Harraseeket Inn
Whitehall Inn

## Massachusetts
Blantyre
Wheatleigh

## Michigan
Grand Hotel

## Minnesota
Arrowwood, A Radisson Resort

## Montana
Grouse Mountain Lodge
Kandahar Lodge

## DRAMATIC PUBLIC SPACES

### New Hampshire

Balsams

### New York State

Doral Arrowwood
Mohonk Mountain House

### Pennsylvania

Evermay on-the-Delaware
Hotel Hershey
Nemacolin Woodlands

### South Carolina

John Rutledge House Inn
Sea Pines
Westin Resort

### Texas

Barton Creek

### Utah

Cliff Lodge
Stein Eriksen Lodge

### Washington

Salish Lodge
Sun Mountain Lodge

### West Virginia

Greenbrier

### Spas

Doral Saturnia
Golden Door
Greenhouse
La Costa Hotel & Spa
Loews Ventana Canyon Resort
Maine Chance
Mario's International Hotel
Murrieta Hot Springs Resort
Sonoma Mission Inn & Spa

# ELITE STATUS

**Atlanta**
Hotel Nikko
J.W. Marriott at Lenox
Ritz-Carlton, Atlanta
Ritz-Carlton, Buckhead
Swissotel Atlanta

**Austin**
Four Seasons Hotel

**Baltimore**
Harbor Court Hotel
Peabody Court Hotel
Stouffer Harborplace

**Birmingham**
Tutwiler
Wynfrey Hotel

**Boston**
Boston Harbor Hotel
Bostonian Hotel
Charles Hotel in Harvard Square
Four Seasons Hotel
Le Meridien Boston
Ritz-Carlton, Boston
Swissotel Boston
Westin Hotel Copley Place

**Chicago**
Drake Hotel
Fairmont Hotel
Four Seasons Hotel
Hotel Nikko
Hotel Sofitel
Le Meridien Hotel Chicago
Mayfair
Park Hyatt
Ritz-Carlton, Chicago
Stouffer Riviere
Swissotel Chicago

**Cincinnati**
Cincinnatian Hotel

**Cleveland**
Cleveland Marriott Society Center
Ritz-Carlton, Cleveland

**Dallas**
Adolphus
Fairmont Hotel
Four Seasons Resort & Club
Hotel Crescent Court
Loews Anatole Hotel
Mansion on Turtle Creek
Omni Mandalay Hotel

Plaza of the Americas Hotel
Sheraton Suites
Westin Galleria

**Denver**
Brown Palace Hotel
Cambridge Hotel
Loews Giorgio Hotel
Oxford Hotel
Westin Hotel Tabor Center

**Detroit**
Atheneum Suites
Ritz-Carlton, Dearborn
River Place Inn
Townsend Hotel

**Fort Lauderdale**
Westin Hotel, Cypress Creek

**Fort Worth**
Worthington

**Hartford**
Goodwin Hotel

**Honolulu**
Halekulani
Hawaii Prince Hotel Waikiki
Kahala Hilton

**Houston**
Four Seasons Hotel
La Colombe d'Or
Lancaster
Omni
Ritz-Carlton, Houston
Wyndham Greenspoint
Wyndham Warwick Hotel

**Indianapolis**
Canterbury Hotel
Westin Hotel Indianapolis

**Kansas City**
Ritz-Carlton, Kansas City

**Los Angeles**
BelAge Hotel
Beverly Hills Hotel
Biltmore Los Angeles
Century Plaza Hotel
Checkers Hotel Kempinski
Four Seasons Hotel
Hotel Bel-Air
Hotel Nikko
J.W. Marriott at Century City
L'Ermitage Hotel

# ELITE STATUS

Loews Santa Monica Beach Hotel
Peninsula Beverly Hills
Regent Beverly Wilshire
Ritz-Carlton, Huntington Hotel
Ritz-Carlton, Marina del Rey
St. James's Club & Hotel
Tower at Century Plaza
Westwood Marquis Hotel

## Memphis
Peabody Memphis

## Miami/Miami Beach
Colonnade Hotel
Grand Bay Hotel
Mayfair House Hotel Grand Luxe
Turnberry Isle Club

## Milwaukee
Pfister Hotel
Wyndham Milwaukee Center

## Minneapolis/St. Paul
Saint Paul Hotel

## New Orleans
Hotel Maison de Ville
Le Meridien Hotel
Pontchartrain Hotel
Westin Canal Place
Windsor Court Hotel

## New York City
Carlyle Hotel
Essex House, Hotel Nikko
Helmsley Palace
Hotel Macklowe
Hotel Millenium
Hotel Plaza Athenee
Le Parker Meridien
Lowell New York
Mark
Mayfair Hotel Baglioni
Michelangelo
Peninsula New York
Pierre
Regency
Rihga Royal
Ritz-Carlton, New York
Stanhope
St. Regis
U.N. Plaza - Park Hyatt
Waldorf-Astoria/Towers
Westbury Hotel

## Oklahoma City
Waterford Hotel

## Orange County, CA
Dana Point Resort
Four Seasons Hotel
Le Meridien Newport
Ritz-Carlton, Laguna Niguel

## Orlando
Disney's Grand Floridian
Hyatt Regency Grand Cypress
Peabody Orlando

## Palm Springs
Hyatt Grand Champions Resort
La Quinta Hotel
Ritz-Carlton, Rancho Mirage
Stouffer Esmeralda
Westin Mission Hills Resort

## Philadelphia
Four Seasons Hotel
Hotel Atop the Bellevue
Rittenhouse
Ritz-Carlton, Philadelphia

## Phoenix/Scottsdale
Hyatt Regency Scottsdale
Phoenician
Ritz-Carlton, Phoenix
Scottsdale Princess

## Pittsburgh
Westin William Penn

## Portland, OR
Heathman Hotel
Hotel Vintage Plaza
River Place Alexis Hotel

## Raleigh-Durham
Siena Hotel

## Richmond
Commonwealth Park Suites Hotel

## San Antonio
Fairmount Hotel
Marriott Rivercenter
Plaza San Antonio

## San Diego
Hyatt Regency La Jolla
Le Meridien San Diego
Loews Coronado Bay Resort
Pan Pacific

Rancho Bernardo Inn
Rancho Valencia
Sheraton Grande at Torrey Pines
U.S. Grant Hotel
Westgate Hotel

### San Francisco

Archbishops Mansion Inn
Campton Place Kempinski
Donatello
Four Seasons Clift Hotel
Hotel Nikko
Huntington Hotel Nob Hill
Mandarin Oriental
Pan Pacific
Park Hyatt
Ritz-Carlton, San Francisco
Sheraton Palace
Sherman House
Stouffer Stanford Court Hotel

### San Jose, CA

Fairmont Hotel

### Seattle

Alexis Hotel
Four Seasons Olympic
Sorrento Hotel

### St. Louis

Adam's Mark
Hotel Majestic
Ritz-Carlton, St. Louis

### Tampa Bay

Stouffer Vinoy Resort
Wyndham Harbour Island Hotel

### Washington, DC

Carlton
Four Seasons Hotel
Grand Hotel
Grand Hyatt Washington
Hay-Adams Hotel
Jefferson Hotel
Madison Hotel
Morrison House
Park Hyatt
Pullman-Highland Hotel
Ritz-Carlton, Pentagon City
Ritz-Carlton, Tysons Corner
Ritz-Carlton, Washington DC
Watergate Hotel
Willard Inter-Continental

### Wilmington

Hotel du Pont

### Alaska

King Salmon Lodge
Tikchik Narrows Lodge

### Arizona

Boulders Resort
L'Auberge de Sedona

### California

Auberge du Soleil
Carmel Valley Ranch Resort
Four Seasons Biltmore
Highlands Inn
Inn at Spanish Bay
Lodge at Pebble Beach
Meadowood Resort
Post Ranch Inn
San Ysidro Ranch
Stonepine Estate Resort
Timberhill Ranch
Ventana - Big Sur

### Colorado

Doral Telluride
Hotel Jerome
Hyatt Regency Beaver Creek
Little Nell
Lodge at Cordillera
Ritz-Carlton, Aspen
Sardy House

### Connecticut

Mayflower Inn

### Florida

Boca Raton Resort & Club
Breakers
Indian River Plantation Resort
Inn at Fisher Island
Little Palm Island
Ocean Grand Hotel
Ritz-Carlton, Amelia Island
Ritz-Carlton, Naples
Ritz-Carlton, Palm Beach

### Georgia

Cloister
Sea Palms Golf & Tennis Resort

# ELITE STATUS

## Hawaii

Four Seasons Resort Wailea
Grand Hyatt Wailea
Hotel Hana-Maui
Hyatt Regency Kauai
Hyatt Regency Maui
Hyatt Regency Waikoloa
Kapalua Bay Hotel & Villas
Lodge at Koele
Manele Bay Hotel
Maui Prince Hotel
Mauna Kea Beach Hotel
Mauna Lani Bay Hotel
Princeville Hotel
Ritz-Carlton, Mauna Lani
Westin Kauai

## Massachusetts

Charlotte Inn

## Mississippi

Monmouth Plantation

## New Mexico

Inn of the Anasazi

## New York State

Point, The

## North Carolina

Fearrington House Inn
Pinehurst Hotel & Country Club

## South Carolina

John Rutledge House Inn
Westin Resort

## Tennessee

Inn at Blackberry Farm

## Texas

Tremont House

## Utah

Stein Eriksen Lodge

## Vermont

Inn at Essex

## Virginia

Inn at Little Washington

## West Virginia

Greenbrier

## Wisconsin

American Club

## Spas

Canyon Ranch
Canyon Ranch in the Berkshires
Doral Saturnia
Golden Door
Greenhouse
La Costa Hotel & Spa
Loews Ventana Canyon Resort
Maine Chance

# ENTERTAINMENT
## (Major Stars and Shows)

**Atlantic City**
Bally's Grand Hotel & Casino
Bally's Park Place
Caesars Atlantic City
Claridge Casino Hotel
Harrah's Marina Hotel & Casino
Merv Griffin's Resorts
Sands Hotel & Casino
Showboat Hotel
TropWorld
Trump Castle Resort
Trump Plaza Hotel & Casino
Trump Taj Mahal

**Boston**
Charles Hotel in Harvard Square

**Honolulu**
Hilton Hawaiian Village

**Houston**
Houston Marriott West Loop

**Las Vegas**
Aladdin Hotel
Bally's
Caesars Palace
Circus Circus Hotel
Desert Inn Hotel & Country Club
Dunes Hotel & Country Club
Excalibur Hotel
Fitzgerald's Casino Hotel
Flamingo Hotel
Four Queens Hotel & Casino
Golden Nugget Hotel & Casino
Hacienda Hotel & Casino
Imperial Palace Hotel & Casino
Lady Luck Casino Hotel
Las Vegas Hilton
Mirage
Plaza Hotel
Riviera Hotel & Casino
Sahara Hotel & Casino
Sands Hotel & Casino
Showboat Hotel
Stardust Resort & Casino
Tropicana Hotel & Country Club

**Little Rock**
Arkansas' Excelsior Hotel

**Los Angeles**
Barnabey's Hotel

**New York City**
Algonquin Hotel

**Philadelphia**
Four Seasons Hotel

**San Diego**
Bahia Hotel

**St. Louis**
Radisson Hotel Clayton

**California**
Villa Royale

**Florida**
Inn at Fisher Island

**Hawaii**
Hyatt Regency Kauai
Kaanapali Beach Hotel
Princeville Hotel

**Illinois**
Marriott's Lincolnshire Resort
Pheasant Run Resort

**Maine**
Nonantum Resort

**Montana**
Glacier Park Lodge
Lake McDonald Lodge
Many Glacier Hotel

**Nevada**
Caesars Lake Tahoe
Harrah's Lake Tahoe

**New York State**
Concord Resort Hotel

**Pennsylvania**
Mount Airy Lodge

**Texas**
Tremont House

**Utah**
Cliff Lodge

**Washington**
Lake Quinault Lodge

# EUROPEAN STYLE

## Atlanta
Ansley Inn
Biltmore Suites
Ritz-Carlton, Atlanta
Ritz-Carlton, Buckhead
Swissotel Atlanta

## Baltimore
Admiral Fell Inn
Doubletree Inn at the Colonnade
Harbor Court Hotel
Peabody Court Hotel
Stouffer Harborplace

## Boston
Boston Harbor Hotel
Bostonian Hotel
Copley Plaza Hotel
Copley Square Hotel
Eliot Hotel
Four Seasons Hotel
Le Meridien Boston
Lenox Hotel
Omni Parker House
Ritz-Carlton, Boston
Swissotel Boston

## Charlotte
Dunhill Hotel

## Chicago
Chicago Claridge Hotel
Chicago Hilton & Towers
Drake Hotel
Fairmont Hotel
Four Seasons Hotel
Hotel Inter-Continental
Hotel Sofitel
Hyatt Printers Row
Hyatt Regency Suites
Knickerbocker Chicago Hotel
Le Meridien Hotel Chicago
Mayfair
Omni Ambassador East
Park Hyatt
Radisson Plaza Ambass. West
Ritz-Carlton, Chicago
Swissotel Chicago
Talbott Hotel

## Cincinnati
Cincinnatian Hotel
Omni Netherland Plaza

## Cleveland
Glidden House
Ritz-Carlton, Cleveland
Stouffer Tower City Plaza Hotel

## Dallas
Adolphus
Aristocrat Hotel
Fairmont Hotel
Four Seasons Resort & Club
Grand Kempinski Dallas
Hotel Crescent Court
Hotel St. Germain
Mansion on Turtle Creek
Melrose Hotel
Plaza of the Americas Hotel
Stoneleigh Hotel

## Denver
Brown Palace Hotel
Burnsley Hotel
Cambridge Hotel
Loews Giorgio Hotel
Oxford Hotel
Warwick Hotel

## Detroit
Atheneum Suites
Ritz-Carlton, Dearborn
River Place Inn
Townsend Hotel

## Fort Lauderdale
Riverside Hotel

## Hartford
Goodwin Hotel

## Honolulu
Hawaii Prince Hotel Waikiki

## Houston
Hotel Sofitel
La Colombe d'Or
Lancaster
Omni
Plaza Hilton
Ritz-Carlton, Houston

## Indianapolis
Canterbury Hotel

## Kansas City
Hotel Savoy
Radisson Suite Hotel
Raphael Hotel
Ritz-Carlton, Kansas City

**Little Rock**
Arkansas' Excelsior Hotel

**Los Angeles**
Barnabey's Hotel
BelAge Hotel
Beverly Hills Hotel
Biltmore Los Angeles
Century Plaza Hotel
Chateau Marmont
Checkers Hotel Kempinski
Four Seasons Hotel
J.W. Marriott at Century City
Le Parc Hotel
L'Ermitage Hotel
Ma Maison Sofitel
Peninsula Beverly Hills
Regent Beverly Wilshire
Ritz-Carlton, Huntington Hotel
Ritz-Carlton, Marina del Rey
St. James's Club & Hotel
Tower at Century Plaza

**Louisville**
Seelbach Hotel

**Memphis**
Peabody Memphis

**Miami/Miami Beach**
Alexander All-Suite Luxury Hotel
Betsy Ross Hotel
Biltmore Hotel
Colonnade Hotel
David William Hotel
Grand Bay Hotel
Grove Isle Yacht & Tennis Club
Hotel Inter-Continental
Hotel Place St. Michel
Hyatt Regency Coral Gables
Mayfair House Hotel Grand Luxe
Occidental Parc Hotel
Turnberry Isle Club

**Milwaukee**
Astor Hotel
Pfister Hotel
Wyndham Milwaukee Center

**Minneapolis/St. Paul**
Northland Inn
Radisson Hotel & Conf. Ctr.
Saint Paul Hotel
Whitney

**Nashville**
Loews Vanderbilt Plaza Hotel
Union Station Hotel

**New Orleans**
Dauphine Orleans Hotel
Fairmont Hotel
Hotel Inter-Continental
Hotel Maison de Ville
Hotel Ste. Helene
Hotel St. Marie
Le Meridien Hotel
Le Pavillon Hotel
Le Richelieu
Omni Royal Orleans
Place d'Armes Hotel
Royal Sonesta
Saint Louis Hotel
Soniat House
Windsor Court Hotel

**New York City**
Algonquin Hotel
Barbizon
Box Tree
Carlyle Hotel
Doral Court Hotel
Doral Tuscany
Dorset
Essex House, Hotel Nikko
Helmsley Palace
Helmsley Park Lane Hotel
Hotel Kimberly
Hotel Plaza Athenee
Hotel Wales
Inter-Continental
Le Parker Meridien
Lowell New York
Mark
Mayfair Hotel Baglioni
Michelangelo
Morgans
Peninsula New York
Pierre
Plaza Hotel
Regency
Rihga Royal
Ritz-Carlton, New York
Royalton
Sheraton Park Avenue
Stanhope
St. Moritz on-the-Park
St. Regis

# EUROPEAN STYLE

Surrey Hotel
U.N. Plaza - Park Hyatt
Waldorf-Astoria/Towers
Westbury Hotel
Wyndham Hotel

## Oklahoma City
Waterford Hotel

## Orange County, CA
Four Seasons Hotel
Le Meridien Newport
Ritz-Carlton, Laguna Niguel

## Orlando
Park Plaza Hotel

## Palm Springs
La Quinta Hotel
Ritz-Carlton, Rancho Mirage
Two Bunch Palms Resort

## Philadelphia
Chestnut Hill Hotel
Hotel Atop the Bellevue
Independence Park Inn
Latham Hotel
Omni Hotel at Independence Park
Penn's View Inn
Rittenhouse
Ritz-Carlton, Philadelphia

## Phoenix/Scottsdale
Phoenician
Ritz-Carlton, Phoenix

## Pittsburgh
Pittsburgh Vista
Priory - A City Inn
Westin William Penn

## Portland, OR
Heathman Hotel
Hotel Vintage Plaza
River Place Alexis Hotel

## Raleigh-Durham
Siena Hotel

## Richmond
Commonwealth Park Suites Hotel

## San Antonio
Fairmount Hotel
Sheraton Gunter Hotel

## San Diego
Gaslamp Plaza Suites
Hyatt Regency La Jolla
La Valencia Hotel
Le Meridien San Diego
Rancho Bernardo Inn
U.S. Grant Hotel

## San Francisco
Archbishops Mansion Inn
Campton Place Kempinski
Cartwright Hotel
Chancellor Hotel
Donatello
Four Seasons Clift Hotel
Galleria Park Hotel
Harbor Court Hotel
Hotel Bedford
Hotel Diva
Hotel Vintage Court
Huntington Hotel Nob Hill
Inn at the Opera
Inn at Union Square
Juliana Hotel
Kensington Park
Majestic
Mark Hopkins Inter-Continental
Orchard Hotel
Pan Pacific
Park Hyatt
Prescott Hotel
Queen Anne
Raphael Hotel
Sheraton Palace
Sherman House
Stouffer Stanford Court Hotel
Tuscan Inn
Villa Florence Hotel
Washington Square Inn
Westin St. Francis
York Hotel

## Seattle
Alexis Hotel
Four Seasons Olympic
Inn at the Market
Mayflower Park Hotel
Sorrento Hotel
Warwick Hotel

## St. Louis
Daniele Hotel
Hotel Majestic

Ritz-Carlton, St. Louis
Seven Gables Inn

**Tampa Bay**
Belleview Mido Resort Hotel
Don Ce-Sar Registry Resort
Heritage Hotel
Hyatt Regency Westshore

**Washington, DC**
Canterbury Hotel
Capital Hilton
Carlton
Embassy Row Hotel
Four Seasons Hotel
Georgetown Inn
Grand Hotel
Hay-Adams Hotel
Henley Park Hotel
Jefferson Hotel
Latham Hotel
Madison Hotel
Morrison-Clark Inn
Morrison House
Park Hyatt
Phoenix Park Hotel
Pullman-Highland Hotel
Radisson Park Terrace Hotel
Ritz-Carlton, Pentagon City
Ritz-Carlton, Tysons Corner
Ritz-Carlton, Washington DC
River Inn
Tabard Inn
Watergate Hotel
Willard Inter-Continental
Wyndham Bristol Hotel

**Wilmington**
Hotel du Pont

**Arizona**
Arizona Inn
L'Auberge de Sedona

**California**
Auberge du Soleil
Claremont Resort
Harvest Inn
La Playa Hotel
Lodge at Pebble Beach
Los Olivos Grand Hotel
Monterey Plaza Hotel
Portofino Hotel & Yacht Club
Stonepine Estate Resort

St. Orres
Timberhill Ranch
Villa Royale
Vintners Inn
Wine Country Inn

**Colorado**
Antlers Doubletree
Broadmoor
Hotel Jerome
Hyatt Regency Beaver Creek
Lodge at Cordillera
Lodge at Vail
Pines Lodge at Beaver Creek
Ritz-Carlton, Aspen
Snowmass Lodge & Club
Stanley Hotel
Westin Resort Vail

**Connecticut**
Mayflower Inn

**Florida**
Breakers
Chalet Suzanne
Inn at Fisher Island
Lodge at Ponte Vedra Beach
Marquesa Hotel
Ocean Grand Hotel
Resort at Longboat Key Club
Ritz-Carlton, Naples

**Georgia**
Eliza Thompson
Foley House Inn
Mulberry Inn
Planter's Inn
President's Quarters

**Hawaii**
Kapalua Bay Hotel & Villas
Lodge at Koele
Manele Bay Hotel
Princeville Hotel
Ritz-Carlton, Mauna Lani

**Louisiana**
Nottoway Plantation

**Maine**
Black Point Inn Resort
White Barn Inn

# EUROPEAN STYLE

## Maryland

Imperial Hotel
Maryland Inn

## Massachusetts

Blantyre
Charlotte Inn
Orchards
Red Lion Inn
Summer House
Wheatleigh

## Minnesota

Fitgers Inn
Schumacher's New Prague
St. James Hotel

## Montana

Kandahar Lodge

## New Mexico

Hotel Edelweiss
Hotel Plaza Real
Hotel St. Francis
Inn on the Alameda
St. Bernard Hotel

## New York State

Clarion Inn at Saratoga
Geneva on the Lake
Guest House
Old Drovers Inn
Point, The
Troutbeck Inn

## North Carolina

Fearrington House Inn
Greystone Inn

## Ohio

Quail Hollow Resort

## Oregon

Columbia Gorge Hotel
Sylvia Beach Hotel

## Pennsylvania

Evermay on-the-Delaware

## Rhode Island

1661 Inn

## South Carolina

Indigo Inn
Jasmine House Inn
John Rutledge House Inn
Lodge Alley Inn
Mills House Hotel
Planters Inn
Vendue Inn

## South Dakota

Franklin Hotel
Hotel Alex Johnson

## Texas

Barton Creek

## Utah

Cliff Lodge
Stein Eriksen Lodge
Washington School Inn

## Vermont

Topnotch at Stowe
Trapp Family Lodge
Woodstock Inn & Resort

## Virginia

Inn at Little Washington
Williamsburg Inn

## Washington

Inn at Semiahmoo

## Wisconsin

American Club

## Spas

Cal-A-Vie
Doral Saturnia
Greenhouse
La Costa Hotel & Spa
Mario's International Hotel
National Institute of Fitness
Palm-Aire Hotel & Spa
Russell House
Sans Souci Resort
Sonoma Mission Inn & Spa

# FAMILY PLACES

## Atlanta
Atlanta Hilton & Towers
Embassy Suites Perim. Ctr.
Marque of Atlanta
Marriott Suites Atlanta Midtown
Marriott Suites Perimeter
Summerfield Suites Hotel

## Atlantic City
Holiday Inn Diplomat
Marriott's Seaview Resort
Merv Griffin's Resorts
Showboat Hotel
Trump Taj Mahal

## Baltimore
Admiral Fell Inn
Hyatt Regency Baltimore
Johns Hopkins Inn
Omni Inner Harbor Hotel
Tremont Hotel
Tremont Plaza Hotel

## Boston
Boston Harbor Hotel
Copley Plaza Hotel
Guest Quarters Suite Hotel
Hyatt Regency Cambridge
Marriott Hotel Long Wharf
Royal Sonesta
Sheraton Boston Hotel & Towers
Sheraton Commander Hotel

## Chicago
Barclay Chicago
Chicago Marriott Downtown
Chicago Marriott Suites O'Hare
Holiday Inn City Centre
Ritz-Carlton, Chicago
Sheraton Chicago Hotel & Towers
Sheraton Plaza Hotel

## Cincinnati
Kings Island Inn & Conf. Ctr.

## Cleveland
Holiday Inn Lakeside City Center

## Corpus Christi
Corpus Christi Marriott Bayfront

## Dallas
Embassy Suites
Four Seasons Resort & Club
Hyatt Regency Dallas at Reunion

## Denver
Embassy Suites Denver Dtwn.
Residence Inn

## Detroit
Dearborn Inn Marriott

## Fort Lauderdale
Bahia Mar Resort
Crown Sterling Suites Cypress
Fort Lauderdale Marina Marriott
Fort Lauderdale Marriott North
Lago Mar Resort & Club
Marriott's Harbor Beach Resort
Ocean Manor Resort Hotel
Pier 66 Resort & Marina
Sheraton Design Center
Sheraton Yankee Clipper
Westin Hotel, Cypress Creek

## Honolulu
Hawaiian Regent
Hawaiian Waikiki Beach Hotel
Hilton Hawaiian Village
Hyatt Regency Waikiki
Ilikai Hotel Nikko Waikiki
Kahala Hilton
New Otani Kaimana Beach Hotel
Outrigger Waikiki
Pacific Beach Hotel
Royal Hawaiian Hotel
Sheraton Makaha Resort
Sheraton Princess Kaiulani
Sheraton Waikiki Hotel
Turtle Bay Hilton

## Houston
Guest Quarters
Holiday Inn Crowne Plaza
Holiday Inn Houston West
Holiday Inn West Loop
Houston Marriott Astrodome
Nassau Bay Hilton & Marina
Ramada Kings Inn
Sheraton Astrodome Hotel

## Indianapolis
Holiday Inn Union Station
Indianapolis Marriott
Radisson Plaza & Suites Hotel

## Kansas City
Allis Plaza Hotel
Sheraton Suites

# FAMILY PLACES

## Las Vegas
Alexis Park Resort
Circus Circus Hotel
Excalibur Hotel
Mirage
Showboat Hotel
St. Tropez
Tropicana Hotel & Country Club

## Little Rock
Arkansas' Excelsior Hotel

## Los Angeles
Barnabey's Hotel
Century Plaza Hotel
Hotel Inter-Continental
Loews Santa Monica Beach Hotel
Malibu Beach Inn
Sportsmen's Lodge Hotel

## Miami/Miami Beach
Betsy Ross Hotel
Biltmore Hotel
Biscayne Bay Marriott
Doral Ocean Beach Resort
Doral Resort & Country Club
Fontainebleau Hilton
Grove Isle Yacht & Tennis Club
Hyatt Regency Coral Gables
Sheraton Bal Harbour Hotel
Sonesta Beach Hotel
Turnberry Isle Club

## Milwaukee
Embassy Suites, West
Milwaukee Marriott - Brookfield

## Minneapolis/St. Paul
Crown Sterling Suites (Minn/St. Paul)
Hotel Luxeford Suites
Northland Inn

## Nashville
Embassy Suites
Opryland Hotel

## New Orleans
Doubletree Hotel New Orleans
Holiday Inn Crowne Plaza
New Orleans Hilton Riverside
New Orleans Marriott
Radisson Suite Hotel
Sheraton New Orleans Hotel

## New York City
Dumont Plaza Hotel
Embassy Suites Hotel
Flatotel International
Gorham New York
Holiday Inn Crowne Plaza
Hotel Beverly
Hotel Wales
Murray Hill East Suite Hotel
New York Marriott Marquis
Novotel New York
Salisbury Hotel
Surrey Hotel
Waldorf-Astoria/Towers

## Orange County, CA
Anaheim Hilton & Towers
Anaheim Marriott Hotel
Casa Laguna Inn
Costa Mesa Marriott Suites
Dana Point Resort
Disneyland Hotel
Hilton Suites In Orange
Hyatt Newporter
Hyatt Regency Alicante
Inn at the Park
Irvine Marriott
Marriott Suites Newport Beach
Newport Beach Marriott Hotel
Ritz-Carlton, Laguna Niguel
Sheraton Anaheim Hotel
Surf & Sand Hotel

## Orlando
Buena Vista Palace
Clarion Plaza Hotel
Disney's Caribbean Beach Resort
Disney's Contemporary Resort
Disney's Grand Floridian
Disney's Polynesian Resort
Disney's Village Resort
Forte Travelodge Hotel
Grosvenor Resort at WDW
Guest Quarters Disney Village
Hilton at WDW Village
Hotel Royal Plaza
Hyatt Orlando
Hyatt Regency Grand Cypress
Marriott
Marriott's Orlando World Center
Orange Lake Country Club
Orlando Heritage Inn
Peabody Orlando

Radisson Inn International Dr.
Sheraton World Resort
Sonesta Villa Resort
Stouffer Orlando Resort
Walt Disney World Dolphin
Walt Disney World Swan

**Palm Springs**
Autry Resort
Doubletree Resort Palm Springs
Hyatt Grand Champions Resort
La Quinta Hotel
Marriott's Desert Springs Resort
Marriott's Rancho Las Palmas
Palm Springs Hilton Resort
Palm Springs Riviera Resort
Shadow Mountain Resort
Stouffer Esmeralda
Westin Mission Hills Resort

**Philadelphia**
Barclay Hotel

**Phoenix/Scottsdale**
Arizona Biltmore
Crown Sterling Suites
Fountains Suite Hotel
Hyatt Regency Scottsdale
Lexington Hotel & City Square
Marriott's Camelback Inn
Marriott Suites Scottsdale
Phoenician
Pointe at Tapatio Cliffs
Red Lion La Posada Resort
Registry Resort
Scottsdale Hilton
Scottsdale Plaza Resort
Scottsdale Princess
Sheraton San Marcos Golf Resort
Wyndham Paradise Valley Resort

**Pittsburgh**
Ramada
Sheraton Hotel Station Square

**Raleigh-Durham**
Washington Duke Inn

**San Antonio**
Best Western Historical Crockett
Hilton Palacio del Rio
Hyatt Regency San Antonio
Marriott Rivercenter
Menger Hotel
Saint Anthony Hotel

San Antonio Riverwalk Marriott
Wyndham San Antonio

**San Diego**
Bahia Hotel
Catamaran Resort Hotel
Doubletree Hotel at Horton Plaza
Embassy Suites
Hanalei Hotel
Hotel del Coronado
Humphrey's Half Moon Inn
Hyatt Islandia
Hyatt Regency San Diego
La Jolla Marriott
Loews Coronado Bay Resort
Rancho Bernardo Inn
San Diego Hilton
San Diego Marriott
San Diego Princess Resort
Sea Lodge

**San Francisco**
Harbor Court Hotel
Hyatt at Fisherman's Wharf
Hyatt Regency San Francisco
Hyde Park Suites
San Francisco Downtown Marriott
San Francisco Hilton
Seal Rock Inn
Sheraton at Fisherman's Wharf
Stanyan Park Hotel
Tuscan Inn
Westin St. Francis

**Seattle**
Mayflower Park Hotel
Red Lion Hotel Bellevue
Sheraton Seattle Hotel & Towers

**St. Louis**
Adam's Mark
Drury Inn Union Station
Embassy Suites
Holiday Inn Clayton Plaza
Holiday Inn Downtown/Conv. Ctr.
Holiday Inn Downtown/Riverfront
Hyatt Regency St. Louis

**Tampa Bay**
Adam's Mark Caribbean Gulf
Crown Sterling Suites
Embassy Suites Tampa Airport
Heritage Hotel
Innisbrook Resort

# FAMILY PLACES

Radisson Bay Harbor Inn
Sheraton Sand Key Resort
Trade Winds

## Washington, DC

Embassy Suites Chevy Chase
Guest Quarters
Hay-Adams Hotel
Holiday Inn Crowne Plaza
Hotel Washington
Hyatt Regency Reston
Inn at Foggy Bottom
J.W. Marriott Hotel
Loews L'Enfant Plaza
One Washington Circle Hotel
Radisson Plaza Hotel
River Inn

## Alabama

Marriott's Grand Hotel

## Alaska

Camp Denali
Denali National Park Hotel
Gustavus Inn at Glacier Bay
King Salmon Lodge

## Arizona

Arizona Inn
El Conquistador
El Tovar Hotel
Enchantment Resort
Grand Canyon Lodge
Los Abrigados
Rancho de los Caballeros
Tanque Verde Ranch
Ventana Canyon
Westin La Paloma
Westward Look Resort
Wickenburg Inn
Wigwam

## Arkansas

Arlington Resort
Gaston's White River Resort

## California

Ahwahnee Hotel
Alisal Ranch
Alta Mira
Big Sur Lodge
Casa Sirena Marina Resort
Claremont Resort

Eureka Inn
Four Seasons Biltmore
Furnace Creek Inn
Inn at Rancho Santa Fe
Inn at the Tides
La Casa del Zorro
La Playa Hotel
Little River Inn
Northstar-at-Tahoe
Ojai Valley Inn
Portofino Hotel & Yacht Club
Quail Lodge Resort & Golf Club
Santa Barbara Miramar
Squaw Valley Inn

## Colorado

Aspen Club Lodge
Breckenridge Hilton
Broadmoor
Charter at Beaver Creek
C Lazy U Ranch
Club Med, Copper Mountain
Doral Telluride
Grande Butte Hotel
Home Ranch
Hotel Boulderado
Hot Springs Lodge
Hyatt Regency Beaver Creek
Inn at Aspen
Inn at Beaver Creek
Iron Horse Resort Retreat
Keystone Lodge
Limelite Lodge
Pines Lodge at Beaver Creek
Radisson Resort Vail
Sheraton Steamboat Resort
Silver Tree Hotel
Sitzmark Lodge
Snowmass Lodge & Club
Sonnenalp Resort
Stanley Hotel
Tamarron Resort
Vista Verde Guest Ranch
Westin Resort Vail

## Connecticut

Water's Edge Inn & Resort

## Florida

Amelia Island Plantation
Breakers
Captiva Beach Resort

Chalet Suzanne
Cheeca Lodge
Club Med Sandpiper
Colony Beach & Tennis Resort
Don Shula's Hotel & Golf Club
Grenelefe Resort
Hawk's Cay Resort & Marina
Hyatt Key West
Indian River Plantation Resort
Inn at Fisher Island
Lakeside Inn
Lodge at Ponte Vedra Beach
Marriott at Sawgrass Resort
Marriott's Bay Point Resort
Marriott's Casa Marina Resort
Marriott's Marco Island Resort
Moose Head Ranch
Ocean Reef Club
PGA National
Pier House Resort
Plantation Inn
Ponce de Leon Resort
Ponte Vedra Inn & Club
Registry Resort
Resort at Longboat Key Club
Ritz-Carlton, Amelia Island
Sheraton Key Largo Resort
Sonesta Sanibel Harbour
South Seas Plantation Resort
Sundial Beach & Tennis Resort
'Tween Waters Inn
Windjammer Resort

## Georgia

Callaway Gardens Resort
Cloister
Evergreen Conference Center
Jekyll Island Club Hotel
King & Prince Beach Resort
Sea Palms Golf & Tennis Resort
Sheraton Savannah Resort

## Hawaii

Embassy Suites Resort Maui
Hyatt Regency Kauai
Hyatt Regency Maui
Hyatt Regency Waikoloa
Kaanapali Beach Hotel
Kanaloa at Kona
Kapalua Bay Hotel & Villas
Kona Village Resort
Manele Bay Hotel
Maui Inter-Continental Resort

Maui Marriott
Maui Prince Hotel
Mauna Kea Beach Hotel
Princeville Hotel
Ritz-Carlton, Mauna Lani
Royal Lahaina Resort
Stouffer Wailea Beach Resort
Stouffer Waiohai Beach Resort
Westin Kauai
Westin Maui

## Idaho

Coeur d'Alene Resort
Idaho Rocky Mountain Ranch
Sun Valley Lodge

## Illinois

Clock Tower Resort & Conf. Ctr.
Eagle Ridge Inn & Resort
Indian Lakes Resort
Marriott's Lincolnshire Resort
Nordic Hills Resort & Conf. Ctr.
Pheasant Run Resort

## Indiana

Four Winds Clarion
French Lick Springs Resort

## Kentucky

Beaumont Inn
Inn at Shaker Village

## Maine

Bethel Inn & Country Club
Black Point Inn Resort
Cliff House
Colony Resort
High Tide Inn on the Ocean
Samoset Resort
Whitehall Inn

## Maryland

Inn at Mitchell House
Loews Annapolis

## Massachusetts

Chatham Bars Inn
Daggett House
Nantucket Inn & Conf. Ctr.
New Seabury Cape Cod
Ocean Edge Resort & Conf. Ctr.
Ship's Knees Inn
White Elephant Inn

# FAMILY PLACES

## Michigan

Grand Hotel
Grand Traverse Resort
Shanty Creek - Schuss Mountain
Stafford's Bay View Inn
Sugar Loaf Resort
Treetops Sylvan Resort

## Minnesota

Arrowwood, A Radisson Resort
Breezy Point Resort
Grand View Lodge
Lutsen Resort
Madden's on Gull Lake

## Missouri

Lodge of Four Seasons
Marriott's TanTarA Resort

## Montana

Chico Hot Springs Lodge
Flathead Lake Lodge
Gallatin Gateway Inn
Glacier Park Lodge
Holland Lake Lodge
Huntley Lodge
Izaak Walton Inn
Kandahar Lodge
Lake McDonald Lodge
Lone Mountain Ranch
Many Glacier Hotel
Mountain Sky Guest Ranch
9 Quarter Circle Ranch

## Nevada

Hyatt Regency Lake Tahoe

## New Hampshire

Balsams
Christmas Farm Inn
Mount Washington Hotel & Resort
Snowy Owl Inn
Whitney's Inn Jackson

## New Jersey

Chalfonte Hotel

## New Mexico

Bishop's Lodge
Hotel Edelweiss
Hotel Santa Fe
Inn of the Mountain Gods
Lodge at Cloudcroft

Quail Ridge Inn
Rancho Encantado Resort
Sagebrush Inn
St. Bernard Hotel

## New York State

Concord Resort Hotel
Elk Lake Lodge
Mohonk Mountain House
Montauk Yacht Club
Omni Sagamore

## North Carolina

Green Park Inn
Grove Park Inn Resort
High Hampton Inn & Country Club
Pinehurst Hotel & Country Club

## Ohio

Quail Hollow Resort
Sawmill Creek Resort

## Oklahoma

Lake Texoma Resort
Shangri-La Resort

## Oregon

Kah-Nee-Ta Resort
Rock Springs Guest Ranch
Salishan Lodge
Sunriver Lodge & Resort
Timberline Lodge
Tu Tu' Tun Lodge

## Pennsylvania

Historic Strasburg Inn
Hotel Hershey
Mount Airy Lodge
Nemacolin Woodlands
Pocono Manor Inn & Golf Resort
Seven Springs Mountain Resort
Skytop Lodge
Split Rock Resort
Sweetwater Farm

## Rhode Island

Doubletree Hotel
Newport Harbor Hotel & Marina
1661 Inn

## South Carolina

Hilton Head Island Hilton Resort
Hyatt Regency Hilton Head

Kiawah Island Resort
Marriott's Hilton Head Resort
Seabrook Island Resort
Sea Pines
Vendue Inn
Westin Resort
Wild Dunes Resort

## South Dakota

Franklin Hotel
Hotel Alex Johnson
Palmer Gulch Lodge

## Tennessee

Fairfield Glade Resort

## Texas

Barton Creek
Flying L Guest Ranch
Lakeway Inn & Conf. Ctr.
Mayan Dude Ranch
Radisson South Padre Island
Tremont House

## Utah

Bryce Canyon Lodge
Cliff Lodge
Grand Canyon Lodge

## Vermont

Basin Harbor Club
Cortina Inn
Equinox
Hawk Inn & Mountain Resort
Inn at Essex
Inn at Manchester
Rabbit Hill Inn
Stratton Mountain Inn
Sugarbush Inn
Topnotch at Stowe
Trapp Family Lodge

Woods at Killington
Woodstock Inn & Resort

## Virginia

Boar's Head Inn
Homestead
Kingsmill Resort & Conf. Ctr.
Tides Inn
Williamsburg Inn

## Washington

Kalaloch Lodge
Lake Quinault Lodge
Sun Mountain Lodge

## West Virginia

Greenbrier

## Wisconsin

Abbey
Heidel House Resort
Lake Lawn Lodge
Lakewoods Resort & Lodge

## Wyoming

Colter Bay Village
Jackson Hole Racquet Club
Jackson Lake Lodge
Mammoth Hot Springs Hotel
Moose Head Ranch
Old Faithful Inn
Paradise Guest Ranch
Ranch at Ucross
R Lazy S Ranch
Roosevelt Lodge
Teton Pines Resort

## Spas

Loews Ventana Canyon Resort
Harbor Island Spa Resort
La Costa Hotel & Spa
Sans Souci Resort

# FIREPLACE IN ROOMS

**Atlanta**
Ansley Inn

**Birmingham**
Tutwiler

**Boston**
Bostonian Hotel
Lenox Hotel
Ritz-Carlton, Boston

**Chicago**
Drake Hotel

**Cleveland**
Glidden House

**Dallas**
Hotel St. Germain

**Hartford**
Goodwin Hotel

**Kansas City**
Hotel Savoy

**Los Angeles**
Barnabey's Hotel
Beverly Hills Hotel
Chateau Marmont
Hotel Bel-Air
Le Dufy
Le Parc Hotel
L'Ermitage Hotel
Malibu Beach Inn
Peninsula Beverly Hills
Sunset Marquis Hotel

**New Orleans**
Cornstalk Hotel
Dauphine Orleans Hotel
Soniat House

**New York City**
Box Tree
Lowell New York
Mayfair Hotel Baglioni
Royalton

**Orange County, CA**
Casa Laguna Inn

**Palm Springs**
Hyatt Grand Champions Resort
La Quinta Hotel
Shadow Mountain Resort
Two Bunch Palms Resort

**Philadelphia**
Barclay Hotel
Penn's View Inn

**Phoenix/Scottsdale**
John Gardiner's Tennis Ranch
Scottsdale Plaza Resort
Stouffer Cottonwoods Resort

**Portland, OR**
River Place Alexis Hotel

**San Diego**
Horton Grand
Rancho Valencia

**San Francisco**
Archbishops Mansion Inn
Majestic
Mansions Hotel
Petite Auberge
Prescott Hotel
Queen Anne
Rancho Valencia
Seal Rock Inn
Sherman House
Victorian Inn on the Park

**Seattle**
Alexis Hotel

**St. Louis**
Doubletree Mayfair
Radisson Hotel Clayton

**Washington, DC**
Hay-Adams Hotel
Morrison House

**Alaska**
Red Quill Lodge

**Arizona**
Boulders Resort
Grand Canyon Lodge
L'Auberge de Sedona
Poco Diablo Resort
Rancho de los Caballeros
Tanque Verde Ranch
Wickenburg Inn

**Arkansas**
Gaston's White River Resort

**California**
Ahwahnee Hotel
Alisal Ranch

Auberge du Soleil
Benbow Inn
Big Sur Lodge
Carmel Valley Ranch Resort
Casa Madrona Hotel
Deetjen's Big Sur Inn
El Encanto Hotel
Four Seasons Biltmore
Harvest Inn
Heritage House
Highlands Inn
Hill House Inn
Inn at Morro Bay
Inn at Rancho Santa Fe
Inn at Spanish Bay
Inn at the Tides
John Gardiner's Tennis Ranch
La Casa del Zorro
La Playa Hotel
Little River Inn
Lodge at Pebble Beach
Los Olivos Grand Hotel
Madonna Inn
Madrona Manor
Meadowood Resort
Mendocino Hotel
Northstar-at-Tahoe
Petersen Village Inn
Post Ranch Inn
Quail Lodge Resort & Golf Club
Santa Barbara Miramar
San Ysidro Ranch
Silverado Country Club & Resort
St. Orres
Timberhill Ranch
Ventana - Big Sur
Villa Royale
Vintage Inn
Vintners Inn
Wine Country Inn

## Colorado

Broadmoor
Charter at Beaver Creek
Club Med, Copper Mountain
Grande Butte Hotel
Home Ranch
Hotel Lenado
Hyatt Regency Beaver Creek
Iron Horse Resort Retreat
Little Nell
Lodge at Cordillera

Lodge at Vail
Mountain Haus at Vail
Sitzmark Lodge
Tall Timber
Vista Verde Guest Ranch
Westin Resort Vail

## Connecticut

Boulders
Griswold Inn
Interlaken Inn
Mayflower Inn

## Florida

Lodge at Ponte Vedra Beach
Mission Inn Golf & Tennis Resort
Moose Head Ranch
Ponte Vedra Inn & Club

## Georgia

Foley House Inn
Gastonian
Jekyll Island Club Hotel
King & Prince Beach Resort
Planter's Inn
President's Quarters
Sea Palms Golf & Tennis Resort
Stouffer Pineisle Resort

## Hawaii

Lodge at Koele

## Idaho

Idaho Rocky Mountain Ranch
Sun Valley Lodge

## Illinois

Eagle Ridge Inn & Resort

## Iowa

Redstone Inn

## Kentucky

Inn at Shaker Village

## Louisiana

Asphodel Plantation Inn
Nottoway Plantation

## Maine

Bayview Hotel & Inn
Bethel Inn & Country Club
Captain Lord Mansion

# FIREPLACE IN ROOMS

Harraseeket Inn
Nonantum Resort
White Barn Inn

## Maryland

Inn at Mitchell House
Maryland Inn

## Massachusetts

Blantyre
Charlotte Inn
Chatham Bars Inn
Ocean Edge Resort & Conf. Ctr.
Orchards
Queen Anne
Summer House
Village Inn
Wauwinet
Westmoor Inn
Wheatleigh
Whistler's Inn
White Elephant Inn

## Michigan

Botsford Inn
Shanty Creek - Schuss Mountain
Stafford's Bay View Inn

## Minnesota

Breezy Point Resort
Grand View Lodge
Madden's on Gull Lake
Schumacher's New Prague

## Montana

Chico Hot Springs Lodge
Flathead Lake Lodge
Huntley Lodge
Lone Mountain Ranch
9 Quarter Circle Ranch
Triple Creek Mountain Hideaway

## North Carolina

Fearrington House Inn
Greystone Inn
Richmond Hill Inn

## New Hampshire

Stonehurst Manor
Whitney's Inn Jackson

## New Mexico

Bishop's Lodge

Dos Casas Viejas
Eldorado Hotel
Historic Taos Inn
Hotel Plaza Real
Inn of the Anasazi
Inn on the Alameda
La Posada de Santa Fe
Lodge at Cloudcroft
Quail Ridge Inn
Rancho Encantado Resort
Sagebrush Inn
St. Bernard Hotel

## New York State

Beekman Arms
Doral Arrowwood
Elk Lake Lodge
Geneva on the Lake
Mohonk Mountain House
Old Drovers Inn
Point, The
Three Village Inn
Troutbeck Inn

## Oregon

Columbia Gorge Hotel
Embarcadero Resort Hotel
Rock Springs Guest Ranch
Salishan Lodge
Sunriver Lodge & Resort
Sylvia Beach Hotel
Timberline Lodge
Tu Tu' Tun Lodge

## Pennsylvania

Bridgeton House
Mount Airy Lodge
Nemacolin Woodlands
Split Rock Resort
Sweetwater Farm

## Rhode Island

1661 Inn

## South Carolina

John Rutledge House Inn
Lodge Alley Inn
Planters Inn
Seabrook Island Resort
Vendue Inn

## South Dakota

Palmer Gulch Lodge

# FIREPLACE IN ROOMS

## Tennessee

Buckhorn Inn
Inn at Blackberry Farm

## Texas

Barton Creek
Flying L Guest Ranch
Lakeway Inn & Conf. Ctr.
Mayan Dude Ranch

## Utah

Brigham Street Inn
Bryce Canyon Lodge
Grand Canyon Lodge
Shadow Ridge Hotel
Stein Eriksen Lodge
Washington School Inn

## Vermont

Basin Harbor Club
Cortina Inn
Hawk Inn & Mountain Resort
Hermitage Inn
Inn at Essex
Inn at Manchester
Inn at Sawmill Farm
Sugarbush Inn
Topnotch at Stowe
Woods at Killington
Woodstock Inn & Resort

## Virginia

Ashby Inn
Boar's Head Inn
Kingsmill Resort & Conf. Ctr.

Manor House at Ford's Colony
Williamsburg Inn

## Washington

Captain Whidbey Inn
Inn at Semiahmoo
Kalaloch Lodge
Salish Lodge
Sun Mountain Lodge

## Wisconsin

Gordon Lodge
Heidel House Resort
Lakewoods Resort & Lodge

## Wyoming

Jackson Hole Racquet Club
Jenny Lake Lodge
Moose Head Ranch
Paradise Guest Ranch
R Lazy S Ranch
Snow King Resort
Spring Creek Ranch
Teton Pines Resort

## Spas

Greenhouse
Gurney's Inn Resort & Spa
Heartland Retreat
Kripalu Center
Maine Chance
Mario's International Hotel
Norwich Inn, Spa & Villas
Sans Souci Resort
Sonoma Mission Inn & Spa

# FREQUENT FLYER AFFILIATIONS

**Air Canada**
Airlines
  Austrian Air
  Cathay Pacific
  Finnair
  Sabena
  Singapore
  Swissair
Hotels
  Hilton
  Holiday Inn
  Radisson
  Sheraton
  Westin
Car Rentals
  Avis
  Budget

**Air France**
Airlines
  United
  USAir

**Alitalia**
Airlines
  Continental
  United
  USAir

**American**
Airlines
  Alaska Airlines
  Qantas
  Singapore
Hotels
  Hilton
  Inter-Continental
  Marriott
  Sheraton
  Wyndham
Car Rentals
  Avis
  Hertz

**British Airways**
Airlines
  Alaska Airlines
Hotels
  Hilton

**Continental**
Airlines
  Alitalia
  KLM
  SAS

Hotels
  Doubletree
  Marriott
  Radisson
Car Rentals
  General
  National
  Thrifty

**Delta**
Airlines
  Lufthansa
  Swissair
Hotels
  Hilton
  Hyatt
  Marriott
  Preferred Hotels
  Trusthouse Forte
Car Rentals
  Alamo
  Avis
  National

**KLM**
Airlines
  Continental
  Delta
  Northwest
  United
  USAir

**Lufthansa**
Airlines
  Delta
  United
  USAir

**Northwest**
Airlines
  Alaska Airlines
  KLM
  USAir
Hotels
  Holiday Inn
  Hyatt
  Marriott
  Westin
Car Rentals
  Budget
  National
  Hertz

**Qantas**
Airlines
  Alaska Airlines
  American

**SAS**
Airlines
  American
  Delta

**Singapore**
Airlines
  American
  Delta

**Swissair**
Airlines
  Air Canada
  Delta
  United
  USAir

**TWA**
Hotels
  Adam's Mark
  Doubletree
  Marriott

**United**
Airlines
  Air Canada
  Air France
  Alaska Airlines
  Alitalia
  Aloha
  Iberia
  KLM
  Lufthansa
  Sabena

  SAS
  Swissair
Hotels
  Hilton
  Hyatt
  Inter-Continental
  Kempinski
  Sheraton
  Westin
Car Rentals
  Alamo
  Hertz
  National

**USAir**
Airlines
  Air France
  Alitalia
  British Airways
  KLM
  Lufthansa
  Northwest
  Swissair
Hotels
  Hilton
  Hyatt
  Marriott
  Omni
  Radisson
  Stouffer
  Westin
Car Rentals
  Hertz
  National

**Virgin Atlantic**
Car Rentals
  Avis

# GAMBLING

## Atlantic City

Bally's Grand Hotel & Casino
Bally's Park Place
Caesars Atlantic City
Claridge Casino Hotel
Harrah's Marina Hotel & Casino
Merv Griffin's Resorts
Sands Hotel & Casino
Showboat Hotel
TropWorld
Trump Castle Resort
Trump Plaza Hotel & Casino
Trump Taj Mahal

## Las Vegas

Aladdin Hotel
Bally's
Binion's Horseshoe
Caesars Palace
Circus Circus Hotel
Desert Inn Hotel & Country Club
Dunes Hotel & Country Club
Excalibur Hotel
Fitzgerald's Casino Hotel
Flamingo Hotel
Four Queens Hotel & Casino
Frontier Hotel
Golden Nugget Hotel & Casino
Hacienda Hotel & Casino

Imperial Palace Hotel & Casino
Lady Luck Casino Hotel
Las Vegas Hilton
Maxim Hotel
Mirage
Plaza Hotel
Riviera Hotel & Casino
Sahara Hotel & Casino
Sam Boyd's Fremont Hotel
Sands Hotel & Casino
Showboat Hotel
Stardust Resort & Casino
Tropicana Hotel & Country Club
Vegas World Hotel & Casino

## Iowa

Redstone Inn

## Montana

Chico Hot Springs Lodge
Grouse Mountain Lodge

## Nevada

Caesars Lake Tahoe
Harrah's Lake Tahoe
Hyatt Regency Lake Tahoe

## South Dakota

Franklin Hotel
Palmer Gulch Lodge

# GARDEN SETTING
## (Outstanding Grounds)

**Atlanta**
Aberdeen Woods Conf. Ctr.
Holiday Inn Crowne Plaza
Hotel Nikko
Peachtree Executive Conf. Ctr.
Wyndham Garden Hotel - Vinings

**Atlantic City**
Marriott's Seaview Resort

**Baltimore**
Cross Keys Inn

**Dallas**
Four Seasons Resort & Club
Loews Anatole Hotel
Omni Mandalay Hotel

**Denver**
Cambridge Hotel

**Honolulu**
Colony Surf Hotel
Halekulani
Hawaiian Regent
Hilton Hawaiian Village
Ilikai Hotel Nikko Waikiki
Kahala Hilton
Royal Hawaiian Hotel
Sheraton Makaha Resort
Sheraton Moana Surfrider
Turtle Bay Hilton

**Houston**
Allen Park Inn
Houstonian Hotel & Conf. Ctr.

**Las Vegas**
Alexis Park Resort
Desert Inn Hotel & Country Club
Dunes Hotel & Country Club
Mirage
Tropicana Hotel & Country Club

**Los Angeles**
Beverly Hills Hotel
Chateau Marmont
Hotel Bel-Air
Le Parc Hotel
New Otani Hotel & Garden
Peninsula Beverly Hills
Ritz-Carlton, Huntington Hotel
Sunset Marquis Hotel
Westwood Marquis Hotel

**Miami/Miami Beach**
Alexander All-Suite Luxury Hotel
Biltmore Hotel
Doral Ocean Beach Resort
Doral Resort & Country Club
Fontainebleau Hilton
Grove Isle Yacht & Tennis Club
Sheraton Bal Harbour Hotel
Turnberry Isle Club

**Nashville**
Opryland Hotel

**New Orleans**
Place d'Armes Hotel

**Orange County, CA**
Casa Laguna Inn
Dana Point Resort
Four Seasons Hotel
Hyatt Newporter
Ritz-Carlton, Laguna Niguel
Sheraton Anaheim Hotel

**Orlando**
Courtyard at Lake Lucerne
Disney's Caribbean Beach Resort
Disney's Grand Floridian
Hyatt Orlando
Hyatt Regency Grand Cypress
Stouffer Orlando Resort

**Palm Springs**
Autry Resort
Doubletree Resort Palm Springs
Hyatt Grand Champions Resort
La Quinta Hotel
Marriott's Desert Springs Resort
Marriott's Rancho Las Palmas
Ritz-Carlton, Rancho Mirage
Shadow Mountain Resort
Stouffer Esmeralda
Westin Mission Hills Resort

**Phoenix/Scottsdale**
Arizona Biltmore
Buttes
Camelview Resort
Crescent Hotel
Fountains Suite Hotel
Hyatt Regency Scottsdale
John Gardiner's Tennis Ranch
Marriott's Camelback Inn
Marriott's Mountain Shadows

## GARDEN SETTING

Orange Tree Golf & Conf. Resort
Phoenician
Pointe at South Mountain
Pointe at Squaw Peak
Pointe at Tapatio Cliffs
Red Lion La Posada Resort
Regal McCormick Ranch
Registry Resort
Scottsdale Conference Resort
Scottsdale Plaza Resort
Scottsdale Princess
Sheraton San Marcos Golf Resort
Wyndham Paradise Valley Resort

### San Antonio
Plaza San Antonio

### San Diego
Catamaran Resort Hotel
Hanalei Hotel
Hotel del Coronado
Humphrey's Half Moon Inn
Hyatt Islandia
Kona Kai Resort
Le Meridien San Diego
Rancho Bernardo Inn
Rancho Valencia
San Diego Hilton
San Diego Princess Resort

### San Francisco
Miyako Hotel

### Tampa Bay
Belleview Mido Resort Hotel
Innisbrook Resort
Saddlebrook
Trade Winds

### Alabama
Marriott's Grand Hotel

### Arizona
Arizona Inn
Boulders Resort
El Conquistador
L'Auberge de Sedona
Sheraton San Marcos Golf Resort
Ventana Canyon
Westin La Paloma
Westward Look Resort

### California
Auberge du Soleil
Carmel Valley Ranch Resort

El Encanto Hotel
Fess Parker's Red Lion Resort
Four Seasons Biltmore
Harvest Inn
Heritage House
Highlands Inn
Inn at Morro Bay
Inn at Rancho Santa Fe
Inn at Spanish Bay
John Gardiner's Tennis Ranch
La Playa Hotel
Little River Inn
Lodge at Pebble Beach
Los Olivos Grand Hotel
Madrona Manor
Meadowood Resort
Ojai Valley Inn
Quail Lodge Resort & Golf Club
San Ysidro Ranch
Silverado Country Club & Resort
Stonepine Estate Resort
Ventana - Big Sur
Vintage Inn

### Colorado
Broadmoor
Doral Telluride

### Connecticut
Mayflower Inn
Water's Edge Inn & Resort

### Florida
Amelia Island Plantation
Boca Raton Resort & Club
Brazilian Court
Breakers
Colony Beach & Tennis Resort
Don Shula's Hotel & Golf Club
Lakeside Inn
Little Palm Island
Marriott at Sawgrass Resort
Marriott's Bay Point Resort
Marriott's Marco Island Resort
Mission Inn Golf & Tennis Resort
Palm Beach Polo & Country Club
PGA National
Pier House Resort
Ponte Vedra Inn & Club
Registry Resort
Resort at Longboat Key Club
Ritz-Carlton, Amelia Island
Ritz-Carlton, Naples

Sonesta Sanibel Harbour
South Seas Plantation Resort
Stouffer Vinoy Resort

## Georgia

Callaway Gardens Resort
Cloister
Evergreen Conference Center
Jekyll Island Club Hotel
King & Prince Beach Resort
Sea Palms Golf & Tennis Resort

## Hawaii

Four Seasons Resort Wailea
Grand Hyatt Wailea
Hotel Hana-Maui
Hyatt Regency Kauai
Hyatt Regency Maui
Hyatt Regency Waikoloa
Kapalua Bay Hotel & Villas
Kona Village Resort
Lodge at Koele
Manele Bay Hotel
Maui Inter-Continental Resort
Maui Marriott
Maui Prince Hotel
Mauna Kea Beach Hotel
Mauna Lani Bay Hotel
Princeville Hotel
Ritz-Carlton, Mauna Lani
Royal Lahaina Resort
Royal Waikoloan
Stouffer Wailea Beach Resort
Stouffer Waiohai Beach Resort
Westin Kauai
Westin Maui

## Idaho

Coeur d'Alene Resort

## Indiana

French Lick Springs Resort

## Kentucky

Inn at Shaker Village

## Maine

Samoset Resort

## Massachusetts

Beach Plum Inn
Blantyre
Charlotte Inn
Coonamessett Inn
Daggett House
Harbor View Hotel
Kelley House
Seacrest Manor
Ship's Knees Inn
Summer House
Wheatleigh
White Elephant Inn
Yankee Clipper Inn

## Michigan

Grand Hotel
Grand Traverse Resort
Shanty Creek - Schuss Mountain

## Minnesota

Breezy Point Resort
Grand View Lodge
Madden's on Gull Lake

## Mississippi

Burn
Monmouth Plantation

## New Hampshire

Balsams
Christmas Farm Inn

## New Mexico

Bishop's Lodge

## New York State

Clarion Inn at Saratoga
Concord Resort Hotel
Doral Arrowwood
Elk Lake Lodge
Geneva on the Lake
Mohonk Mountain House
Omni Sagamore
Otesaga Hotel
Point, The
Troutbeck Inn

## North Carolina

Grove Park Inn Resort
High Hampton Inn & Country Club
Pinehurst Hotel & Country Club

## Ohio

Quail Hollow Resort

# GARDEN SETTING

## Oregon

Columbia Gorge Hotel
Salishan Lodge

## Pennsylvania

Evermay on-the-Delaware
Hotel Hershey
Nemacolin Woodlands
Skytop Lodge

## Rhode Island

Atlantic Inn
Doubletree Hotel

## South Carolina

Hilton Head Island Hilton Resort
Hyatt Regency Hilton Head
Kiawah Island Resort
Marriott's Hilton Head Resort
Seabrook Island Resort
Sea Pines
Westin Resort
Wild Dunes Resort

## Texas

Barton Creek
Horseshoe Bay Resort
Lakeway Inn & Conf. Ctr.
Woodlands Executive Conf. Ctr.

## Vermont

Basin Harbor Club

Shelburne House
Topnotch at Stowe
Woodstock Inn & Resort

## Virginia

Boar's Head Inn
Homestead
Inn at Little Washington
Kingsmill Resort & Conf. Ctr.
Tides Inn

## Washington

Salish Lodge

## West Virginia

Greenbrier

## Wisconsin

Abbey
Americana Lake Geneva Resort
American Club
Lake Lawn Lodge

## Spas

Cal-A-Vie
Heartland Retreat
La Costa Hotel & Spa
Loews Ventana Canyon Resort
Maine Chance
Phoenix Health Spa
Sonoma Mission Inn & Spa

# GRANDE DAMES

**Boston**
Boston Park Plaza
Copley Plaza Hotel
Omni Parker House

**Chicago**
Blackstone Hotel
Chicago Hilton & Towers
Drake Hotel
Palmer House Hilton

**Cincinnati**
Omni Netherland Plaza

**Dallas**
Adolphus

**Denver**
Brown Palace Hotel

**Honolulu**
Royal Hawaiian Hotel

**Houston**
Wyndham Warwick Hotel

**Los Angeles**
Beverly Hills Hotel
Biltmore Los Angeles

**Louisville**
Seelbach Hotel

**Memphis**
Peabody Memphis

**Miami/Miami Beach**
Biltmore Hotel

**Milwaukee**
Pfister Hotel

**Minneapolis**
Saint Paul Hotel

**New Orleans**
Fairmont Hotel
Pontchartrain Hotel

**New York City**
Algonquin Hotel
Carlyle Hotel
Holiday Inn Downtown
Hotel Kimberly
Marriott Financial Center Hotel
Mayfair Hotel Baglioni
Peninsula New York
Plaza Hotel
St. Regis
Waldorf-Astoria/Towers

**Phoenix/Scottsdale**
Arizona Biltmore

**Pittsburgh**
Westin William Penn

**San Diego**
Hotel del Coronado
U.S. Grant Hotel

**San Francisco**
Fairmont Hotel
Four Seasons Clift Hotel
Huntington Hotel Nob Hill
Mark Hopkins Inter-Continental
Westin St. Francis

**Seattle**
Four Seasons Olympic

**St. Louis**
Doubletree Hotel & Conf. Center
Hyatt Regency St. Louis
St. Louis Marriott West

**Tampa Bay**
Don Ce-Sar Registry Resort

**Washington, DC**
Willard Inter-Continental

**Wilmington**
Hotel du Pont

**Colorado**
Broadmoor

**Florida**
Boca Raton Resort & Club
Breakers

**Michigan**
Grand Hotel

**New Hampshire**
Balsams

**New York State**
Omni Sagamore

**North Carolina**
Pinehurst Hotel & Country Club

**Virginia**
Homestead

**West Virginia**
Greenbrier

# HISTORIC

**Atlanta**
Ansley Inn
Biltmore Suites

**Atlantic City**
Marriott's Seaview Resort
Merv Griffin's Resorts

**Baltimore**
Admiral Fell Inn
Inn at Henderson's Wharf
Peabody Court Hotel
Society Hill Hotel

**Birmingham**
Tutwiler

**Boston**
Boston Park Plaza
Copley Plaza Hotel
Copley Square Hotel
Eliot Hotel
Le Meridien Boston
Lenox Hotel
Omni Parker House
Ritz-Carlton, Boston

**Charlotte**
Dunhill Hotel

**Chicago**
Allerton Hotel
Bismarck Hotel
Blackstone Hotel
Chicago Claridge Hotel
Chicago Hilton & Towers
Congress Hotel
Drake Hotel
Hotel Inter-Continental
Hyatt Printers Row
Knickerbocker Chicago Hotel
Lenox House Suites
Mayfair
Midland Hotel
Omni Ambassador East
Palmer House Hilton
Radisson Plaza Ambass. West
Raphael Hotel
Talbott Hotel
Tremont Hotel

**Cincinnati**
Cincinnatian Hotel
Omni Netherland Plaza
Vernon Manor Hotel

**Cleveland**
Glidden House
Stouffer Tower City Plaza Hotel

**Columbus**
Worthington Inn

**Dallas**
Adolphus
Hotel St. Germain
Mansion on Turtle Creek
Melrose Hotel
Stoneleigh Hotel

**Denver**
Brown Palace Hotel
Oxford Hotel

**Detroit**
Dearborn Inn Marriott
Mayflower Bed & Breakfast
River Place Inn

**Fort Worth**
Stockyards Hotel

**Hartford**
Goodwin Hotel

**Honolulu**
Royal Hawaiian Hotel
Sheraton Moana Surfrider

**Houston**
La Colombe d'Or
Lancaster
Wyndham Warwick Hotel

**Indianapolis**
Canterbury Hotel
Omni Severin

**Kansas City**
Hotel Savoy
Radisson Suite Hotel
Raphael Hotel

**Little Rock**
Capital Hotel

**Los Angeles**
Beverly Hills Hotel
Biltmore Los Angeles
Chateau Marmont
Checkers Hotel Kempinski
Hollywood Roosevelt Hotel
Regent Beverly Wilshire
Ritz-Carlton, Huntington Hotel
St. James's Club & Hotel

**Louisville**
Seelbach Hotel

**Memphis**
Peabody Memphis

**Miami/Miami Beach**
Biltmore Hotel
Colonnade Hotel
Hotel Place St. Michel

**Milwaukee**
Astor Hotel
Marc Plaza Hotel
Pfister Hotel

**Minneapolis/St. Paul**
Saint Paul Hotel
Whitney

**Nashville**
Hermitage Hotel
Union Station Hotel

**New Orleans**
Bourbon Orleans Hotel
Columns Hotel
Cornstalk Hotel
Fairmont Hotel
Hotel Maison de Ville
Hotel Ste. Helene
LaMothe House
Le Pavillon Hotel
Le Richelieu
Monteleone Hotel
Place d'Armes Hotel
Pontchartrain Hotel
Soniat House
St. Pierre

**New York City**
Algonquin Hotel
Barbizon
Beekman Tower Hotel
Box Tree
Doral Inn
Doral Park Avenue
Dorset
Drake Swissotel
Gorham New York
Gramercy Park Hotel
Helmsley Palace
Hotel Beverly
Hotel Elysee
Hotel Lexington

Hotel Pickwick Arms
Hotel Plaza Athenee
Hotel Wales
Inter-Continental
Lowell New York
Mark
Mayfair Hotel Baglioni
Mayflower Hotel
Michelangelo
Milford Plaza Hotel
Morgans
New York Marriott Eastside
Omni Berkshire Place
Paramount
Park Central
Peninsula New York
Plaza Hotel
Radisson Empire Hotel
Ramada Hotel
Ritz-Carlton, New York
Roger Smith
Roosevelt Hotel
Royalton
Sheraton Park Avenue
Sherry-Netherland Hotel
Southgate Tower Suite Hotel
Stanhope
St. Regis
Surrey Hotel
Waldorf-Astoria/Towers
Warwick
Westbury Hotel
Wyndham Hotel

**Orlando**
Courtyard at Lake Lucerne
Park Plaza Hotel

**Palm Springs**
La Quinta Hotel

**Philadelphia**
Barclay Hotel
Chestnut Hill Hotel
Hotel Atop the Bellevue
Independence Park Inn
Latham Hotel
Penn's View Inn
Society Hill Hotel
Warwick Hotel

**Phoenix/Scottsdale**
Arizona Biltmore
Sheraton San Marcos Golf Resort

# HISTORIC

## Pittsburgh
Priory - A City Inn
Westin William Penn

## Portland, OR
Heathman Hotel
Hotel Vintage Plaza

## Raleigh-Durham
Carolina Inn

## Richmond
Commonwealth Park Suites Hotel

## San Antonio
Best Western Historical Crockett
Emily Morgan
Fairmount Hotel
La Mansion del Rio
Menger Hotel
Saint Anthony Hotel
Sheraton Gunter Hotel

## San Diego
Colonial Inn
Gaslamp Plaza Suites
Horton Grand
Hotel del Coronado
La Valencia Hotel
U.S. Grant Hotel

## San Francisco
Andrews Hotel
Archbishops Mansion Inn
Beresford Arms
Best Western Canterbury
Campton Place Kempinski
Cartwright Hotel
Chancellor Hotel
Fairmont Hotel
Four Seasons Clift Hotel
Galleria Park Hotel
Harbor Court Hotel
Hotel Diva
Hotel Vintage Court
Huntington Hotel Nob Hill
Inn at the Opera
Juliana Hotel
Kensington Park
Majestic
Mansions Hotel
Mark Hopkins Inter-Continental
Orchard Hotel
Petite Auberge
Prescott Hotel

Queen Anne
Raphael Hotel
Ritz-Carlton, San Francisco
Sheraton Palace
Sherman House
Sir Francis Drake
Stanyan Park Hotel
Stouffer Stanford Court Hotel
Victorian Inn on the Park
Villa Florence Hotel
Washington Square Inn
Westin St. Francis
York Hotel

## Seattle
Alexis Hotel
Four Seasons Olympic
Mayflower Park Hotel
Sorrento Hotel

## St. Louis
Doubletree Mayfair
Hotel Majestic
Hyatt Regency St. Louis
Seven Gables Inn

## Tampa Bay
Belleview Mido Resort Hotel
Don Ce-Sar Registry Resort
Heritage Hotel
Stouffer Vinoy Resort

## Washington, DC
Carlton
Henley Park Hotel
Hotel Washington
Jefferson Hotel
Morrison-Clark Inn
Phoenix Park Hotel
Pullman-Highland Hotel
Ritz-Carlton, Washington DC
Stouffer Mayflower Hotel
Tabard Inn
Willard Inter-Continental

## Wilmington
Hotel du Pont

## Alabama
Marriott's Grand Hotel

## Alaska
Waterfall Resort

## Arizona

Arizona Inn
El Tovar Hotel
Grand Canyon Lodge
Hassayampa Inn
Sheraton San Marcos Golf Resort
Tanque Verde Ranch
Wigwam

## Arkansas

Arlington Resort
Palace Hotel & Bath House

## California

Ahwahnee Hotel
Alta Mira
Benbow Inn
Casa Madrona Hotel
Claremont Resort
El Encanto Hotel
Eureka Inn
Four Seasons Biltmore
Furnace Creek Inn
Highlands Inn
Inn at Rancho Santa Fe
La Casa del Zorro
La Playa Hotel
Little River Inn
Lodge at Pebble Beach
Madrona Manor
Mendocino Hotel
Ojai Valley Inn
San Ysidro Ranch
Silverado Country Club & Resort
Stonepine Estate Resort
Wawona Hotel

## Colorado

Broadmoor
C Lazy U Ranch
Hotel Boulderado
Hotel Jerome
Sardy House
Stanley Hotel

## Connecticut

Boulders
Griswold Inn
Homestead Inn
Interlaken Inn
Mayflower Inn
Riverwind Inn
Stonehenge

Under Mountain Inn
Water's Edge Inn & Resort

## Florida

Boca Raton Resort & Club
Brazilian Court
Breakers
Lakeside Inn
Marquesa Hotel
Marriott's Casa Marina Resort
Ponte Vedra Inn & Club

## Georgia

Cloister
Eliza Thompson
Foley House Inn
Gastonian
Greyfield Inn
Jekyll Island Club Hotel
Mulberry Inn
Planter's Inn
President's Quarters
Sheraton Savannah Resort

## Indiana

French Lick Springs Resort

## Iowa

Redstone Inn

## Kentucky

Beaumont Inn
Inn at Shaker Village

## Louisiana

Asphodel Plantation Inn
Madewood Plantation
Nottoway Plantation

## Maine

Asticou Inn/Cranberry Lodge
Bethel Inn & Country Club
Black Point Inn Resort
Captain Lord Mansion
Cliff House
Colony Resort
Harraseeket Inn
High Tide Inn on the Ocean
Nonantum Resort
Pilgrim's Inn
Poland Spring Inn
White Barn Inn
Whitehall Inn

# HISTORIC

## Maryland

Atlantic Hotel
Imperial Hotel
Inn at Mitchell House
Inn at Perry Cabin
Maryland Inn
Robert Morris Inn

## Massachusetts

Beach Plum Inn
Blantyre
Charlotte Inn
Chatham Bars Inn
Coonamessett Inn
Daggett House
Harbor View Hotel
Jared Coffin House
Kelley House
Publick House
Queen Anne
Seacrest Manor
Ship's Knees Inn
Summer House
Village Inn
Wauwinet
Wequassett Inn
Westmoor Inn
Wheatleigh
Whistler's Inn
White Elephant Inn
Yankee Clipper Inn

## Michigan

Botsford Inn
Grand Hotel
Stafford's Bay View Inn

## Minnesota

Fitgers Inn
Grand View Lodge
Schumacher's New Prague
St. James Hotel

## Mississippi

Burn
Monmouth Plantation
Natchez Eola Hotel

## Montana

Chico Hot Springs Lodge
Flathead Lake Lodge

Gallatin Gateway Inn
Glacier Park Lodge
Holland Lake Lodge
Izaak Walton Inn
Lake McDonald Lodge
Lone Mountain Ranch
Many Glacier Hotel
Mountain Sky Guest Ranch

## New Hampshire

Balsams
Christmas Farm Inn
Mount Washington Hotel & Resort
Stonehurst Manor

## New Jersey

Abbey
Chalfonte Hotel
Inn at Millrace Pond
Mainstay Inn & Cottage
Queen Victoria
Virginia

## New Mexico

Bishop's Lodge
Dos Casas Viejas
Hotel St. Francis
Historic Taos Inn
La Fonda Hotel on the Plaza
La Posada de Albuquerque
La Posada de Santa Fe
Lodge at Cloudcroft
Sagebrush Inn

## New York State

Beekman Arms
Clarion Inn at Saratoga
Elk Lake Lodge
Geneva on the Lake
Guest House
Mohonk Mountain House
Old Drovers Inn
Omni Sagamore
Otesaga Hotel
Three Village Inn
Troutbeck Inn

## North Carolina

Green Park Inn
Greystone Inn
Grove Park Inn Resort
High Hampton Inn & Country Club

Pinehurst Hotel & Country Club
Richmond Hill Inn

## Oregon

Columbia Gorge Hotel
Sylvia Beach Hotel
Timberline Lodge

## Pennsylvania

Black Bass Hotel
Bridgeton House
Evermay on-the-Delaware
Historic Strasburg Inn
Hotel Hershey
Pocono Manor Inn & Golf Resort
Skytop Lodge
Sweetwater Farm

## Rhode Island

Atlantic Inn
Hotel Manisses
Inn at Castle Hill
1661 Inn

## South Carolina

Indigo Inn
Jasmine House Inn
John Rutledge House Inn
Lodge Alley Inn
Mills House Hotel
Planters Inn
Vendue Inn

## South Dakota

Franklin Hotel
Hotel Alex Johnson

## Tennessee

Buckhorn Inn

## Texas

Tremont House

## Utah

Brigham Street Inn

Bryce Canyon Lodge
Grand Canyon Lodge
Washington School Inn

## Vermont

Basin Harbor Club
Equinox
Hermitage Inn
Inn at Manchester
Inn at Sawmill Farm
Middlebury Inn
Rabbit Hill Inn
Shelburne House

## Virginia

Ashby Inn
Homestead
Inn at Little Washington

## Washington

Captain Whidbey Inn
Lake Quinault Lodge

## West Virginia

Greenbrier

## Wisconsin

American Club
Lakewoods Resort & Lodge

## Wyoming

Jenny Lake Lodge
Paradise Guest Ranch
Roosevelt Lodge

## Spas

Kerr House
Mario's International Hotel
Murrieta Hot Springs Resort
New Age Health Spa
Norwich Inn, Spa & Villas
Safety Harbor Spa
Sonoma Mission Inn & Spa

# HOMEY FEELING

**Atlanta**
Ansley Inn

**Baltimore**
Admiral Fell Inn
Celie's Waterfront

**Boston**
Charles Hotel in Harvard Square

**Cleveland**
Glidden House

**Denver**
Scanticon

**Detroit**
Mayflower Bed & Breakfast

**New Orleans**
Columns Hotel
Cornstalk Hotel
Hotel Maison de Ville
Hotel Ste. Helene
LaMothe House
Soniat House
St. Pierre

**New York City**
Box Tree
Wyndham Hotel

**Orange County, CA**
Casa Laguna Inn

**Orlando**
Courtyard at Lake Lucerne
Sonesta Villa Resort

**Pittsburgh**
Priory - A City Inn

**Portland, OR**
River Place Alexis Hotel

**San Diego**
Horton Grand

**San Francisco**
Archbishops Mansion Inn
Majestic
Mansions Hotel
Petite Auberge
Queen Anne
Stanyan Park Hotel
Victorian Inn on the Park
Washington Square Inn

**Washington, DC**
Tabard Inn

**Alaska**
Brooks Lodge
Camp Denali
Denali National Park Hotel
Gustavus Inn at Glacier Bay
Yes Bay Lodge

**Arizona**
El Tovar Hotel
Grand Canyon Lodge
Hassayampa Inn
Rancho de los Caballeros
Tanque Verde Ranch
Wickenburg Inn

**Arkansas**
Gaston's White River Resort
Palace Hotel & Bath House

**California**
Alisal Ranch
Alta Mira
Big Sur Lodge
Casa Madrona Hotel
Deetjen's Big Sur Inn
Heritage House
Little River Inn
Madrona Manor
Mendocino Hotel
Stonepine Estate Resort
Wine Country Inn

**Colorado**
C Lazy U Ranch
Home Ranch
Hotel Boulderado
Hotel Jerome
Hotel Lenado
Sardy House
Tall Timber
Vista Verde Guest Ranch

**Connecticut**
Boulders
Griswold Inn
Homestead Inn
Riverwind Inn
Stonehenge
Under Mountain Inn

**Florida**
Lakeside Inn
Marquesa Hotel

## Georgia

Eliza Thompson
Foley House Inn
Gastonian
Greyfield Inn
Jekyll Island Club Hotel
Planter's Inn
President's Quarters

## Iowa

Redstone Inn

## Kentucky

Inn at Shaker Village

## Louisiana

Asphodel Plantation Inn
Madewood Plantation
Nottoway Plantation

## Maine

Asticou Inn/Cranberry Lodge
Bayview Hotel & Inn
Bethel Inn & Country Club
Captain Lord Mansion
High Tide Inn on the Ocean
Poland Spring Inn
White Barn Inn
Whitehall Inn

## Maryland

Atlantic Hotel
Imperial Hotel
Inn at Mitchell House
Inn at Perry Cabin
Maryland Inn
Robert Morris Inn

## Massachusetts

Beach Plum Inn
Charlotte Inn
Coonamessett Inn
Daggett House
Harbor View Hotel
Jared Coffin House
Kelley House
Orchards
Queen Anne
Seacrest Manor
Ship's Knees Inn
Summer House
Village Inn

Wauwinet
Wequassett Inn
Westmoor Inn
Whistler's Inn
Yankee Clipper Inn

## Michigan

Botsford Inn
Stafford's Bay View Inn

## Minnesota

Grand View Lodge
Lutsen Resort
Madden's on Gull Lake
Schumacher's New Prague
St. James Hotel

## Mississippi

Burn

## Montana

Chico Hot Springs Lodge
Flathead Lake Lodge
Holland Lake Lodge
Izaak Walton Inn
Lone Mountain Ranch
9 Quarter Circle Ranch
Triple Creek Mountain Hideaway

## New Hampshire

Christmas Farm Inn
Stonehurst Manor

## New Jersey

Abbey
Chalfonte Hotel
Inn at Millrace Pond
Mainstay Inn & Cottage
Queen Victoria
Virginia

## New Mexico

Dos Casas Viejas
Historic Taos Inn
Lodge at Cloudcroft

## New York State

Beekman Arms
Elk Lake Lodge
Point, The
Three Village Inn
Troutbeck Inn

# HOMEY FEELING

## North Carolina

Fearrington House Inn
Green Park Inn
High Hampton Inn & Country Club
Richmond Hill Inn

## Oregon

Columbia Gorge Hotel
Rock Springs Guest Ranch
Tu Tu' Tun Lodge

## Pennsylvania

Black Bass Hotel
Bridgeton House
Evermay on-the-Delaware
Historic Strasburg Inn
Sweetwater Farm

## Rhode Island

Atlantic Inn
Hotel Manisses
Inn at Castle Hill
1661 Inn

## South Carolina

Indigo Inn
Jasmine House Inn
John Rutledge House Inn
Lodge Alley Inn
Planters Inn

## South Dakota

Palmer Gulch Lodge

## Tennessee

Buckhorn Inn
Inn at Blackberry Farm

## Texas

Mayan Dude Ranch

## Utah

Brigham Street Inn
Grand Canyon Lodge
Stein Eriksen Lodge
Washington School Inn

## Vermont

Equinox
Hermitage Inn
Inn at Manchester
Inn at Sawmill Farm
Mountain Top Inn
Shelburne House
Trapp Family Lodge
Woodstock Inn & Resort

## Virginia

Williamsburg Inn

## Wisconsin

Gordon Lodge

## Wyoming

Colter Bay Village
Jackson Lake Lodge
Jenny Lake Lodge
Paradise Guest Ranch
Ranch at Ucross
R Lazy S Ranch
Roosevelt Lodge
Spring Creek Ranch
Teton Pines Resort

## Spas

Heartland Retreat
Kerr House
New Age Health Spa

# HONEYMOON

**Atlanta**
Ansley Inn
French Quarter Suites
J.W. Marriott at Lenox
Stouffer Waverly Hotel

**Baltimore**
Admiral Fell Inn
Harbor Court Hotel
Peabody Court Hotel

**Boston**
Le Meridien Boston

**Chicago**
Drake Hotel
Fairmont Hotel
Four Seasons Hotel
Park Hyatt
Ritz-Carlton, Chicago

**Cleveland**
Glidden House
Ritz-Carlton, Cleveland

**Dallas**
Adolphus
Four Seasons Resort & Club
Hotel Crescent Court
Hotel St. Germain
Mansion on Turtle Creek

**Denver**
Cambridge Hotel
Oxford Hotel

**Detroit**
Ritz-Carlton, Dearborn
Townsend Hotel

**Honolulu**
Halekulani
Hawaii Prince Hotel Waikiki
Hilton Hawaiian Village
Hyatt Regency Waikiki
Kahala Hilton
Royal Hawaiian Hotel
Sheraton Moana Surfrider
Turtle Bay Hilton

**Houston**
La Colombe d'Or
Ritz-Carlton, Houston

**Indianapolis**
Canterbury Hotel

**Kansas City**
Ritz-Carlton, Kansas City

**Las Vegas**
Caesars Palace
Desert Inn Hotel & Country Club
Excalibur Hotel
Golden Nugget Hotel & Casino
Mirage

**Little Rock**
Arkansas' Excelsior Hotel

**Los Angeles**
Barnabey's Hotel
Century Plaza Hotel
Checkers Hotel Kempinski
Four Seasons Hotel
Hotel Bel-Air
Hotel Nikko
L'Ermitage Hotel
Peninsula Beverly Hills
Regent Beverly Wilshire
Ritz-Carlton, Huntington Hotel
Ritz-Carlton, Marina del Rey

**Louisville**
Seelbach Hotel

**Miami/Miami Beach**
Biltmore Hotel
Grand Bay Hotel

**Milwaukee**
Pfister Hotel
Wyndham Milwaukee Center

**Minneapolis/St. Paul**
Saint Paul Hotel

**Nashville**
Opryland Hotel

**New Orleans**
Hotel Maison de Ville
Hotel St. Marie
Soniat House
Windsor Court Hotel

**New York City**
Box Tree
Hotel Plaza Athenee
Lowell New York
Mayfair Hotel Baglioni
Michelangelo
Pierre
Plaza Hotel
Waldorf-Astoria/Towers

# HONEYMOON

## Orange County, CA
Dana Point Resort
Disneyland Hotel
Four Seasons Hotel
Ritz-Carlton, Laguna Niguel
Surf & Sand Hotel

## Orlando
Buena Vista Palace
Courtyard at Lake Lucerne
Disney's Grand Floridian
Hyatt Regency Grand Cypress
Park Plaza Hotel
Peabody Orlando

## Palm Springs
La Quinta Hotel
Marriott's Desert Springs Resort
Ritz-Carlton, Rancho Mirage
Stouffer Esmeralda
Westin Mission Hills Resort

## Philadelphia
Four Seasons Hotel
Rittenhouse
Ritz-Carlton, Philadelphia

## Phoenix/Scottsdale
Arizona Biltmore
Hyatt Regency Scottsdale
Phoenician
Scottsdale Princess
Sheraton San Marcos Golf Resort

## Pittsburgh
Pittsburgh Vista

## Portland, OR
Heathman Hotel
Hotel Vintage Plaza

## Richmond
Commonwealth Park Suites Hotel

## San Antonio
Fairmount Hotel
Plaza San Antonio

## San Diego
Horton Grand
Hotel del Coronado
Le Meridien San Diego
Loews Coronado Bay Resort
Rancho Bernardo Inn
Rancho Valencia

## San Francisco
Archbishops Mansion Inn
Four Seasons Clift Hotel
Majestic
Mansions Hotel
Petite Auberge
Queen Anne
Ritz-Carlton, San Francisco
Sherman House
Victorian Inn on the Park

## Seattle
Alexis Hotel
Four Seasons Olympic
Sorrento Hotel

## St. Louis
Hotel Majestic
Ritz-Carlton, St. Louis
Seven Gables Inn
St. Louis Marriott West

## Washington, DC
Grand Hotel
Hay-Adams Hotel
Henley Park Hotel
Jefferson Hotel
Morrison-Clark Inn
Morrison House
Ritz-Carlton, Washington DC
Watergate Hotel
Willard Inter-Continental

## Alabama
Marriott's Grand Hotel

## Alaska
Gustavus Inn at Glacier Bay

## Arizona
Boulders Resort
El Conquistador
Enchantment Resort
L'Auberge de Sedona
Poco Diablo Resort
Sheraton San Marcos Golf Resort
Westin La Paloma
Westward Look Resort

## Arkansas
Palace Hotel & Bath House

## California
Auberge du Soleil

Carmel Valley Ranch Resort
Casa Madrona Hotel
Claremont Resort
Eureka Inn
Four Seasons Biltmore
Heritage House
Highlands Inn
Inn at Spanish Bay
La Casa del Zorro
Little River Inn
Lodge at Pebble Beach
Los Olivos Grand Hotel
Madrona Manor
Meadowood Resort
Northstar-at-Tahoe
Post Ranch Inn
San Ysidro Ranch
Squaw Valley Inn
Stonepine Estate Resort
St. Orres
Timberhill Ranch
Ventana - Big Sur
Villa Royale
Vintners Inn

## Colorado

Breckenridge Hilton
Doral Telluride
Home Ranch
Hotel Jerome
Hotel Lenado
Hyatt Regency Beaver Creek
Little Nell
Ritz-Carlton, Aspen
Sardy House
Snowmass Lodge & Club
Vista Verde Guest Ranch

## Connecticut

Boulders
Mayflower Inn
Riverwind Inn
Under Mountain Inn
Water's Edge Inn & Resort

## Florida

Amelia Island Plantation
Boca Raton Resort & Club
Brazilian Court
Chalet Suzanne
Colony Beach & Tennis Resort
Hawk's Cay Resort & Marina

Hyatt Key West
Inn at Fisher Island
Lakeside Inn
Little Palm Island
Lodge at Ponte Vedra Beach
Marquesa Hotel
Marriott at Sawgrass Resort
Marriott's Bay Point Resort
Marriott's Marco Island Resort
Ocean Reef Club
Ponte Vedra Inn & Club
Reach Resort
Ritz-Carlton, Amelia Island
Ritz-Carlton, Naples
Ritz-Carlton, Palm Beach
Sonesta Sanibel Harbour
South Seas Plantation Resort
Sundial Beach & Tennis Resort

## Georgia

Cloister
Evergreen Conference Center
Gastonian
Jekyll Island Club Hotel

## Hawaii

Embassy Suites Resort Maui
Four Seasons Resort Wailea
Grand Hyatt Wailea
Hotel Hana-Maui
Hyatt Regency Maui
Hyatt Regency Waikoloa
Kapalua Bay Hotel & Villas
Kona Village Resort
Lodge at Koele
Manele Bay Hotel
Maui Inter-Continental Resort
Maui Marriott
Maui Prince Hotel
Mauna Kea Beach Hotel
Mauna Lani Bay Hotel
Princeville Hotel
Ritz-Carlton, Mauna Lani
Stouffer Wailea Beach Resort
Stouffer Waiohai Beach Resort
Westin Kauai
Westin Maui

## Iowa

Redstone Inn

# HONEYMOON

## Idaho

Coeur d'Alene Resort

## Louisiana

Nottoway Plantation

## Maine

Captain Lord Mansion
Harraseeket Inn
Pilgrim's Inn
Samoset Resort
White Barn Inn
Whitehall Inn

## Maryland

Atlantic Hotel
Inn at Perry Cabin
Maryland Inn

## Massachusetts

Blantyre
Charlotte Inn
Kelley House
Ocean Edge Resort & Conf. Ctr.
Red Lion Inn
Seacrest Manor
Summer House
Wequassett Inn
Westmoor Inn
Wheatleigh
Whistler's Inn

## Michigan

Grand Hotel
Grand Traverse Resort
Shanty Creek - Schuss Mountain
Stafford's Bay View Inn

## Minnesota

Grand View Lodge
Schumacher's New Prague

## Mississippi

Burn
Monmouth Plantation

## Missouri

Lodge of Four Seasons
Marriott's TanTarA Resort

## Montana

Kandahar Lodge

## Nevada

Harrah's Lake Tahoe
Hyatt Regency Lake Tahoe

## New Hampshire

Whitney's Inn Jackson

## New Jersey

Abbey
Inn at Millrace Pond
Mainstay Inn & Cottage
Queen Victoria
Virginia

## New Mexico

Dos Casas Viejas
Inn of the Anasazi
Sagebrush Inn

## New York State

Mohonk Mountain House
Old Drovers Inn
Omni Sagamore
Point, The
Three Village Inn
Troutbeck Inn

## North Carolina

Fearrington House Inn
Grove Park Inn Resort
Pinehurst Hotel & Country Club
Richmond Hill Inn

## Oregon

Columbia Gorge Hotel
Salishan Lodge
Sylvia Beach Hotel

## Pennsylvania

Bridgeton House
Mount Airy Lodge
Nemacolin Woodlands

## Rhode Island

Inn at Castle Hill
1661 Inn

## South Carolina

Hilton Head Island Hilton Resort
Hyatt Regency Hilton Head
Indigo Inn
Jasmine House Inn
John Rutledge House Inn
Kiawah Island Resort

Lodge Alley Inn
Marriott's Hilton Head Resort
Planters Inn
Seabrook Island Resort
Sea Pines
Westin Resort

## South Dakota

Palmer Gulch Lodge

## Tennessee

Inn at Blackberry Farm

## Utah

Brigham Street Inn
Cliff Lodge
Stein Eriksen Lodge
Washington School Inn

## Vermont

Equinox
Hawk Inn & Mountain Resort
Hermitage Inn
Inn at Essex
Inn at Sawmill Farm
Mountain Top Inn
Shelburne House
Sugarbush Inn
Topnotch at Stowe
Trapp Family Lodge

## Virginia

Homestead
Inn at Little Washington
Tides Inn
Williamsburg Inn

## Washington

Inn at Semiahmoo
Salish Lodge
Sun Mountain Lodge

## West Virginia

Greenbrier

## Wisconsin

American Club
Heidel House Resort

## Wyoming

Jackson Lake Lodge
Spring Creek Ranch

## Spas

Gurney's Inn Resort & Spa
La Costa Hotel & Spa
Loews Ventana Canyon Resort
Mario's International Hotel
Sans Souci Resort
Sonoma Mission Inn & Spa

# "IN" PLACES

**Anchorage**
Captain Cook Hotel

**Atlanta**
Atlanta Marriott Marquis
Hotel Nikko
J.W. Marriott at Lenox
Ritz-Carlton, Atlanta
Ritz-Carlton, Buckhead
Swissotel Atlanta

**Atlantic City**
Bally's Grand Hotel & Casino
Marriott's Seaview Resort

**Austin**
Four Seasons Hotel

**Baltimore**
Harbor Court Hotel
Peabody Court Hotel
Stouffer Harborplace

**Boston**
Boston Harbor Hotel
Bostonian Hotel
Charles Hotel in Harvard Square
Four Seasons Hotel
Le Meridien Boston
Ritz-Carlton, Boston

**Charlotte**
Dunhill Hotel

**Chicago**
Fairmont Hotel
Four Seasons Hotel
Hotel Nikko
Le Meridien Hotel Chicago
Mayfair
Park Hyatt
Ritz-Carlton, Chicago

**Cincinnati**
Cincinnatian Hotel

**Cleveland**
Ritz-Carlton, Cleveland

**Dallas**
Adolphus
Four Seasons Resort & Club
Hotel Crescent Court
Loews Anatole Hotel
Mansion on Turtle Creek
Omni Mandalay Hotel

**Denver**
Cambridge Hotel
Loews Giorgio Hotel
Oxford Hotel

**Detroit**
Ritz-Carlton, Dearborn
River Place Inn
Townsend Hotel

**Fort Lauderdale**
Westin Hotel, Cypress Creek

**Honolulu**
Halekulani
Hawaii Prince Hotel Waikiki
Kahala Hilton

**Houston**
Four Seasons Hotel
La Colombe d'Or
Omni
Ritz-Carlton, Houston

**Indianapolis**
Canterbury Hotel
Westin Hotel Indianapolis

**Kansas City**
Ritz-Carlton, Kansas City

**Las Vegas**
Desert Inn Hotel & Country Club
Golden Nugget Hotel & Casino
Mirage

**Los Angeles**
BelAge Hotel
Beverly Hills Hotel
Checkers Hotel Kempinski
Hotel Bel-Air
Hotel Nikko
L'Ermitage Hotel
Peninsula Beverly Hills
Regent Beverly Wilshire
Ritz-Carlton, Huntington Hotel
Ritz-Carlton, Marina del Rey
St. James's Club & Hotel
Sunset Marquis Hotel
Tower at Century Plaza
Westwood Marquis Hotel

**Louisville**
Seelbach Hotel

**Memphis**
Peabody Memphis

**Miami/Miami Beach**
Grand Bay Hotel
Hyatt Regency Coral Gables
Mayfair House Hotel Grand Luxe
Turnberry Isle Club

**Milwaukee**
Wyndham Milwaukee Center

**Minneapolis/St. Paul**
Saint Paul Hotel
Whitney

**Nashville**
Opryland Hotel

**New Orleans**
Hotel Maison de Ville
Le Meridien Hotel
Pontchartrain Hotel
Soniat House
Westin Canal Place
Windsor Court Hotel

**New York City**
Box Tree
Carlyle Hotel
Hotel Millenium
Hotel Plaza Athenee
Lowell New York
Mark
Mayfair Hotel Baglioni
Michelangelo
Peninsula New York
Pierre
Rihga Royal
Royalton
Stanhope
St. Regis

**Oklahoma City**
Waterford Hotel

**Orange County, CA**
Dana Point Resort
Four Seasons Hotel
Le Meridien Newport
Ritz-Carlton, Laguna Niguel

**Orlando**
Disney's Grand Floridian
Hyatt Regency Grand Cypress
Peabody Orlando
Walt Disney World Swan

**Palm Springs**
Hyatt Grand Champions Resort
La Quinta Hotel
Ritz-Carlton, Rancho Mirage

**Philadelphia**
Four Seasons Hotel
Hotel Atop the Bellevue
Rittenhouse
Ritz-Carlton, Philadelphia

**Phoenix/Scottsdale**
Hyatt Regency Scottsdale
Phoenician
Ritz-Carlton, Phoenix
Scottsdale Princess

**Pittsburgh**
Priory - A City Inn

**Portland, OR**
Heathman Hotel
Hotel Vintage Plaza
River Place Alexis Hotel

**Raleigh-Durham**
Siena Hotel

**Richmond**
Commonwealth Park Suites Hotel

**San Antonio**
Fairmount Hotel
Marriott Rivercenter

**San Diego**
Le Meridien San Diego
Loews Coronado Bay Resort
Pan Pacific
Rancho Bernardo Inn
Rancho Valencia
Sheraton Grande at Torrey Pines
Westgate Hotel

**San Francisco**
Archbishops Mansion Inn
Campton Place Kempinski
Donatello
Four Seasons Clift Hotel
Huntington Hotel Nob Hill
Mandarin Oriental
Pan Pacific
Park Hyatt
Petite Auberge
Ritz-Carlton, San Francisco
Sherman House
Stouffer Stanford Court Hotel

# "IN" PLACES

## San Jose, CA
Fairmont Hotel

## Seattle
Alexis Hotel
Four Seasons Olympic
Inn at the Market
Sorrento Hotel

## St. Louis
Hotel Majestic
Ritz-Carlton, St. Louis
Seven Gables Inn

## Tampa Bay
Wyndham Harbour Island Hotel

## Washington, DC
Four Seasons Hotel
Grand Hotel
Hay-Adams Hotel
Henley Park Hotel
Jefferson Hotel
Morrison-Clark Inn
Morrison House
Park Hyatt
Ritz-Carlton, Pentagon City
Ritz-Carlton, Tysons Corner
Ritz-Carlton, Washington DC
Watergate Hotel
Westfield's Intl. Conf. Ctr.
Willard Inter-Continental

## Arizona
Boulders Resort
Westin La Paloma

## California
Auberge du Soleil
Carmel Valley Ranch Resort
Four Seasons Biltmore
Highlands Inn
Inn at Spanish Bay
John Gardiner's Tennis Ranch
Lodge at Pebble Beach
Meadowood Resort
Stonepine Estate Resort
Timberhill Ranch
Ventana - Big Sur

## Colorado
C Lazy U Ranch
Doral Telluride
Home Ranch

Hotel Jerome
Hyatt Regency Beaver Creek
Little Nell
Lodge at Vail
Ritz-Carlton, Aspen
Sardy House
Tall Timber

## Connecticut
Boulders
Mayflower Inn

## Florida
Little Palm Island
Marriott's Bay Point Resort
Ocean Grand Hotel
Ocean Key House
Palm Beach Polo & Country Club
Resort at Longboat Key Club
Ritz-Carlton, Naples
Ritz-Carlton, Palm Beach

## Georgia
Cloister
Mulberry Inn

## Hawaii
Four Seasons Resort Wailea
Grand Hyatt Wailea
Hotel Hana-Maui
Kapalua Bay Hotel & Villas
Lodge at Koele
Manele Bay Hotel
Mauna Kea Beach Hotel
Mauna Lani Bay Hotel
Princeville Hotel
Ritz-Carlton, Mauna Lani

## Idaho
Coeur d'Alene Resort

## Maine
Bayview Hotel & Inn
Captain Lord Mansion
White Barn Inn

## Maryland
Atlantic Hotel

## Massachusetts
Beach Plum Inn
Blantyre
Charlotte Inn

Orchards
Summer House

**Michigan**
Grand Traverse Resort

**Minnesota**
Schumacher's New Prague

**Mississippi**
Monmouth Plantation

**Montana**
Lone Mountain Ranch
Mountain Sky Guest Ranch

**New Jersey**
Mainstay Inn & Cottage
Virginia

**New Mexico**
Dos Casas Viejas
Hotel Santa Fe
Inn of the Anasazi

**New York State**
Point, The

**North Carolina**
Fearrington House Inn
Greystone Inn
Pinehurst Hotel & Country Club
Sanderling Inn Resort

**South Carolina**
Mills House Hotel
Westin Resort

**Texas**
Barton Creek

**Utah**
Stein Eriksen Lodge

**Vermont**
Inn at Sawmill Farm
Topnotch at Stowe

**Virginia**
Inn at Little Washington
Williamsburg Inn

**West Virginia**
Greenbrier

**Wisconsin**
American Club

**Spas**
Canyon Ranch
Doral Saturnia
Golden Door
Greenhouse
La Costa Hotel & Spa
Loews Ventana Canyon Resort

# KITCHENETTES
## All-suites, plus the following:

**Atlanta**
Ansley Inn
Hyatt Regency
Marque of Atlanta

**Baltimore**
Omni Inner Harbor Hotel
Peabody Court Hotel
Tremont Hotel

**Boston**
Best Western Boston
Copley Plaza Hotel
Royal Sonesta

**Chicago**
Allerton Hotel
Mayfair
Park Hyatt
Radisson Plaza Ambass. West
Talbott Hotel

**Cincinnati**
Vernon Manor Hotel

**Cleveland**
Cleveland Marriott Society Center

**Dallas**
Dallas Grand
Stoneleigh Hotel

**Fort Lauderdale**
Lago Mar Resort & Club
Ocean Manor Resort Hotel

**Honolulu**
Ilikai Hotel Nikko Waikiki
New Otani Kaimana Beach Hotel
Waikiki Joy Hotel

**Houston**
Allen Park Inn
Harvey Suites
Ritz-Carlton, Houston
Wyndham Warwick Hotel

**Indianapolis**
Indianapolis Hilton Downtown
University Place

**Las Vegas**
Desert Inn Hotel & Country Club

**Los Angeles**
Barnabey's Hotel
Beverly Hills Hotel
Beverly Hilton

Chateau Marmont
Hotel Bel-Air
Peninsula Beverly Hills
Shangri-La
Tower at Century Plaza

**Memphis**
Peabody Memphis

**Miami/Miami Beach**
Marlin

**Milwaukee**
Astor Hotel
Marc Plaza Hotel

**Minneapolis/St. Paul**
Minneapolis Marriott City Center
Saint Paul Hotel

**Nashville**
Stouffer Nashville Hotel

**New Orleans**
Hotel Inter-Continental
Hotel Ste. Helene
Windsor Court Hotel

**New York City**
Carlyle Hotel
Doral Court Hotel
Dorset
Gorham New York
Gramercy Park Hotel
Helmsley Palace
Hotel Beverly
Hotel Elysee
Hotel Kimberly
Hotel Plaza Athenee
Hotel Wales
Inter-Continental
Le Parker Meridien
Lowell New York
Mark
Mayfair Hotel Baglioni
Michelangelo
Ramada Hotel
Regency
Royalton
St. Moritz on-the-Park
St. Regis
U.N. Plaza - Park Hyatt
Waldorf-Astoria/Towers
Westbury Hotel
Wyndham Hotel

## Orange County, CA
Casa Laguna Inn
Le Meridien Newport

## Orlando
Courtyard at Lake Lucerne
Disney's Village Resort
Marriott
Residence Inn by Marriott

## Palm Springs
Doubletree Resort Palm Springs
Racquet Club Resort
Shadow Mountain Resort
Spa Hotel & Mineral Springs

## Philadelphia
Barclay Hotel
Rittenhouse
Warwick Hotel

## Phoenix/Scottsdale
John Gardiner's Tennis Ranch
Royal Palms Inn
Scottsdale Hilton
Stouffer Cottonwoods Resort

## Pittsburgh
Pittsburgh Vista

## San Diego
Bahia Hotel
Catamaran Resort Hotel
Horton Grand
Humphrey's Half Moon Inn
La Valencia Hotel
San Diego Princess Resort
Sea Lodge

## San Francisco
Seal Rock Inn
Stanyan Park Hotel

## Seattle
Alexis Hotel

## St. Louis
Holiday Inn Downtown/Riverfront
Radisson Hotel Clayton

## Tampa Bay
Holiday Inn Ashley Plaza
Saddlebrook
Trade Winds

## Washington, DC
Embassy Row Hotel
Guest Quarters

Radisson Park Terrace Hotel
Residence Inn Bethesda
Ritz-Carlton, Washington DC
River Inn
Sheraton Premiere
Sheraton Washington Hotel
Stouffer Mayflower Hotel
Watergate Hotel
Wyndham Bristol Hotel

## Alaska
Waterfall Resort

## Arizona
Poco Diablo Resort
Rancho de los Caballeros
Wickenburg Inn

## Arkansas
Gaston's White River Resort

## California
Big Sur Lodge
Casa Madrona Hotel
Casa Sirena Marina Resort
El Encanto Hotel
Eureka Inn
Harvest Inn
Highlands Inn
Inn at Rancho Santa Fe
John Gardiner's Tennis Ranch
La Casa del Zorro
La Playa Hotel
Northstar-at-Tahoe
Santa Barbara Miramar
Squaw Valley Inn
Ventana - Big Sur
Villa Royale

## Colorado
Broadmoor
Charter at Beaver Creek
Grande Butte Hotel
Hyatt Regency Beaver Creek
Inn at Aspen
Iron Horse Resort Retreat
Lodge at Vail
Mountain Haus at Vail
Sheraton Steamboat Resort
Stanley Hotel
Tamarron Resort
Vail Athletic Club

# KITCHENETTES

## Connecticut

Interlaken Inn
Mayflower Inn
Water's Edge Inn & Resort

## Florida

Amelia Island Plantation
Captiva Beach Resort
Chalet Suzanne
Cheeca Lodge
Grenelefe Resort
Indian River Plantation Resort
Inn at Fisher Island
Lodge at Ponte Vedra Beach
Marriott at Sawgrass Resort
Marriott's Bay Point Resort
Marriott's Marco Island Resort
Mission Inn Golf & Tennis Resort
Ocean Reef Club
Palm Beach Polo & Country Club
Ponte Vedra Inn & Club
Sonesta Sanibel Harbour
South Seas Plantation Resort
'Tween Waters Inn
Windjammer Resort

## Georgia

Callaway Gardens Resort
King & Prince Beach Resort
Sea Palms Golf & Tennis Resort

## Hawaii

Hyatt Regency Waikoloa
Kaanapali Beach Hotel
Kapalua Bay Hotel & Villas
Royal Lahaina Resort

## Idaho

Coeur d'Alene Resort

## Kentucky

Inn at Shaker Village

## Maine

Bayview Hotel & Inn
Bethel Inn & Country Club
High Tide Inn on the Ocean
Nonantum Resort

## Maryland

Imperial Hotel
Maryland Inn

## Massachusetts

Daggett House
New Seabury Cape Cod
Ocean Edge Resort & Conf. Ctr.
Red Lion Inn
Summer House
Westmoor Inn
White Elephant Inn

## Michigan

Boyne Mountain Hotel
Grand Traverse Resort
Shanty Creek - Schuss Mountain
Sugar Loaf Resort
Treetops Sylvan Resort

## Minnesota

Breezy Point Resort
Grand View Lodge

## Missouri

Lodge of Four Seasons
Marriott's TanTarA Resort

## Montana

Chico Hot Springs Lodge
Grouse Mountain Lodge
Holland Lake Lodge
Huntley Lodge
Kandahar Lodge
Mountain Sky Guest Ranch
Triple Creek Mountain Hideaway

## Nevada

Hyatt Regency Lake Tahoe

## New Mexico

Hotel Edelweiss
Inn on the Alameda
La Posada de Santa Fe
Quail Ridge Inn
Rancho Encantado Resort
St. Bernard Hotel

## New York State

Elk Lake Lodge

## North Carolina

Green Park Inn
Sanderling Inn Resort

## Oklahoma

Lake Texoma Resort
Shangri-La Resort

## Oregon

Embarcadero Resort Hotel
Inn at Spanish Head
Rock Springs Guest Ranch
Sunriver Lodge & Resort

## Pennsylvania

Nemacolin Woodlands
Seven Springs Mountain Resort
Split Rock Resort

## Rhode Island

1661 Inn

## South Carolina

Hilton Head Island Hilton Resort
Lodge Alley Inn

## South Dakota

Palmer Gulch Lodge

## Tennessee

Buckhorn Inn
Fairfield Glade Resort

## Texas

Flying L Guest Ranch
Horseshoe Bay Resort
Lakeway Inn & Conf. Ctr.
Radisson South Padre Island
Sheraton South Padre Island
Woodlands Executive Conf. Ctr.

## Utah

Brigham Street Inn
Shadow Ridge Hotel
Stein Eriksen Lodge

## Vermont

Equinox
Mountain Top Inn
Sugarbush Inn
Topnotch at Stowe

## Virginia

Kingsmill Resort & Conf. Ctr.
Manor House at Ford's Colony

## Washington

Captain Whidbey Inn
Kalaloch Lodge
Rosario Resort & Spa
Sun Mountain Lodge

## Wisconsin

Abbey
Heidel House Resort
Olympia Resort

## Wyoming

Paradise Guest Ranch
Spring Creek Ranch

## Spas

Norwich Inn, Spa & Villas
Palm-Aire Hotel & Spa

# MARINA

**Atlantic City**
Harrah's Marina Hotel & Casino
Trump Castle Resort

**Baltimore**
Harbor Court Hotel
Inn at Henderson's Wharf

**Boston**
Boston Harbor Hotel
Marriott Hotel Long Wharf

**Fort Lauderdale**
Bahia Mar Resort
Fort Lauderdale Marina Marriott
Pier 66 Resort & Marina
Riverside Hotel

**Honolulu**
Hawaii Prince Hotel Waikiki
Ilikai Hotel Nikko Waikiki

**Houston**
Nassau Bay Hilton & Marina

**Los Angeles**
Ritz-Carlton, Marina del Rey

**Miami/Miami Beach**
Alexander All-Suite Luxury Hotel
Biscayne Bay Marriott
Doubletree Hotel Coconut Grove
Eden Roc Hotel & Marina
Grand Bay Hotel
Grove Isle Yacht & Tennis Club
Turnberry Isle Club

**Orange County, CA**
Dana Point Resort
Disneyland Hotel
Four Seasons Hotel
Hyatt Newporter
Surf & Sand Hotel

**Orlando**
Buena Vista Palace
Disney's Contemporary Resort
Disney's Grand Floridian
Disney's Village Resort

**Portland, OR**
River Place Alexis Hotel

**San Diego**
Bahia Hotel
Humphrey's Half Moon Inn
Hyatt Islandia
Hyatt Regency San Diego

Kona Kai Resort
Le Meridien San Diego
Loews Coronado Bay Resort
San Diego Marriott
San Diego Princess Resort
Sheraton Grande Harbor Island
Sheraton - Harbor Island East

**Tampa Bay**
Belleview Mido Resort Hotel
Hyatt Regency Westshore
Stouffer Vinoy Resort
Wyndham Harbour Island Hotel

**Alabama**
Marriott's Grand Hotel

**Alaska**
Gustavus Inn at Glacier Bay
King Salmon Lodge
Waterfall Resort

**Arizona**
Wahweap Lodge & Marina

**Arkansas**
Gaston's White River Resort

**California**
Casa Sirena Marina Resort
Inn at Morro Bay
Lodge at Pebble Beach
Portofino Hotel & Yacht Club

**Florida**
Boca Raton Resort & Club
Captiva Beach Resort
Club Med Sandpiper
Grenelefe Resort
Hawk's Cay Resort & Marina
Hyatt Key West
Indian River Plantation Resort
Inn at Fisher Island
Lakeside Inn
Little Palm Island
Marriott's Bay Point Resort
Mission Inn Golf & Tennis Resort
Ocean Key House
Ocean Reef Club
Plantation Inn
Resort at Longboat Key Club
Sonesta Sanibel Harbour
South Seas Plantation Resort
Sundial Beach & Tennis Resort
'Tween Waters Inn

**Georgia**
Jekyll Island Club Hotel
Sheraton Savannah Resort
Stouffer Pineisle Resort

**Hawaii**
Manele Bay Hotel

**Idaho**
Coeur d'Alene Resort

**Illinois**
Eagle Ridge Inn & Resort

**Indiana**
Four Winds Clarion
French Lick Springs Resort

**Maine**
Black Point Inn Resort

**Maryland**
Inn at Mitchell House

**Massachusetts**
Harbor View Hotel
Wequassett Inn
White Elephant Inn

**Minnesota**
Arrowwood, A Radisson Resort
Breezy Point Resort
Grand View Lodge
Madden's on Gull Lake

**Missouri**
Lodge of Four Seasons
Marriott's TanTarA Resort

**New York State**
Geneva on the Lake
Montauk Yacht Club
Omni Sagamore
Three Village Inn

**North Carolina**
Greystone Inn
High Hampton Inn & Country Club
Pinehurst Hotel & Country Club

**Ohio**
Sawmill Creek Resort

**Oklahoma**
Lake Texoma Resort
Shangri-La Resort

**Oregon**
Embarcadero Resort Hotel
Sunriver Lodge & Resort
Tu Tu' Tun Lodge

**Rhode Island**
Doubletree Hotel
Newport Harbor Hotel & Marina

**South Carolina**
Hyatt Regency Hilton Head
Seabrook Island Resort
Sea Pines
Wild Dunes Resort

**Tennessee**
Fairfield Glade Resort

**Texas**
Horseshoe Bay Resort
Lakeway Inn & Conf. Ctr.

**Vermont**
Basin Harbor Club
Hawk Inn & Mountain Resort
Mountain Top Inn

**Virginia**
Kingsmill Resort & Conf. Ctr.
Tides Inn

**Washington**
Captain Whidbey Inn
Inn at Semiahmoo
Rosario Resort & Spa

**Wisconsin**
Abbey
Heidel House Resort
Lake Lawn Lodge
Lakewoods Resort & Lodge

**Wyoming**
Colter Bay Village
Jackson Lake Lodge

**Spas**
Harbor Island Spa Resort
Lake Austin Resort

# MOUNTAIN SETTING

**Anchorage**
Captain Cook Hotel

**Honolulu**
Sheraton Makaha Resort

**Palm Springs**
Autry Resort
Doubletree Resort Palm Springs
Hyatt Grand Champions Resort
Hyatt Regency Suites
La Quinta Hotel
Marriott's Rancho Las Palmas
Palm Springs Hilton Resort
Palm Springs Riviera Resort
Ritz-Carlton, Rancho Mirage
Shadow Mountain Resort
Spa Hotel & Mineral Springs
Stouffer Esmeralda
Westin Mission Hills Resort
Wyndham Palm Springs

**Phoenix/Scottsdale**
Buttes
John Gardiner's Tennis Ranch
Marriott's Camelback Inn
Marriott's Mountain Shadows
Phoenician
Pointe at South Mountain
Pointe at Squaw Peak
Pointe at Tapatio Cliffs
Red Lion La Posada Resort
Regal McCormick Ranch
Royal Palms Inn
Scottsdale Plaza Resort
Scottsdale Princess
Stouffer Cottonwoods Resort
Wyndham Paradise Valley Resort

**Alaska**

Brooks Lodge
Camp Denali
Denali National Park Hotel
Gustavus Inn at Glacier Bay
Harper Lodge Princess
Red Quill Lodge
Tikchik Narrows Lodge
Waterfall Resort
Yes Bay Lodge

**Arizona**

El Conquistador
Enchantment Resort
Grand Canyon Lodge
L'Auberge de Sedona

Los Abrigados
Poco Diablo Resort
Rancho de los Caballeros
Tanque Verde Ranch
Ventana Canyon
Westin La Paloma

**Arkansas**

Arlington Resort
Gaston's White River Resort
Palace Hotel & Bath House

**California**

Ahwahnee Hotel
Benbow Inn
Big Sur Lodge
Carmel Valley Ranch Resort
El Encanto Hotel
Madonna Inn
Northstar-at-Tahoe
Ojai Valley Inn
Post Ranch Inn
Quail Lodge Resort & Golf Club
San Ysidro Ranch
Squaw Valley Inn
Stonepine Estate Resort
Timberhill Ranch
Ventana - Big Sur
Villa Royale
Wawona Hotel

**Colorado**

Antlers Doubletree
Aspen Club Lodge
Breckenridge Hilton
Broadmoor
Charter at Beaver Creek
Cheyenne Mountain Conf. Resort
C Lazy U Ranch
Doral Telluride
Grande Butte Hotel
Home Ranch
Hotel Jerome
Hotel Lenado
Hot Springs Lodge
Hyatt Regency Beaver Creek
Inn at Aspen
Inn at Beaver Creek
Iron Horse Resort Retreat
Keystone Lodge
Limelite Lodge
Little Nell
Lodge at Cordillera
Lodge at Vail

Mountain Haus at Vail
Pines Lodge at Beaver Creek
Radisson Resort Vail
Ritz-Carlton, Aspen
Sardy House
Sheraton Steamboat Resort
Silver Tree Hotel
Sitzmark Lodge
Snowmass Lodge & Club
Sonnenalp Resort
Stanley Hotel
Tall Timber
Tamarron Resort
Vail Athletic Club
Vista Verde Guest Ranch
Westin Resort Vail

## Connecticut

Boulders
Interlaken Inn
Under Mountain Inn

## Georgia

Callaway Gardens Resort
Evergreen Conference Center

## Hawaii

Hotel Hana-Maui
Hyatt Regency Waikoloa
Lodge at Koele
Maui Marriott
Mauna Kea Beach Hotel
Princeville Hotel
Royal Lahaina Resort
Volcano House

## Idaho

Coeur d'Alene Resort
Idaho Rocky Mountain Ranch
Sun Valley Lodge

## Maine

Bayview Hotel & Inn
Bethel Inn & Country Club
High Tide Inn on the Ocean
Poland Spring Inn

## Massachusetts

Red Lion Inn
Village Inn
Wheatleigh
Whistler's Inn

## Michigan

Boyne Highlands Inn
Boyne Mountain Hotel
Shanty Creek - Schuss Mountain
Sugar Loaf Resort

## Montana

Chico Hot Springs Lodge
Gallatin Gateway Inn
Glacier Park Lodge
Grouse Mountain Lodge
Holland Lake Lodge
Huntley Lodge
Izaak Walton Inn
Kandahar Lodge
Lake McDonald Lodge
Lone Mountain Ranch
Many Glacier Hotel
Mountain Sky Guest Ranch
9 Quarter Circle Ranch
Triple Creek Mountain Hideaway

## Nevada

Harrah's Lake Tahoe
Hyatt Regency Lake Tahoe

## New Hampshire

Balsams
Mount Washington Hotel & Resort
Snowy Owl Inn
Stonehurst Manor
Whitney's Inn Jackson

## New Jersey

Inn at Millrace Pond

## New Mexico

Bishop's Lodge
Historic Taos Inn
Hotel Edelweiss
Inn of the Mountain Gods
Lodge at Cloudcroft
Quail Ridge Inn
Rancho Encantado Resort
Sagebrush Inn
St. Bernard Hotel

## New York State

Concord Resort Hotel
Elk Lake Lodge
Guest House
Mohonk Mountain House

# MOUNTAIN SETTING

Old Drovers Inn
Omni Sagamore
Point, The
Troutbeck Inn

## North Carolina

Green Park Inn
Greystone Inn
Grove Park Inn Resort
High Hampton Inn & Country Club
Richmond Hill Inn

## Oregon

Columbia Gorge Hotel
Rock Springs Guest Ranch
Sunriver Lodge & Resort
Timberline Lodge

## Pennsylvania

Black Bass Hotel
Mount Airy Lodge
Nemacolin Woodlands
Pocono Manor Inn & Golf Resort
Seven Springs Mountain Resort
Skytop Lodge
Split Rock Resort

## South Dakota

Hotel Alex Johnson
Palmer Gulch Lodge

## Tennessee

Buckhorn Inn
Fairfield Glade Resort
Inn at Blackberry Farm

## Utah

Bryce Canyon Lodge
Cliff Lodge
Grand Canyon Lodge
Shadow Ridge Hotel
Stein Eriksen Lodge
Washington School Inn

## Vermont

Cortina Inn
Equinox
Hawk Inn & Mountain Resort
Hermitage Inn
Inn at Essex
Inn at Manchester
Inn at Sawmill Farm
Mountain Top Inn

Rabbit Hill Inn
Stratton Mountain Inn
Sugarbush Inn
Topnotch at Stowe
Trapp Family Lodge
Woods at Killington
Woodstock Inn & Resort

## Virginia

Ashby Inn
Boar's Head Inn
Homestead
Inn at Little Washington

## Washington

Lake Quinault Lodge
Sun Mountain Lodge

## West Virginia

Greenbrier

## Wyoming

Colter Bay Village
Jackson Hole Racquet Club
Jackson Lake Lodge
Jenny Lake Lodge
Mammoth Hot Springs Hotel
Moose Head Ranch
Old Faithful Inn
Paradise Guest Ranch
Ranch at Ucross
R Lazy S Ranch
Roosevelt Lodge
Snow King Resort
Spring Creek Ranch
Teton Pines Resort

## Spas

Ashram Retreat
Canyon Ranch
Canyon Ranch in the Berkshires
Deerfield Manor Spa
Green Mountain at Fox Run
Jimmy Le Sage's
Lake Austin Resort
Loews Ventana Canyon Resort
Maine Chance
National Institute of Fitness
New Age Health Spa
Oaks at Ojai
Palms at Palm Springs
Vista Clara Spa

# NO CREDIT CARDS ACCEPTED

**Alaska**
Camp Denali
Yes Bay Lodge

**Arizona**
Rancho de los Caballeros

**California**
Deetjen's Big Sur Inn
Little River Inn
Madonna Inn

**Colorado**
Tall Timber
Vista Verde Guest Ranch

**Georgia**
Cloister

**Idaho**
Middle Fork Lodge

**Maine**
Pilgrim's Inn

**Montana**
9 Quarter Circle Ranch

**New Jersey**
Mainstay Inn & Cottage

**New Mexico**
Bishop's Lodge
St. Bernard Hotel

**New York State**
Elk Lake Lodge

**Pennsylvania**
Seven Springs Mountain Resort

**Wyoming**
R Lazy S Ranch

**Spas**
Ashram Retreat
Golden Door
Maine Chance

# NOTEWORTHY NEWCOMERS

**Atlanta**
Swissotel Atlanta

**Chicago**
Hyatt Regency Suites
Sheraton Chicago Hotel & Towers
Stouffer Riviere

**Cleveland**
Cleveland Marriott Society Center

**Dallas**
Hotel St. Germain
Sheraton Suites

**Denver**
Atheneum Suites

**Kansas City**
Sheraton Suites

**Los Angeles**
Hotel Inter-Continental
Hotel Nikko
Peninsula Beverly Hills

**New York City**
Flatotel International
Hotel Millenium
Michelangelo
Ramada Renaissance

**Orlando**
Clarion Plaza Hotel

**Portland, OR**
Hotel Vintage Plaza

**Philadelphia**
Omni Hotel at Independence Park
Penn's View Inn
Ritz-Carlton, Philadelphia

**San Diego**
Hyatt Regency San Diego
Loews Coronado Bay Resort
Pan Pacific

**San Francisco**
Hyatt at Fisherman's Wharf
Ritz-Carlton, San Francisco
Tuscan Inn

**Tampa Bay**
Stouffer Vinoy Resort

**Washington, DC**
Hyatt Regency Reston
Ritz-Carlton, Pentagon City
Ritz-Carlton, Tysons Corner

**California**
Post Ranch Inn

**Colorado**
Doral Telluride
Pines Lodge at Beaver Creek
Ritz-Carlton, Aspen

**Florida**
Ritz-Carlton, Amelia Island
Ritz-Carlton, Palm Beach

**Hawaii**
Grand Hyatt Wailea
Manele Bay Hotel
Ritz-Carlton, Mauna Lani

**New Mexico**
Dos Casas Viejas
Hotel Plaza Real
Hotel Santa Fe
Inn of the Anasazi

# OFFBEAT/FUNKY

**Atlantic City**
Trump Taj Mahal

**Indianapolis**
Holiday Inn Union Station

**Fort Worth**
Stockyards Hotel

**Las Vegas**
Caesars Palace
Circus Circus Hotel
Excalibur Hotel
Mirage

**Los Angeles**
Chateau Marmont
Mondrian Hotel
Shangri-La

**Nashville**
Union Station Hotel

**New York City**
Morgans
Paramount
Royalton

**Orlando**
Disney's Contemporary Resort

**San Francisco**
Hotel Diva
Mansions Hotel
Miyako Hotel

**St. Louis**
Hyatt Regency St. Louis

**California**
Furnace Creek Inn
Madonna Inn

**Montana**
Izaak Walton Inn

# OLD-WORLD CHARM

**Atlanta**
Ansley Inn
Ritz-Carlton, Atlanta
Ritz-Carlton, Buckhead

**Atlantic City**
Marriott's Seaview Resort

**Baltimore**
Admiral Fell Inn
Harbor Court Hotel
Peabody Court Hotel
Society Hill Hotel

**Boston**
Boston Park Plaza
Copley Plaza Hotel
Four Seasons Hotel
Le Meridien Boston
Omni Parker House
Ritz-Carlton, Boston

**Chicago**
Chicago Claridge Hotel
Chicago Hilton & Towers
Drake Hotel
Four Seasons Hotel
Knickerbocker Chicago Hotel
Mayfair
Omni Ambassador East
Palmer House Hilton
Tremont Hotel

**Cincinnati**
Vernon Manor Hotel

**Columbus**
Worthington Inn

**Dallas**
Adolphus
Four Seasons Resort & Club
Hotel Crescent Court
Hotel St. Germain
Mansion on Turtle Creek
Melrose Hotel
Stoneleigh Hotel

**Denver**
Brown Palace Hotel
Loews Giorgio Hotel
Oxford Hotel

**Detroit**
Townsend Hotel

**Fort Worth**
Stockyards Hotel

**Houston**
Four Seasons Hotel
La Colombe d'Or
Lancaster
Ritz-Carlton, Houston
Wyndham Warwick Hotel

**Indianapolis**
Canterbury Hotel

**Kansas City**
Radisson Suite Hotel
Raphael Hotel
Ritz-Carlton, Kansas City

**Los Angeles**
Beverly Hills Hotel
Biltmore Los Angeles
Chateau Marmont
Four Seasons Hotel
Hotel Bel-Air

**Louisville**
Seelbach Hotel

**Memphis**
Peabody Memphis

**Miami/Miami Beach**
Biltmore Hotel
Hotel Place St. Michel

**Milwaukee**
Pfister Hotel

**Minneapolis/St. Paul**
Saint Paul Hotel
Whitney

**Nashville**
Hermitage Hotel

**New Orleans**
Bourbon Orleans Hotel
Columns Hotel
Cornstalk Hotel
Fairmont Hotel
Hotel Maison de Ville
Le Richelieu
Monteleone Hotel
Omni Royal Orleans
Pontchartrain Hotel
Saint Louis Hotel
Soniat House
Windsor Court Hotel

**New York City**
Algonquin Hotel
Box Tree
Carlyle Hotel
Dorset
Helmsley Palace
Hotel Plaza Athenee
Inter-Continental
Mayfair Hotel Baglioni
Peninsula New York
Pierre
Plaza Hotel
Ritz-Carlton, New York
Sherry-Netherland Hotel
Stanhope
Waldorf-Astoria/Towers
Westbury Hotel

**Orange County, CA**
Ritz-Carlton, Laguna Niguel

**Orlando**
Park Plaza Hotel

**Palm Springs**
Ritz-Carlton, Rancho Mirage

**Philadelphia**
Barclay Hotel
Four Seasons Hotel
Hotel Atop the Bellevue
Latham Hotel
Penn's View Inn
Rittenhouse
Ritz-Carlton, Philadelphia

**Pittsburgh**
Priory - A City Inn

**Portland, OR**
Heathman Hotel

**Raleigh-Durham**
Carolina Inn
Siena Hotel

**Richmond**
Commonwealth Park Suites Hotel

**San Antonio**
Menger Hotel
Saint Anthony Hotel
Sheraton Gunter Hotel

**San Diego**
Colonial Inn
Horton Grand

Hotel del Coronado
U.S. Grant Hotel
Westgate Hotel

**San Francisco**
Archbishops Mansion Inn
Fairmont Hotel
Four Seasons Clift Hotel
Hotel Vintage Court
Huntington Hotel Nob Hill
Inn at Union Square
Juliana Hotel
Kensington Park
Majestic
Mansions Hotel
Prescott Hotel
Queen Anne
Sheraton Palace
Sherman House
Victorian Inn on the Park
Washington Square Inn

**Seattle**
Four Seasons Olympic
Mayflower Park Hotel
Sorrento Hotel

**St. Louis**
Hotel Majestic
Ritz-Carlton, St. Louis

**Washington, DC**
Carlton
Henley Park Hotel
Madison Hotel
Morrison-Clark Inn
Morrison House
Radisson Park Terrace Hotel
Ritz-Carlton, Washington DC
Stouffer Mayflower Hotel
Tabard Inn
Watergate Hotel
Willard Inter-Continental

**Wilmington**
Hotel du Pont

**Arizona**
Hassayampa Inn

**California**
Alta Mira
Eureka Inn
Four Seasons Biltmore
Madrona Manor

537

# OLD-WORLD CHARM

## Colorado
Broadmoor
Hotel Jerome
Little Nell
Sardy House

## Connecticut
Boulders
Mayflower Inn

## Florida
Boca Raton Resort & Club
Breakers
Lakeside Inn

## Georgia
Cloister
Eliza Thompson
Gastonian
Jekyll Island Club Hotel
President's Quarters

## Louisiana
Nottoway Plantation

## Maine
Bayview Hotel & Inn
Captain Lord Mansion
White Barn Inn

## Maryland
Inn at Perry Cabin

## Massachusetts
Blantyre
Charlotte Inn
Daggett House
Orchards
Whistler's Inn

## Michigan
Grand Hotel

## Minnesota
Schumacher's New Prague
St. James Hotel

## Mississippi
Monmouth Plantation

## New Hampshire
Balsams
Mount Washington Hotel & Resort

## New Jersey
Mainstay Inn & Cottage
Virginia

## New York State
Clarion Inn at Saratoga
Gideon Putnam Hotel
Otesaga Hotel
Troutbeck Inn

## North Carolina
Grove Park Inn Resort
Pinehurst Hotel & Country Club
Richmond Hill Inn

## Oregon
Columbia Gorge Hotel

## Pennsylvania
Bridgeton House

## Tennessee
Inn at Blackberry Farm

## Vermont
Equinox
Shelburne House

## Virginia
Homestead
Inn at Little Washington

## West Virginia
Greenbrier

## Wisconsin
American Club

# OUTSTANDING BARS

**Boston**
Charles Hotel in Harvard Square
Eliot Hotel
Guest Quarters Suite Hotel

**Chicago**
Drake Hotel

**Dallas**
Mansion on Turtle Creek

**Denver**
Cambridge Hotel

**Los Angeles**
Beverly Hills Hotel
Biltmore Los Angeles
Four Seasons Hotel

**Louisville**
Seelbach Hotel

**Miami/Miami Beach**
Hyatt Regency Coral Gables

**Milwaukee**
Hyatt Regency Milwaukee

**Minneapolis/St. Paul**
Saint Paul Hotel

**New York City**
Algonquin Hotel
Beekman Tower
Carlyle
Essex House
Grand Hyatt
Helmsley Palace
Hotel Elysee
Le Parker Meridien
Loews New York
Mark
Paramount
Plaza Hotel
Regency
Ritz-Carlton
Stanhope
St. Regis
Waldorf

**Philadelphia**
Penn's View Inn

**Phoenix/Scottsdale**
Hyatt Regency Phoenix
Phoenician

**Portland, OR**
Heathman Hotel

**San Antonio**
Fairmount Hotel

**San Francisco**
Campton Place Kempinski
Fairmont Hotel
Four Seasons Clift Hotel
Hotel Bedford
Inn at the Opera
Mark Hopkins Inter-Continental
Sir Francis Drake
Villa Florence Hotel
Westin St. Francis

**Seattle**
Sorrento Hotel

**St. Louis**
Hotel Majestic

**Washington, DC**
Phoenix Park Hotel

**Colorado**
Hotel Jerome
Little Nell
Sardy House

**Florida**
Ocean Key House

**Maryland**
Maryland Inn

**Michigan**
Boyne Mountain Hotel

**Montana**
Chico Hot Springs Lodge

**Texas**
Flying L Guest Ranch

**Wyoming**
Wort Hotel

# OUTSTANDING RESTAURANTS

**Anchorage**
Captain Cook Hotel

**Atlanta**
Atlanta Hilton & Towers
  Nikolai's Roof
  Trader Vic's
Hotel Nikko
  Cassis
  Kamogawa
J.W. Marriott at Lenox
Ritz-Carlton, Atlanta
  Cafe, The
  Restaurant, The
Ritz-Carlton, Buckhead
  Cafe, The
  Dining Room
Stouffer Waverly Hotel
Swissotel Atlanta

**Atlantic City**
Bally's Grand Hotel & Casino
  Caruso's
  Oaks, The
Marriott's Seaview Resort
Merv Griffin's Resorts
  Ivana's
  Max's
  Roberto's
Trump Plaza Hotel & Casino
  Capriccio
  Le Palais

**Austin**
Four Seasons Hotel

**Baltimore**
Doubletree Inn at the Colonnade
Harbor Court Hotel
  Hamptons
Peabody Court Hotel
  Conservatory, The
  Peabody's
Stouffer Harborplace

**Boston**
Boston Harbor Hotel
  Rowes Wharf
Bostonian Hotel
  Seasons
Charles Hotel in Harvard Square
  Bennett Street Cafe
  Rarities

Copley Plaza Hotel
  Copley's
  Plaza Dining Room
Four Seasons Hotel
  Aujourd'hui
  Bristol Lounge
Le Meridien Boston
  Cafe Fleuri
  Julien
Ritz-Carlton, Boston
  Cafe
  Dining Room
Westin Hotel Copley Place
  Ten Huntington
  Turner Fisheries

**Chicago**
Drake Hotel
  Cape Cod Room
  Oak Terrace
Fairmont Hotel
  Entre Nous
  Primavera
Four Seasons Hotel
  Seasons
Hotel Inter-Continental
  Boulevard Room
Hotel Nikko
  Benkay
  Celebrity Cafe
Hotel Sofitel
Mayfair
  Le Ciel Bleu
  Palm, The
Omni Ambassador East
  Pump Room
Park Hyatt
  La Tour
Ritz-Carlton, Chicago
  Cafe
  Dining Room
Tremont Hotel
  Cricket's

**Cincinnati**
Cincinnatian Hotel
Omni Netherland Plaza

**Cleveland**
Ritz-Carlton, Cleveland

**Columbus**
Worthington Inn

**Dallas**
Adolphus
  French Room
Fairmont Hotel
  Brasserie
  Pyramid Room
Four Seasons Resort & Club
Hotel Crescent Court
  Beau Nash
  Conservatory
  Crescent Gourmet
  East Wind
Loews Anatole Hotel
  L'Entrecote
  Nana Grill
Mansion on Turtle Creek
  Mansion
  Promenade
Omni Mandalay Hotel
Plaza of the Americas Hotel
Sheraton Park Central
  Laurels

**Denver**
Brown Palace Hotel
Cambridge Hotel
Hyatt Regency Denver
Loews Giorgio Hotel

**Detroit**
Ritz-Carlton, Dearborn
Townsend Hotel

**Fort Worth**
Worthington
  Reflections

**Hartford**
Goodwin Hotel

**Honolulu**
Colony Surf Hotel
  Michel's
Halekulani
  La Mer
  Orchids
Hawaiian Regent
  Secret, The
Hawaii Prince Hotel Waikiki
  Hakone
  Prince Court
  Takanawa

Kahala Hilton
  Hala Terrace
  Maile
  Plumeria Cafe

**Houston**
Four Seasons Hotel
  De Ville
La Colombe d'Or
  La Colombe d'Or
Omni
Ritz-Carlton, Houston
  Ritz-Carlton
Wyndham Warwick Hotel
  Hunt Room

**Indianapolis**
Canterbury Hotel

**Kansas City**
Hyatt Regency Crown Center
  Peppercorn Duck Club
  Skies
  Terrace, The
Ritz-Carlton, Kansas City
  Cafe, The
  Grill, The
Westin Crown Center
  Benton's
  Brasserie
  Kabuki
  Trader Vic's

**Las Vegas**
Caesars Palace
Desert Inn Hotel & Country Club
Four Queens Hotel & Casino
Golden Nugget Hotel & Casino
Mirage

**Los Angeles**
BelAge Hotel
  Diaghilev
Beverly Hills Hotel
Beverly Hilton
  L'Escoffier
Beverly Pavilion Hotel
Biltmore Los Angeles
  Bernard's
Checkers Hotel Kempinski
  Checkers
Four Seasons Hotel
Hotel Bel-Air
L'Ermitage Hotel

## OUTSTANDING RESTAURANTS

Los Angeles Hilton & Towers
  Cardini
Peninsula Beverly Hills
  Belvedere
Regent Beverly Wilshire
Ritz-Carlton, Huntington Hotel
  Ritz-Carlton
Ritz-Carlton, Marina del Rey
  Ritz-Carlton
St. James's Club & Hotel
  St. James's
Tower at Century Plaza
Westwood Marquis Hotel
  Dynasty Room

### Louisville
Seelbach Hotel

### Memphis
Peabody Memphis

### Miami/Miami Beach
Grand Bay Hotel
  Grand Cafe
Hotel Inter-Continental
Hotel Place St. Michel
  Rest. St. Michel
Mayfair House Hotel Grand Luxe
  Mayfair Grill
Turnberry Isle Club
  Veranda

### Milwaukee
Pfister Hotel
  English Room
Wyndham Milwaukee Center
  Kilbourn Cafe

### Minneapolis/St. Paul
Hotel Sofitel
Marquette
Omni Northstar Hotel
Saint Paul Hotel
Whitney

### New Orleans
Fairmont Hotel
  Bailey's
  Sazerac
Hotel Inter-Continental
  Veranda
Hotel Maison de Ville
  Maison de Ville Bistro
Le Meridien Hotel
  Henri
  La Gauloise

Omni Royal Orleans
  Rib Room
Pontchartrain Hotel
  Cafe Pontchartrain
  Caribbean Room
Saint Louis Hotel
  Louis XVI
Westin Canal Place
  Le Jardin
Windsor Court Hotel
  Grill Room

### New York City
Box Tree
  Box Tree
Carlyle Hotel
  Carlyle Dining Room
Drake Swissotel
  Lafayette
Essex House
  Cafe Botanica
  Les Celebrites
Hotel Plaza Athenee
  La Regence
Lowell New York
  Pembroke Room
  Post House
Mark
  Mark's
Mayfair Hotel Baglioni
  Le Cirque
  Lounge
Paramount
  Brasserie des Theatres
  Mezzanine
Pierre
  Cafe Pierre
Plaza
  Edwardian Room
  Oak Room
  Palm Court
  Plaza Oyster Bar
Regency
  Regency
Righa Royal
  Halcyon
Royalton
  44
St. Regis
  King Cole Room
  Lespinasse
U.N. Plaza - Park Hyatt
Westbury Hotel
  Polo

**Oklahoma City**
Waterford Hotel

**Orange County, CA**
Four Seasons Hotel
  Pavilion, The
Le Meridien Newport
  Antoine
Ritz-Carlton, Laguna Niguel
  Dining Room, The

**Orlando**
Buena Vista Palace
  Arthur's 27
  Outback Restaurant
Disney's Grand Floridian
  Flagler's
  Narcoossee's
  Victoria & Albert's
Hyatt Regency Grand Cypress
  Hemingway's
  La Coquina
Park Plaza Hotel

**Palm Springs**
Ritz-Carlton, Rancho Mirage
  Ritz-Carlton

**Philadelphia**
Four Seasons Hotel
  Fountain, The
  Swan Lounge
Hotel Atop the Bellevue
  Barrymore Room
  Founders
Omni Hotel at Independence Park
  Azalea
Penn's View Inn
  Ristorante Panorama
Rittenhouse
  Cassatt Tea Room
  Restaurant 210
  Treetops Restaurant
Ritz-Carlton, Philadelphia
  Dining Room, The
  Grill, The

**Phoenix/Scottsdale**
Arizona Biltmore
  Gold Room Grille
  Orangerie
Hyatt Regency Scottsdale
  Golden Swan
John Gardiner's Tennis Ranch

Phoenician
  Mary Elaine's
Ritz-Carlton, Phoenix
  Grill at Ritz-Carlton
  Restaurant, The
Scottsdale Princess
  Grill at the TPC
  La Hacienda
  Marquesa

**Portland, OR**
Heathman Hotel
  Heathman Hotel
River Place Alexis Hotel
  Esplanade

**Raleigh-Durham**
Siena Hotel

**Richmond**
Commonwealth Park Suites Hotel

**San Antonio**
Fairmount Hotel

**San Diego**
Le Meridien San Diego
  Marius
Rancho Bernardo Inn
  El Bizcocho
Rancho Valencia
  Rancho Valencia Restaurant
U.S. Grant Hotel
  Grant Grill

**San Francisco**
Campton Place Kempinski
  Campton Place
Donatello
  Donatello
Four Seasons Clift Hotel
  French Room
Hotel Vintage Court
  Masa's
Huntington Hotel Nob Hill
  Big Four
Inn at the Opera
  Act IV
Mandarin Oriental
  Silks
Mark Hopkins Inter-Continental
  Nob Hill Restaurant
Prescott Hotel
  Postrio
Rancho Valencia

## OUTSTANDING RESTAURANTS

Ritz-Carlton, San Francisco
  Dining Room, The
  Restaurant, The
Sherman House
  Sherman House
Stouffer Stanford Court Hotel
  Fournou's Oven
Villa Florence Hotel
  Kuleto's

### San Jose, CA
Fairmont Hotel
  Les Saisons

### Seattle
Alexis Hotel
  Cafe Alexis
  Cajun Corner
  92 Madison
Four Seasons Olympic
  Chartwell
Hyatt Regency Bellevue
Sheraton Seattle Hotel & Towers
  Fuller's
Sorrento Hotel
  Hunt Club, The
Westin Hotel Seattle
  Palm Court, The

### St. Louis
Daniele Hotel
  London Grill
Hotel Majestic
  Richard Perry
Ritz-Carlton, St. Louis
  Dining Room, The
  Grill, The
Seven Gables Inn
  Bernard's
  Chez Louis

### Tampa Bay
Hyatt Regency Westshore
  Armani's
  Oystercatchers
Saddlebrook
Wyndham Harbour Island Hotel

### Washington, DC
Embassy Row Hotel
  Lucie
Four Seasons Hotel
  Aux Beaux Champs

Hay-Adams Hotel
  Hay-Adams Dining Rm.
Henley Park Hotel
  Coeur de Lion
Jefferson Hotel
  Jefferson Restaurant
Madison Hotel
  Montpelier Restaurant
Morrison-Clark Inn
  Morrison-Clark Restaurant
Park Hyatt
  Melrose
Phoenix Park Hotel
  Powerscourt
Ritz-Carlton, Pentagon City
  Dining Room, The
  Grill, The
Ritz-Carlton, Tysons Corner
  Grill, The
  Restaurant, The
Ritz-Carlton, Washington DC
  Jockey Club
Watergate Hotel
  Jean-Louis
  Riverview
Willard Inter-Continental
  Willard Room

### Wilmington
Hotel du Pont
  Brandywine Room
  Green Room, The

### Arizona
Boulders Resort
L'Auberge de Sedona
Poco Diablo Resort
Ventana Canyon
Westin La Paloma
Westward Look Resort

### California
Auberge du Soleil
Carmel Valley Ranch Resort
Casa Madrona Hotel
Eureka Inn
Four Seasons Biltmore
Highlands Inn
Inn at Spanish Bay
John Gardiner's Tennis Ranch
Lodge at Pebble Beach
Madrona Manor
Meadowood Resort

Quail Lodge Resort & Golf Club
San Ysidro Ranch
Stonepine Estate Resort
St. Orres
Timberhill Ranch
Ventana - Big Sur

### Colorado

Broadmoor
C Lazy U Ranch
Home Ranch
Hotel Jerome
Hyatt Regency Beaver Creek
Little Nell
Lodge at Vail
Sardy House

### Connecticut

Homestead Inn
Mayflower Inn

### Florida

Breakers
Colony Beach & Tennis Resort
Lakeside Inn
Little Palm Island
Marquesa Hotel
Ocean Grand Hotel
Ritz-Carlton, Amelia Island
Ritz-Carlton, Naples
Ritz-Carlton, Palm Beach

### Georgia

Cloister

### Hawaii

Four Seasons Resort Wailea
Hotel Hana-Maui
Hyatt Regency Maui
Kapalua Bay Hotel & Villas
Lodge at Koele
Manele Bay Hotel
Maui Prince Hotel
Mauna Kea Beach Hotel
Mauna Lani Bay Hotel
Ritz-Carlton, Mauna Lani
Westin Maui

### Kentucky

Inn at Shaker Village

### Louisiana

Nottoway Plantation

### Maine

Pilgrim's Inn
White Barn Inn

### Maryland

Atlantic Hotel
Imperial Hotel

### Massachusetts

Beach Plum Inn
Blantyre
Charlotte Inn
Wauwinet
Wheatleigh

### Michigan

Grand Traverse Resort

### Minnesota

Schumacher's New Prague

### Montana

Chico Hot Springs Lodge

### New Hampshire

Balsams
Christmas Farm Inn

### New Jersey

Inn at Millrace Pond
Virginia

### New Mexico

Inn of the Anasazi

### New York State

Point, The
Troutbeck Inn

### North Carolina

Fearrington House Inn

### Oregon

Columbia Gorge Hotel
Tu Tu' Tun Lodge

### Pennsylvania

Evermay on-the-Delaware

### Rhode Island

Atlantic Inn
Hotel Manisses

## OUTSTANDING RESTAURANTS

### South Carolina

Hyatt Regency Hilton Head
Mills House Hotel
Westin Resort

### Utah

Stein Eriksen Lodge

### Vermont

Hermitage Inn
Inn at Essex
Inn at Sawmill Farm
Shelburne House

### Virginia

Ashby Inn
Inn at Little Washington

### Wisconsin

American Club

### Wyoming

Jenny Lake Lodge

### Spas

Loews Ventana Canyon Resort

# OUTSTANDING VIEWS

**Albuquerque**
Marriott Albuquerque

**Anchorage**
Captain Cook Hotel

**Atlanta**
Atlanta Hilton & Towers
Atlanta Marriott Marquis
Doubletree Hotel at Concourse
Holiday Inn Crowne Plaza
Hyatt Regency
J.W. Marriott at Lenox
Sheraton Colony Square Hotel
Westin Peachtree Plaza

**Atlantic City**
Bally's Grand Hotel & Casino
Bally's Park Place
Caesars Atlantic City
Claridge Casino Hotel
Harrah's Marina Hotel & Casino
Holiday Inn Diplomat
Marriott's Seaview Resort
Merv Griffin's Resorts
Sands Hotel & Casino
Showboat Hotel
TropWorld
Trump Castle Resort
Trump Plaza Hotel & Casino
Trump Regency Hotel
Trump Taj Mahal

**Austin**
Four Seasons Hotel

**Baltimore**
Admiral Fell Inn
Brookshire Hotel
Clarion Hotel - Inner Harbor
Harbor Court Hotel
Hyatt Regency Baltimore
Inn at Henderson's Wharf
Peabody Court Hotel
Sheraton Inner Harbor Hotel
Stouffer Harborplace
Tremont Hotel

**Boston**
Back Bay Hilton
Boston Harbor Hotel
Cambridge Center Marriott
Charles Hotel in Harvard Square
Colonnade Hotel
Four Seasons Hotel
Guest Quarters Suite Hotel

Hyatt Regency Cambridge
Marriott Copley Place
Marriott Hotel Long Wharf
Ritz-Carlton, Boston
Royal Sonesta
Sheraton Boston Hotel & Towers
Westin Hotel Copley Place

**Chicago**
Allerton Hotel
Barclay Chicago
Blackstone Hotel
Chicago Marriott Downtown
Congress Hotel
Drake Hotel
Executive Plaza
Fairmont Hotel
Four Seasons Hotel
Holiday Inn City Centre
Hotel Inter-Continental
Hotel Nikko
Hyatt Regency Chicago
Hyatt Regency Suites
Le Meridien Hotel Chicago
Mayfair
McCormick Center Hotel
Ritz-Carlton, Chicago
Sheraton Chicago Hotel & Towers
Swissotel Chicago

**Cincinnati**
Cincinnati Terrace Hilton
Clarion Hotel Cincinnati
Hyatt Regency Cincinnati
Omni Netherland Plaza

**Cleveland**
Cleveland Marriott Society Center
Glidden House
Holiday Inn Lakeside City Center
Sheraton City Centre
Stouffer Tower City Plaza Hotel

**Corpus Christi**
Corpus Christi Marriott Bayfront

**Dallas**
Four Seasons Resort & Club
Hyatt Regency Dallas at Reunion
Omni Mandalay Hotel
Sheraton Park Central
Stouffer Dallas Hotel

**Denver**
Burnsley Hotel
Doubletree Hotel Denver

## OUTSTANDING VIEWS

Embassy Suites Denver Dtwn.
Hyatt Regency Denver
Hyatt Regency Tech Center
Loews Giorgio Hotel
Marriott Southeast
Radisson Hotel
Red Lion
Scanticon
Sheraton Denver Tech Center
Warwick Hotel
Westin Hotel Tabor Center

### Detroit
Hyatt Regency Dearborn
Omni
Radisson Hotel Pontchartrain
Radisson Plaza Hotel
River Place Inn
Townsend Hotel

### Florham Park
Hamilton Park

### Fort Lauderdale
Bahia Mar Resort
Fort Lauderdale Marina Marriott
Marriott's Harbor Beach Resort
Ocean Manor Resort Hotel
Pier 66 Resort & Marina
Sheraton Yankee Clipper
Westin Hotel, Cypress Creek

### Hartford
Goodwin Hotel

### Honolulu
Colony Surf Hotel
Halekulani
Hawaiian Regent
Hawaiian Waikiki Beach Hotel
Hawaii Prince Hotel Waikiki
Hilton Hawaiian Village
Hyatt Regency Waikiki
Ilikai Hotel Nikko Waikiki
Kahala Hilton
New Otani Kaimana Beach Hotel
Outrigger Waikiki
Pacific Beach Hotel
Ritz-Carlton Kapalua
Royal Hawaiian Hotel
Sheraton Makaha Resort
Sheraton Moana Surfrider
Sheraton Princess Kaiulani
Sheraton Waikiki Hotel

Turtle Bay Hilton
Waikiki Beachcomber Hotel

### Houston
Guest Quarters
Holiday Inn Houston West
La Colombe d'Or
Nassau Bay Hilton & Marina
Omni
Plaza Hilton
Ritz-Carlton, Houston
Stouffer Presidente Hotel
Woodlands Executive Conf. Ctr.
Wyndham Warwick Hotel

### Indianapolis
Westin Hotel Indianapolis

### Kansas City
Allis Plaza Hotel
Doubletree Hotel
Hyatt Regency Crown Center
Raphael Hotel
Sheraton Suites

### Las Vegas
Aladdin Hotel
Excalibur Hotel
Fitzgerald's Casino Hotel
Four Queens Hotel & Casino
Lady Luck Casino Hotel
Las Vegas Hilton
Mirage
Riviera Hotel & Casino

### Little Rock
Arkansas' Excelsior Hotel

### Los Angeles
BelAge Hotel
Beverly Hilton
Beverly Pavilion Hotel
Century Plaza Hotel
Chateau Marmont
Four Seasons Hotel
Hotel Bel-Air
Hotel Inter-Continental
Hyatt on Sunset
Industry Hills Sheraton Resort
L'Ermitage Hotel
Loews Santa Monica Beach Hotel
Los Angeles Airport Hilton
Malibu Beach Inn
Ma Maison Sofitel
Mondrian Hotel

New Otani Hotel & Garden
Radisson Bel-Air Summit
Ritz-Carlton, Huntington Hotel
Ritz-Carlton, Marina del Rey
Shangri-La
St. James's Club & Hotel
Tower at Century Plaza
Westin Bonaventure
Westwood Marquis Hotel
Wilshire Plaza Hotel

## Miami/Miami Beach
Alexander All-Suite Luxury Hotel
Betsy Ross Hotel
Biltmore Hotel
Biscayne Bay Marriott
Doral Ocean Beach Resort
Doral Resort & Country Club
Doubletree Hotel Coconut Grove
Eden Roc Hotel & Marina
Fontainebleau Hilton
Grand Bay Hotel
Grove Isle Yacht & Tennis Club
Hotel Inter-Continental
Hyatt Regency Miami
Occidental Parc Hotel
Omni International Hotel
Sheraton Bal Harbour Hotel
Sonesta Beach Hotel
Turnberry Isle Club

## Milwaukee
Marc Plaza Hotel

## Minneapolis/St. Paul
Crown Sterling (Minn/St. Paul)
Minneapolis Marriott City Center
Radisson Hotel St. Paul
Saint Paul Hotel
Whitney

## Nashville
Holiday Inn Crowne Plaza
Loews Vanderbilt Plaza Hotel

## New Orleans
Doubletree Hotel New Orleans
Holiday Inn Crowne Plaza
Hyatt Regency New Orleans
Royal Sonesta
Sheraton New Orleans Hotel
Westin Canal Place
Windsor Court Hotel

## New York City
Beekman Tower Hotel
Carlyle Hotel
Dumont Plaza Hotel
Embassy Suites Hotel
Essex House, Hotel Nikko
Flatotel International
Gramercy Park Hotel
Grand Hyatt
Helmsley Park Lane Hotel
Holiday Inn Crowne Plaza
Hotel Pickwick Arms
Hotel Wales
Le Parker Meridien
Loews New York Hotel
Marriott Financial Center Hotel
Mayflower Hotel
New York Marriott Marquis
New York Vista
Peninsula New York
Pierre
Plaza Hotel
Regency
Rihga Royal
Ritz-Carlton, New York
Shelburne Suite Hotel
Stanhope
St. Moritz on-the-Park
St. Regis
U.N. Plaza - Park Hyatt

## Orange County, CA
Casa Laguna Inn
Dana Point Resort
Disneyland Hotel
Four Seasons Hotel
Hyatt Newporter
Irvine Marriott
Le Meridien Newport
Marriott Suites Newport Beach
Newport Beach Marriott Hotel
Ritz-Carlton, Laguna Niguel
Surf & Sand Hotel
Westin South Coast Plaza

## Orlando
Buena Vista Palace
Disney's Caribbean Beach Resort
Disney's Contemporary Resort
Disney's Polynesian Resort
Disney's Village Resort
Forte Travelodge Hotel

# OUTSTANDING VIEWS

Grosvenor Resort at WDW
Harley Hotel
Hotel Royal Plaza
Hyatt Regency Grand Cypress
Marriott's Orlando World Center
Peabody Orlando
Walt Disney World Dolphin
Walt Disney World Swan

## Palm Springs
Autry Resort
Doubletree Resort Palm Springs
Hyatt Grand Champions Resort
Hyatt Regency Suites
La Quinta Hotel
Marriott's Rancho Las Palmas
Palm Springs Hilton Resort
Palm Springs Marquis
Palm Springs Riviera Resort
Ritz-Carlton, Rancho Mirage
Shadow Mountain Resort
Stouffer Esmeralda
Two Bunch Palms Resort
Westin Mission Hills Resort
Wyndham Palm Springs

## Philadelphia
Barclay Hotel
Four Seasons Hotel
Hyatt Cherry Hill
Omni Hotel at Independence Park
Rittenhouse
Society Hill Hotel

## Phoenix/Scottsdale
Arizona Biltmore
Buttes
Camelview Resort
Crescent Hotel
Crown Sterling Suites
Fountains Suite Hotel
Hyatt Regency Phoenix
Hyatt Regency Scottsdale
John Gardiner's Tennis Ranch
Marriott's Camelback Inn
Marriott's Mountain Shadows
Marriott Suites Scottsdale
Orange Tree Golf & Conf. Resort
Phoenician
Pointe at South Mountain
Pointe at Squaw Peak
Pointe at Tapatio Cliffs
Red Lion La Posada Resort

Regal McCormick Ranch
Registry Resort
Ritz-Carlton, Phoenix
Royal Palms Inn
Scottsdale Hilton
Scottsdale Plaza Resort
Scottsdale Princess
Sheraton Mesa Hotel
Sheraton San Marcos Golf Resort
Stouffer Cottonwoods Resort
Wyndham Paradise Valley Resort

## Pittsburgh
Hyatt Regency Pittsburgh
Pittsburgh Hilton & Towers
Pittsburgh Vista
Sheraton Hotel Station Square

## Portland, OR
River Place Alexis Hotel

## Richmond
Commonwealth Park Suites Hotel

## San Antonio
Hilton Palacio del Rio
La Mansion del Rio
San Antonio Riverwalk Marriott

## San Diego
Bahia Hotel
Catamaran Resort Hotel
Colonial Inn
Embassy Suites
Gaslamp Plaza Suites
Horton Grand
Hotel del Coronado
Humphrey's Half Moon Inn
Hyatt Islandia
Hyatt Regency La Jolla
Hyatt Regency San Diego
Kona Kai Resort
La Valencia Hotel
Le Meridien San Diego
Loews Coronado Bay Resort
Pan Pacific
Rancho Bernardo Inn
Rancho Valencia
San Diego Hilton
San Diego Marriott
San Diego Princess Resort
Sea Lodge
Sheraton Grande at Torrey Pines
Sheraton Grande Harbor Island

Sheraton - Harbor Island East
U.S. Grant Hotel

## San Francisco
ANA Hotel
Archbishops Mansion Inn
Campton Place Kempinski
Chancellor Hotel
Fairmont Hotel
Grand Hyatt
Harbor Court Hotel
Hotel Bedford
Hotel Nikko
Huntington Hotel Nob Hill
Hyatt Regency San Francisco
Hyde Park Suites
Mandarin Oriental
Mark Hopkins Inter-Continental
Park Hyatt
San Francisco Downtown Marriott
Seal Rock Inn
Sherman House
Sir Francis Drake
Stouffer Stanford Court Hotel
Westin St. Francis

## San Jose, CA
Fairmont Hotel

## Seattle
Edgewater
Holiday Inn Crowne Plaza
Hyatt Regency Bellevue
Inn at the Market
Seattle Hilton
Sheraton Seattle Hotel & Towers
Stouffer Madison
Warwick Hotel
Westin Hotel Seattle

## St. Louis
Adam's Mark
Clarion Hotel St. Louis
Holiday Inn Downtown/Riverfront
Marriott Pavilion Hotel
Ritz-Carlton, St. Louis
St. Louis Marriott West

## Tampa Bay
Adam's Mark Caribbean Gulf
Don Ce-Sar Registry Resort
Embassy Suites Tampa Airport
Hyatt Regency Westshore
Radisson Bay Harbor Inn

Saddlebrook
St. Petersburg Beach Hilton
Trade Winds
Wyndham Harbour Island Hotel

## Washington, DC
Embassy Row Hotel
Hay-Adams Hotel
Hotel Washington
Hyatt Arlington at Key Bridge
Hyatt Fair Lakes
Hyatt Regency Washington
J.W. Marriott Hotel
Key Bridge Marriott
Loews L'Enfant Plaza
One Washington Circle Hotel
Ritz-Carlton, Tysons Corner
Ritz-Carlton, Washington DC
River Inn
Sheraton Premiere
Washington Court Hotel
Washington Hilton & Towers
Watergate Hotel

## Alabama
Marriott's Grand Hotel

## Alaska
Brooks Lodge
Camp Denali
Denali National Park Hotel
Glacier Bay Lodge
Gustavus Inn at Glacier Bay
Harper Lodge Princess
King Salmon Lodge
Red Quill Lodge
Tikchik Narrows Lodge
Waterfall Resort
Yes Bay Lodge

## Arizona
Boulders Resort
El Conquistador
El Tovar Hotel
Enchantment Resort
Grand Canyon Lodge
L'Auberge de Sedona
Los Abrigados
Poco Diablo Resort
Rancho de los Caballeros
Tanque Verde Ranch
Ventana Canyon
Wahweap Lodge & Marina

# OUTSTANDING VIEWS

Westin La Paloma
Westward Look Resort
Wickenburg Inn

## Arkansas

Arlington Resort
Gaston's White River Resort
Palace Hotel & Bath House

## California

Ahwahnee Hotel
Alisal Ranch
Alta Mira
Auberge du Soleil
Benbow Inn
Big Sur Lodge
Carmel Valley Ranch Resort
Casa Madrona Hotel
Casa Sirena Marina Resort
Claremont Resort
Deetjen's Big Sur Inn
El Encanto Hotel
Four Seasons Biltmore
Furnace Creek Inn
Harvest Inn
Heritage House
Highlands Inn
Hill House Inn
Inn at Morro Bay
Inn at Rancho Santa Fe
Inn at Spanish Bay
Inn at the Tides
La Casa del Zorro
La Playa Hotel
Little River Inn
Lodge at Pebble Beach
Madonna Inn
Madrona Manor
Mendocino Hotel
Monterey Plaza Hotel
Northstar-at-Tahoe
Ojai Valley Inn
Portofino Hotel & Yacht Club
Post Ranch Inn
Quail Lodge Resort & Golf Club
Santa Barbara Miramar
San Ysidro Ranch
Sheraton Universal Hotel
Silverado Country Club & Resort
Squaw Valley Inn
Stonepine Estate Resort
St. Orres

Timberhill Ranch
Ventana - Big Sur
Villa Royale
Vintage Inn
Vintners Inn
Wawona Hotel
Wine Country Inn

## Colorado

Antlers Doubletree
Aspen Club Lodge
Breckenridge Hilton
Broadmoor
Charter at Beaver Creek
Cheyenne Mountain Conf. Resort
C Lazy U Ranch
Doral Telluride
Home Ranch
Hotel Jerome
Hotel Lenado
Hot Springs Lodge
Hyatt Regency Beaver Creek
Inn at Aspen
Inn at Beaver Creek
Iron Horse Resort Retreat
Keystone Lodge
Limelite Lodge
Little Nell
Lodge at Cordillera
Lodge at Vail
Mountain Haus at Vail
Pines Lodge at Beaver Creek
Radisson Resort Vail
Ritz-Carlton, Aspen
Sardy House
Sheraton Steamboat Resort
Silver Tree Hotel
Snowmass Lodge & Club
Sonnenalp Resort
Stanley Hotel
Tall Timber
Tamarron Resort
Vail Athletic Club
Vista Verde Guest Ranch
Westin Resort Vail

## Connecticut

Boulders
Homestead Inn
Mayflower Inn
Under Mountain Inn
Water's Edge Inn & Resort

# OUTSTANDING VIEWS

## Florida

Amelia Island Plantation
Boca Raton Resort & Club
Breakers
Captiva Beach Resort
Cheeca Lodge
Club Med Sandpiper
Colony Beach & Tennis Resort
Grenelefe Resort
Hawk's Cay Resort & Marina
Hyatt Key West
Indian River Plantation Resort
Inn at Fisher Island
Lakeside Inn
Little Palm Island
Lodge at Ponte Vedra Beach
Marriott's Bay Point Resort
Marriott's Casa Marina Resort
Marriott's Marco Island Resort
Mission Inn Golf & Tennis Resort
Moose Head Ranch
Ocean Grand Hotel
Ocean Key House
Ocean Reef Club
Palm Beach Polo & Country Club
PGA National
Pier House Resort
Ponce de Leon Resort
Ponte Vedra Inn & Club
Reach Resort
Resort at Longboat Key Club
Ritz-Carlton, Amelia Island
Ritz-Carlton, Naples
Sheraton Key Largo Resort
Sonesta Sanibel Harbour
South Seas Plantation Resort
Sundial Beach & Tennis Resort
'Tween Waters Inn

## Georgia

Callaway Gardens Resort
Cloister
Evergreen Conference Center
Greyfield Inn
Jekyll Island Club Hotel
King & Prince Beach Resort
Sea Palms Golf & Tennis Resort
Sheraton Savannah Resort
Stouffer Pineisle Resort

## Hawaii

Embassy Suites Resort Maui
Four Seasons Resort Wailea

Grand Hyatt Wailea
Hotel Hana-Maui
Hyatt Regency Kauai
Hyatt Regency Maui
Hyatt Regency Waikoloa
Kaanapali Beach Hotel
Kapalua Bay Hotel & Villas
Kona Hilton Resort
Kona Village Resort
Lodge at Koele
Manele Bay Hotel
Maui Inter-Continental Resort
Maui Marriott
Maui Prince Hotel
Mauna Kea Beach Hotel
Mauna Lani Bay Hotel
Princeville Hotel
Ritz-Carlton, Mauna Lani
Royal Lahaina Resort
Royal Waikoloan
Stouffer Wailea Beach Resort
Stouffer Waiohai Beach Resort
Volcano House
Westin Kauai
Westin Maui

## Idaho

Coeur d'Alene Resort
Idaho Rocky Mountain Ranch
Middle Fork Lodge
Sun Valley Lodge

## Illinois

Eagle Ridge Inn & Resort
Indian Lakes Resort

## Indiana

Four Winds Clarion

## Kentucky

Inn at Shaker Village

## Louisiana

Nottoway Plantation

## Maine

Asticou Inn/Cranberry Lodge
Bayview Hotel & Inn
Bethel Inn & Country Club
Black Point Inn Resort
Cliff House
Colony Resort
Harraseeket Inn
High Tide Inn on the Ocean

# OUTSTANDING VIEWS

Poland Spring Inn
Samoset Resort
Whitehall Inn

## Maryland

Inn at Perry Cabin
Maryland Inn
Robert Morris Inn

## Massachusetts

Beach Plum Inn
Blantyre
Chatham Bars Inn
Daggett House
Harbor View Hotel
New Seabury Cape Cod
Ocean Edge Resort & Conf. Ctr.
Seacrest Manor
Ship's Knees Inn
Summer House
Village Inn
Wauwinet
Wequassett Inn
Westmoor Inn
Wheatleigh
Whistler's Inn
White Elephant Inn
Yankee Clipper Inn

## Michigan

Boyne Highlands Inn
Boyne Mountain Hotel
Grand Hotel
Grand Traverse Resort
Shanty Creek - Schuss Mountain
Sugar Loaf Resort
Treetops Sylvan Resort

## Minnesota

Arrowwood, A Radisson Resort
Fitgers Inn
Grand View Lodge
Lutsen Resort
Madden's on Gull Lake

## Missouri

Lodge of Four Seasons
Marriott's TanTarA Resort

## Montana

Chico Hot Springs Lodge
Gallatin Gateway Inn
Glacier Park Lodge
Grouse Mountain Lodge

Holland Lake Lodge
Huntley Lodge
Izaak Walton Inn
Kandahar Lodge
Lake McDonald Lodge
Lone Mountain Ranch
Many Glacier Hotel
Mountain Sky Guest Ranch
9 Quarter Circle Ranch
Triple Creek Mountain Hideaway

## North Carolina

Green Park Inn
Greystone Inn
Grove Park Inn Resort
High Hampton Inn & Country Club
Richmond Hill Inn

## Nevada

Harrah's Lake Tahoe
Hyatt Regency Lake Tahoe

## New Hampshire

Balsams
Christmas Farm Inn
Mount Washington Hotel & Resort
Snowy Owl Inn
Stonehurst Manor
Whitney's Inn Jackson

## New Jersey

Inn at Millrace Pond

## New Mexico

Bishop's Lodge
Hotel Edelweiss
Inn of the Mountain Gods
Quail Ridge Inn
Rancho Encantado Resort
Sagebrush Inn
St. Bernard Hotel

## New York State

Concord Resort Hotel
Doral Arrowwood
Elk Lake Lodge
Geneva on the Lake
Gideon Putnam Hotel
Mohonk Mountain House
Montauk Yacht Club
Omni Sagamore
Point, The
Three Village Inn

## Ohio

Quail Hollow Resort

## Oklahoma

Lake Texoma Resort
Shangri-La Resort

## Oregon

Columbia Gorge Hotel
Embarcadero Resort Hotel
Inn at Spanish Head
Kah-Nee-Ta Resort
Rock Springs Guest Ranch
Salishan Lodge
Sunriver Lodge & Resort
Sylvia Beach Hotel
Timberline Lodge
Tu Tu' Tun Lodge

## Pennsylvania

Bridgeton House
Hotel Hershey
Mount Airy Lodge
Nemacolin Woodlands
Pocono Manor Inn & Golf Resort
Seven Springs Mountain Resort
Skytop Lodge
Split Rock Resort
Sweetwater Farm

## Rhode Island

Atlantic Inn
Doubletree Hotel
Inn at Castle Hill
Newport Harbor Hotel & Marina
1661 Inn

## South Carolina

Hyatt Regency Hilton Head
Kiawah Island Resort
Marriott's Hilton Head Resort
Seabrook Island Resort
Sea Pines
Westin Resort
Wild Dunes Resort

## South Dakota

Franklin Hotel
Hotel Alex Johnson
Palmer Gulch Lodge

## Tennessee

Buckhorn Inn
Fairfield Glade Resort
Inn at Blackberry Farm

## Texas

Barton Creek
Flying L Guest Ranch
Horseshoe Bay Resort
Lakeway Inn & Conf. Ctr.
Mayan Dude Ranch
Radisson South Padre Island
Sheraton South Padre Island

## Utah

Bryce Canyon Lodge
Cliff Lodge
Grand Canyon Lodge
Shadow Ridge Hotel
Stein Eriksen Lodge
Washington School Inn

## Vermont

Basin Harbor Club
Cortina Inn
Equinox
Hawk Inn & Mountain Resort
Hermitage Inn
Inn at Manchester
Inn at Sawmill Farm
Mountain Top Inn
Rabbit Hill Inn
Stratton Mountain Inn
Sugarbush Inn
Topnotch at Stowe
Trapp Family Lodge
Woods at Killington

## Virginia

Ashby Inn
Boar's Head Inn
Homestead
Inn at Little Washington
Kingsmill Resort & Conf. Ctr.
Manor House at Ford's Colony
Tides Inn

## Washington

Captain Whidbey Inn
Inn at Semiahmoo
Kalaloch Lodge
Lake Quinault Lodge

# OUTSTANDING VIEWS

Rosario Resort & Spa
Salish Lodge
Sun Mountain Lodge

**West Virginia**
Greenbrier

**Wisconsin**
Abbey
Americana Lake Geneva Resort
Gordon Lodge
Heidel House Resort
Lakewoods Resort & Lodge

**Wyoming**
Colter Bay Village
Jackson Hole Racquet Club
Jackson Lake Lodge
Jenny Lake Lodge
Mammoth Hot Springs Hotel
Moose Head Ranch
Old Faithful Inn
Paradise Guest Ranch
Ranch at Ucross
R Lazy S Ranch

Roosevelt Lodge
Snow King Resort
Spring Creek Ranch
Teton Pines Resort
Wort Hotel

**Spas**
Canyon Ranch
Canyon Ranch in the Berkshires
Golden Door
Gurney's Inn Resort & Spa
Heartland Retreat
La Costa Hotel & Spa
Lake Austin Resort
Loews Ventana Canyon Resort
Maine Chance
National Institute of Fitness
New Age Health Spa
Norwich Inn, Spa & Villas
Oaks at Ojai
Palms at Palm Springs
Sans Souci Resort
Vista Clara Spa

# PEOPLE-WATCHING

## Atlanta
Atlanta Marriott Marquis
Hotel Nikko
Hyatt Regency
J.W. Marriott at Lenox
Omni Hotel at CNN Center
Ritz-Carlton, Atlanta
Ritz-Carlton, Buckhead
Stouffer Waverly Hotel
Westin Peachtree Plaza

## Atlantic City
Bally's Grand Hotel & Casino
Bally's Park Place
Caesars Atlantic City
Claridge Casino Hotel
Harrah's Marina Hotel & Casino
Merv Griffin's Resorts
Sands Hotel & Casino
Showboat Hotel
TropWorld
Trump Castle Resort
Trump Plaza Hotel & Casino
Trump Regency Hotel
Trump Taj Mahal

## Austin
Four Seasons Hotel

## Baltimore
Harbor Court Hotel
Hyatt Regency Baltimore
Peabody Court Hotel
Stouffer Harborplace

## Birmingham
Tutwiler
Wynfrey Hotel

## Boston
Boston Harbor Hotel
Charles Hotel in Harvard Square
Le Meridien Boston
Marriott Copley Place
Ritz-Carlton, Boston
Swissotel Boston
Westin Hotel Copley Place

## Charlotte
Dunhill Hotel

## Chicago
Chicago Hilton & Towers
Chicago Marriott Downtown
Drake Hotel
Fairmont Hotel
Four Seasons Hotel
Hotel Nikko
Hyatt Regency Chicago
Le Meridien Hotel Chicago
Mayfair
Omni Ambassador East
Park Hyatt
Ritz-Carlton, Chicago
Sheraton Chicago Hotel & Towers
Stouffer Riviere
Swissotel Chicago

## Cincinnati
Cincinnatian Hotel

## Cleveland
Ritz-Carlton, Cleveland

## Dallas
Adolphus
Dallas Marriott Quorum
Fairmont Hotel
Hotel Crescent Court
Hyatt Regency Dallas at Reunion
Loews Anatole Hotel
Mansion on Turtle Creek
Omni Mandalay Hotel
Stouffer Dallas Hotel
Westin Galleria

## Denver
Brown Palace Hotel
Cambridge Hotel
Loews Giorgio Hotel
Westin Hotel Tabor Center

## Detroit
Ritz-Carlton, Dearborn
River Place Inn
Westin Hotel

## Fort Lauderdale
Bahia Mar Resort
Marriott's Harbor Beach Resort
Sheraton Yankee Clipper

## Fort Worth
Stockyards Hotel

## Honolulu
Colony Surf Hotel
Halekulani
Hawaiian Regent
Hawaiian Waikiki Beach Hotel
Hawaii Prince Hotel Waikiki
Hilton Hawaiian Village

# PEOPLE-WATCHING

Hyatt Regency Waikiki
Ilikai Hotel Nikko Waikiki
Kahala Hilton
New Otani Kaimana Beach Hotel
Outrigger Waikiki
Park Plaza Waikiki
Royal Hawaiian Hotel
Sheraton Moana Surfrider
Sheraton Princess Kaiulani
Sheraton Waikiki Hotel

## Houston
Four Seasons Hotel
Houstonian Hotel & Conf. Ctr.
J.W. Marriott Hotel
Omni
Ritz-Carlton, Houston
Wyndham Warwick Hotel

## Indianapolis
Westin Hotel Indianapolis

## Kansas City
Hyatt Regency Crown Center
Ritz-Carlton, Kansas City
Westin Crown Center

## Las Vegas
Aladdin Hotel
Bally's
Caesars Palace
Circus Circus Hotel
Desert Inn Hotel & Country Club
Dunes Hotel & Country Club
Excalibur Hotel
Frontier Hotel
Golden Nugget Hotel & Casino
Imperial Palace Hotel & Casino
Las Vegas Hilton
Mirage
Plaza Hotel
Riviera Hotel & Casino
Sahara Hotel & Casino
Sands Hotel & Casino
Showboat Hotel
Tropicana Hotel & Country Club
Vegas World Hotel & Casino

## Los Angeles
BelAge Hotel
Beverly Hills Hotel
Beverly Hilton
Beverly Rodeo Hotel
Biltmore Los Angeles

Century Plaza Hotel
Chateau Marmont
Checkers Hotel Kempinski
Four Seasons Hotel
Hollywood Roosevelt Hotel
Hotel Bel-Air
Hotel Nikko
Hyatt on Sunset
L'Ermitage Hotel
Loews Santa Monica Beach Hotel
Los Angeles Hilton & Towers
Peninsula Beverly Hills
Regent Beverly Wilshire
Ritz-Carlton, Huntington Hotel
Ritz-Carlton, Marina del Rey
Sheraton Grande Hotel
Sunset Marquis Hotel
Tower at Century Plaza
Westin Bonaventure
Westwood Marquis Hotel

## Memphis
Peabody Memphis

## Miami/Miami Beach
Alexander All-Suite Luxury Hotel
Doral Ocean Beach Resort
Fontainebleau Hilton
Grand Bay Hotel
Grove Isle Yacht & Tennis Club
Hotel Inter-Continental
Hyatt Regency Miami
Mayfair House Hotel Grand Luxe
Turnberry Isle Club

## Milwaukee
Hyatt Regency Milwaukee
Wyndham Milwaukee Center

## Minneapolis/St. Paul
Minneapolis Marriott City Center
Radisson Plaza Hotel
Whitney

## Nashville
Opryland Hotel

## New Orleans
Dauphine Orleans Hotel
Fairmont Hotel
Hyatt Regency New Orleans
Inn on Bourbon
Le Meridien Hotel
New Orleans Hilton Riverside
New Orleans Marriott

Omni Royal Orleans
Pontchartrain Hotel
Radisson Suite Hotel
Royal Sonesta
Sheraton New Orleans Hotel
Westin Canal Place
Windsor Court Hotel

**New York City**
Algonquin Hotel
Carlyle Hotel
Essex House, Hotel Nikko
Grand Hyatt
Helmsley Palace
Holiday Inn Crowne Plaza
Hotel Plaza Athenee
Le Parker Meridien
Lowell New York
Mark
Mayfair Hotel Baglioni
Mayflower Hotel
Michelangelo
Morgans
New York Vista
Paramount
Peninsula New York
Pierre
Plaza Hotel
Ramada Renaissance
Regency
Rihga Royal
Royalton
Sheraton New York
Stanhope
St. Moritz on-the-Park
St. Regis
U.N. Plaza - Park Hyatt
Waldorf-Astoria/Towers

**Orange County, CA**
Anaheim Hilton & Towers
Anaheim Marriott Hotel
Disneyland Hotel
Four Seasons Hotel
Ritz-Carlton, Laguna Niguel

**Orlando**
Buena Vista Palace
Disney's Caribbean Beach Resort
Disney's Contemporary Resort
Disney's Grand Floridian
Disney's Polynesian Resort
Disney's Village Resort

Grosvenor Resort at WDW
Guest Quarters Disney Village
Hilton at WDW Village
Hyatt Orlando
Hyatt Regency Grand Cypress
Marriott
Marriott's Orlando World Center
Sheraton World Resort
Stouffer Orlando Resort
Walt Disney World Dolphin
Walt Disney World Swan

**Palm Springs**
Hyatt Grand Champions Resort
Marriott's Desert Springs Resort
Palm Springs Marquis
Ritz-Carlton, Rancho Mirage
Stouffer Esmeralda

**Philadelphia**
Four Seasons Hotel
Hotel Atop the Bellevue
Omni Hotel at Independence Park
Rittenhouse
Ritz-Carlton, Philadelphia

**Phoenix/Scottsdale**
Hyatt Regency Scottsdale
Phoenician
Ritz-Carlton, Phoenix
Scottsdale Princess

**Portland, OR**
Heathman Hotel

**Raleigh-Durham**
Siena Hotel

**San Antonio**
Fairmount Hotel
Hilton Palacio del Rio
Hyatt Regency San Antonio
La Mansion del Rio
Marriott Rivercenter
Menger Hotel
San Antonio Riverwalk Marriott

**San Diego**
Doubletree Hotel at Horton Plaza
Hotel del Coronado
Hyatt Regency La Jolla
La Valencia Hotel
Le Meridien San Diego
Loews Coronado Bay Resort
Rancho Bernardo Inn

## PEOPLE-WATCHING

Rancho Valencia
San Diego Marriott
U.S. Grant Hotel
Westgate Hotel

### San Francisco
Campton Place Kempinski
Donatello
Fairmont Hotel
Four Seasons Clift Hotel
Grand Hyatt
Hotel Nikko
Hyatt Regency San Francisco
Hyde Park Suites
Inn at the Opera
Mandarin Oriental
Pan Pacific
Park Hyatt
Prescott Hotel
Ritz-Carlton, San Francisco
San Francisco Downtown Marriott
San Francisco Hilton
Stouffer Stanford Court Hotel
Tuscan Inn
Villa Florence Hotel
Westin St. Francis

### Seattle
Hyatt Regency Bellevue
Sorrento Hotel

### St. Louis
Adam's Mark
Clarion Hotel St. Louis
Hotel Majestic
Hyatt Regency St. Louis
Ritz-Carlton, St. Louis

### Tampa Bay
Adam's Mark Caribbean Gulf
Don Ce-Sar Registry Resort
Hyatt Regency Westshore
Wyndham Harbour Island Hotel

### Washington, DC
Carlton
Four Seasons Hotel
Georgetown Inn
Grand Hotel
Grand Hyatt Washington
Hay-Adams Hotel
Jefferson Hotel
J.W. Marriott Hotel
Madison Hotel

Park Hyatt
Ramada Renaissance
Ritz-Carlton, Pentagon City
Ritz-Carlton, Tysons Corner
Ritz-Carlton, Washington DC
Sheraton Washington Hotel
Watergate Hotel
Willard Inter-Continental

### Wilmington
Hotel du Pont

### Arizona
Arizona Inn
Boulders Resort

### California
Auberge du Soleil
Carmel Valley Ranch Resort
Four Seasons Biltmore
Highlands Inn
Inn at Rancho Santa Fe
Inn at Spanish Bay
Lodge at Pebble Beach
Meadowood Resort
Northstar-at-Tahoe
Quail Lodge Resort & Golf Club
San Ysidro Ranch
Ventana - Big Sur

### Colorado
Broadmoor
Doral Telluride
Hotel Jerome
Hotel Lenado
Hyatt Regency Beaver Creek
Inn at Beaver Creek
Little Nell
Lodge at Vail
Mountain Haus at Vail
Ritz-Carlton, Aspen
Sardy House
Vail Athletic Club
Westin Resort Vail

### Connecticut
Mayflower Inn

### Florida
Amelia Island Plantation
Boca Raton Resort & Club
Brazilian Court
Breakers

Club Med Sandpiper
Don Shula's Hotel & Golf Club
Hyatt Key West
Marriott at Sawgrass Resort
Marriott's Marco Island Resort
Ocean Grand Hotel
Palm Beach Polo & Country Club
Pier House Resort
Reach Resort
Registry Resort
Ritz-Carlton, Amelia Island
Ritz-Carlton, Naples
Ritz-Carlton, Palm Beach
South Seas Plantation Resort

## Georgia

Cloister

## Hawaii

Embassy Suites Resort Maui
Four Seasons Resort Wailea
Grand Hyatt Wailea
Hotel Hana-Maui
Hyatt Regency Maui
Hyatt Regency Waikoloa
Kapalua Bay Hotel & Villas
Manele Bay Hotel
Maui Inter-Continental Resort
Maui Marriott
Mauna Lani Bay Hotel
Ritz-Carlton, Mauna Lani
Westin Kauai
Westin Maui

## Idaho

Sun Valley Lodge

## Maine

White Barn Inn

## Massachusetts

Charlotte Inn
Ocean Edge Resort & Conf. Ctr.

## Michigan

Grand Hotel

## Montana

Huntley Lodge

## Nevada

Caesars Lake Tahoe
Harrah's Lake Tahoe
Hyatt Regency Lake Tahoe

## New Mexico

Eldorado Hotel
Hotel Santa Fe
Inn of the Anasazi

## New York State

Concord Resort Hotel

## Oregon

Hotel Vintage Plaza
River Place Alexis Hotel

## South Carolina

Hilton Head Island Hilton Resort
Hyatt Regency Hilton Head
Kiawah Island Resort
Marriott's Hilton Head Resort
Seabrook Island Resort
Sea Pines
Westin Resort
Wild Dunes Resort

## Texas

Radisson South Padre Island
Sheraton South Padre Island

## Utah

Stein Eriksen Lodge

## Virginia

Inn at Little Washington
Williamsburg Inn

## West Virginia

Greenbrier

## Wisconsin

Olympia Resort

## Spas

Canyon Ranch
La Costa Hotel & Spa
Loews Ventana Canyon Resort

# POWER SCENES

**Anchorage**
Captain Cook Hotel

**Atlanta**
Hotel Nikko
J.W. Marriott at Lenox
Ritz-Carlton, Atlanta
Ritz-Carlton, Buckhead
Swissotel Atlanta

**Austin**
Four Seasons Hotel

**Baltimore**
Harbor Court Hotel
Peabody Court Hotel
Stouffer Harborplace

**Birmingham**
Tutwiler
Wynfrey Hotel

**Boston**
Boston Harbor Hotel
Bostonian Hotel
Charles Hotel in Harvard Square
Four Seasons Hotel
Le Meridien Boston
Ritz-Carlton, Boston
Swissotel Boston

**Charlotte**
Dunhill Hotel

**Chicago**
Drake Hotel
Fairmont Hotel
Four Seasons Hotel
Hotel Nikko
Le Meridien Hotel Chicago
Mayfair
Omni Ambassador East
Park Hyatt
Ritz-Carlton, Chicago
Swissotel Chicago

**Cincinnati**
Cincinnatian Hotel

**Cleveland**
Ritz-Carlton, Cleveland

**Dallas**
Adolphus
Four Seasons Resort & Club
Hotel Crescent Court
Mansion on Turtle Creek
Omni Mandalay Hotel

Plaza of the Americas Hotel
Westin Galleria

**Denver**
Cambridge Hotel
Hyatt Regency Denver
Loews Giorgio Hotel
Westin Hotel Tabor Center

**Detroit**
Hotel St. Regis
Ritz-Carlton, Dearborn
River Place Inn

**Fort Worth**
Worthington

**Houston**
Four Seasons Hotel
Houstonian Hotel & Conf. Ctr.
La Colombe d'Or
Lancaster
Omni
Ritz-Carlton, Houston
Wyndham Warwick Hotel

**Indianapolis**
Canterbury Hotel
Westin Hotel Indianapolis

**Kansas City**
Ritz-Carlton, Kansas City
Westin Crown Center
Woodlands Executive Conf. Ctr.

**Las Vegas**
Caesars Palace

**Los Angeles**
BelAge Hotel
Beverly Hills Hotel
Biltmore Los Angeles
Century Plaza Hotel
Checkers Hotel Kempinski
Hotel Bel-Air
Hotel Nikko
L'Ermitage Hotel
Peninsula Beverly Hills
Regent Beverly Wilshire
Ritz-Carlton, Huntington Hotel
Ritz-Carlton, Marina del Rey
Sheraton Grande Hotel
St. James's Club & Hotel
Sunset Marquis Hotel
Tower at Century Plaza
Westwood Marquis Hotel

**Louisville**
Seelbach Hotel

**Memphis**
Peabody Memphis

**Miami/Miami Beach**
Grand Bay Hotel
Grove Isle Yacht & Tennis Club
Mayfair House Hotel Grand Luxe
Turnberry Isle Club

**Milwaukee**
Pfister Hotel
Wyndham Milwaukee Center

**Minneapolis/St. Paul**
Marquette
Saint Paul Hotel
Whitney

**New Orleans**
Le Meridien Hotel
Pontchartrain Hotel
Westin Canal Place
Windsor Court Hotel

**New York City**
Carlyle Hotel
Hotel Macklowe
Hotel Plaza Athenee
Le Parker Meridien
Lowell New York
Mark
Mayfair Hotel Baglioni
Michelangelo
Pierre
Plaza Hotel
Regency
Rihga Royal
Stanhope
U.N. Plaza - Park Hyatt
Waldorf-Astoria/Towers

**Oklahoma City**
Waterford Hotel

**Orange County, CA**
Four Seasons Hotel
Le Meridien Newport
Ritz-Carlton, Laguna Niguel

**Palm Springs**
Ritz-Carlton, Rancho Mirage

**Philadelphia**
Four Seasons Hotel
Hotel Atop the Bellevue
Rittenhouse
Ritz-Carlton, Philadelphia

**Phoenix/Scottsdale**
Phoenician
Ritz-Carlton, Phoenix
Scottsdale Princess

**Portland, OR**
Heathman Hotel
River Place Alexis Hotel

**Raleigh-Durham**
Siena Hotel

**Richmond**
Commonwealth Park Suites Hotel

**San Antonio**
Plaza San Antonio

**San Diego**
Kona Kai Resort
Le Meridien San Diego
Pan Pacific
Rancho Bernardo Inn
U.S. Grant Hotel
Westgate Hotel

**San Francisco**
Campton Place Kempinski
Donatello
Four Seasons Clift Hotel
Hotel Nikko
Huntington Hotel Nob Hill
Mandarin Oriental
Pan Pacific
Park Hyatt
Prescott Hotel
Ritz-Carlton, San Francisco
Stouffer Stanford Court Hotel
Westin St. Francis

**Seattle**
Alexis Hotel
Four Seasons Olympic
Sorrento Hotel

**St. Louis**
Ritz-Carlton, St. Louis

**Tampa Bay**
Wyndham Harbour Island Hotel

# POWER SCENES

## Washington, DC
Carlton
Four Seasons Hotel
Grand Hotel
Hay-Adams Hotel
Jefferson Hotel
Madison Hotel
Park Hyatt
Pullman-Highland Hotel
Ritz-Carlton, Pentagon City
Ritz-Carlton, Tysons Corner
Ritz-Carlton, Washington DC
Watergate Hotel
Willard Inter-Continental

## Wilmington
Hotel du Pont

## California
Four Seasons Biltmore

## Colorado
Hotel Jerome

Little Nell
Ritz-Carlton, Aspen

## Florida
Boca Raton Resort & Club
Breakers Hotel
Indian River Plantation Resort
Ocean Grand Hotel
Ritz-Carlton, Naples
Ritz-Carlton, Palm Beach

## Maryland
Loews Annapolis

## New York State
Doral Arrowwood

## Wisconsin
American Club

## Spas
Loews Ventana Canyon Resort

# PETS ALLOWED

## Atlanta
Ansley Inn
Holiday Inn Buckhead
Marriott Suites Perimeter
Peachtree Executive Conf. Ctr.
Radisson Hotel
Ramada Hotel Dunwoody
Sheraton Colony Square Hotel
Summerfield Suites Hotel
Westin Peachtree Plaza

## Atlantic City
TropWorld
Trump Castle Resort

## Austin
Four Seasons Hotel

## Baltimore
Baltimore Marriott Inner Harbor
Johns Hopkins Inn
Marriott's Hunt Valley Inn
Sheraton Inner Harbor Hotel
Society Hill Hotel
Tremont Hotel
Tremont Plaza Hotel

## Boston
Back Bay Hilton
Boston Harbor Hotel
Charles Hotel in Harvard Square
Copley Plaza Hotel
Four Seasons Hotel
Le Meridien Boston
Marriott Copley Place
Midtown Hotel
Ritz-Carlton, Boston
Swissotel Boston

## Chicago
Bismarck Hotel
Blackstone Hotel
Chicago Claridge Hotel
Chicago Marriott Downtown
Chicago Marriott O'Hare
Chicago Marriott Suites O'Hare
Four Seasons Hotel
Hotel Sofitel
McCormick Center Hotel
Palmer House Hilton
Ritz-Carlton, Chicago
Sheraton Plaza Hotel
Stouffer Riviere
Westin Hotel, Chicago

## Cincinnati
Cincinnati Marriott
Clarion Hotel Cincinnati
Holiday Inn I-275

## Cleveland
Cleveland Marriott East
Cleveland South Hilton Inn

## Corpus Christi
Corpus Christi Marriott Bayfront

## Dallas
Aristocrat Hotel
Dallas Grand
Dallas Marriott Park Central
Dallas Marriott Quorum
Doubletree Hotel Campbell Ctr.
Embassy Suites
Melrose Hotel
Omni Mandalay Hotel
Plaza of the Americas Hotel
Southland Center Hotel
Stoneleigh Hotel
Stouffer Dallas Hotel
Westin Galleria

## Denver
Burnsley Hotel
Marriott Southeast
Red Lion
Residence Inn
Sheraton Denver Tech Center
Warwick Hotel
Westin Hotel Tabor Center

## Detroit
Hotel St. Regis
Mayflower Bed & Breakfast
Novi Hilton
Westin Hotel

## Fort Lauderdale
Fort Lauderdale Marriott North
Sheraton Design Center
Westin Hotel, Cypress Creek

## Houston
Four Seasons Hotel
Guest Quarters
Holiday Inn Crowne Plaza
Holiday Inn Houston West
Holiday Inn West Loop
Houston Marriott Astrodome
Houston Marriott West Loop
Hyatt Regency Houston

## PETS ALLOWED

J.W. Marriott Hotel
La Colombe d'Or
Lancaster
Plaza Hilton
Ramada Kings Inn
Ritz-Carlton, Houston
Stouffer Presidente Hotel
Westin Galleria
Westin Oaks

### Indianapolis
Canterbury Hotel
Indianapolis Marriott
Radisson Plaza & Suites Hotel
Woodlands Executive Conf. Ctr.

### Kansas City
Americana Hotel on Convention
Doubletree Hotel
Marriott Overland Park
Radisson Suite Hotel
Westin Crown Center

### Los Angeles
Century Plaza Hotel
Chateau Marmont
Checkers Hotel Kempinski
Four Seasons Hotel
Hotel Bel-Air
Hotel Nikko
Le Parc Hotel
Loews Santa Monica Beach Hotel
Los Angeles Airport Hilton
Ma Maison Sofitel
Mondrian Hotel
Sheraton Los Angeles Airport
St. James's Club & Hotel
Westwood Marquis Hotel

### Miami/Miami Beach
Grand Bay Hotel
Grove Isle Yacht & Tennis Club
Marlin
Radisson Mart Plaza
Sheraton Bal Harbour Hotel
Warner Center Marriott

### Milwaukee
Marc Plaza Hotel
Milwaukee Marriott - Brookfield

### Minneapolis/St. Paul
Crown Sterling (Minn/St. Paul)
Minneapolis Marriott City Center
Omni Northstar Hotel
Radisson Hotel & Conf. Ctr.

Radisson Hotel Metrodome
Radisson Hotel St. Paul
Radisson Plaza Hotel

### Nashville
Embassy Suites
Hermitage Hotel
Holiday Inn Crowne Plaza
Nashville Airport Marriott
Regal Maxwell House
Sheraton Music City Hotel

### New Orleans
Dauphine Orleans Hotel
New Orleans Hilton Riverside
St. Pierre

### New York City
Box Tree
Carlyle Hotel
Dorset
Essex House, Hotel Nikko
Gramercy Park Hotel
Holiday Inn Crowne Plaza
Holiday Inn Downtown
Hotel Kimberly
Hotel Plaza Athenee
Inter-Continental
Lowell New York
Mayfair Hotel Baglioni
Mayflower Hotel
New York Hilton & Towers
New York Marriott Marquis
New York Vista
Novotel New York
Pierre
Plaza Hotel
Rihga Royal
Royalton
Sheraton Park Avenue
Surrey Hotel
Westbury Hotel

### Orange County, CA
Anaheim Marriott Hotel
Costa Mesa Marriott Suites
Irvine Marriott
Marriott Suites Newport Beach
Newport Beach Marriott Hotel
Westin South Coast Plaza

### Orlando
Orlando Heritage Inn
Radisson Plaza Hotel
Sheraton World Resort

## Palm Springs
Doubletree Resort Palm Springs
Hyatt Regency Suites
La Quinta Hotel
Palm Springs Hilton Resort
Palm Springs Riviera Resort
Stouffer Esmeralda

## Philadelphia
Barclay Hotel
Chestnut Hill Hotel
Four Seasons Hotel
Rittenhouse
Sheraton Society Hill
Sheraton University City

## Phoenix/Scottsdale
Buttes
Fountains Suite Hotel
Lexington Hotel & City Square
Marriott's Camelback Inn
Marriott Suites Scottsdale
Omni Adams Hotel
Pointe at South Mountain
Pointe at Squaw Peak
Pointe at Tapatio Cliffs
Red Lion La Posada Resort
Registry Resort
Royal Palms Inn
Scottsdale Hilton
Sheraton San Marcos Golf Resort
Stouffer Cottonwoods Resort

## Pittsburgh
Pittsburgh Green Tree Marriott
Pittsburgh Vista
Westin William Penn

## Portland, OR
Hotel Vintage Plaza
River Place Alexis Hotel

## Richmond
Commonwealth Park Suites Hotel

## San Antonio
Marriott Rivercenter

## San Diego
Marriott Mission Valley
Rancho Bernardo Inn
San Diego Hilton
San Diego Marriott
San Diego Princess Resort
Town & Country Hotel

## San Francisco
Campton Place Kempinski
Four Seasons Clift Hotel
Hotel Nikko
Majestic
Mansions Hotel
Marriott Fisherman's Wharf
Pan Pacific
Sheraton at Fisherman's Wharf
Westin St. Francis

## Seattle
Alexis Hotel
Four Seasons Olympic
Inn at the Market
Red Lion Hotel Bellevue
Sheraton Seattle Hotel & Towers
Westin Hotel Seattle

## St. Louis
Clarion Hotel St. Louis
Daniele Hotel
Drury Inn Union Station
Holiday Inn Clayton Plaza
Holiday Inn Downtown/Conv. Ctr.
Holiday Inn Downtown/Riverfront
Seven Gables Inn

## Tampa Bay
Belleview Mido Resort Hotel
Courtyard by Marriott
Hyatt Regency Westshore

## Washington, DC
Canterbury Hotel
Capital Hilton
Carlton
Embassy Row Hotel
Embassy Suites Chevy Chase
Four Seasons Hotel
Guest Quarters
Holiday Inn Crowne Plaza
Hotel Washington
Loews L'Enfant Plaza
One Washington Circle Hotel
Park Hyatt
Ramada Renaissance
Residence Inn Bethesda
Sheraton Premiere
Sheraton Washington Hotel
Stouffer Mayflower Hotel
Tabard Inn
Washington Hilton & Towers
Washington Marriott

# PETS ALLOWED

Watergate Hotel
Willard Inter-Continental

## Arizona

Boulders Resort
El Conquistador
Wahweap Lodge & Marina
Westward Look Resort

## Arkansas

Arlington Resort
Gaston's White River Resort

## California

Auberge du Soleil
Eureka Inn
Fess Parker's Red Lion Resort
Four Seasons Biltmore
Harvest Inn
Inn at Rancho Santa Fe
Lodge at Pebble Beach
Madrona Manor
Ojai Valley Inn
Quail Lodge Resort & Golf Club
San Ysidro Ranch
Sheraton Universal Hotel
Vintage Inn

## Colorado

Antlers Doubletree
Broadmoor
Cheyenne Mountain Conf. Resort
Doral Telluride
Limelite Lodge
Little Nell

## Connecticut

Griswold Inn

## Florida

Brazilian Court
Chalet Suzanne
Plantation Inn
'Tween Waters Inn

## Georgia

Callaway Gardens Resort
Sea Palms Golf & Tennis Resort
Sheraton Savannah Resort

## Hawaii

Four Seasons Resort Wailea
Ritz-Carlton, Mauna Lani

## Idaho

Middle Fork Lodge
Sun Valley Lodge

## Illinois

Indian Lakes Resort
Marriott's Lincolnshire Resort

## Maine

Bayview Hotel & Inn
Bethel Inn & Country Club
Colony Resort

## Maryland

Imperial Hotel
Loews Annapolis
Tidewater Inn

## Massachusetts

Jared Coffin House
Nantucket Inn & Conf. Ctr.

## Minnesota

Fitgers Inn

## Mississippi

Natchez Eola Hotel

## Montana

Chico Hot Springs Lodge
Holland Lake Lodge

## New Mexico

Eldorado Hotel
Inn of the Anasazi
Inn on the Alameda
Sagebrush Inn

## New York State

Beekman Arms
Old Drovers Inn
Point, The

## North Carolina

Green Park Inn
High Hampton Inn & Country Club

## Ohio

Quail Hollow Resort

## Oklahoma

Lake Texoma Resort

## Oregon

Columbia Gorge Hotel
Salishan Lodge
Tu Tu' Tun Lodge

## Pennsylvania

Black Bass Hotel
Historic Strasburg Inn
Sweetwater Farm

## South Carolina

Indigo Inn
Mills House Hotel

## South Dakota

Palmer Gulch Lodge

## Vermont

Basin Harbor Club
Cortina Inn
Middlebury Inn

## Virginia

Boar's Head Inn
Tides Inn

## Washington

Kalaloch Lodge

## Wisconsin

Lakewoods Resort & Lodge

## Wyoming

Ranch at Ucross
Snow King Resort

# RESTFUL

**Atlantic City**
Marriott's Seaview Resort

**Baltimore**
Admiral Fell Inn
Celie's Waterfront
Inn at Henderson's Wharf
Society Hill Hotel

**Boston**
Charles Hotel in Harvard Square

**Cleveland**
Glidden House

**Columbus**
Worthington Inn

**Dallas**
Four Seasons Resort & Club
Hotel St. Germain
Mansion on Turtle Creek
Omni Mandalay Hotel

**Denver**
Oxford Hotel

**Detroit**
Townsend Hotel

**Fort Lauderdale**
Lago Mar Resort & Club
Ocean Manor Resort Hotel

**Honolulu**
Colony Surf Hotel
Halekulani
Hawaii Prince Hotel Waikiki
Kahala Hilton
Royal Hawaiian Hotel
Sheraton Makaha Resort
Sheraton Moana Surfrider
Turtle Bay Hilton

**Houston**
Woodlands Executive Conf. Ctr.

**Los Angeles**
Chateau Marmont
Four Seasons Hotel
Shangri-La

**Miami/Miami Beach**
Doral Ocean Beach Resort
Doral Resort & Country Club
Hotel Place St. Michel

**New Orleans**
Columns Hotel
Cornstalk Hotel

Hotel Maison de Ville
Le Richelieu
Soniat House

**Orange County, CA**
Casa Laguna Inn
Dana Point Resort
Ritz-Carlton, Laguna Niguel
Surf & Sand Hotel

**Orlando**
Courtyard at Lake Lucerne

**Palm Springs**
Doubletree Resort Palm Springs
Hyatt Grand Champions Resort
Hyatt Regency Suites
La Quinta Hotel
Marriott's Desert Springs Resort
Marriott's Rancho Las Palmas
Palm Springs Hilton Resort
Palm Springs Marquis
Palm Springs Riviera Resort
Racquet Club Resort
Ritz-Carlton, Rancho Mirage
Spa Hotel & Mineral Springs
Stouffer Esmeralda
Two Bunch Palms Resort
Westin Mission Hills Resort

**Philadelphia**
Chestnut Hill Hotel
Society Hill Hotel

**Phoenix/Scottsdale**
Buttes
Hyatt Regency Scottsdale
Marriott's Camelback Inn
Phoenician
Pointe at South Mountain
Pointe at Squaw Peak
Pointe at Tapatio Cliffs
Registry Resort
Royal Palms Inn

**Pittsburgh**
Priory - A City Inn

**Raleigh-Durham**
Washington Duke Inn

**San Diego**
Horton Grand
Hotel del Coronado
La Valencia Hotel
Le Meridien San Diego
Loews Coronado Bay Resort

Rancho Bernardo Inn
Rancho Valencia

## San Francisco

Archbishops Mansion Inn
Huntington Hotel Nob Hill
Kensington Park
Lombard Hotel
Majestic
Mansions Hotel
Petite Auberge
Queen Anne
Sherman House
Stanyan Park Hotel
Victorian Inn on the Park
Washington Square Inn

## Tampa Bay

Adam's Mark Caribbean Gulf
Innisbrook Resort
Saddlebrook
Stouffer Vinoy Resort
Trade Winds

## Washington, DC

Henley Park Hotel
Morrison-Clark Inn
Tabard Inn

## Alabama

Marriott's Grand Hotel

## Alaska

Brooks Lodge
Camp Denali
Denali National Park Hotel
Glacier Bay Lodge
Gustavus Inn at Glacier Bay
Yes Bay Lodge

## Arizona

Arizona Inn
Boulders Resort
El Conquistador
El Tovar Hotel
Grand Canyon Lodge
L'Auberge de Sedona
Los Abrigados
Poco Diablo Resort
Rancho de los Caballeros
Ventana Canyon
Westin La Paloma
Westward Look Resort
Wickenburg Inn
Wigwam

## Arkansas

Gaston's White River Resort
Palace Hotel & Bath House

## California

Ahwahnee Hotel
Alisal Ranch
Alta Mira
Auberge du Soleil
Benbow Inn
Big Sur Lodge
Carmel Valley Ranch Resort
Casa Madrona Hotel
Claremont Resort
Deetjen's Big Sur Inn
El Encanto Hotel
Fess Parker's Red Lion Resort
Four Seasons Biltmore
Furnace Creek Inn
Harvest Inn
Heritage House
Highlands Inn
Hill House Inn
Inn at Morro Bay
Inn at Rancho Santa Fe
Inn at Spanish Bay
Inn at the Tides
La Casa del Zorro
La Playa Hotel
Little River Inn
Lodge at Pebble Beach
Los Olivos Grand Hotel
Madrona Manor
Meadowood Resort
Mendocino Hotel
Ojai Valley Inn
Post Ranch Inn
Quail Lodge Resort & Golf Club
Santa Barbara Miramar
San Ysidro Ranch
Silverado Country Club & Resort
Squaw Valley Inn
Stonepine Estate Resort
St. Orres
Timberhill Ranch
Ventana - Big Sur
Vintage Inn
Wine Country Inn

## Colorado

Broadmoor
Charter at Beaver Creek
C Lazy U Ranch

# RESTFUL

Grande Butte Hotel
Home Ranch
Hotel Boulderado
Hotel Jerome
Hotel Lenado
Keystone Lodge
Little Nell
Lodge at Cordillera
Mountain Haus at Vail
Ritz-Carlton, Aspen
Sardy House
Snowmass Lodge & Club
Tall Timber
Tamarron Resort
Vista Verde Guest Ranch

## Connecticut

Boulders
Griswold Inn
Homestead Inn
Interlaken Inn
Mayflower Inn
Riverwind Inn
Stonehenge
Under Mountain Inn
Water's Edge Inn & Resort

## Florida

Amelia Island Plantation
Boca Raton Resort & Club
Club Med Sandpiper
Colony Beach & Tennis Resort
Don Shula's Hotel & Golf Club
Grenelefe Resort
Hawk's Cay Resort & Marina
Hyatt Key West
Lakeside Inn
Little Palm Island
Lodge at Ponte Vedra Beach
Marquesa Hotel
Marriott at Sawgrass Resort
Marriott's Bay Point Resort
Marriott's Casa Marina Resort
Marriott's Marco Island Resort
Mission Inn Golf & Tennis Resort
Ocean Reef Club
Palm Beach Polo & Country Club
PGA National
Pier House Resort
Plantation Inn
Ponce de Leon Resort
Ponte Vedra Inn & Club

Registry Resort
Resort at Longboat Key Club
Ritz-Carlton, Amelia Island
Ritz-Carlton, Naples
Ritz-Carlton, Palm Beach
Sonesta Sanibel Harbour
South Seas Plantation Resort
Sundial Beach & Tennis Resort
'Tween Waters Inn

## Georgia

Callaway Gardens Resort
Cloister
Eliza Thompson
Evergreen Conference Center
Foley House Inn
Gastonian
Greyfield Inn
Jekyll Island Club Hotel
King & Prince Beach Resort
President's Quarters
Sea Palms Golf & Tennis Resort
Sheraton Savannah Resort
Stouffer Pineisle Resort

## Hawaii

Embassy Suites Resort Maui
Four Seasons Resort Wailea
Grand Hyatt Wailea
Hotel Hana-Maui
Hyatt Regency Kauai
Hyatt Regency Maui
Hyatt Regency Waikoloa
Kanaloa at Kona
Kapalua Bay Hotel & Villas
Kona Hilton Resort
Kona Village Resort
Lodge at Koele
Manele Bay Hotel
Maui Marriott
Maui Prince Hotel
Mauna Kea Beach Hotel
Mauna Lani Bay Hotel
Princeville Hotel
Ritz-Carlton, Mauna Lani
Royal Lahaina Resort
Royal Waikoloan
Stouffer Wailea Beach Resort
Stouffer Waiohai Beach Resort
Volcano House
Westin Kauai

## Idaho

Coeur d'Alene Resort
Idaho Rocky Mountain Ranch
Middle Fork Lodge

## Illinois

Eagle Ridge Inn & Resort
Indian Lakes Resort
Nordic Hills Resort & Conf. Ctr.

## Indiana

French Lick Springs Resort

## Iowa

Redstone Inn

## Louisiana

Asphodel Plantation Inn
Madewood Plantation
Nottoway Plantation

## Maine

Asticou Inn/Cranberry Lodge
Bayview Hotel & Inn
Bethel Inn & Country Club
Black Point Inn Resort
Captain Lord Mansion
Cliff House
Colony Resort
Harraseeket Inn
High Tide Inn on the Ocean
Nonantum Resort
Pilgrim's Inn
Poland Spring Inn
Samoset Resort
White Barn Inn
Whitehall Inn

## Maryland

Atlantic Hotel
Imperial Hotel
Inn at Mitchell House
Inn at Perry Cabin
Maryland Inn
Robert Morris Inn
Tidewater Inn

## Massachusetts

Beach Plum Inn
Blantyre
Charlotte Inn
Coonamessett Inn
Daggett House

Harbor View Hotel
Jared Coffin House
Kelley House
Nantucket Inn & Conf. Ctr.
New Seabury Cape Cod
Ocean Edge Resort & Conf. Ctr.
Orchards
Red Lion Inn
Seacrest Manor
Ship's Knees Inn
Summer House
Village Inn
Wauwinet
Wequassett Inn
Westmoor Inn
Wheatleigh
Whistler's Inn
White Elephant Inn
Yankee Clipper Inn

## Michigan

Botsford Inn
Boyne Highlands Inn
Boyne Mountain Hotel
Grand Hotel
Shanty Creek - Schuss Mountain
Stafford's Bay View Inn
Sugar Loaf Resort
Treetops Sylvan Resort

## Minnesota

Breezy Point Resort
Grand View Lodge
Lutsen Resort
Madden's on Gull Lake
Schumacher's New Prague
St. James Hotel

## Mississippi

Burn
Monmouth Plantation
Natchez Eola Hotel

## Missouri

Lodge of Four Seasons

## Montana

Chico Hot Springs Lodge
Flathead Lake Lodge
Gallatin Gateway Inn
Holland Lake Lodge
Kandahar Lodge
Lake McDonald Lodge
Lone Mountain Ranch

# RESTFUL

Many Glacier Hotel
Mountain Sky Guest Ranch
9 Quarter Circle Ranch
Triple Creek Mountain Hideaway

## New Hampshire

Balsams
Christmas Farm Inn
Mount Washington Hotel & Resort
Snowy Owl Inn
Stonehurst Manor

## New Jersey

Abbey
Chalfonte Hotel
Inn at Millrace Pond
Mainstay Inn & Cottage
Queen Victoria
Virginia

## New Mexico

Bishop's Lodge
Dos Casas Viejas
Historic Taos Inn
Inn of the Mountain Gods
Lodge at Cloudcroft
Rancho Encantado Resort

## New York State

Concord Resort Hotel
Elk Lake Lodge
Geneva on the Lake
Gideon Putnam Hotel
Mohonk Mountain House
Montauk Yacht Club
Old Drovers Inn
Omni Sagamore
Otesaga Hotel
Point, The
Three Village Inn
Troutbeck Inn

## North Carolina

Fearrington House Inn
Green Park Inn
Greystone Inn
Grove Park Inn Resort
High Hampton Inn & Country Club
Pinehurst Hotel & Country Club
Richmond Hill Inn
Sanderling Inn Resort

## Ohio

Quail Hollow Resort
Sawmill Creek Resort

## Oklahoma

Lake Texoma Resort
Shangri-La Resort

## Oregon

Columbia Gorge Hotel
Rock Springs Guest Ranch
Salishan Lodge
Sylvia Beach Hotel
Timberline Lodge
Tu Tu' Tun Lodge

## Pennsylvania

Black Bass Hotel
Bridgeton House
Evermay on-the-Delaware
Hotel Hershey
Mount Airy Lodge
Nemacolin Woodlands
Seven Springs Mountain Resort
Skytop Lodge
Split Rock Resort
Sweetwater Farm

## Rhode Island

Atlantic Inn
Doubletree Hotel
Hotel Manisses
Inn at Castle Hill
1661 Inn

## South Carolina

Hilton Head Island Hilton Resort
Hyatt Regency Hilton Head
Indigo Inn
Jasmine House Inn
John Rutledge House Inn
Kiawah Island Resort
Lodge Alley Inn
Marriott's Hilton Head Resort
Mills House Hotel
Planters Inn
Seabrook Island Resort
Sea Pines
Westin Resort
Wild Dunes Resort

## South Dakota

Franklin Hotel
Hotel Alex Johnson

## Tennessee

Buckhorn Inn
Fairfield Glade Resort
Inn at Blackberry Farm

## Texas

Barton Creek
Horseshoe Bay Resort
Lakeway Inn & Conf. Ctr.
Mayan Dude Ranch
Radisson South Padre Island
Sheraton South Padre Island
Tremont House

## Utah

Bryce Canyon Lodge
Cliff Lodge
Grand Canyon Lodge
Shadow Ridge Hotel
Stein Eriksen Lodge
Washington School Inn

## Vermont

Basin Harbor Club
Cortina Inn
Equinox
Hawk Inn & Mountain Resort
Hermitage Inn
Inn at Essex
Inn at Manchester
Inn at Sawmill Farm
Middlebury Inn
Mountain Top Inn
Rabbit Hill Inn
Shelburne House
Stratton Mountain Inn
Sugarbush Inn
Topnotch at Stowe
Trapp Family Lodge
Woods at Killington
Woodstock Inn & Resort

## Virginia

Ashby Inn
Boar's Head Inn

Homestead
Inn at Little Washington
Kingsmill Resort & Conf. Ctr.
Tides Inn

## Washington

Captain Whidbey Inn
Inn at Semiahmoo
Kalaloch Lodge
Rosario Resort & Spa
Salish Lodge
Sun Mountain Lodge

## West Virginia

Greenbrier

## Wisconsin

Abbey
Americana Lake Geneva Resort
American Club
Gordon Lodge
Heidel House Resort
Lake Lawn Lodge
Lakewoods Resort & Lodge
Olympia Resort

## Wyoming

Colter Bay Village
Jackson Lake Lodge
Jenny Lake Lodge
Moose Head Ranch
Paradise Guest Ranch
R Lazy S Ranch
Ranch at Ucross
Roosevelt Lodge
Spring Creek Ranch
Teton Pines Resort

## Spas

Heartland Retreat
Kripalu Center
Lake Austin Resort
Loews Ventana Canyon Resort
Northern Pines
Norwich Inn, Spa & Villas
Russell House
Sonoma Mission Inn & Spa

# ROMANTIC

**Baltimore**
Admiral Fell Inn
Harbor Court Hotel

**Chicago**
Four Seasons Hotel
Park Hyatt
Ritz-Carlton, Chicago

**Dallas**
Adolphus
Four Seasons Resort & Club
Hotel Crescent Court
Hotel St. Germain
Mansion on Turtle Creek

**Denver**
Cambridge Hotel

**Detroit**
Townsend Hotel

**Honolulu**
Halekulani
Hawaii Prince Hotel Waikiki
Kahala Hilton
Royal Hawaiian Hotel
Sheraton Makaha Resort
Sheraton Moana Surfrider
Turtle Bay Hilton

**Houston**
La Colombe d'Or
Ritz-Carlton, Houston
Woodlands Executive Conf. Ctr.

**Los Angeles**
Beverly Hills Hotel
Checkers Hotel Kempinski
Hotel Bel-Air
L'Ermitage Hotel
Peninsula Beverly Hills
Regent Beverly Wilshire
Ritz-Carlton, Huntington Hotel
Ritz-Carlton, Marina del Rey

**Louisville**
Seelbach Hotel

**Miami/Miami Beach**
Biltmore Hotel
Grand Bay Hotel
Mayfair House Hotel Grand Luxe

**Milwaukee**
Pfister Hotel
Wyndham Milwaukee Center

**New Orleans**
Columns Hotel
Hotel Maison de Ville
Soniat House
Windsor Court Hotel

**New York City**
Box Tree
Lowell New York

**Orange County, CA**
Dana Point Resort
Four Seasons Hotel
Ritz-Carlton, Laguna Niguel
Surf & Sand Hotel

**Orlando**
Courtyard at Lake Lucerne

**Palm Springs**
Hyatt Grand Champions Resort
La Quinta Hotel
Marriott's Desert Springs Resort
Ritz-Carlton, Rancho Mirage
Stouffer Esmeralda
Westin Mission Hills Resort

**Philadelphia**
Rittenhouse

**Phoenix/Scottsdale**
Arizona Biltmore
Hyatt Regency Scottsdale
Phoenician
Ritz-Carlton, Phoenix
Scottsdale Princess
Stouffer Cottonwoods Resort

**Portland, OR**
Heathman Hotel
Hotel Vintage Plaza

**Richmond**
Commonwealth Park Suites Hotel

**San Antonio**
Fairmount Hotel
Plaza San Antonio

**San Diego**
Horton Grand
Hotel del Coronado
Kona Kai Resort
Le Meridien San Diego
Loews Coronado Bay Resort
Rancho Bernardo Inn
Rancho Valencia

## San Francisco
Archbishops Mansion Inn
Four Seasons Clift Hotel
Inn at the Opera
Majestic
Mansions Hotel
Petite Auberge
Queen Anne
Ritz-Carlton, San Francisco
Sherman House
Victorian Inn on the Park

## Seattle
Four Seasons Olympic
Inn at the Market
Sorrento Hotel

## St. Louis
Hotel Majestic
Ritz-Carlton, St. Louis
Seven Gables Inn

## Washington, DC
Grand Hotel
Henley Park Hotel
Jefferson Hotel
Morrison-Clark Inn
Morrison House
Ritz-Carlton, Washington DC
Willard Inter-Continental

## Alabama
Marriott's Grand Hotel

## Arizona
Arizona Inn
Boulders Resort
El Conquistador
Enchantment Resort
L'Auberge de Sedona
Westin La Paloma

## Arkansas
Palace Hotel & Bath House

## California
Alta Mira
Auberge du Soleil
Carmel Valley Ranch Resort
Casa Madrona Hotel
Deetjen's Big Sur Inn
El Encanto Hotel
Four Seasons Biltmore
Harvest Inn

Heritage House
Highlands Inn
Inn at Rancho Santa Fe
Inn at Spanish Bay
Inn at the Tides
John Gardiner's Tennis Ranch
La Casa del Zorro
Little River Inn
Lodge at Pebble Beach
Los Olivos Grand Hotel
Madrona Manor
Meadowood Resort
Mendocino Hotel
Ojai Valley Inn
Post Ranch Inn
San Ysidro Ranch
Squaw Valley Inn
Stonepine Estate Resort
St. Orres
Timberhill Ranch
Ventana - Big Sur
Vintage Inn
Wine Country Inn

## Colorado
Doral Telluride
Hotel Jerome
Hotel Lenado
Inn at Beaver Creek
Little Nell
Ritz-Carlton, Aspen
Sardy House

## Connecticut
Boulders
Mayflower Inn
Riverwind Inn
Stonehenge
Water's Edge Inn & Resort

## Florida
Amelia Island Plantation
Boca Raton Resort & Club
Hyatt Key West
Lakeside Inn
Little Palm Island
Marquesa Hotel
Marriott at Sawgrass Resort
Marriott's Bay Point Resort
Marriott's Casa Marina Resort
Ocean Key House
Pier House Resort

## ROMANTIC

Ritz-Carlton, Amelia Island
Ritz-Carlton, Naples
Ritz-Carlton, Palm Beach
Sonesta Sanibel Harbour
South Seas Plantation Resort

### Georgia

Cloister
Foley House Inn
Gastonian
Jekyll Island Club Hotel
Planter's Inn

### Hawaii

Embassy Suites Resort Maui
Four Seasons Resort Wailea
Grand Hyatt Wailea
Hotel Hana-Maui
Hyatt Regency Kauai
Hyatt Regency Maui
Hyatt Regency Waikoloa
Kapalua Bay Hotel & Villas
Kona Village Resort
Lodge at Koele
Manele Bay Hotel
Maui Marriott
Maui Prince Hotel
Mauna Kea Beach Hotel
Mauna Lani Bay Hotel
Princeville Hotel
Ritz-Carlton, Mauna Lani
Royal Waikoloan
Stouffer Wailea Beach Resort
Stouffer Waiohai Beach Resort
Westin Kauai
Westin Maui

### Idaho

Idaho Rocky Mountain Ranch

### Iowa

Redstone Inn

### Louisiana

Asphodel Plantation Inn
Madewood Plantation
Nottoway Plantation

### Maine

Captain Lord Mansion
Pilgrim's Inn
White Barn Inn

### Maryland

Inn at Mitchell House
Inn at Perry Cabin
Maryland Inn
Robert Morris Inn

### Massachusetts

Beach Plum Inn
Blantyre
Charlotte Inn
Jared Coffin House
Orchards
Red Lion Inn
Seacrest Manor
Summer House
Village Inn
Wauwinet
Wequassett Inn
Wheatleigh
Whistler's Inn
Yankee Clipper Inn

### Michigan

Grand Hotel

### Minnesota

Schumacher's New Prague
St. James Hotel

### Mississippi

Burn
Monmouth Plantation

### Montana

Gallatin Gateway Inn
Holland Lake Lodge
Kandahar Lodge

### Nevada

Harrah's Lake Tahoe

### New Jersey

Abbey
Inn at Millrace Pond
Mainstay Inn & Cottage
Queen Victoria
Virginia

### New Mexico

Dos Casas Viejas
Inn of the Anasazi
Rancho Encantado Resort

## New York State

Mohonk Mountain House
Old Drovers Inn
Omni Sagamore
Point, The
Three Village Inn
Troutbeck Inn

## North Carolina

Fearrington House Inn
Pinehurst Hotel & Country Club
Richmond Hill Inn

## Oregon

Columbia Gorge Hotel
Salishan Lodge

## Pennsylvania

Black Bass Hotel
Bridgeton House
Evermay on-the-Delaware
Sweetwater Farm

## Rhode Island

Hotel Manisses
Inn at Castle Hill
1661 Inn

## South Carolina

Indigo Inn
Jasmine House Inn
John Rutledge House Inn
Lodge Alley Inn
Mills House Hotel
Planters Inn
Seabrook Island Resort
Sea Pines
Westin Resort

## Tennessee

Buckhorn Inn
Inn at Blackberry Farm

## Texas

Tremont House

## Utah

Brigham Street Inn
Cliff Lodge
Stein Eriksen Lodge
Washington School Inn

## Vermont

Hawk Inn & Mountain Resort
Hermitage Inn
Inn at Sawmill Farm
Rabbit Hill Inn
Shelburne House
Topnotch at Stowe
Woodstock Inn & Resort

## Virginia

Homestead
Inn at Little Washington

## Washington

Captain Whidbey Inn
Inn at Semiahmoo
Salish Lodge
Sun Mountain Lodge

## West Virginia

Greenbrier

## Wisconsin

American Club

## Wyoming

Spring Creek Ranch

## Spas

Loews Ventana Canyon Resort
Sonoma Mission Inn & Spa

# RUSTIC

**Honolulu**
Sheraton Makaha Resort

**Palm Springs**
Two Bunch Palms Resort

**Raleigh-Durham**
Washington Duke Inn

**San Diego**
Rancho Bernardo Inn

**Seattle**
Edgewater

**Alaska**

Brooks Lodge
Camp Denali
Denali National Park Hotel
Glacier Bay Lodge
Harper Lodge Princess
King Salmon Lodge
Tikchik Narrows Lodge
Waterfall Resort
Yes Bay Lodge

**Arizona**

El Tovar Hotel
Grand Canyon Lodge
L'Auberge de Sedona
Wickenburg Inn

**California**

Ahwahnee Hotel
Alisal Ranch
Auberge du Soleil
Big Sur Lodge
Deetjen's Big Sur Inn
Furnace Creek Inn
Madonna Inn
Mendocino Hotel
Northstar-at-Tahoe
Ojai Valley Inn
Quail Lodge Resort & Golf Club
Squaw Valley Inn
Ventana - Big Sur

**Colorado**

Broadmoor
Cheyenne Mountain Conf. Resort
C Lazy U Ranch
Hyatt Regency Beaver Creek
Lodge at Vail
Radisson Resort Vail
Tall Timber

Vista Verde Guest Ranch

**Connecticut**
Interlaken Inn

**Florida**
'Tween Waters Inn

**Georgia**
Callaway Gardens Resort
Greyfield Inn

**Hawaii**
Hotel Hana Maui
Volcano House

**Idaho**
Idaho Rocky Mountain Ranch
Middle Fork Lodge

**Illinois**
Indian Lakes Resort

**Indiana**
Four Winds Clarion

**Kentucky**
Inn at Shaker Village

**Maine**
Black Point Inn Resort
Poland Spring Inn
White Barn Inn

**Massachusetts**
Coonamessett Inn
Red Lion Inn
Whistler's Inn

**Michigan**
Botsford Inn
Boyne Highlands Inn
Boyne Mountain Hotel

**Minnesota**
Arrowwood, A Radisson Resort
Breezy Point Resort
Grand View Lodge
Lutsen Resort
Madden's on Gull Lake

**Missouri**
Lodge of Four Seasons
Marriott's TanTarA Resort

## Montana

Chico Hot Springs Lodge
Flathead Lake Lodge
Glacier Park Lodge
Holland Lake Lodge
Huntley Lodge
Izaak Walton Inn
Kandahar Lodge
Lake McDonald Lodge
Lone Mountain Ranch
Many Glacier Hotel
Mountain Sky Guest Ranch
9 Quarter Circle Ranch
Triple Creek Mountain Hideaway

## New Jersey

Inn at Millrace Pond

## New Mexico

Inn of the Mountain Gods
Sagebrush Inn

## New York State

Elk Lake Lodge
Guest House
Mohonk Mountain House
Old Drovers Inn
Point, The

## North Carolina

Grove Park Inn Resort
High Hampton Inn & Country Club

## Ohio

Sawmill Creek Resort

## Oregon

Sunriver Lodge & Resort
Timberline Lodge

## Pennsylvania

Black Bass Hotel
Historic Strasburg Inn
Nemacolin Woodlands
Seven Springs Mountain Resort
Split Rock Resort
Sweetwater Farm

## Rhode Island

Newport Harbor Hotel & Marina

## South Carolina

Seabrook Island Resort

## South Dakota

Palmer Gulch Lodge

## Texas

Mayan Dude Ranch

## Utah

Grand Canyon Lodge

## Vermont

Hawk Inn & Mountain Resort
Hermitage Inn
Inn at Sawmill Farm

## Washington

Captain Whidbey Inn
Kalaloch Lodge
Salish Lodge
Sun Mountain Lodge

## Wisconsin

Abbey
Gordon Lodge
Heidel House Resort
Lake Lawn Lodge

## Wyoming

Colter Bay Village
Jackson Hole Racquet Club
Jackson Lake Lodge
Jenny Lake Lodge
Old Faithful Inn
Paradise Guest Ranch
Ranch at Ucross
R Lazy S Ranch
Snow King Resort
Spring Creek Ranch

## Spas

Ashram Retreat
Lake Austin Resort
New Age Health Spa
Northern Pines
Oaks at Ojai
Sans Souci Resort

# SPORTS FACILITIES

(**Bi** = Bicycling; **Bo** = Boating; **Bl** = Bowling; **E** = Exercise, Health
Club and/or Spa Facilities; **F** = Fishing; **G** = Golf;
**Hi** = Hiking; **Ho** = Horseback Riding; **Hu** = Hunting; **I** = Ice Skating;
**J** = Jogging; **S** = Skiing; **Si** = Swimming Pool - Indoors;
**So** = Swimming Pool - Outdoors; **T** = Tennis)

### Albuquerque
Doubletree Albuquerque (S)
Hyatt Reg. Albuquerque (E,So)
Marriott Albuquerque (E,Si,So)

### Anchorage
Captain Cook Hotel

### Atlanta
Aberdeen Woods Conf. Ctr. (E,Si,T)
Atlanta Hilton & Towers (E,J,So,T)
Atlanta Marriott Marquis (E,Si,So)
Atlanta Marriott Perim. (E,Si,So,T)
Atlanta Penta Hotel (E,So)
Courtyard by Marriott (E,So)
Doubletree Hotel at Concourse (J,So)
Embassy Suites Perim. Ctr. (E,J,Si)
French Quarter Suites (E,So)
Holiday Inn Buckhead (So)
Holiday Inn Crowne Plaza (E,J,Si,T)
Hotel Nikko (E,So)
Hyatt Regency (E,So)
J.W. Marriott at Lenox (E,Si)
Lanier Plaza Hotel & Conf. Ctr. (So)
Marque of Atlanta (Bi,E,J,So)
Marriott Suites Midtown (E,Si,So)
Marriott Suites Perimeter (E,Si,So)
Omni Hotel at CNN Center (E,J,Si)
Peachtree (Bi,E,G,Si,So,T)
Radisson Hotel (E,Si,So)
Ramada Hotel Dunwoody (So,T)
Ritz-Carlton, Atlanta (E)
Ritz-Carlton, Buckhead (E,Si)
Sheraton Colony Square Hotel (So)
Stouffer Waverly Hotel (E,J,Si,So)
Summerfield Suites Hotel (So)
Swissotel Atlanta (E,Si)
Terrace Garden Inn (E,Si,So,T)
Westin Peachtree Plaza (E,Si)
Wyndham Garden Vinings (E,So)
Wyndham Garden - Mtwn. (E,Si)
Wyndham Perimeter Center (E)

### Atlantic City
Bally's Grand (E,Si)
Bally's Park Place (E,Si)
Caesars Atlantic City (E,So,T)
Claridge Casino Hotel (E,Si)

Harrah's Marina (Bo,E,Si,T)
Holiday Inn Diplomat (Bi,So)
Marriott's Seaview (E,G,J,Si,So,T)
Merv Griffin's Resorts (E,Si,So)
Sands Hotel & Casino (Bi,E,F,Si)
Showboat Hotel (Bi,Bl,E,So)
TropWorld (E,J,Si,So,T)
Trump Castle Resort (E,J,So,T)
Trump Plaza (E,Si,T)
Trump Regency Hotel (E,Si)
Trump Taj Mahal (Bi,E,Si)

### Austin
Four Seasons Hotel

### Baltimore
Baltimore Marriott (B,E,Si)
Clarion Hotel - Inner Harbor (E)
Cross Keys Inn (E,J,So)
Doubletree Inn (Si)
Harbor Court Hotel (Bo,E,Si,T)
Hyatt Regency (B,E,I,J,So,T)
Inn at Henderson's Wharf (Bo,E,F)
Johns Hopkins Inn (So)
Marriott's Hunt Valley (Bi,E,Si,So,T)
Omni Inner Harbor Hotel (E,So)
Sheraton Baltimore North (E,J,Si)
Sheraton Inner Harbor Hotel (E,Si)
Stouffer Harborplace (E,Si)
Tremont Plaza Hotel (E,So)

### Birmingham
Wynfrey Hotel (E,So)

### Boston
Back Bay Hilton (Si)
Best Western Boston (E)
Boston Harbor Hotel (Bo,E,Si)
Boston Marriott Peabody (E,Si)
Boston Park Plaza (E)
Cambridge Center Marriott (E,Si)
Charles Hotel (Bi,Bo,E,J,Si)
Colonnade Hotel (E,So)
Eliot Hotel (J)
Four Seasons Hotel (E,Si)
Guest Quarters Suite Hotel (E,Si)
Hyatt Regency Cambridge (Bi,E,Si)
Le Meridien Boston (E,Si)
Lenox Hotel (E)

Marriott Copley Place (E,Si)
Marriott Hotel Long Wharf (E,Si)
Midtown Hotel (So)
Ritz-Carlton, Boston (E)
Royal Sonesta (Bi,Bo,E,Si,So)
Sheraton Boston (E,J,Si,So)
Sheraton Commander Hotel (E)
Swissotel Boston (E,Si)
Westin Hotel Copley Place (E,Si)

## Chicago

Barclay Chicago (E,So)
Chicago Claridge Hotel (E)
Chicago Hilton & Towers (E,J,Si)
Chicago Marriott Downtown (E,Si,T)
Chicago Marriott O'Hare (E,Si,So,T)
Chicago Marriott Stes. O'Hare (E,Si)
Drake Hotel (E)
Executive Plaza (E)
Four Seasons Hotel (E,Si)
Holiday Inn City Ctr. (Bi,E,Si,So,T)
Hotel Inter-Continental (E,Si)
Hotel Nikko (E)
Hotel Sofitel (E,Si)
Hyatt Regency O'Hare (E,J,Si)
Hyatt Regency Suites (E,Si)
Mayfair (E)
McCormick Center Hotel (E,Si)
Midland Hotel (E)
Palmer House Hilton (E,Si)
Park Hyatt (E)
Quality Inn (E,Si,So)
Radisson Suite Hotel (E,Si)
Ritz-Carlton, Chicago (E,Si)
Sheraton Chicago (E,J,Si)
Sheraton Plaza Hotel (So)
Stouffer Riviere (E,Si)
Swissotel Chicago (E,Si)
Westin Hotel, Chicago (E)
Westin Hotel O'Hare (E,Si)

## Cincinnati

Cincinnatian Hotel (E)
Cincinnati Marriott (Si,So)
Cincinnati Terrace Hilton (E)
Clarion Hotel Cincinnati (E,So)
Holiday Inn I-275 (E,Si)
Hyatt Regency Cincinnati (E,Si)
Kings Island Inn (E,F,Si,So,T)
Omni Netherland Plaza (E,Si)
Vernon Manor Hotel (E)
Westin Hotel (E,Si)

## Cleveland

Cleveland Marriott East (E,Si,So)
Cleveland Marriott (Bi,Bo,E,F)
Cleveland South Hilton (E,Si,So,T)
Holiday Inn Lakeside (E,Si)
Pierre Radisson Inn (E,So)
Radisson Plaza Hotel (E,Si)
Ritz-Carlton, Cleveland (E,Si)
Sheraton City Centre (E)
Stouffer Tower City Plaza Hotel (E,Si)

## Corpus Christi

Corp. Christi Marriott (Bo,E,F,Si,So)

## Dallas

Adolphus (E)
Aristocrat Hotel (E)
Dallas Grand (E)
Dallas Marriott Park Central (E,So)
Dallas Marriott Quorum (E,Si,So)
Dallas Parkway Hilton (Si,So)
Doubletree Hotel at Park West (E,So)
Doubletree Hotel Campbell Ctr. (E,T)
Doubletree Hotel Lincoln Ctr. (So)
Embassy Suites (E,Si)
Fairmont Hotel (So)
Four Seasons (E,G,J,Si,So,T)
Grand Kempinski Dallas (E,Si,So,T)
Hotel Crescent Court (E,So)
Hyatt Regency Reunion (E,J,So,T)
Loews Anatole Hotel (E,J,Si,So,T)
Mansion on Turtle Creek (E,So)
Melrose Hotel (J)
Omni Mandalay Hotel (E,J,So)
Plaza of the Americas Hotel (E,I,J,T)
Sheraton Park Central (So)
Sheraton Suites (E,Si,So)
Southland Center Hotel (E)
Stoneleigh Hotel (So,T)
Stouffer Dallas Hotel (E,So)
Westin Galleria (I,J,So)
Wyndham Garden Hotel (Si)

## Denver

Burnsley Hotel (So)
Denver Marriott City Center (E,Si)
Doubletree Hotel Denver (E,Si)
Embassy Suites (E,So)
Hyatt Regency Denver (J,So,T)
Hyatt Reg. Tech Ctr. (Bi,E,J,Si,T)
Marriott Southeast (E,J,Si,So)
Radisson Hotel (E,So)
Red Lion (E,Si)

# SPORTS FACILITIES

Residence Inn (E,So)
Scanticon (E,G,J,Si,So,T)
Sheraton Denver (E,J,Si,So)
Stouffer Concourse Hotel (E,Si,So)
Warwick Hotel (So)
Westin Tabor Center (E,Si,So)

## Detroit
Dearborn Inn Marriott (E,So,T)
Hotel St. Regis (E)
Hyatt Regency Dearborn (Bi,E,Si)
Novi Hilton (E,Si)
Omni (E,J,Si,T)
Radisson Pontchartrain (E,So)
Radisson Plaza Hotel (E,So)
Ritz-Carlton, Dearborn (E,J,Si,T)
River Place Inn (E,Si,T)
Townsend Hotel (Bi)
Westin Hotel (E,J,Si)

## Florham Park
Hamilton Park (Bi,E,J,Si,So,T)

## Fort Lauderdale
Bahia Mar Resort (Bo,F,So,T)
Crown Sterling Stes. Cypress (So)
Ft. Lauderdale Mar. (E,F,So,T)
Ft. Lauderdale Marriott N. (E,So)
Lago Mar Resort & Club (Bo,So,T)
Marriott's Hrbr. (Bi,Bo,E,F,S,So,T)
Ocean Manor Resort Hotel (So)
Pier 66 (Bo,E,F,So,T)
Riverside Hotel (So)
Sheraton Design Center (E,So,T)
Sheraton Yankee Clipper (E,So)
Westin Cypress Creek (Bo,E,J,So)

## Fort Worth
Worthington (E,Si,T)

## Hartford
Goodwin Hotel (E)

## Honolulu
Ala Moana Hotel (So)
Colony Surf Hotel (Bi,F,Hi,J,T)
Halekulani (E,So)
Hawaiian Regent (So,T)
Hawaiian Waikiki Beach (So)
Hawaii Prince (Bi,E,F,So,T)
Hilton Hawaiian Village (Bo,E,So)
Hyatt Regency Waikiki (Bo,So)
Ilikai Hotel Nikko Waikiki (E,So,T)
Kahala Hilton (E,So,T)
Outrigger Waikiki (E,So)
Pacific Beach Hotel (So,T)

Park Plaza Waikiki (E,So)
Ritz-Carlton (Bi,Bo,E,G,Si,T)
Royal Hawaiian Hotel (So)
Sheraton Makaha (G,Hi,Ho,J,So,T)
Sheraton Moana Surfrider (So)
Sheraton Princess Kaiulani (So)
Sheraton Waikiki Hotel (Bo,So)
T.B. Hilton (Bi,Bo,E,F,G,Hi,Ho,J,So,T)
Waikiki Beachcomber Hotel (So)
Waikiki Joy Hotel (So)

## Houston
Adam's Mark (E,Si,So)
Allen Park Inn (E,So)
Doubletree at Post Oak (So)
Doubletree Hotel at Allen Center (E)
Fit Inn Charlie Club (E,J,Si,So)
Four Seasons Hotel (E,So)
Guest Quarters (E,So)
Harvey Suites (So)
Holiday Inn Crowne Plaza (E,Si)
Holiday Inn Houston West (Bi,E,J,Si)
Holiday Inn West Loop (E,So)
Hotel Sofitel (E,So)
Houstonian (E,J,So,T)
Houston Marriott Astrodome (E,So)
Houston Marriott West Loop (E,Si)
Houston Marriott Westside (E,So,T)
Hyatt Regency Houston (E,So)
J.W. Marriott Hotel (E,Si,So)
Marriott Medical Center (E,J,Si)
Nassau Bay Hilton (Bo,E,F,J,S,So)
Omni (E,J,So,T)
Plaza Hilton (E,J,So)
Ramada Kings Inn (So)
Ritz-Carlton, Houston (E,So)
Sheraton Astrodome Hotel (E,So)
Sheraton Grand Hotel (E,So)
Stouffer Presidente Hotel (E,So)
Westin Oaks (I,J,So)
Woodlands (Bi,E,F,G,Hi,J,So,T)
Wyndham Greenspoint (So)
Wyndham Warwick Hotel (E,So)

## Indianapolis
Adam's Mark (E,Si,So)
Embassy Suites Hotel (Si)
Holiday Inn Union Station (Si)
Hyatt Regency Indianapolis (E,Si)
Indianapolis Hilton Downtown (So)
Indianapolis Marriott (E,Si,So)
Omni Severin (E,Si)
Radisson Plaza (Si)
University Place (Si)

Westin Hotel Indianapolis (E,Si)
Wyndam Garden Hotel (E,Si)

## Kansas City
Adam's Mark (E,Si,So,T)
Allis Plaza Hotel (E,J,Si,T)
Americana Hotel (E,J,So)
Doubletree Hotel (E,J,Si)
Hilton Plaza Inn (E,So)
Holiday Inn Crowne Plaza (E,Si)
Hyatt Regency Crown Ctr. (E,I,So,T)
Marriott Overland Park (E,Si,So)
Quarterage Hotel (E)
Radisson Suite Hotel (E)
Ritz-Carlton, Kansas City (E,So)
Sheraton Suites (E,Si,So)
Westin Crown Center (E,J,So,T)

## Las Vegas
Aladdin Hotel (So,T)
Alexis Park Resort (E,So)
Bally's (E,So,T)
Binion's Horseshoe (So)
Caesars Palace (E,So,T)
Circus Circus Hotel (So)
Desert Inn (E,G,J,So,T)
Dunes Hotel (G,So)
Excalibur Hotel (So)
Fitzgerald's Casino Hotel (E)
Flamingo Hotel (E,So,T)
Frontier Hotel (So,T)
Golden Nugget (E,So)
Hacienda Hotel & Casino (So)
Imperial Palace (E,So)
Lady Luck Casino Hotel (So)
Las Vegas Hilton (E,So,T)
Maxim Hotel (So)
Mirage (E)
Plaza Hotel (J,So,T)
Riviera Hotel & Casino (E,So,T)
Sahara Hotel & Casino (So)
Sands Hotel & Casino (E,So)
Showboat Hotel (Bl,So)
Stardust Resort & Casino (So)
St. Tropez (E,So)
Tropicana (E,Si,So)
Vegas World Hotel & Casino (So)

## Little Rock
Arkansas' Excelsior (E,F,G,Hu,J,T)

## Los Angeles
Barnabey's Hotel (Bi,F,G,J,Si,T)
BelAge Hotel (So)
Beverly Hills Hotel (E,So,T)

Beverly Hilton (E,So)
Beverly Pavilion Hotel (So)
Biltmore Los Angeles (E,Si)
Century Plaza Hotel (E,J,So)
Chateau Marmont (So)
Checkers Hotel Kempinski (E,So)
Four Seasons Hotel (E,J,So)
Hollywood Roosevelt Hotel (So)
Hotel Bel-Air (J,So)
Hotel Inter-Continental (Bi,E,So)
Hotel Nikko (E,So)
Hyatt at Los Angeles Airport (E,So)
Hyatt on Sunset (So)
Hyatt Regency Los Angeles (E)
Industry Hills Sheraton (E,J,So,T)
J.W. Marriott (E,Si,So)
Le Dufy (So)
Le Parc Hotel (E,So,T)
L'Ermitage Hotel (So)
Loews Santa Monica (Bi,E,Si,So)
Los Angeles Airport Hilton (E,J,So)
Los Angeles Hilton & Towers (E,So)
Malibu Beach Inn (Bo,E,F,Hi,J)
Ma Maison Sofitel (E,So)
Marriott LAX (E,So)
Mondrian Hotel (E,So)
Peninsula Beverly Hills (E,So)
Radisson Bel-Air Summit (So,T)
Radisson Plaza (Bi,E,G,So)
Regent Beverly Wilshire (E,So)
Ritz-Carlton, Huntington (Bi,E,So,T)
Ritz, Marina (Bi,Bo,E,J,So,T)
Sheraton Grande Hotel (So)
Sheraton LAX (E,So)
Sportsmen's Lodge Hotel (E,So)
St. James's Club & Hotel (E,So)
Stouffer Los Angeles (E,So)
Sunset Marquis Hotel (E,So)
Tower at Century Plaza (E,J,So)
Warner Center Marriott (E,Si,So)
Westin Bonaventure (So)
Westwood Marquis Hotel (E,So)
Wilshire Plaza Hotel (E,So)

## Memphis
Peabody Memphis (E,Si)

## Miami/Miami Beach
Alexander (Bo,E,So)
Betsy Ross Hotel (Bi,So)
Biltmore Hotel (Bi,E,G,So,T)
Biscayne Bay Marriott (Bo,F,So)
Colonnade Hotel (E,So)
David William Hotel (So)

## SPORTS FACILITIES

Doral Ocean (Bi,Bo,E,F,S,So,T)
Doral Resort (Bi,E,G,J,So,T)
Doubletree (Bo,E,F,So,T)
Eden Roc Hotel & Marina (So)
Fontainebleau Hilton (E,So,T)
Grand Bay Hotel (E,So)
Grove Isle (Bo,E,F,J,So,T)
Hotel Inter-Continental (Si)
Hyatt Reg. Coral Gables (E,So)
Hyatt Regency Miami (So)
Marlin (Bi,Bo,F,Hi,So)
Mayfair House (So)
Occidental Parc Hotel (E,So)
Omni International Hotel (So)
Radisson Mart Plaza (E,So,T)
Sher Bal Harbour (Bo,E,F,J,So,T)
Sheraton River House (E,So)
Sonesta Bch. (Bi,Bo,E,So,T)
Turnberry Isle (Bo,E,F,G,So,T)

### Milwaukee

Embassy Suites, West (E,Si)
Hyatt Regency Milwaukee (Bi,Bo,F)
Marc Plaza Hotel (Si)
Milwaukee Marriott (E,Si,So)
Milwaukee River Hilton Inn (Si)
Pfister Hotel (E,Si)
Wyndham Milwaukee Center (E)

### Minneapolis/St. Paul

Crown Sterling (Minn/St. Paul) (Si)
Hotel Sofitel (E,Si)
Hyatt Regency (E,J,Si,T)
Minneapolis Marriott City Center (E)
Northland Inn (E,Si)
Radisson Hotel (E,Hi,I,J,Si)
Radisson Hotel Metrodome (E)
Radisson Hotel St. Paul (E,Si)
Radisson Plaza Hotel (E)
Registry Hotel (E,Si)
Saint Paul Hotel (E)
Sheraton Park Place (E,J,Si)

### Nashville

Doubletree Hotel Nashville (E,Si)
Embassy Suites (E,Si)
Holiday Inn Crowne Plaza (E,Si)
Loews Vanderbilt Plaza Hotel (E)
Nashville Airport Marriott (E,Si,So,T)
Opryland Hotel (E,G,So,T)
Regal Maxwell House (E,J,So,T)
Sheraton Music City (E,Si,So,T)
Stouffer Nashville Hotel (E,Si)

### New Orleans

Avenue Plaza Suite & Eurovita (E,So)
Bourbon Orleans Hotel (So)
Clarion Hotel New Orleans (E,So)
Dauphine Orleans Hotel (E,So)
Doubletree (E,F,So)
Fairmont Hotel (E,So,T)
Holiday Inn Crowne Plaza (E,So)
Hotel Inter-Continental (E,So)
Hotel Maison de Ville (So)
Hotel Ste. Helene (So)
Hotel St. Marie (So)
Hyatt Regency New Orleans (E,So)
Inn on Bourbon (So)
Le Meridien Hotel (E,So)
Le Pavillon Hotel (So)
Le Richelieu (So)
Maison Dupuy Hotel (E,So)
Monteleone Hotel (So)
New Orleans Hilton (E,F,J,So,T)
New Orleans Marriott (E,So)
Omni Royal Orleans (E,So)
Place d'Armes Hotel (So)
Radisson Suite Hotel (J,So)
Royal Sonesta (E,So)
Sheraton New Orleans (E,So)
Soniat House (Bi)
St. Pierre (So)
Westin Canal Place (E,So)
Windsor Court Hotel (E,So)

### New York City

Beekman Tower Hotel (E)
Carlyle Hotel (E)
Doral Inn (E)
Dumont Plaza Hotel (E)
Embassy Suites Hotel (E)
Essex House, Hotel Nikko (Bi,E)
Flatotel International (E)
Holiday Inn Crowne Plaza (E,Si)
Hotel Kimberly (E,Si,T)
Hotel Macklowe (E)
Hotel Millenium (E,Si)
Hotel Plaza Athenee (E)
Inter-Continental (E)
Le Parker Meridien (E,J,Si)
Loews New York Hotel (E)
Marriott Financial Center Hotel (E,Si)
Mayfair Hotel Baglioni (E)
Mayflower Hotel (E)
Milford Plaza Hotel (E)
New York Hilton & Towers (E)
New York Marriott Eastside (E)

New York Marriott Marquis (E)
New York Vista (E,J,Si)
Paramount (E)
Peninsula New York (E,Si)
Ramada Midtown (So)
Ramada Renaissance (E)
Regency (E)
Rihga Royal (E)
Ritz-Carlton, New York (E)
Royalton (E)
Shelburne Suite Hotel (E)
Sheraton Manhattan (E,Si)
Southgate Tower Suite Hotel (E)
Stanhope (E)
St. Regis (E)
Surrey Hotel (E)
U.N. Plaza - Park Hyatt (E,Si,T)
Waldorf-Astoria/Towers (E)
Westbury Hotel (E)

## Oklahoma City
Waterford Hotel (E,J,So,T)

## Orange County, CA
Anaheim Hilton & Towers (E,Si,So)
Anaheim Marriott Hotel (E,Si,So)
Casa Laguna Inn (So)
Costa Mesa Marriott (Bi,E,So)
Dana Pt. (Bi,Bo,E,F,Hi,Ho,J,So,T)
Disneyland Hotel (E,J,So,T)
Doubletree Orange County (E,So,T)
Four Seasons (Bi,Bo,E,F,J,So,T)
Hilton Suites In Orange (E,Si)
Hyatt Newporter (E,G,J,So,T)
Hyatt Regency Alicante (E,So,T)
Hyatt Regency Irvine (E,So,T)
Inn at the Park (E,So)
Irvine Marriott (Bi,E,Si,So,T)
Le Meridien Newport (Bi,E,So,T)
Marriott Stes. (E,Si,So)
Newport Beach Marriott (E,So,T)
Red Lion Orange County (E,So)
Ritz-Carlton, Laguna (E,Hi,So,T)
Sheraton Anaheim Hotel (So)
Sheraton Newport Beach (E,So,T)
Surf & Sand Hotel (So)
Westin South (E,J,So,T)

## Orlando
Buena Vista (Bo,E,G,J,Si,So,T)
Clarion Plaza Hotel (So)
Disney's Caribbean (Bo,E,So,T)
Disney's Contemp. (Bo,E,G,J,S,So,T)
Disney's Gr. Florid. (E,F,G,J,S,So,T)

Disney's Polynesian (Bi,E,J,So,T)
Disney's Village (Bi,Bo,E,F,G,J,So,T)
Forte Travelodge Hotel (So)
Grosvenor (G,So,T)
Guest Quarters (E,J,So,T)
Harley Hotel (E,So)
Hilton at WDW Village (Bi,Bo,E,So,T)
Hotel Royal Plaza (G,So,T)
Hyatt Orlando (E,J,So,T)
Hyatt Reg. Grand
   (Bi,Bo,E,G,Hi,J,So,T)
Marriott (E,J,So,T)
Marriott's World Ctr. (E,G,J,Si,So,T)
Omni (E,So)
Orange Lake (Bi,Bo,E,F,G,So,T)
Orlando Heritage Inn (So)
Park Plaza Hotel (J)
Peabody Orlando (E,So,T)
Radisson Inn (E,Si,So,T)
Radisson Plaza Hotel (E,J,S,So,T)
Residence Inn by Marriott (G,Si,T)
Sheraton World Resort (E,So,T)
Sonesta Villa (Bi,Bo,E,F,S,So,T)
Stouffer Orlando (E,J,So,T)
Walt Disney Dolphin
   (Bo,E,F,G,J,So,T)
Walt Disney Swan (Bo,E,G,J,So,T)

## Palm Springs
Autry Resort (Bi,E,Hi,So,T)
Doubletree (Bi,E,G,J,So,T)
Hyatt Gr. Champ. (Bi,E,G,Hi,J,So,T)
Hyatt Regency Suites (So)
La Quinta Hotel (Bi,G,Hi,So,T)
Marr. Desert Spgs. (Bo,E,G,Hi,J,So,T)
Marriott's Rancho (Bi,E,G,So,T)
Palm Springs Hilton (E,So,T)
Palm Springs Marquis (E,So)
Palm Springs Riviera (E,So,T)
Racquet Club Resort (E,Si,So,T)
Ritz-Carlton (Bi,E,Hi,J,So,T)
Shadow Mountain (Bi,E,Hi,So,T)
Spa Hotel & Mineral Springs (E,So)
Stouffer Esmeralda (E,G,So,T)
Two Bunch Palms (Bi,E,J,So,T)
Westin Mission (Bi,E,G,Hi,So,T)
Wyndham (Bi,E,Hi,J,So)

## Philadelphia
Adam's Mark (E,Si,So)
Four Seasons Hotel (E,Si)
Hotel Atop the Bellevue (E,Si)
Hyatt Cherry Hill (E,J,So,T)
Omni Independence Park (E,Si)

## SPORTS FACILITIES

Philadelphia Hilton (E,J,Si)
Rittenhouse (E,Si)
Ritz-Carlton, Philadelphia (E)
Sheraton Society Hill (E,Si)
Sheraton University City (So)
Wyndham (Bi,E,J,Si,T)

### Phoenix/Scottsdale
Arizona Biltmore (Bi,E,G,Hi,So,T)
Buttes (E,Hi,So,T)
Camelview Resort (So)
Crescent Hotel (Bi,E,So,T)
Crown Sterling Suites (Bi,J,So)
Fountains Suite Hotel (E,So,T)
Hyatt Regency Phoenix (E,J,So)
Hyatt Reg. Scottsdale (Bi,E,G,So,T)
John Gardiner's (E,J,So,T)
Lexington Hotel (E,So)
Marriott's Camelback (E,G,J,So,T)
Marr. Mtn. Shadows (E,G,Hi,So,T)
Marriott Suites Scottsdale (E,So)
Omni Adams Hotel (E,J,So)
Orange Tree (E,G,So,T)
Phoenician (Bi,E,G,Hi,J,So,T)
Pointe S. Mtn. (E,G,Hi,Ho,So,T)
Pointe Squaw Pk. (E,Hi,Ho,J,So,T)
Pointe Tapatio (E,Hi,Ho,J,So,T)
Red Lion La Posada (Bi,E,So,T)
Regal McCormick (Bi,Bo,F,G,So,T)
Registry Resort (Bi,E,G,So,T)
Ritz-Carlton, Phoenix (Bi,E,So,T)
Royal Palms Inn (G,So,T)
Scottsdale Conf. (Bi,E,J,So,T)
Scottsdale Hilton (E,So,T)
Scottsdale Plaza (E,J,So,T)
Scottsdale Princess (E,G,J,So,T)
Sheraton Mesa Hotel (E,So,T)
Sher. San Marcos (Bi,Bl,E,G,J,So,T)
Stouffer Cottonwoods (J,So,T)
Sunburst Hotel & Conf. Ctr. (So)
Wyndham Paradise (E,J,So,T)

### Pittsburgh
Hyatt Regency Pittsburgh (E,Si)
Pittsburgh Green Tree (E,Si,So,T)
Pittsburgh Hilton & Towers (E,J)
Pittsburgh Vista (E,Si)
Ramada (E,J,Si)
Sheraton Station Square (E,Si)
Westin William Penn (E)

### Portland, OR
Heathman Hotel (J)
Hotel Vintage Plaza (E)

### Raleigh-Durham
Washington Duke Inn (G,Hi,J,So,T)

### San Antonio
Best Western Crockett (So)
Emily Morgan (E,So)
Hilton Palacio del Rio (E,So)
Hyatt Reg. San Antonio (E,So)
La Mansion del Rio (So)
Marriott Rivercenter (E,Si,So)
Menger Hotel (E,So)
Plaza San Antonio (Bi,E,J,So,T)
Saint Anthony Hotel (E,So)
San Antonio River. Marriott (E,Si,So)
Sheraton Gunter Hotel (E,So)
Wyndham San Antonio (E,Si,So)

### San Diego
Bahia Hotel (Bi,Bo,E,F,J,So,T)
Catamaran (Bi,Bo,E,J,So,T)
Colonial Inn (So)
Doubletree Hotel (E,So,T)
Embassy Suites (E,Si)
Hanalei Hotel (So)
Hotel del Coronado (Bi,Bo,E,So,T)
Humphrey's Half Moon Inn (Bi,So)
Hyatt Islandia (Bi,Bo,F,So)
Hyatt Regency La Jolla (E,So,T)
Hyatt Regency S.D. (Bo,E,J,T,So)
Kona Kai Resort (Bi,Bo,E,J,So,T)
La Jolla Marriott (E,Si,So)
La Valencia Hotel (E,J,So)
Le Meridien (Bi,Bo,E,J,So,T)
Loews Coronado (Bi,Bo,E,F,J,So,T)
Marriott Mission Valley (E,So,T)
Pan Pacific (E,So)
Radisson La Jolla (E,So,T)
Rancho Bernardo (Bi,E,G,J,So,T)
Rancho Valencia (Bi,E,J,So,T)
San Diego Hilton (Bi,Bo,E,J,So,T)
San Diego Marriott (Bi,Bo,E,F,So,T)
San Diego Princess (Bi,Bo,E,J,So,T)
Sea Lodge (So,T)
Sheraton Torrey (E,G,J,So,T)
Sheraton Grande (Bo,E,J,So,T)
Sheraton Hbr. Isl. E. (Bo,E,J,So,T)
Town & Country Hotel (E,So)
U.S. Grant Hotel (E)
Westgate Hotel (E)

### San Francisco
ANA Hotel (J)
Best Western Canterbury (E)
Cathedral Hill (So)

Fairmont Hotel (E)
Four Seasons Clift Hotel (E)
Galleria Park Hotel (J)
Grand Hyatt (E)
Harbor Court Hotel (E,Si)
Hotel Diva (E)
Hotel Nikko (E,Si)
Hyatt at Fisherman's Wharf (E,So)
Mark Hopkins (E)
Marriott Fisherman's Wharf (E)
Parc 55 (E)
Queen Anne (E)
Ritz-Carlton, San Francisco (E,Si)
San Francisco Dtwn. Marriott (E,Si)
San Francisco Hilton (E,So)
Seal Rock Inn (So)
Sheraton Fisherman's Wharf (So)
Sheraton Palace (E,Si)
Sir Francis Drake (E)
Westin St. Francis (E)
York Hotel (E)

### San Jose, CA
Fairmont Hotel (E,So)
Marriott Glenpointe (E,SI)

### Seattle
Doubletree Seattle Inn (So)
Doubletree Suites Seattle (Si)
Edgewater (E)
Four Seasons Olympic (Bi,E,Si)
Holiday Inn Crowne Plaza (E)
Red Lion Hotel Bellevue (E,So)
Sheraton Seattle (E,Si)
Stouffer Madison (E,Si)
Warwick Hotel (E,Si)
Westin Hotel Seattle (E,Si)

### St. Louis
Adam's Mark (E,Si,So)
Cheshire Inn (E,Si,So)
Clarion Hotel St. Louis (E,J,Si,So)
Daniele Hotel (So)
Doubletree Hotel (E,Si,T)
Doubletree Mayfair (E,So)
Drury Inn Union Station (Si)
Embassy Suites (E,Si)
Holiday Inn Clayton Plaza (E,Si)
Holiday Inn Conv. Ctr. (E,Si)
Holiday Inn Riverfront (So)
Hyatt Regency St. Louis (E,J,So)
Marriott Pavilion Hotel (E,Si)
Radisson Hotel Clayton (E,Si,So)

Ritz-Carlton, St. Louis (E,J,Si)
St. Louis Marriott West (E,J,Si)

### Tampa Bay
Adam's Mark (Bi,Bo,S,So,T)
Belleview (Bi,Bo,E,F,G,Si,So,T)
Courtyard by Marriott (E,So)
Crown Sterling Suites (So)
Don Ce-Sar (Bo,E,F,So,T)
Embassy Suites (Bo,E,F,So)
Heritage Hotel (So)
Holiday Inn Ashley Plaza (E,So)
Hyatt Reg. (Bo,E,Hi,J,So,T)
Innisbrook Resort (Bi,E,F,G,J,So,T)
Radisson Bay Harbor Inn (Bo,E,So,T)
Saddlebrook (Bi,E,F,G,So,T)
Sheraton Grand Hotel (J,So)
Sheraton Sand Key (Bi,Bo,F,So,T)
Stouffer Vinoy Resort (E,G,So,T)
St. Petersburg Hilton (Bo,F,So)
Tampa Marriott (E,J,Si,So)
Trade Winds (Bo,E,F,Si,So,T)
Wyndham Harbour (Bo,E,J,So,T)

### Washington, DC
ANA Hotel (E,Si)
Capital Hilton (E,J)
Carlton (E)
DuPont Plaza Hotel (E,Si)
Embassy Row Hotel (So)
Embassy Suites (E,Si)
Four Seasons Hotel (E,J,Si)
Grand Hotel (E,So)
Grand Hyatt Washington (E,Si)
Hay-Adams Hotel (E)
Holiday Inn Crowne Plaza (E,Si)
Hotel Washington (E)
Hyatt Arlington at Key Bridge (E)
Hyatt Fair Lakes (Bi,E,J,Si)
Hyatt Regency Bethesda (E,I)
Hyatt Regency Reston (Bi,E,J,Si)
Hyatt Regency Washington (E,Si)
J.W. Marriott Hotel (E,Si)
Key Bridge Marriott (E,Si,So)
Latham Hotel (So)
Loews L'Enfant Plaza (E,So)
Madison Hotel (E)
Omni Georgetown (E,So)
Omni Shoreham (E,So,T)
One Washington Circle Hotel (So)
Park Hyatt (E,Si)
Radisson Park Terrace Hotel (E)
Radisson Plaza (Bi,E,J,Si,So,T)

## SPORTS FACILITIES

Ramada Renaissance (E,Si)
Residence Inn Bethesda (Si)
Ritz-Carlton, Pent. Cty. (E,Si,T)
Ritz-Carlton, Tysons Corner (E,Si)
Ritz-Carlton, Washington DC (E)
Sheraton Premiere (E,J,Si,So)
Sheraton Washington (E,So)
Washington Court Hotel (E)
Washington Hilton (Bi,J,So,T)
Washington Marriott (E,Si)
Washington Vista Hotel (E)
Watergate Hotel (E,J,Si)
Westfield's Intl. Conf. Ctr. (E,Si,T)
Willard Inter-Continental (E,I)
Wyndham Bristol Hotel (J)

### Wilmington
Hotel du Pont (E)

### Alabama
Marriott's (Bi,Bo,E,F,G,Hi,Ho,J,So,T)

### Alaska
Brooks Lodge (Bo,F,Hi)
Camp Denali (Bi,Hi)
Denali National Park Hotel (Hi)
Glacier Bay Lodge (Bo,F)
Gustavus Inn (Bi,Bo,F,Hi)
Harper Lodge (Bi,Bo,F,Hi)
King Salmon Lodge (Bo,F,Hi)
Red Quill Lodge (Bo,F)
Tikchik Narrows Lodge (Bo,F)
Waterfall Resort (F,Hi)
Yes Bay Lodge (Bo,E,F,Hi)

### Arizona
Arizona Inn (So,T)
Boulders (Bi,E,G,Hi,Ho,J,So,T)
El Conq. (Bi,E,G,Hi,Ho,J,So,T)
El Tovar Hotel (Hi,Ho)
Enchantment Resort (Bi,E,Hi,So,T)
Grand Canyon Lodge (Hi,Ho)
L'Auberge de Sedona (Bi,F,Hi,So)
Los Abrigados (E,So,T)
Poco Diablo Resort (G,Hi,So,T)
Rancho Caballeros (G,Ho,So,T)
Tanque Verde (E,F,Hi,Ho,Si,So,T)
Ventana Canyon (E,G,J,So,T)
Wahweap Lodge & Marina (Bo,F,So)
Westin La Paloma (Bi,E,G,J,So,T)
Westward Look Resort (Hi,J,So,T)
Wickenburg Inn (Ho,So,T)
Wigwam (Bi,E,G,Ho,J,So,T)

### Arkansas
Arlington Resort (E,Hi,So)
Gaston's (Bo,F,Hi,So)
Palace Hotel & Bath House (E)

### California
Ahwahnee Hotel (F,Hi,So,T)
Alisal Ranch (Bo,F,G,Hi,Ho,So,T)
Auberge du Soleil (E,So,T)
Benbow Inn (Bi,Hi)
Big Sur Lodge (Hi,So)
Carmel Valley Ranch Resort (G,So,T)
Casa Sirena (Bi,Bo,E,F,J,So,T)
Claremont Resort (E,Hi,J,So,T)
Deetjen's Big Sur Inn (Hi)
El Encanto Hotel (So,T)
Eureka Inn (So)
Fess Parker's (Bi,E,So,T)
Four Seasons Biltmore (Bi,E,J,So,T)
Furnace Creek (E,G,Hi,Ho,J,So,T)
Harvest Inn (Bi,So)
Highlands Inn (Bi,Hi,So)
Inn at Morro Bay (Bi,Hi,So)
Inn at Rancho Santa Fe (E,So,T)
Inn at Spanish Bay (E,G,Hi,Ho,So,T)
Inn at the Tides (Bo,F,Hi,So)
John Gardiner's (So,T)
La Casa del Zorro (Bi,E,Hi,So,T)
La Playa Hotel (Bi,So)
Little River (Bi,Bo,F,G,Hi,Ho,J,T)
Lodge Peb. Bch.
    (Bi,Bo,E,F,G,Hi,Ho,So,T)
Los Olivos Grand Hotel (Bi,Hi,So)
Madrona Manor (So)
Meadowood (Bi,E,G,Hi,J,So,T)
Monterey Plaza Hotel (E)
Northstar (Bi,E,G,Hi,Ho,S,So,T)
Ojai Valley Inn (Bi,E,G,Hi,J,So,T)
Portofino Hotel (Bi,E,F,J,So)
Post Ranch Inn (So)
Quail Lodge (Bi,G,Hi,J,So,T)
San Luis Bay Inn (Bi,Bo,Hi,So,T)
Santa Barb. Miramar (Bi,E,So,T)
San Ysidro (Bi,E,Hi,Ho,J,So,T)
Sheraton Universal Hotel (E,So)
Silverado Country (Bi,G,J,So,T)
Squaw Valley (Bi,G,Hi,Ho,I,S,So,T)
Stonepine (Bi,E,Hi,Ho,J,So,T)
Timberhill Ranch (Hi,So)
Ventana - Big Sur (E,Hi,J,So)
Villa Royale (Bi,G,Hi,Ho,S,Si,T)
Vintage Inn (Bi,So,T)
Vintners Inn (Bi)

Wawona Hotel (G,So,T)
Wine Country Inn (So)

## Colorado

Antlers Doubletree (E,Si)
Aspen Club Lodge (Hi,S,So)
Breckenridge Hilton (E,Hi,S,Si,So)
Broadmoor (Bi,Bo,E,G,Hi,I,J,So,T)
Charter Beaver (E,G,Hi,I,S,Si,So)
Chey. Mtn. (Bo,E,F,G,Si,So,T)
C Lazy U (F,G,Ho,Hu,I,S,So,T)
Club Med, Copper Mountain (S)
Doral (Bi,E,F,G,Hi,Ho,Hu,I,S,Si,So,T)
Grande Butte Hotel (Bi,F,Hu,S,Si)
Home Ranch (Bi,F,Hi,Ho,S,So,T)
Hotel Boulderado (Bi)
Hotel Jerome (Bi,So)
Hotel Lenado (S)
Hot Springs Lodge (E,So)
Hyatt (Bi,E,F,G,Hi,Ho,I,J,S,Si,So,T)
Inn at Aspen (E,Hi,Ho,I,J,S,So,T)
Inn at Beaver Creek (Hi,S,So)
Iron Hrs. (Bi,E,F,G,Hi,Ho,Hu,I,S,Si,So)
Keystone (Bi,E,G,Hi,Ho,I,S,So,T)
Limelite Lodge (Hi,S,So)
Little Nell (Bi,E,Hi,S,So)
Lodge Cordillera (Bi,E,Hi,S,Si,So,T)
Lodge at Vail (Bi,Bo,E,Hi,S,So)
Mountain Haus at Vail (Hi,S,So)
Pines (Bi,E,F,G,Hi,Ho,Hu,I,J,S,So,T)
Radisson Vail (E,Hi,S,Si,So,T)
Ritz-Carlton, Aspen (E,So)
Sardy House (S,So)
Sheraton Steamboat (G,S,So,T)
Silver Tree Hotel (Bi,E,S,So)
Sitzmark Lodge (S,So)
Snowmass (Bi,E,G,Hi,J,S,So,T)
Sonnenalp (Bi,E,G,Hi,I,J,S,So,T)
Stanley Hotel (E,So)
Tall Timber (F,G,Hi,Ho,J,S,So,T)
Tamarron (E,F,G,Hi,Ho,Si,So,T)
Vail Athletic Club (E,Hi,S,Si)
Vista Verde (Bi,E,F,Hi,Ho,Hu,S)
Westin Resort Vail (Bi,Hi,S,So)

## Connecticut

Boulders (Bi,Bo,F,Hi,Ho,I,S,T)
Homestead Inn (Bi,Hi)
Interlaken (Bi,Bo,E,F,Hi,Ho,J,S,So,T)
Mayflower Inn (Bl,E,Hi,So,T)
Stonehenge (So)
Water's Edge (Bo,E,Si,So,T)

## Florida

Amelia Isl. (Bi,Bo,E,F,G,Hi,J,Si,So,T)
Boca Raton Club (Bo,E,F,G,So,T)
Brazilian Court (Bi,So)
Breakers Hotel (Bi,E,G,So,T)
Captiva Beach (Bi,Bo,F,So)
Chalet Suzanne (F,Hi,So)
Cheeca Lodge (Bi,Bo,F,G,So,T)
Club Med (Bi,Bo,E,F,G,S,So,T)
Colony Beach Resort (Bi,Bo,E,F,So,T)
Don Shula's (E,G,J,So,T)
Grenelefe (Bi,E,F,G,J,So,T)
Hawk's Cay (Bi,Bo,F,J,So,T)
Hyatt Key West (E,So)
Indian River (Bi,Bo,E,F,G,Hi,S,So,T)
Inn at Fisher Island (Bi,Bo,E,F,G,Si,T)
Lakeside (Bi,Bo,E,F,G,Hi,So,T)
Little Palm Island (Bo,E,F,So)
Lodge at Ponte Vedra (Bi,Bo,E,So)
Marquesa Hotel (So)
Marr. Sawgrass (Bi,Bo,E,F,G,J,So,T)
Marr. Bay Point (Bi,Bo,E,F,G,Si,So,T)
Marr. Casa Marina (Bi,Bo,E,F,So,T)
Marr. Marco Island (Bi,Bo,E,F,G,So,T)
Mission Inn (Bi,Bo,E,F,G,J,So,T)
Ocean Grand Hotel (Bi,E,So,T)
Ocean Key House (Bi,Bo,F,So)
Ocean Reef (Bi,Bo,E,F,G,J,So,T)
Palm Beach (Bi,E,G,Ho,J,So,T)
PGA National (Bi,Bo,E,F,G,J,So,T)
Pier House Resort (Bi,Bo,E,F,S,So)
Plantation Inn (Bo,G,So,T)
Ponce de Leon Resort (F,G,J,So,T)
Ponte Vedra (Bi,Bo,E,F,G,So,T)
Reach Resort (E,So)
Registry Resort (Bo,E,F,G,S,So,T)
Rst. at Longboat (Bi,Bo,F,G,J,So,T)
Ritz, Am. Isl. (Bi,E,G,Si,So,T)
Ritz, Naples (Bi,Bo,E,F,So,T)
Ritz-Carlton, Palm Beach (E,So,T)
Sheraton Key Largo (Bo,E,F,So,T)
Sonesta (Bo,E,F,J,Si,So,T)
South Seas (Bi,Bo,E,F,G,J,S,So,T)
Sundial (Bi,Bo,E,F,J,So,T)
'Tween Waters Inn (Bi,Bo,F,So,T)
Windjammer Resort (F,So)

## Georgia

Callaway (Bi,Bo,E,F,G,Hu,J,S,Si,So,T)
Cloister (Bi,Bo,E,F,G,Ho,So,T)
Evergreen
   (Bi,Bo,E,F,G,Hi,Ho,I,J,Si,So,T)
Greyfield Inn (Bi,Bo,F,Hi,Hu)

## SPORTS FACILITIES

Jekyll (Bi,Bo,F,G,Hi,Ho,J,So,T)
King & Prince (Bi,Bo,E,F,Si,So,T)
Mulberry Inn (So)
Sea Palms (Bi,E,G,Ho,J,Si,So,T)
Sheraton (Bi,Bo,E,F,G,J,So,T)
Stouffer (Bo,E,F,G,Si,So,T)

### Hawaii

Embassy Stes. Maui (Bo,E,So)
Four Seasons (Bi,Bo,E,So,T)
Grand Hyatt Wailea (Bi,E,F,So)
Hotel Hana-Maui (Bi,E,Hi,Ho,J,So,T)
Hyatt Reg. Kauai (E,So,T)
Hyatt Regency Maui (Bi,Bo,E,So,T)
Hyatt Waikoloa
  (Bi,Bo,E,F,G,Ho,J,So,T)
Kaanapali Beach Hotel (So)
Kanaloa at Kona (So)
Kapalua Bay (Bo,E,F,G,So,T)
Kona Hilton Resort (F,So,T)
Kona Village (Bo,F,Hi,So,T)
Lodge/Koele
  (Bi,Bl,Bo,E,F,G,Hi,Ho,Hu,So,T)
Manele Bay
  (Bi,Bo,E,F,G,Hi,Ho,Hu,So,T)
Maui Inter-Cont. (Bo,E,F,G,Hi,J,So)
Maui Marriott (Bo,E,J,So,T)
Maui Prince (Bo,E,F,G,Ho,So,T)
Mauna Kea
  (Bo,E,F,G,Hi,Ho,Hu,J,So,T)
Mauna Lani (Bi,Bo,E,F,G,Hi,Ho,So,T)
Princeville (Bi,Bo,E,F,G,Hi,Ho,So,T)
Ritz, Mauna Lani
  (Bi,Bo,E,F,G,Hi,Ho,J,So,T)
Royal Lahaina Resort (Bo,F,So,T)
Royal Waikoloan
  (Bi,Bo,E,F,G,Hi,Ho,J,So,T)
Stouffer Wailea (E,G,So,T)
Stouffer Waiohai (E,So,T)
Westin Kauai (E,G,J,So,T)
Westin Maui (Bo,E,F,J,So)

### Idaho

Coeur d'Alene
  (Bi,Bl,Bo,E,F,G,Hi,Hu,J,Si,So,T)
Idaho Rocky Mountain Ranch
  (Bi,Bo,F,Hi,Ho,S,Si)
Middle Fork (E,F,Ho,Hu,So)
Sun Valley Lodge (I,S,Si,So)

### Illinois

Clock Tower (Bi,E,Si,So,T)
Eagle (Bi,Bo,E,F,G,Hi,Ho,I,S,Si,T)

Indian Lakes (E,G,J,S,Si,So,T)
Marriott (Bo,E,G,J,Si,So,T)
Nordic Hills (Bl,E,G,Si,So,T)
Pheasant Run Resort (E,G,Si,So,T)

### Indiana

Four Winds (Bo,E,Hi,J,Si,So,T)
French Lick (Bi,Bl,E,G,Hi,Ho,Si,So,T)

### Kentucky

Inn at Shaker Village (Bo,Hi)

### Louisiana

Asphodel Plantation Inn (Hi,So)
Madewood Plantation (Hi)
Nottoway Plantation (So)

### Maine

Asticou Inn (Bi,Hi,So,T)
Bayview Hotel & Inn (E,Si,So,T)
Bethel Inn (Bo,E,F,G,Hi,I,J,S,So,T)
Black Point (Bi,Bo,E,F,G,Hi,Si,So,T)
Captain Lord (Bi,Bo,F,Hi,Ho)
Cliff House (E,F,Si,So,T)
Colony Resort (Bi,So)
Nonantum Resort (So)
Pilgrim's Inn (Bi,Bo,Hi)
Poland Spring Inn (Bo,F,G,Hi,So,T)
Samoset (Bi,E,F,G,Hi,J,Si,So,T)
White Barn Inn (Bi,Hi,J)
Whitehall Inn (Hi,T)

### Maryland

Imperial Hotel (Bi)
Inn at Mitchell House (Bi,Bo,F,Hi)
Inn at Perry Cabin (Bi,Bo,E,F,Si)
Robert Morris Inn (Bi,Bo)
Tidewater Inn (So)

### Massachusetts

Blantyre (F,Hi,So,T)
Chatham Bars (Bi,Bo,E,F,G,H,J,So)
Harbor View Hotel (Bo,So,T)
Jared Coffin House (Bi)
Kelley House (So)
Nantucket Inn (E,Si,So,T)
New Seabury (Bi,Bo,E,F,G,J,So,T)
Ocean Edge (Bi,E,G,J,Si,So,T)
Orchards (Bi,E,So)
Publick House (So,T)
Queen Anne (Bi,Bo,F,T)
Red Lion Inn (E,Si)
Seacrest Manor (Bi)
Ship's Knees Inn (So)

Summer House (Bi,Bo,F,Hi,So)
Village Inn (Bi,Hi,I)
Wauwinet (Bi,Bo,E,F,Hi,T)
Wequassett Inn (Bi,Bo,E,F,So,T)
Westmoor Inn (Bi)
Wheatleigh (Hi,So,T)
White Elephant Inn (So)
Yankee Clipper Inn (So)

## Michigan

Botsford Inn (T)
Boyne High. Inn (Bi,E,G,Hi,S,So,T)
Boyne (Bi,Bo,E,F,G,Hi,Hu,I,J,S,So,T)
Grand (Bi,Bo,E,F,G,Hi,Ho,J,So,T)
Grand Traverse (Bi,E,G,I,J,S,Si,So,T)
Shanty (Bi,E,G,Hi,Hu,I,J,S,Si,So,T)
Stafford's Bay View Inn (Bi)
Sugar Loaf (Bi,E,G,S,Si,So,T)
Treetops (E,G,Hi,I,S,Si,So,T)

## Minnesota

Arrowwood
    (Bi,Bo,E,F,G,Hi,Ho,I,J,S,Si,So,T)
Breezy Point (Bi,Bo,F,G,Hi,I,S,Si,T)
Grand View (Bi,Bo,F,G,Hi,Ho,Si,So,T)
Lutsen (Bi,Bo,F,G,Hi,Ho,Hu,S,Si,T)
Madden's (Bi,Bo,E,F,G,Hi,Si,So,T)

## Mississippi

Burn (So)

## Missouri

Lodge of Four Seasons
    (Bi,Bl,Bo,E,F,G,Hi,Ho,J,S,Si,So,T)
Marriott's TanTarA Resort
    (Bl,Bo,E,F,G,Hi,Ho,I,J,Si,So,T)

## Montana

Chico Hot Springs (Bi,F,Hi,Ho,So)
Flathead Lake (Bo,Hi,Ho,S,So,T)
Gallatin Gateway Inn (Bi,F,Hi,So,T)
Glacier Park Lodge (G,So)
Grouse Mountain Lodge (Si)
Holland Lake (Bi,Bo,F,Hi,Ho,Hu,I,S)
Huntley (Bi,E,F,G,Hi,Ho,S,So,T)
Izaak Walton Inn (Bi,Bo,F,Hi,S)
Kandahar Lodge (Hi,Ho,Hu,I,S,T)
Lake McDonald Lodge (Hi)
Lone Mountain Ranch (F,Hi,Ho,S)
Many Glacier Hotel (Bo,F,Hi,Ho)
Mountain Sky (F,Hi,Ho,So,T)
9 Quarter Circle Ranch (F,Ho)
Triple Creek (Bo,F,G,Hi,Ho,S,So,T)

## Nevada

Harrah's Lake Tahoe (Bi,Bl,E,Hi,Si)
Hyatt Lake Tah. (Bi,Bo,E,G,Hi,S,So,T)

## New Hampshire

Balsams (Bi,Bo,F,G,Hi,I,S,So,T)
Christmas Farm Inn (Hi,So)
Mt. Wash. (Bi,G,Hi,S,Si,So,T)
Snowy Owl Inn (Bi,Bo,Hi,S,Si,So)
Stonehurst Manor (Hi,So,T)
Whitney's Inn Jackson (F,Hi,I,S,T)

## New Jersey

Inn at Millrace Pond (T)

## New Mexico

Bishop's Lodge (E,Hi,Ho,So,T)
Dos Casas Viejas (S,So)
Eldorado Hotel (So)
Historic Taos Inn (So)
Hotel Edelweiss (S,T)
Hotel Santa Fe (So)
Inn of the Anasazi (Bi,E)
Inn Mtn. Gods
    (Bi,Bo,F,G,Hi,Ho,Hu,J,S,So,T)
La Fonda Hotel on the Plaza (So)
La Posada de Santa Fe (So)
Lodge at Cloudcroft (G,Hi,S,So)
Quail Ridge Inn (Bi,E,F,Hi,J,So,T)
Rancho Encantado (Hi,Ho,Si,So,T)
Sagebrush Inn (So)
Sheraton Old Town (E,So)
St. Bernard Hotel (S)

## New York State

Concord (Bo,E,G,Ho,I,J,S,Si,So,T)
Doral (Bi,E,G,Hi,J,Si,So,T)
Elk Lake Lodge (Bo,F,Hi,Hu)
Geneva (Bi,Bo,F,J,So)
Gideon Putnam (E,Hi,I,S,So,T)
Guest House (Bi,E,F,Hi,So)
Harrison Conf. Ctr. (Bl,E,Si,So,T)
Mohonk Mtn. (Bo,E,F,G,Hi,Ho,I,J,S,T)
Montauk (Bi,Bo,E,F,Si,So,T)
Omni (Bi,Bo,E,F,G,Hi,Ho,I,S,Si,T)
Otesaga Hotel (G,So,T)
Point (Bi,Bo,F,Hi,Hu,I,J,S)
Three Village Inn (Bi,Bo,F,Hi)
Troutbeck Inn (E,F,Hi,I,Si,So,T)

## North Carolina

Fearrington House Inn (Bi,So)
Green Park Inn (So)

## SPORTS FACILITIES

Greystone (Bo,F,G,Hi,Ho,S,So,T)
Grove Park (E,G,Si,So,T)
High Hampton (Bo,E,F,G,J,T)
Pinehurst (Bi,Bo,E,F,G,J,So,T)
Sanderling (Bi,E,J,Si,So,T)

### Ohio

Quail Hollow (E,G,J,S,Si,So,T)
Sawmill Creek (Bo,E,G,Hi,Si,So,T)

### Oklahoma

Lake Texoma
(Bi,Bo,E,F,G,Hi,Ho,So,T)
Shangri-La (Bl,Bo,E,F,G,J,S,Si,So,T)

### Oregon

Columbia Gorge (Bi,F,Hi,Ho,S)
Embarcadero Resort Hotel (Bo,F,Si)
Inn at Spanish Head (So)
Kah-Nee-Ta (Bi,E,F,G,Hi,Ho,So,T)
Rock Springs (Bi,F,Ho,I,S,So,T)
Salishan Lodge (E,F,G,Hi,J,Si,T)
Sunriver
(Bi,Bo,E,F,G,Hi,Ho,I,J,S,Si,So,T)
Sylvia Beach Hotel (Bo,F,Hi)
Timberline Lodge (S,So)
Tu Tu' Tun Lodge (Bo,F,Hi,So)

### Pennsylvania

Bridgeton House (Bi,Hi,J)
Evermay (Bi,Bo,F,Hi)
Historic Strasburg Inn (Bi,So)
Hotel Hershey (Bi,E,G,Hi,J,S,Si,So,T)
Mt. Airy (Bi,Bo,E,F,G,Hi,Ho,I,S,Si,So,T)
Nemacolin
(Bi,Bo,E,F,G,Hi,Ho,J,S,Si,So,T)
Poc. Manor (Bi,E,F,G,Ho,I,S,Si,So,T)
Seven (Bi,Bo,Bl,E,F,G,Hi,Ho,J,S,Si,So,T)
Skytop Lodge (E,F,G,Hi,S,Si,So,T)
Split Rock
(Bi,Bl,Bo,E,F,G,Hi,Hu,I,S,Si,So,T)
Sweetwater Farm (Bi,Hi,So)

### Rhode Island

Atlantic Inn (T)
Doubletree Hotel (Bo,E,Si,So,T)
Hotel Manisses (Bi,Bo,F,Hi)
Inn at Castle Hill (F)
Newport Harbor Hotel (Bi,Bo,F,Si)

### South Carolina

Hilton head(Bi,Bo,E,F,G,Hi,J,So,T)
Hyatt Reg. (Bi,Bo,E,F,Si,So,T)

Kiawah Island (Bi,Bo,F,G,So,T)
Marriott's (Bi,E,F,Hi,Si,So,T)
Mills House Hotel (So)
Seabrook (Bi,Bo,E,F,G,Hi,Ho,J,So,T)
Sea Pines (Bi,Bo,E,F,G,Hi,Ho,Si,So,T)
Westin Resort (Bi,Bo,E,G,Si,So,T)
Wild Dunes (Bi,Bo,F,G,Hi,So,T)

### South Dakota

Hotel Alex Johnson (E,Hi)
Palmer Gulch (Bi,F,Hi,Ho,So)

### Tennessee

Buckhorn Inn (Bi,F,Hi)
Fairfield Glade
(Bo,E,F,G,Ho,J,Si,So,T)
Inn/Blackberry (Bi,F,Hi,J,So,T)

### Texas

Barton
(Bi,Bo,E,F,G,Hi,Ho,Hu,J,S,Si,So,T)
Flying L Guest (G,Hi,Ho,So,T)
Horseshoe (Bo,F,G,Ho,J,S,So,T)
Lakeway (Bo,E,F,G,S,So,T)
Mayan Dude (E,F,Hi,Ho,So,T)
Radisson (Bo,F,So,T)
Sheraton (Si,So,T)

### Utah

Bryce Canyon Lodge (Bi,F,Hi,Ho)
Cliff Lodge (Bi,E,F,Hi,S,So,T)
Grand Canyon Lodge (Hi,Ho)
Shadow Ridge Hotel (Bi,E,S,So)
Stein Eriksen
(Bi,E,F,G,Hi,Ho,I,S,So,T)

### Vermont

Basin Harbor (Bi,Bo,F,G,Hi,So,T)
Cortina Inn (Bi,E,F,Hi,I,Si,T)
Equinox
(Bi,Bo,E,F,G,Hi,Ho,Hu,Si,So,T)
Hawk Inn (Bi,Bo,E,F,Hi,Ho,I,S,Si,T)
Hermitage Inn (Bi,Hi,Hu,S,So,T)
Inn at Manchester (Bi,Hi,S,So)
Inn at Sawmill
(Bi,F,Hi,Ho,Hu,I,J,S,So,T)
Mtn. Top
(Bi,Bo,F,G,Hi,Ho,Hu,I,J,S,So,T)
Rabbit Hill Inn (Bo,F,Hi,So)
Shelburne House (Bo,F,Hi,J,T)
Stratton (Bi,F,Hi,Hu,I,S,So,T)
Sugarbush
(Bi,E,G,Hi,Ho,I,J,S,Si,So,T)

Topnotch (Bi,E,Hi,Ho,Hu,S,Si,So,T)
Trapp (E,F,Hi,S,Si,So,T)
Woods (B,E,F,G,Hi,Ho,I,S,Si,T)
Woodstock (Bi,E,G,Hi,I,S,Si,So,T)

## Virginia

Ashby Inn (Hi)
Boar's Head (Bi,E,F,G,Hi,J,So,T)
Homestead
　(Bl,E,F,G,Hi,Ho,I,J,S,Si,So,T)
Inn at Little Washington (Bi,F)
Kingsmill (Bo,E,F,G,J,Si,So,T)
Lansdowne (E,G,Si,So,T)
Manor House (E,G,J,So,T)
Tides Inn (Bi,Bo,E,F,G,So,T)
Williamsburg Hosp. House (So)
Wmsbg. Inn (Bi,E,G,J,Si,So,T)

## Washington

Captain Whidbey Inn (Bi,Bo)
Inn/Semiahmoo
　(Bi,E,F,G,Hi,J,Si,So,T)
Kalaloch Lodge (Bi,F,Hi)
Lake Quinault Lodge (Si)
Rosario (E,F,Hi,Si,So,T)
Salish Lodge (Bi,E,Hi,T)
Sun Mtn. (Bi,Bo,E,F,Hi,Ho,I,S,So,T)

## West Virginia

Greenbrier
　(Bi,Bl,E,F,G,Hi,Ho,I,J,Si,So,T)

## Wisconsin

Abbey (Bi,Bo,E,F,G,Hi,I,J,Si,So,T)
Americana (Bi,Bo,E,G,Ho,S,Si,So,T)
American Club
　(Bi,Bo,E,F,G,Hi,Ho,Hu,I,J,S,Si,T)
Gordon (Bi,Bo,E,F,Hi,J,So,T)
Heidel (Bi,Bo,E,F,G,Hi,I,Si,So,T)
Lake Lawn
　(Bi,Bo,E,F,G,Ho,I,S,Si,So,T)
Lakewoods
　(Bi,Bo,E,F,Hi,Hu,I,S,Si,So,T)
Olympia Resort (E,G,I,S,Si,So,T)

## Wyoming

Colter Bay Village (Bi,Bo,F,Hi,Ho)
Jackson Hole R.C. (Bi,E,J,So,T)
Jackson Lake (F,G,Hi,Ho,So,T)
Jenny Lake (Bi,Bo,F,G,Hi,Ho,T)
Mammoth (F,Hi,Ho,I,S)
Moose Head Ranch (F,Hi,Ho)

Old Faithful Inn (F,Hi)
Paradise Guest Ranch (F,Hi,Ho,So)
Ranch at Ucross (Bi,Hi,Ho,Hu,So,T)
R Lazy S Ranch (F,Hi,Ho,S)
Roosevelt Lodge (F,Hi,Ho)
Snow King (Bi,F,Hi,Ho,Hu,I,S,So,T)
Spring Creek (Bi,F,Hi,Ho,I,S,So,T)
Teton Pines Resort (F,G,Hi,S,So,T)
Wort Hotel (E)

## Spas

Ashram Retreat (E,Hi,J,So)
Bonaventure (Bl,E,G,Ho,J,So,T)
Bon Reussite Resort (Bi,E,J,Si,So,T)
Cal-A-Vie (E,Hi,So,T)
Canyon/Berkshires
　(Bi,Bo,E,Hi,J,S,Si,So,T)
Canyon Ranch (Bi,E,Hi,Si,So,T)
Deerfield Manor Spa (E,Hi,So,T)
Doral Saturnia (Bi,Bo,E,F,G,J,Si,So,T)
Golden Door (E,Hi,So,T)
Greenhouse (E,J,Si,So,T)
Green Mountain (Bi,E,Hi,J,S,T)
Gurney's Inn Resort & Spa (E,Si)
Harbor Island (E,F,So,T)
Heartland (Bi,E,Hi,J,S,Si,T)
Hilton Head Health Inst. (Bi,E,Hi,So)
Jimmy Le Sage's (E,Hi,Ho,Si,So,T)
Kerr House (E,Hi)
Kripalu Center (So)
La Costa (Bi,E,G,Hi,J,So,T)
Lake Austin
　(Bi,Bo,E,F,G,Hi,Ho,J,Si,So)
Loews Ventana (Bi,E,G,Hi,So,T)
Maine Chance (Bi,E,Hi,J,Si,So,T)
Mario's (Bi,E,Hi,Si,So,T)
Murrieta (Bi,E,G,So,T)
National Inst. (Bi,E,Hi,Si,T)
New Age (E,Hi,S,Si,So,T)
Northern Pines (Bo,E,Hi,S)
Norwich Inn (E,F,J,Si,So,T)
Oaks at Ojai (Bi,E,Hi,J,So,T)
Palm-Aire (E,G,J,So,T)
Palms (Bi,E,Hi,So)
Phoenix Health Spa (E,J,So,T)
Rancho La Puerta (E,Hi,J,So)
Russell House (E,So)
Safety Harbor Spa (Bi,E,Si,So,T)
Sans Souci Resort (E,Hi,Ho,So)
Shangri-La Health Spa (So,T)
Sonoma Mission (Bi,E,Hi,J,So,T)
Vista Clara Spa (E,Hi,J,So)

# STUDENT BUDGET

## Atlanta
Biltmore Suites
Courtyard by Marriott
French Quarter Suites
Holiday Inn Buckhead
Lanier Plaza Hotel & Conf. Ctr.
Ramada Hotel Dunwoody
Terrace Garden Inn - Buckhead
Wyndham Garden Hotel - Vinings
Wyndham Perimeter Center

## Atlantic City
Holiday Inn Diplomat
Merv Griffin's Resorts
Trump Regency Hotel

## Baltimore
Johns Hopkins Inn
Marriott's Hunt Valley Inn
Tremont Hotel
Tremont Plaza Hotel

## Boston
Best Western Boston
Harvard Manor House
Midtown Hotel

## Chicago
Allerton Hotel
Best Western Inn
Bismarck Hotel
Lenox House Suites
Palmer House Hilton
Quality Inn & Clarion Hotel
Richmont Hotel

## Cincinnati
Cincinnati Terrace Hilton
Clarion Hotel Cincinnati
Holiday Inn I-275
Kings Island Inn & Conf. Ctr.

## Cleveland
Holiday Inn Lakeside City Center

## Dallas
Aristocrat Hotel
Dallas Grand
Dallas Marriott Park Central
Embassy Suites

## Detroit
Mayflower Bed & Breakfast

## Fort Lauderdale
Crown Sterling Suites Cypress
Lago Mar Resort & Club

Ocean Manor Resort Hotel
Riverside Hotel
Sheraton Yankee Clipper

## Honolulu
Ala Moana Hotel
Hawaiian Waikiki Beach Hotel
Outrigger Waikiki
Waikiki Beachcomber Hotel
Waikiki Joy Hotel

## Houston
Allen Park Inn
Fit Inn Charlie Club
Harvey Suites
Holiday Inn Houston West
Holiday Inn West Loop
Houston Marriott Astrodome
Nassau Bay Hilton & Marina
Ramada Kings Inn
Sheraton Astrodome Hotel

## Indianapolis
Indianapolis Hilton Downtown

## Kansas City
Adam's Mark
Americana Hotel on Convention
Hilton Plaza Inn
Hotel Savoy
Quarterage Hotel

## Las Vegas
Aladdin Hotel
Bally's
Binion's Horseshoe
Circus Circus Hotel
Dunes Hotel & Country Club
Excalibur Hotel
Fitzgerald's Casino Hotel
Flamingo Hotel
Four Queens Hotel & Casino
Frontier Hotel
Hacienda Hotel & Casino
Imperial Palace Hotel & Casino
Lady Luck Casino Hotel
Maxim Hotel
Plaza Hotel
Riviera Hotel & Casino
Sahara Hotel & Casino
Sam Boyd's Fremont Hotel
Sands Hotel & Casino
Showboat Hotel
Stardust Resort & Casino
St. Tropez

Tropicana Hotel & Country Club
Vegas World Hotel & Casino

**Los Angeles**
Hollywood Roosevelt Hotel
Hyatt on Sunset
Industry Hills Sheraton Resort
Shangri-La
Sportsmen's Lodge Hotel

**Miami/Miami Beach**
Betsy Ross Hotel
David William Hotel
Eden Roc Hotel & Marina
Occidental Parc Hotel

**Milwaukee**
Astor Hotel
Manchester Suites - Airport
Milwaukee River Hilton Inn
Park East Hotel

**Minneapolis/St. Paul**
Radisson Hotel Metrodome
Radisson Hotel St. Paul
Registry Hotel
Sheraton Park Place

**New Orleans**
Avenue Plaza Suite & Eurovita
Clarion Hotel New Orleans
Columns Hotel
LaMothe House
St. Pierre

**New York City**
Edison Hotel
Gramercy Park Hotel
Hotel Beverly
Hotel Elysee
Hotel Pickwick Arms
Hotel Wales
Journey's End Hotel
Milford Plaza Hotel
Novotel New York
Radisson Empire Hotel
Ramada Midtown
Ramada Hotel
Roosevelt Hotel
Sheraton Park Avenue
Southgate Tower Suite Hotel
Wyndham Hotel

**Orange County, CA**
Inn at the Park
Sheraton Anaheim Hotel

**Orlando**
Clarion Plaza Hotel
Forte Travelodge Hotel
Harley Hotel
Orlando Heritage Inn
Radisson Inn International Dr.
Sheraton World Resort

**Palm Springs**
Palm Springs Riviera Resort
Racquet Club Resort
Shadow Mountain Resort
Spa Hotel & Mineral Springs

**Philadelphia**
Penn Tower Hotel

**Phoenix/Scottsdale**
Camelview Resort
Crescent Hotel
Fountains Suite Hotel
Lexington Hotel & City Square
Royal Palms Inn
Sheraton Mesa Hotel
Sunburst Hotel & Conf. Ctr.

**Pittsburgh**
Pittsburgh Green Tree Marriott
Priory - A City Inn
Ramada

**Raleigh-Durham**
Carolina Inn

**San Antonio**
Best Western Historical Crockett
Emily Morgan

**San Diego**
Bahia Hotel
Hanalei Hotel
Humphrey's Half Moon Inn
Radisson La Jolla
Town & Country Hotel

**San Francisco**
Andrews Hotel
Beresford Arms
Best Western Canterbury
Cartwright Hotel
Chancellor Hotel
Hotel Bedford
Hotel Diva
Hotel Vintage Court
Juliana Hotel
Lombard Hotel
Orchard Hotel

## STUDENT BUDGET

Raphael Hotel
Seal Rock Inn
Stanyan Park Hotel
Victorian Inn on the Park

**Seattle**
Doubletree Seattle Inn

**St. Louis**
Cheshire Inn Motor Hotel
Clarion Hotel St. Louis
Drury Inn Union Station
Holiday Inn Clayton Plaza
Holiday Inn Downtown/Conv. Ctr.
Holiday Inn Downtown/Riverfront

**Tampa Bay**
Courtyard by Marriott
Heritage Hotel
Holiday Inn Ashley Plaza
Radisson Bay Harbor Inn
Sheraton Grand Hotel

**Washington, DC**
Inn at Foggy Bottom
Tabard Inn

**Alaska**
Denali National Park Hotel

**Arizona**
Grand Canyon Lodge
Hassayampa Inn
Wahweap Lodge & Marina
Westward Look Resort

**Arkansas**
Arlington Resort
Gaston's White River Resort
Palace Hotel & Bath House

**California**
Benbow Inn
Big Sur Lodge
Casa Sirena Marina Resort
La Casa del Zorro
Madonna Inn
Mendocino Hotel
Northstar-at-Tahoe
Wawona Hotel

**Colorado**
Hot Springs Lodge
Limelite Lodge
Sitzmark Lodge

**Connecticut**
Griswold Inn

**Florida**
Captiva Beach Resort
Grenelefe Resort
Indian River Plantation Resort
Ponce de Leon Resort
'Tween Waters Inn
Windjammer Resort

**Georgia**
Jekyll Island Club Hotel
Mulberry Inn
Planter's Inn
Sea Palms Golf & Tennis Resort

**Hawaii**
Kona Hilton Resort
Royal Lahaina Resort
Royal Waikoloan
Volcano House

**Indiana**
French Lick Springs Resort

**Kentucky**
Beaumont Inn
Inn at Shaker Village

**Louisiana**
Asphodel Plantation Inn

**Maine**
Bethel Inn & Country Club
High Tide Inn on the Ocean
Poland Spring Inn
Whitehall Inn

**Maryland**
Atlantic Hotel

**Massachusetts**
Kelley House
Publick House
Seacrest Manor
Ship's Knees Inn

**Michigan**
Botsford Inn
Stafford's Bay View Inn
Treetops Sylvan Resort

## Minnesota

Breezy Point Resort
Fitgers Inn
St. James Hotel

## Mississippi

Burn

## Montana

Chico Hot Springs Lodge
Gallatin Gateway Inn
Glacier Park Lodge
Grouse Mountain Lodge
Holland Lake Lodge
Izaak Walton Inn
Kandahar Lodge
Lake McDonald Lodge
Many Glacier Hotel

## New Hampshire

Snowy Owl Inn

## New Jersey

Inn at Millrace Pond

## New Mexico

Historic Taos Inn
Hotel Plaza Real
Inn of the Mountain Gods
Sagebrush Inn

## New York State

Beekman Arms
Clarion Inn at Saratoga
Three Village Inn

## North Carolina

High Hampton Inn & Country Club

## Ohio

Quail Hollow Resort

## Oklahoma

Lake Texoma Resort

## Oregon

Kah-Nee-Ta Resort
Sylvia Beach Hotel

## Pennsylvania

Black Bass Hotel
Historic Strasburg Inn
Mount Airy Lodge

## Rhode Island

Atlantic Inn

## South Carolina

Hilton Head Island Hilton Resort

## South Dakota

Franklin Hotel
Hotel Alex Johnson
Palmer Gulch Lodge

## Tennessee

Fairfield Glade Resort

## Texas

Flying L Guest Ranch

## Utah

Bryce Canyon Lodge
Grand Canyon Lodge

## Vermont

Mountain Top Inn

## Virginia

Williamsburg Hospitality House

## Washington

Lake Quinault Lodge
Rosario Resort & Spa

## Wisconsin

Americana Lake Geneva Resort
Lakewoods Resort & Lodge

## Wyoming

Colter Bay Village
Mammoth Hot Springs Hotel
Old Faithful Inn
Ranch at Ucross
Roosevelt Lodge

## Spas

Murrieta Hot Springs Resort

# TEAS

**Atlanta**
Ansley Inn
Hotel Nikko
Ritz-Carlton, Atlanta
Ritz-Carlton, Buckhead

**Baltimore**
Harbor Court Hotel
Stouffer Harborplace

**Boston**
Boston Harbor Hotel
Boston Park Plaza
Charles Hotel in Harvard Square
Four Seasons Hotel
Ritz-Carlton, Boston

**Chicago**
Chicago Hilton & Towers
Drake Hotel
Fairmont Hotel
Four Seasons Hotel
Hotel Inter-Continental
Hotel Nikko
Mayfair
Park Hyatt
Ritz-Carlton, Chicago
Sheraton Chicago Hotel & Towers
Stouffer Riviere

**Cincinnati**
Cincinnatian Hotel

**Cleveland**
Cleveland Marriott Society Center
Glidden House

**Dallas**
Adolphus

**Denver**
Brown Palace Hotel

**Detroit**
Hyatt Regency Dearborn
Ritz-Carlton, Dearborn
Townsend Hotel

**Honolulu**
Halekulani
Hawaii Prince Hotel Waikiki
Kahala Hilton
Ritz-Carlton Kapalua
Sheraton Moana Surfrider

**Houston**
Omni
Ritz-Carlton, Houston

**Indianapolis**
Canterbury Hotel

**Kansas City**
Ritz-Carlton, Kansas City

**Los Angeles**
Barnabey's Hotel
Beverly Hilton
Beverly Pavilion Hotel
Biltmore Los Angeles
Century Plaza Hotel
Checkers Hotel Kempinski
Four Seasons Hotel
Hotel Bel-Air
J.W. Marriott at Century City
Le Parc Hotel
Peninsula Beverly Hills
Regent Beverly Wilshire
Ritz-Carlton, Huntington Hotel
Ritz-Carlton, Marina del Rey
Shangri-La
St. James's Club & Hotel
Tower at Century Plaza
Westwood Marquis Hotel

**Memphis**
Peabody Memphis

**Miami/Miami Beach**
Biltmore Hotel
Grand Bay Hotel
Hotel Place St. Michel
Mayfair House Hotel Grand Luxe

**New Orleans**
Columns Hotel
Dauphine Orleans Hotel
Hotel Maison de Ville
Royal Sonesta
Soniat House
Windsor Court Hotel

**New York City**
Algonquin Hotel
Carlyle Hotel
Helmsley Palace
Helmsley Park Lane Hotel
Hotel Macklowe
Hotel Plaza Athenee
Inter-Continental
Lowell New York
Mark
Mayfair Hotel Baglioni
Morgans
Omni Berkshire Place

Peninsula New York
Pierre
Plaza Hotel
Royalton
Sheraton New York
Stanhope
St. Regis
Waldorf-Astoria/Towers

**Orange County, CA**
Casa Laguna Inn
Dana Point Resort
Four Seasons Hotel
Ritz-Carlton, Laguna Niguel

**Orlando**
Peabody Orlando

**Palm Springs**
Autry Resort
La Quinta Hotel
Ritz-Carlton, Rancho Mirage
Two Bunch Palms Resort
Westin Mission Hills Resort

**Philadelphia**
Four Seasons Hotel
Hotel Atop the Bellevue
Independence Park Inn
Rittenhouse
Ritz-Carlton, Philadelphia

**Phoenix/Scottsdale**
Fountains Suite Hotel
Phoenician
Ritz-Carlton, Phoenix

**Pittsburgh**
Westin William Penn

**Portland, OR**
Heathman Hotel

**San Diego**
Horton Grand
Hyatt Regency La Jolla
La Valencia Hotel
Rancho Bernardo Inn
Sheraton Grande at Torrey Pines
U.S. Grant Hotel

**San Francisco**
Archbishops Mansion Inn
Campton Place Kempinski
Fairmont Hotel
Four Seasons Clift Hotel
Grand Hyatt

Hotel Diva
Inn at the Opera
Inn at Union Square
Juliana Hotel
Kensington Park
Lombard Hotel
Mandarin Oriental
Mansions Hotel
Mark Hopkins Inter-Continental
Miyako Hotel
Park Hyatt
Petite Auberge
Queen Anne
Ritz-Carlton, San Francisco
Sheraton Palace
Stanyan Park Hotel
Stouffer Stanford Court Hotel
Tuscan Inn
Victorian Inn on the Park
Washington Square Inn
Westin St. Francis

**San Jose, CA**
Fairmont Hotel

**Seattle**
Four Seasons Olympic
Holiday Inn Crowne Plaza
Sheraton Seattle Hotel & Towers
Sorrento Hotel

**St. Louis**
Adam's Mark
Ritz-Carlton, St. Louis

**Washington, DC**
Carlton
Four Seasons Hotel
Hay-Adams Hotel
Henley Park Hotel
Hotel Washington
Jefferson Hotel
Madison Hotel
Morrison House
Park Hyatt
Ritz-Carlton, Pentagon City
Ritz-Carlton, Tysons Corner
Ritz-Carlton, Washington DC
Stouffer Mayflower Hotel
Tabard Inn
Watergate Hotel
Willard Inter-Continental

**Alabama**
Marriott's Grand Hotel

# TEAS

## Alaska
Gustavus Inn at Glacier Bay

## Arizona
L'Auberge de Sedona

## California
Ahwahnee Hotel
Benbow Inn
Four Seasons Biltmore
Furnace Creek Inn
Heritage House
Meadowood Resort
Quail Lodge Resort & Golf Club
Ventana - Big Sur
Vintage Inn

## Colorado
Broadmoor
Doral Telluride
Inn at Beaver Creek
Limelite Lodge
Little Nell
Pines Lodge at Beaver Creek
Ritz-Carlton, Aspen

## Connecticut
Boulders
Mayflower Inn
Under Mountain Inn

## Florida
Boca Raton Resort & Club
Brazilian Court
Breakers Hotel
Lodge at Ponte Vedra Beach
Ritz-Carlton, Amelia Island
Ritz-Carlton, Naples
Ritz-Carlton, Palm Beach

## Georgia
Cloister
Gastonian
Eliza Thompson
Foley House Inn
Jekyll Island Club Hotel
Planter's Inn
President's Quarters

## Hawaii
Kapalua Bay Hotel & Villas
Lodge at Koele

Manele Bay Hotel
Princeville Hotel

## Idaho
Coeur d'Alene Resort

## Indiana
French Lick Springs Resort

## Iowa
Redstone Inn

## Kentucky
Inn at Shaker Village

## Maine
Asticou Inn/Cranberry Lodge
Black Point Inn Resort
Captain Lord Mansion
Harraseeket Inn
White Barn Inn
Whitehall Inn

## Maryland
Imperial Hotel
Inn at Mitchell House
Inn at Perry Cabin

## Massachusetts
Charlotte Inn
Orchards
Seacrest Manor
Village Inn
Wauwinet
Whistler's Inn

## Michigan
Grand Hotel
Stafford's Bay View Inn

## New Hampshire
Stonehurst Manor

## New Jersey
Abbey
Mainstay Inn & Cottage
Queen Victoria

## New Mexico
Hotel Edelweiss
Hotel St. Francis
Rancho Encantado Resort

**New York State**

Mohonk Mountain House
Old Drovers Inn
Omni Sagamore
Troutbeck Inn

**North Carolina**

Fearrington House Inn
Greystone Inn
High Hampton Inn & Country Club
Richmond Hill Inn

**Oregon**

Salishan Lodge
Sylvia Beach Hotel

**Pennsylvania**

Bridgeton House
Evermay on-the-Delaware
Nemacolin Woodlands

**Rhode Island**

Inntowne Inn
1661 Inn

**South Carolina**

Indigo Inn
Jasmine House Inn
John Rutledge House Inn
Planters Inn
Vendue Inn
Westin Resort

**Utah**

Brigham Street Inn
Stein Eriksen Lodge
Washington School Inn

**Vermont**

Cortina Inn
Inn at Manchester
Inn at Sawmill Farm
Middlebury Inn
Rabbit Hill Inn
Sugarbush Inn
Topnotch at Stowe
Trapp Family Lodge
Woodstock Inn & Resort

**Virginia**

Boar's Head Inn
Homestead
Inn at Little Washington
Williamsburg Inn

**Washington**

Captain Whidbey Inn
Salish Lodge

**West Virginia**

Greenbrier

**Wisconsin**

American Club

**Wyoming**

Spring Creek Ranch

**Spas**

Greenhouse
Harbor Island Spa Resort
Loews Ventana Canyon Resort
Maine Chance
New Age Health Spa
Russell House
Sans Souci Resort

# WEEK OR MORE STAY

## Atlanta
Ansley Inn
Atlanta Marriott Perim. Ctr.
Biltmore Suites
Embassy Suites Perim. Ctr.
French Quarter Suites
Lanier Plaza Hotel & Conf. Ctr.
Marque of Atlanta
Marriott Suites Atlanta Midtown
Marriott Suites Perimeter
Peachtree Executive Conf. Ctr.
Summerfield Suites Hotel

## Atlantic City
Harrah's Marina Hotel & Casino
Trump Castle Resort

## Baltimore
Admiral Fell Inn
Brookshire Hotel
Peabody Court Hotel
Tremont Hotel
Tremont Plaza Hotel

## Birmingham
Tutwiler

## Boston
Best Western Boston
Copley Plaza Hotel
Eliot Hotel
Guest Quarters Suite Hotel

## Chicago
Allerton Hotel
Barclay Chicago
Chicago Marriott Suites O'Hare
Hyatt Regency Suites
Lenox House Suites
Mayfair
Radisson Suite Hotel
Raphael Hotel
Talbott Hotel

## Cincinnati
Kings Island Inn & Conf. Ctr.
Vernon Manor Hotel

## Cleveland
Radisson Plaza Hotel

## Dallas
Aristocrat Hotel
Dallas Grand
Embassy Suites
Sheraton Suites
Stoneleigh Hotel

## Denver
Burnsley Hotel
Cambridge Hotel
Embassy Suites Denver Dtwn.
Residence Inn
Scanticon

## Detroit
Townsend Hotel

## Florham Park
Hamilton Park

## Fort Lauderdale
Crown Sterling Suites Cypress
Ocean Manor Resort Hotel

## Honolulu
Colony Surf Hotel
Halekulani
Hawaii Prince Hotel Waikiki
Ilikai Hotel Nikko Waikiki
Kahala Hilton
New Otani Kaimana Beach Hotel
Waikiki Joy Hotel

## Houston
Allen Park Inn
Fit Inn Charlie Club
Guest Quarters
Harvey Suites
Plaza Hilton

## Indianapolis
Embassy Suites Hotel
Radisson Plaza & Suites Hotel
University Place

## Kansas City
Hotel Savoy
Radisson Suite Hotel
Raphael Hotel
Sheraton Suites

## Las Vegas
Alexis Park Resort
Desert Inn Hotel & Country Club
Frontier Hotel
St. Tropez

## Los Angeles
BelAge Hotel
Beverly Hills Hotel
Chateau Marmont
Hotel Bel-Air
Le Dufy
Le Parc Hotel

L'Ermitage Hotel
Mondrian Hotel
Peninsula Beverly Hills
Shangri-La
St. James's Club & Hotel
Sunset Marquis Hotel
Westwood Marquis Hotel

## Miami/Miami Beach
Alexander All-Suite Luxury Hotel
David William Hotel
Doral Ocean Beach Resort
Doral Resort & Country Club
Marlin
Mayfair House Hotel Grand Luxe
Occidental Parc Hotel

## Milwaukee
Astor Hotel
Embassy Suites, West
Manchester Suites - Airport

## Minneapolis/St. Paul
Crown Sterling Suites (Minn/St. Paul)
Hotel Luxeford Suites
Northland Inn
Saint Paul Hotel
Whitney

## Nashville
Embassy Suites
Hermitage Hotel

## New Orleans
Avenue Plaza Suite & Eurovita
Columns Hotel
Hotel Ste. Helene
Radisson Suite Hotel
Soniat House
Windsor Court Hotel

## New York City
Algonquin Hotel
Beekman Tower Hotel
Carlyle Hotel
Doral Court Hotel
Dorset
Dumont Plaza Hotel
Eastgate Tower Suite Hotel
Flatotel International
Gorham New York
Gramercy Park Hotel
Helmsley Palace
Hotel Beverly
Hotel Elysee

Hotel Plaza Athenee
Hotel Wales
Le Parker Meridien
Lowell New York
Mark
Mayfair Hotel Baglioni
Mayflower Hotel
Michelangelo
Murray Hill East Suite Hotel
Plaza Fifty Suite Hotel
Regency
Rihga Royal
Salisbury Hotel
Shelburne Suite Hotel
Southgate Tower Suite Hotel
St. Moritz on-the-Park
Surrey Hotel
U.N. Plaza - Park Hyatt
Westbury Hotel
Wyndham Hotel

## Orange County, CA
Casa Laguna Inn
Costa Mesa Marriott Suites
Four Seasons Hotel
Hilton Suites In Orange
Marriott Suites Newport Beach

## Orlando
Disney's Village Resort
Guest Quarters Disney Village
Hilton at WDW Village
Sonesta Villa Resort

## Palm Springs
Hyatt Grand Champions Resort
Hyatt Regency Suites
Racquet Club Resort
Shadow Mountain Resort
Wyndham Palm Springs

## Philadelphia
Barclay Hotel
Rittenhouse

## Phoenix/Scottsdale
Crown Sterling Suites
Fountains Suite Hotel
John Gardiner's Tennis Ranch
Marriott Suites Scottsdale
Pointe at South Mountain
Pointe at Squaw Peak
Pointe at Tapatio Cliffs
Registry Resort

## WEEK OR MORE STAY

Royal Palms Inn
Scottsdale Conference Resort
Scottsdale Hilton
Scottsdale Plaza Resort
Stouffer Cottonwoods Resort
Sunburst Hotel & Conf. Ctr.

### Pittsburgh
Pittsburgh Vista
Ramada

### Richmond
Commonwealth Park Suites Hotel

### San Diego
Bahia Hotel
Catamaran Resort Hotel
Embassy Suites
Gaslamp Plaza Suites
Horton Grand
Humphrey's Half Moon Inn
Hyatt Islandia
Radisson La Jolla
Rancho Valencia
San Diego Princess Resort

### San Francisco
Beresford Arms
Huntington Hotel Nob Hill
Hyde Park Suites
Seal Rock Inn
Stanyan Park Hotel

### Seattle
Alexis Hotel
Doubletree Suites Seattle
Stouffer Madison

### St. Louis
Doubletree Mayfair
Embassy Suites
Holiday Inn Downtown/Riverfront

### Tampa Bay
Crown Sterling Suites
Embassy Suites Tampa Airport
Innisbrook Resort
Saddlebrook
Trade Winds

### Washington, DC
Canterbury Hotel
Embassy Suites Chevy Chase
Hyatt Fair Lakes
Inn at Foggy Bottom
One Washington Circle Hotel

Park Hyatt
Watergate Hotel
Wyndham Bristol Hotel

### Alabama
Marriott's Grand Hotel

### Alaska
Brooks Lodge
Camp Denali
Denali National Park Hotel
King Salmon Lodge
Red Quill Lodge
Tikchik Narrows Lodge
Yes Bay Lodge

### Arizona
Boulders Resort
El Conquistador
Los Abrigados
Rancho de los Caballeros
Tanque Verde Ranch
Ventana Canyon
Wickenburg Inn
Wigwam

### Arkansas
Gaston's White River Resort

### California
Alisal Ranch
Carmel Valley Ranch Resort
Casa Sirena Marina Resort
Inn at Rancho Santa Fe
John Gardiner's Tennis Ranch
La Casa del Zorro
Northstar-at-Tahoe
Santa Barbara Miramar
Silverado Country Club & Resort

### Colorado
Charter at Beaver Creek
C Lazy U Ranch
Club Med, Copper Mountain
Grande Butte Hotel
Home Ranch
Lodge at Vail
Snowmass Lodge & Club
Tall Timber
Tamarron Resort
Vista Verde Guest Ranch

## Connecticut

Boulders

## Florida

Amelia Island Plantation
Captiva Beach Resort
Cheeca Lodge
Colony Beach & Tennis Resort
Grenelefe Resort
Little Palm Island
Marriott's Bay Point Resort
Marriott's Casa Marina Resort
Marriott's Marco Island Resort
Moose Head Ranch
Palm Beach Polo & Country Club
Pier House Resort
Ponte Vedra Inn & Club
Reach Resort
Resort at Longboat Key Club
Ritz-Carlton, Amelia Island
Ritz-Carlton, Naples
Ritz-Carlton, Palm Beach
Sonesta Sanibel Harbour
South Seas Plantation Resort
Sundial Beach & Tennis Resort
'Tween Waters Inn
Windjammer Resort

## Georgia

Cloister
Gastonian
King & Prince Beach Resort

## Hawaii

Embassy Suites Resort Maui
Four Seasons Resort Wailea
Grand Hyatt Wailea
Hotel Hana-Maui
Hyatt Regency Kauai
Hyatt Regency Maui
Hyatt Regency Waikoloa
Kanaloa at Kona
Kapalua Bay Hotel & Villas
Kona Village Resort
Lodge at Koele
Manele Bay Hotel
Maui Inter-Continental Resort
Maui Marriott
Maui Prince Hotel
Mauna Kea Beach Hotel
Mauna Lani Bay Hotel
Princeville Hotel

Ritz-Carlton, Mauna Lani
Royal Lahaina Resort
Royal Waikoloan
Stouffer Wailea Beach Resort
Stouffer Waiohai Beach Resort
Westin Kauai
Westin Maui

## Idaho

Coeur d'Alene Resort
Middle Fork Lodge

## Maine

Bayview Hotel & Inn
Black Point Inn Resort
Captain Lord Mansion
High Tide Inn on the Ocean
Poland Spring Inn
Samoset Resort

## Maryland

Imperial Hotel

## Massachusetts

Charlotte Inn
Harbor View Hotel
New Seabury Cape Cod
Ocean Edge Resort & Conf. Ctr.
Summer House
Westmoor Inn
White Elephant Inn

## Michigan

Boyne Highlands Inn
Boyne Mountain Hotel
Grand Traverse Resort
Shanty Creek - Schuss Mountain
Sugar Loaf Resort

## Minnesota

Breezy Point Resort
Grand View Lodge
Lutsen Resort
Madden's on Gull Lake

## Missouri

Lodge of Four Seasons
Marriott's TanTarA Resort

## Montana

Chico Hot Springs Lodge
Flathead Lake Lodge
Holland Lake Lodge

## WEEK OR MORE STAY

Huntley Lodge
Kandahar Lodge
Lone Mountain Ranch
Mountain Sky Guest Ranch
9 Quarter Circle Ranch

### New Hampshire

Snowy Owl Inn

### New Jersey

Abbey

### New Mexico

Hotel Edelweiss
Hotel Santa Fe
Rancho Encantado Resort
St. Bernard Hotel

### New York State

Elk Lake Lodge
Geneva on the Lake
Harrison Conference Center
Troutbeck Inn

### North Carolina

Pinehurst Hotel & Country Club

### Oklahoma

Shangri-La Resort

### Oregon

Embarcadero Resort Hotel
Inn at Spanish Head
Rock Springs Guest Ranch
Salishan Lodge
Sunriver Lodge & Resort
Sylvia Beach Hotel
Timberline Lodge

### Pennsylvania

Nemacolin Woodlands
Split Rock Resort

### Rhode Island

Atlantic Inn
Inn at Castle Hill

### South Carolina

Indigo Inn
Jasmine House Inn
John Rutledge House Inn
Kiawah Island Resort
Lodge Alley Inn

Planters Inn
Seabrook Island Resort
Sea Pines
Wild Dunes Resort

### Tennessee

Buckhorn Inn

### Texas

Flying L Guest Ranch
Horseshoe Bay Resort
Lakeway Inn & Conf. Ctr.
Radisson South Padre Island
Sheraton South Padre Island
Woodlands Executive Conf. Ctr.

### Utah

Brigham Street Inn
Shadow Ridge Hotel
Stein Eriksen Lodge
Washington School Inn

### Vermont

Basin Harbor Club
Hawk Inn & Mountain Resort
Hermitage Inn
Inn at Sawmill Farm
Mountain Top Inn
Stratton Mountain Inn
Topnotch at Stowe
Woods at Killington

### Virginia

Homestead
Inn at Little Washington
Kingsmill Resort & Conf. Ctr.
Tides Inn

### Washington

Kalaloch Lodge

### West Virginia

Greenbrier

### Wisconsin

Abbey
Gordon Lodge
Lakewoods Resort & Lodge

### Wyoming

Colter Bay Village
Jackson Hole Racquet Club
Jackson Lake Lodge

Jenny Lake Lodge
Moose Head Ranch
Paradise Guest Ranch
Ranch at Ucross
R Lazy S Ranch
Roosevelt Lodge
Snow King Resort
Spring Creek Ranch
Teton Pines Resort

### Spas

Ashram Retreat
Bon Reussite Resort
Cal-A-Vie

Deerfield Manor Spa
Doral Saturnia
Golden Door
Greenhouse
Heartland Retreat
Kerr House
Lake Austin Resort
Maine Chance
National Institute of Fitness
New Age Health Spa
Rancho La Puerta
Russell House
Sans Souci Resort
Vista Clara Spa

# YOUNG AND LIVELY

**Atlanta**
Atlanta Marriott Marquis
Hyatt Regency

**Atlantic City**
Bally's Grand Hotel & Casino
Bally's Park Place
Caesars Atlantic City
Claridge Casino Hotel
Harrah's Marina Hotel & Casino
Holiday Inn Diplomat
Sands Hotel & Casino
Showboat Hotel
TropWorld
Trump Castle Resort
Trump Plaza Hotel & Casino
Trump Regency Hotel
Trump Taj Mahal

**Boston**
Marriott Hotel Long Wharf

**Chicago**
Hyatt Regency Chicago

**Dallas**
Dallas Marriott Quorum
Dallas Parkway Hilton
Hyatt Regency Dallas at Reunion
Loews Anatole Hotel

**Denver**
Doubletree Hotel Denver
Embassy Suites Denver Dtwn.
Hyatt Regency Tech Center
Sheraton Denver Tech Center

**Detroit**
Westin Hotel

**Fort Lauderdale**
Marriott's Harbor Beach Resort
Ocean Manor Resort Hotel
Sheraton Yankee Clipper

**Fort Worth**
Stockyards Hotel

**Honolulu**
Colony Surf Hotel
Hawaiian Regent
Hawaiian Waikiki Beach Hotel
Hawaii Prince Hotel Waikiki
Hilton Hawaiian Village
Ilikai Hotel Nikko Waikiki
Outrigger Waikiki
Park Plaza Waikiki
Sheraton Princess Kaiulani
Sheraton Waikiki Hotel

**Houston**
Houstonian Hotel & Conf. Ctr.
Houston Marriott West Loop

**Indianapolis**
Holiday Inn Union Station

**Kansas City**
Adam's Mark

**Las Vegas**
Bally's
Caesars Palace
Circus Circus Hotel
Dunes Hotel & Country Club
Excalibur Hotel
Flamingo Hotel
Golden Nugget Hotel & Casino
Mirage
Riviera Hotel & Casino
Sahara Hotel & Casino
Sam Boyd's Fremont Hotel
Tropicana Hotel & Country Club

**Los Angeles**
Mondrian Hotel
Shangri-La
Sportsmen's Lodge Hotel
Sunset Marquis Hotel

**Miami/Miami Beach**
Alexander All-Suite Luxury Hotel
Turnberry Isle Club

**Milwaukee**
Milwaukee Marriott - Brookfield

**Minneapolis/St. Paul**
Crown Sterling Suites (Minn/St. Paul)

**Nashville**
Embassy Suites
Opryland Hotel

**New Orleans**
Dauphine Orleans Hotel
Doubletree Hotel New Orleans
Inn on Bourbon
New Orleans Hilton Riverside
New Orleans Marriott
Royal Sonesta
Sheraton New Orleans Hotel

**New York City**
Mayflower Hotel
Morgans
New York Marriott Marquis
Paramount

Ramada Hotel
Royalton

## Orange County, CA
Anaheim Hilton & Towers
Anaheim Marriott Hotel
Disneyland Hotel
Hyatt Newporter
Hyatt Regency Alicante
Sheraton Anaheim Hotel

## Orlando
Buena Vista Palace
Clarion Plaza Hotel
Disney's Caribbean Beach Resort
Disney's Contemporary Resort
Disney's Grand Floridian
Disney's Polynesian Resort
Disney's Village Resort
Forte Travelodge Hotel
Grosvenor Resort at WDW
Guest Quarters Disney Village
Hilton at WDW Village
Hotel Royal Plaza
Hyatt Orlando
Hyatt Regency Grand Cypress
Marriott
Marriott's Orlando World Center
Orange Lake Country Club
Orlando Heritage Inn
Peabody Orlando
Radisson Inn International Dr.
Sheraton World Resort
Sonesta Villa Resort
Stouffer Orlando Resort
Walt Disney World Dolphin
Walt Disney World Swan

## Palm Springs
Hyatt Grand Champions Resort
Shadow Mountain Resort

## Phoenix/Scottsdale
Hyatt Regency Scottsdale
Lexington Hotel & City Square

## San Antonio
Hilton Palacio del Rio
Hyatt Regency San Antonio
La Mansion del Rio
Marriott Rivercenter
Menger Hotel
San Antonio Riverwalk Marriott
Wyndham San Antonio

## San Diego
Hyatt Regency La Jolla
San Diego Marriott
Sea Lodge

## San Francisco
Marriott Fisherman's Wharf
Sheraton at Fisherman's Wharf
Tuscan Inn

## St. Louis
Embassy Suites
Holiday Inn Downtown/Conv. Ctr.
Holiday Inn Downtown/Riverfront
Hyatt Regency St. Louis
Marriott Pavilion Hotel

## Tampa Bay
St. Petersburg Beach Hilton

## Alabama
Marriott's Grand Hotel

## Arizona
Boulders Resort
El Conquistador
Tanque Verde Ranch

## Arkansas
Gaston's White River Resort

## California
Alisal Ranch
Monterey Plaza Hotel
Northstar-at-Tahoe
Sheraton Universal Hotel
Squaw Valley Inn

## Colorado
Aspen Club Lodge
Breckenridge Hilton
Charter at Beaver Creek
C Lazy U Ranch
Club Med, Copper Mountain
Doral Telluride
Grande Butte Hotel
Home Ranch
Hotel Jerome
Hotel Lenado
Hyatt Regency Beaver Creek
Inn at Aspen
Inn at Beaver Creek
Iron Horse Resort Retreat
Keystone Lodge
Little Nell

# YOUNG AND LIVELY

Lodge at Vail
Mountain Haus at Vail
Pines Lodge at Beaver Creek
Radisson Resort Vail
Sardy House
Sheraton Steamboat Resort
Sitzmark Lodge
Snowmass Lodge & Club
Sonnenalp Resort
Vail Athletic Club
Westin Resort Vail

## Florida

Amelia Island Plantation
Captiva Beach Resort
Club Med Sandpiper
Colony Beach & Tennis Resort
Hawk's Cay Resort & Marina
Hyatt Key West
Marriott at Sawgrass Resort
Marriott's Casa Marina Resort
Pier House Resort
Reach Resort
Resort at Longboat Key Club
Sheraton Key Largo Resort
Sonesta Sanibel Harbour
South Seas Plantation Resort

## Georgia

Cloister
Sea Palms Golf & Tennis Resort

## Hawaii

Embassy Suites Resort Maui
Four Seasons Resort Wailea
Grand Hyatt Wailea
Hyatt Regency Kauai
Hyatt Regency Maui
Hyatt Regency Waikoloa
Kanaloa at Kona
Maui Inter-Continental Resort
Maui Marriott
Royal Lahaina Resort
Royal Waikoloan
Stouffer Waiohai Beach Resort
Westin Maui

## Idaho

Coeur d'Alene Resort
Sun Valley Lodge

## Illinois

Eagle Ridge Inn & Resort

## Massachusetts

New Seabury Cape Cod
Ocean Edge Resort & Conf. Ctr.

## Michigan

Boyne Highlands Inn
Boyne Mountain Hotel
Grand Traverse Resort
Shanty Creek - Schuss Mountain
Sugar Loaf Resort
Treetops Sylvan Resort

## Minnesota

Arrowwood, A Radisson Resort
Grand View Lodge
Lutsen Resort
Madden's on Gull Lake

## Missouri

Lodge of Four Seasons
Marriott's TanTarA Resort

## Montana

Flathead Lake Lodge
Huntley Lodge
Izaak Walton Inn
Kandahar Lodge
Lone Mountain Ranch

## Nevada

Caesars Lake Tahoe
Harrah's Lake Tahoe
Hyatt Regency Lake Tahoe

## New Mexico

Bishop's Lodge
Inn of the Mountain Gods

## North Carolina

Pinehurst Hotel & Country Club

## Oregon

Salishan Lodge
Sunriver Lodge & Resort
Timberline Lodge

## South Carolina

Hilton Head Island Hilton Resort
Hyatt Regency Hilton Head
Kiawah Island Resort
Marriott's Hilton Head Resort
Seabrook Island Resort
Sea Pines

Westin Resort
Wild Dunes Resort

**Texas**
Flying L Guest Ranch
Radisson South Padre Island
Sheraton South Padre Island

**Utah**
Cliff Lodge
Shadow Ridge Hotel
Stein Eriksen Lodge

**West Virginia**
Greenbrier

**Wisconsin**

Olympia Resort

**Wyoming**

Jackson Hole Racquet Club
Mammoth Hot Springs Hotel
Old Faithful Inn
R Lazy S Ranch
Snow King Resort
Spring Creek Ranch
Teton Pines Resort

# ALPHABETICAL PAGE INDEX

# RATING SHEETS

**To aid in your participation in our next *Survey*.**

## RATING SHEETS

| R | S | D | P | $ |
|---|---|---|---|---|

|   |   |   |   |   |   |
|---|---|---|---|---|---|

**Hotel, etc. Name** _____ **City** _____
**Phone: (800)** _____ **Local (    )** _____
**Address** _____
**Comments** _____
_____
_____

|   |   |   |   |   |   |
|---|---|---|---|---|---|

**Hotel, etc. Name** _____ **City** _____
**Phone: (800)** _____ **Local (    )** _____
**Address** _____
**Comments** _____
_____
_____

|   |   |   |   |   |   |
|---|---|---|---|---|---|

**Hotel, etc. Name** _____ **City** _____
**Phone: (800)** _____ **Local (    )** _____
**Address** _____
**Comments** _____
_____
_____

|   |   |   |   |   |   |
|---|---|---|---|---|---|

**Hotel, etc. Name** _____ **City** _____
**Phone: (800)** _____ **Local (    )** _____
**Address** _____
**Comments** _____
_____
_____

|   |   |   |   |   |   |
|---|---|---|---|---|---|

**Hotel, etc. Name** _____ **City** _____
**Phone: (800)** _____ **Local (    )** _____
**Address** _____
**Comments** _____
_____
_____

**RATING SHEETS**

| R | S | D | P | $ |
|---|---|---|---|---|

| | | | | | |
|---|---|---|---|---|---|

Hotel, etc. Name _____ City _____
Phone: (800) _____ Local ( ) _____
Address _____
Comments _____
_____
_____

| | | | | | |
|---|---|---|---|---|---|

Hotel, etc. Name _____ City _____
Phone: (800) _____ Local ( ) _____
Address _____
Comments _____
_____
_____

| | | | | | |
|---|---|---|---|---|---|

Hotel, etc. Name _____ City _____
Phone: (800) _____ Local ( ) _____
Address _____
Comments _____
_____
_____

| | | | | | |
|---|---|---|---|---|---|

Hotel, etc. Name _____ City _____
Phone: (800) _____ Local ( ) _____
Address _____
Comments _____
_____
_____

| | | | | | |
|---|---|---|---|---|---|

Hotel, etc. Name _____ City _____
Phone: (800) _____ Local ( ) _____
Address _____
Comments _____
_____
_____

## RATING SHEETS

| R | S | D | P | $ |

| | | | | | |
Hotel, etc. Name _____ City _____
Phone: (800) _____ Local ( ) _____
Address _____
Comments _____
_____
_____

| | | | | | |
Hotel, etc. Name _____ City _____
Phone: (800) _____ Local ( ) _____
Address _____
Comments _____
_____
_____

| | | | | | |
Hotel, etc. Name _____ City _____
Phone: (800) _____ Local ( ) _____
Address _____
Comments _____
_____
_____

| | | | | | |
Hotel, etc. Name _____ City _____
Phone: (800) _____ Local ( ) _____
Address _____
Comments _____
_____
_____

| | | | | | |
Hotel, etc. Name _____ City _____
Phone: (800) _____ Local ( ) _____
Address _____
Comments _____
_____
_____

**RATING SHEETS**
| R | S | D | P | $ |

| | | | | |

Hotel, etc. Name _____ City _____
Phone: (800) _____ Local ( ) _____
Address _____
Comments _____
_____
_____

| | | | | |

Hotel, etc. Name _____ City _____
Phone: (800) _____ Local ( ) _____
Address _____
Comments _____
_____
_____

| | | | | |

Hotel, etc. Name _____ City _____
Phone: (800) _____ Local ( ) _____
Address _____
Comments _____
_____
_____

| | | | | |

Hotel, etc. Name _____ City _____
Phone: (800) _____ Local ( ) _____
Address _____
Comments _____
_____
_____

| | | | | |

Hotel, etc. Name _____ City _____
Phone: (800) _____ Local ( ) _____
Address _____
Comments _____
_____
_____

## RATING SHEETS

| R | S | D | P | $ |

|   |   |   |   |   |

**Hotel, etc. Name** _____ **City** _____
**Phone: (800)** _____ **Local (** ) _____
**Address** _____
**Comments** _____
_____
_____

| R | S | D | P | $ |

|   |   |   |   |   |

**Hotel, etc. Name** _____ **City** _____
**Phone: (800)** _____ **Local (** ) _____
**Address** _____
**Comments** _____
_____
_____

| R | S | D | P | $ |

|   |   |   |   |   |

**Hotel, etc. Name** _____ **City** _____
**Phone: (800)** _____ **Local (** ) _____
**Address** _____
**Comments** _____
_____
_____

| R | S | D | P | $ |

|   |   |   |   |   |

**Hotel, etc. Name** _____ **City** _____
**Phone: (800)** _____ **Local (** ) _____
**Address** _____
**Comments** _____
_____
_____

| R | S | D | P | $ |

|   |   |   |   |   |

**Hotel, etc. Name** _____ **City** _____
**Phone: (800)** _____ **Local (** ) _____
**Address** _____
**Comments** _____
_____
_____

**RATING SHEETS**

| R | S | D | P | $ |
|---|---|---|---|---|

| | | | | | |
|---|---|---|---|---|---|

Hotel, etc. Name _____ City _____

Phone: (800) _____ Local ( ) _____

Address _____

Comments _____

_____

_____

| | | | | | |
|---|---|---|---|---|---|

Hotel, etc. Name _____ City _____

Phone: (800) _____ Local ( ) _____

Address _____

Comments _____

_____

_____

| | | | | | |
|---|---|---|---|---|---|

Hotel, etc. Name _____ City _____

Phone: (800) _____ Local ( ) _____

Address _____

Comments _____

_____

_____

| | | | | | |
|---|---|---|---|---|---|

Hotel, etc. Name _____ City _____

Phone: (800) _____ Local ( ) _____

Address _____

Comments _____

_____

_____

| | | | | | |
|---|---|---|---|---|---|

Hotel, etc. Name _____ City _____

Phone: (800) _____ Local ( ) _____

Address _____

Comments _____

_____

_____

**RATING SHEETS** | R | S | D | P | $ |

| | | | | |

**Hotel, etc. Name** _____ **City** _____
**Phone: (800)** _____ **Local (** ) _____
**Address** _____
**Comments** _____
_____
_____

| | | | | |

**Hotel, etc. Name** _____ **City** _____
**Phone: (800)** _____ **Local (** ) _____
**Address** _____
**Comments** _____
_____
_____

| | | | | |

**Hotel, etc. Name** _____ **City** _____
**Phone: (800)** _____ **Local (** ) _____
**Address** _____
**Comments** _____
_____
_____

| | | | | |

**Hotel, etc. Name** _____ **City** _____
**Phone: (800)** _____ **Local (** ) _____
**Address** _____
**Comments** _____
_____
_____

| | | | | |

**Hotel, etc. Name** _____ **City** _____
**Phone: (800)** _____ **Local (** ) _____
**Address** _____
**Comments** _____
_____
_____